2nd Edition

Choosing Democracy
A Practical Guide to Multicultural Education

Duane E. Campbell
California State University, Sacramento

With contributions by

Dolores Delgado-Campbell

Forrest Davis

Diane Cordero de Noriega

Kathryn Singh

Eric Vega

Velma Villegas

Pia Linquist Wong

Merrill
an imprint of Prentice Hall
Upper Saddle River, New Jersey   *Columbus, Ohio*

Library of Congress Cataloging-in-Publication Data

Campbell, Duane E.

    Choosing democracy : a practical guide to multicultural education / Duane E. Campbell: with contributions by Dolores Delgado-Campbell . . . [et al.].—2nd ed.

      p. cm.

    Includes bibliographical references and index.

    ISBN 0-13-096102-7

    1. Multicultural education—United States. 2. Education—Social aspects—United States. 3. Pluralism (Social sciences)—United States. 4. Racism—United States. 5. United States—Race relations. 6. Social classes—United States. 7. Sex differences in education—United States.   I. Delgado-Campbell, Dolores. II. Title.

   LC1099.3.C36 2000

   370.117—dc21

                             99-31550

                                CIP

Editor: Debra A. Stollenwerk
Assistant Editor: Heather Doyle Fraser
Editorial Assistant: Penny S. Burleson
Production Editor: Mary Harlan
Copy Editor: Robert L. Marcum
Design Coordinator: Diane C. Lorenzo
Text Designer: Ed Horcharik/Pagination
Photo Coordinator: Sherry Mitchell
Cover Designer: Dan Eckel
Cover Art: Stephan Schildbach
Production Manager: Pamela D. Bennett
Electronic Text Management: Marilyn Wilson Phelps, Karen L. Bretz, Melanie N. King
Illustrations: Barry Bell Graphics
Director of Marketing: Kevin Flanagan
Marketing Manager: Meghan Shepherd
Marketing Coordinator: Krista Groshong

This book was set in Life and AvantGarde by Prentice Hall and was printed and bound by R. R. Donnelley & Sons Company. The cover was printed by Phoenix Color Corp.

©2000, 1996 by Prentice-Hall, Inc.
Pearson Education
Upper Saddle River, New Jersey 07458

Printed in the United States of America

10 9 8 7 6 5 4 3

ISBN: 0-13-096102-7

Prentice-Hall International (UK) Limited, *London*
Prentice-Hall of Australia Pty. Limited, *Sydney*
Prentice-Hall of Canada, Inc., *Toronto*
Prentice-Hall Hispanoamericana, S. A., *Mexico*
Prentice-Hall of India Private Limited, *New Delhi*
Prentice-Hall of Japan, Inc., *Tokyo*
Prentice-Hall (Singapore) Pte. Ltd., *Singapore*
Editora Prentice-Hall do Brasil, Ltda., *Rio de Janeiro*

Foreword

By Henry T. Trueba

The democratic foundations of the United States of America seem to be under enormous pressure by the persistent earthquakes engineered by the conservative radical right in California and other states, and the defensive strategies of some European Americans. Public opinion on immigrants of color and on the future of American democracy is colored by myths and sensationalized in the context of "the American Dream." It is very likely that the United States will continue to attract large numbers of Latino and Asian immigrants, judging from current population trends and immigration patterns, due primarily to demand for cheap labor, our economy, and other socio-political events around the globe. It is inevitable that immigrants will be called upon to play a very important role in the making of our "new" democracy and "new" global economy. The need to re-invent our democratic institutions within our cultural diversity is unavoidable.

In May of 1996, the population of the United States was 265,022,000. Among persons 65 years of age and over, whites comprised 85%, blacks 8%, Hispanics 4%, and Asian and Pacific Islanders 2% (*Population Today*, 1996, pp. 4–6). Blacks, Hispanics, Asian & Pacific Islanders, and American Indians accounted for 34% of the U.S. population under 18 years of age. Fifty years ago the United States was 87% white, 10% black, 2.5% Hispanic and 0.5% Asian. Fifty years from now the U.S. population will be 52.8% white, 13.6% black, 24.5% Hispanic, and 8.2% Asian (U.S. Bureau of the Census, 1996). What is amazing is that these changes are taking place in scarcely one hundred years, and will have produced vast and lasting consequences for the nation and for the world.

Immigration studies show differential academic achievement among various ethnic groups (see Suárez-Orozco, 1998; Cornelius, 1995, 1996, 1998; Delgado-Gaitan, 1994; Hondagneu-Sotelo, 1994; Delgado-Gaitan & Trueba, 1991; Ogbu, 1974, 1978, 1982, 1991, 1992; Patthey-Chavez, 1993; Portes, 1996; Trueba, 1999; Trueba, Cheng & Ima, 1993; Trueba, Jacobs & Kirton, 1990; and Zou & Trueba, 1998). The marginalization of some immigrant families seems to start long before they arrive to this country, and is accelerated under oppression and isolation. Immigrants' naïve notions about the politics of employment and of schools (with their "hidden curriculum" of instruction for newcomers of color) can result in shock and profound disappointment for the family, especially if the family comes from a rural area (Suárez-Orozco & Suárez-Orozco, 1995a; Trueba, 1999; Valencia, 1991; Valenzuela, in press). There seems to be a possible "deterioration" in academic performance among certain immigrant groups (Latinos, for example), and consequently their progress is of great concern (Portes, 1996; Orfield & Eaton, 1996; Orfield, Bachmeier, James & Eitle, 1997). What we need to know is what are the specific factors and agencies that determine the actual performance levels of individual minority students, beyond any general structural, historical, and socio-economic characteristics of the entire ethnic population? For example, to what type of family support, home literacy practices, academic socialization, mentoring, and reward systems are these students exposed? How do these factors translate into different learning strategies, cognitive skills, achievement motivation, and long-term commitment to achieve? To what extent do cognitive and motivational assets translate into opportunities to play a significant role in higher education? If indeed cultural ecological explanations of differential performance are deemed to be insufficient or excessively inflexible, what theoretical modifications are required in order to increase their explanatory power vis-à-vis the lack of representation of minority persons in higher education positions?

Ethnic resilience and assimilation are the two sides of the immigration coin. Common opinion has it that in order to become a "real" ("assimilated") American, one must forget his/her ethnic identity. Yet, often racial or ethnic identification becomes pivotal in American society to determine a person's relative status and chances for success. Sheer statistical, demographic, and residential information serves to predict educational achievement, income, dropout and suspension rates, size of family, mortality trends, incarceration, tendencies to violence, use of welfare, and other presumed dysfunctional characteristics that configure the American justice system, investment and banking policies and operation, and even the distribution of resources and liabilities (from the location of banks, grocery stores, movie theaters, to that of waste disposal facilities, prisons, and nuclear sites). Additionally, the racial and/or ethnic prejudice in the society at large is reflected not only in the elementary and secondary public schools, but also in higher education institutions, and extended to the most critical areas: the hiring, promotion, and retention norms and procedures. In a broader historical perspective, the pendulum-like cycle of intolerance for racial and ethnic diversity in the United States is often associated with military, socio-economic, cultural, and political crises. These crises bring an intensity to the stereotyping, scapegoating, and persecuting of immigrants, rationalized as a legitimate concern for national security or crime prevention, or the protection of our economic interests or cultural purity. Yet, in recent years, in spite of our economic bonanza and generally healthy international diplomatic climate for the United States, there is a renewed xenophobia. For a critical analysis of these currents and malaise affecting our view of immigration in Europe and the United States, see M. Suárez-Orozco (1998).

Over the years the struggle for social justice in California has produced unusual powerful statements that revisit the democratic foundations of America as a free country with justice for all. This book belongs to that category but in a strict sense deserves to be seen as a foundational volume in teacher education for three reasons: (1) it places "multicultural" education as pivotal to retain the democratic fabric of American society; (2) it refocuses on "culture" (without neglecting social class and sociological theories on equity and stratification) as a crucial factor cementing ethnic and racial harmony in our modern pluralistic world; and (3) it addresses the reality of poverty in North America, and especially poverty of school-age children. There are important implications of these three issues for a practical pedagogical approach to "multicultural" education, for educational reform, and for social transformation.

Education is crucial to the realization of the American dream. The reason is that it is primarily through the acquisition of knowledge and skills associated with formal education that immigrant and low-income students become empowered and a part of mainstream America. It is particularly relevant to speak of multicultural education as the kind of education that will permit Americans to become aware of "democracy at work," realize their full potential, and live in harmony. The obstacle to a good education for racial and ethnic minority groups and others who become marginalized is the use of white mainstream culture as a vehicle for classroom instruction; that is, as a mediating tool or agent in the transmission and acquisition of knowledge. The use of white mainstream culture also tends to devalue the cultures of people who have been excluded from educational opportunities. Multicultural education brings us back to understand the democratic philosophy that has permitted all citizens in this country to pursue the goals of freedom and economic prosperity without prejudice, at least, prejudice *de jure*.

I find *Choosing Democracy* to be a very clear, pragmatic, and powerful statement guiding teachers, educators, and scholars to engage in substantive reflection about our educational philosophy, policies, and practices. I find it refreshing and useful. Most of all, I find this book extremely timely. The fact that American democracy is at risk because of the "revivalistic" or "nativistic" tendencies of the 1980s and 1990s (identical to those of a century ago) is not dissimilar to the events faced by this country during the Industrial Revolution and the increasing immigrant waves of the last century. Social unrest, rapid cultural change, economic crises around the world, and cultural confusion about what America is all about have resulted in scapegoating immigrants and attempting to exclude them from the social benefits of this country, in spite of the fact that those immigrants help build the economic strength of America. Some people refer to these historical parallels as "malaise" but others see these cyclical crises as normal reactions and adjustment in American values. This "malaise" is not unique to this country. Indeed, France, Spain, Belgium and Germany have seen their share of anti-immigrant currents, now politically strong, that have won a good portion of the European populations on issues about exiling non-Europeans, or at least excluding them from receiving employment. Nativism has led to xenophobia and even to hysteria in some countries. Even in California the hysteria about undocumented immigrants and their children has had a serious detrimental impact on many other children of the same ethnic groups who are legal.

In the face of irrational behavior and prejudice, *Choosing Democracy* reaffirms our philosophical position that for this country to remain democratic, it must embrace the principles of multicultural education, including respect and appreciation of languages and cultures of other immigrants. It is not enough to embrace these principles. We must act on these principles as well. What this means is that education is intrinsically a political act that creates awareness of how democracy works and what its fundamental components are. We must start from what Freire (1993) has called the "ontological" need for hope, or the essential commitment to pursue human existence with dignity even in the worst of circumstances:

> Hope is an ontological need. As a program [for action], lack of hope paralyzes us and makes us fall into fatalism where it is impossible to muster the necessary strength in order to fight for the recreation of the world. (p. 10)

American society is prey to currents and counter-currents that occur in cycles. In the late nineteenth century with the sentiment against "foreigners," there was a hysteria surrounding the use of languages other than English. In the 1980s there was a hysteria about brown people and the use of Spanish and other "foreign" languages in California, Texas, and Florida. For individuals who were born here and treated like unwanted people, hope must be ontological, essential to existence, in order to pursue democratic ideals. Yet, as Paulo Freire (1993) explains, hope is not enough:

> Hope alone cannot win a struggle, but without hope we will be weak and hesitate in the struggle. We need critical hope, in the same way that a fish needs clean water. (ibid.)

The philosophical and theoretical foundations, as well as the actual content of this book, are clearly marked by Freire's critical pedagogy and pedagogy of hope. In fact, there are very few books that have accomplished both: the presentation of a solid theoretical basis for critical pedagogy and the presentation of a content congruent in practice with its theoretical basis. The examples, the approach to the various issues, the suggestions made, the way various audiences are handled (teachers, educators, parents, etc.) respect the principles established by Freire. The author, having recognized the need for critical pedagogy in the schooling of linguistically and culturally diverse student populations, proceeds to teach the content exemplifying the pedagogical principles of respect and appreciation to all groups.

This book not only provides a better idea of what multicultural education is all about, but also an even more profound understanding of how schooling can integrate multicultural education in the curriculum. This book does a great deal, because it

1. Invites serious reflection about the nature of American society and the role of schools.

2. Shows teachers and students the way to heal from prejudice and racial/ethnic biases.

3. Provides clear guidelines to regain a sense of purpose and resolve ethnic/racial conflicts.

4. Engages teachers and students in more effective classroom organization and meaningful curriculum exercises that will heal the wounds opened by conflict.

5. Suggests the creation of support groups to promote better teaching/learning skills and strategies to enhance human relations.

6. Emphasizes cooperation and integration beyond the "melting pot."

7. Offers a guide for a democratic school reform.

I believe that teacher educators, teachers, and students will find this book extremely useful and a constant companion as they discover the importance of healing from prejudice and of linking democratic ideals with pragmatic school reform. They will find the book written in a clear and simple style, well organized and practical for daily use and for serious reflection. There is an extensive section of extremely useful references and sources for those individuals who want to pursue a more in-depth knowledge of specific subjects. In the end, the main contribution of this book will be to understand better the relationship between our historical past as a democratic society and the politics of culture and education today. The danger in ignoring this relationship is to permit prejudice and cultural hegemony to become pervasive and destructive in schools. In turn, the serious recognition of the need to respect ethnic identities, linguistic and cultural heritages, and the rich variety of contributions by all the groups who form modern America is crucial for the future democracy of our country and its survival as a free and powerful country. Giroux (1994) has clearly pointed out that

> The relationship between history and identity is a complex one and cannot be reduced to unearthing hidden histories that are then mined for positive images. On the contrary, educators need to understand and develop in their pedagogies how identities are produced differently, how they take up narratives of the past through the stories and experiences of the present. (p. 50)

Critical pedagogy (McLaren, 1995) is indispensable in order to establish an adequate learning environment, congruent with American democratic principles and hence with multicultural education and one in which ethnic identification of students paves the way for their empowerment in schools, a positive self-image, and the motivation to achieve academically. "Critical pedagogy situates itself in the intersection of language, culture and history—the nexus in which students' subjectivities are formed, contested and played out" (McLaren, 1989, p. 233). Theoretically, we accept the role of critical pedagogy and advocate it. In practice, we are not sure how to pursue it. McLaren (1989) insists that

The struggle is one that involves their history, their language, and their culture, and the pedagogical implications are such that students are given access to a critical discourse or are conditioned to accept the familiar as the inevitable. Worse still, they are denied a voice with which to be present in the world; they are made invisible to history and rendered powerless to shape it. (p. 233)

Multicultural education is the only hope immigrants have to get their families out of poverty. In this context, racial and ethnic intolerance in higher education affects profoundly the access and quality of education for racial and ethnic minority students. In the final instance, an institution primarily created and maintained by white faculty will present perspectives and values that exclude, penalize, or ignore students of color. The consistent reluctance of higher education institutions to diversify its faculty is clearly impinging upon the quality of education offered for all students. Even European American students need to understand ethnically and racially diverse populations in this country. Their insulation from exposure to minorities perpetuates their prejudice and inability to deal with populations of color.

Ethnic identification and the creation of cultural bridges for students to acquire new knowledge (both cultural and subject-matter related to traditional schooling) are processes intimately related and mutually interdependent. In the end, cultural bridges will be required to live up to our ideal of human solidarity in a society which demands respect for racial, ethnic, linguistic, cultural, and socioeconomic diversity. Duane Campbell makes an important contribution to education and educational reform as he strongly advocates for multicultural education as an expression of critical pedagogy in the service of human solidarity and genuine democracy.

Henry T. Trueba, Ph.D.
University of Texas, Austin

References

Cornelius, W. (1995). Educating California's immigrant children: Introduction and overview. In R. G. Rumbaut and W. A. Cornelius (Eds.), *California's immigrant children: Theory, research, and implications for educational policy* (pp. 1–16). San Diego, CA: Center for U.S.–Mexican Studies.

Cornelius, W. (1996). Economics, culture, and the politics of restricting immigration. *The Chronicle of Higher Education, XLIII*(12), pp. B4–B5.

Cornelius, W. (1998). The structural embeddedness of demand for Mexican immigrant labor: New evidence from California. In M. M. Suárez-Orozco (Ed.), *Crossings: Mexican immigration in interdisciplinary perspectives* (p. xx). Cambridge, MA: Harvard University Press and the D. Rockefeller Center for Latin American Studies.

Delgado-Gaitan, C. (1994). Russian refugee families: Accommodating aspirations through education. *Anthropology and Education Quarterly* 25(2), 137–155.

Delgado-Gaitan, C., & Trueba, H. T. (1991). *Crossing cultural borders: Education for immigrant families in America.* London: Falmer Press.

Freire, P. (1973). *Pedagogy of the oppressed.* New York: Seabury.

Freire, P. (1993). *Pedagogia da Esperança: Um reencontro com a pedagogia do oprimido.* São Paulo, Brazil: Editora Paz e Terra, S.A.

Giroux, H. A. (1994). Living dangerously: Identity, politics and the new cultural racism. In H. A. Giroux & P. McLaren (Eds.), Between borders: Pedagogy and the politics of cultural studies (pp. 29–55). New York: Routledge.

Hondagneu-Sotelo, P. (1994). Gendered transitions: Mexican experiences of immigration. Berkeley, CA: University of California Press.

McLaren, P. (1995). Critical pedagogy and predatory culture. New York: Routledge.

Ogbu, J. (1974). The next generation: An ethnography of education in an urban neighborhood. New York: Academic Press.

Ogbu, J. (1978). Minority education and caste: The American system in cross-cultural perspective. New York: Academic Press.

Ogbu, J. (1982). Cultural discontinuities and schooling. Anthropology and Education Quarterly, 13(4), 290–307.

Ogbu, J. (1991). Immigrant and involuntary minorities in comparative perspective. In Gibson & J. Ogbu, (Eds.), Minority status and schooling: A comparative study of immigrant and involuntary minorities (pp. 3–33). New York: Garland Publishing, Inc.

Ogbu, J. (1992). Understanding cultural diversity. Educational Researcher 21(8), 5–24.

Orfield, G., & Eaton, S. E. (Eds.) (1996). Dismantling desegregation: The quiet reversal of Brown v. Board of Education. New York: The New Press.

Orfield, G., Bachmeier, M., James, D., and Eitle, T. (1997). Deepening segregation in American public schools. Harvard Project on School Desegregation. Harvard University. Unpublished manuscript.

Patthey-Chavez, G. (1993). High school as an arena for cultural conflict and acculturation for Latino angelinos. Anthropology and Education Quarterly 24(1), 33–60.

Population Today: News, Numbers and Analysis (August 1996) 24(8).

Portes, A. (1996). Introduction: Immigration and its aftermath. In A. Portes (Ed.) The new second generation (pp. 1–7). New York: Russell Sage Foundation.

Suárez-Orozco, C., & Suárez-Orozco, M. (1995a). Transformations: Immigration, family life and achievement motivation among Latino adolescents. Stanford, CA: Stanford University Press.

Suárez-Orozco, C., & Suárez-Orozco, M. (1995b). Migration: Generational discontinuities and the making of Latino identities. In L. Romanucci-Ross and G. DeVos (Eds.), Ethnic identity: Creation, conflict, and accommodation (3d ed.)(pp. 321–347). Walnut Creek, CA: AltaMira Press.

Suárez-Orozco, M. (1998). State terrors: Immigrants and refugees in the post-national space. In Y. Zou & H. T. Trueba (Eds.), Ethnic identity and power: Cultural contexts of political action in school and society (pp. 283–319). New York: SUNY Press.

Trueba, H. T. (1989). Raising silent voices: Educating linguistic minorities for the 21st century. New York: Harper & Row.

Trueba, H. T. (1991). Linkages of macro-micro analytical levels. Journal of Psychohistory, 18(4) 457–468.

Trueba, H. T. (1999). Latinos unidos: Socio-cultural diversity in ethnic solidarity. Lanham, MD: Rowman & Littlefield.

Trueba, H. T., Cheng, L., & Ima, K. (1993). Myth or reality: Adaptive strategies of Asian Americans in California. London: Falmer Press.

Trueba, H. T., Jacobs, L., & Kirton, E. (1990). Cultural conflict and adaptation: The case of the Hmong children in American society. London: Falmer Press.

Trueba, H. T., Rodriguez, C., Zou, Y., & Cintrón, J. (1993). Healing multicultural America: Mexican immigrants rise to power in rural California. London: Falmer Press.

Trueba, H., & Zou, Y. (1994). Power in education: The case of Miao university students and its significance for American culture. London: Falmer Press.

U.S. Bureau of the Census. Current Population Reports published by the U.S. Department of Commerce, Economics and Statistics Administration, June 1996.

Valencia, R. R. (1991). The Plight of Chicano students: An overview of schooling conditions and outcomes. In R. R. Valencia (Ed.) Chicano school failure: An analysis through many windows (pp. 3-26). London, England: Falmer Press).

Valenzuela, A. (in press). Subtractive Schooling: U.S.-Mexican Youth and the Politics of Caring. New York: SUNY Press.

Zou, Y. & Trueba, E. (Eds.) (1998). Ethnic identity and power: Cultural contexts of political action in school and society. New York: SUNY Press.

Foreword

By Cornel West

Duane Campbell is an organic intellectual with a deep commitment to a substantive democratic vision. He understands education as a critical activity that unsettles our presuppositions and unstiffens our prejudices such that we can bond with others to alleviate social misery. His acute sense of history enables him to view schooling within a broad multilayered context in which the harsh realities of race, class, and gender as well as the sweet possibilities of freedom, equality, and democracy loom large.

This magisterial treatment of our contemporary crisis in American society, culture, and education takes us step-by-step through the treacherous terrains that impede our efforts to examine critically and expand effectively democracy in our time. His powerful text is the most comprehensive analysis we have of sharpening the practical strategies for multicultural education in America.

Like the exquisite poetry of Walt Whitman and the exhilarating music of Louis Armstrong, Duane Campbell's empowering pedagogy is shot through with profound democratic sentiments. In our frightening moment of class polarization and racial balkanization, his themes of social reconstruction, cultural innovation, and political transformation—themes that link any talk about diversity to the expansion of democracy—are refreshing and uplifting. They also present the principal means by which we can link order to justice, civility to mutual respect, and merit to fairness.

His radical democratic analysis and vision is a voice of sanity at a time of irrationality—a voice that understands rage yet transforms bitterness into bonding. This bonding is neither naive nor utopian; rather it is rooted in a candid encounter with the sources of our rage and an unleashing of the best in us for serious democratic engagement that goes far beyond our hostilities.

The best of American life has always been embodied and enacted by courageous figures who chose democracy—from Thomas Paine, Harriet Tubman, César Chávez, Ronald Takaki to Dolores Huerta. Duane Campbell makes it clear what it means to choose democracy in our classrooms, workplaces, homes, and civic life. In short, like James Baldwin, he frightfully reminds us that we either choose democracy now or ultimately witness the fire this time!

Cornel West
Harvard University

Preface

As teachers, readers of this second edition will participate in the construction of the future of our society. In deciding what future is constructed, I anticipate that substantive school reform, including the development of multicultural education, will be necessary for the preservation of our democratic community. *Choosing Democracy: A Practical Guide to Multicultural Education* seeks to assist future teachers to analyze their own cultural frames of reference and to develop a second, multicultural perspective. It further seeks to ally teachers' commitments to democratic opportunity and to expand that value position to include cultural democracy in school and equal educational opportunity.

In *Choosing Democracy: A Practical Guide to Multicultural Education,* Second Edition, I share the concerns of teachers struggling to develop multicultural curriculum and school practices. As a consequence of the dialogues between our students and the several co-authors, and the developmental usage of this text material with hundreds of students over the years, I remain convinced that "a nature of culture" approach, as developed in this text, provides most students with positive alternatives to continuing "Business as usual" and allows them to participate in re-conceptualizing their own basic assumptions and frames of reference.

Text Organization

Part One of this text combines a critical analysis of race, class, gender, and poverty as they apply in school. Chapters 1 through 5 include research evidence and conclusions about societal crises, culture, economics, racism, and gender discriminations to demonstrate how they impact classrooms, teachers, and schools. Armed with this information teachers can begin to understand how these matters affect their own classrooms. Dr. Manning Marable, co-author of Chapter 3 in the first edition, was unable to participate in the revision. The work in Chapter 3 has been revised by Drs. Forrest Davis and Eric Vega.

Part Two of the text then provides practical strategies for teachers to use in responding to problem areas. In Chapter 6 students consider the importance of developing quality interpersonal relationships with students and between students; an issue seldom addressed in other texts. It also offers ideas on promoting positive self-esteem and serving as a cultural mediator. The second edition has new teaching ideas on conflict resolution.

Chapter 7, "Teaching to Empower Students," has a number of teaching strategies that pursue goal empowerment and the philosophy of social reconstructionism. In response to reviewers' suggestions, Chapter 8 has been significantly revised to add more descriptions of the interaction between classroom management and democracy. Chapter 9 has new material on constructivism and defines more precisely the differences between critical thinking and critical theory. These chapters present more than five major approaches and one hundred concrete suggestions on how to change the classroom to adapt to our rapidly changing society. These include descriptions of strategies, objectives, and lesson plans on classroom management, guidance and lesson plans to initiate cooperative learning, and theory and practice of bilingual education and second language acquisition. Chapter 11 on Teaching Language Minority Children has been updated with the assistance of Dr. Kathryn Singh and Dr. Diane Cordero de Noriega.

By Part Three, readers will have developed both a theory and practice for multicultural education. They will have the background to examine the controversies and enter the dialogue on school reform. Chapter 12 describes the battle of the textbooks in California and New York and phonics battles in California. This chapter includes new materials on the accountability and standards efforts as major directions for school reform. With the assistance of Dr. Velma Villegas, this chapter also includes a description of how two Texas school districts used standards and accountability to dramatically improve student achievement. Chapter 13 has been substantially rewritten, with co-author Dr. Pia Wong, to report on several of the major efforts at school reform. It critiques most reform efforts for inadequate attention to the problems of the marginalized, students of color, and the poor. It concludes with a vision for pluralistic democracy and a description of some of the successful efforts of school reform including "Accelerated Schools" and the Comer model.

Using This Text

When I use this book with practicing teachers or in the preservice program while students are practice teaching, I often begin with Chapter 10 on cooperative learning and then proceed immediately to Chapter 8 on classroom management. These chapters help readers get started with practical strategies to resolve immediate class-room issues. After experiencing success with these strategies, readers often are more open to considering the alternative perspectives presented in other chapters.

In working with preservice teachers, I have found that most of them have little preparation in economics, and what they do have is only of limited usefulness, yet economics is central to arguments about school renewal. I have found the work of Nancy Folbre and the Center for Popular Economics particularly helpful in explaining complex economic issues. You will find their graphs used often in this text. This second edition has updated economic data throughout the text. These graphs and others as well as economic cartoons are included in an excellent work, *A Field Guide to the U.S. Economy* (1995, Amherst, MA: Center for Popular Economics). I recommend that you get a copy of it so you can photocopy graphs and transfer them to transparencies for use on an overhead projector. A second excellent source for economics is the publication *Social Stratification in the United States, The American Profile Poster* (1992, New York: The New Press). Its poster of U.S. social class and the many readable one- to two-page essays explaining aspects of the poster provide excellent preparation for teaching.

Activities and Teaching Strategies

At the ends of several chapters, you will find activities for further study of the subject covered in the chapter. These suggestions are drawn from how we teach this material in our basic Introduction to Multicultural Education class. I hope you find these useful.

These activities are followed by teaching strategies, which are written for your students to use as teachers in K through grade 12 classrooms. In Chapters 9, 10, and 11, these strategies include actual lesson plans that are designed to introduce readers to issues such as critical thinking and cooperative learning. I encourage you to add to and amend these lessons. Often in dealing with complex issues such as critical thinking, I find that students agree with the concept in general, but have only a limited understanding of how to implement the strategies in the classsroom. Students better understand the strategies and the need for advance planning of the strategies when they see them applied in lesson plans and lessons.

Conclusion

We have the skills, abilities, opportunities, and the hopes necessary to sustain one of the greatest social experiments in history, a democratic republic where wealth and a high quality of life are shared. It is the hope of the authors that *Choosing Democracy: A Practical Guide to Multicultural Education,* Second Edition, will contribute to teachers' opportunities to create a society where all students receive a quality education to prepare them to produce for the world, to compete in the world economy, to trade with the world, and to build a world with a diverse, democratic community.

Acknowledgments

Choosing Democracy is a product of years of dialogue with my students and former students. They consistently reteach me and remind me to respect the invaluable contributions that teachers make to the nation and to social justice. I have tried to pass on some of their wisdom. Particularly helpful since the first edition have been colleagues who have used the book in their classes, and former students Julieta Mendoza, Marcella Enriquez, Miguel Hernandez, Melinda Melendez, Enrique Sepulveda, and Marta Rodriguez.

I want to thank Dolores Delgado-Campbell for her co-authorship of Chapter 5, How Society and Schools Shortchange Girls and Boys. Her Chicana, feminist perspective added wisdom and insight to this important chapter. I also want to thank Manning Marable, Director of the Center on African American Studies at Columbia University, for his co-authorship of Chapter 3 in the first edition.

Although I graduated from a fine university, I learned more about the commitment to justice and equality by my own participation in several of the social justice movements of the last two decades. These continuing struggles for economic justice and social democracy provided organic intellectuals as tutors, coaches, guides, and teachers. Particularly important to my own education has been working with César Chávez, Bert Corona, Br. Ed Dunn, Dolores Huerta, and Philip Vera Cruz. Movements are more than the individual names. I owe much of my political education and respect for discipline and the working people to service with DSA and the United Farmworkers of America (AFL-CIO).

I am grateful to have worked with and learned from Michael Harrington, Shakoor Aljuwani, Cornel West, Barbara Ehrenreich, Manning Marable, Jose La Luz, Eric Vega and Joe Schwartz, among others. Their insights and critical reflections are found throughout this book.

I am fortunate to have a position within a community of scholars who have worked together for over a decade and in 1994 became the Department of Bilingual Multicultural Education at CSU, Sacramento—a people's university. The collective efforts and integrity of this group sustain me and guide me to resist the individualism and to avoid the narcissism and self-indulgence of many university departments. I particularly thank José Cintrón, Thomas P. Carter, Diane Cordero de Noriega, Forrest Davis, Richard Figueroa, Sue Heredia, Victoria Jew, Harold Murai, John McFadden, Nadeen Ruiz, Pia Wong, René Merino, Miguel Martinez, Leo Maestas, Carmen Sacco-Pollit, Ricardo Torres, and my students for their support at crucial moments, their insights, and their challenges.

The list of other scholars and friends who have helped me, supported me, and encouraged me to refine ideas is too long to enumerate. But particularly helpful have been Rudy Acuña, Henry T. Trueba of the University of Texas at Austin, Stephen Krashen, Carlos Muñoz, Armando Ayala, Patricia Gandara, and Denis Minamora.

I also wish to acknowledge the contribution of the reviewers, who offered many helpful suggestions: John Attinasi, California State University, Long Beach; Beverly E. Cross, University of Wisconsin, Milwaukee; Virginia Lazenby Pierce, Gustavus Adolphus College; and Pia Lindquist Wong, California State University, Sacramento.

The César E. Chávez Foundation and Marc Grossman assisted me with research, as did Nancy Folbre of the Center for Popular Economics, Lawrence Michel of the Economic Policy Institute, Norm Gold of the California Department of Education and staff of the library at California State University-Sacramento. Katy Romo has been an endless source of support.

To Dolores Delgado-Campbell, your more than twenty years' instruction from a Chicana feminist perspective informs all that I say and write. You have helped me to cross the borders of culture and to appreciate the dialectics of change.

To Javier Sean Campbell, your sense of conscience and integrity about your issues reteaches me to treat young people with dignity and respect. Hay que pensar en el futuro—y el futuro pertenece a su generacíon.

Brief Contents

Contents

Part 2
Teaching Strategies to Promote Democracy and Multicultural Education

Part 3

The Dialogue Between Democracy and Multicultural Education

Introduction

May the truth of my tale speak for me.

This book addresses teachers at a remarkable time in this country's history: the dramatic birth and development of a new, more culturally and linguistically diverse society. In the last two decades, economic turmoil and unprecedented levels of immigration have filled the public schools of the United States with a rich rainbow of faces. Many classrooms include dozens of cultures, and the use of three, four, or even five languages among students. Few societies have classrooms and schools as diverse as those faced by teachers in the United States each day.

In 1993, the U.S. Congress passed the Goals 2000: Educate America Act (see Chapter 13), among whose established goals were, "By the year 2000 U.S. students will be first in the world in science and math achievement," and "Every school in America will be free of drugs and violence and will offer a disciplined environment conducive to learning."

Spend time in our urban schools and you will quickly learn that we have achieved neither these nor the other goals set by Congress. In many ways, we are not even making progress toward them. This lack of progress requires an explanation, particularly for you as a future teacher.

Schools and teaching reflect society, and also participate in constructing future society. New forms of knowledge and new approaches to teaching have emerged in response to changes in our economy, in our society, and in our schools. Teachers have forged a variety of new strategies to respond to the demands for economic relevancy, democracy, equal opportunity, and this remarkable cultural and linguistic diversity.

In this book I share the insights gained by dozens of teachers working with bilingual and multicultural education as they developed new cross-cultural perspectives, new pedagogies and curricula, and new strategies and programs to respond both to the continuing social crises of schools that are failing and to educating students in these schools. Innovative teachers have found ways to validate students' diverse cultures while preparing them to participate in the social, economic, and political mainstream of U.S. society.

Teachers dedicated to multicultural education hope to build on the cultural diversity of our nation to create a new, dynamic, democratic—and fair—society, one not racked by the problems of poverty, homelessness, unemployment, community dislocations, and racial division. It is teachers and students in our urban centers who feel the brunt of demographic and economic changes in the United States. It is teachers who are developing the strategies to respond to the poverty and educational crises in our society.

What are these crises?

1. It is increasingly difficult for students and teachers alike to deal with and respond positively to cultural diversity, cross-cultural and class conflicts, violence, and oppression.

2. The stress students bring to school is aggravated by rapidly changing demographics and turbulent economic conditions, particularly in low-income communities.

3. More than one-third of all schools in major cities and rural poverty areas fail to provide a positive educational environment for an increasing number of poor and racial- and ethnic-minority students.

Teachers now know a great deal more about teaching in a cross-cultural environment than we knew in previous years. Effective teaching strategies and programs have been identified, clarified, and developed to take advantage of classroom diversity and to weave stronger, more united communities.

We know that teachers can make a difference. Dedicated teachers from all racial, ethnic, and cultural backgrounds can learn to be effective cross-cultural teachers and brokers of information that provides students with greater access to economic opportunity and social equality. We know a great deal about teaching. New teachers are fortunate to be able to learn from the experiences of their predecessors.

We now know that schools are not politically neutral. Teachers and schools are situated in specific economic, political environments. Study and reflection on that reality help teachers to select strategies that empower their students and help them succeed. Studies on the nature of race, class, and gender relations in our society provide teachers with a theoretical framework for selecting and evaluating teaching strategies (see Part One of this text).

But theoretical analysis of the problems of urban and problem schools is not enough. Teachers—particularly new teachers—need practical strategies for responding to the dozens of problems they face each day in the classroom, complex problems that have no one solution. In fact, the complexity of teacher decision making often baffles and, at times, overwhelms new teachers. While working through the problems of critical thinking, for example (see Chapter 9), teachers will also need clear, descriptive assistance on issues such as cooperative learning, classroom management, and helping students to learn English (see Part Two of this text).

On Objectivity

We know that study of race, class, and gender issues presents some readers with strong conflicts between what they are reading and their own worldviews. This raises the question of objectivity. Objectivity is a very important issue, and requires a serious response.

In this book I avoid the artificial "neutrality" often claimed by those who write using "academic" language. *Choosing Democracy* is written from the perspective that universities and textbooks are not neutral; they in fact present a point of view. Some texts are Eurocentric, some are male centered, some promote the status quo of economic and educational inequality as normal, natural, and inevitable. This work, like all textbooks, has a point of view.

Historian Howard Zinn, in *Declarations of Independence: Cross-examining American Ideology* (1990), deals with the question quite well:

> Writing this book, I do not claim to be neutral, nor do I want to be. There are things I value and things I don't. I am not going to present ideas objectively if that means I don't have strong opinions on which ideas are right and which are wrong. I will try to be fair to opposing ideas by accurately representing them. But the reader should know that what appears here are my own views on the world as it is and as it should be.
>
> I do want to influence the reader. But I would like to do this by the strength of argument and fact, by presenting ideas and ways of looking at issues that are outside of the orthodox. I am hopeful that given more possibilities people will come up with wiser conclusions. (p. 7)

I do not expect that readers will agree with every statement in this book. Rather, I and my coauthors encourage you to engage the ideas, to argue with the text, to prepare yourself to debate the conclusions.

We say more about dubious academic claims of objectivity in Chapter 7. The concepts of positivism and critical theory and the idea of the maintenance of ideological domination are important aspects of the general idea of academic objectivity. We discuss these concepts in Chapters 3 and 4.

Rather than hide our point of view, in *Choosing Democracy* we try to make our viewpoint explicit, so that you, the reader, can evaluate the point of view and make up your own mind.

As the spiritual says, "May the truth of my tale speak for me." I seek to share a view of our society as I and my colleagues in the schools have come to know it. We recognize both the hope and the problems of our schools.

A Few Words About Words

Language use is constantly changing. Since 1960, the most common term for one group of people has changed from *Negro* to *Black* to *African American.* In the same period, the most common term for another group changed from *Latin* to *Mexican American* to *Chicano* to *Latino.* These changes reflect substantial redefinition of the problems of race and ethnic conflict occurring in the curriculum, the schools, and U.S. society.

The purpose of language and of books is to communicate. In *Choosing Democracy,* I use terms based on two primary criteria:

1. What terms do the leaders, the intellectuals, and the community itself prefer?
2. What terms most precisely describe the group?

African Americans

I use the term *African American* for the nation's largest minority group, reflecting the preferred current usage. Ron Daniels, a leading African American political activist, argues that the effort to encourage the use of this term over *black* goes back to the early 1980s.

Black is a racial term that attempts to describe a racial group. Biologists encourage us to avoid use of race because the concept is so imprecise, while sociologists have documented the social importance of race (see Chapter 3).

Race and ethnicity are not the same. In the classic work, *They and We,* sociologist Peter Rose (1974) states:

> Groups whose members share a unique social and cultural heritage passed on from one generation to the next are known as ethnic groups. Ethnic groups are frequently identified by distinctive patterns of family life, language, recreation, religion and other customs that cause them to be differentiated from others. (p. 13)

The racial term *black* includes significant new immigrant groups of Haitians, Dominicans, and many Puerto Ricans. These groups share "blackness" and are treated as black by the larger U.S. society. They are, however, distinct ethnic and cultural groups.

Asian Americans

I use the term *Asian American* to describe the common experiences of Asian peoples in the United States. The enormous differences among the groups in language, culture, and immigration histories will lead more often to my referring to the specific group—for example, Vietnamese or Korean—rather than using the often-misleading general term. The discussion of population numbers for the Asian/Pacific Islander census subcategory in Chapter 3 illustrates the diversity.

European Americans

In this book I use the term *European American* to describe persons commonly referred to as *white*. Like the decision to use *African American* over *black*, the term *European American* describes the complex cultural heritage of the majority group and macroculture in the United States.

Most European Americans come from a mixture of a variety of cultural and national groups, such as German, Italian, Greek, Irish, and English. Members of these groups have been in the United States for generations, and most have little contact with their originating societies. They tend to consider themselves *Americans*. I do not use the designation *American* in this way in this text, as it excludes non-Europeans by implication.

I use the term *European American* in part to encourage members of this group to recognize their own ethnicity and cultural roots. The European American culture is substantially derived from Anglo-Saxon and English culture in language, common law, and Protestant denomination. Many immigrant groups, such as Greeks, Poles, Scandinavians, and Irish, have added to the developing common culture, as have the Catholic Church and the Jewish religion. European Americans, often conceptualized as a single group, are in fact a diverse population.

Native Americans

I have chosen to use the term *Native Americans* and *Indians* interchangeably within the text. Both terms are in popular usage and both have drawbacks. It is most important to recognize the tribal and historical diversity of members of the several native nations. Whenever possible, I refer to a group by its tribal name, for example, the Dineh, Cree, or Lakota nation.

Latinos

I use the term *Latino* to describe people who are descendants of immigrants from Latin American countries and the Caribbean and those persons of Spanish-Indian mixed heritage present in the Southwest when U.S. armies first moved into the area in the 1840s. The U.S. Census Bureau and many people use the term *Hispanic* for this group. Neither term is perfect, but *Hispanic* seems to overemphasize the influence of Spain and to deemphasize the major contributions of Native American and African cultures. Preference for either term varies by region. In the eastern half of the United States, *Hispanic* is more often used; in the West, *Latino* is more common.

Latinos share some cultural characteristics, yet are widely diverse. Sixty-two and one-third percent of Latinos are of Mexican ancestry; 12.7 percent are Puerto Ricans, 5.3 percent are descendants of Cubans, and the remaining 19.7 percent are from a variety of other Latin American and Caribbean nations.

The term *Latino* unfortunately connotes the male gender even when used in the plural to describe both males and females. When referring to females only, we will use the specific term *Latina* or *Chicana*. While most Latinos are of mixed race, the U.S. Census Bureau attempts to count Hispanics separately by racial categories: Indian, White, and Black. We discuss the variety within Latino culture in more detail in Chapter 2.

People of Color

In referring to the collective experiences of racial groups in the United States, I refer to *people of color* rather than to *minority groups*. This deliberate choice highlights the fact that in many urban areas, and in some rural regions such as Texas, Mississippi, and New Mexico, people of color are the majority, not minority, group.

Americans

I deliberately use the term *people of the United States* to refer to U.S. residents and citizens. As noted previously, the common term *American* is a misnomer in this context, and seems arrogant to some of the millions of people who live in the Americas. *American* refers to the residents of both North and South America (although it is true that it is primarily colloquially used to refer to residents of the United States). Thus, Brazilians, Peruvians, Costa Ricans, and Canadians are all Americans. The many indigenous groups in these nations are all Native Americans.

In spite of this, citizens of the United States of several racial and ethnic groups commonly refer to themselves as Americans. I do not. When other authors have used the term *American* to describe U.S. citizens, I have respected their word choice.

The Poor

The United States has a large poverty class. Official statistics number this group around 13 percent, while more careful studies show that as many as 20 percent of the U.S. population is poor in any one year. Poverty among children is growing.

When we use the term *poor* in this text, the reference is to people's economic status, not to their lifestyles, morals, values, or family stability. The term *low income* hides the gravity and permanence of poverty in our society. The many euphemisms developed to avoid saying "the poor" significantly obscure the magnitude of poverty in influencing school opportunities. At times, authors are so polite that they refuse to name reality.

The Problem of Categories

The formation of categories of people encourages social scientists to fit everyone into a category. Allegedly racial categories are particularly misleading. P. Rose (1974) illustrates the issue:

Mexican-Americans are largely the children of Spanish and Indian parentage; Puerto Ricans are the offspring of white and black as well as Indian ancestors; and many people who we call black are very white indeed. (p. 11)

Each person is both an individual and a member of several groups. We may fit into several categories: an individual may be Latino, Catholic, middle class, and a teacher, for example. Each individual's worldview is a complex compilation of diverse influences. Even within a single group such as Guatemalans, there are Indians, Latinos, men, women, children, immigrants, poor, and rich. Categories are necessary for analysis, but they are only transitional starting points for coming to understand the complex varieties of human experience.

Part 1

The Social, Economic, and Cultural Foundations of the Current School Crisis

Chapter 1

The Need for Multicultural Education

Why *Choosing Democracy?*

Our society and our schools are in rapid transition from the old to the new. Business and corporations have propelled our nation into a worldwide market, a place of economic and social instability. Meanwhile our governmental structures and schools remain pretty much as they were in the 1950s. The gap between the private, corporate society—growing, dynamic, starkly unequal—and the public institutions—underfunded, criticized, and under attack—grows each day. Yet the private society depends on the public sector to provide roads, schools, fire departments, water and electricity systems (infrastructure), educated workers, and domestic order.

We in the United States have created one of the most free and democratic societies in human history, but at great cost to Native Americans, African slaves, and many immigrant workers. Though far from perfect, we nonetheless offer our citizens more freedom and self-governance, and a higher standard of living, than is found in most of the world. Today, however, we stand in danger of losing this cherished freedom, self-governance, and standard of living both to domestic prejudice and intolerance and to chaotic and uncertain global market competition.

Schools and teachers promote either inequality or equality. Schools, whether public or private, may reinforce antidemocratic values and increase the hostile divi-

Figure 1.1   Laura's Story

The Sacramento Bee   Dateline: Monday, November 2, 1987

Tracking a Poor Reader's Stumbling Steps Through School

By Deb Kollars [Bee Staff Writer]

In an unruly classroom at California Middle School, a dark-eyed seventh-grader named Laura Montero sits quietly, day after day, stumbling over simple words like "justice," rarely finishing her work before the bell rings.

She is 13 years old, has average intelligence and reads at a third-grade level. At a time when many junior high students are bracing for algebra, compositions and "Romeo and Juliet," Laura has arrived at a different crossroads. She can barely read, spell, multiply or divide. Her teacher holds little hope she will ever catch up. She doesn't like school much anymore.

"I work as hard as I can, but I feel so behind," she said, looking down at her hands. "I'm scared of high school. I don't think I can do it."

The road Laura will follow is almost assured. She has spent her entire academic life on it and there's no turning back. When she emerges from public school within the next few years, Laura will likely join millions of adults who have serious literacy problems.

Her journey is not unique. California schools are failing to educate at least one-third of all students, according to test results, dropout rates and research by leading educational experts in the state.

Although test scores and graduation requirements indicate schools are doing better these days, many children who are poor, who live in big cities, who are minority members are coming through school without ever learning to read, to write, to understand history or math or science.

Laura's report cards show that year after year she was passed into the next grade at Oak Ridge Elementary School in Sacramento without having adequate reading and language skills for her age. The older she got, the further behind she fell.

Teachers in Laura's past said during interviews that they either didn't realize she was so far behind or did their best and could not do anything more about her low skills because of large class sizes and the serious home problems of many of their students.

Brooks Cassidy, her teacher now, said she probably won't progress much this year, either.

"I have a room full of students who are as far behind as Laura. I'll be lucky if I can raise her reading level by one year," he said. "I have so many behavior problems in this class right now that I just don't have the time to give her the individual help she needs."

Laura is known as a remedial student. She is not alone.

In the Sacramento City Unified School District, 872 of 2,951, or 30 percent of all seventh-graders, are two or more years below grade level in reading. Another 874 eighth-graders are similarly behind. In Los Angeles, 13,000 or 37 percent, of all seventh-graders are two or more years behind. In Oakland, in San Francisco, in San Diego, the story is the same.

These children reach middle school with severely low skills. They can't multiply five by six. They can't spell the names of the states. They can't use a ruler. They don't know what the plot of a story is. They have no idea where Israel lies on a map.

"I get kids who don't know that California is a state and Sacramento is a city," Luther Burbank High School teacher Barbara Johnson said, shaking her head.

'I don't think I can do it,' says Laura, looking ahead to high school.

Note. From "Tracking a Poor Reader's Stumbling Steps Through School," by D. Kollars, *Sacramento Bee*, 2 November 1987, p. 1. Copyright 1994 the *Sacramento Bee*. Reprinted by permission.

sions in our society, or teachers can reconstruct schools to become laboratories for democratic life.

We need to learn to live and work together, to at least tolerate one another, or we may yet tear our society apart. Public schools are the one institution in which we all participate, and where we need to teach young people tolerance, cooperation, and the skills of working together. Teaching is where we touch the future. In schools we have an opportunity to teach the coming generations to preserve and extend the United States as an experiment in building a democratic community. The task is far from over, and victory for democratic pluralism is far from certain.

What is the current state of public education in the United States? The answer you get to this question depends a great deal on where you look.

Many of our schools work quite well—students learn to read, to do math, and to write—but in a significant number of schools children are failing to master such basic skills and are failing to develop the commitments toward work, self-sufficiency, and self-government that preserving our democratic society requires.

In a special issue of *Education Week*, titled "Quality Counts: A Report Card on the Condition of Public Education in the 50 States," Olsen (1997) states the following:

> Contrary to popular belief, U.S. students generally outperform students from other large countries on international assessments of basic literacy. Our 8th graders score above average on international assessments in science but below average in mathematics.
>
> Meanwhile, millions of students attend school each day in crumbling facilities, to learn from teachers who have not majored in the subject areas they teach, in schools that are too big for them to be known well.
>
> Many children in our poorest urban and rural areas attend schools that lack even the barest necessities, from up-to-date textbooks to functioning toilets. Some of these schools systems spend thousands of dollars less per child than those in more affluent suburbs. (p. 7)

In the 36 states participating in the National Assessment of Educational Progress, a majority of fourth- and eighth-grade students perform at the "basic" level or below in reading and math ("Quality Counts," 1997, p. 26). Performers at the "basic" level only partially master the knowledge and skills needed for grade-level work (Table 1.1).

Table 1.1   Comparison Scores on 1994 NAEP Reading Exam, Percentage of Fourth Graders by State

State	At Proficient Level	At Basic Level	Below Basic Level
California	18	56	26
Arizona	24	48	28
Florida	23	50	27
New York	27	43	30
Texas	26	32	42
National average	28	41	31

Note. Adapted from "Quality Counts: A Report Card on the Condition of Public Education in the 50 States," *Education Week* (1997, 22 January), pp. 30–31.

All states have a large number of students performing "below basic level." These students would have difficulty with grade-level student work. The great majority of these students are found in specific schools in specific districts. As reported in Brown and Haycock (1984),

> there is considerable evidence that our system denies minority youngsters an education of the same quality as that provided to other youngsters. When predominantly minority schools are compared to predominantly white schools, certain systematic differences begin to appear. By virtually every measure of quality, predominantly minority schools are the losers: teacher quality, staffing ratios, college prep classes, overcrowding, and instructional materials. (p. 8)

With the publication of *A Nation At Risk* (National Commission on Excellence in Education, 1983), the United States began one of its periodic decades of school reform. However, as we approach the twenty-first century, not much has changed. I contend that schools and districts that were successful in 1983 remain so today, except in those locations where the economy of the community itself has changed from middle class to marginalized and poverty stricken. Schools and districts that were failing in 1983, including most of our large urban school districts, continue to fail students today. There have been no substantive changes in student achievement levels in the last 30 years. In the National Assessment of Educational Progress, performers at the "basic" level are defined as students who only partially master the knowledge and skills needed for grade-level work ("Quality Counts," 1997). A debilitating achievement gap continues between white, black, and Latino students (Ravitch, 1997).

Not only do schools fail, entire school systems fail. Conservative critic Diane Ravitch describes the New York City system as follows (Ravitch & Viteritti, 1997):

New York: The Obsolete Factory

> It is difficult to imagine an organizational structure as hapless or incorrigible as the New York City public school system. By any reasonable measure of educational effectiveness, the system is not working well. Sprawling, rigid, machinelike, uncompromising, it is the premiere [sic] example of factory model schooling. Its centennial in 1996 passed uncelebrated and unremarked, possibly because its multitude of embarrassments made celebration unseemly. The school system has become a symbol of unresponsive bureaucracy that somehow rebuffs all efforts to change it. It is the creature of another era, designed as a machine in which orders flowed from the top and were quickly implemented below with no regard for the ideas or opinions of either its workers or customers.
>
> The system worked well enough in an earlier age. In its first half century, the percentage of graduates increased in each decade, and steady progress seemed the order of the day. The economy also had good jobs for students who left school without graduating. But today, progress has stalled: little more than 50 percent of the youngsters who start high school reach graduation, and the economy has few places for high school dropouts. (pp. 17–18)

Although most citizens believe that we must reform our schools, teachers, administrators, education professors, and other school workers have generally been unwilling to rethink old assumptions and prior ways of teaching and learning. During the last decade, school reform advocates in many states have been unable to convince voters and political leaders to invest the time, funds, and discipline necessary to reform failing systems.

What once seemed liked a consensus in society is breaking down. One would think that we could all agree that children ought to be able to attend public schools that are safe, where gangs and narcotics are not common, where roofs don't leak and plaster doesn't fall from the ceilings. We ought to be able to at least assure our students that the toilets work and fresh water is available. But we cannot. Elected officials and voters repeatedly and consistently refuse to make this choice, by declining to adequately fund schools in low-income areas. As a result, "millions of students attend school each day in crumbling facilities, to learn from teachers who have not majored in the subject area they teach, in schools that are too big for them to be known well" (Olsen, 1997, p. 7).

And while in 1954 the U.S. Supreme Court in *Brown v. Board of Education* determined that racially separate school systems and schools were inherently unequal, the best evidence indicates that at present schools and the teaching profession are becoming more segregated by race than they were in the 1950s. In *Dismantling Desegregation: The Quiet Reversal of Brown v. Board of Education* (Orfield, Eaton, & the Harvard Project, 1996), Orfield argues, "National data show that most segregated African American and Latino schools are dominated by poor children but that 96 percent of white schools have middle-class majorities. The extremely strong relationship between racial segregation and concentrated poverty in the nation's schools is a key reason for the educational differences between segregated and integrated schools" (p. 53).

What is going on here? Do we have a school crisis or a racial crisis? Or is the school crisis a racial crisis?

As you enter the teaching profession, it is important to develop your own position on the vital matter of equal educational opportunity. You will soon directly experience one or more aspects of the issue. Will you find your first job in a clean, well-built, modern school with high standards for professional conduct and high student achievement? Or will you be assigned to a segregated school, or to a segregated program within an integrated school, where students lack the basic conditions of safety and security, where some teachers are just marking time and controlling kids? Will your first school have clean windows and modern computers, or broken windows and locked bathrooms? And how did we get to the present situation, where those schools with mostly European American students have decent learning conditions and those with primarily African American and/or Latino students do not?

Schools do not exist in a vacuum. They are not isolated from their neighborhoods and communities. Inequality in schooling reflects inequality in society. Schools reflect and re-create our society and its values. To understand the particular failure of schools serving poor children and many students belonging to ethnic, language, and cultural minorities, we must first consider the context, the environment within which these schools exist.

The Structural Crisis in Our Society

Both our society and our schools are in crisis. In many areas, crime and street gangs make travel unsafe at night. Funds have been cut for basic government services, such as police and fire protection, emergency medical response, public safety, and schools. Unemployment and homelessness have continued at recession levels for decades for certain populations. Families are stressed and often destroyed by poverty, crime, and violence.

How do you view wealth and income in our society? Many authors and the media in general typically portray the United States as a classless society (Luhman, 1996). In this work I present a perspective, based on actual census data and as described in the writings of Michael Harrington, Cornel West, Manning Marable, Howard Zinn, and others, that U.S. society in fact consists of three societies, or classes: an upper (affluent), a middle, and a lower (poor).

Forbes magazine reports that Bill Gates III (Microsoft Corp.) is worth $58.4 billion, Paul Gardner Allen (Microsoft Corp.) is worth $22 billion, and the Walton family (Wal Mart Stores) is worth over $55 billion, but most of us are not billionaires or millionaires (*Forbes*, 1999). Income distribution for the middle class and poor is discussed in Chapter 4.

The rich, with incomes exceeding $250,000 per year, are affluent, comfortable, and successful. They have access to cars, the latest technology, excellent health care and schools, and spacious homes. The largest class, the middle class, itself is divided, as we shall see in Chapter 4. Some live well and have good health care and schools. Bartlett and Steele (1992) argue that others in the middle class are struggling to keep their jobs, their income, and their standard of living in a rapidly changing economy. Most teachers, and most future teachers, come from the economically stressed middle class.

The third society is made up of the chronic poor and those temporarily forced into poverty by loss of jobs, health crises, or economic recession (West, 1993a). In this tier, we find levels of poverty, crime, and health hazards that are typical of underdeveloped nations (Hacker, 1992). As I will detail in Chapter 4, this society of poverty is growing the fastest, particularly among children. Where would you place yourself in this diagram of class division in the United States?

The extremes of wealth and poverty among neighborhoods lead directly to extreme differences in the quality of schooling offered to children. Schools on one side of town serve children of the affluent and middle classes, many of whom can look forward to a bright economic future. In poor neighborhoods, middle-class teachers face overcrowded classrooms filled with children from immigrant groups and from African American and Latino communities. The quality of instruction and school experience in middle-class schools varies dramatically from that of schools serving poor and working-class children (Darling-Hammond, 1995). As Laura's story reveals (see Figure 1.1), school failure is endemic in many poor neighborhoods in our major cities.

A related problem, and one of the ironies arising from the growing race–class divisions in our society, is that while the middle class provides most of the teachers, most new teaching positions are in districts and schools filled with poor children from a variety of racial, cultural, national, and linguistic backgrounds. Many of these children have no reasonable opportunity to achieve the same social and economic privileges enjoyed by the person instructing them (Darling-Hammond, 1995).

Bartlett and Steele (1992) describe the destruction of economic opportunity for millions of middle-class and formerly middle-class families:

Worried that you are falling behind, not living as well as you once did? Or expected to?

Worried that the people who represent you in Congress are taking care of themselves and their friends at your expense?

You are right. Keep worrying.

For those people in Congress that wrote the complex tangle of rules by which the economy operates have, over the last twenty years, rigged the game—by design and default—to favor the privileged, the powerful and the influential. At the expense of everyone else.

Seizing the opportunity, an army of business buccaneers began buying and selling and trading companies the way most Americans buy, sell and trade knickknacks at a yard sale. They borrowed money to destroy, not to build. They constructed the financial houses of cards, then vanished before they collapsed.

Caught between the lawmakers in Washington and the dealmakers on Wall Street have been millions of American workers forced to move from jobs that once paid $15 per hour into jobs that now pay $7. If, that is, they aren't already victims of mass layoffs, production halts, shuttered factories and owners who enrich themselves by doing the damage and then walking away.

As a result, the already rich are richer than ever; there has been an explosion in overnight new rich: life for the working class is deteriorating, and those at the bottom are trapped. For the first time in this century, members of the generation entering adulthood will find it impossible to achieve a better lifestyle than their parents. Most will be unable to even match their parents' middle-class status.

Indeed the growth of the middle class—one of the underpinnings of democracy in this country—has been reversed. By government action. (p. 2)

As stated in a recent report from the Annie E. Case Foundation (1997), "The 7.1 million children growing up in poor communities today face tough odds. Research predicts that they are at a greater risk of being sick and having inadequate health care; of being parents before they complete school; of being users of available drugs; of being exposed to violence; and of being incarcerated before they are old enough to vote" (p. 5).

As the gap between the lower and upper classes grows, our secondary schools, particularly in the cities, are increasingly ineffective in preparing non-college-bound students for entrance into a workforce that requires advanced education and computer skills. Some middle-class children have access to higher education, enabling them to move into well-paying professional careers. But the majority of children of the working class will end up in the service sector as fast-food employees, service workers, and maintenance personnel earning (using the prevailing wages of today's economy) less than $8.00 per hour (Reich, 1991b). Unless education gives working-class students access to new careers, knowledge systems, and technology, they will join the working poor.

In Chapter 4 we will demonstrate that from the point of view of the unemployed, the underemployed, and the poor, our society is deeply troubled and divided. As described there, the official poverty level is artificially low. Realistically, life is difficult for families living at 200 percent of the poverty level, at about what the U.S. Census Bureau considers the "low budget" line. There are some 31 million people trapped in this lower strata of our economy. (U.S. Bureau of the Census, 1996b; Children's Defense Fund, 1997). As jobs move out of the cities, the poverty and desperation of these families increase. Their lives become increasingly brutal. Some young people turn to crime, violence, and acts of rage that make battlegrounds of schools and neighborhoods in some cities (West, 1993b).

A Day in the Life

The Children's Defense Fund has earned a national reputation for its advocacy work. *The State of America's Children: Yearbook, 1997* (Children's Defense Fund, 1998) describes a day in the lives of children in the United States (Figure 1.2).

Mishel and Bernstein (1995) report that over 25.6 percent of all children come from a family in poverty. For African American children, the figure is 51 percent; for Latinos, 43 percent (Children's Defense Fund, 1997). And poverty among the young is rapidly increasing. As West (1993b) notes, "The tragic plight of our children clearly reveals our deep disregard for public well being" (p. 7).

Families living in poverty participate less economically and politically. Their children attend understaffed, poorly financed schools. Robert Reich (1991a), then a Harvard economist and soon to be secretary of labor in the Clinton administration, used examples from Massachusetts to demonstrate this division:

Figure 1.2   Every Day in the United States

Note. From *The State of America's Children: Yearbook 1997* (back cover) by the Children's Defense Fund, 1998, Washington, DC: Author. Reprinted by permission.

3	young people under age 25 die from HIV infection
6	children commit suicide
13	children are homicide victims
14	children are killed by firearms
81	babies die
280	children are arrested for violent crimes
443	children are born to mothers who had late or no prenatal care
781	children are born of low birthweight
1,403	children are born to teenage mothers
1,827	children are born without health insurance
2,430	children are born into poverty
2,756	children drop out of high school every day
3,436	children are born to unmarried mothers
5,753	children are arrested
8,470	children are reported abused or neglected
11.3 million	children have no health insurance
14.5 million	children live in poverty

In Belmont, an affluent suburb of Boston, the average teacher earned $36,100 per year, only 3% of the eighteen-year-olds dropped out of school, and 80% of the seniors chose to go on to college. In nearby Chelsea, a more impoverished town, the average teacher earned $26,200, more than half of the eighteen-year-olds did not graduate, and only 10% planned to attend college. (p. 44)

If you were a parent in Chelsea or in one of the hundreds of other impoverished areas, would you not resent the lack of opportunity for future success offered your children? When you become a teacher, how will you feel about the differences in pay, working conditions, and student attitudes, and about your own opportunities for success?

The Emerging Diversity of Students

Cultural diversity is increasing in our society and in our schools (Figure 1.3). The case of California illustrates the impact of immigration on schools. Since 1977, the number of students who struggle to learn English has increased steadily and sharply. According to the *Language Census Report for California Public Schools* (California Department of Education, 1997) these students now comprise over 24.6 percent of the total school population in the state, up from 15 percent of the student population in 1988. The single largest group of limited-English students is Spanish speaking (80%), followed by those who speak Vietnamese (3%), Cantonese (2%), Hmong

Figure 1.3   U.S. Population by Ethnicity, 1985 and 1998

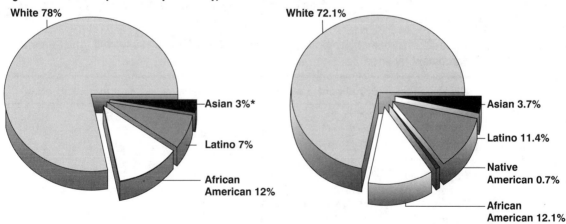

White 78%

Asian 3%*

Latino 7%

African American 12%

White 72.1%

Asian 3.7%

Latino 11.4%

Native American 0.7%

African American 12.1%

* Includes Asian, Pacific Islander, American Indian, Eskimo, Aleut

* Includes Asian, Pacific Islander, Eskimo, Aleut

(a)   (b)

Note. From *Resident Population of the United States* by U.S. Bureau of the Census, 1998, retrieved 21 January 1999 from the World Wide Web: http://www.census.gov:80/population/estimates/

(2%), Pilipino (2%), Cambodian (Khmer), and dozens of other languages including Farsi, Russian, and Polish.

So, if you take a teaching position in California, New York, Illinois, Texas, or in most other urban school districts, you can expect that out of a class of 28 students, up to 7 will not speak English fluently. How are you going to teach them in your subject if they do not completely understand English?

Students from these minority language groups are concentrated in specific school districts and in the elementary grades. While a few benefit from high-quality bilingual education programs, the great majority of teachers assigned to these students are unprepared to help them (Gándara, 1997). Most immigrant students receive inadequate English instruction and little academic support in their native language (Gándara, 1997).

In the 1970s, 1980s, and 1990s, the Latino population became the largest of the nation's refugee and immigrant groups. More than one-third of all Latino children live in poverty (Children's Defense Fund, 1997; U.S. Bureau of the Census, 1996b). High school completion rates for most students have improved, but remain lowest for Latino youth, and Latinos are less likely to attend college than other young people (U.S. Bureau of the Census, 1997). Latino males have a substantially higher unemployment rate than the national average, while Latinas (Latino women) suffer more of a wage disparity between men's and women's wages than any other group (Amott & Matthaei, 1991).

In California, Hawaii, New Mexico, Texas, and Mississippi, the sum of all "minority" students now constitute a majority of the total student population (U.S. Department of Education, 1996). At the same time in urban areas throughout the country, European Americans students are becoming a minority (Table 1.2). In

Table 1.2   Enrollment of Ten Largest Central City Districts 1994–1995, and Percent of Enrollment by Race

City	Enrollment	White	Black	Latino	Asian
New York	953,535	17.6	36	36.5	9.5
Los Angeles	613,192	11.4	14	67.2	7.2
Chicago	402,136	11.3	54.7	30.6	3.2
Dade (Miami)	314,881	15.1	33.8	49.7	1.3
Philadelphia	202,387	21.1	63.1	10.9	4.7
Houston	197,722	11.7	35.2	50.3	2.7
Detroit	164,258	6.3	89.7	2.8	0.9
Dallas	142,630	12.8	43.5	41.6	1.7
San Diego	125,389	30.7	16.7	32.3	19.7
Memphis	109,611	16.8	81.8	.4	1.1

Note. From "Deepening Segregation in American Public Schools: A Special Report from the Harvard Project on School Segregation" by G. Orfield, M. Bachmeier, D. R. James, and T. Eitle, Harvard Project on School Desegregation, 1997, *Equity and Excellence in Education* (September), p. 33, Table 11. Reprinted by permission.

other states such as Maine, Minnesota, Indiana, Utah, and Wyoming, the population remains over 80 percent European American (U.S. Department of Education, 1996). Students from all of these areas, schools, ethnic groups, and classes will have to work together and cooperate in the twenty-first-century workforce.

The rapid changes in the ethnic and cultural composition of our society worry many adults, particularly those who presently enjoy power, influence, and privilege. In April 1990, *Time* magazine devoted a special issue to what they considered the "crisis" of a changing nation. Its editors wrote, "In the 21st Century—and that's not far off—racial and ethnic groups in the U.S. will outnumber whites for the first time. The 'browning of America' will alter everything in our society, from politics and education, to industry, values, and culture" (Henry, 1990, p. 28).

The Fire This Time

In the absence of quality educational opportunities and enlightened social policy, increased racial diversity interacts with painful changes in the economy to produce racial polarization and an increase in violence. In 1963, James Baldwin published an essay entitled "The Fire Next Time," predicting widespread violence if racial justice was further delayed. In 1965, 1967, and 1968, major U.S. cities were, in fact, rocked by race riots as economic conditions declined in urban areas. Cornel West claims that there were "329 revolts in 257 cities between 1964 and 1968" (West, 1993a, p. 21). In 1985, 1990, and 1992, race disturbances returned to plague our cities, the largest insurrection occurring in Los Angeles from April 29 through May 1, 1992 (Figures 1.4 and 1.5).

The cost of the 1992 Los Angeles riots: 51 dead, 1,032 injured, 3,000 arrested, $1.5 billion in property damage. The people hurt most by this rebellion and riot were the residents of the neighborhoods where the rioting took place: the people of South Central Los Angeles—a predominantly African American neighborhood—and the people of the Pico Union district—a predominantly Latino immigrant neighborhood (West, 1993a).

Racial prejudice had divided neighborhood against neighborhood, African American families against Korean shop owners ("America on Trial," 1992). The children watched this racial polarization going on around them and on their television screens at night. It frightened and confused them.

On Monday, 4 May 1992, Los Angeles's 800,000 students returned to school in their devastated communities. In many schools, teachers focused discussion on the events. Students wanted to talk, to share their own stories. Some students wrote, some spoke up, some listened. In Compton, near the riot area, a group of parents went to the child care center and protected "their school" from arsonists.

The rebellion in Los Angeles and simultaneous disturbances in Seattle, San Francisco, and Atlanta confirmed that living conditions for many poor, disenfranchised African Americans and Latinos had deteriorated in the decades of the 1970s and 1980s. The lesson of the riots is that our society once again is moving toward racial

Figure 1.4   Los Angeles, 1992
Source: AP/Wide World Photos

Figure 1.5 **Selected Race Riots in U.S. History**

Date	Place	Results
1866	Memphis, TN	48 dead
December, 1874	Vicksburg, MS	70 dead
July, 1917	East St. Louis, IL	49 dead
May, 1921	Tulsa, OK	36 dead
June 3–5, 1943	Los Angeles, CA	Thousands of U.S. sailors attack Mexican youth
July 23, 1943	Detroit, MI	43 dead
August 11, 1965	Los Angeles, CA	35 dead
July 23, 1967	Detroit, MI	43 dead
April 4, 1968	Pittsburgh, PA Chicago, IL and other U.S. cities	Riots erupt after the assassination of Martin Luther King, Jr.
August 29, 1969	Los Angeles, CA	3 dead; Chicano anti-war march becomes a three-day battle with police.
May 17, 1980	Miami, FL	15 dead and 743 arrested, mostly African American men.
April 28–May 1, 1992	Los Angeles, CA	51 dead

and ethnic polarization. Angry, alienated young people—African Americans, Latinos, and members of other ethnic groups—cluster and stagnate in our inner cities. As I will show in Chapters 3 and 4, economic opportunity for the working class declined in the 1980s and remained stagnant in the 1990s. This stalled economy does not provide working-class children with entry-level jobs, and the schools have not reached them. Many feel abandoned by the economic system and oppressed by entrenched authority, represented on the streets as police power.

Unlike the substantial response to the riots of the 1960s, the 1992 riots sparked no national-level investigatory commissions, nor were substantial new programs funded to combat poverty, racial division, and alienation. Outside of Los Angeles, most of the political leadership went back to business as usual and tried to forget that the riots had occurred, ignoring the root causes of the violence. School leaders and teachers were left to deal with the continuing crises of racial division, crime, and poverty.

By 1995 the U.S. economy had improved for all except the poor, but racial division in the society continued to fester. In 1994, California voters passed Proposition 187, which banned illegal immigrants, including students in schools, from receiving public education, prenatal care, and other social services and required that teachers and other school personnel report any children they suspected of lacking proper immigration papers. In 1996, a majority of Californians voted to abolish affirmative action. Legislative campaigns against immigrants, against gays and lesbians, and against affirmative action programs became unifying themes for conservative political victories around the nation. On 11 September 1997, a group of Asian American organizations issued a report describing growing hate crimes against Asian immigrants in our nation and filed a 27-page petition with the U.S. Commission on Civil Rights, calling on the Commission to investigate widespread bias (King & Jackson, 1997).

In September 1998, the Advisory Board to the President's Initiative on Race, chaired by distinguished historian John Hope Franklin, wrote in *One America in the 21st Century: Forging a New Future*:

> At the dawn of a new century, America is once again at a crossroads on race. The eminent African American scholar W. E. B. DuBois noted decades ago that the main problem of the 20th century would be the color line. Indeed, at the end of the 20th century, the color of one's skin still has a profound impact on the extent to which a person is fully included in American society and provided the equal opportunity and equal protection promised to all Americans in our chartering documents. The color of one's skin continues to affect an individual's opportunities to receive a good education, acquire the skills to get and maintain a good job, have access to adequate health care, and receive equal justice under the law. . . .
>
> The path toward racial progress has had a difficult, sometimes bloody history: Our early treatment of American Indians and Alaska Natives, followed by the enslavement and subsequent segregation of African Americans and then the conquest and legal oppression of Mexican Americans and other Hispanics, the forced labor of Chinese Americans, the internment of Japanese Americans, and the harassment of religious minorities is a history of which many Americans are not fully aware and no American should be proud. (pp. 35–36)

But then when the Advisory Board turned to recommendations, they began as follows: "Enhance early childhood learning [and] [s]trengthen teacher preparation and equity. There is a strong consensus that high-quality teachers are our most valuable educational resource, and the need for high-quality teachers is increasing; an estimated 2 million new teachers will be hired in the next decade. . . . " The board continued: "If we are serious about ensuring that all children have access to high-quality education and high standards, the Nation must make a national priority the task of increasing the number of high-quality teachers with high expectations for all students" (President's Initiative on Race, 1998, p. 61).

As you will read in the following chapters, the contradictions within our society, the positive elements of our great democratic experiment and the troubling legacy of racial, gender, and class conflict, will in many ways shape both the resources available to you as a teacher and your daily decisions of what and how to teach.

One measure of the differences in our society is clearly visible in the data shown in Table 1.3.

The Crisis in Our Schools

Citizens of the United States have long believed in education. For over 100 years, parents have trusted the public schools to provide a better future for their children. Today, however, public schooling is in crisis, particularly for children living in

Table 1.3   U.S. Average Annual Income 1996 (in dollars)

Household median income	$35,492
Family households	$43,082
Female head of household	$21,564
Race of householder	
White	$37,161
White, not Hispanic	$38,787
Black	$23,482
Asian and Pacific Islander	$43,276
Hispanic origin	$24,906

Note. From *Poverty in the United States 1995* by U.S. Bureau of the Census, 1996, retrieved 17 February 1999 from the World Wide Web: http://www.census.gov:80/prod/2/poverty95/p60-194

poverty. At least 14.7 million children live below the poverty line set by the U.S. government (U.S. Bureau of the Census, 1996b). This line is set artificially low and understates the real gravity of poverty in our society (Mishel & Bernstein, 1995).

Of these poor children living below the official poverty line—41 percent of all African American children, 39.5 percent of all Latino children, 19.2 percent of all Asian children, 41.4 percent of Native American children, 16 percent of all European American children—most attend underfunded, poverty-stricken schools (Children's Defense Fund, 1997). The government-established poverty level in 1995 was $12,158 per year for three-person families and $15,569 per year for four-person families (U.S. Bureau of the Census, 1996b; Children's Defense Fund, 1997).

A debate on educational reform raged during the 1980s and 1990s, but there was widespread disagreement on the cause of the education crisis. As the authors of *A Nation at Risk* (National Commission on Excellence in Education, 1983) dramatically warned, "Our nation is at risk. Our once-unchallenged preeminence in commerce, industry, science, and technological innovation is being overtaken by competitors throughout the world. . . . The educational foundations of our society are presently being eroded by a rising tide of mediocrity that threatens our very future as a nation and a people" (p. 5).

Presidents, the U.S. Congress, and numerous state legislatures passed reform plans, including President Clinton's *American Schools 2000* initiative. Several states have discussed dramatic program changes. However, by the most basic measures, after 20-plus years of political posturing, the quality of education for schools in poverty-stricken areas remains essentially the same—dismal ("Quality Counts," 1997).

From the conservative point of view, the problem in the 1980s was mediocrity. But from the point of view of advocates for the poor and those monitoring the growing urban crisis, the nature of the problem was quite different. Reviewing the major arguments about the source of the crisis in education, Bastian, Fruchter, Gittell, Greer, and Hoskins (1985) described the problem in these terms:

There is, however, a far more fundamental crisis in our schools. It is located where it has always been, in the bottom layers of a multi-tiered system, in our failure to provide even minimal levels of quality to the school population that is working class and poor. This crisis can be measured in some stark statistics: 50–80% of all inner-city teenagers drop out of high school, 1 million teenagers cannot read above the third-grade level, 13% of all seventeen-year-olds are functionally illiterate, 28% of all students do not get high school diplomas. (p. 26)

These authors made this claim in 1985. In 1996, the Harvard Project convincingly argued that matters had not improved. Many African American, Latino, and other minority children are concentrated in de facto segregated schools where low expectations are the norm. Orfield, Eaton, and the Harvard Project (1996) demonstrate that our nation is becoming increasingly divided by race and class, and that this resegregation destroys the educational opportunities for millions of school children.

When schools are segregated by race and class, those in poor areas have more problems of control, more broken windows, fewer high-level classes and fewer well-prepared teachers (Colvin, 1998). Perhaps not surprisingly, as a new teacher in a district, you may well be assigned to just such a school, while experienced teachers transfer out in search of more reasonable teaching and learning conditions.

Problems in elementary schools become crises in middle schools and high schools. Dropout rates soar. The gap widens in the quality of curriculum and student retention between schools serving the rich and middle class and schools serving the poor. A major problem is the use of a system called *tracking*, wherein individuals are identified according to specified physiological, cultural, socioeconomic, or academic criteria and placed in academic course schedules (tracks) designed to fulfill select educational prerequisites or to develop a specific skill set. Tracking students on the basis of alleged "ability groups" and sometimes hostile teacher attitudes deprives many young people of an enriched, relevant, and motivating school experience (see Chapter 10). The chaos and destruction of life in certain areas of our cities make it difficult for students to study and to learn in school (see Chapter 8).

For some young people, the results are catastrophic. Hacker (1992) points out that a young African American child born in the United States is as likely to go to prison as to college. "A man living in New York's Harlem is less likely to reach sixty-five than is a resident of Bangladesh. . . . Black men outnumber whites as murder victims by a factor of seven" (p. 46). Economic and educational opportunities for many Latinos, Native Americans, and poor European Americans are similarly bleak.

In some schools, teaching and learning conditions are an outright scandal. In Los Angeles, California, schools cannot hire enough credentialed teachers to face classrooms already overcrowded with more than 35 students per class. In 1998 the district had 20,000 teachers per day serving as long-term substitutes, indicating that they are not sufficiently prepared to legally be in charge of a class for more than monthlong temporary assignments. The district has over 6000 teachers on emergency credentials, indicating that they do not have a credential for the subject which they are teaching (Colvin, 1998). The Los Angeles situation is an extreme, but similar conditions exist in the schools of New York, Boston, Chicago, Dallas, Detroit, Philadelphia, Dallas, Denver, and many other urban centers ("Quality Counts," 1998).

Schools without prepared and stable teaching faculties do not provide safe or productive environments for learning ("High Standards," 1998). The persistence of these inadequate and disruptive conditions clearly indicates that society accepts the failure of many of its children, particularly the failure of minority children in urban areas. Although many dedicated teachers continue to struggle against the scandal of urban public schooling, individual efforts are not enough. We need substantial and effective reform. The large percentage of African American and Hispanic students who score "below basic" on the national *Reading Report Card* (Figure 1.6) clearly reveal the urgency of the problem.

Schools and Democracy

Ideally, all citizens of the United States consent to a social contract by which we agree to work together to improve our common standard of living, particularly for

Figure 1.6   1998 "Below Basic" Reading Level by Ethnicity

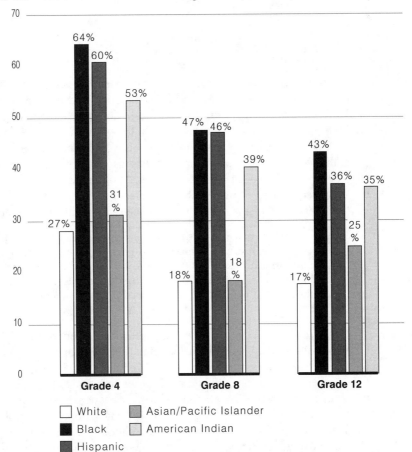

Note. Data from *1998 Reading Report Card* by National Center for Education Statistics, National Assessment of Educational Progress, Washington, DC: U.S. Department of Education.

our children. We all benefit from a society in which children learn to read and write, to be productive in the workforce, and to participate in democratic decision making. But only one portion of U.S. society, the middle class, receives quality public education. (Most children of the upper class attend private schools.) The children of the poor are often excluded from a high-quality public education experience. They are failed in school and too often leave without graduating. School failure makes most of them ineligible or not interested in college preparation. This exclusion, this marginalization, damages not only their future, but also endangers the economy and the democratic community.

In this book I argue that multicultural education is an integral part of the effort to create a more democratic society. We must then define democracy. Dahl (1985) lists the following criteria to describe the democratic process:

1. Equal votes
2. Effective participation
3. Enlightened understanding
4. Final control of the agenda by the people
5. Inclusiveness

A democratic society encourages maximum citizen participation in political decision making, respects the rule of the majority, and protects the rights of minorities. Fundamental values of our constitutional form of democracy include justice, equality, protection of individual rights, and the promotion of the common good.

Many people believe that public schools were created in part to promote these democratic ideals. Others see public schooling as primarily preparation for work. As a new teacher, you will need to consider these two perspectives. John Dewey (1859–1952), the preeminent U.S. philosopher of education, described in the "Democratic Conception of Education" the relationship between schools and democracy:

> A society which makes provisions for participation in its good of all its members on equal terms and which secures flexible readjustment of its institutions through interaction of the different forms of associated life is in so far democratic. Such a society must have a type of education which gives individuals a personal interest in social relationships and control, and the habits of mind which secure social changes without introducing disorder. (Dewey, 1916/1966, p. 90)

Civitas: A Framework for Civic Education (Center for Civic Education, 1991) elaborates on the U.S. constitutional heritage and applies it to teaching. The authors argue that schools must prepare all citizens for equal participation and responsibility in society. Schools, as public institutions, must also provide equal preparation and equal opportunity for entrance into a prosperous economic life. Despite these democratic goals, however, inequities among schools are a reality. Extreme inequalities in public funding and quality of schooling exist and act to deny, thwart, and obstruct democratic opportunity in our society (Kozol, 1991).

The preservation of prosperity and democracy depends on a system of education that prepares *all* children (majority and minority) equally to achieve high standards of success in the basic skills of reading, writing, and arithmetic, and that fully moti-vates them to participate in maintaining our democratic community. Democracy requires quality education for all, not just for a favored few.

Today, groups that have been historically excluded (African Americans, Latinos, Native Americans, some immigrants) seek opportunity throughout society for jobs, housing, health, and schooling. Their struggle focuses most immediately on U.S. public schools because, although these individuals often cannot undo the hardship and depri-vation of their own lives, they can and do insist on equal opportunity for their children.

Democracies are characterized by a formal equality of political power for each citizen. In landmark court cases in 1896 (*Plessy v. Ferguson*) and 1954 (*Brown v. Board of Education*), the U.S. Supreme Court decided that schools, as public insti-tutions financed by tax dollars, have an obligation to provide equal opportunity for all students. For a democracy to achieve its promise, schools must provide an arena where all students are equally prepared to fully participate in the economic and political life of society.

From the 1970s through the 1990s, a new antipolitical force emerged in the United States. Darling-Hammond and Ancess (1996) argue that a sort of electoral apartheid has combined with increased segregation of schools by race and class to produce starkly unequal educational opportunities. The decline in schools and the abandonment of adequate educational funding reflect a similar abandonment of public life in other spheres: feeding the poor, protecting our communities from gangs and crime, controlling and eliminating drug abuse.

Building democracy requires more than frequent elections and two or more politi-cal parties. Ultimately, government is about power. Democracy is about the equal dis-tribution of power. To focus on elections as the primary definition of democracy dis-connects parents in poor communities from real power and hides the manner in which many communities, abandoned and impoverished by the new economy, are losing their power. While the voting public has become increasingly cynical about elections, parents in these communities care very much about their children. As you will read in Chapter 13, organizations affiliated with the Industrial Areas Foundation in Dallas and Albuquerque have taught parents to have a real say in their children's schools.

Teachers can promote democracy by engaging parents as equals in real-world dialogue. Teachers and parents can work together on, and learn from each other about, schools, student achievement, and educational reform. Citizens create com-munity by working together to solve real problems, such as hunger, unemployment, and homelessness. Students in schools should be introduced to building democracy by working together to resolve problems in their lives: racial conflict, violence, alien-ation, even an antiseptic and irrelevant curriculum.

A fundamental purpose of schools is to prepare future citizens to be stakeholders in society. Arnstine (1995) argues that young people should become active partici-pants in building a democratic community. Public schools are the primary institu-tion designed to produce a public, civic community. Schools distribute knowledge. Unequal schools distribute knowledge unequally. When schools distribute knowl-edge unequally, they contribute to the decline of democratic opportunity and the continuing oppression of marginalized citizens.

But just as there are prodemocracy forces in our society, so are there antidemocratic forces. Antidemocratic forces seek to maintain balances of power based on race and class. In recent elections in Louisiana (the David Duke campaign), in the campaigns on Proposition 2 in Colorado (1992) and Propositions 187 (1994) and 209 (1996) in California, and in other issues, antidiversity and antidemocracy forces have divided communities along racial, gender, and class lines. This divide-and-conquer electoral strategy maintains present power and privileges. In school curriculum terms, antidemocratic forces promote excellence for a few students without concern for building a mutually supportive school community and educating all children to high standards.

Arnstine (1995) argues that to participate in building a democratic community, curricula and school practices need to provide young people with the skills and the disposition to advance democratic values. Curricula can change to openly teach democratic values. Chapter 6 gives examples of how students, parents, and teachers can learn to work together to resolve conflicts, to respect the right of minority opinions. In Chapter 10, I argue that for democracy to flourish, schools should be restructured to produce equal opportunity, rather than maintaining tracking and inequality.

Unequal opportunity is promoted in the schools through unequal government spending. States differ widely in the amount of financial support they provide for their schools. For example, one of the points of comparison in a study by the non-partisan California Legislative Analysts Office (Hall, 1994) was expenditure per pupil. The results of this comparison in five states, shown in the last row in Table 1.4, reveal expenditures per student as low as $4,451 (in California) and as high as $8,452 (in New York).

The quality of schooling in many ways depends on the adequacy of funds for schools. Yet the adequacy of school funds ranges dramatically from state to state and from district to district. Inequality of school funding between districts in a state is a major focus of school reform efforts in Ohio, New Jersey, Tennessee, Texas, Maryland, Michigan, and in other states (*School Finance*, 1997).

Conservative political and antitax efforts have seriously reduced school funding in many states. The report, "Quality Counts: A Report Card on the Condition of Public

Table 1.4   Measures of Diversity in Five States (Percentages except as noted)

	CA	AZ	FL	NY	TX	National Average
Home language other than English	31.5%	20.8%	17.3%	23.3%	25.4%	13.8%
Nonwhite students	46.3	37.8	34.6	31.6	49.0	30.0
Adults without a high school degree	23.8	21.3	25.6	25.2	27.9	24.8
Children living in poverty	18.2	22.0	18.7	19.1	24.3	18.3
Expenditures per pupil	$4,451	$4,625	$5,280	$8,452	$4,457	$5,241

Note. From *California K–12 Report Card* (p. 14) by Elizabeth E. Hall, 1994, Sacramento, CA: California Legislative Analyst's Office.

Education in the 50 States" (1997) shows that while the legislatures of some relatively wealthy states, such as Massachusetts and California, have chosen to tax their citizens and their corporations less rather than invest in their public schools, other, more poverty-stricken states such as West Virginia have made enormous efforts to adequately fund their schools. The report ranked six states—Alaska, California, Massachusetts, New Jersey, Rhode Island, and Texas—at a "D" rating for their wide disparities in education spending. That is, schools in wealthy areas were well funded while schools in poverty areas were dramatically underfunded.

Studies done at the Washington-based Economic Policy Institute show that in per capita funds spent on public education for grades K–12, the United States ranks fourteenth out of sixteen modern industrialized nations (Rasell & Mishel, 1990). Underfunded schools cannot provide equal opportunity within an unequal society. They cannot prepare workers for the high-tech industries of the future or for full participation in a political or economic democracy.

School Reform

In the 1970s and 1980s, Ron Edmonds and others located, described, and analyzed so-called "effective schools" (Edmonds, 1982). They found that approximately 2 percent of schools in low-income areas function well. Planned school interventions involving parents, teachers, and administrators have slowly increased the number of effective schools serving poor and impoverished neighborhoods in the last 20 years. These schools show that effective schools are at least possible in poor areas. Students in these schools learn basic skills and enjoy academic enrichment (see Chapter 12). The schools work in spite of the economic chaos in the surrounding neighborhoods. Graduates of these schools are as well prepared for college and our new information-based economy as are graduates of suburban schools (Carter & Chatfield, 1986; Levine & Lezotte, 1995).

We know how to improve our schools. The report, "Making Schools Work for Children in Poverty" (Commission on Chapter 1, 1993), states the following:

> The fact is that we know how to educate poor and minority children of all kinds—racial, ethnic, and language—to high levels. Some teachers and entire schools do it every day, year in and year out. But the nation as a whole has not yet acted on that knowledge, even though we need each and every one of our young people to master high-level knowledge and skills.
>
> Instead, to those who need the best our education system has to offer, we give the least. The least well-trained teachers. The lowest level curriculum. The oldest books. The least instructional time. Our lowest expectations. Less, indeed, of everything we believe makes a difference.
>
> Of course these children perform less well on standardized tests; the whole system conspires to teach them less. But when the results come in, we are only too happy to excuse ourselves, and turn around to blame the children and their parents. (pp. 46–47)

There are several keys to quality schools and quality teaching. Critical elements include high expectations for all students (high standards, eliminating tracking), protection of academic learning time, a high degree of direct instruction and on-task behavior, and maintenance of a safe and orderly learning environment. Latinos attending many Catholic parochial schools have enjoyed these advantages for years. In Cleveland and Milwaukee, African American parents have organized to leave the public schools in search of private schools that will deliver quality educational opportunities to their children through tax-supported vouchers (Lowe & Miner, 1996).

In other areas, such as the Central Park East complex in Harlem of New York City and in schools in Corpus Christi and El Paso, Texas (discussed in Chapter 12), public schools provide an environment where academic success and personal support are integral parts of the curriculum for cultural and linguistic minorities. Research and practices described in *The Good Common School* (National Coalition of Advocates for Students, 1991) and in *School Reform and Student Diversity* (McLeod, 1996) demonstrate that well-run, orderly schools with an academic focus, higher expectations, and high achievement levels make a difference in the lives of children.

Teachers Touch the Future

We need multicultural educational reform to improve the quality of school life for all of our children. Multicultural school reform is directly linked to the pursuit of democratic opportunities. Developing democratic opportunities and dispositions in students is a formidable task in a society divided by inequality and economic insecurity. But democratic practices and economic behaviors are learned, not inherited. Middle-class students—around whose needs the present public school system is designed—learn to exercise their democratic rights and assume their responsibilities. It should come as no surprise, then, that the perspectives and agendas of the middle class permeate the schools. Middle-class families provide most of the teachers and administrators for our schools. For democracy to continue, middle-class professionals need to learn to work with the poor to reform those schools that are currently failing. If our working class and poor become convinced that they are not expected to participate in the political, social, and economic processes that run our society, then democracy itself becomes at risk. Improving the quality of educational opportunity for these students is the central task of multicultural education and is essential to the survival of our democratic society.

Multicultural education assumes that the future of our society is pluralistic. It proposes to restore and fulfill the promise made in the establishment of public schools: to prepare all young people for full participation in the economy and in the democratic community. It also proposes to validate the humanity and cultural life of diverse peoples.

Multicultural education assumes that teachers want all their students to succeed and that they are looking for positive and effective democratic responses to the economic and demographic changes taking place in U.S. classrooms. We assume that the future of our society is attending our schools today. We need teachers who are willing to search out the potential of all children. A significant percentage of the U.S. labor force for the next decade will pass through our urban schools. These citizens must be prepared to work, investigate, explore, and decide on public policy that will benefit the entire community. If the schools fail, even if only the urban schools continue to fail, then the U.S. economy will fail. Linda Wong of California Tomorrow, a research group committed to educational reform and supporting racial and ethnic diversity, invokes the frequently used lifeboat analogy to describe our choices:

> California—eventually the nation, if the demographic projections are correct—is a life boat. If the boat is springing leaks because of inadequate and poor quality education, because of deepening poverty . . . the people who are sitting in the boat are going to figure out some ways of plugging those leaks and working together if they value their lives. (quoted in Njeri, 1991, p. E9)

The debate and dialogue in our society over justice, freedom, and equality is a part of our democratic heritage. Now, a new wave of immigrants is adding to the populations of historically dominated cultures and ethnic groups. Faith and hope in democratic opportunity are currently on trial in the public schools.

Multicultural Education—A Definition

Multicultural educational strategies were developed to assist teachers trying to solve the diverse problems imposed on their classrooms by rapidly changing and, at times, crisis-filled society.

Today, teachers in most urban areas face students from a variety of social classes and cultural and language groups. Often, European American children are a minority group. In many rural areas, such as the Rio Grande Valley of Texas, the central valleys of California, Arizona, New Mexico, Georgia, and Mississippi, and the Appalachian region, the majority of students do not share the middle-class, European American culture common to most college-educated teachers.

We must substantially reform schools to give these diverse students an equal chance in school, in the job market, and in contributing to building healthy communities. Banks (1989), one of the leaders in the field of multicultural education, offers this definition of the term:

> Multicultural education is at least three things: an idea or concept, an educational reform movement, and a process. Multicultural education incorporates the idea that all students—regardless of their gender and social class, and their ethnic, racial, and cultural characteristics—should have an equal opportunity to learn in school. (pp. 2–3)

In 1995, Banks helped document multicultural education as a discipline by coediting *Handbook of Research in Multicultural Education*, in which he notes that "a major goal of multicultural education, as stated by specialists in the field, is to reform the school and other educational institutions so that students from diverse racial, ethnic, and social-class groups will experience educational equality" (Banks, 1995, p. 3).

Teachers, as they work with and motivate the young, must serve as community leaders who observe reality and recognize the gap between the stated ideals of society and actual living conditions. Democratic citizens respect the rights of their neighbors, including language and cultural rights. In our roles as teachers, we participate in the struggle to extend democracy to students from populations and cultures previously excluded. We must not allow the growing poverty, violence, and anarchy in some of our neighborhoods to overcome our schools and destroy their contribution to the American dream.

In this book I argue that multicultural education builds on democratic theory to promote the dignity of the individual, the possibility of human progress, and the fundamental equality of all people. Teachers have a responsibility to both teach and reflect these values. We already know how to improve schools. Effective school reform begins with you, the teacher. We need to end tracking, to hold high expectations for all students, to promote success and self-esteem, and to empower students.

In the following chapters, we elaborate and extend this preliminary definition of multicultural education. Sleeter and Grant (1999) describe five teaching approaches: teaching for cultural diversity, human relations, single-group studies, multicultural education, and multicultural education that is social reconstructionist (see Chapter 7). Each of these approaches is described in the following chapters with a somewhat different emphasis. The categories described by Sleeter and Grant (1999)—and earlier by Gibson (1976)—were important, but no longer adequately encompass the rapidly emerging field. We begin in Chapter 2 with a detailed discussion on the nature of culture.

Summary

Schools did not create, and cannot resolve, the racial, class, and gender divisions in U.S. society. But schools and teachers can and do affect individual students' lives every day. Our multicultural society requires multicultural schooling. Students from all cultural and ethnic groups must learn to get along and to respect each other's cultural traditions. Schools must change, and must recognize and draw on the background knowledge and languages of all children. Teachers and the curriculum both must validate the home and community knowledge that all children bring to school. To do this, teachers should know about, respect, and draw strength from diverse cultural traditions present in our society. Teachers must learn new strategies so that African Americans, Latinos, Asians, Pacific Islanders, Native Americans, working-class whites, and others achieve equal educational opportunity.

Questions Over the Chapter

1. Compare the ethnic and gender composition of the students in your own teacher preparation program with the population of your region. How do you explain what, if any, differences you find?

2. Some consider the disturbances of April 29 through May 1, 1992, in Los Angeles as a riot; others describe what occurred as a rebellion.

What are the differences in point of view between these two positions?

3. Examine Table 1.3. How would you explain the differences in average income by race? How would you explain the difference in income between "family household" and "female head of household"?

4. Give your personal definitions of the following terms. Explain how they function in schools.

a. Economic crisis
b. Ethnic diversity
c. Language diversity
d. Mediocrity
e. Equal opportunity
f. Democratic responsibility

Chapter 2

Culture and Schooling

Political changes, changing immigration patterns, and the growth of minority student populations have led to renewed interest in multicultural education and bilingualism. In fact, school populations have changed so much that most students in urban classrooms share histories and experiences that differ dramatically from those represented in the curriculum or lived by their teachers. Students in more homogenous rural areas will also grow up and seek employment in a society and an economy that have been reshaped by demographic changes. As a result, teachers and schools are struggling to find ways to bring success to new and diverse student populations.

When properly understood, the concept of culture explains a great deal about school success and failure for both students and teachers. Unfortunately, many teachers and future teachers have an inadequate understanding of culture. Cultures are often presented as fixed, static, homogeneous; they are not. Nor are cultures sufficiently understood by looking at artifacts, eating ethnic food, or by participating in idealized celebrations and dances.

This chapter seeks to help you to recognize, understand, and evaluate the concept of culture—your own and the cultures of your students. The perspective has been developed from the field of anthropology, particularly from the works of Henry Trueba and George and Louise Spindler.

Your active reading and working toward a sophisticated comprehension of culture will provide you with the foundation for developing new teaching strategies and understanding the process of school change.

The Nature of Culture

A *culture* is a complex web of information that a person learns, and which guides each person's actions, experiences, and perceptions of events. We all learn a culture as children. Through it, we learn a broad series of assumptions about people and the world, and then perceive new incidents and new people through the lens of these assumptions (Hansen, 1979). Culture includes the acquired knowledge that people use to interpret their world and to generate social behavior (Spradley & McCurdy, 1994). As we grow and learn, we reinterpret and modify our assumptions based on our experiences and our perceptions. James Banks, an authority in the field of multicultural education, defines *culture* as "the behavior, patterns, symbols, institutions, values, and other human made components of the society" (Banks, 1984, p. 52). For further elaboration see Valentine (1968), Münch and Smelser (1992), and McDermott and Varenne (1995).

New facts, opinions, and interpretations are presented to us each day. We use the knowledge we have, our culture, to construct meaning from these facts, to define and explain these new events. Some of these events cause us to refine and to reflect on our prior cultural knowledge. King (1995), in developing her own views on multicultural curricula, refers to a people's particular way of interpreting and perceiving reality— their social thought and folk wisdom—as a component of their cultural knowledge.

All human beings learn a culture. All parents teach a culture to their children. A great deal of cultural knowledge is encoded, recorded, and transmitted to the young through language. Culture is also learned and transmitted through the organizations and institutions of a society. That is, cultures are not individuals. Individuals experience and transmit culture uniquely, but culture itself transcends individual experience. Individuals within a culture share an interactive, learned perspective on "appropriate" social conduct.

A culture is the way of life of a group of people. Explicitly and implicitly, a culture teaches its members how to organize their experience. To learn a culture is to learn how to perceive, judge, and act in ways that are recognizable, predictable, and understandable to others in the same community.

Children bring these cultural values—including language—with them when they enter school, where they may suddenly find themselves in an entirely new community with new values, and perhaps even a new language.

The School Culture

In U.S. society, the job of training children to participate in the dominant culture of the society has been assigned to the schools. Spindler and Spindler (1991) write, "As a teacher, a student, a delinquent, a superlatively good student, or a miserably inept student, we are all caught up in a cultural process" (p. 1). They identify the school system as a "mandated cultural process" and the teacher as a "cultural agent" (p. 1).

The multicultural environment of most urban schools is a culture in its own right; the authority structure of teachers and administrators, the sealed-off quality of the campus, the grade-by-grade hierarchy of the students, and the rich mix of ethnic home cultures create a unique cultural arena. For a minority-culture child, entering a public school is similar to being thrust suddenly into a foreign country. Even if the child knows the native language (and many don't), the habits, rules, customs, and expectations encountered at school can all be dramatically different from those learned at home.

Hoffman (1996) follows the lead of Gibson (1976) to criticize oversimplified views of culture and to argue that there is a need to clarify and extend anthropological conceptions of culture to better inform teachers.

Teachers who have developed a complex comprehension of the role of culture can assist students of diverse cultures as they grapple with the public school experience. They can guide and advocate for these students as they adapt to the school culture and begin to learn the dimensions of the *macroculture* (the surrounding, general, inclusive culture) beyond. From a multicultural perspective, a teacher's task is to respect the cultures children bring from home, to guide students' learning of the basic skills, language, and attitudes of the macroculture, and to nourish each student's self-esteem.

To be guides to culture, teachers must be able to communicate with students. The most appropriate and effective means of guiding children is to build on what they already know. Effective teachers use those concepts and strategies children have acquired at home to teach new concepts and strategies. The need to build on knowledge acquired at home before a student starts school is most apparent in language acquisition. Languages are central to cultures. When teaching a child a second language, such as English, teachers are most effective when they can provide instruction in the child's home language.

Few issues in education are more controversial than bilingual instruction and English-language acquisition by non-English-speaking students. In Chapter 11 we explore in detail bilingual education (including the Ebonics debate), and offer useful teaching strategies for English as a second language (ESL) instruction.

Students have a need and a right to learn about their own culture as well as the macroculture. For students from minority-status cultures, studying their own culture (including language) can empower them to make important life choices, such as whether to complete high school or college. Studying the culture and historical experience of their people validates minority students' background knowledge and converts it into an accessible base for further learning activities. Incorporating this background information into the official school curriculum gives status to students' parents and communities.

With the security and self-confidence provided by self-knowledge, students can begin to learn about both the school culture and the macroculture, which they must do to gain entry into the political and economic institutions of the larger society. However, if the school system simply imposes the dominant culture's values with little recognition or use of students' home cultures, students may become confused, frustrated, hostile, resistant, and frequently, educational casualties.

Imagine a young boy who enters kindergarten knowing how to read. This student delights in reading, in discovering new stories in books. What would happen to him if the teacher begins presenting prereading skills without acknowledging the unique skills the child brings from home? He would feel that his own skills are being devalued, and he would be bored and frustrated with the material.

Many children from Latino, African American, and other minority cultures experience such devaluation of their languages and cultures. Some schools insist that children must immediately integrate into the dominant European American culture of the school. But this has proven to be counterproductive. To pull children (or adults) from one culture and place them in another, produces anxiety, frustration, and culture shock; it seldom produces learning. In a similar manner, when the dominant culture's language is imposed with little recognition or use of students' home languages to encourage communication, students frequently fail to acquire basic academic skills of reading and writing (Perry & Delpit, 1997). Children respond in a number of ways to rejection of their home language and culture. Some fail to learn, others withdraw and become passive; still others engage in open power struggles and resistance against teachers and the school.

Worldview

All people develop a worldview as a part of learning their culture. A *worldview* is the set of *a priori* judgments and expectations with which we perceive other people, history, our own culture, other cultures, and daily events. Components of our worldview are taught to us by our parents, family, friends, and later, teachers.

We also have social experiences and unique individual experiences that shape our worldview. For example, the oldest child in a family will experience some aspects of childhood differently than will the youngest child. The oldest child cannot look to older siblings for guidance, while the youngest child will not have younger siblings on whom to practice parenting behavior.

Our worldview is composed of all the things we have learned, all of our previous experiences. Our culture defines and directs the ways in which we interpret this information and thus how we may react to new experiences. To clarify this point, imagine a family gathering at which a 9-year-old child contradicts the statement of a grandparent. In one culture, this might be interpreted as an expression of self-confidence and independence. The child is learning facts in school that the grandparent does not have. In another culture, however, the same event is seen as disrespectful, as showing a lack of education (the child has not yet learned respect for the wisdom of elders). The significance of the event differs depending on the worldview and the culture of those involved.

This process of learning a worldview also applies to students' school experience. Various cultural groups develop their own analysis of schools, which they teach to their young. U.S. schools have developed based primarily on the cultural practices of the dominant European American culture. Rules, strategies, curricula, methods of evaluation, and systems of discipline derive primarily from teachers of this culture. Students reared in the dominant culture take these school rules for granted. To them, our school patterns seem natural, normal, and logical. For example, the pressure to compete for grades and attention is often assumed to be a part of universal human experience.

However, if we view schools through the experiences and perceptions of some urban ghetto residents, a different analysis of schools emerges. The real experience of generations of African Americans, particularly those from the lower classes in urban ghettos, is that school is often a place of frustration and failure. Over 50 percent of these students do not complete high school (Wilson, 1996). Many of those who do have difficulty finding a secure job.

Many African American families have experienced school as a place where their child is measured, tested, and judged to be inadequate. Hard work in school does not always lead to success. In spite of the nation's formal commitment to democracy in schools, the experience of a lower-class, African American child is likely to be significantly different from her middle-class European American counterpart. School may be a frightening, cold intrusion into the child's life, or, conversely, may be a zone of safety from the street violence in some neighborhoods.

Ogbu (1978; 1995) has argued that some students from subjugated minority groups may believe that teachers and successful students in the school promote "acting white" (see also Fordham, 1988). Such students may perceive that teachers criticize their family members for not monitoring homework or for not attending back-to-school nights. Children who are already defensive about their home culture and who perceive their cultural or ethnic group as under assault may respond to these school messages with withdrawal, distrust, or resistance. Ogbu argues that some students are forced to choose between "acting white," which also means adopting attitudes and behavior associated with academic success, and building peer group unity, membership, and support. Such cultural conflict between teachers from the dominant culture and students from subjugated cultures extends also to many rural Appalachian areas, where European American students often suffer educational neglect similar to that of racial and ethnic minority groups (Eller-Powell, 1994).

The conflict between cultures and worldviews begins when children from a minority culture enter school and may continue throughout their years of schooling. These students learn about the macroculture's values at school, but continue to live within, experience, and learn their home culture's worldviews and values.

Keep in mind that culture is complex and multifaceted. Some children within a family may learn resistance to school culture while other children in the same family may learn to comply based on their experiences in the complex cultural milieu of intercultural conflict at school.

Children's cultural experiences are reconstructed and redefined based on their school experience. For example, parents may teach, "Go to school, get a good education, get a good job." But the lived experience of many young people may be that school is an alienating, struggle-filled scene of conflict and even degradation. These students learn a different view of school than that intended by parents or teachers. As they mature, students may enter a youth culture with values and views that conflict with both the home culture and the macroculture. This continuing cultural conflict can have a cumulative eroding effect on their confidence and commitment to schooling.

Many young African American and Latino students experience failure and frustration in school. As described in Chapter 1, schools are frequently segregated, underfunded, and poorly equipped. Children in these schools, overwhelmingly from cultural minorities, fall behind in basic study skills. Persistent failure breaks down their self-esteem until some begin to believe that they cannot learn, that school failure is normal and inevitable for children like them. Once a negative attitude is internalized, the pattern of school failure repeats itself. Students who doubt their own capacity to learn will not learn well. They become in-school casualties, or they leave.

The Macroculture and U.S. Schools

The dominant worldview in U.S. society, and therefore in U.S. schools, has been defined by the values, attitudes, beliefs, and folkways of the European American majority.[1] These patterns of communication and life are used as criteria by which to judge right and wrong behavior. In the classroom, this cultural domination is reinforced by the preponderance of middle-class, usually female, European American teachers who unconsciously use their cultural values to judge their students' work and behavior.

The precise term for this majority view in U.S. society is *dominant culture*. While the dominant culture in the United States dominates our social, political, and educational perceptions, in the aggregate U.S. society is in fact *multicultural*. It includes European Americans, Mexican Americans, African Americans, Asian-Pacific Islanders, Puerto Ricans, and dozens more. It includes Christians, Jews, Muslims, and others. U.S. society, in fact, is made up of all of us, and thus is not only English speaking, and is not only composed of white people. We will use the term *macroculture* when referring to those cultural patterns common to all peoples living in the United States.

Students from minority cultures and from the working class are generally respected and accepted by school authorities only when they imitate the cultural traits of the dominant culture, particularly its middle-class language and customs; that is, when they become assimilated, accepting their socialization with little resistance. They thus learn that the middle-class, European American culture represents the preferred way of living, working, and learning.

Using the schools to teach a preferred way of living is called *socialization*. In addition to teaching basic skills, such as English, one of the primary functions of schools has been socialization. Public schools have prepared students to "conform" to the existing social structures of the school and of the society. Socialization is one of several ideological functions of schooling (Arnstine, 1995; Grelle & Metzger, 1996).

---

[1]The dominant culture in the modern urban United States is referred to in this text as "European American." It is composed of the contributions of several ethnic cultural groups (Italian, Irish, German, Greek, and others). At times, the culture is referred to as Anglo or Anglo European because much of it has been drawn from English language, laws, religion, and customs.

Cultural Pluralism

One form of democracy is *pluralism*, the belief that multiple viewpoints exist and that each deserves the right to vie for the approval of the majority. *Political pluralism* is the theory that society operates through the interaction of competing interest groups: business, labor, the military, corporations, the finance industry, environmentalists, civil rights advocates, the elderly, and so on. These groups organize and advance their own interests through the political parties and other organizations. The government provides an arena for these competing interests to work out solutions to everyday problems (Carnoy & Levin, 1985).

Political pluralism can provide a model for cultural pluralism. The United States has been pluralist since its founding, composed of several distinct immigrant communities.

It has been recognized throughout U.S. history that European American immigrants may be good citizens even while maintaining their own cultural groupings. Each person had a right to their own culture, and also had the expectation of participating in a common civic culture. German-Americans had their own schools, Finns and Italians had their own neighborhoods and newspapers, the Irish had their own schools, unions, and political organizations. Throughout the nineteenth century, nativist members of the current dominant culture accused each successive immigrant group of being different, separatist, and at times disloyal. Historian Oscar Handlin described pluralism in 1957: "In a free society such as the United States the groups which devoted themselves to such nongovernmental functions tended to follow an ethnic pattern. Men with common antecedents and ideas were usually disposed to join together to further their religious, charitable, and social interests through churches and a multitude of other organizations; and through such activities many individuals became conscious of the fact that, while they were all Americans, some were also Swedes or Jews or Dutch or Quakers" (p. 171). If, as Handlin argued, it has been acceptable to be Swedish, Dutch, or Jewish throughout the nation's history, why then is it today controversial to be Mexican American, Hmong, Puerto Rican, or African American?

Realistically, violence, slavery, terrorism, forced subjugation, annihilation, and attempts at forced assimilation have existed alongside the clearly visible cultural pluralism of our society. The Mormons were driven from their homes in Illinois and Missouri to the Utah desert due to their religious beliefs and practices, Native American children were kidnapped and forced into boarding schools such as one in Carlisle, Pennsylvania, in an attempt to root out their native cultures, and Japanese Americans in California and Oregon were placed in "relocation camps" during World War II based on their ethnicity even though Japanese Americans in Hawaii were not incarcerated. "Pluralism" was usually reserved for Christian white people.

The Civil Rights Movement of 1954–1968, and the changes to eliminate racial quotas from our immigration laws in 1966 extended the rights of political pluralism and cultural pluralism already recognized for European immigrant groups to non-European groups. The Civil Rights struggle insisted that race could no longer serve as a factor in determining political and cultural rights. Individuals now must be recognized as having the right to be bicultural (and bilingual)—they have the right to both identify with a specific cultural heritage group and to be active citizens of the United States.

The Melting Pot Boils Over   Elected officials and public school administrators stressed a "melting pot" point of view or ideology from 1900 until the 1980s. This viewpoint was based upon the experiences of European immigrants. It held that distinctions between Swedes, Germans, Irish, Italians, Jews and others would gradually melt away in the creation of a new "American" culture.

Common observation demonstrates that the melting pot has not worked for many groups, particularly those visibly identifiable "racial" groups. People have not melted into one "model American." In fact, the melting pot viewpoint was often damaging to students from minority cultures in schools. Dramatic achievement gaps emerged between students from the dominant group and minority students, as shown in Figure 1.6. Members of certain racially visible minority cultures could not easily assimilate. Their performance in school suffered; to some, this lower achievement was proof of the inferiority of the racial and cultural origins of these students.

Even though racial integration became a national goal and ultimately the law of the land in the 1950s, today's schools are in many ways more isolated, more segregated, and more unequal than those of previous generations (Orfield, Eaton, & the Harvard Project, 1996). Both schools and society are moving methodically away from equality. Today schools prepare African Americans, Latinos, Native Americans, and working-class European Americans for unequal, lower-status positions in the economy. Far from melting into one common culture, U.S. society is rapidly dividing into multiple racial, class, ethnic, cultural groups who increasingly regard each other with suspicion and hostility (Carnoy, 1994).

Not melting pot
Now tossed salad

Cultural Democracy

By the late 1960s, a new theory had emerged to contend with the melting pot theory. Termed *cultural democracy*, this new approach drew from different perspectives on our nation's history, developments in the social sciences, and a different analysis of the educational process.

Cultural democracy argues that our society consists of several cultures. In this multicultural society, each culture has its own childrearing practices, languages, learning styles, and emotional support systems. These cultures contribute to and participate in a common culture (the macroculture), which includes such features as watching the same television programs, making a commitment to a democratic political system, and attending a public or private school system. Groups may have different views on specific issues, such as secular versus religious schooling, but schooling itself is seldom questioned.

For those raised to believe in the melting pot, the change to a culturally democratic view involves a major conceptual shift. The worldview of childhood no longer adequately frames society. More precisely, the melting pot view fails to explain the persistent lack of school success by children from dominated ethnic groups and cultures. As the explanatory power of the melting pot view declines, and as teachers shift to cultural pluralism, fundamental ideas about schools that were based on the melting pot viewpoint—including curriculum practices, teaching strategies, bilingualism, teacher recruitment, measurement, and motivational assumptions—require reexamination.

In the new multicultural worldview, cultures and cultural values are analyzed relatively. That is, they are investigated by considering the group's own vantage point. This is not, however, cultural relativism. *Cultural relativism* is a perspective adopted by anthropologists to enhance their research abilities. They seek to achieve objective (that is, value free) research by adopting the view that there are no universal values, rather researchers should respect and work within the values of each culture in order to understand that culture.

Public school teachers have a different task than research anthropologists, particularly in the elementary grades. The tasks of public schools include teaching literacy and basic skills, socializing students to the norms of society, and advocating for and promoting democratic values. These goals for schools are not value free or value neutral. The multicultural teacher, as opposed to the anthropologist, should not adopt the perspective of cultural relativism. Teachers need to promote democracy, to obey the law, and to respect the rights of individuals. These are value-laden obligations.

For example, an immigrant cultural group from Afghanistan may have practiced the forced subordination of women, and the early contracting of marriage partners. But when a young girl enters school in our society, she has a right to equal treatment and respect. Practices from other countries such as arranged youthful marriages can violate U.S. laws.

While developing a cross-cultural perspective does not presume ethical relativism, it does require that teachers become precise observers of culture. Rejecting both the past practices of melting pot cultural domination and the hands-off, *laissez faire*, value-neutrality approach, democratic teachers become cultural mediators and present models of ethical behavior that encourage equality and respect.

Teachers and the Concept of Culture

Helping teachers understand the nature of culture provides a direct way to help them diminish the effects of prejudice in the classroom. Understanding the complexity of culture helps teachers to work against ethnocentrism and provides a central strategy for reform of schools. Most of us are so immersed in our own cultures that we fail to recognize how much of our behavior derives from cultural patterns. Teachers need to understand how their own cultures affect their lives, their teaching strategies, and the lives of their students. (See exercise 1 of the "Activities for Further Study of Culture" at the end of this chapter.)

Each person learns a series of strategies, perceptions, and responses during their childhood. Culture, gender, and socioeconomic class overlap within the home to produce behavior patterns, attitudes, and values. For example, some children are reared with a great deal of criticism, others with little criticism but a great deal of modeling, and still others with little or no direction at all. These patterns, learned before the age of 4, provide a subconscious framework for much of what children will learn later.

Cultural patterns are not absolute, but do produce tendencies toward certain behaviors or beliefs within a group. For example, Mexican Americans tend to speak both English and Spanish. Some members of the group speak Spanish almost exclusively, some speak a balance of English and Spanish, and some speak almost no Spanish. A few Mexican Americans also speak German or other languages. A cultural pattern, then, is a possibility—a probability—but not a certainty. Individuals within each group also have their own histories and experiences.

Latino, Hispanic, Chicano, or Cultural Diversity?

It is important for teachers to be aware of the variations of experiences within cultural groups and to not assume that all members of a group have similar background experiences. A description of the complexity of the Latino cultural heritage will illustrate this point.

Latinos comprise all of those people who are descendants of immigrants from Latin American countries and those persons of Spanish-Indian heritage present in the Southwest when the U.S. Army arrived in the 1830s and 1840s. As Figure 2.1 shows, there is wide diversity within the Latino (also called Hispanic) culture.

The largest component (62.6%) of the Latino population in the United States is descended from Mexican parents. In the Southwestern United States, descendants

Figure 2.1 **Percentage of Ethnic Groups Within the Latino Population in the United States, 1990**

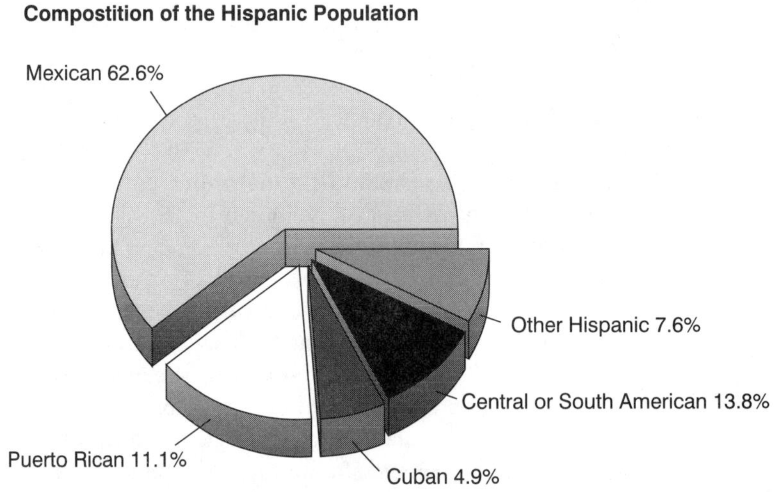

Compostition of the Hispanic Population

Mexican 62.6%

Other Hispanic 7.6%

Central or South American 13.8%

Cuban 4.9%

Puerto Rican 11.1%

Note. From *The Hispanic Population of the United States* by U.S. Bureau of the Census, March 1991. Washington, DC: U.S. Government Printing Office.

of Mexicans predominate, making up over 80 percent of the Latino population (McCarthey & Vernez, 1997; Shorris, 1992). In northern New Mexico, this population arrived before Mexico was established as an independent nation, and members often describe themselves as "Hispanos," a term that retains some sense of historical linkage with European-Spanish culture.

The Mexican American population in the United States is diverse. Some lived as Indians on what is now U.S. territory before first Spain and then the United States arrived to conquer the land. Others immigrated during the major periods of migration: 1911–1924, 1945–1954, and 1965–present. Some of the most recent immigrants are bringing modern urban Mexican cultural traditions, while others continue the rural traditions. In recent years, large numbers of Mixtec Indians from the southern Mexican state of Oaxaca have arrived to perform farm labor.

Puerto Ricans constitute another part of the Latino population (11.1%). Puerto Rico's native population was decimated by the Spanish invasion and colonization prior to 1800. They were replaced with African slave laborers who, after abolition, were integrated into the society. The United States conquered Puerto Rico in 1898 and gave it Commonwealth status in 1924. However, in the early 1950s, new "economic development" plans drove many Puerto Rican families from their farms. As a result, millions migrated to the U.S. mainland in search of work, often settling in cities along the East Coast.

Cuban Americans comprise a third ethnic Latino group in the United States. The one million Cuban Americans living in Florida have become a powerful social and political force in that state. They make up about 4.9% of the total Latino population in the country. Their genetic heritage is similar to that of Puerto Ricans, but their history is quite different. After the War of 1898, Cuba achieved a limited independence. Unlike Puerto Rico, it was not integrated as a part of the United States. Governed by a series of U.S.-supported military dictators, Cuba in the 1950s was in a state of economic and social crisis. Gambling, poverty, prostitution, and underdevelopment were severe. In 1959, a nationalist guerrilla group led by Fidel Castro seized power, turned to the former Soviet Union for support and assistance, and adopted communism as their economic and political system.

A large segment of educated middle-class Cubans fled the island at the time of the 1959 revolution. With U.S. government assistance, they established an effective Cuban American community in Florida that later supported subsequent immigrants fleeing poverty in Cuba. While Mexican Americans and Puerto Rican families experienced decades of economic hardships in the United States, many Cubans were able to move into successful businesses within a single generation. Eventually they established majority status in the economy and government in parts of Florida. Thus, though the decades of Cuban immigration were difficult, they did not last for generations, and Cuban Americans did not suffer the cultural disruption experienced by both Mexican Americans and Puerto Ricans. Assimilation was the major experience for Cuban Americans, while domination by the host culture was the major experience for Mexicans and Puerto Ricans (Crawford, 1992; Llanes, 1982).

In the 1980s and 1990s, large numbers of immigrants arrived from El Salvador, Nicaragua, Guatemala, and Peru, fleeing deteriorating economies and extended wars in these areas. The 2.2 million recent immigrants from Latin America make up only 13.8% of the total Latino population in the United States, but they add even more diversity to the Latino population. Some areas of Latin America (Costa Rica, Uruguay, and Argentina) were so thoroughly shaped by Spanish and European cultures that little of their native cultures or native peoples remains. Other areas (Mexico, Guatemala, El Salvador, and Peru) had such strong Indian cultures and so few Spanish immigrants (and these mostly male) that areas of their societies remain substantially Indian even today.

Recently hundreds of thousands of Latinos from the Dominican Republic, Haiti, Cuba, and other islands have been landing on the east coast of the United States, fleeing the political and economic chaos of their countries. They bring yet another distinct cultural heritage.

As these communities live in the United States and adapt to the social and economic conditions they find here, they often metamorphose into another kind of cultural group, one neither native to their country of origin nor imitative of the European American macroculture. Second- and third-generation descendants of Mexicans and Puerto Ricans tend to speak only English (Trueba, 1989). For some, their formative years were spent in communities and schools where being perceived as Latino put them at a social disadvantage. Others lived in barrios and attended de facto segregated schools where, despite being the majority in their own neighborhoods, they were still regarded as a second-class minority by government and school authorities. These groups have developed new cultural experiences based on their lives in the United States. Unlike recent immigrants, who tend to view the school system as a vehicle for assimilation into U.S. life, Chicano (descendants of Mexican Americans) and Puerto Rican students may see their schools as run-down and shabby, symbols of their oppression and second-class status in U.S. society. These dominated cultural groups have developed new cultural traits, such as bilingualism, and dramatic new poetry and art in the process of creating a culture of resistance to domination.

For many parents from earlier generations, the schools were the sites of disempowerment. The conflict between home and school at times produced alienation, at other times, failure. The culture of the Latino communities is currently in transition. New immigrants arrive each year to reinforce more traditional values, such as respect for home, family, and teacher.

The current Latino culture emerged from peoples' experiences and the diverse communities' responses. For example, some Latinos have turned to Catholic schools to guard their children from urban violence. Another portion of the community has turned to Evangelical religious experiences, while a third group has been overwhelmed by failing schools, gangs, and street violence. These experiences, and others, have continually reconstructed Latino culture.

All of these diverse elements make up the groups that the U.S. Census Bureau (1991) calls "Hispanics." Similar diversity exists within most cultures, be it Asian, Native American, or African American. The diversity of Asian Americans is indicated by the data shown in Chapter 3, Table 3.2. Teachers who pursue a cross-cultural perspective take years to learn the complexities of interaction within this cultural diversity. Often by the time one group is familiar, a new group will arrive (for example, Filipino, Hmong, Thai).

Because culture is constantly changing, teachers need to be cautious about all generalizations concerning cultural groups. Most generalizations apply to only one part of a population, and many are overdrawn. While teachers should not generalize, they should learn to observe, listen, and learn. Teachers need to be aware of the differences between ideal and real (lived) culture and foster mutual respect in the classroom. Teachers help students navigate the troublesome terrain between their home culture, with all of its changes and complexities, and the macroculture's traumas, including gangs, crime, poverty, and social dissolution.

Figure 2.2 summarizes the multiple perspectives on culture useful for teachers working in multicultural education.

Cultural Politics and Cultural Ethics

European Americans, like all cultural groups, continually reevaluate and recreate their culture. Like those in most modern societies, we in the United States have chosen to use schools to introduce students to dominant cultural patterns. Over many years the idea arose that all students should learn a common civic culture and that schools should teach that culture. Schools are therefore a primary site of cultural transmission. In the process of transmitting cultural patterns—through both formal and informal curricula—the U.S. macroculture is itself redefined.

Current European American culture is being forced to change in response to economic transitions and urban crises. The melting pot model assumed that over time and with proper instruction people from diverse cultures could be molded into an approximation of an "ideal American." The characteristics and values of that ideal person were assumed to be those of the English-speaking, European American culture. But in California, New York, Illinois, Florida, New Mexico, and Texas, total English dominance can no longer be assumed. In many border and urban areas, the bilingual high school graduate has an advantage for business and educational success.

A Multicultural Worldview

In place of the single idealized "American," the worldview of the multicultural education movement sees a society in which members of several different cultures are all equally valued and respected. Most people are not even aware they have a worldview. They assume that all people see reality through a perspective similar to their own. Persians (Iranians) have a saying for this myopia: "It is difficult for the fish to see the stream." In schools, the assumption that "my way is the right way" is revealed when teachers state, "I just want to get beyond this ethnic divisiveness. I treat everyone as an individual. I am tired of having to deal with this ethnic, cultural thing."

Persons making this choice usually fail to recognize that denying the significance of ethnicity and cultural differences is a privilege reserved primarily for members of the dominant group. In our society, the primacy of the individual's rights and needs

Figure 2.2 Perspectives on Culture for Teachers

What Culture Is

- Dynamic, neither fixed nor static.
- A continuous and cumulative process.
- Learned and shared by a people.
- Behavior and values exhibited by a people.
- Creative and meaningful to our lives.
- Symbolically represented through language and people interacting.
- A guide to people in their thinking, feeling, and acting.

What Culture Is Not   *But can be manifested*

- Artifacts or material used by a people.
- A "laundry list" of traits and facts.
- Biological traits such as race.
- The ideal and romantic heritage of a people as seen through music, dance, holidays, etc.
- Higher class status derived from a knowledge of the arts, manners, literature, etc.
- Something to be bought, sold, or passed out.

Why It Is Important To Know About Culture

- Culture is a means of survival.
- All people are cultural beings and need to be aware of how culture affects peoples' behavior.
- Culture is at work in every classroom.
- Culture affects how learning is organized, how school rules and curriculum are developed, and how teaching methods and evaluation procedures are implemented.
- Schools can prepare students for effective participation in dealing with the cultures of the world.

- Understanding cultural differences can help solve problems and conflicts in the school and in the community.

Developing a Crosscultural Perspective: Becoming Aware of Culture in Ourselves

- Involves perception or knowledge gained through our senses and interpreted internally.
- Helps in understanding and avoiding areas of unnecessary conflict and allows us to learn through contrast.
- Calls attention to value positions and value hierarchies of our culture which may be different from the value structures of other cultures.

Becoming Aware of Culture in Others

- Involves a certain degree of ethnocentrism, which is the belief that our own cultural ways are correct and superior to others. Ethnocentrism is natural and occurs in each of us.
- While ethnocentrism helps to develop pride and a positive self-image, it can also be harmful if carried to the extreme of developing an intolerance for people of other cultures.
- Is, in part, based upon the value of cultural relativity, the belief that there are many cultural ways that are correct, each in its own location and context.
- Analyses based on cultural relativity are essential to building respect for cultural differences and appreciation for cultural similarities.
- Cultural relativity as an analytical system is not the same as ethical neutrality in teaching.

Note. From Perspectives on Culture for Teachers, p. 36, by Cross Cultural Resource Center, California State University—Sacramento, 1996, Sacramento, CA: Author. Reprinted with permission

("I've got to do what's right for me") derives from cultural patterns rooted in the Protestant tradition of European American culture. In this tradition, individuals—not groups—are the significant elements of a society, and the individual's primary responsibility is to seek personal salvation. Of course, achieving salvation means obeying certain laws and carrying out certain social admonitions such as those found in the Bible's Ten Commandments. But the focus is on the private and personal relationship between an individual and God. Thus, admiration for strong individualism is an attribute of the dominant culture in our society, but it is only a culturally specific choice, not a human universal.

Multicultural educators believe that teachers do not have the right to insist that students from other cultural traditions abandon their less individualistic, more communal values. For example, a young Mexican American child may be taught from an early age to respect the family first, prior to individual advancement. Rural Irish children are taught a roughly similar hierarchy of values based on their shared rural, Catholic culture. African American teenagers may well have learned to stick together to defend their neighborhood friends against the intrusion of drug dealers, police, social workers, landlords, and the political powers of a city.

These students have learned a less individualistic value structure, and the teacher using a culturally democratic approach will recognize and respect these values. Teachers, as cultural mediators who reduce conflict and help children succeed in school, can help students to better comprehend both their own cultures and the demands of the macroculture.

Teaching About Culture

Students first learn about culture at home. Lessons about families and roles in the primary grades help students to draw on their home experiences. We know that the very young are often aware of ethnic differences. Students can be empowered by studying the groups and institutions closest to them, including family and school. Studies of concepts including kinship, education, health, leadership, and community help young children to understand the more general concept of culture.

Children at very young ages can begin to analyze the facets of culture that they have learned from their families. Later, after ages 10 to 12, when peer groups become more important, students can begin to analyze the differences between the values that their parents taught them and the new values encouraged and advocated by television and their peer groups.

Beginning in about fourth grade, children can study themselves in the context of their cultural patterns. Children can begin to see that they have *learned* to be who they are. They can study the process of learning, and the traits and languages taught at home. It is very important for children to see that they are active participants in the process of acquiring their culture. For example, an African American girl should understand that in her home she is a product of the African American culture. Yet the same child deserves to know that she is also being trained to be a part of the macroculture in school. Some conflict about this is unavoidable, but in a culturally democratic classroom it can be discussed and analyzed, and may become the source of new insight and strategies for survival. If unexamined, cultural conflict creates anxiety that, once internalized, hardens into dysfunctional responses such as a chronic expectation of failure.

For example, U.S.-born children of Mexican descent (Chicanos or Mexican Americans), U.S.-born Puerto Rican children, and African American children frequently do not perform well in English or in reading (Carter & Segura, 1979; Gándara, 1995). Bilingual education has served immigrant students well but has done little to resolve the cultural conflicts of English-speaking Chicano, Puerto Rican, Hawaiian, African American or Filipino students. Drill and practice alone will not change the pattern of school failure. Difficulty mastering English and acquiring reading skills are frequently related to students' conflicts of existing in two cultures—one dominant and one subordinate. Some students attempt to overcome this conflict by abandoning their native culture and totally adopting the macroculture. This cultural abandonment strategy has proven to be disastrous for many. It leads to low reading and math scores, withdrawal, passivity, a high rate of school failure, and leaving school before graduation. Rather than accept failure, students can study those aspects of their culture that determined their language acquisition patterns and try to understand how those patterns conflict with the job of mastering American English (Trueba, 1989).

Cultural conflict is an important subject of study in the multicultural classroom. Students need to be aware that they have learned many cultural patterns from their family and others from their formal education. Students also need to see themselves not only as products of the decisions of others but also as competent individuals who are in charge of the direction of their lives. When students learn that they can analyze and overcome educational problems, their self-confidence and self-control increase. By studying the school culture and students' roles, teachers can encourage students to be responsible for and in control of their future.

Schools can offer students the unique opportunity to study themselves and their classmates in the safe context of the classroom. Problems that emerge in the classroom, such as weakness in reading and math, can be treated as obstacles for the student to overcome. When children experience failure, the study of cultural conflict may help them to analyze the difficulties and to select ways to overcome educational problems. They will be able to overcome some obstacles by individual effort, such as acquiring new learning skills; other problems may require group work. The experience of being part of a team that successfully completes a project can help a student develop the courage and confidence to overcome educational and psychological barriers.

Cultural Conflicts   One frequent type of cultural conflict in classrooms concerns language. Conflict over bilingual education versus English-only language instruction and the 1997 California Ebonics episode (Figure 2.3) reveal the intense cultural and world view battles over language (Perry & Delpit, 1997).

Primary teachers and English teachers have taught formal or Standard English as their primary task almost since the founding of public schools. They are teaching

Figure 2.3   Case Study, Oakland, California, 1997

African American children in Oakland public schools, 53% of the total school population, were suffering from educational failure. Their reading and writing scores averaged below the 25th percentile. African American children accounted for over 80% of the district's school suspensions, and their average grade point in high school was a D+.

In one school in the district, Prescott Elementary, a majority of the teachers had been participating in a Standard English proficiency program provided by the State of California. This program acknowledges that many African American children learn to speak a dialect of English called Black English. Linguists have studied the origins and codified the rules of Black English, and it has taken its place as a full-fledged *dialect,* or internally consistent, rule-based lingustic variant.

A group of teachers at Prescott believed that if they were to study this dialect, its history and its patterns, they might come to better understand African American culture. This knowledge of a major African American communication system would assist them to serve as cultural mediators and help students learn Standard English. Lisa Delpit, Michele Foster, Gloria Ladson-Billings, and other authors have termed the process of considering the language, communications styles, and culture of students in selecting teaching strategies *culturally responsive pedagogy.*

The Oakland School Board had a task force searching for ways to improve the school achievement of African American children. They recommended that all schools in the district participate in California's Standard English proficiency program. In writing their resolution for the board, the task force included some of the definitions of Black English. They asserted that Black English (then termed Ebonics) is a dialect, and like other dialects is systematic and rule governed. The resolution argued that Ebonics should be affirmed by teachers, not stigmatized, and could be used to help children learn standard English.

The simple action of the Oakland School Board in encouraging teachers to know about the language use, and thus the culture, of their students, led to a national media frenzy in 1997. Editorial writers, political leaders, and the conservative radio talk show circuit became incensed. Ultimately Congress held investigatory hearings and the School Board repealed its resolution. Throughout this episode, the opponents of the new program seldom researched the nature of language or the children's dialect, listened to the children's teachers, or considered how to improve school achievement for African American children.

Editorial writers, talk show hosts, and political pundits, with virtually no reasonable discussion of the research, all assumed that they knew best how to teach these children. They argued that teachers should ignore or correct the children's home language and immerse them in Standard English. This strategy already had been tried with little success with African American children in urban districts around the nation. It was also tried unsuccessfully in Native American boarding schools earlier in the century and with language-minority children throughout the Southwestern United States.

Similar episodes of media panic and campaigns of misinformation occur from time to time about the issue of bilingual education.

the "standard" communication system of the middle-class members of the dominant culture, and this produces conflicts with other cultures and social classes. African American teachers in the rural south used strategies similar to the Oakland teachers successfully for decades prior to the 1970s.

Languages are usually learned at home (not in school) and they are based on culture. Heath (1986) has well argued that "all language learning is cultural learning"

(p. 145). As children learn a second language, they encounter cultural conflict and require assistance with these conflicts. Learning a second language also introduces teachers to learning a second culture. Strategies for teaching limited-English-speaking students are found in Chapter 11.

Languages also carry cultural assumptions within their expressions. For example, languages influence the manner in which we greet or criticize one another. Languages and cultures differ on how dialogue is initiated (do elders speak first?) and how it is completed. They also vary considerably in the manner in which they deal with silence and nonverbal expression. Languages permeate and influence most of our social relationships. They both reveal and mark status and education levels. Language and language use within a community and within a school reveal a great deal about power and authority relationships.

Keeping Up with Cultural Change

All cultures are dynamic. As students learn about their culture, the culture itself is changing. Some approaches to multicultural education completely fail to consider this. For example, primary teachers have frequently approached multicultural education by introducing young children to a variety of culturally specific foods. Such an approach teaches that variety exists and little else. Many units on teaching the culture of Mexican children present idealized pictures of people eating tortillas, tamales, and similar traditional foods. Studies of Chinese Americans focus on the use of chopsticks, rice, and fortune cookies. However, if students actually looked at the most frequently eaten food of young Mexican or Chinese American students, they would probably find it is a McDonald's hamburger. Cultures are dynamic, including, as noted previously, the macroculture.

Many students in a macroculture-based school system are not only in the process of learning how to operate in the dominant culture, but they are also adapting to continuing change within their own home culture. Acquiring new patterns does not necessarily mean abandoning home culture; acculturation can be additive. Engaging in and studying this process under the guidance of a teacher skilled in multicultural education help students to make sense of what is happening to them. Understanding cultural conflict empowers students to make effective choices about how to pursue their education, their careers, and ultimately, their lives. When schools do not help students sort out this conflict, street gangs and the criminal justice system may offer more violent alternatives.

Summary

Culture is a complex concept central to understanding multicultural education. Culture includes learned behavior, and attitudes. Great variety of behaviors and values exists within and between cultures. Understanding cultural patterns and cultural differences assists teachers to understand student behavior, motivate students, and resolve conflicts in school. Schools and teachers play an important role in preparing students for cultural pluralism.

Culture is a powerful force in the lives of both students and teachers. By developing a cross-cultural perspective, teachers can guide students toward creating a more democratic society. A cross-cultural perspective will also assist teachers in designing and implementing school and curriculum reforms.

Questions Over the Chapter

1. Do you think that there is a common "American" culture? Describe it.
2. What role does the school play in teaching a common culture?
3. What role does television play in teaching children a common culture?
4. What are some of the values taught by typical U.S. holidays, such as the Fourth of July, Thanksgiving, or Christmas?
5. What are at least three examples of how the U.S. macroculture is currently changing?
6. The chapter provided an example of the diversity within the Hispanic culture. What are examples of diversity within the dominant European American culture?
7. Would you prefer to be called European American or American? Explain.

Activities for Further Study of Culture

1. Conduct an Individual's View of Culture Interview

Part One
Conduct a life history interview of a person from a major cultural group distinctly different from your own (for example, if you are Chinese American, interview a person of Polish descent; if Native American, interview an African American; if European American, interview a Latino; etc.). Choose from a group often represented in the students of your school.

The interview should include a brief biography and proceed through a series of questions that highlight the person's cultural views and perspectives. Your goal is to understand how this person's specific cultural perspectives help to determine how he or she perceives your common society. Typical probing questions might include the following:

a. To what ethnic or minority group (such as Hispanic or African American) would you describe yourself as belonging? Why do you identify yourself as being part of this group?
b. When did you or your family first arrive in the United States? If you are a recent arrival to this country, how would you describe your first impressions of the dominant U.S. culture?
c. Describe your early school experiences. Were they positive? D⁀d ̶̶̶̶̶ conflict?

Part Two
Now consider your with these same issu tion of your own life with your subject's e ics. Then answer the t

a. How is your worldview similar to your subject's? How is it different?
b. What experiences in your life were distinctly different than those of your subject?
c. What conclusions can you draw about the process of learning culture from comparing these experiences?

Part Three
a. What are the limitations of interviewing a single individual as an informant about a culture?
b. Did your subject have experiences or viewpoints that differed from the generalizations you have heard about members of this cultural group? Be specific.

c. On completing this comparison, what conclusions can you draw about the nature of culture, and the differences between your own culture and that of your interviewee?
Note: this exercise is loosely based on work of the Cross Cultural Resource Center. A brief exercise such as this is only an introduction to life histories. See Chapter 3, Figure 3.3 for a life history example.
2. Share the results of your interview with your class.
3. Play BAFA-BAFA, a cross-cultural simulation.
4. Since you are entering the profession of teaching, consider teachers as a cultural group. What are the norms of this culture? How are they enforced? What sanctions are used?

Teaching Strategies

1. Recognize that schooling is only one form of education. Plan lessons that incorporate and build on the informal educational systems of home and community.
2. In teaching new concepts, use concepts, strategies, and language students already know.
3. Study the nature of culture and of cultural conflict.
4. Study both positive and negative cultural conflict.
5. Study the concepts of kinship, education, health, leadership, language, beliefs, and community prior to the concept of culture.
6. Study and analyze the learning process in school and in the home.
7. Do not assume that students accept your management rules. Use direct instruction to teach school-appropriate behavior.

Chapter 3

Racism and Schools

with Forrest Davis and Eric Vega

We find ourselves threatened by hordes of Yankee emigrants . . . whose progress we cannot arrest.

—Jose Sepulveda (last Mexican Governor of California, 1846)
San Francisco Examiner, 23 February 1986

You may well encounter in your classroom the growing cultural, racial, and ethnic diversity of our society. Until 2000, the majority of people in the United States were European Americans. In most of our major urban areas, however, a new majority is emerging—one composed of people of color: African Americans, Latinos, Asian/Pacific Islanders, and many others.

The New Majority

Who is this emerging new majority? It includes the 33 million (as of 1994) African Americans, many of them descendants of slaves, who today struggle against segregation, ghettoization, poverty, failing schools, high rates of unemployment, and police brutality.

57

It includes the Latino population of (as of 1993) 22.8 million, which is projected to reach 35 million by the year 2000, more than double the 1980 U.S. Census figure. Nearly two-thirds of the Latino population is Chicano (that is, U.S.-born persons of Mexican heritage). Like African Americans, Latinos experience systematic racial and class oppression. In 1996, 26.4 percent of all Latino households were below the federal government's poverty line, compared to just 8.6 percent for European Americans (U.S. Bureau of the Census, 1998b). While the average annual family income for European Americans was $35,975 in 1990, the average annual family income for Chicano families was only $22,200 and for Puerto Rican households, $19,900 per year (U.S. Bureau of the Census, 1991). Latinos and African Americans also suffered double the rate of unemployment and triple the rate of homelessness experienced by European Americans (U.S. Bureau of the Census, 1998b).

The new majority includes the Asian/Pacific American population, which has doubled in size over the past decade to more than 6 million people (Marable, 1992). Though portions of this community are economically less disadvantaged than other people of color, Asian Americans have had to endure their full share of exploitation and oppression by the European American macroculture. The continuing ethnic harassment of Asian people throughout the country and efforts to undercut their educational opportunities link their struggle with that of African Americans and Latinos.

The new majority also includes approximately 3.5 million Arab American citizens, who are subjected to political harassment, media abuse, and ethnic discrimination, and over 2 million Native Americans, who have survived genocide and cultural domination for more than 200 years (Al-Qazzaz, 1996). The struggle of Native Americans is simultaneously political, cultural, and spiritual. It is a struggle for national self-determination, for the reclamation of land, and for the renewal of the strength and vision of a people (Marable, 1992).

The statistics for the six cities shown in Table 3.1 illustrate how past demographic changes have increased national diversity.

The emerging majority is also evident in small towns and rural areas of the South and Southwest, where Mexican Americans, African Americans, or Native Americans often constitute a majority population within their communities. In Chapter 2, I described some of the diversity within the group identified as "Hispanic" by the U.S. Census. Similar diversity exists within the Census Bureau's Asian or Pacific Islander category. Table 3.2 presents data from the Los Angeles metropolitan area that illustrate the complexity that exists within these two broad census subcategories.

The emerging diversity is even more pronounced among young people and students. The 1990 U.S. Census revealed that in New York City, whites made up 40 percent of the population, blacks 28.7 percent, Hispanics 24.4 percent, Asian/Pacific Islanders 7 percent, and Native Americans 0.4 percent (see Table 3.1). However, in 1990 the New York City schools served a student population that was 38 percent black, 35 percent Hispanic, 19 percent white, and 7.9 percent Asian/Pacific Islander (National Center for Education Statistics, 1998). Thus, in New York City as in many urban centers, African American, Latino, and Asian students each represent a higher percentage of the student population than do the same groups in the total population.

Table 3.1   National Diversity in Six Cities, 1990

				Racial Origin						
	White	Black	%	American Indian, Eskimo, or Aleut	%	Asian or Pac. Islanders	%	Other Race	Hispanic Origin	%
Chicago, IL	1,263,524	1,087,711	39.1	7,064	0.3	104,118	3.7	321,309	545,852	19.6
Los Angeles, CA	1,841,182	487,674	14.0	16,379	0.5	341,807	9.8	798,356	1,391,411	39.9
Sacramento, CA	221,963	56,521	15.3	4,561	1.2	55,426	15.0	30,894	60,007	16.2
Seattle, WA	388,858	51,948	10.1	7,326	1.4	60,819	11.8	7,308	18,349	3.6
Honolulu, HI	97,527	4,821	1.3	1,126	0.3	257,552	70.5	4,246	16,704	4.6
New York, NY	3,827,088	2,102,512	28.7	27,531	0.4	512,719	7.0	852,714	1,783,511	24.4

Note: % = percent of total population

Note. From U.S. Bureau of the Census, 1990.

Table 3.2 Racial Diversity in Los Angeles, California, 1990

Detailed Race	Population
White	1,841,182
Black	487,674
American Indian, Eskimo, or Aleut:	
• American Indian	15,641
• Eskimo	299
• Aleut	439
Asian or Pacific Islander:	
• Asian	
• Chinese	67,196
• Filipino	87,625
• Japanese	45,370
• Asian Indian	17,227
• Korean	72,970
• Vietnamese	18,674
• Cambodian	4,257
• Hmong	30
• Laotian	1,083
• Thai	9,270
• Other Asian	10,672
• Pacific Islander	
• Polynesian	
Hawaiian	2,635
Samoan	1,790
Tongan	225
Other Polynesian	155
• Micronesian	
Guamanian	2,140
Other Micronesian	32
• Melanesian	301
• Pacific Islander, not specified	155
Other Race	798,356
Hispanic Origin:	
• Not of Hispanic Origin	2,093,987
• Hispanic Origin	
• Mexican	936,507
• Puerto Rican	14,367
• Cuban	15,225
• Other Hispanic	425,312

Note. From U.S. Bureau of the Census, 1990. By U.S. Census definition, those of Hispanic origin may be of any race. Figures shown here do not add to 100% of the Los Angeles population.

In many states and school districts, the increased diversity of the student population has resulted in the districts' having no single majority group. *All* cultural groups, including European Americans, are minorities. Since there is no majority group, what does the term *minority* mean? In nontechnical writing, such as newspapers, authors usually mean minority-status individuals, or subjugated individuals. As a means of addressing the new reality of the diverse populations in their towns and cities, community activists at times refer to African Americans, Asians, Latinos, and Native Americans collectively as "people of color" rather than as minorities.

Race and Racism

Race is the term used to describe a large group of people with a somewhat similar genetic history. Many observers believe that they can describe a racial group based on hair color and texture, skin color, eye color, and body type. In Chapter 2, I noted that we learn culture but we inherit race. *Racial prejudice* is the *pre*judgment that members of a race are in some way inferior, dangerous, or repugnant to others.

Most biologists and physical anthropologists recognize the futility of previous attempts to "scientifically" define race and believe that there are no pure races on earth. In 1997, following the publication of the notorious book, *The Bell Curve: Intelligence and Class Structure in American Life* (Herrnstein & Murray, 1994), the American Anthropological Association responded to the confusion on race as follows:

> For several hundred years before this time, both scholars and the public had been conditioned to viewing purported "races" as natural, distinct, and exclusive divisions among human populations based on visible physical differences. However, with the vast expansion of scientific knowledge in this century, it is clear that human populations are not unambiguous, clearly demarcated, biologically distinct groups. As a result, we conclude that the concept of "race" has no validity as a biological category in the human species. Because it homogenizes widely varying individuals into limited categories, it impedes research and understanding of the true nature of human variation. (American Anthropological Association, 1997, p. 1)

Only 0.012 percent of the differences between individuals can be attributed to racial differences (Cameron & Wycoff, 1998). Thus race makes little biological difference in our lives, but in the United States it may make a great deal of social difference. In popular discussion, persons often incorrectly refer to national groups (such as Mexicans) or to cultural or language groups as races.

Race is more of a social category than a reliable biological classification. Racial categories have long been used to describe a group, a culture, or an ethnic group. These social definitions have changed over time, often based on the relative power of the group in question. In early Greece and Rome, for example, it was important to be a Greek or Roman citizen because such people were accorded the privileges of a superior group. Genetic lineage was of little importance. The attempt to create racial definitions based on observed physical characteristics became important in the European-dominated part of the world and in the United States between 1490 and 1850.

The *American Journal of Physical Anthropology* (American Association of Physical Anthropologists, 1996) describes the emergence of the idea of race in the United States: "As they were constructing this society, white Americans fabricated the cultural/behavioral characteristics associated with each "race" linking superior traits to Europeans and negative and inferior traits to blacks and Indians. Thus arbitrary beliefs about the different peoples were institutionalized and deeply embedded in American thought" (pp. 569–570).

Race is a social category created by persons, and thus carries with it the perspectives of those who create and use it. For example, as reported in Omi and Winant (1986): "Pro-slavery physician Samuel George Morton (1799–1851) compiled a collection of 800 crania from all parts of the world which formed the sample for his studies of race. He assumed that the larger the size of cranium translated into greater intelligence. In 1849 one of his studies included the following results: the English skulls in his collection proved to be the largest, with an average cranial capacity of 96 cubic inches. The Americans and Germans were poor seconds, both with cranial capacities of 90 cubic inches. At the bottom of the list were the Negroes with 83 cubic inches, the Chinese with 82 and the Indians with 79" (p. 163).

Ethnic Groups and Ethnicity

Some sociologists seek to deal with the limits of racial theory by describing the role of ethnic groups. P. Rose (1974) states, "Groups whose members share a unique social and cultural heritage passed on from one generation to the next are known as ethnic groups. Ethnic groups are frequently identified by distinctive patterns of family life, language, recreation, religion and other customs that cause them to differentiate from others. . . . Above all else, members of such groups feel a consciousness of kind and an interdependence of fate" (p. 13). In the United States, Mexican Americans, Puerto Ricans, the Hmong, Vietnamese, Chinese Americans, and others are each considered an ethnic group even though their biological differences are mixed.

While reference to ethnic groups are common in sociology, history, and the popular press, Omi and Winant (1986) have written an extensive criticism of ethnic group theory, arguing that it tends to blur together European immigrants and racial groups as if racial differences were not significant. They argue for a racial formation position, rather than an ethnic group analysis. That is, they argue that the United States's particular preoccupation with race creates racial distinctions between groups, whether those groups are in fact racial, ethnic, or national. Ignatiev (1995) illustrates the creation of a racial group (whites) out of an ethnic group (Irish immigrants). See Padilla and Lindholm (1995) for more on the problems of definition and measurement in conducting social science research, and arriving at social science conclusions on areas of ethnicity.

Pluralism, ethnocentrism, prejudice, and racism are ideologies that exist on a continuum (Figure 3.1). Pluralism and ethnocentrism were defined in Chapter 2. *Pluralism* is a belief in and respect for cultural diversity. *Ethnocentrism* is the belief that one's own cultural ways of doing things are the most appropriate and best.

Figure 3.1   A Continuum of Ideologies

Pluralism   Tolerance   Ethnocentrism   Prejudice   Discrimination   Racism

Prejudice is a negative attitude toward a person or group of people. For example, some individuals are prejudiced toward young or old people. In our society, many children learn prejudice against members of racial, cultural, and ethnic groups. *Racial prejudice* is the prejudgment that members of a group are in some way inferior, dangerous, or repugnant to others. Racial *discrimination* refers to one's actual behavior and actions when treating people of a different racial or ethnic group in an inferior manner. Prejudice and discrimination allow one social group to preserve a superior position by prohibiting other groups from living, working, and learning together as equals. *Racism* is the extreme point on the continuum, where a dominant group uses its power and often its legal authority to enforce differences and prejudice.

Racism

The danger to our democracy is not race, but racism, the oppression of a group of people based on their perceived race. Racism is both a belief system and the domination of a people based on these beliefs. The Spanish, Portuguese, and European conquest of the Americas provides an excellent example of racism.

As the Spanish and Portuguese conquered, enslaved, and dominated coastal areas in Africa and certain population centers in the Americas, Catholic religious leaders wrestled with the question of whether Africans and "Indians" (Native Americans) were human. After a furious debate, these leaders decided that both groups had souls and could become Christians. This theology-based decision had important consequences in shaping the nature of conquest and slavery in the Americas.

Spain and Portugal's bloody conquest of Latin America (1492–1811) in search of gold was brutal beyond description. The conquerors sought economic and political, as well as spiritual, goals. The Catholic church spent enormous effort to convert native populations to Christianity. The Indian population of most of the territory survived, although their cultures suffered. The conquerors raped and intermarried with them on a large scale.

In the English-speaking colonies, intermarriage was not as common for Native Americans and slaves. In contrast to Catholic law, primarily Protestant European settlers moving west in the territory of the present United States justified their murder of Native Americans (including women and children) and their enslavement of Africans by declaring them to be two separate, not truly human, species.

This expansion and domination of the Americas fostered its own logic of self-justification. Thus, over time the physical characteristics of various non-European people (Africans, Native Americans, Mexicans) came to be associated with lower or subordinate status. This subordination was both a matter of ideas (ideologies) and of power relationships, and had economic and political consequences. For example, in 1849–1850, Mexican and Chinese miners were run out of the new gold mines in California, and Native Americans were forced into slave labor, even though many had been there before European immigrants from France, Scotland, Ireland, and Germany arrived in the gold fields.

Racism has produced a tortuous history in the U.S. intellectual community. Approaches based on an alleged "science" of race derived from distorted Darwinism developed theories of superiority that found not only African Americans and Native Americans inferior, but at various times also "proved" the inferiority of women, the Irish, Jews, Italians, and Slavs. Theorists sought to demonstrate the historical inevitability and moral superiority of Anglo-European Americans as a race, arguing for genetic explanations of African American and Native American behavior while ignoring the violence and terrorism of slavery, genocide, and imperialism as causal factors (Omi & Winant, 1986).

Between 1840 and 1860 the press and the dominant political groups in the United States actually believed that the Irish immigrants were a separate, substandard race. During the early 1900s, the first IQ tests, administered in English and allegedly "scientific," were used to demonstrate that immigrant Jews, Slavs, and people from Eastern Europe were a racial group of inferior intellectual stock. In the 1930s, a California court ruled that Mexicans could not be assigned to segregated schools since they were legally Caucasians, while other courts permitted segregation of black, Native American, and Asian children on allegedly racial grounds (*Westminster School District v. Méndez et al.*, 1947).

Although racial definitions are vague and imprecise, racism continues to divide our society and our schools. Most scientists agree that humans cannot usefully be distinguished physiologically by race, but for a racist nothing could be easier: A race is "them," "those people," the "others"—any group the racist hates and fears. At times, racism is directed at nationality groups (such as Irish, Mexicans, Russians, or Armenians), language groups (such as Spanish, Creole, or Hawaiian), and cultural groups (such as "hillbillies" or "Okies"). *Institutional racism* uses the power and authority of a dominant group to enforce prejudice and to prevent the subjugated group from gaining equal access to employment, quality housing, health care, and education.

Racism and Schools

As shown in Figure 1.6 in Chapter 1, students of different ethnic groups (Latinos, Asians, Native Americans, African Americans, and European Americans) succeed and fail at dramatically different rates in our schools.

The ethnic group you belong to makes a substantial difference in school achievement. Mexican Americans leave school at a higher rate than other Hispanics, and Hispanics drop out at a higher rate than do whites (National Center for Education Statistics, 1995). There is a dramatic increase in the rate of segregation of black and Latino students from white students in the nation's public schools (Orfield, Eaton, & the Harvard Project, 1996). We are becoming a more divided nation.

The reason is relatively straightforward: Schools for poor children and children of color are inadequately funded. Economic choices—the unequal and inadequate funding of schools—produce most of the differences in achievement that are used as evidence of racial superiority and inferiority. Kozol (1991) describes school conditions that would never be accepted in adequately funded European American schools:

"We work under difficult circumstances. The school was built to hold one thousand students. We have 1,550. We are badly overcrowded. We need smaller classes, but to do this, we would need more space. I can't add five teachers. I would have no place to put them," says a principal of a New York City school.

"I can't set up a computer lab. I have no room. I had to put a class into the library. I have no librarian. There are two gymnasiums upstairs, but they cannot be used for sports. We hold more classes there. It's unfair to measure us against the suburbs. They have 17–20 children in a class. Average class size at this school is thirty."

"We have no science room. The science teachers carry their equipment with them." (p. 89)

Kozol describes one of the schools he visited:

The school is 29% black, 70% Hispanic. . . . We sit and talk in the nurse's room. The window is broken. There are two holes in the ceiling. About a quarter of the ceiling has been patched and covered with a plastic garbage bag.

"Will these children ever get what white kids in the suburbs take for granted? I don't think so," says the principal. "If you ask me why, I'd have to speak of race and social class. I don't think that the powers that be in New York City understand, or want to understand, that if they do not give these children a sufficient education to lead healthy, productive lives, we will be their victims later on. We'll pay the price someday—in violence, in economic costs." (p. 89)

Our country's history of race relations has been mired in tragedy, including the enslavement of Africans, the murder of Native Americans, and the seizing of one third of Mexico's arable land in addition to seizing all of Puerto Rico and Hawaii, making these people domestic, conquered, subjugated minority groups. We must recognize that, despite decades of resistance and struggle, only limited progress has been made toward ending racial stratification and oppression. Martin Luther King, Jr., a major campaigner for human rights and recipient of the Nobel Peace Prize, commented on the centrality of the struggle against racism in his famous "Beyond Vietnam" speech (King, 1986):

We must rapidly begin the shift from a "thing-oriented" to a person-oriented society. When machines and computers, profit motives and property rights are considered more important than people, then the giant triplets of racism, materialism, and militarism are incapable of being conquered. (p. 629)

Racism and Privilege

As we shall explore in detail in Chapter 4, a poor African American or Latino faces oppression, both as a poor person and as a member of an ethnic group. These two forms of oppression interact and reinforce each other. Families who live in poverty belong to a social class. Class relationships influence and affect the status of racial groups.

Racism interacts with class, gender, and other variables to construct a complex fabric of intergroup relations. For example, while the African American middle class has achieved significant advancement in the last three decades of the twentieth century, the African American lower class suffers increased poverty and unemployment. Robert Reich, former U.S. Secretary of Labor, writes:

> Between 1977 and 1990 the average income of the poorest fifth of Americans declined by about five percent, while the richest fifth became about nine percent wealthier. During these years, the average income of the poorest fifth of American families declined by about seven percent, while the average income of the richest fifth of American families increased by 15 percent. . . .
>
> Among blacks, whose earnings at all levels continued to trail whites, the gap is wider still. Between 1978 and 1988, the average income of the lowest fifth of black families declined by 24%, while that of the top five percent of black families received 47% of total black income, compared with 42.9% of total white income received by the top five percent of white families. (Reich, 1991b, p. 197)

Affirmative Action

Racism produces privileges for some and oppression for others. The beneficiaries of racism often are taught not to recognize their personal participation in an unjust system. Let us take the example of a European American teacher candidate in California. "Jane" is in a teacher education program at a publicly financed university. Racial privilege provides her with an easy admission to the program. Nearly 50 percent of all African American, Latino, and Native American students dropped out of high school. Of those who graduated, another 50 percent decided not to go on to college or were tracked to a nonacademic program in community college. Jane received admission to the teacher preparation program without recognizing the privileges granted to her (and withheld from others) by this high school tracking system.

Jane notices that there are only a few Latinos, African Americans, Native Americans, and Asians in the teacher preparation program, even though over 50 percent of the students in the schools where she completes her teacher training are from these cultural groups. She relies on folk knowledge to explain this gap. She assumes, incorrectly, that African American and Mexican Americans must not recognize the importance of education nor value the career goal of being a teacher, or perhaps they are unwilling to work as hard as she had to get through the university. She has heard that many fail the admissions screening.

Jane does not recognize that her own admission to the program benefited from a quality high school education that others were denied. Instead, she assumes that her admission to the teacher preparation program was the result of a fair and equitable system based on merit. (In California, it would be college grade-point average or a passing score on a standardized teachers' exam.) She also is taught to assume that her college preparation provides her with the appropriate knowledge needed to teach and motivate all children. During student teaching, she will be puzzled and confused when some students from these same cultures do not respond enthusiastically to the Euro-centric viewpoint and teaching strategies she took for granted in her own preparation.

When Jane completes the teacher preparation program, she looks for a job. The first districts she applies to are seeking minority applicants. Jane feels she worked hard to earn her degree and her teaching credential, and she did. Affirmative action programs that recruit bilingual teachers and members of cultural minorities seem to give them an unfair advantage. Many job seekers resent these programs. Her own job search convinces Jane that some minorities are given preferential treatment that they do not deserve. She may even assume, without evidence, that she is better pre-pared for teaching than the minority person who gets the job.

Rather than recognize her own privileges (quality public schools, low-cost public universities), Jane resents minorities getting jobs and assumes they are less qualified. She believes that good test scores and good grades obtained within the European American–centered university system are proof of superior preparation—an ideo-logical position now challenged by affirmative action policies. The truth is, Jane may be well prepared to present the curriculum, but she is poorly prepared to teach chil-dren whose cultures and communication styles are different from her own.

Jane's privileges and her consequent problems reflect the experiences and fears of some prospective teachers. Public employment and publicly funded employment, such as teaching, now operate under the scrutiny of affirmative action programs as a counterbalance to the racial privileges granted to European Americans. Affirmative action programs designed to remedy historical social problems sound just in the abstract, but individuals such as Jane end up experiencing the frustration of employ-ment insecurity in hard times. These frustrated job seekers begin to resent programs that benefit minorities and to blame minorities for the loss of economic opportunity. A growing majority of European Americans oppose affirmative action policies and refer to affirmative action programs as "reverse discrimination."

An additional problem is that affirmative action programs, while helpful to some, have primarily benefited middle-class ethnic minorities and professional women. They have even benefited some minorities who have suffered very little discrimination in their own lives. Affirmative action programs have benefited working-class minori-ties less. A second example clarifies this point. A Latino candidate, "Joe" comes from a middle-class home, benefits from quality public schooling, and is admitted to the state university. Because of the recognized shortage of Latino teachers, Joe receives priority treatment in admission to the teacher preparation program. After the pro-gram, he receives numerous employment offers. Yet Joe fails to recognize the *class* privileges he receives. His preferential admission and preferred position in interviews were produced because there were few Latinos graduating. The massive failure of working-class Latinos to excel in schools, the more than 50 percent dropout rate of Mexican Americans in high school, and the only 9.2 percent college completion rate place Joe at an advantage. He competes from a sharply reduced pool of applicants.

Twenty-five applicants seek the teaching position in which Jane and Joe are inter-ested. However, neither Jane nor Joe get the job; Carmen does. Carmen was born and raised in Arizona. Her home language is Spanish. No bilingual education was available in her school in the 1960s. At age 16, she left school and married. Carmen raised three children who are now grown. She and her family performed back-breaking labor in the lettuce, grape, and tomato fields for over 15 years. Finally, because of a death in the family, the family settled in Sacramento, California.

Carmen begins to attend community college at age 36. She studies very hard while continuing to raise her children. Learning to read and write English at a college level is difficult; most of her communication for the previous 15 years has been in Spanish. After six years of study, she finally receives her B.A. degree and is admitted to the teacher preparation program. Carmen speaks English and Spanish well, but her college grades are lower than Jane's.

Carmen is an outstanding student teacher. She draws on her skills and competence as a mother, her maturity, and her bilingualism. The school district is under pressure from Mexican American parents to improve the poor quality of education for their children. The teacher selection committee consists of a principal and one bilingual teacher. They select Carmen because 50 percent of the children in grades 1 through 3 speak Spanish as their first language.

Twenty-one of the 25 applicants for the teaching position now believe that they were passed over because of preferential hiring. They each assume that they were superior to Carmen. But clearly there was only one job opening. If a European American female (Jane) had received the job, the other 24 would still be left without a job.

In 1996 California began to reduce its teacher–pupil ratio in grades K–3 from over 30 to 1 down to 20 to 1 ("Quality Counts," 1998).[1] This created an immediate shortage of over 16,000 teachers. Now all credentialed teachers receive jobs and the resentment previously caused by minority teachers receiving a limited number of jobs has disappeared.

A growing political movement, primarily European American and organized within the Republican Party, angrily opposes "affirmative action" and now opposes bilingual education. They believe that less qualified females and persons of color are receiving privileges in hiring and bidding on contracts. In 1994 and 1995 only 11 percent of California's public contracting dollars went to minorities and only 7.5 percent went to women-owned businesses (California Senate Office of Research, 1995). In 1996 the voters of California, in an emotional and divisive electoral campaign, voted 54 percent to 46 percent to end affirmative action programs in their state (Chávez, 1998).

How would you judge Carmen's case? Was the hiring committee correct or practicing "reverse discrimination"? How realistic is this case compared to your own experiences?

---

[1]Teacher–pupil ratios are arrived at by dividing the total number of teachers by the total number of students. Because many teachers, such as those in special education, work in small special classes, these ratios do not reflect actual class size. While California's teacher–pupil ratio was 25 to 1 in elementary schools in 1993, its average class size was actually 29.5 students to 1 teacher (California Department of Education, 1994–1995).

Institutional Racism

As the previous example illustrates, racism, poverty, and gender discrimination are interactive, complex, and often misunderstood. During the 1980s and 1990s, racial hate groups increased in number and size, and more incidents of racially motivated violence were reported than in prior years.

Many teachers find the discussion of race and racism uncomfortable. Well-meaning people have very diverse perceptions of the issue. Some believe that racial discrimination and racism are dated and repugnant doctrines that no longer affect our daily lives. Persons holding this view, for example, voted in 1996 in California to repeal affirmative action laws they believed no longer necessary. In contrast, voters in Houston, Texas, in 1997 voted to keep their affirmative action programs.

Racism is much more than acts of violence, expressions of individual prejudice, and the preservation of demeaning stereotypes. Racial discrimination includes many habits, decisions, and procedures that result in keeping racial and ethnic groups at the bottom of the social and economic order. For example, examine the racial and ethnic composition of your own teacher preparation program and compare it with the student population in nearby school districts. In most cases, even in urban areas, the teaching force is over 85 percent European American and middle class, while the student population is much more diverse. How did this unusual selection of a largely white teaching population get created? How was it re-created in your own teacher preparation program?

Racism does its greatest damage in our institutions, where well-meaning people preserve a seldom-examined social structure that benefits some people while frequently harming others. Current discrimination in wages, schooling, health care, housing, and employment opportunities continue the historical pattern of racism into the present. In these areas, institutions such as schools reinforce and recreate racism.

Our educational institutions work for some students and don't work for others. Schools for middle-class European American, Latino, and African American children fundamentally fulfill their purposes. But schools for poor African American, Latino, and European American children often fail. While this institutional failure harms all poor children, it disproportionately affects the children of ethnic minorities. In 1995 the nation had 20.5 percent of its children living in poverty. Sixteen percent of white students, 41.3 percent of blacks, 41.4 percent of American Indians, 19.2 percent of Asians, and 39.5 percent of Hispanics lived in poverty (Figure 3.2).

The differences in income and poverty levels among racial and cultural groups are not accidental. They are a result of our economic, social, and educational systems. Extreme poverty is a direct result of a lack of employment skills. Educational discrimination and failure in one generation often lead to poverty and school crises in the next. These are cycles that a functioning democracy ought to be able to interrupt and remedy.

Low-quality education in prior generations led to a concentration of African American and Latino workers in low-skilled industrial labor fields. With the growth in power of labor unions, these industrial jobs began paying substantial wages and

Figure 3.2 Percentage of U.S. Children Living Below the Poverty Line, 1995

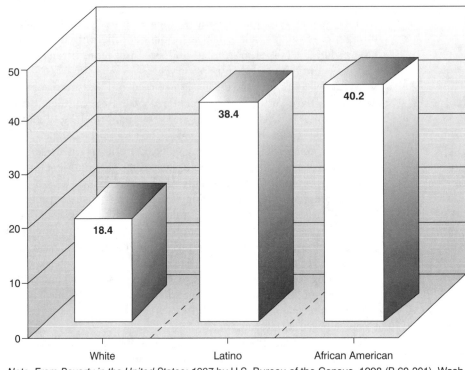

Note. From *Poverty in the United States: 1997* by U.S. Bureau of the Census, 1998 (P 60-201), Washington, DC: U.S. Government Printing Office.

benefits. From the 1970s through the mid 1990s, however, as the U.S. economy began to shift from a reliance on these fields to a demand for higher-level, more technical skills, millions of jobs in the steel, automotive, and other heavy industries were eliminated. As a result, even workers who once had secure and relatively high-paying industrial jobs were at risk. Today, the children of these endangered workers are in school. They must either prepare for new jobs in knowledge-based industries or suffer the poverty of the working poor in low-skilled, low-paying service industries.

As a result of decades of poverty within minority communities, forms of racist behavior became embedded in our institutions. African American and Latino children in urban areas have few teachers who understand their cultural reality. They attend overcrowded and understaffed schools, and immigrant children are measured by standardized tests biased against persons whose primary language is not English and whose home culture is not that of the dominant culture.

Institutional racism seeps into schools through unequal funding and a curriculum that focuses primarily on the European American view of history, literature, and language, largely ignoring multicultural views and contributions. It enters schools when teachers and curricula validate and support one group's language and learning styles while ignoring or even repressing the languages and learning styles of other groups. Institutional racism is embedded in teacher folk knowledge about teaching strategies and in inaccurate assumptions about student potential. Its existence is implicit when universities select over 85 percent of future teachers from European American candidates, excluding people of color and language minorities.

Racism and African Americans

The African American story is the best known of the many devastating histories of racism in our country. The work of Du Bois, Douglass, and others provides a substantial scholarly tradition of African American history. W. E. B. Du Bois was a leading scholar-activist in the African American community from 1890 until his death in 1963. He wrote the following:

> We can no longer regard Western Europe and North America as the world for which civilization exists; nor can we look upon European culture as the norm for all peoples. Henceforth the majority of the inhabitants of the earth, who happen for the most part to be colored, must be regarded as having the right and the capacity to share in human progress and to become copartners in that democracy which alone can ensure peace among men, by the abolition of poverty, the education of the masses, protection from disease, and the scientific treatment of crime. [So long as] the majority of men can be regarded mainly as sources of profit for Europe and North America . . . we are planning not peace but war, not democracy but the continued oligarchical control of civilization by the white race. (Du Bois, 1975, p. 249)

Accurately including the African American contribution to U.S. history would substantially alter the interpretation of much of the United States's past. Africa, prior to the slave trade, had rich and diverse cultures, major cities, and advanced civilizations. Slavery existed in other societies, including Greek, Egyptian, Roman, and several Arab and African societies. But the British and American slave trade assumed a particularly brutal racial context. Slave traders used their superior firepower to capture, rape, and murder Africans. Many Africans brought to the United States as slaves came from advanced, sophisticated societies, yet were treated like animals. Their capture was followed by the horrors of the slave ships, where as many as half of the human cargo died in passage. The African American experience of slavery—the breaking up of families, the erasure of African culture and history, the forced labor, two and a half centuries of being regarded as less than human—gives a dimension to their suffering different than that of any other immigrant group.

The domination by the slave-owning class in the southern part of the United States created a slave culture. Slaveowners developed ideologies of racial superiority, and their apologists defended and extended their brutal system. Together with the European immigrants' genocidal assault on the native populations, the institution of slavery established the racial foundations of present U.S. society.

The Civil War and the end of slavery did not end the terror of racism against African American people. Legal segregation, inadequate schooling, ideologies of racism, lynching, and other forms of open terrorism prevented African Americans from achieving equal opportunity until well into the 1960s (Figure 3.3). The struggle to maintain "white supremacy" in the United States has shaped and distorted the labor movement, the populist movement, our political parties, and our economic system.

Marable (1985) argues that although the United States prides itself on having a two-party system, African Americans faced a one-party system in the South well

Figure 3.3   The Life Story of Mr. Charlie Evans as Told by Forrest Davis, November 1997

In November of 1997 I had the opportunity to travel to Birmingham, Alabama, where I grew up from 1943 to 1964. I had visited my home only three times since relocating to California.

I had the impulse to pay a visit to Mr. Charlie Evans, who was a positive role model and who hired me when I was thirteen years old to work on his vegetable truck. During the hot, humid days of the summer I would assist him in delivering produce to areas in Brighton, Westfield and Fairfield. He was surprised but overwhelmed with joy to see me and was even more ecstatic after I told him I was a professor at Sacramento State University. His eyes filled with tears, and he interrupted our conversation and went into his bedroom, then presented me with a manuscript that contained details of his personal life growing up in Alabama.

Mr. Evans's manuscript revealed that he was born in 1914 in Grove Hill, Alabama. His family relocated to Fairfield to work for the Tennessee Iron and Coal Company. Mr. Evans was happy about the move because it presented him with the opportunity to attend Westfield School. This was a company school considered to be the best in the area. A few select black students could attend if their parents were employees of the company. The school was a multigrade classroom from the first through the sixth grade. After completion of these grades, you could not go further because the whites controlled access to the available educational facilities. James Anderson, in *The Education of Blacks in the South, 1860–1935,* documents the influence of the "planter class" and their use of child labor as a major barrier to the education of African Americans. On the other hand, the growth of the coal and iron industry represented a change in the local economy, and competition between these economic forces resulted in an increase in educational facilities. Mr. Evans indicated that his math teacher recognized his potential and offered to pay for his college education because she thought he was one of the smartest students in the class.

Unfortunately the Depression came (1929–1936) and his dream was deferred. Mr. Evans had to work to help support his family. Despite economic hardships, he managed to persevere and save enough money to graduate from Westfield High in 1936. While discussing and reading his personal accounts I was reminded of the accounts of Charles Marden, Gladys Meyer, and Madeline Engel in *Minorities in American Society* (1992) on the social milieu in the South from 1875 to 1954. These researchers describe the caste system in which the two groups were physically separated. Segregation was predicated on the idea that whites were innately superior. African Americans were denied equal opportunities to compete for employment, housing, and education and denied access to public lodging.

Figure 3.3 *Continued*

This socially sanctioned caste system was enforced by terrorist acts of the Ku Klux Klan. Mr. Evans described an incident in which his boss, a white man, was good to him and so familiar with his proficiency with numbers that he would make bets with other whites, who would put up money to prove Mr. Evans's mental inferiority. "One night we were working and my boss and two other men came to me. My boss called me over and said, 'Charlie, take this damn flashlight and go out there to the railroad cars and bring me those numbers off the three cars out there and don't carry any pencil or paper.' Each car had eight numbers. I wondered why he wanted me to do that. He had made a bet with the other two men that I could do it. So I got the flashlight, went out to the cars, shined the light on them about three times and put the numbers in my mind. I came back and called the numbers out on each car at a time. My boss said 'I knew damn well that he could do this without paper and pencil.' He won the bet because he knew I had a photographic memory."

After World War II, Mr. Evans initiated numerous business ventures, including purchasing a vegetable truck for six hundred dollars. Then he went to a vegetable garden and bought sixteen dollars worth of produce. He said, "I had only two dollars left for gas and two left to make change. On this day I sold twenty-five dollars worth of vegetables from my truck. I built a route that was paying me about three hundred dollars a month. At this time my oldest child was ready for college, so I was able to send her to Alabama State University. Her room, board, and tuition was sixty dollars a month. I would take every half dollar I collected and put it in one pocket. When I got home I would put it in a cigar box. So when it came time for me to pay the tuition I would take the money in half dollars from this box. This is the way I put her through college."

Later, Mr. Evans supplemented his income by buying and selling houses and then focused his energy on constructing a gas station on Highway 11 between Birmingham and Bessemer, Alabama. He negotiated a joint venture project with a local white businessman who could also see the potential profits. However, the project was immediately aborted after the Ku Klux Klan discovered that the station was going to be owned by a black man. Mr. Evans converted the gas station into a confectionery where he sold Piper Ice Cream, from a company based in Birmingham.

The Evans family had increased to nine girls by 1958, so the business activities were diversified to buying, selling, and renting houses and farming vegetables. He used the income to support his family, and eight out of nine daughters graduated from college.

into the 1960s. The Civil Rights Movement of the 1950s and 1960s grew up outside of the traditional political parties. The movement broke the monopoly of power held by European American Democrats in the South and finally brought a two-party system to the region. When blacks gained new power in the Democratic Party, large numbers of European Americans in the South became Republicans.

The growth of a Republican voting majority in the southern congressional districts, along with major transformations of the Southern economy, helped Republicans gain control of the U.S. presidency from 1968 until 1992, except for 1976–1980. In 1994 and 1996, Republicans won over half of all congressional seats in the South, a major change in the politics of the region (DeWitt, 1994).

The Civil Rights Movement also produced major changes in the relationship between African Americans and the dominant society. Omi and Winant (1986) argue that the Civil Rights Movement produced a change in African American self-perception from an earlier colonized view to a recognition that their poverty and powerlessness were the products of systems of oppression. This change of viewpoint produced some improvement in race relationships, and the dominant culture lost its ideological power to define the boundaries of race relations.

The political ideology, behavior, and cultural consciousness of several genera-tions of African Americans evolved into the idealism of the Civil Rights Movement. Marable (1985) argues that the worldview of most African American leaders, with the exception of the Black Power period of the late 1960s and early 1970s, could be termed *integrationist.* Integrationists called for the elimination of structural barriers that prohibited African Americans from full participation in the mainstream of American life.

Integrationists had an implicit faith in U.S. democracy. The political system could be made to work, they believed, if only people of color and others victimized by discrimination and poverty were brought to the table as full partners. This could be realized by expanding the number of African Americans, Latinos, women, low-income wage earners, and others into positions of authority within the existing structures of power in business, labor, government, and the media. When one encountered resistance, the integrationist strategy relied heavily on the intervention of a "benevolent" federal judiciary, which could be counted on to defend civil rights and civil liberties. With the passage of the Voting Rights Act of 1965 and other civil rights legislation—the result of a sustained campaign of nonviolent direct action—all members of society supposedly had equal access to the process of democratic decision making.

Though notably successful in the political and legal arenas, the integrationist strategy lacked a method for advancing democracy against the many means avail-able to those in economic power to dominate and thwart electoral participation.

New forms of racism developed during the 1980s. In the wake of the Civil Rights Movement, it was no longer possible or viable for white elected officials, administra-tors, and corporate executives to attack African Americans openly. The Ku Klux Klan and other racist vigilante groups still existed, but did not represent a mass movement.

Instead, many racists developed a new strategy that attributed the source of racial tensions to the actions of people of color. For example, David Duke, former mem-ber of the American Nazi Party and leader of the Ku Klux Klan, received the major-ity of European American votes in his senatorial race in Louisiana by arguing that "affirmative action" programs discriminated unfairly against innocent European Americans. African American college students were attacked as "racists" for advo-cating academic programs in African American studies academic programs or proposing African American cultural centers. African American workers were accused of racism for supporting affirmative action programs.

African American political leaders had to defend themselves against charges of "reverse racism." In this context, *racism* had begun to be defined by some European Americans as any behavior by individuals or groups that empowered Latinos, African Americans, or other people of color, or an agenda that took away long-held privileges of European American elite groups. Conservatives academics and think tanks promoted a theory of "reverse discrimination." Frustrated low-income workers often blamed affirmative action programs, special admissions, and other remedial programs for their loss of educational and economic opportunity (Joint Economic Committee, 1992; Tate, 1992).

In 1996 the voters of California voted 54 percent to 46 percent to ban affirmative action programs for minorities and for women (Chávez, 1998). The campaign was led by African American Ward Connerly, a regent of the University of California. As a result of the ban, the number of African American and Latino students enrolling in the University of California at Berkeley dropped more than 50 percent in 1998. The admission of Asian American students, and students who declined to state their ethnicity, increased (Johnston, 1998). Similar declines occurred at other University of California campuses (230,000 students). The ban on affirmative action had less effect on the California State University system (360,000 students)—which produces 60 percent of all the state's teachers—and the California Community colleges (1.4 million students).

Although conservatives charge that affirmative action is reverse discrimination, such "discrimination" could exist on an institutional level only if African Americans, Native Americans, Latinos, and other people of color actually controlled the institutional resources that could affect European Americans' life chances and opportunities. If people of color owned the banks and financial institutions, the systems of transportation, communication, housing and health services, even in numbers commensurate with their percentages in the population, then one might theoretically perceive a pattern of institutional prejudice aimed at European Americans.

In spite of affirmative action programs, institutional racism, discrimination, and prejudice continue to be present within the U.S. economy and U.S. schools. Far from implementing a policy of reverse discrimination, affirmative action plans and programs have had minimal impact on entrenched patterns of power and privilege.

While many European Americans in the United States say that they believe that racism and related violence have declined and that great progress has been made, leaders in the African American, Latino, and Native American communities regularly state the opposite. Speakers who testify to the continued violence of institutional racism are often dismissed or marginalized by the media and in educational institutions.

Derrick Bell, a prominent African American professor of law, states in *Faces at the Bottom of the Well* (1992):

> But the fact of slavery refuses to fade, along with the deeply imbedded personal attitudes and public policy assumptions that supported it for so long. Indeed, the racism that made slavery feasible is far from dead in the last decade of 20th Century America. . . .
>
> What we now call the "inner city" is, in fact, the American equivalent of the South African homelands. . . .
>
> Consider: In this last decade of the 20th Century, color determines the social and economic status of all African-Americans, both those who have been highly successful and

their poverty-bound brethren whose lives are grounded in misery and despair. We rise and fall less as a result of our efforts than in response to the needs of a white society that condemns all blacks to quasi-citizenship as surely as it segregated our parents and enslaved their forebears. The fact is that, despite what we designate as progress wrought through struggle over many generations, we remain what we were in the beginning: a dark and foreign presence, always the designated "other." Tolerated in good times, despised when things go wrong, as a people we are scapegoated and sacrificed as distraction or catalyst for compromise to facilitate resolution of political differences or relieve economic adversity. (pp. 3, 10)

By the 1980s, a profound social crisis—a deep sense of fragmentation and collective doubt—had developed within the African American community. The symptoms of this internal crisis were the widespread drug epidemic, black-against-black violence, the growth of urban youth gangs, and the destruction of black social institutions. By the 1990s, about 12,000 African Americans were being murdered annually. For young African American males in their twenties, the murder rate was more than 1 in 20 (West, 1993b).

Violence inevitably influenced community relationships. People concerned with street violence, robbery, or death were reluctant to attend neighborhood political meetings after dark. Black-owned businesses in the central cities lost patrons and support, making it even harder for small entrepreneurs to survive. Churches and community centers located in drug-infested areas found it difficult to attract many middle-class African Americans. Large sections of major cities such as Detroit, Newark, and Chicago were depopulated as hundreds of thousands of African American working-class and middle-income people fled to the suburbs.

The internal crisis within contemporary African American life was aggravated by corporate and governmental decisions. In the 1970s, many corporations, searching for higher profits, abandoned their plants in the central cities and relocated to nonunionized, low-wage states and countries. W. J. Wilson has detailed this decline extensively in his book, *When Work Disappears* (1996), which we discuss in Chapter 4. The refusal of the federal government to initiate economic reconstruction programs opened many new neighborhoods to the illegal economies of crack and crime.

Somewhat paradoxically, at the same time that the economic crisis has grown, the political empowerment of African American leaders also continues to grow. Elected officials now commonly incorporate an African American agenda in political programs. In 1989, Virginia became the first state to have an African American governor. African American mayors lead several major U.S. cities. In 1992, an African American woman, Carol Moseley Braun, was elected to the U.S. Senate from Illinois (although she was subsequently defeated in 1998), and the Black Caucus of the U.S. House of Representatives, including both women and men, reached 27 members.

This was followed in October 1995 by the Million Man March; African American men from throughout the country converged on the nation's capitol. Significant aspects of this event were directed by very conservative nationalist forces led by Louis Farrakhan of the Nation of Islam.

New forms of organizing developed as established political organizations failed to provide adequate leadership to address the crises within the African American community: high unemployment, high incarceration rates, violence in schools, and the collapse of human services programs. One new form was the Million Women March in Philadelphia, a nonexclusive gathering (not led by the Nation of Islam) that sought to define a broader social agenda and gender equality. In 1998, in response to a decline in progressive politics within the African American community, political activists assembled a Black Radical Congress in Chicago to draft a "Black Freedom Agenda" for further struggle against racism and poverty (for information, look on the World Wide Web at http://www.blackradicalcongress.com).

Racism and Ethnic Conflict in a Nation of Immigrants

Since its founding in 1776, the United States has been a pluralistic society—a society of immigrants. In spite of this diversity, members of the majority culture have often held somewhat xenophobic attitudes toward foreigners, persons who speak other languages, and native peoples. A brief history of immigration to the United States provides a context for understanding how successive populations entered and transformed a racially stratified society. The specific historical experiences of each group illuminate a part of our current racial divisiveness.

The present territory of the United States was first colonized by the Spanish (St. Augustine, Florida, in 1565, and Santa Fe, New Mexico, in 1610), English settlers (Jamestown, Virginia, in 1607, and Plymouth, Massachusetts, in 1620), Germans, Swedes, and Dutch (the Middle Colonies from 1624 to1640), the French (Louisiana in 1800), and Spanish-Indian Mestizos (the Southwest from 1610 to 1784).

Immigration from Europe

From 1840 to 1920, there was an enormous influx of immigrants from Europe to the "New World." They came in hopes of building a new, more prosperous life. Poor, hungry, adventurous, and at times desperate, they fled European poverty, wars, and oppression. They settled in Canada, the United States, Mexico, and throughout the Americas. Between 1860 and 1920, 28.5 million people arrived in the United States, 74.1 percent of them from Europe (Fix & Passel, 1994). During this same period, the Native American population in the United States was decimated from over 4 million to less than 1 million and Chinese immigration was banned, first by terrorism and then by law (Almaguer, 1994).

From 1840 to 1870, the European migration consisted mainly of English, Scotch-Irish, Irish, and later, German settlers. Immigrants entered primarily through East Coast ports, spoke a variety of languages, and became both the working class for an emerging U.S. industry as well as farmers in the Midwest. In the 1880s and 1890s, thousands of Swedes, Norwegians, and Finns arrived, most often settling in the upper Midwest.

The first two decades of the twentieth century produced the largest immigration wave in U.S. history. Between 1860 and 1900, the total number of immigrants was

14 million, but between 1900 and 1915 alone, another 14.5 million arrived (National Center for Immigrants' Rights, 1979; U.S. Immigration and Naturalization Service, 1997). This massive influx set off in current citizens waves of fear and concern about immigration similar in many ways to those of the present. The anxiety of U.S.-born citizens was intensified by the varied cultural character of immigrants arriving after 1890. By the 1890s, large numbers of immigrants were pouring into the country from Southern and Eastern Europe: Poles, Italians, Greeks, and Slavs. Unlike the previous immigrants, who generally assimilated quickly into the U.S. population, these latter groups created ethnic enclaves in major cities and across the farming areas of the upper Midwest. These "new immigrants" from Southern and Eastern Europe were Catholic, in desperate economic straits, and often poorly educated. An anti-immigrant, or nativist, movement grew to oppose the influx of immigrants and to maintain the "European American" lifestyle. Power, politics, cultural suppression, and the schools were used to create a myth that all "Americans" were white, Anglo Saxon, and Protestant (discussed in Chapter 4).

Migration and Immigration from Mexico

Florida and Louisiana were once territories of Spain. Texas was a territory of Mexico prior to 1835, when Anglo-American immigrants rebelled and created the Texas Republic. Parts of the present states of Utah, Colorado, California, New Mexico, and Nevada were seized from Mexico in 1848. The Mestizo peoples in this area did not emigrate from Mexico, but were living in the Southwest when the U.S. Army arrived.

The border between the United States and Mexico was neither defended nor restricted from 1850 to 1924. Persons of Mexican and Native American ancestry moved freely back and forth. Major cities in the Southwest such as Los Angeles were often predominantly Mexican in population well into the 1870s (Acuña, 1972; Grisold del Castillo, 1979).

From 1850 to 1870, a landowning population of communities of Mexicans, Native Americans, and Spanish immigrants existed in California, Texas, and New Mexico. After the area was seized in the war of 1848, the Land Law of 1851 forced this population off its lands and into manual labor. Mexicans worked as miners, ranch hands, and on the railroads. A few assimilated into the dominant European American society through marriage.

The Mexican Revolution of 1910–1917 became a bloody, extended civil war. Under the leadership of the brothers Enrique and Ricardo Flores-Magón, a significant movement in support of the revolutionaries was organized in the U.S. Southwest. Mexican residents raised funds and protected family members who fled from Mexico into the United States.

These refugees dramatically increased the size of the Mexican populations, creating large communities in El Paso, Los Angeles, and South Texas. European American immigrants had only recently managed to dominate the area, and they perceived the rapidly increasing Mexican population as a threat. In an effort to control these groups, some law enforcement organizations, such as the Texas Rangers, became notorious for eliminating "Indians" and "keeping Mexicans in their place" (Limerick, 1988; Weber, 1973). In the Southwest, many Ku Klux Klan chapters focused on what they termed the "Mexican problem."

Resistance to European American (also called "Anglo" or "Norteamericano") domination of the area was a constant aspect of Southwest U.S. history prior to 1890. By the 1930s, Mexican and Chicano workers actively formed their own unions in mining and agriculture to protect their rights under expanding corporate capitalism. The companies and the press accused many of these union leaders of being communists as a means to defeat their organizing efforts. In the 1950s, a program of deportations known as "Operation Wetback" arrested and deported hundreds of local Mexican and Mexican American leaders, terrorizing the community and depriving many areas of effective local leaders for over a decade. Local community organizations, the training ground for political empowerment, were decimated (M. T. Garcia, 1994).

From 1952 to 1962, the political progress of the Mexican and Chicano communities was set back. No single, notable national leader emerged. More than six major attempts were made to organize the largely Mexican, Mexican American, and Filipino population of agricultural workers. Finally in 1964, these efforts unified in the United Farm Workers Union (AFL-CIO) under the leadership of Cesar Chavez, Dolores Huerta, Philip Vera Cruz, and others. The African American civil rights struggle occurring at the same time gave renewed hope to Mexican and Chicano organizing.

In 1968, conditions in schools in Los Angeles and other cities led thousands of Mexican American students to walk out and strike. The Chicano student movement was born in these walkouts. This movement quickly spread to Crystal City, Texas; Denver, Colorado; and other locations (Acuña, 1981).

Chicano/Latino civil rights struggles developed in a highly dispersed manner. Union organizing and educational struggles were major focuses of activity. By 1972, Chicana/Latinas were asserting their own distinct demands for gender equality within the movement. In the 1980s, Chicano/Latino efforts began to merge with Puerto Rican and other "Hispanic" efforts in the Midwest and East.

The Civil Rights Movement (1954–1968) shook the political and social structure of the United States and produced a reevaluation of the role of racial, ethnic, and gender identity in the country. Although popularly understood as primarily the struggle of African Americans in the South, the Civil Rights Movement also fundamentally changed the status and participation of Chicano and Mexican American people in the Southwest, raising long ignored and suppressed issues of conquest and subordination. Challenges of land ownership, workers rights, language use, and immigration were renewed, often by student activists. These volatile struggles led to a bold assertion of a Chicano identity by many activists.

The Treaty of Guadalupe Hidalgo (1848) that ended the Mexican American War and ceded over one third of Mexican territory to the United States created the territories of California, New Mexico, Arizona, Nevada, and parts of Colorado and Utah, and raised the question of the status and legal rights of the people living on the land. Mexicans thought they were promised in the treaty that they would be treated equally. They believed their property rights would be protected and their language and culture would be respected. Instead, they were quickly deprived of their land. In spite of resistance, most Mexicans were reduced to cheap and exploitable labor or driven from the country. California, which was a bilingual state by its original constitution, rewrote its constitution in the 1870s to make English the only official language (E. D. Wilson, 1994). In New Mexico, land long held by New Mexican settlers was taken and sold to European American ranchers and merchants.

During the era of the Civil Rights Movement, Mexican American activists led by Reies Lopez Tijerina seized lands in New Mexico they claimed had been illegally stolen from them over a hundred years before. They were jailed and imprisoned and their organizations destroyed. Native Americans in California seized Alcatraz island and other disputed pieces of land in the Pitt River area. Other young militants led by Jose Angel Gutierrez and Maria Hernandez organized politically and took control of Crystal City, Texas, and began to challenge the domination of Texas politics by European American Democrat officeholders (Acuña, 1981).

Language rights and immigration continue to divide voters in the Southwest and in Florida today. In 1986 California passed an "English as the Official Language" act, as did several other Southwest states. In 1998, California voters decided to eliminate bilingual education, which served immigrant children in schools.

Chicano-led labor unions and community organizations developed organizing strategies to empower Mexican American communities. The most famous of these efforts was the United Farm Workers Union, mentioned previously. Although there have been many victories in labor organizing, the low-wage economy of the Southwest constantly re-creates conditions of worker oppression. In the 1990s, campaigns to organize strawberry workers in California, apple workers in Washington, tomato workers in Ohio, and garment workers and janitors in major cities helped labor organizing evolve to become a major source of community organizing among Mexican Americans.

Civil rights struggles changed in the 1980s when a new middle class of Latino professionals and merchants emerged and advocated a less confrontative style of leadership. Many adopted the term *Hispanic* as a description of their identity. Often beneficiaries of admission to college education through affirmative action programs, a similar layer of middle-class government employees and elected officials developed within the African American community. In both cases, members of this new middle class politically engaged more cautiously and with more focus on individual advancement and electing candidates to office and evinced less interest in building community organizations and challenging an unequal political and economic structure.

From 1990 to 1996, the Latino population grew six times faster than the general population, and is expected to reach 35 million people by the year 2000 (U.S. Bureau of the Census, 1997). Latinos will be the largest minority group in the nation in about 2005 (U.S. Bureau of the Census, 1997). In this same period over 1 million Latinos registered to vote for the first time, fundamentally re-shaping elections in several key states including California, Texas, Florida, and New York.

In spite of new political power, and electing Hispanic officials in key states, the Latino dropout rate from high school remains the highest in the nation (U.S. Bureau of the Census, 1997a). Gangs and youth crime, along with low wages and unemployment, contribute to urban decay. There are 19 Hispanic members of Congress; 16 Democrats and 3 Republicans. The major increase in Latino teachers and Hispanic elected officials has not significantly improved schools, employment, or health conditions for the growing Mexican American and Latino population.

Chinese and Asian Immigration

The Chinese—and later, other Asians—had yet a different and distinct experience of immigration. The Chinese began coming to California while it was still a part of Mexico in the 1840s, primarily because of economic hardships and violence in China. California's vast riches were taken from Mexico and incorporated into the United States after the war of 1848. By 1850, when California became a state, some 25,000 Chinese were working in the gold mines and providing basic laundry and cooking services to the rapidly growing immigrant population rushing to the gold fields of northern California. Exploited with xenophobic cruelty rooted in the racial ideology of the times, Chinese workers quickly learned to live in defensive enclaves, separate from the mining communities.

Anti-Chinese campaigns grew as the gold rush ended. The Chinese, who comprised 10 percent of California's population, became the target of political hate campaigns, terrorism, murder, and violence. These anti-Asian pressures culminated in 1882, when the U.S. Congress passed the first openly racial restriction on immigration, the Chinese Exclusion Act. While immigration from Europe was open and encouraged at this time, immigration from China was made illegal.

Between 1885 and 1894, the Japanese government supported emigration to Hawaii, sending over 29,000 workers to labor on sugar cane plantations. These Japanese workers were followed by Filipinos. Many of these workers soon moved on to the U.S. mainland. By 1910, there were over 72,000 (mostly male) Japanese working, often under brutal conditions, in California, Oregon, Washington, and Alaska (Takaki, 1989).

Japanese workers saved money and bought land to begin farming. They imported brides from Japan and established families and family farms. The economic success of the Japanese in the face of severe prejudice and discrimination led to increased hostility from the European American majority population. When the United States and Japan went to war in 1941, anti-Japanese hostility became so intense that all Japanese Americans on the West Coast were arrested and placed in detention camps for the duration of the war (Takaki, 1989). Of all racial and ethnic groups, only Japanese and Native Americans have faced this kind of forced incarceration.

As Takaki (1989) describes, anti-Asian discrimination climaxed during World War II and then slowly receded. Chinese and Filipinos, who had joined the United States in the war, achieved more acceptance in U.S. society after the war. According to the U.S. Bureau of the Census (1992), Filipinos (1,419,711), Koreans (797,304), Asian/Pacific Islanders (354,000), Vietnamese (593,213), and numerous other groups have moved to the United States in the last 40 years, often in connection with our military installations and operations in the Pacific (Figure 3.4).

While some Japanese Americans, Chinese Americans, Koreans, Filipinos, and the first wave of Vietnamese refugees have achieved economic prosperity, Takaki (1989) shows that other Asian/Pacific immigrants and their children continue to face hostility and discrimination. The stereotype of a "model minority" hides the poverty inflicted on many. Anti-Asian attacks, discrimination, even murders, have grown as Japan has become a major economic competitor with the United States in the 1980s and 1990s. The May 1992 racial rebellion and looting in Los Angeles particularly involved attacks on Korean immigrant store owners by African American youths ("Siege of L.A.," 1992).

The Asian American community became an increasing political force in the 1990s, mobilized both to defend immigrants' rights and to protect programs for children to learn English in public school. The welfare and immigration reforms of 1996 impacted these communities particularly severely. Union campaigns were developed to challenge such outrageously exploitative conditions as workers sewing high-priced designer clothes while being paid far below the minimum wage.

In 1997, President Clinton appointed Angela Oh and Linda Chavez-Thompson to his National Commission on Race, where they insisted that race in the United States could not be properly understood within only a black–white paradigm as commonly presented in the media.

Figure 3.4   Who Are Asians and Pacific Islanders? (Resident population by separated ethnic categories, 1990.)

Note. From *Population and Housing, 1990* by U.S. Bureau of the Census, 1992 (Summary Tape File 3c [CD-ROM]), Washington, DC: U.S. Government Printing Office.

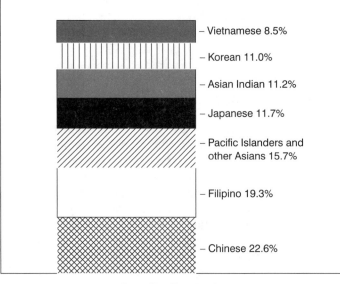

– Vietnamese 8.5%

– Korean 11.0%

– Asian Indian 11.2%

– Japanese 11.7%

– Pacific Islanders and other Asians 15.7%

– Filipino 19.3%

– Chinese 22.6%

Asian/Pacific Islanders

The Hmong and the Mien

The Hmong and the Mien are cultural groups from Laos and the mountains of Vietnam. Beginning in 1976, the first of over 145,000 Hmong refugees came to the United States. The great numbers came under the Indochina Migration and Refugee Assistance Act of 1975 (PL 94-23). Thousands of Hmong had acted as special guerilla units, mostly in Laos, helping the United States in the war in Vietnam and Laos. The Hmong became particular targets of repression after the Communists won control of Laos and Vietnam.

The first Hmong to arrive were refugees from war. Thousands suffered incredible terror and hardship, with entire families being killed, in trying to reach refugee camps in Thailand. Many had to stay in the camps for up to six years. The extended and brutal terror, along with the extended periods spent in refugee camps, divided families and broke up traditional family support systems.

As refugees, Hmong received several kinds of financial support and assistance denied to other immigrants. The Hmong and the Mien suffered more cultural dislocation in coming to the United States than did Vietnamese and most other immigrants. Some of the Hmong were from a tribal, almost preliterate, society. One refugee described the experience as getting on an airplane in the sixteenth century and then landing in the twentieth century. Others received up to three years of education in Laos prior to leaving.

Many U.S. teachers had as their first Asian students the more successful, school-oriented, middle-class Vietnamese refugees of the 1975 immigration wave. These teachers were shocked when the Hmong began to arrive. The languages and cultures of these groups are distinctly different. In part because of the extreme cultural incongruities and the lack of bilingual assistance, Hmong and Mien students in U.S. schools often began with difficult transitions.

Over 60,000 Hmong came to many parts of the United States, often sponsored by U.S. church groups and charitable organizations. Large concentrations were found in California (more than 47,000), Wisconsin (13,200), and Minnesota (10,500). After their original settlement, many moved a second time to be near other Hmong. The largest groups moved to the Central Valley of California. Such large Hmong migrations heavily affected a few schools in a brief time, causing stress to these school systems.

Hmong families tend to have many children. The children born in the United States are U.S. citizens, entitled to all of the rights of citizens but not to the special assistance given to refugees.

The current Hmong and Mien students in school have usually been in the United States for a number of years. Years of acculturation and assimilation have produced conflicts within Hmong families. Children raised in the United States have faced increased cultural conflict, at times leading them to join gangs. School authorities have been drawn into several disputes between young people adjusting to the U.S. system and families wishing to maintain older systems of respect and family loyalty (Bliatout, Downing, Lewis, & Yang, 1988).

Anti-Immigrant Politics

As each immigrant group grew, so did fear, strong prejudice, and hostility in the majority European American population. Irish, Jewish, Chinese, and Japanese immigrants were each described at one time with stereotypes characterizing them as dirty, uneducated, secretive, and subversive. Racial stereotyping, scapegoating, and violence have continued as a sustained theme in U.S. history, often encouraged by the press and so-called "fraternal organizations."

The U.S. economy passed through a difficult recession and stagnation from 1991 to 1993, and the nation faces a prolonged period of economic restructuring and transformation for the next decade. Historically, immigrants have often become targets and scapegoats during recessions and depressions, and the 1990s repeated that pattern (Figure 3.5 presents immigration patterns for the previous century).

Figure 3.5   Legal Immigration in the United States by Area of Origin, 1891–1996

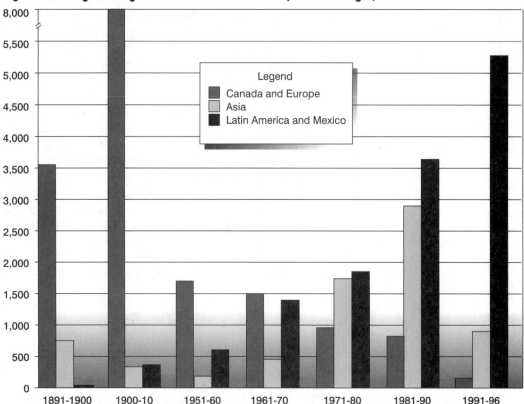

Note. Numbers are expressed in thousands. 1891–1910 data are from U.S. Bureau of the Census (n.d.). 1951–1990 data are from *A Field Guide to the U.S. Economy, 1985–1995* (graph 4.4) by Center for Popular Economics, 1995, Amherst, MA. Reprinted with permission. 1991–1996 data are from *Statistical Yearbook, 1996* (pp. 14–17) by U.S. Immigration and Naturalization Service, 1997, Washington, DC: U.S. Government Printing Office.

By the summer of 1993, a recession plagued the economy and combined with government cutbacks to make California Governor Pete Wilson the most unpopular governor in recent history. He was able to recover and win election with over 56 percent of the California vote in 1994 by attacking immigrants and blaming the federal government for the state's economic problems. Wilson won in large part by using a hostile, divisive campaign that blamed the state's economic woes on the Mexican and Mexican American populations (Adams, 1995; Chávez, 1998).

European Americans made up only 56.3 percent of the population but represented over 80 percent of California voters in the 1994 elections. Latinos, on the other hand, make up 26.3 percent of the population but were only about 9 percent of California's voters. Californians voted 62 percent to 38 percent in favor of Proposition 187, which bans illegal immigrants from receiving social services, and in almost the same percentages in favor of Governor Wilson, who campaigned for the initiative. Voter exit polls revealed that the electorate was polarized along ethnic lines: Latinos opposed the initiative 3 to 1, African Americans and Asians split about 50 percent to 50 percent, and European Americans supported the measure by over 64 percent. (Adams, 1995; Chávez, 1998. See also California's 1998 voting patterns, discussed in Chapter 11.)

This 1994 California election demonstrated that anti-immigrant campaigns can mobilize angry voters. Such campaigns have quickly spread to a number of border states, increasing anti-immigrant sentiments in the country. In several border states, immigrants were inaccurately blamed for economic problems, even though numerous studies demonstrate that immigrants contribute far more to the economy in taxes and productivity than they allegedly cost in human services such as education for children.

In contrast, in New York and Texas in 1994 and 1998, both also led by Republican governors, immigrant bashing never became as popular, and anti-immigrant fervor was marginalized to extremist groups such as the Ku Klux Klan rather than becoming part of the mainstream political debate.

Scapegoating campaigns are not about facts; they are about seeking a temporary political advantage at the cost of a weaker group. In the California campaigns political opportunists created and capitalized on misinformation and commonly accepted stereotypes to blame immigrant school children for the problems of a rapidly changing economy. Anti-immigrant politics continue as a popular theme in U.S. political life with the Immigration Reform Act of 1996, the Welfare Reform Act of 1996, and California's 1998 Proposition 227, which banned bilingual education.

Native Americans

Native Americans, of course, were not immigrants, although in their own lands they have often been treated worse than immigrants.

By 1840, the U.S. government had driven Native American tribes from most of the arable lands east of the Mississippi, but the native peoples of the Southwest and Florida resisted domination well into the twentieth century. The growing Spanish and Mexican population of the Southwest intermingled with Native Americans to establish cities and some farming areas, but Native Americans continued to dominate large areas of land. The Navajo (Dineh), the largest remaining tribe, survives in regions of Arizona and New Mexico. The 19 Pueblo tribes have maintained their culture and civilization despite Spanish, Mexican, and European American attempts to defeat them. The Cherokee were forced from their lands in the East and resettled in Oklahoma, beside the Kiowa. The Lakota Sioux maintain established societies and cultures in the Dakotas. A host of other tribes maintain their societies in the intermountain regions. Along the coast in California and Oregon, Native American peoples such as the Chumash and Miwok were virtually eliminated (Figure 3.6).

One by one, the diverse Native American societies signed treaties and became domestic dependent nations. They signed these treaties to protect the limited land and water rights assigned to them, but few of these rights have been honored by the states or the U.S. government. For decades, the European American majority has maintained a continual military presence on or near the reservations and ignored terrorism against and exploitation of this population.

Gradually, political control of Native American nations was established and maintained through the Bureau of Indian Affairs. The bureau penetrated the tribes by control of schooling, allocation of "missionary" rights, and through deliberate policies aimed at terminating tribes or confining them to reservations on unproductive land.

Today approximately 38 percent of Native American people live on reservations (National Geographic Society, 1993). With few exceptions, they live in extreme economic poverty. Reservation economies and standards of living often resemble the economies of the most exploited regions of the world.

Figure 3.6   Who Are Native Americans? (Resident population by separated ethnic categories, 1990.)

Note. Graphic from *A Field Guide to the U.S. Economy, 1985–1995* (graph 4.3) by Center for Popular Economics, 1995, Amherst, MA. Reprinted with permission. Data from *Population and Housing, 1990* by U.S. Bureau of the Census, 1992 (Summary Tape File 3c [CD-ROM]), Washington, DC: U.S. Government Printing Office.

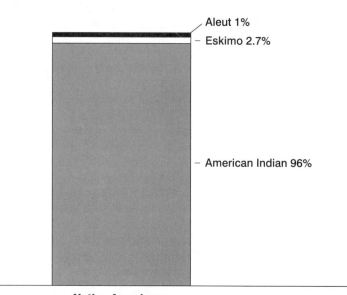

Aleut 1%

Eskimo 2.7%

American Indian 96%

Native Americans

A few tribal nations—the Cherokee, the Navajo, some of the Pueblo, and the Cree—have successfully pursued economic development through education and extended legal struggles to control and profit from the vast natural resources (oil, coal, uranium, etc.) located on their reservations. Recently, other tribes have sought economic opportunity by operating gambling casinos on their land. Their struggle for economic development continues in dozens of Native American nations, at times assisted by and coordinated with urban Native Americans through organizations such as the Inter-Tribal Council. Nevertheless, for many Native American children, extreme poverty, degradation, disease, and both cultural and physical suicide are the legacy of the conquest of their people by the European American culture.

Public schooling, whether on or off the reservation, often serves a contradictory function in Native American communities. Clearly, schooling provides opportunities to enter the macroculture and to seek economic progress. But even more than other subjugated groups, Native American societies continue to experience cultural repression in the public school system. Many schools and teachers have imposed a colonized perspective on Native American children, with all of the attendant cultural conflicts and problems. Only in the last 20 years have some tribes achieved control over their own schools and colleges, providing needed cross-cultural educational experiences.

Multicultural Education and Racial Ideology

The specific and diverse historical experiences of each group explain a part of our present racial divisiveness and crisis. Although seldom recorded in public school history books and university courses, popular struggles against racism and toward cultural democracy have also occurred throughout our history. An accurate and comprehensive understanding of history and current race relations will help teachers and this generation of students to build a more appropriate curriculum and more supportive classroom relationships.

Schools teach ideas. Systems of ideas are called *ideologies*. Teachers model either an ideology of racism or pluralism, an ideology of equality or inequality. The dominant ideology in our society supports the present social structure and the resulting stratification of opportunity. Most school curricula reinforce ideas that legitimize the present distribution of power and money. Since present U.S. society is stratified by race, gender, and class, schools tend to legitimize the present racial divisions as normal and natural, even logical and scientific. But logic and science are not responsible for the low quality of education that children from poor and minority neighborhoods receive. These children, who most need education, are often assigned to attend underfinanced, poorly equipped, and often rundown schools. Only a few of them will be able to overcome the economic consequences of a poorly funded education. Power and money—not logic, not science—determine that some students receive a quality education and others a poor education. Multicultural education is a school reform process that challenges the continuing domination of inherited privilege.

Multicultural education offers an alternative worldview, an alternative ideology. It argues that schools, along with church and family, are potential sources of knowledge and thus sources of power in a democratic society. Schools should promote the growth and extension of democracy rather than maintain the status quo. Advocates of multicultural education emphasize the values inherent and unique to democratic societies: citizenship participation, liberty, and equality of opportunity. We recognize that developing a democratic worldview of mutual respect and shared opportunity is difficult in a society divided by race and class. Yet, limited as it is, the school system is one of the few vehicles we presently have that permit us to work toward political, economic, social, and cultural democracy.

Our once resource-based economy is evolving into a knowledge-based economy increasingly dependent on international trade (and therefore valuing and rewarding bilingualism). Knowledge of diverse cultures has ever-increasing financial value. As economic changes accelerate, people who have knowledge will gain financial and political power. Children who acquire knowledge and skills in school will get ahead. Children who suffer in low-quality schools and receive a low-quality education will suffer permanent underemployment and limited economic opportunities.

The European American ideological bias, or *Eurocentrism*, in present curricula maintains inappropriate privileges for European American children. Children from all ethnic and cultural backgrounds deserve to see themselves and their families represented in the curriculum in order to see schooling as a path toward a prosperous future. Many young African American and Latino students experience failure and frustration in school; they fall behind in basic study skills. Omission from the curriculum and consistent school failure lead to erosion of students' self-esteem. Many students of color internalize the opinion that they can't learn, that failure is their fault. Thus, a cycle of failure begins. Students who doubt their own capacity do not learn well. Their anxiety and frustration as they constantly face failure reinforces self-doubt and soon leads them to question the value of staying in school. The persistent academic failure of African Americans, Latinos, and Native Americans leads some of these students to conclude that schools are negative, intrusive institutions rather than gateways out of poverty and discrimination.

As economic crises in urban areas continues to cause specific neighborhoods to decline and schools to deteriorate, some students turn to resistance. They respond to school failure with open hostility. Some black, Latino, and alienated white youth have developed cultures of resistance to school authority, rebelling against the school's negative view of themselves. At times resistance is necessary and positive, such as in the development of a Chicano identity distinct from a Mexican identity. Unfortunately, many of these young people are choosing destructive forms of resistance such as gangs, violence, and drugs. Schools become war zones. Gangs and youth culture make instruction difficult in many urban schools, depriving all students of their future economic opportunities.

Each individual and family experiences school domination or empowerment in their own manner. The ethnic and racial experiences of African Americans are substantially different from those of Latinos. The experiences of racial minorities such as African Americans, Chicanos, and Puerto Ricans can be significantly different from the experiences of immigrant minorities from Latin America or Asia such as the Japanese, Chinese, and Vietnamese (Ogbu, 1978; Almaguer, 1994).

As a consequence of the increasing hostility, divisiveness, and racial conflict in our society, schools, when not segregated, become cauldrons of individual and intergroup conflict, sometimes leading to positive outcomes, sometimes leading to negative outcomes. Figure 3.7 illustrates the complex interrelationships between race, class, gender, culture, and personal histories.

The struggle against racism and for multicultural education calls on teachers and schools to participate in the painful creation of a new, more democratic society. Democratic teachers seek to claim the promise of the American dream of equal opportunity for all. In part, the struggle calls for a change in worldview. The view of cultural democracy and pluralism presented in this chapter replaces stereotypes of racial ideology and challenges Eurocentric views of history.

The United States is and has been an immigrant and pluralistic society. The current struggle for multicultural education is one more step in the 200-year-old effort to build a more democratic society. Multicultural education poses this challenge: Will teachers and schools recognize that we are a pluralistic, multilingual society in curriculum, testing, ability grouping, and hiring? Will teachers choose to empower children from all communities and races, and both sexes? Or will schools continue to deliver knowledge, power, and privilege primarily to members of the European American majority culture at the expense of students from other cultures?

When students study the ideals of the Declaration of Independence and the U.S. Constitution, they learn a worldview that includes a commitment to democratic

Figure 3.7 Interrelationships of Race, Class, Gender, Culture, and Personal History

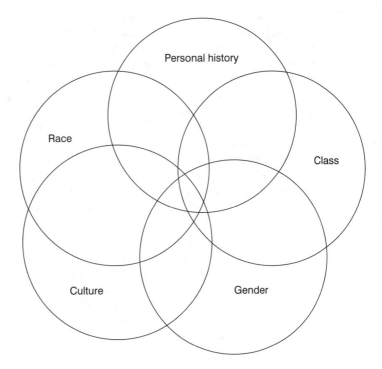

opportunity. They are taught an ideology of the "American creed." Multicultural education insists that schools serve as an arena where we achieve the promises of the Declaration of Independence:

> We hold these truths to be self evident, That all men are created equal and are endowed by their creator with certain unalienable rights, that among these rights are life, liberty and the pursuit of happiness. . . .

Throughout the nation's history, citizens have faced conflicts between our ideals and our national reality. Important battles have been won, such as the fight to end slavery and the campaign to recognize women's right to vote. Some of the battles have been lost, such as the survival of several diverse Native American nations. But the struggle to create a democratic society continues, and the manner in which we instruct our young people is crucial to that struggle.

The Attacks on Multicultural Education

Achieving political change toward democracy is not a smoothly continuous process. After the advances made by the Civil Rights Movement during the 1960s and 1970s, including an emphasis on more equal educational opportunity and the development of multicultural education, the end of the civil rights era brought attacks on these advances in the 1980s and 1990s. As conservatives gained national, state, and local political power in the 1980s and 1990s, they began to advance their social agenda, which includes a particular view of history and schooling.

An ideology of conservative educational "reform" dominated public discussion from 1982 to 1992, emphasizing excellence for a few students and pushing aside discussions of equality. Public support for funding education to advance equal opportunity declined. School segregation returned to many cities. Public education itself came under attack from the political right.

Conservatives labeled the crisis in public education as a crisis of mediocrity. The federal document, *A Nation at Risk* (National Commission on Excellence in Education, 1983), describes the crisis of school mediocrity as equivalent to a war. Schools were blamed for not preparing students adequately for the rapidly changing economy. Then-President Ronald Reagan and his second secretary of education, William Bennett, signaled their long-range goals by attacking bilingual education (Crawford, 1991). In California and other states, new Republican governors vetoed bilingual education laws. Business and corporate interests, faced with new international business competition, blamed the schools for failing to prepare workers adequately.

In times of economic crisis, some people have turned to racial scapegoating. Racism, stereotyping, and scapegoating are often still used to explain economic and school failure. The national economic crisis of the 1980s and early 1990s—with its business failures, enormous federal deficits, corruption, and loss of competitiveness—was disingenuously presented to the public as an educational crisis. But racial scapegoating cannot explain why nine billion dollars were plundered in savings and loan scandals, leaving the U.S. government with over $21 billion in bad debts and overpriced real estate, and resulting in the indictments of five U.S. senators for their participation.

As a consequence of the conservative political climate of the 1980s and 1990s, funding for public schooling and other social services remained stagnant until 1996 while student enrollment climbed. Already underfunded schools in poverty areas were devastated by budget cuts. The federal government transferred substantial costs for immigrants, health care, and education to the states to save money for the defense budget (Sawicky, 1991). Low-income schools, school districts, and even some cities went bankrupt in the recessions of 1988 and 1994.

As economic conditions continued to worsen, many teachers' salaries and school budgets were cut back. By 1987, in response to weaknesses in their own reform strategies, conservatives began to blame the multicultural education movement for declining student performance, an attack that began with Alan Bloom's *The Closing of the American Mind* (1987) and continues in works such as Arthur Schlesinger's *The Disuniting of America* (1992).

Conservatives at the university level (in think tanks and advocacy groups such as the Educational Excellence Network, the Bradley Commission on History in the Schools, the *Social Studies Review,* the Olin Foundation, the American Textbook Council, and the Committee on Economic Opportunity), in the media, and among textbook authors attack and distort efforts at multicultural education in an effort to regain control of the discussion about race, racism, schools, and democracy (Adler, 1982; California Department of Education, 1987; Gitlin, 1995; Ravitch, 1990; Schlesinger, 1992). The current efforts of multicultural education challenge conservatives' hegemony of ideas and power.

The Way Ahead

The long struggle against racism and cultural oppression continues today. Multicultural education is a part of that struggle. Neoconservative educational leaders, including Alan Bloom, E. D. Hirsch, Diane Ravitch, Chester Finn, and William Bennett, promote their own careers and resist the change to a more inclusive curriculum. They assert that multicultural education is political and divisive. Other conservatives, such as Shelby Steele, Linda Chavez, Richard Rodrigues, Ward Connerly, and Thomas Sowell, demonstrate that persons of all races can favor the traditional curriculum.

This time attacks against the idea of equal educational opportunity will fail. As the Rev. Dr. Martin Luther King, Jr., said, "I am convinced that we shall overcome because the arc of the universe is long, but it bends toward justice" (Washington, 1986, p. 207). The demographics of a young, immigrant population assure us that students will be more diverse. These students will speak more languages, not fewer. All of the students in our schools need to study diversity to understand and to participate productively in our dynamic economic changes. Multicultural education is an ideological project to move the schools toward cultural democracy. It reasserts the traditional role of the common school to provide economic opportunity for all. This effort necessarily operates within the current contested and disputed worldview of the appropriate role and functions of public schools in a democratic society.

Control of schools and curricula was central to the effort of neoconservatives to maintain a dominance of the European American agenda against the demands for cultural pluralism. Operating out of fear of losing their leadership, these critics argue that national unity requires the reassertion of dated, European American–centered culture (Ravitch, 1990; Schlesinger, 1992). But by 1998 even traditionalists such as Oscar Handlin were recognizing that we all are multicultural. Multicultural education advocates respond that national unity comes from respecting our diversity and developing a free, democratic allegiance to a common nationhood (Banks & Banks, 1995; Ladson-Billings, 1992).

The election of Bill Clinton to the presidency in 1992 began the process of pushing back conservative political control on a national level, including conservative dominance of school reform efforts. Political debate (as epitomized by the 1998–1999 Presidential impeachment proceedings) and school debate have moved back and forth since that date. The neoconservative agenda produced its own problems. Businesses need well-trained workers—not high school dropouts. Unless education improves its ability to prepare many more students, including students from diverse cultures, the economy will suffer a skills shortage. School failure reinforces institutionalized racism and deepens the divisions in our society. Meanwhile the welfare system and the penal system are increasingly expensive and overloaded. Without quality educational opportunities for all, there will be no economic justice. Without economic justice, there will be no social peace. Multicultural education offers a positive alternative to current divisions in our society by preparing all students for productive employment and democratic participation.

Summary

U.S. public school classrooms commonly encompass a cultural, linguistic, and ethnic diversity found in few nations. The United States has suffered a long and troubled history of racial conflicts and oppressions. The diverse historical experiences of African Americans, Latinos, Asians, Native Americans, and European Americans explain a part of our present racial divisiveness and crises.

A racial ideology emerged in the United States from the cauldron of expansion, settlement, slavery, displacement, migration, and immigration. This racial ideology permeates our history, our view of ourselves, and our society and distorts efforts at school reform. Multicultural education is a part of the 200-year-old struggle to foster democratic opportunity in this society. Multicultural education combats racial ideology with an ideology of cultural pluralism and equal educational opportunity.

Questions Over the Chapter

1. Define the difference between *race* and *culture*.
2. Define *racism*.
3. Give three examples of racial inequality in schools.
4. In what ways did Jane, one of the teachers discussed in the section, "Affirmative Action," receive privilege?
5. How is institutionalized racism different from prejudice?

6. How did racism affect the U.S. tradition of a two-party political system?
7. Explain factors that contributed to social fragmentation in the African American political leadership in the 1980s.
8. List four ways that public schools reflect the macroculture.

Activities for Further Study of Race and Racism

1. Make a list of the advantages or privileges you enjoy because you were born and educated in the United States. Seek out a student in your program who was born and educated in another country. Ask them to make a similar list, reflecting their own background. Compare your answers. (For further information on this topic, see *The State of the World's Children*, UNICEF, the United Nations Children's Fund, 1997.)
2. Compare the ethnic and gender makeup of your own teacher preparation program with the population of the region and with the student populations in local schools. Explain whatever differences you find.
3. In cooperative groups, describe your most vivid memory of racial or ethnic differences. Who was the "other" group? What were their characteristics? Who was the source of information about this "other"?

4. In cooperative groups, describe a time when you were separated into racial, ethnic, class, ability, or gender groups. Describe your memory of that event.
5. In a group or individually, assume the points of view of the following different Native American tribes: (a) a Plains tribe (Sioux, Crow, etc.), (b) a Pueblo tribe, and (c) a Cherokee tribe. Describe the arrival and settlement of European Americans into the territory of each group.
6. Since 1965, immigration to the United States has increased significantly from Mexico, Central America, South America, Asia, and the Middle East. Immigration reform and control have been major political issues. What is your own view on this increase in immigration? What is good about it? What is bad about it? Should immigration be controlled more?

Teaching Strategies

1. Present accurate, truthful information on the role of race and the separate role of class in determining school and economic opportunity.

2. Teach students necessary school knowledge as an addition to, not in place of, community knowledge.

3. Study racism and the forces that sustain racial privilege.
4. Plan strategies to develop prodemocratic values of equality and the dignity of each individual.
5. Reorganize your teaching of history and the social studies to present a multiethnic point of view.

6. Help students to analyze the interactive and complex nature of race, gender, and class oppression.
7. Provide all students with instruction in a language they comprehend.

Chapter 4

With Liberty and Justice for Some: Class Relations and Schools

You ought to be marching with us. You're just as poor as the Negro. . . . You are put in the position of supporting your oppressor. Because through prejudice and blindness, you fail to see that the same forces that oppress Negroes in American society oppress poor white people. And all you are living on is the satisfaction that you are somebody big because you are white. And you are so poor you can't send your children to school. . . .

Now that's a fact. That the poor white has been put into this position—where through blindness and prejudice, he is forced to support his oppressors, and the only thing he has going for him is the false feeling that he is superior because his skin is white.

—Dr. Martin Luther King, Jr., February 1968

The Crisis of Poverty

In *The Work of Nations*, former U.S. Secretary of Labor Robert Reich (1991b) demonstrated that our society was increasingly divided along economic lines. The wealthy live in luxury housing in affluent neighborhoods, professional workers live

Dr. Martin Luther King, Jr., gives his "I Have a Dream" speech during the March on Washington, August 28, 1963.
Photo: National Archives.

in comfortable middle-class suburbs, and working-class and poverty-stricken people make do with deteriorating and substandard housing in the central cities and many rural areas. By the mid 1980s, federal policy toward low-income housing had changed. Most forms of subsidy were eliminated, and now at least 3 million people have no homes at all.

By 1997 the economy had recovered from the recession and economic restructuring of the 1980s and the early 1990s. Political leaders told us that our standard of living was improving. But as *The State of Working America, 1998–1999* (Mishel, Bernstein, & Schmitt, 1999) reveals, although the economy was expanding, the economic problems that emerged in the 1980s continued to produce growing inequality. The median family income in 1997 finally reached $44,568, or $284 more per family per year than it had been in 1989 (Mishel et al., 1999). The growth in median income was produced by the wealthy doing much better, the middle class working longer hours, but with the poor doing significantly worse (Figure 4.1).

The immense economic growth of the 1990s benefited the upper class while the average family's situation remained stagnant, and the income of the poor actually declined, continuing a pattern that goes back to 1979. From 1979 until 1996, the latest period for which we have figures, the income of the lowest 20 percent of working people declined. Between 1989 and 1996, the period covered by Figure 4.1, the income of 40 percent of people either remained stagnant or declined, while

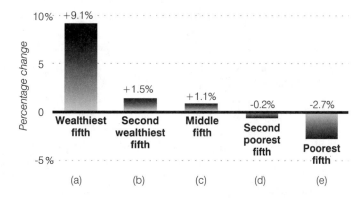

Figure 4.1   U.S. Household Income Growth, 1989–1996

Note. Data from Economic Policy Institute, 1998. Reprinted by permission.

the income of the top 20 percent of persons grew by 9.1 percent and that of the top 1 percent grew by 10 percent per year (Mishel et al., 1999). Figure 4.2. illustrates the growing inequality in our society.

While their wages have remained stagnant, many working people have lost health benefits and job security in the growing global market economy.

Economists call each 20 percent segment of the population shown in Figure 4.1 a *quintile* (one fifth). The top one-fifth of persons (a) is doing quite well. In the period covered by the chart their income improved by 9.1 percent. The middle quin-

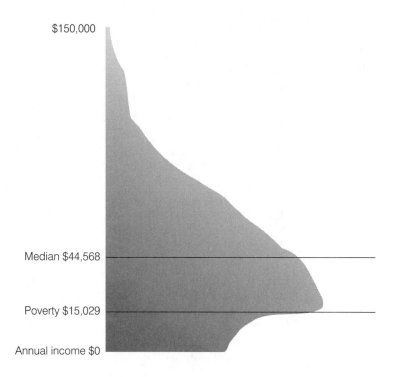

Figure 4.2   Median and Poverty-level Income for a Family of Four in 1996 (1997 dollars)

Note. Data from *Income 1997* by U.S. Bureau of the Census, 1997, Washington D.C., U.S. Government Printing Office.

tiles (b & c), the heart of the middle class, are having a more difficult time. Their income remained essentially stagnant. Working longer and working harder did not lead to economic growth. Members of this group, which includes most teachers, nurses, and other professionals, are working ever harder to maintain their current standard of living.

Only a generation ago, in the 1950s, it was common in most families to have only one adult working in the paid labor force. One income was enough to buy a home and to raise a family. Today many in the middle class achieve a higher standard of living by having husband and wife both working for pay outside of the home. The average worker in the United States, the person in quintile c, worked 129 hours, or three weeks, more, in 1997 than in 1989 (Mishel et al., 1999). Stressed families have an important impact on children in school.

The fourth quintile of the middle class (d), which would include many teachers who are single-parent heads of households, has experienced an overall decline in their standard of living over the last twenty years. From 1989 to 1996, they experienced 0.2 percent decline. This is not enough to cause a crisis, but it does make it difficult to buy a home or a new car. This the lower part of the middle class, at times referred to as the *working class*. They watch as their jobs are sent over seas, their job security is lost, their taxes remain high, and the economic opportunities for their children erode (Mishel et al., 1999).

The growing divisions in our society between economic winners and losers occurs because the economy in which we live and work is changing dramatically. For example, most jobs created during the 1990s have been in the service sector (teaching assistants, truck drivers nurse assistants, custodial workers) (Bartlett & Steele, 1992). These workers, whose jobs are often part time or temporary, provide services to people and to corporations. Even many manufacturing jobs, such as some in the clothing and computer industries, pay poor wages and often do not include job security, health benefits, and retirement plans. As Bartlett and Steele note, these low-wage jobs do not allow working people to provide for their families, to buy homes, or to save for their children to go to college.

Some of these low-wage workers are threatened by poverty. The loss of a job or a serious illness in the family could quickly destroy their home and lifestyle. Twenty-five percent do not have health insurance (U.S. Bureau of the Census, 1998b). This is the strata most hurt by the flight of well-paying union jobs to other countries. Women in Haiti were paid only 6 cents for every $19.99 Disney garment they made, while teenagers in El Salvador were paid 12 cents for every $20 Gap shirt they sewed (National Labor Committee, 1996). This kind of global competition regularly drives jobs out of the United States to other countries where unions are almost nonexistent. U.S. workers who lose their jobs understandably resent the loss of opportunity for themselves and their families. In recent years political campaigns among the middle and working classes have blamed immigrants and affirmative action programs for these problems rather than recognizing the effects of the new global economy.

As we shall see in this chapter, economic changes dramatically effect our work lives and the educational opportunities for our children. The economy is working quite well for the upper class and the top quintile of the middle class.

Reich (1997) notes that economic opportunities change with business cycles, and describes a pattern of disparity:

> The national economy is growing at a healthy clip, and we are currently blessed by a combination of low unemployment and low inflation. . . . But it is important to note the unevenness of this benign picture. Most of the growth is going to people at the top, whose incomes have soared, but the median wage is barely inching upward, and even this measure hides the fact that a substantial portion of the workforce still losing ground—following a trend that began in the late 1970s. (pp. 27–35)

More than one out of five children in the United States live in poverty—a higher rate than that tolerated by other industrialized nations. Despite our idealism about equal educational opportunity, poor children generally attend poor schools. This is because schools frequently mirror the neighborhoods around them. After detailed studies of five large metropolitan areas, Orfield and Ashkinage (1991) concluded that because poor neighborhoods usually have poorly financed schools, class is a major determinant of educational opportunity.

Yet working people have a faith in education. They have been among the primary supporters of public education since the growth of state-supported schools in the 1840s. Through good times and economic crises, working people have insisted on improving public schools. They expect schools to teach their children how to participate in a democracy, prepare them for employment, and show them how they can improve the quality of their lives. They expect equal opportunity for their children.

But our schools are not living up to these expectations, especially for children of the poor. Forty-one percent of African American children, 39.5 percent of Latino children, 19.2 percent of Asian children, and 16 percent of European American children live in poverty (U.S. Bureau of the Census, 1996b). Too many of them attend inadequate and even failing schools.

Four social crises have devastated teachers and schools, particularly in urban America, during the last decade. As described in Chapter 1, an economic crisis began developing in 1972 as the U.S. economy lost its domination of world markets. In the 1980s, confusing cause and effect, business leaders blamed this decline on the schools. The economic policies of the 1980s created a second crisis in which public financial support for all social programs, including schools, was severely cut.

A third crisis was the societal abandonment of responsibility to care for and guide our children. Adults without children pursued their own wealth. They demanded tax reductions while increasing their own public benefits. Reversing a 100-year pattern, voters refused to pay taxes to fund schools sufficiently. The voting majority of the adult population and their political leaders, particularly in urban areas, abandoned schools, children, and the future in favor of buying a new car, a new home, or a new missile system. The financial and physical condition of urban schools sank into a state of chronic crisis. At the same time, many parents, squeezed by a slow, hidden economic decline of working-class incomes between 1970 and 1996, were working more hours and consequently shifting more of the responsibility for childrearing onto the schools. Poverty continues to grow. Increases in poverty particularly affect women heads of households and their families, as shown in Table 4.1 and Figure 4.3.

Table 4.1 **Changes in Wages by Gender, 1973–1997**	Year	Male	Female	Ratio
	1973	$14.08	8.89	63.1%
	1979	$14.39	9.03	62.8%
	1989	$13.07	9.55	73.1%
	1997	$12.19	9.63	79.0

Note: The change in the gap between men and women's wages is due to both increases in women's wages and decreases in men's wages.

Note. From *The State of Working America 1998–1999* (p. 135) by L. Mishel, J. Bernstein, and J. Schmitt, 1999, Ithaca, NY: Cornell University Press. Reprinted by permission.

Ehrenreich (1989) summarizes decades of research to describe a fourth crisis produced by these social changes: the abandonment of the cities by the middle class. With the rapid growth in the ranks of the poor and consequent increases in homelessness, street gangs, drug abuse, and prostitution, many middle-class professionals no longer find cities safe environments to raise a family. They may have to work in the city, but increasingly they choose to live in the suburbs. The cities, with their declining tax base and decaying school systems, are being left to the working poor (white, black, and Latino) (Jargowsky & Bane, 1991: Orfield, Eaton, & the Harvard Project, 1996).

These crises in society have produced crises in the schools. Today's parents are working more hours and earning less money. More than ever they are looking to the schools to bring up the next generation of children. But schools have been unable to respond to these momentous changes. With shrinking budgets, decaying physical facilities, and a deteriorating social environment, they are falling behind. The burden of this failure weighs most heavily on the children of people of color, because their parents can escape neither the public school system nor the cities where the problem is most acute.

Social Class as an Analytical Concept

The racial and cultural analyses of school achievement described in prior chapters reveal only part of the story. Social class and gender interact with race and culture to influence each individual child's school achievement.

Social class is a concept, an intellectual construct, a tool that helps us to categorize, store, and retrieve information. In Chapter 2, we used the concept of culture to organize a variety of information about how groups of people live. We may not remember all of the particulars of a group, but we recognize the general concept of culture. Having learned this concept, we can approach learning about new groups using the same organizing principle.

Another attribute of concepts is that they shape the thinking of their users. Thomas Kuhn, in his landmark work, *The Structure of Scientific Revolutions*

Figure 4.3 **Percentage of All Poor Families Maintained by Women in the United States, 1959–1985**

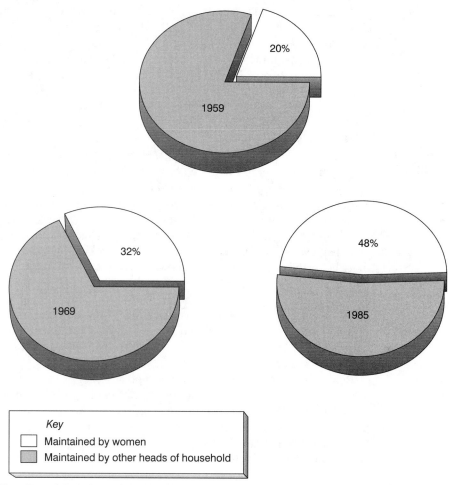

Note. From *A Field Guide to the U.S. Economy, 1985–1995* by Center for Popular Economics, 1995, Amherst, MA. Reprinted with permission.

(1970), describes how the selection of basic concepts for research strongly influences researchers' methodologies and results. For example, a researcher seeking explanations for school failure by examining the concept of social class (usually a sociologist or economist) would pay attention to different evidence than a researcher who uses the concepts of psychology or the neoconservative philosophies of the 1982–1998 school reform movement.

As a result of the personal histories, worldviews, and cultures of most professional educators and many U.S. sociologists and psychologists, the literature of education pays only limited attention to class issues or avoids discussing them entirely.[1] Instead, researchers refer to *socioeconomic status* (SES). This approach, one of two approaches commonly taught in university sociology courses (the other is social class), follows the tradition of W. Lloyd Warner (1898–1970). SES blends both economic issues of jobs and income (or lack of work) with status issues of role relationships, consumption patterns, and implied values to determine a prescribed "socioeconomic status." Educational research usually follows the Warner tradition and uses the concept of SES rather than the concept of social class to describe differences among families, neighborhoods, and schools. While SES studies explain some issues, the concept, as Kuhn (1970) notes, also shapes the perceptions of social scientists and teachers.

The use of SES as an analytical tool emphasizes the role of the individual in determining success or failure. SES can be improved, for example, by getting more education or earning a big promotion at one's workplace. Researchers using SES as an organizational concept usually assume that people improve their position in society primarily by individual effort and that schools serve as vehicles for economic and social advancement. The SES approach rarely challenges the inequality of the system. The use of the concept of status leads to seeking incremental improvements in the schools to benefit those students who appear to be willing to try harder.

The assumptions behind status research reinforce the position that it is individuals who need to change, not schools. Decades of educational research and policy development from this perspective have described the deterioration of educational opportunities for students placed at risk by declining economic opportunities in many regions, but the research has not led to the development of democratic alternatives for teachers and students (W. J. Wilson, 1996).

Research organized around the concept of social class works from substantially different assumptions. From a class perspective, our society is made up of an upper class that includes the owners and managers of businesses and corporations; a middle/working class that includes a professional stratum, many service workers, and blue-collar workers; and a lower class characterized by social isolation, often irregular employment, welfare, and family disruption.

Some of the difficulties that result from using the idea of SES rather than class are revealed in the common use of the term *middle class*. The media and people in casual conversation use the term to mean a variety of living situations. S. Rose (1992) gives examples of two people who would probably be considered middle class:

> The term *middle class* is widely used—most Americans consider themselves part of it—but rarely defined. People usually reject the alternative categorizations, lower or upper class, because no one wants to be poor and few consider themselves wealthy enough to be classified as rich.

[1]The complexity of definitions of social class in the United States and the rapid changes in professional jobs in the middle class lead some researchers to avoid class issues. But the difficulty of arriving at a clear definition of *class* is not an adequate reason to avoid using it as an analytical concept (Ehrenreich & Ehrenreich, 1979; Parker, 1972; Walker, 1979).

Consider the following two families. In the first, the family income is $22,000: the husband works as a forklift operator at an assembly plant while the wife stays at home caring for their two children. The other family is a suburban couple, a dentist and psychologist, with a combined income of $110,000; they own a $250,000 house and three cars, one child is in college, and another attends a local private school. Both families might describe themselves as being "strapped" for money and as having little left over for frills. Both would probably consider themselves part of the middle class—though, the first family might add the adjective "lower" and the second add "upper."

In other words, "middle class" has become a nearly all-inclusive category, one so broad that it not only blurs real distinctions in income, lifestyle, and well-being but often clouds public discussion as well. (p. 15)

Most people in this society work for someone else. Managers direct workers and owners control the jobs. Over 50 percent of all U.S. families depend on wages (as opposed to being self-employed) for their income. The jobs, the income, and the class position of the parents of students largely determine where students will live. In turn, where a student lives significantly affects the quality of the school the student will attend.

Bowles and Gintis (1976), Carnoy and Levin (1985), and others whose research is based on a social-class perspective argue that our economic system produces social classes and that these classes are group phenomena, not individual choices. Changes in class composition occur as a result of changes in the economic system. The structural changes presently occurring in our economy are having this effect. Well-paying union jobs in the auto, steel, electronics, and other industries are being transferred to other countries and are being replaced by low-paying service jobs. These are class changes—not individual changes.

Attention to social class rather than SES yields additional insights into the functions of schooling in our racially and class-polarized society. Scholars, teachers, and researchers interested in promoting equality in schooling use the concept of social class to explain how the gaps in school achievement among students from the upper, middle, working, and poor classes reproduce and maintain inequality in society. According to Bowles and Gintis (1976), only when we grasp the role of class in our educational system can we begin to counteract its effects:

Understanding the dynamics of class relationships is important to an adequate appreciation of the connection between economics and education. For the institutions of economic life (including schools) do not work mechanistically and mindlessly to produce social outcomes, but rather change and develop through the types of class relationships to which they give rise. The educational system is involved in reproducing and changing these class relationships and cannot be understood by simply "adding up" the effects of schooling on each individual to arrive at a total social impact. (p. 67)

Researchers such as Orfield (Orfield & Ashkinage, 1991; Orfield et al., 1996) and W. J. Wilson (1978, 1987, 1988, & 1996), who pay attention to class issues, view the way in which education is presently dispensed as a part of the system of maintaining class relationships. Tracking, ability grouping, teacher expectations, counseling services, and inequitable school expenditures reinforce already existing social class differences (Carnoy & Levin, 1985). Researchers who approach these problems from the perspective of social class usually have different goals for schools than those using a status-based approach. They argue that democratic schools should produce more equality rather than advance a few individuals within the present unequal system. This viewpoint regards schools as a product of public policy and as an institution that is subject to change based on the democratic demands of the majority.

Formation of the European American Working Class

To have an accurate understanding of culture in the United States, it is important to know that the majority of the population is not only "white", but that most "white" people belong to a working class. Each part of the macroculture has its own history and identity. As an example, consider the Irish in the United States. (I have drawn data for the following section from Aronowitz, 1973; Davis, 1986; and Ignatiev, 1973. Please see these works for more detailed discussion and further suggested reading.)

Irish Americans are immigrants who trace their roots to Ireland. Ireland had always produced a surplus of food, but the imposition of an English aristocracy changed agricultural production and the rural Irish were forced into extreme poverty. In 1846 and 1847 the Irish potato crop failed, and over 1 million people faced starvation. During this time Ireland produced sufficient food for all of its people, but the control of the food production was in the hands of English nobility.

When the potato famine hit, starvation was so severe that human bodies piled up beside the roads. There were not enough healthy people to bury the dead. Over 50 percent of the male population either fled or died. Some moved to England to earn a few dollars, and then fled to Australia, Latin America, or the United States. Families survived by sending their young men, and later young women, to the United States looking for work.

Irish workers were recruited in England, Ireland, and in the cities of New York and Boston to build railroads, work in coal mines, and dig canals. By 1850 a majority of people in many of the major cities in the United States were immigrants, predominantly Irish.

Irish immigrants enjoyed a few advantages; they spoke English, they had a history of political organizing, and they brought several community organizations with them, notably the Catholic Church. Irish immigrants used these skills to create labor unions in the United States and political organizations to defend themselves from factory owners. The Irish had long developed resistance societies in Ireland, and political organizations soon arose in the United States. The Irish developed their own schools and universities, incorporated today into the Catholic school system.

In the United States, the new Irish immigrants faced racism and prejudice. Irish workers and their unions were attacked as subversive. But the Irish entered an economy with a rapidly growing job market. Factories, mines, railroads, and the U.S. Army needed workers. Immigrants could get jobs without an education.

Their children went to school, some even to college. Better-paying jobs, and public service jobs such as police and fire, jobs that required training, were opened to the Irish through kinship networks, political patronage, and Catholic schools.

Factories and mines grew in the north after the Civil War. More unskilled and menial workers were needed to do the dangerous and exhausting work. Unions began to form in the mines and on the railroads and to spread to more industries. Factory owners responded by recruiting new immigrant workers in Europe, sending recruiters to Poland, Germany, Lithuania, and Italy.

When Irish and U.S. workers went on strike, Polish workers were imported to do the work, or Italians or Finns. These workers were brought here by labor contractors and did not speak English. Like the Irish before them, they were fleeing the poverty of peasant life in Europe. They came to earn money and to feed their families, and could be used to break the strikes of the Irish and Germans.

Not all immigrants reached U.S. cities alive. They crossed the ocean as cargo. They had to bring their own food and water, and were packed below decks in large groups. Diseases and epidemics killed tens of thousands on their way to the United States.

These migrants hoped to find farm land in the West, but many got no further than Cleveland, Detroit, or Milwaukee, wherever the most desperate jobs could be found. Men, women, and children worked 12 to 14 hours per day, earning barely enough to eat. Living conditions in the urban immigrant communities (called *ghettos* after their counterparts in Europe) were almost subhuman. Housing was unbearable. Workers in factories often could only rent a bed, which they shared with workers on other shifts. Children went to work around 12 years of age. Women worked as hard as men. If they couldn't find a position in a mill, they would be forced to work as servants. Losing that job, many were forced into prostitution. After 10 years of hard labor, many immigrants were too diseased or mutilated to continue to work, so they were thrown out on the street. Criminal behavior and drunkenness were common.

Slowly, painfully, each community was able to get its children into schools. It took over 80 years of struggle to create unions, in part because each immigrant group could be used against the next. In many communities, economic stability was not achieved until World War II.

Throughout the East and Midwest, ethnic communities developed around industries: the Irish in Boston, New York, and the coal fields of Pennsylvania; Poles, Italians, and Irish in Pittsburgh; Slovaks and Italians in Cleveland and Buffalo; Germans in Milwaukee and Chicago; Finns in the iron mines of Minnesota; German and Russian Jews in New York.

People in these immigrant communities worked hard. They sent their children to school. Public schooling offered the families a hope for a better life. The schools were vehicles to "Americanize" the children, to teach them English. After decades a new fiercely "American" culture developed among these working-class descendants of immigrants.

After World War II, these communities began to redefine themselves as "Americans" rather than as Irish or Polish, and working people began to move out of the central cities to the new places called *suburbs*. Federal veterans' home loans (subsidies) helped them purchase homes, and the G.I. Bill (financial aid) allowed many veterans to attend college. During and after both World War I and II a large number of African Americans moved from the South to the North, often coming into conflict and economic competition with the working-class descendants of European immigrants.

In their own communities' view of history, these descendants of immigrants believed that they worked hard, built their unions, played by the rules, educated their children and became "good Americans." This European American working-class culture, like other cultures, passed on a perspective, a worldview, of the melting pot to its children, a worldview they believed to be accurate history.

Each new immigrant group became economic competition for those already here, and they were often faced with hatred. Immigrant groups were easily turned against one another. In the 1830s "native" working people rioted when the Irish began to arrive in large numbers. Political parties were created to keep the Irish out. In 1846 Irish immigrants became the soldiers for the United States invasion of Mexico. In the 1860s, Irish workers in New York rioted rather than be drafted to fight in the Civil War. In the 1870s the new Republican Party campaigned against the Irish with opposition to "Rum, Romanism (Catholicism) and Rebellion" (Ignatiev, 1995).

Although they had been treated as "outsiders" themselves, by the 1850s Irish workers and other "natives" used both the courts and terrorism to demand that Mexican workers be driven out of the gold fields of California and their land seized. In the 1880s, Irish political leaders led the Workingman's Party and demanded that the Chinese workers be kept out of California (Almaguer, 1994). The Irish, Czechs, Poles, Italians, Russians, and Jews were each in turn considered aliens, foreigners, a threat to the "American way" of life by nativist forces.

In the 1920s and again in the 1940s, unions, political forces, and terrorism were used to keep African Americans from gaining political power as they migrated from the South to take jobs in factories in the North. Unity between Protestant and Catholic European immigrants could often be achieved within the working class by uniting against African Americans; or, more recently, against Mexican and Latino immigrants, who seem to pose a threat of economic competition.

These European immigrant groups, along with others, built the railroads, dug the coal, produced the steel, and made the automobiles. As they achieved economic stability, they created schools and universities and enrolled their children. The formerly separate Irish, Italian, Polish, and other subgroups have widely intermarried; as a result, their children have a substantially mixed and new cultural heritage. Having benefited from education, the children, particularly the women, of these European American working-class families seek secure jobs in such professions as teaching and nursing. At present many European American working-class families are under severe financial pressure to keep a secure job. International economic restructuring has replaced many well-paying, unionized, industrial jobs.

An American Dilemma: Poor Children in Poor Schools

There often exists a direct relationship between poverty and school failure. Under our present structure of schooling, poor kids fail more often than kids from middle-income families. The number of poor people in our society is growing. We can therefore predict that a growing number of children will fail in school. *Why* they are failing is a more complex question.

To understand the crisis of poor children in urban and rural schools, we need more information about the growth of poverty in our society and how poverty, schools, and cultural minority groups interact to produce school failure.

As described previously, substantial economic transformations are causing rapid changes in our society and our schools. The U.S. economy has lost its dominant position in the world (Bartlett & Steele, 1992). Figure 4.1 reveals a decline in standard of living and job opportunities of many young people from the working class. Bartlett and Steele describe trends indicating that both the absolute and relative size of the poverty class will grow. As poverty increases, school problems increase.

During the 1960s, as a result of economic growth and government programs known as "the War on Poverty," there was an overall decline in poverty in the United States. In the 1970s, the poverty rate stopped declining, but remained stable despite the fact that the poverty level increased with each recession and decreased in each recovery (Figure 4.4).

As the economy entered the current period of structural change, poverty levels have increased in recessions and remained high during recoveries. Clearly, some segments of society do not benefit significantly from current economic recoveries.

Figure 4.4   Number of Poor and Poverty Rate, 1959–1997

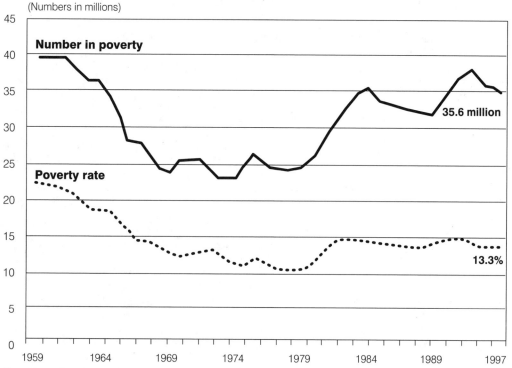

Note. From *Current Population Survey* by U.S. Bureau of the Census, March 1998, Washington, DC: U.S. Government Printing Office.

According to the U.S. Bureau of the Census (1998b), the total number of people living below the official poverty line, with an annual income of $15,569 for a family of four, climbed to 36.5 million in 1996. Over 13 percent of the total population lives below this index of poverty. Poverty levels in the United States remain higher than they have been at any time since 1961 (Figures 4.4 and 4.5).

Poverty is still increasing during the current time of economic prosperity. In 1970, 15 percent of children in the United States lived in poverty, while in 1995, 20.5 percent lived in such severe poverty that their basic needs for nutrition, health, and housing were not reliably met (Children's Defense Fund, 1997; UNESCO, 1993).

The Children's Defense Fund, a respected source of information on income levels of children, writes, "In 1995, the number of children living in families with incomes below the poverty line ($15,569 for a family of four in 1995) declined. In 1995, 14.7 million children (21 percent of America's children) were living in poverty, 2.1 million more than in 1989" (Children's Defense Fund, 1997, p. 12). Over 15 percent of the total population lives below this index of poverty.

While the total poverty rate for children in 1995 was 21 percent, the rate for white children was 16 percent, for blacks 41.3 percent, for Native Americans, 41.4 percent, for Asians, 19.2 percent, and for Hispanics, 39.5 percent (U.S. Bureau of the Census, 1998b).

In past business cycles poverty declined during times of prosperity. The 1994–1998 business cycle was one of the longest, most sustained times of progress

Figure 4.5   Percentages of Persons Below Poverty Level, 1997

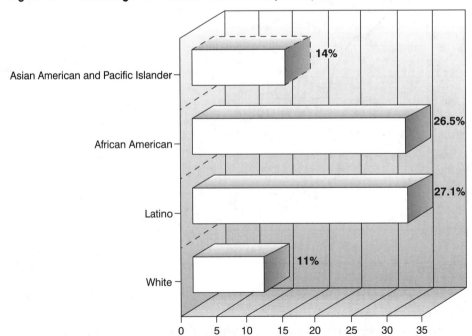

Note. From *Poverty in the United States: 1997* (P 60-201) by U.S. Bureau of the Census, 1998, Washington, DC: U.S. Government Printing Office.

in the nation's history, yet poverty rates remained stable in 1995 and 1996, the last year for which data is available (U.S. Bureau of the Census, 1998b).

In 1996, the Republican Party–controlled U.S. Congress passed, and President Clinton signed, welfare reform in the shape of the Temporary Assistance to Needy Families Act of 1996, a law that again substantially reduced federal spending for the poor, and significantly changed the 60-year-old program for assistance to poor families. Since the new law includes both two-year and five-year phase-in plans, we will begin to see the consequences of this "reform" on the national level by the year 2000.

Finally, in 1998, as a consequence of the longest sustained economic expansion in over 50 years, the poverty rate stopped climbing. The passage of a raise in the federal minimum wage actually reduced poverty levels slightly in 1998 (Mishel et al., 1999).

At present our society, unlike other modern industrialized societies, does not have a policy to prevent poverty or to help families escape from poverty. Certainly any plan would include quality public schooling. Without such a policy, we pay the enormous social and human costs of creating a poverty class (for a discussion of this topic, see Thurow, 1996).

One of the very real human costs is that poverty affects whether children live or die. San Francisco, California, for example, has an infant mortality rate of 7 per 1,000 births—the same as Norway or Switzerland. The rate in Detroit, Michigan, on the other hand, with its higher percentage of urban poor, ranks below that of Cuba, and Washington, DC, has the same infant mortality rate as Jamaica. When infant mortality is compared by race, white infant mortality is 8 per 1,000 births—one of the best in the world. Black infant mortality in the United States is 18 per 1,000—higher than that of Bulgaria, Poland, or Cuba (Children's Defense Fund, 1997; UNICEF, 1997).

One fact that official unemployment statistics often do not reveal is that most of the poor work. Mishel and Bernstein (1995) show that between 1979 and 1990, the number of poor who worked yet remained poor grew from 6.5 million to 8.5 million people. Hard work does not necessarily keep families out of poverty. The exceptions are the disabled, elderly, and single parents of small children. About two-thirds of all other poor people work full or parttime. Many parttime workers would prefer to work fulltime but are unable to find jobs.

As you can see in Figure 4.1, between 1989 and 1996, real family income for the poorest fifth of our people declined by 2.7 percent while that of the richest fifth increased by 9.1 percent. But it is not just the poorest who are in trouble. According to Marshall and Tucker (1992),

> The middle class, the key to social stability in the United States, is also in difficulty. Overall, the top 30 percent of our people in terms of income distribution are getting richer while the bottom 70 percent are getting poorer. (p. xv–xvi)

Poor Children in the Classroom

When a child comes to school from a middle-class family, that child already has learned values at home that closely match the school values advocated by teachers. The child knows much of the culture of the school upon entering. Further, middle-class children have social skills, behaviors, and attitudes that teachers find appropriate. The children are similar to the teachers' own children in most respects. Because the middle-class child's culture is similar to the teacher's culture, most teachers react positively to their middle-class students, and supportive bonds develop between them. In elementary school most of the teachers are female, producing particularly supportive bonds for girls.

A child from a poor, marginalized family is more likely to enter school with a different set of behaviors and attitudes (Carnoy, 1989). While the school expects children to know the themes of mainstream children's literature—such as Cinderella and other European folktales—some children come from homes where few people read. Other children's language skills may be extensive in Spanish or Vietnamese, but limited in English. Yet the school culture expects performance in English. Some children come from homes where computers and the Internet are often used, while others come from homes dominated by television. The punishment and reward systems used by schools are often confusing and different for some children.

Some children arrive at school from homes where poverty or divorce has disrupted stable living arrangements, although disruption and disorganization of home life are not unique or universal to families living in poverty. Middle- and upper-class families also frequently experience disruption and can be made dysfunctional by divorce, alcoholism, drug abuse, and physical or psychological abuse.

Poor but stable families usually prepare their children well for school success. The safety and security of a stable home environment enhance children's ability to view the new environment of school without undue fear. Getting a good start in school in a safe, protected environment helps children learn the culture of school and the new ways of doing things. Children who fail to learn these new behaviors and values required for school success may encounter conflict at school.

The high rate of children moving from school to school in poor neighborhoods degrades the quality of their school experience. Poor people often lose their jobs and their apartments. Poverty, health, and economic crises require them to move. Some even become homeless. For children, frequent moving produces a pattern of health problems and school disruption with a constant array of new teachers, new classmates, and new curriculum.

The truly poor have severe financial problems simply getting through the month. A doctor's appointment can require two days of waiting for service at a public health clinic. For recipients of Temporary Assistance to Needy Families (TANF), contacts with governmental institutions are intrusive, overwhelming, and full of dangers. In poor neighborhoods, a simple school request for family information may cause fear and alarm at home. Parents may fear that yet another social worker is going show up to reduce their already inadequate benefits.

In spite of the problems of poverty, most poor parents still look to school as the best hope for their children's future economic opportunity. They believe in the ideals of our school system. They recognize schooling as the best available route to ending their own cycle of poverty. These parents sacrifice for their children.

When poor children come to school, too often they encounter frustration and failure. Large urban school districts with bureaucratic authoritarian structures and intrusive cultural demands seldom ensure success for poor children (Darling-Hammond, 1997; Ravitch, 1997). Not one of the major cities provides a quality education to all of its students. Up to 50 percent real dropout rates are common. Over 30 percent of the schools in these urban areas fail to educate these children even to basic levels of literacy (Children's Defense Fund, 1997; Orfield et al., 1996). Children fail to learn the rules of the school and find it difficult to meet the school's expectations. Middle-class psychologists and educators may label the students "bad" or "unmotivated."

Even in "difficult" neighborhoods, most parents are struggling to achieve an education for their children. These efforts are sometimes counteracted by overworked and burned-out school staff workers whose main focus is to maintain control of the school campus. Tired school staff too often hold low expectations for children, routinely practice tracking, and ultimately blame the children, their parents, and their communities for existing problems. Parents blame the schools and schools blame the parents. None of this helps the children. Rather than continue this fruitless cycle, teachers need to accept their responsibility to work with parents to educate children and to maintain high standards for all children.

In the face of such school conditions, families can lose hope and confidence in themselves and in schools. Other families, who recognize the violence happening to their children and see their own dreams of opportunity fade, become defensive or hostile toward schools. They vote for tax limitation plans and "choice" or voucher plans that reduce school funding. Some parents make enormous financial sacrifices to place their children in tuition-based private schools. Some frustrated parents avoid school entirely. Others, angry at a society that seems to have abandoned their children, encourage students to engage in open conflict with school authorities.

Society's Obligations to Its Children

The interaction between poverty and schooling is complex and changing. Teachers have always needed to control and redirect a few children in each class who fail in their schoolwork or who refuse to adjust to reasonable standards for social behavior. In many poverty neighborhoods today, however, matters are much worse than in prior years. While a teacher in the 1950s might have faced 2 disruptive children per class, today's teacher may face 8 or, in some classes, up to 20.

Two worldviews of society's obligations to its children are contending for support. Voters and taxpayers have long insisted that our democratic society promote the common good. Our federal constitution and most state constitutions assign the government the task of promoting the "general welfare." One view holds that a society needs to arrange itself so that children are cared for, their health protected, and their education provided. This view has been the mainstream opinion since at least the 1850s and provides the justification for establishing schools as a public responsibility.

A "theory of the common good" recognizes that if a society stops caring for its children, all parts of society suffer. Even a family that is responsible, protective, and nurturing can lose children to the war zones found in some urban neighborhoods.

Society as a whole loses when a child is shot in random gang violence, killed as a bystander at school, or kidnapped by a person who ought to be receiving mental health care and perhaps hospitalization. Parents in marginalized neighborhoods recognize the danger to their families, and they resent the refusal of political leaders to respond to their children's most basic needs of security and educational opportunity.

Unfortunately for children, the ideology of conservative political activists of the 1980s and 1990s promoted an alternative view of society. Conservatives convinced a majority of voters that by saving money and not paying taxes they would be promoting the common good. This was a reversal of traditional conservative thinking. As Reich (1991b) describes, the wealthy secede from the cities, buy beautiful homes in suburbs, wall off their neighborhoods, hire private security forces, and richly fund their children's schools. They promote their individual wealth rather than the public good. They try to blame the deterioration of life in poverty areas on welfare recipients, immigrants, and minorities. Their flight from poverty into walled enclosures has replaced concern for the common good.

Yet no part of society remains healthy when the other parts are sick. Violence and drug abuse in one part of the community endanger us all. Even in the suburbs, runaway and suicide rates of teens have reached epidemic proportions. The conservative strategy of withdrawing into the suburbs worked only until gangs, violence, and drug abuse appeared there, too.

In the bottom tier of our society—the semipermanent poverty areas—the decline in well-paying jobs has substantially damaged family life. Families are divided and some are destroyed by crime, drugs, health crises, divorce, abandonment, and permanent underemployment.

These are not crises that most people choose to acknowledge. W. J. Wilson (1996) describes how unemployment, economic decay, and the deindustrialization of society rob the lower tier of workers of hope and economic opportunity. Neither the schools nor the police are adequately funded or prepared to handle this growing crisis.

Kozol (1991) records how children bring their crises to school each day. Poor and middle-class children mix in some schools. The deterioration of life opportunities among the poor adds to a deterioration of schools. Some students bring to school the same disorder, crime, and gang violence they see in their neighborhoods. Dealing with these problems inevitably takes away from instructional time. Tax cuts and the demand to spend extra funds on school security, plus the need for remediation of basic skills, stress many urban school budgets.

Only major increases in public spending will improve the schools and promote the common good. But the rich and most corporations paid a higher percentage of taxes in the 1960s than they do today. As a result of the tax cuts in the 1980s, the corporate tax burden was shifted from corporations to the middle-class voter. The rich, the middle class, and the elderly are assiduous voters and as a group have fewer children in public schools than do the poor and working class.

The economically privileged tend to vote to limit taxes and to limit school spending. Taxation wars and tax rebellions over school funding have rocked numerous states, including New Jersey, Massachusetts, California, and Ohio. Elected officials have responded to the demands of mobilized voters. The poor seldom vote, and children cannot vote. Consequently, the needs of poor children have low priority among many elected officials, who place little value on arguments for promoting the public good when aroused voters are demanding tax relief.

Interaction of Race, Class, and Poverty

Research on race, class, and poverty in the United States and their cumulative effect on schools is notoriously inadequate. Media descriptions of poverty with their emphasis on gangs, drugs, and violence produce distorted images of inner-city youth. Multiple experiences and race, class, gender, age, and ethnicity factors combine to create an individual's cultural perspective. The isolation of teachers (many of whom live in the suburbs) from the communities surrounding their schools combines with a lack of parental participation to produce misunderstandings and the perpetuation of harmful stereotypes.

The subjects of stereotyping are not limited to racial and ethnic groups. There is class stereotyping as well. Michael Harrington (1928–1990) spent much of his life studying the poor and wrote dozens of books and articles on the subject. His *The Other America* (1963) is a landmark work on poverty in the United States. His research led directly to the war on poverty of the 1960s and influence the perspectives of this chapter. Harrington reviewed decades of research on poverty and pointed out that the average poor family is white and headed by a person working fulltime at a low-paying job. Many of the poor are former middle-class women and children whose poverty is due primarily to divorce or spousal neglect to pay child support (Harrington, 1989).

One particularly large portion of the poor studied by Harrington were the people of Appalachia and other rural areas. Rural poverty is often not considered when considering social class. Yet, according to the U.S. Census Bureau, the states with the highest levels of poverty in 1993 were usually rural, beginning with Louisiana at 26.4 percent, Mississippi at 24.7 percent, West Virginia at 22.2 percent, Kentucky at 20.4 percent, and Arkansas at 20 percent. Other states with large rural areas followed closely, including Tennessee at 19.6 percent, Oklahoma at 19.9 percent, and New Mexico at 17.4 percent (U.S. Bureau of the Census, 1997b).

Appalachian children, among the most Anglo-Saxon in heritage in our nation, also have a distinct culture that at times clashes with school expectations. The example of an "Appalachian" culture reveals the interaction of culture and class. A leader of the Urban Appalachian Council in Cincinnati, Ohio, describes the history of the group as follows:

> Over half a century ago the mechanization of the coal mining industry caused a mass migration from Kentucky, West Virginia, and other Appalachian states. Coal miners, farmers, and railroad men came with their families to nearby industrial cities to look for work. In the early years, work was easy to find. But the labor market was soon saturated with people who had little more to offer than willing hands and strong backs. . . .

>Urban Appalachians are called the "Invisible Minority" because, by such socio-economic measures as educational attainment, occupational status, income, and housing, Appalachians in urban areas are a distinct group that researchers have found to be significantly less advantaged than members of the majority community. But they are not easily identifiable as a minority, since race, sex, or surname in and of themselves do not set urban Appalachians apart from others. (Sullivan & Miller, 1990, p. 112)

Race and Class

Misunderstandings about the causal factors of school achievement occur because in our society there is a strong congruence between race and class. Educational failure by students from the lower class is often reported as a racial issue. But school failure is, in fact, a race–class problem. We collect clear data on race and confusing, indirect data on class. Each year the Economic Policy Institute, in *The State of Working America*, publishes data on the interaction between poverty and race.

Middle-class African American students and Chicano students succeed remarkably like their middle-class European American peers. Meanwhile poor and working class European American students fail remarkably like their poor African American and Chicano peers (MacLeod, 1987; Mehan, 1992). Decades of research reveal the significance and complexity of the interactions between race, class, gender, and culture. These variables interact to influence the home and peer environments and school success.

Cultural and Linguistic Deficit Explanations of School Failure

Early writings on "disadvantaged" young people in the 1960s focused on their alleged cultural and educational "deprivation" or deficits. To early writers, students from the African American minority group came from deprived homes, spoke a limited language, and had few cultural opportunities (Bruner & Cole, 1973). Jensen (1969) and others argued that these students may even have a genetic deficit. These researchers focused on the environment of the young child in search of causal factors of school failure. One group of researchers, following the research of Basil Bernstein, examined the alleged language deficiencies of working-class children in England (Bernstein, 1977). Compensatory education programs such as Head Start and Distar Reading were designed to overcome students' alleged "deficits."

This line of educational research was refuted by most persons working in schools, based in part on the careful linguistic research of William Labov and Noam Chomsky. A more adequate early description of the relationship between culture and poverty was developed by the pioneering anthropologist Oscar Lewis.

Lewis (1968) originally developed the "culture of poverty" thesis to explain the relationship between economic conditions and cultural resistance patterns. He noted that culture was the product of a specific historical situation and the dynamic interaction between families and their environment. He argued that living in extreme and chronic poverty produces defensive behaviors such as distrust of schools and government agencies. In Lewis's studies, these defensive, apathetic, or hostile behaviors were not a product of a specific cultural heritage, but were learned in the interactions between families living in poverty and social institutions, including schools.

Unfortunately, middle-class educational researchers and policy advocates created harmful myths of cultural and language deprivation to explain the school failure of some children (Labov, 1970). The cultural and language deprivation theses became incorporated into teacher folk knowledge and curriculum plans.

Compensatory education program services based on the culture of poverty thesis continue as important elements in school curriculum today through a federal program known as Chapter 1. But three decades of these programs have made only marginal improvements in the achievement gap between middle-class students and students living in poverty. The programs have never been adequately funded, but an additional problem is conceptual. Compensatory education programs and the culture of poverty thesis—as interpreted by a generation of mainly European American, mainly middle-class educational theorists—often worked from the unexamined assumption that there must be something wrong with poor people or they wouldn't be poor. The researchers of the 1960s studied students and found fault with their cultures. They did not study the structures of schooling and therefore did not identify school practices as contributing to student failure. They failed to challenge fundamental practices within the educational system, such as tracking and low teacher expectations, that tend to restrict poor students to a school life of low aspirations and few opportunities.

In 1976, the sociologist William Julius Wilson began using the term *underclass* to describe the reality he saw in urban African American communities in inner-city Chicago. A serious scholar, he argues that class divisions are increasing between middle-class African Americans, working poor African Americans, and a very poor, marginalized, and isolated stratum of some African Americans in urban ghettos— the group to which he applied the term (Raymond, 1991; W. J. Wilson, 1987).

In Wilson's view, the Civil Rights Movement of the 1960s and the governmental policies that followed resulted mainly in the strengthening of the black middle class. The Civil Rights Movement secured political equality, and new government policies assisted some African Americans in leaving poor neighborhoods and finding good jobs, housing, and schooling. The African American middle class grew as a result of these gains. New opportunities were created in government, in education, and later in private industry for well-educated African Americans. Unfortunately, the African American lower class did not share in this prosperity. The rural farmer moving north from Georgia, the marginally employed resident of Harlem, Chicago, Gary, or Los Angeles gained the right to vote, but did not gain economic opportunity.

Wilson's emphasis on the importance of economics in race relations followed the lead of Dr. Martin Luther King, Jr. Early on, King recognized the need for a broad, inclusive movement to promote economic justice as well as racial equality. The Southern Christian Leadership Conference (SCLC), along with others, promoted a multiracial struggle for economic justice with the Poor People's Campaign of 1967–1968. King and the SCLC developed their movement based in part on a critical awareness of the relationship between economic justice and political equality. King united the struggle for civil rights with union struggles and other efforts to end class oppression. Unfortunately, King was assassinated on 4 April 1968, before the Poor People's Campaign could organize a sustainable movement for economic justice.

The U.S. economy has changed since the 1970s. Major corporations closed their plants in the industrialized and unionized northeastern United States, depriving hundreds of thousands of working-class African Americans and Latinos of good jobs and steady income. Plants moved to nonunion areas in the South and Southwest, and to Third World nations, devastating the economic base of African American and Latino communities and the lives of many in the working class. In 1977, General Motors corporation had 77,000 jobs for hourly workers in Flint, Michigan. By 1998, there were only 33,000 ("Man of Flint," 1998). Working-class union families lost their jobs or were pushed into marginal employment in low-paying service industries. The economic crisis of the 1970s and 80s destroyed many African American families. W. J. Wilson (1987) describes the consequences of this economic shift in urban areas.

Wilson contends that since the 1970s the deterioration of central cities and the loss of union-wage jobs to the South and Sunbelt regions and to foreign competition left a marginally employed underclass behind in urban ghettos (W. J. Wilson, 1987, 1996). He argues, for example, that the flight of the middle class from Chicago left behind weakened neighborhood institutions and schools. A portion of society was set aside—apartheid style—as an area where drugs, crime, and neglect were considered normal and were tolerated. Today, children from these areas attend inferior schools and enjoy few opportunities for success.

Wilson's most recent work, *When Work Disappears: The World of the New Urban Poor* (1996), offers an explanation of how race, class, and lack of government policy of economic growth work together to reinforce school failure. He recommends government policies to promote economic growth and change for the entire lower class. In his view, general programs for the poor, such as jobs and quality education, are preferable to racially specific programs, such as affirmative action.

Wilson does not argue that race is unimportant, only that race–class variables interact. Unfortunately, educational researchers and the media have a long history of oversimplifying and of rushing to apply new ideas. Predictably, the discussion of the underclass has not remained focused on the precise group described by Wilson. For example, the media should—but often don't—distinguish between the working poor and members of the marginally employed underclass who, at times, find intermittent work in an illegal economy of theft, prostitution, and drugs. The two are separate groups; they are not all a part of a single "underclass" and their children have distinct educational experiences.

Hacker (1992) accurately describes the diversity among today's black families. He notes that over 40 percent of African American children live in a family with both parents. Both the growth of the black middle class and the continuation of the poor but stable African American family challenge stereotypic notions of the underclass.

Further reading about the very poor in areas such as Chicago, New York, Boston, Philadelphia, and Los Angeles does not tell teachers much about the life experiences of a child in such midsize cities as Sacramento, Toledo, Seattle, or Denver. Nor does the concept of underclass adequately describe the experiences of those in Atlanta, Birmingham, New Orleans, or other large cities of the South.

As constructed by Wilson, the underclass thesis describes conditions in large, northern urban ghettos where social institutions have failed and where some communities are dominated by gangs and the drug culture. Even in these devastated areas, not all families have lost the battle to guide their children. For these reasons, it is important that teachers avoid stereotypes about poor and low-income students. Descriptions of family life need to be tested to see if they match the reality of an actual neighborhood served by an actual school.

African American and Mexican American children have routinely been inappropriately placed in special education classrooms. Schools have established tracking systems and placed children based on inaccurate psychological attributions of culturally specific information (Oakes, 1985). Some ultraconservative foundations, such as the Ollin Foundation, have generously funded a branch of "research" that purports to demonstrate genetic differences by class and by race. *The Bell Curve: Intelligence and Class Structure in American Life*, by Herrnstein and Murray (1994) is the most recent of several such publications on this subject. The authors have sought to revalidate discredited theories of the 1960s of genetic and cultural deprivation. Murray's previous book, *Losing Ground: American Social Policy 1950–1980* (1984), helped to set the agenda for current attacks on the welfare system. A range of social scientists has demonstrated the flaws in argument and psychological measurement found in *The Bell Curve*. In spite of the numerous errors, a number of policy organizations continue to promote these ideas. Interested readers can find more on the advocacy of this line of argument on the World Wide Web at the Committee on Economic Opportunity's website (http://www.ceo.org), chaired by Linda Chavez.

Minimally, teachers should be wary of conclusions drawn about childrearing behavior in one cultural group or class when these conclusions are based on the observations by members of a distinctly different cultural group. Moore (1988), in a paper on Hispanic poverty, demonstrates that Wilson's findings about urban black families should *not* be extended to describe urban Hispanics. While Latino poverty has grown substantially—and Latino family poverty is as acute as African American family poverty—the characteristics of community dissolution that are part of the underclass model are not present in most Latino families and neighborhoods (Moore, 1988; Tienda & Stier, 1991).

While Wilson noted that the flight of the black middle class left the largest urban ghettos with few supporting institutions intact, Moore observes that the family and community institutions in most Latino communities have not crumbled. Mexican and Mexican American family life, for example, is comparatively unified, stable, and supportive of education. The Catholic church has remained in the barrios and at times has become an immigrant church influenced by and receptive to Latino cultures. The steady flow of new immigrants with their folk culture and expectations of success has also positively influenced the Mexican American community. Moore (1988) concludes that the underclass thesis does not adequately describe poverty in the Hispanic community. In a similar manner, the responses of the predominantly Puerto Rican neighborhoods in New York, Newark, Chicago, and Milwaukee are not necessarily similar to the Mexican American experiences in San Antonio, El Paso, Los Angeles, San Diego, and Oakland.

School Responses to Poverty

As a response to the dramatic growth of poverty among children in the past 15 years, teachers need to improve on present school curricula and work closely with community institutions. Classrooms need fewer disruptions. Teachers need more time to work with children. Special compensatory education programs must not interrupt the normal flow of classroom instruction. Children need a safe and orderly environment in order to learn basic skills (Institute for Puerto Rican Policy, 1991; Olsen, 1988; Quality Education for Minorities Project, 1990; U.S. Department of Education, 1987). Current supplementary federal and state programs designed to teach basic skills to poor children are underfunded and inadequate to meet the crisis of the rapidly growing population of the poor.

Schools could serve to promote democracy instead of recycling a society divided into the rich, the middle and the poor. They could serve as a response to poverty. Schools in marginalized neighborhoods and cities could provide safe, clean, well-constructed schools, with counselors, nurses, security, and high quality instruction. The children of the poor could be offered education as a way out of poverty—but they are not. Legislators and school administrators fail when they create new programs instead of using their resources to improve the teaching and leaning conditions.

It is harmful and inaccurate to assume that children in poverty-stricken neighborhoods or from poor families have "characteristic" problems in school. Living in a poor neighborhood does not necessarily affect reading and math, although living in a violent and disruptive family or attending a violent and disruptive school might. A variety of people and families live in poverty. Some are chronically unemployed, low skilled, or even criminals. Most are not. The children of these families require quality public schools. Under the existing political and economic systems, they are usually denied them.

Summary

A growing crisis of poverty, particularly among children, contributes to many of the failures in our school system. Multicultural education employs the concept of social class along with race, ethnicity, culture, and gender in describing, designing, and improving schools.

Schools serving poor communities usually are underfunded, staffed with less-experienced teachers, and frequently practice tracking and accept low standards of achievement. These school practices, not the individual characteristics of children, provide unequal educational opportunity and produce failure. Federally funded and directed compensatory education programs have not remedied the problems of our failing schools in urban areas. Attention to social class helps to explain the persistent failure of students in poverty-stricken schools.

Questions Over the Chapter

1. List factors that contributed to the significant increase in the number of children living in poverty from the 1970s through the 1990s.
2. What are differences between the concepts of *social class* and *socioeconomic status?*
3. List three recommendations for school improvement from each conceptual scheme: (a) socioeconomic status, (b) social class.
4. Explain the differences in poverty rates for African American, Latino, and European American children. Why do these differences occur?
5. From 1967 to 1968, Dr. Martin Luther King, Jr., and the Southern Christian Leadership Council expanded their emphasis from civil rights to include economic justice.
    a. What were the important elements of an economic justice agenda in the 1960s?
    b. Describe the elements of an economic justice agenda today.
6. What are the differences in policy between a racial analysis and a race–class analysis of school achievement?
7. What can schools and teachers do to respond to the rise in poverty among children?

Activities for Further Study of Class Relationships in Schools

1. Observe and document the broad spectrum of diversity found in a classroom of your choice, such as culture, ethnicity, gender, social class, gifted and talented.
    a. What are the different groups in the class?
    b. How many are there of each?
    c. Does the teacher devote more time to certain students or groups?
    d. Are certain students singled out for criticism and punishment?
    e. Are any groups of students treated in a different manner? Are female students treated differently than males? How? Are fast or slow learners treated differently? How?
2. Conduct observations of classes at several school sites. Using the following criteria, work in groups to compare your observations of middle-class schools and schools in poverty areas.
    a. Teacher optimism/teacher stress
    b. School facilities
    c. Discipline systems used
    d. Parent participation, parent respect
3. Take a walking tour of the immediate neighborhood of the school in which you are working. Record your impressions and share them with your classmates.
4. Compare the social class positions of students in your teacher preparation program with those of the school children you serve. List some class differences between teachers and students—for example, attitudes toward fighting, manners, and any other differences you identify.
5. Identify and describe at least three problems of economic achievement that are related to social class.

6. Many colleges and universities have departments of ethnic studies and women's studies. Few, or none, have departments of class studies. Why did ethnic studies departments develop? Interview a sociology professor. Why were departments of sociology not sufficient to examine ethnicity in the United States?

7. Investigate the class connotations of using the term *Hispanic* rather than *Puerto Rican, Mexi-* *can,* or another term. How do persons who use each term see their own class position?

8. Conduct research on the educational success and conflicts of poor, European American children from the Appalachian regions of our country. Contact the Appalachian Educational Laboratory, PO Box 1348, Charleston, West Virginia 25325.

Teaching Strategies

1. Find literature, music, and videos that begin in students' own experiences and reach to universal themes and skills.

2. Validate students' own languages and cultures.

3. Integrate reading, oral, and written language instruction and skills into several subject-matter areas.

4. Include hands-on learning activities whenever possible.

5. Plan and teach specific study skills as a part of the curriculum. Begin at students' actual skill levels. Teach the use of texts, paragraph writing, and other necessary skills.

6. Maintain the goal of reading and writing at the skill level of middle-class, suburban schools (or state standards). Do not lower your expectations for achievement (see Chapter 9).

7. Teach standard appropriate academic English as a valuable system of communication in addition to students' vernacular expressions.

8. Create a classroom climate of safety, trust, and community building.

9. Study and encourage pro-school values.

Chapter 5

How Society and Schools Shortchange Girls and Boys

with Dolores Delgado Campbell

There are strong similarities between sexism and racism. Both teach role relationships that leave one group in a subordinate position. Both are primarily expressed through institutional arrangements of privilege for some and oppression for others. Both are forms of violence: individual and collective, psychological and physical. Just as previous chapters described how African Americans, Latinos, and Native Americans, among others, are harmed by low expectations, being female also leads to subtle forms of tracking—even by female teachers.

Amott and Matthaei (1991) argue that gender, like race, is as much a social as a biological category:

> Gender differences in the social lives of men and women are based on, but not the same thing as, biological differences between the sexes. Gender is rooted in societies' beliefs that the sexes are naturally distinct and opposed social beings. These beliefs are turned into self-fulfilling prophecies through sex-role socialization; the biological sexes are assigned distinct and often unequal work and political positions, and turned into distinct genders. (p. 13)

The school site is a stage on which gender roles are developed in our society, and thus schools contribute to the assignment of unequal status and work opportunity in our rapidly changing economy. Schools serve as "gatekeepers" providing opportunity to some, but not to all.

Between 1983 and 1992, the press, elected officials, and corporate advocacy groups conducted a national debate, loosely termed the "educational reform movement," concerning the role and future of public education in the United States. The leading "experts" in this debate avoided discussions of race, class, and gender issues whenever possible. In 1992, the American Association of University Women (AAUW) issued a report, *How Schools Shortchange Girls,* that responded to the avoidance of gender issues:

> The absence of attention to girls in the current educational debate suggests that girls and boys have identical educational experiences in schools. Nothing could be further from the truth. Whether one looks at achievement scores, curriculum design, self-esteem levels, or staffing patterns, it is clear that sex and gender make a difference in the nation's public elementary and secondary schools. There is clear evidence that the educational system is not meeting girls' needs. Girls and boys enter school roughly equal in measured ability. In some measures of school readiness, such as fine motor control, girls are ahead of boys. Twelve years later, girls have fallen behind their male classmates in key areas such as higher-level mathematics and measures of self-esteem. (AAUW, 1992, p. 2)

Tracking Female Students

For girls, especially middle-class, European American girls, attending school in the United States means getting a head start in the early grades only to be tracked and subsequently held back or diverted into less challenging fields in the higher grades. Recall that in Chapter 1 we defined *tracking* as a system wherein individuals are identified according to specified physiological, cultural, socioeconomic, or academic criteria and placed in academic course schedules [tracks] designed to fulfill select educational prerequisites, develop a specific skill set, or prepare them for specific careers. Oakes (1985) amplifies this definition:

> Tracking is the process whereby students are divided into categories so that they can be assigned in groups to various kinds of classes. Sometimes students are classified as fast, average, or slow learners and placed into fast, average, or slow classes on the basis of their scores on achievement or ability tests. Often teachers' estimates of what students have already learned or their potential for learning more determine how students are identified and placed. Sometimes students are classified according to what seems most appropriate to their future lives. Sometimes, but rarely in any genuine sense, students themselves choose to be in "vocational," "general," or "academic" programs. (p. 3)

Tracking of women occurs in our schools despite the fact that the schools are predominantly female turf. For example, women now constitute a majority of all college students and 73 percent of all teachers, concentrated particularly at the elementary school level. In Los Angeles, California, for example, over 70 percent of the teachers and over half of the administrators in K–6 elementary schools are female (Los Angeles County Office of Education, 1991).

The women in charge of these schools are usually European American. In most elementary schools, girls are not systematically disparaged and criticized for being girls, although they may be disparaged for being lower-class Latinas, African Americans, or Asians. The emotions and turmoil of middle-class European American girls are sympathetically understood by elementary school authorities, both teachers and principals. The female-dominated institution produces female success during the critical early years when the child is defining her own identity and her relationship to learning and schooling (National Education Association, 1990; Sadker, Sadker, & Long, 1989).

Self-Esteem

Although racism and sexism both have damaging effects on the oppressed and on the oppressor, their manifestations in the early years of school are often quite different from their adult forms. While the excellent AAUW report argues that positive cross-sex relationships may be more difficult than cross-race relationships, in elementary schools the problem is more complex. This is because families and schools generally are much better at giving young children positive cross-gender experiences than they are at giving them positive cross-racial experiences. Several examples can be seen in the typical home.

Children develop a view of self in their very early years, usually in the intimate and nurturing surroundings of the home. Evidence indicates that children learn both about themselves and about others by at least age 4. Most learning of "appropriate" role relationships takes place under the guidance of females, either in the home or in child care.

When children or adults work in an intimate relationship with another person in a positive environment, they learn to like and respect that person. This equal-status interaction teaches mutual respect (Buteyn, 1989; National Education Association, 1990; Sadker et al., 1989). Almost all little boys have an intimate, trust-building relationship or an equal-status relationship with at least one female—usually their mother. In the early formative years, most boys learn to respect and love their mother or some other female caregiver, such as a grandmother or aunt. Few young boys learn to dominate their mothers. This early relationship should provide a basis for future learning of mutual respect and cooperation in relationships with women.

Of course, this picture does not match the experience of all children. In a home with an abusive or dominating parent, children may learn abusive and dominating patterns. In homes with a single female head of household, boys may still learn respectful relationships. In some such homes, however, boys may fail to experience positive relationships with males. They then may get guidance from television and the streets—both inadequate substitutes for a caring family. However, generally speaking, prior to age 6, most young boys and girls learn to interact with their peers without male dominance. Their early experience of respect and cooperation provides a basis for future equality-based relationships.

While families provide opportunities for cross-gender respect, they seldom provide opportunities for cross-racial respect. Most U.S. neighborhoods, cities, and families are segregated by race and culture. Most of our cities are more racially segregated in 1990 than they were in 1960 (Orfield, Bachmeier, James, & Eitle, 1997). Too many of our young children do not develop an intimate, loving, caring relationship with persons of other races.

The teaching profession remains female dominated and racially segregated (National Education Association, 1998). As a result, too few young students have a positive relationship with a teacher from a minority culture. The lack of this intimate, perception-shaping experience makes learning mutual respect and cooperation in cross-cultural relationships more difficult. Children learn to fear the "other," the outsider. This fear establishes a basis for future learning of prejudice.

The lack of cultural diversity in the upbringing and schooling of young children hits the children of minority cultures hardest. When African American, Vietnamese, or Latina girls enter school, they enter a new culture, often one where they are regarded as "other," different, and inferior. The shock may be profound. Some of these children may suddenly feel uncertain about themselves and become withdrawn or defensive. Their ability to learn also suffers. Too often failure and frustration in school attacks a student's self-image and distorts her view of her home culture (Au & Kawakami, 1994; Foster, 1994). Young girls (and boys) of color first experience an inferior, castelike status in their neighborhood school.

Entering school is a major, traumatic event in the lives of many girls (and boys) from these cultures. The average African American or Latina student enters school a few months behind her middle-class counterparts in skill development, and falls progressively behind for the next 12 years (National Center for Education Statistics, 1997). Although school may not be the primary source of this society's oppressions, it is often the institution where tracking, labeling, and failing first occur.

Oakes (1988) documents the negative results of tracking African American and Latina youths away from college-bound classes and into general classes, homemaking, and business courses. Evidence indicates that Catholic schools track Latinas less than do public schools (Oakes, 1985).

Research on European American Girls

School failure and intrusion are substantially different for European American girls than for members of racial and linguistic minorities. Studies by Sadker et al. (1989) and others (which focus mainly on European American girls) show that gender-based bias in school is significant and powerful. Some schools still track girls to mothering roles and boys to college. By high school, girls tend to score lower than boys on some math and science measures. Since these courses are prerequisites for entrance into traditionally male, well-paying careers, a society such as ours that promises equal opportunity should not accept these scoring differences.

In the primary grades, the oppression of girls takes different forms. The average girl enters school academically ahead of boys her age and remains ahead (as measured by grades and test scores) through the elementary grades (AAUW, 1992). The research collected by the AAUW is excellent, but the recommendations are limited substantially to European American girls. The major problems of school achievement for these girls occur after they leave the female turf of elementary schools. A multiracial perspective on gender and student achievement leads to quite different conclusions for students of color.

Unlike students of color, young European American girls normally do not come to school and encounter a new environment run by "others." These girls go from a usually female-centered home culture to a female-centered school culture. Schools and teachers have positive expectations for them. Young, middle-class, European American girls do not encounter the substantially destructive attacks on their gender that young minority children (male or female) encounter on their culture. When students share class, race, and gender with the teacher or the counselor, they are usually encouraged to "become the best they can be." Female students from a minority culture often encounter the oppression of race and class in school.

Fortunately, gender-role stereotyping in schools is decreasing, but it remains a problem (AAUW, 1992). The efforts to reduce gender stereotyping among teachers create new questions about school achievement across cultural groups.

It is boys who lack role models for the first six years of schooling, particularly African American, Latino, and Asian boys. While European American girls benefit from their female-centered primary school experience, children of color—particularly boys—fail. It is boys who encounter the most conflicts, receive the most punishments in school, and most often get placed in special education and remedial programs (Sadker et al., 1989).

The positive school experiences of girls begin to change in adolescence. The teenage years in our society are a time of redefining self and roles. Young girls and boys who were once self-confident now search for new identities. Earlier self-definitions shift. For many teenagers, belonging to a group becomes a major goal. Young people look to their peers for guidance through these difficult and troubling years.

Schoolgirls, at least those European American girls studied, suffer significant declines in self-esteem as they move from childhood to adolescence:

> A nation-wide study commissioned by the A.A.U.W. in 1990 found that on average 69 percent of elementary school boys and 60 percent of elementary school girls reported that they were "happy the way I am"; among high school students the percentages were 46 percent for boys and only 29 percent for girls.
>
> The A.A.U.W. survey revealed sharp differences in self-esteem among girls from different racial and ethnic groups. Among elementary school girls, 55 percent of white girls, 65 percent of black girls, and 68 percent of Hispanic girls reported being "happy the way I am." But in high school, agreement statements came from only 22 percent of white girls and 30 percent of Hispanic girls, compared to 58 percent of black girls. However, these black girls did not have high levels of self-esteem in areas related to school. . . . Obviously, self-esteem is a complex construct, and further study of the various strengths and perspectives of girls from many different backgrounds is needed in order to design educational programs that benefit all girls. (AAUW, 1992, pp. 12–13)

Young girls who excelled in elementary school may begin to falter as they enter the middle grades (6 through 8). Particular concern has been expressed by teachers over the falling grades of girls in science and math (AAUW, 1992). One apparent reason for this is that young boys are often more assertive in class than girls, and receive more teacher attention, both positive and negative. Gilligan (1982), in her groundbreaking work, *In a Different Voice,* hypothesizes that many girls acquire feminine ways of learning and relating to others that are distinctly different from the behavior described as universal to boys and girls by psychologists. In critiquing prominent theories of moral behavior, she states, "While the truths of psychological theory have blinded psychologists to the truth of women's experience, that experience illuminates a world psychologists have found hard to trace" (p. 62). Another researcher, Tannen (1990), describes differences in communication styles learned by boys and girls.

The writing and research of feminist authors also provide important insights into classroom differences. Tavris (1992) systematically examines the research on differences between males and females and finds many assumptions and assertions to be overgeneralized beyond the available evidence. Her book, *The Mismeasure of Woman,* provides an excellent analysis of overinterpretation from limited data, criticizing work in learning styles and brain activity, as well as Gilligan's assumptions about value orientations and relationships. We must assume, until proven otherwise, that gender differences do not explain or cause differences in school achievement; these differences can be attributed to how teachers and schools treat children (Tannen, 1990; Tavris, 1992).

Research by Dweck and her associates suggests that girls may learn "helplessness" in math based in part on teacher expectations and on how teachers respond to and evaluate student work. Teachers of either gender could unknowingly concentrate their responses to girls in a way that discourages intellectual effort, particularly in math (Dweck, 1977).

The most recent data we have is from the 1994 for reading and 1996 for mathematics National Assessment of Educational Progress (NAEP). This collection of test results from around the nation indicates that girls significantly outperform boys in grades 4, 8, and 12 in reading (Campbell, Donahue, Reese, & Philips, 1996); and lag 1 to 3 percent behind boys in grades 4, 8, and 12 in math (Reese, Miller, Mazzeo, & Dossey, 1997).

It is in middle school, as adolescents, that many girls crash into cultural expectations, an emphasis on looks, and a perceived lack of power. While most girls make it through adolescence and redefine themselves and their gender roles in healthy ways, too many end up with severe emotional problems.

In middle school and high school, when young women have a peak concern with appearance, some experience harassment for their looks and others are harassed because they avoid sexuality. Peer pressure can lead to drug use, early sexual relations, and leaving school. School can be a harsh and difficult world to negotiate. Depression and eating disorders are frequent introductions to crisis. Young women need coaches and support during this time (Pipher, 1994). We discuss this further in Chapter 6.

Feminist researchers have developed the concept of "silenced voices" among students. Fine (1993), in her study of a major New York City high school, found that systematic "silencing" of girls' voices (by not respecting their opinions) helped teachers to preserve an ideology of equal opportunity while in fact the schooling practices reinforced inequality. Fine's research offers dramatic examples of the conflict between what some teachers want to pursue as democratic goals and the reality of public school experiences.

At the high school level, teachers' discomfort with discussion of sexual issues prevented the school from serving as a source of valid and valuable information, so girls turned elsewhere, to the streets, for information. When schools refuse to deal with the urgent issues of young women—contraception, sexuality, and so on—some women choose to leave school (Fine, 1993).

By high school, girls begin to make career choices. Influenced in part by the ideology of movies, television, teen magazines, and popular culture, some young women learn to prefer nonacademic, unchallenging classes. They come to regard intellectually rigorous classes as "unfeminine." Faludi (1991) describes this as an "undeclared war" on women and feminism, arguing that some current counseling practices continue to track girls to become nurses rather than doctors, legal secretaries rather than lawyers, elementary school teachers rather than college professors. In their immaturity, some young women dream they can escape work by becoming models or movie stars. The American Association of University Women reports that between 40 percent and 50 percent of female dropouts leave school because they are pregnant (AAUW, 1992). Their childcare responsibilities sharply limit their future economic opportunities. Later, deprived of a quality education, they will find themselves laboring long hours doing unfulfilling work for low pay in a gender-stratified workforce.

The Lure of the Beauty Myth

Many girls and young women become preoccupied with their personal image and their relationships with others. Later, by high school, this becomes the "beauty and romance" myth. Television and popular media teach that a girl can achieve success, defined as marriage and wealth, by becoming beautiful and shrewdly using her sexual powers.

Wolf (1991) discusses the destructive effects of the beauty industry and its ideology. As she describes in *The Beauty Myth: How Images of Beauty Are Used Against Women*, the myth is that girls do not need to prepare for a career; they can just be beautiful and become a model, a star, or at least a mother. (The male equivalent of this myth is to plan to become a major league sports figure and make millions of dollars.)

This belief in a magic alternative to hard work misleads both young women and men, but the beauty industry is built on it. Our communications media—especially television and popular magazines—are saturated with the assertion that beauty, popularity, and acceptance can be bought. Wolf argues that girls' self-esteem may be predicated on being admired by boys, usually for their physical beauty or sexual availability.

Many young girls work hard and diet hard in pursuit of physical beauty. Girls who succumb to this myth feel secure only when they have a date or when they establish their value in relationship to a boy. Powerful advertising sells the myths of beauty and romance. Television also sells a current culture of assertive, at times irresponsible, sexuality that successfully competes with school culture. Television, film, and print media and the culture of consumerism shape teenage girls' worldview more than does their school experience. For many, the shopping mall is the campus of choice.

Adolescent Sexuality

Sex and gender orientation are significant issues to many adolescents. Their identities and social roles are frequently in transition. The school curriculum needs to include discussion of these vital issues. Discussion and analysis of teenage sexuality plays an important part in students developing their own identity.

A young woman who is clear about her sexuality is knowledgeable and capable of making important decisions. Young people who are troubled and uncertain about their sexuality and their gender identification are subject to many conflicting pressures from peer groups.

In *Fateful Choices: Healthy Youth for the 21st Century*, Hechinger (1992) gives numerous examples of school-based health clinics providing important information to young adolescents. Although conservatives have attacked such clinics as interfering in the parents' role, the authors of the present text believe that it is better to not have 11- to 14-year-old girls getting pregnant and encountering sexually transmitted diseases. We prefer that young women grow beyond 16 before having children. To make it through adolescence without birthing children requires that young women and men clarify their own views on sex and sexuality and that they be taught adult decision-making skills.

Adolescence is a time of high risk. Peer pressure to participate in sexual relationships at a young age has grown significantly in the last 20 years. Young women need self-confidence and support from others to protect themselves from the peer pressure and the sexual harassment they encounter in school.

When questioned, young women report that the peer pressure to engage in sexual activity, by both boys and girls, and their own desire to love someone and to be loved leads to sexual behavior and pregnancy (Hechinger, 1992). Early pregnancy and childbirth lead many to leave school and face subsequent lifelong poverty. For some, early pregnancy is an introduction to a life of abuse and behavioral problems that are then passed on to their children.

Not all young people become interested in sex at age 11, or 12, or 14, or even 16. Interest in sex is a result of a complex series of social, psychological, biological, and cultural events. In our society, in which television, magazines, and movies regularly define being female primarily in sexual terms, many young women suffer undue pressure to "grow up" fast, to have breasts, to have a boyfriend, and to become sexually active. Many young people are pressured to be sexual—and to be sexually active—while they would still prefer the safety of early adolescence. Girls and boys, particularly in middle schools, deserve the support of empathetic teachers, counselors, and parents in their times of changing identities.

Sexual behavior, particularly by the very young, has severe consequences. Sexually transmitted diseases are on the rise. AIDS due to unprotected sex and drug abuse presents a serious crisis. Sexual education could be included in several areas of the curriculum, including literature, science, health education, and social studies. English literature classes, for example, could use stories or poems dealing with teenage sexuality. Role playing of peer pressure and writing journal entries can further explore these themes.

Assisting Young Women

Women teachers, with their own role identity clear, can assist young women by serving as mentors, encouragers, and providing a sounding board for young women's role and gender questions. Teachers, counselors, coaches, librarians and nurses have opportunities to establish trusting and helping relations with these young women. If a teacher acts in a trusting and friendly way, and respects students' confidences, she will attract students who are looking for support, a smile, and a person with whom they can talk. Often a teacher's small gestures of encouragement and expressions of interest and support can change a student's direction (Figure 5.1). (See also the discussion on coaching in Chapter 7.)

Teachers can be the first to notice such crisis signs as bulimia or anorexia, and to ask for the assistance of the school nurse or counselor. Teachers can bring out into open discussion the commercial overemphasis on looks, dress, and being thin that

Figure 5.1   A Teacher Inspires a Student

Maria's family moved, so she was forced to change schools in sixth grade. She was shy, and insecure about her abilities. Her new teacher, Miss Vernon, taught both English and Spanish classes. She was gentle and encouraged Maria's comments, even though Maria spoke softly and avoided attention. Miss Vernon smiled and encouraged her with comments, a touch on the shoulder, and support.

One day Miss Vernon stood next to Maria's desk and handed her an English paper with a large gold seal on it. She smiled and said, "Maria, you are a smart girl." Maria felt warm, glowing, and proud. This small event continues to inspire Maria to this day. She went on to college and is now a teacher herself. Whenever she faces a difficult problem, a confusing assignment, she remembers the encouragement and the faith that Miss Vernon had in her.

endangers some young women's lives. Many adolescent girls respond to their natural body growth with an unwarranted fear of weight gain.

Young girls are dieting and skipping meals far too often for good health. Schools cannot change the commercial media's emphasis on the "perfect" image, but they can promote a healthy balance of personality development, learning social skills, good health, and physical fitness. Friendly teachers can advise young women on dress and makeup, to counter the sometimes bizarre messages of magazines and television, helping students to develop healthy self-confidence.

The feminist movement of the 1970s and 1980s affected many teachers' views of themselves and of their roles as advocates for young girls. Weiler (1988) argues that feminist sociologists constructed a new way of looking at school success and girls' resistance. Her work offers a detailed analysis of how several women teachers experienced gender issues. These teachers were committed to working with their students to challenge traditional gender roles. They each had a strong sense of social justice and drew from their commitment in selecting teaching strategies. Many believed that they themselves had suffered professionally as a result of the prior generation's rigid gender roles. In this study each teacher's own sense of self, her view of her own relationship to feminist goals, was an important factor in her selection of instructional strategies.

Sexual Orientation

Friend (1993) argues that our schools and society have "a systematic set of institutional and cultural arrangements that reward and privilege people for being or appearing to be heterosexual, and establish potential punishments or lack of privilege for being or appearing to be homosexual" (p. 211).

Adolescents face many crises of identity. Some young people, about 10 percent, face a conflict between their emerging sexual preference and the socially approved norm (Friend, 1993). Deciding on or accepting a sexual orientation other than the socially approved one involves a number of social, psychological, and personality conflicts. Recognizing homosexual preferences can provoke crises in students' lives. Students who acknowledge and exhibit homosexual behaviors are often subject to assauit, harassment, and violence in school. Violence toward homosexual students is a major problem for some students, and deserves to be dealt with in the same manner as other hate crimes (Friend, 1993).

When students face such troubling decisions as whether to acknowledge or hide their sexual preferences, they need to talk with adults, with teachers and with counselors. When the curriculum silences any student voices, and omits coverage of sexual orientation issues, the vulnerable students are left on their own. Failing or leaving school, or even considering suicide, are among the consequences of some schools' unwillingness to stop sexual violence. In addition to protection, students need opportunities to think and rethink their emotions, feelings, and decisions. Human relations lessons on name calling and homophobia provide opportunities for students to explore identity conflicts (see Chapter 6). It is helpful if there are community agencies or support groups that can help them think through these issues.

Divorce in families due to parental sexual orientation conflicts also can cause crises in young people. A divorced parent in a gay or lesbian relationship can trigger an identity crisis for children that requires support and often counseling.

Limited Choices for Non-College-Bound Women

Until recently the typical U.S. high school has had little to offer non-college-bound female students in the way of technical and professional preparation. Business courses, for example, offered little more than secretarial training.

The conservative school reform movement (1982–1992) sought to reestablish a common academic curriculum for all students in high school. Schools concentrated their time, energy, and funds on improving academic programs. Opportunities for college-bound students improved. But in their emphasis on academic excellence, these reformers neglected vocational preparation—a critical omission at a time when job opportunities and the skills needed to take advantage of them were rapidly changing. Thus the post–high school opportunities of non-college-bound students became more restricted than ever (Weis, 1988, 1990).

In 1994, the U.S. Congress passed, and President Clinton signed, the School to Work Opportunities Act (PL 103-239) to encourage states and local schools to develop new, high-technology programs to help students move from school to employment. The law "sunsets" in 2001, when it assumes that the states will have developed and implemented their own programs.

School-to-work programs offer preparation for the new knowledge-based economy to students as part of their high school and community college preparation. Well-developed programs motivate students to remain in school by providing them with workplace experience and introducing them to the adult world of work (Figure 5.2). School-to-work counselors assist students to explore new, emerging industries for their career choices.

Teachers can assist students in taking advantage of school and work opportunities by sharing their own life histories and by encouraging young women to get a good education. Young women 16 to 18 years old often look mature and dress in an adult manner. Many even engage in adult sexual behavior. Yet their consciousness of the reality of the working world remains underdeveloped. Feminist scholarship argues that girls benefit in school from assistance in developing self-confidence, rather than relying on beauty images. Girls should receive praise for their intellectual work, not for their conformity and obedience to marketed images of women. All young women need to be encouraged to pursue a well-rounded, rigorous education. Female teachers sharing experiences from their own lives validate the experiences of younger women. Sharing adds a mature view to questions of career choice and sexual role. In Chapter 6, we present further suggestions and strategies on developing positive self-esteem.

Figure 5.2   A School-to-Work Success Story

Noemi was a troubled teenager. She daily considered leaving school. She was sexually involved and feared that she was pregnant. Her group of friends were into drugs, gang activity, and frequent petty crime. Her grade-point average was 1.5, and she missed more than 20 days of school each semester.

Then, a school-to-work counselor got her a position working in food preparation and catering. The work schedule forced her to be on time and to improve her cleanliness habits. Entering the world of work gave Noemi a feeling of maturity, an exit from her adolescent troubles. Her circle of friends changed as she worked daily and met new people, many of them more mature and with a sense of purpose.

She says, "I feel that I am more prepared for work than the college-bound students. I work in a real hospital, with real patients, employees, and customers. Every day I am learning something new.

"For me, getting an education now means more than just going to school. This program (School to Work) has really helped me to focus. Now I want to finish high school and go on to college."

The new high-skills economy demands that students acquire both academic knowledge and workplace skills. School-to-work placements help students to earn money and to see the immediate application of their school courses. Worksites provide interesting, relevant, and paid experiences to encourage young women toward further training, two-year colleges, and quality entry-level jobs. Often work placement is a major motivation for students, and effective programs provide a guided transition from adolescence to adulthood.

Gender, Race, and Class

The importance of gender issues can change from one generation to the next, and is culture specific. It is often difficult or impossible to separate race, class, and gender discrimination, because the oppressions interact with each other. Research on the school behavior of girls and young women of color has been notably absent, even in the American Association of University Women (AAUW, 1992) report. Most researchers have assumed that young girls have similar experiences across cultures.

Women of color have gained university positions and political leadership in recent decades and have turned their research skills to documenting the conflicts faced by African American, Latina, and working-class girls in schools. Weis and Fine (1993) have documented some of the ways young women face and react to sex education in high schools, collecting powerful essays that begin to move beyond the more restricted early research boundary of European American women.

A particular concern has been voiced concerning the destructive impact on African American children, particularly boys, of common public school practices such as negating children's home cultures and using biased assessment methods, usually carried out in elementary schools by female European American teachers. Researchers King, Foster, Ladson-Billings, and others have documented several basic issues facing African American girls and boys in classrooms in *Teaching Diverse Populations: Formulating a Knowledge Base* (Hollins, King, & Hayman, 1994). They have suggested characteristics and tendencies in the African American culture that teachers can use as background information to reduce the cultural conflicts in the classroom and to improve student achievement.

The predominantly European American teaching profession needs such research to begin to understand the diverse classroom roles of girls and boys within specific cultures. For example, young Latinas who succeed often have supportive parents, particularly mothers (Gándara, 1995). These insights support the importance of schools offering programs to develop parental support for education and for attending college. For example, successful programs of uniting mothers and daughters have developed in San Antonio, Texas, and in the *Adelante Latina* conferences in California (Gándara, 1995).

One persistent social myth is that women do most of the work in the home and men do most of the work outside the home. Amott and Matthaei (1991) provide a multicultural history of how farm and working-class women have labored for wages in increasing numbers since the beginning of the Industrial Revolution in the Unites States in the 1840s. The great historical and social events of the twentieth century—the Great Depression (1929–1939), the shift from a rural to an urban society, the worker shortages caused by World War II—brought even more women into the paid labor force. More recently, the economic stagnation that began in the 1970s has produced a dramatic increase in the number of middle-class women entering the paid workforce (Figures 5.3 and 5.4). While over 50 percent of all women of color have been in the paid labor force since the 1950s, since the 1970s over 50 percent of *all* women over age 16 have worked for wages (Amott & Matthaei, 1991). According to the AFL-CIO

> More women are working than ever before. And they're looking for solutions to the problems of juggling work and family, making ends meet and finding respect and opportunity on the job. . . . Over the past century, women workers have grown steadily in number and as a proportion of the workforce.
>
> • The number of working women has grown from 5.3 million in 1900 to 18.4 million in 1950 and to 63 million in 1997.
> • Women made up 18.3 percent of the labor force in 1900, 29.6 percent in 1950 and 46.2 percent in 1997. (AFL-CIO, 1998, n.p.)

In the United States, many women of color must assume extra responsibilities to protect and advance their community's interests. African American women, for example, are often looked to as the centers of strength and the source of leadership within their communities. Because they are regarded by the macroculture as less threatening than African American men, African American women may be less

Figure 5.3   Labor Force Participation Rates for Women in the United States, 1955–1985

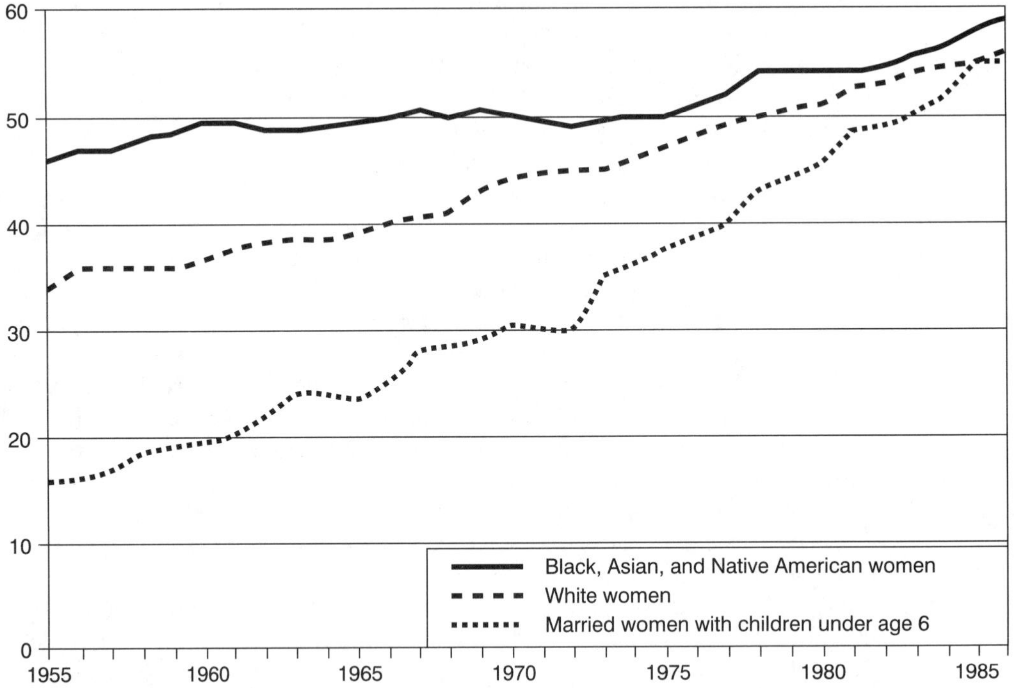

Note. The rates reported are for women age 16 and older. From *A Field Guide to the U.S. Economy, 1985–1995* (p. 3.1) by Center for Popular Economics, Amherst, MA. Reprinted with permission.

impeded and more accepted as they assume positions of responsibility in their communities or seek career advancement in the professional world. West (1993b) describes the fear of black men and the acceptance of African American women as in part a result of "psychosexual racist logic." Yet many African American women are well prepared for their role as economic providers. Many African societies had strong female leadership. Slavery forced a matrifocal family structure on the African American community. The women of many African American families have drawn strength from this long tradition of female leadership.

Latinas share many of the racially based economic burdens of African American women, including the responsibility to care for the elderly and for extended families. Strong female leadership was also common in many Mesoamerican societies prior to the Spanish conquest. Currently, matrifocal family structures have developed in Mexico in response to the migration of millions of male farm workers to labor in U.S. agricultural fields. Most Mexican American and Latino families in the United States remain patriarchal, similar to those in the dominant European American society (for more on this complex issue, see Gándara, 1995; Ramirez & Castañeda, 1974; Váldes, 1996). Girls and young women have paid a price for this continued

Figure 5.4 Women and Men as Percentages of All Employed Workers

Note. From *Working Women* by AFL-CIO, 1998, retrieved 1 February 1999 from the World Wide Web: http://www.aflcio.org/women. Reprinted with permission.

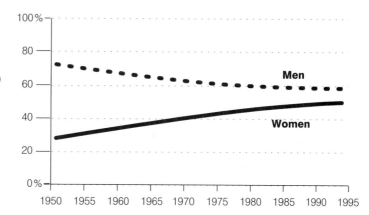

patriarchy, lagging behind African American women in entrance into college and professional schools until the 1990s (Amott & Matthaei, 1991).

The oppression of African American, Latina, and some rural European American women has taught them to work in cooperative communities. Families take care of the elderly, care for children troubled by divorce and abandonment, and take extended family members (cousins, aunts, etc.) into their homes. In these communities, women serve on school–parent advisory councils and keep churches functioning. Women are the primary social service providers in these communities.

School curricula should acknowledge and recognize the extensive contributions of women to the community's health. The female-centered home and community provide a rich and extensive breadth of background knowledge on which to build an educational curriculum. Moll, Vélez-Ibañez, and Greenberg (1992) assert that children gain when classrooms draw on this community knowledge and use it to advance literacy instruction. Multicultural education is important in this context because curriculum and literacy efforts should give more emphasis to women's contributions to provide role models for female students and to counterbalance the devaluation of women by the media and by the patriarchal traditions of the macroculture.

While European American women have attended colleges since the 1840s and African American women have had access to the traditionally black colleges that rose up in the South after Reconstruction, substantial numbers of other women of color did not gain access to higher education until the 1970s. The development of both ethnic studies and women's studies on campuses has opened new doors of scholarship and expression. In a pioneering work, *This Bridge Called My Back* (Moraga & Anzaldúa, 1981), women of color speak eloquently about the nature of male and female roles and the issue of male domination within their respective communities. In *Teaching to Transgress: Education as the Practice of Freedom,* hooks (1994) offers several powerful essays on how race, class, and gender interact in the classroom.

An outpouring of African American, Latina, Native American, and Asian women writers has redefined women's sphere in the United States to include women of color. Amy Tan, Gloria Anzaldúa, Maya Angelou, bell hooks, Olivia Castellano,

Paula Gunn Allen, Wilma Mankiller, Marian Wright Edelman, and others provide insights into the diverse voices and insights of the many peoples of our nation.

Affirmative Action: Again

Affirmative action programs since the 1970s have been effective in promoting women and in breaking down traditional rigid gender roles in many universities. Currently, college-bound students benefit from changing work opportunities and the victories of the feminist movement. There are now more women doctors, lawyers, and college professors than ever before. In 1994, women received 38 percent of medical degrees, compared with 9 percent in 1972; 43 percent of law degrees, compared with 7 percent in 1972; and 44 percent of all doctoral degrees, compared to 25 percent in 1977. Women now make up the majority of the students in U.S. colleges and universities and make up the majority of recipients of master's degrees (Women's Equity Resource Center, 1997).

Women's studies, apprenticeship programs, and mentoring have opened important new opportunities. Title IX (1972) describes the federal commitment to equal gender treatment in matters of federal assistance:

> No person . . . shall, on the basis of sex, be denied the benefits of, or be subjected to, discrimination under any education program or activity receiving federal financial assistance. . . .

As a result of the passage of Title IX in 1972, the role of women and girls in education has changed substantially. Title IX prohibits sexual discrimination and sexual harassment in educational institutions receiving federal funds. The act prohibits discrimination in recruitment, educational programs, activities, financial aid, counseling, athletics, employment assistance and other school functions.

Special programs provide additional counseling and encouragement for Latinas and African American women to attend college. Well-educated young women are choosing careers as doctors, attorneys, and politicians. As yet, however, the benefits and advantages of the feminist revolution of the 1970s are less apparent in the school lives and career opportunities of the 50 percent of women high school graduates who do not go on to college.

Women's Story in the Textbooks

Although feminist scholarship has made strides in the university, this progress is only beginning to have a significant impact on public school textbooks. Tetreault (1989) and Moraga and Anzaldúa (1981) have written about the invisibility and fragmentation of women's history, particularly women of color, in literature and text illustrations.

Some progress is being made. Publishers have started to delete linguistic bias and to use gender-neutral terms. States are requiring that texts move beyond depicting women in stereotypic roles. The National Women's History Project has developed excellent new materials to overcome this invisibility.

Students seem to develop self-esteem and a sense of being socially centered when they see their role models in books and other educational materials. Women's literature, history, and sociology assist female students in evaluating their own experiences and traumas. Readings in these areas can help young women gain perspective on the pressures of surrendering self and goals for temporary status and temporary relationships. Social history and popular histories record the extensive participation of women in building our communities, public schools, and social institutions. Readings from the era in which the "cult of true womanhood" was promoted (1800–1860) help students to reflect on how public images and role models can promote profit-seeking rather than developing human potential. Readings from the Progressive Era (1890–1920) help students to see how immigrant women organized unions and (European American) women made significant advances in attending colleges and entering the professions.

The curriculum should be authentic, realistic, and inspirational. Reform requires more than adding a few new heroines to existing textbooks. The writings and speeches of Dolores Huerta, Fannie Lou Hamer, Shirley Chisholm, and others are important additions to the curriculum.

Women students can keep journals to reflect on their own lives. Recording a journal helps young girls through times of doubt and insecurity, as does developing friendships. Teenage girls can learn to accept themselves as they are and build a positive future instead of dreaming of cosmetic makeovers.

Young women also gain from learning about the leadership and activism of women in their communities. Working-class women and women of color have raised families and survived. They have created a positive life for their children. Presenting guest speakers from the community teaches that average, normal people run unions, institutions, and essential community organizations. Guest speakers bridge the gap between the school and adult reality. The curriculum empowers and motivates students when it presents hope and optimism without presenting a superwoman model of accomplishment.

Wilbur (1992) states that a gender-fair curriculum has six attributes:

1. *Variation,* that is, similarities and differences among and within groups of people

2. *Inclusive,* allowing both females and males to find and identify positively with messages about themselves

3. *Accurate,* presenting information that is data-based, verifiable, and able to withstand critical analysis

4. *Affirmative,* acknowledging and valuing the worth of individuals and groups

5. *Representative,* balancing multiple perspectives

6. *Integrated,* weaving together the experiences, needs, and interests of both males and females

Wilbur and the AAUW (1992) report argue that so far no major curriculum reform efforts have explicitly used gender-fair approaches.

The AAUW report offers a list of over 40 action items for change. Individual teachers may pursue the following 13 items from the list (AAUW, 1992):

1. Teachers must help girls develop positive views of themselves and their futures, as well as an understanding of the obstacles women must overcome in a society where their options and opportunities are still limited by gender stereotypes and assumptions.

2. The formal school curriculum must include the experiences of women and men from all walks of life. Girls and boys must see women and girls reflected and valued in the materials they study.

3. School curricula should deal directly with issues of power, gender politics, and violence against women. Better-informed girls are better equipped to make decisions about their futures. Girls and young women who have a strong sense of themselves are better able to confront violence and abuse in their lives.

4. Curricula for young children must not perpetuate gender stereotypes and should reflect sensitivity to different learning styles.

5. Girls must be educated and encouraged to understand that mathematics and the sciences are important and relevant to their lives. Girls must be actively supported in pursuing education and employment in these areas.

6. Existing equity guidelines should be effectively implemented in all programs supported by the local, state, and federal governments. Specific attention must be directed toward including women on planning committees and focusing on girls and women in the goals, instructional strategies, teacher training, and research components of these programs.

7. Local schools and communities must encourage and support girls studying science and mathematics by showcasing women role models in scientific and technological fields, disseminating career information, and offering "hands-on" experiences and work groups in science and math classes.

8. Continued attention to gender equity in vocational education programs must be a high priority at every level of educational governance and administration. Have students discuss how gender roles are changing in their own generation.

9. Testing and assessment must serve as stepping-stones, not stop signs. New tests and testing techniques must accurately reflect the abilities of both girls and boys.

10. Girls and women must play a central role in educational reform. The experiences, strengths, and needs of girls from every race and social class must be considered in order to provide excellence and equity for all our nation's students.

11. A critical goal of education reform must be to enable students to deal effectively with the realities of their lives, particularly in areas such as sexuality and health.

12. Federal and state funding should be used to promote partnerships between schools and community groups, including social service agencies, youth-serving organizations, medical facilities, and local businesses. The needs of students, particularly as highlighted by pregnant teens and teen mothers, require a multi-institutional response.

13. Child care for the children of teen mothers must be an integral part of all programs designed to encourage young women to pursue or complete educational programs. (pp. 84–87)

Unfortunately, despite the efforts of feminist scholars, educators, and some textbook publishers, self-image and role stereotyping problems for girls continue. Clearly, schools and textbooks are less powerful in their influence than the commercial marketplace is. They are no match for television programs and multimedia advertising campaigns aimed at the youth culture. We are unlikely to make much progress on this front until large companies and the advertising agencies they hire cease to exploit gender stereotyping for profit.

Teaching for Equity

Teachers may use several strategies to improve the success of girls in school. Cooperative and collaborative learning work well (see chapter 10). Teachers can place students in small groups of six to eight to listen and work together for part of the curriculum.

Girls and young women can be assigned the status of experts on a given topic and make presentations to the class. Students can learn to critique and improve the work of their group. Girls should have equal opportunity to be in charge or to assume responsibility in the classrooms. This generation has many young women who are experts on computers, microscopes and other forms of technology. Effective teachers place young women in high-status positions as appropriate.

Many teachers have found success by emphasizing young women's verbal and written communication strengths. Girls often do well on assignments of journal writing. Keeping journal records of their observations in science, history, and biology may produce more success for girls. Establishing a positive, trusting relationship with your students is the first step. This is the subject of Chapter 6.

Teachers can encourage girls to keep journals and to read literature about their many adolescent conflicts. They can make close and consistent contact with the home. While home contact is frequent in elementary school, it usually declines in middle and high school. This decline in contact hurts students. Many adolescent girls and boys prefer to build a wall of separation between the home and the school. The break in communication allows them a space of liberty. However, the communication gap separates young women and men from the consistency of support they need from the adult world. Teachers can extend themselves to get to know families. You can refuse to be a party to young people's attempts to build the wall between school and home.

You can find other excellent teaching ideas at the Web site of the National Women's History Project (www.nwhp.org/) and at www.edc.org/WomensEquity.

The Counterattack

In 1994, Congress passed revisions to the Elementary and Secondary Education Act (ESEA), the two basic federal programs for schools. The decades of feminist scholarship—particularly the work of the AAUW—led to efforts to strengthen the gender equity provisions of ESEA by allocating some $3 million in new money for gender equity activities. A counterattack was launched by Diane Ravitch, former undersecretary of education during the Reagan and Bush administrations, and other critics of feminist and gender-based research. Ravitch claimed that the proposed allocation "takes as findings of Congress that all these flawed research claims were true" (quoted in Schmidt, 1994, p. 1). Senator Nancy Kassebaum argued against the legislation, saying that gender inequity claims were "supported only by a small body of research which has questionable findings" (quoted in Schmidt, 1994, p. 16). Finally, Professor Joseph Adelson of the University of Michigan called the AAUW studies "a propaganda machine that does not seem to respond to any contrary evidence" (quoted in Schmidt, 1994, p. 16).

In 1996, California voters passed Proposition 209, which banned equal opportunity programs in the state. This was a major reversal of gains achieved by women since the 1970s. Conservatives claimed that affirmative action programs amounted to reverse discrimination. Similar legislation was introduced in several other states. Can you measure whether this policy change has affected programs for gender equity in your state?

The counterattack against claims of gender-based failure in school is growing. Like the attacks on multicultural education (see Chapter 12), critics accuse advocates of gender equity of promoting an ideology. (In the following two chapters, we discuss the role of ideology in shaping research perspectives and educational philosophies.)

This chapter concludes the social-political foundations underlying multicultural education. The emphasis in Part Two shifts to concrete teaching strategies to help empower all cultural groups to seek cultural democracy.

Summary

Schools, particularly elementary schools, are primarily female institutions. Young girls do well in elementary school. Recent evidence in the National Assessment of Educational Progress indicates that girls are doing as well or better than boys in reading in grades 4, 8, and 12, and equal to boys in math in grades 4 and 8.

Gender issues interact with race, culture and class to influence the development of young girls and boys. Gender stereotyping and sexual identity become volatile issues in middle and high school. Girls need supportive teachers to deal with dangerous cultural practices, including sexual behavior and dieting. Students need adult assistance and guidance in these difficult years. Feminist research has been valuable in identifying problems and developing responses for teachers to use in making their classrooms more supportive.

Questions Over the Chapter

1. Define *gender-role stereotyping*.
2. How does your gender influence how you learn about culture?
3. Girls tend to be more successful than boys in school in grades K through 6, but many begin to encounter difficulties at grade 7 and above. What factors contribute to this change?
4. List some ways schools may track girls. Why is this practice damaging? (Note that tracking's effects may be either negative or positive.)

5. What is the "beauty myth?" How does it negatively impact girls?
6. List at least four attributes of a gender-fair curriculum.
7. List four teaching strategies that lead to gender fairness.
8. What is the name of the primary federal legislation requiring gender-fair school policies?
9. What evidence supports the thesis that elementary schools are primarily female "turf"?
10. What are some of the effects of female dominance in elementary schools?
11. What factors contribute to a "crisis of self-esteem" in middle and high schools?
12. Describe your own development of self-identity as you recall your adolescent years.
13. List three strategies to support positive self-esteem among girls.
14. What careers for women do not require a college education? What high school classes or subjects prepare students for these careers?
15. List jobs you have held (including parttime). What high school study prepared you for these jobs?
16. How does the absence of strong female role models from textbooks and curricula affect girls?
17. Name at least three major female authors. As a class, compare and discuss your lists.
18. Name at least two major African American female authors. As a class, compare and discuss your lists.
19. How has sexual responsibility changed in the last decade? What evidence do you have for your conclusion?
20. What behaviors are prohibited by Title IX?

Activities for Further Study of Gender Relationships

1. View the film *Union Maids* (1977), which illustrates class and gender relationships during the period 1930–1945. Compare these relationships to those of the present.
2. In a small group of students, discuss and summarize the effect of gender relationships on schooling. Report as a team to the class.
3. Invite a guest speaker from the Women's Studies Department at your local college campus to speak to your class. Compare this person's ideas to the presentation in this chapter.
4. Invite a Chicana or African American feminist to speak on the relationship between ethnic and feminist struggles.
5. In small groups, describe recent experiences in which you were treated unfairly based on your gender or race. Then share your stories with the entire class.
6. Complete a life history interview with a female over age 40. Share your interview with the class.
7. Compare *racism* and *sexism*. How are they similar? How are they different? How does socioeconomic class affect each?
8. In class discussion, predict five major changes in gender role relationships that will take place in the next decade. Discuss how these changes may affect schools.
9. Interview another student. If that student is not going into teaching, what other profession would he or she select? Ask what influences might encourage him or her to select teaching. Share your interviews as a class. Look for patterns in the respondents' choices.
10. Read the entire report, *How Schools Shortchange Girls* (AAUW, 1992). Select three of the authors' recommendations for change. Discuss these suggestions with a person in authority at your school, such as the director of your campus Women's Studies Program or Teacher Preparation Program. Present the results of your discussion to the class.
11. Make a chart of your class's grade-point averages (GPA) in grades 1 through 12. What patterns can you detect? Develop a table of class GPAs arranged by race and gender. What patterns do you detect now?

12. Bring four advertisements from women's magazines that promote "the beauty myth." What
messages are the ads sending to readers?
13. Ask students in your class who are mothers or
fathers to describe the financial difficulties of
graduating from college.

14. Describe to the class the reasons for your choice
to become a teacher. How did the female domination of the profession affect your schooling
and your career choices?

Teaching Strategies

1. Include the study of power and gender equity in
the curriculum.
2. Teach students to recognize and oppose gender
stereotyping.
3. Study stereotyping presented in commercial
media. Identify what values are being advocated,
and develop ways to present alternative values to
students.
4. Use self-esteem-building lessons for girls and
boys to combat the stereotyping messages of
commercial media.
5. Use role playing and role reversal strategies to
resist stereotyping.

6. Use a nonracial definition of women's achieve-
ments. Include the contributions of women of
color.
7. Make the curriculum inclusive, including examples of women in nontraditional careers.
8. Write for and use the excellent materials of the
National Women's History Project.
9. Praise and encourage girls for their academic
excellence and skills in addition to areas such as
neatness and compliance.
10. Use strategies and lessons found in Schniedewind
and Davidson, *Open Minds To Equality* (Needham Heights, MA: Allyn & Bacon, 1998).

Part 2

Teaching Strategies to Promote Democracy and Multicultural Education

Chapter 6

Human Relations and Multicultural Education

Good teachers make a difference. Each year schools, districts, individual states, private corporations, and the President recognize a few of the many excellent teachers working in schools all around the country. Excellent teachers illustrate the truism that the quality of interaction between teachers and students is the single most important element in schools. Quality teaching and coaching occur even in underfunded, racially segregated, or isolated schools. Quality teaching depends on creating trusting and supportive relationships between students and their teachers.

This chapter will introduce five major teaching issues in promoting positive human relations:

1. Serving as a cultural mediator
2. Teaching social skills
3. Promoting positive self-esteem
4. Resolving conflicts
5. Building supportive relationships

Underlying Assumptions of Human Relations

We are, of course, all human—teachers and students. As humans, we are much more alike than we are different, and many teachers begin their approaches to multicultural education by affirming our common humanity. Lessons thus focused are called *human relations* lessons. Some teachers welcome human relations lessons but regard other approaches to multicultural education, such as ethnic studies and women's studies, as divisive because they acknowledge, some say emphasize, uncomfortable differences. Discussions, particularly of race, make many new teachers uncomfortable. They would rather affirm our common humanity, putting aside the histories of race, class, and gender oppression described in prior chapters. Certainly many students in your teacher preparation program hold this view. It is important for new teachers to understand this position, to analyze it, and to develop their own philosophy concerning human relations and the other approaches to multicultural education.

The human relations approach to multicultural education emphasizes our common humanity—the enormous similarities in physical, psychological, and social patterns among humans—and builds lessons to emphasize human similarity. For example, we can see differences in skin color, but well over 98 percent of all human biology is identical—we all have hearts, kidneys, toes, eyes, and so on (Chavez Comeron & Macias Wycoff, 1998).

The human relations approach traces its intellectual roots to efforts during World War II to understand the Holocaust (Sleeter & Grant, 1999). Scholars and activists sought to develop lessons that schools could use to promote an end to prejudice and discrimination in U.S. society. Other important work was done for the U.S. military to assist them with the desegregation of military units as ordered by President Truman.

Applications of human relations research are currently commonplace in public schools, with human relations being the dominant form of multicultural education in grades K through 4. Such approaches remain an important aspect of multicultural education throughout high school and college.

Human relations approaches provide good strategies for new teachers to begin pursuing democracy and equal opportunity in the curriculum. As a new teacher, you enter the profession believing in the positive possibilities of children, looking for strategies to build on children's humanness.

The human relations approach is the least controversial of several approaches to multicultural education and the one that requires the least change of worldview on the part of teachers. However, teaching even human relations can become controversial. In a 1997 case in Vaughn, New Mexico, two Mexican American teachers were encouraged to teach about the Holocaust, but were dismissed from their positions for teaching Mexican American history to their Mexican American students (*Education Week*, 1997). Teaching the students about contributions of their own people is a common human relations strategy.

The Work of Abraham Maslow

Psychologist Abraham Maslow's hierarchy of needs provides a model for understanding the need for human relations in the classroom (Figure 6.1). Needs lower

Figure 6.1   Maslow's Hierarchy of Needs

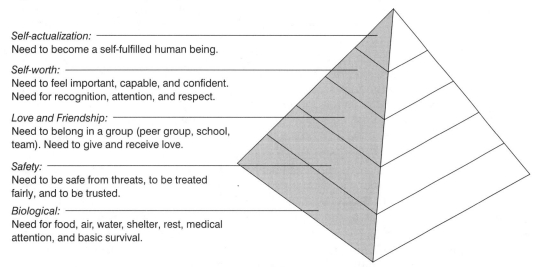

Self-actualization:
Need to become a self-fulfilled human being.

Self-worth:
Need to feel important, capable, and confident.
Need for recognition, attention, and respect.

Love and Friendship:
Need to belong in a group (peer group, school,
team). Need to give and receive love.

Safety:
Need to be safe from threats, to be treated
fairly, and to be trusted.

Biological:
Need for food, air, water, shelter, rest, medical
attention, and basic survival.

Note. From *Motivation and Personality* (3rd ed.) by Abraham H. Maslow. Copyright 1954, 1987 by Harper & Row Publishers, Inc. Copyright 1970 by Abraham H. Maslow. Reprinted by permission of Addison Wesley Educational Publishers, Inc.

on the pyramid, such as physical and safety needs, must be met before an individual will consider higher-level needs.

This hierarchy explains important components of behavior, including school behavior. Teachers often assume that the physical security and safety needs of their students are assured, but in many schools they are not. Increasing numbers of homes and schools are unable to provide simple safety. When physical security and safety are challenged, students will use most of their time, energy, and creativity simply trying to survive. This struggle interferes with learning.

Belonging needs are often strong in school. Children need to know they are a welcomed part of the class. The teacher cannot allow derogatory name calling and other forms of isolation and exclusion to dominate the classroom. These peer-group relations substantially influence school success. It is difficult to learn in hostile, conflict-filled classrooms and schools. Classroom planning and curriculum decisions, such as choosing to teach cooperative learning (see Chapter 10) and peer-group mediation (discussed later in this chapter) can help convert the classroom environment to one of support and belonging.

Maslow did not consider this hierarchy a rigid one. Students will partially fulfill some needs, and thus become prepared to consider higher-level needs. The highest level, self-actualization, is a theoretical position Maslow describes as a goal, usually for adults. *Self-actualization* is, at most, a goal advocated by practitioners of Gestalt therapy—anthropologists would not recognize it as a cross-cultural, universal human experience. Teachers can help students learn to meet their own safety and friendship needs, and to recognize their own self-worth. These basic needs must be met before education can take place in the classroom.

Responding to these basic needs is particularly problematic when schools are the primary location for ethnic integration. Neighborhoods and cities are increasingly segregated by race and class. Many urban school districts and the courts seek to integrate children in schools.

In 1991, Selma, Alabama, was rocked by school conflict when an African American superintendent tried to end school tracking that maintained de facto segregation (Snider, 1990). Kansas City has long been under a court order to provide equal opportunity in its schools (Armor, 1995).

Human relations theory, including the work of Maslow, provides the psychological and sociological basis for the democratic claim that schools should promote equal opportunity. Once accepted, the concept of equal opportunity suggests a need for fundamental changes in school financing, and in curriculum and teaching strategies.

Human relations theory assists teachers to promote a safe and supportive environment at school. However, The Children's Defense Fund points out that our society must also change to support a safe and supportive environment for children, considering both psychological and physical needs. In many schools roofs and windows need repair, buildings need reconstruction, violence needs to be controlled, and the children need sufficient food and safe homes (Children's Defense Fund, 1997).

Current conditions in our streets make the learning of positive self-worth difficult. In human relations lessons, all students are treated as individuals, often ignoring that the student is also a member of a group (gender, cultural, ethnic). Because each person is regarded only as an individual, human relations theory suggests there are no changes nor adaptations in lessons for cultural, gender, or class variables. The same teaching strategies are suggested for diverse racial, ethnic, cultural, language, class, and gender groups. Human relations theory assumes a universal human hierarchy of needs and values that emphasizes individual differences and individual independence. Other cultures emphasize more group solidarity and interdependence with others in the community. In the U.S. macroculture children are encouraged to learn self-esteem and self-worth for themselves. Human relations theory often fails to recognize that self-esteem and self-worth are significantly culturally determined (Ladson-Billings, 1994b).

The central insight of the human relations approach is that creating positive and nurturing human relationships between teachers and students and among students is one of the most important issues of school improvement. Young people do not learn math, reading, or English well if they are intimidated, defensive, and fearful.

Violence and the Urban Crisis

In the 1980s federal budget cuts eliminated many of the antipoverty and urban development programs, leaving the cities to fend for themselves with a dramatically reduced tax base. The federal government's abandonment of parts of the cities to crime, poverty, and decay included abandoning students in inner-city schools. The visible decay of the urban infrastructure teaches hopelessness and helplessness to many children. Violence, shootings, and even death plague some of our schools. Teachers are expected to control increasing numbers of students who have serious physical and emotional problems. Young people are bringing weapons to school to protect themselves and to intimidate others.

The poor suffer the most from cutbacks in police, education, fire, health, and nutritional services. The Children's Defense Fund (1997) states that one out of five children in the United States lives in poverty—over 50 percent of African American children and 43 percent of Latino children. The children live in decaying communities stressed by racism, class and gender prejudice, job loss, crime, and poverty. In 1996 Congress and the President passed new welfare legislation (the Temporary Assistance to Needy Families Act) that ended the 60-year-old guarantee of food and housing for the poorest families. Millions more of the poor, mostly women, are now threatened with hunger and homelessness. In addition, Public Law 104-208, the Illegal Immigration Reform and Immigration Responsibility Act of 1996, restricted most immigrant families, including children, from access to public benefits including health care and prenatal care. These social conditions create conflict and violence in the community and in schools. Virtually abandoned by the society, some children learn violent responses to the violence they endure. And they bring the violence with them to school.

McKenna (1992), an African American school district superintendent in Inglewood, California, and a former high school principal, describes his experience as follows:

> In my 30 years in working in inner-city schools, I have witnessed a decline in student behavior that mirrors the rise of violence in society—the increase in violent assaults on campus, gang involvement, drug use, sexual activity, suicide and other acts that, besides bringing great harm to those involved, leave others in the school community feeling helpless, powerless—and even more disadvantaged than before.
>
> Typically, the schools' response is greater reliance on the police and other campus security agencies. I propose that educators give education a chance: that we teach values and respect for human life through a comprehensive school-based program centered on a nonviolence curriculum at all grade levels. Some of the key ingredients would be . . . parent involvement . . . a nonviolence curriculum . . . peer counseling and community service . . . and antigang education. (p. A11)

Teachers, social workers, and police cannot by themselves stop the violence in society. But schools have an obligation to provide safety and security to children. Schools must become islands of safety in the urban landscape. The teacher's difficult task is to build positive relationships, to organize the curriculum, and to respond to the students in a positive, nurturing, and constructive manner that encourages learning respect and nonviolence. Political leaders—presidents, governors, legislators, mayors, and school administrators from school board to principal—have the responsibility to keep school grounds safe and clean and to keep drugs, gangs, and violence off campus. They often fail.

To reform schools toward multicultural democracy, teachers must improve the quality of respect and interchange in the classroom. Teachers create positive environments by their decisions, choices, expectations, and interactions with students.

The converse is also true. Students do not learn in stressful, failure-filled environments where their physical and emotional safety is threatened.

How Research Limits Our Views of Students and Schools

Unfortunately, present practices in psychology and the social sciences provide only limited insight into the growing crisis of urban decay and in describing and explaining teacher–student relationships and interaction. The dominant approaches in psychology, the social sciences, and educational studies generally accept the present impersonal and control-oriented structures of schools as natural, as the result of "scientific planning." As you have read in prior chapters, multicultural education challenges these basic assumptions, asserting that present school practices are often unequal and discriminatory on racial, gender, and class issues.

Positivism

To understand the problem of accepting an impersonal and, at times, unjust and violent school structure as natural, we must look at the philosophy of positivism that provides the basis for most educational and social science research. *Positivism* derives from the belief that human behavior, including thought, can be adequately understood by isolating variables for study. It includes the assumptions of hypothesis testing research and a belief that natural laws of human behavior may be understood and manipulated in terms of "universal" facts, generalizations, and regularities through use of the "scientific method." Most scholars and teachers in the United States have been educated within the positivist viewpoint.

This philosophy developed during the Age of Enlightenment (1600–1860). Early scientists such as Newton and Descartes developed a scientific method based on a philosophy of realism and sought to isolate variables for study. Other scientists, such as Galileo, created experimental processes to look for natural causes for events. The landmark research of Louis Pasteur and Charles Darwin, based on experimentation and observation, was admired and copied by others.

The social sciences emerged in the late 1800s, following the earlier dramatic developments in the natural sciences. Early social scientists hoped to discover natural laws about human society similar to those laws discovered in the natural sciences by Pasteur, Mendel, Newton, and others. They searched for universal law–like statements and predictive explanations. These scientists hoped to move beyond the moral philosophy of their time by applying a "modern," scientific approach to human behavior. Currently, this "modern" scientific approach dominates educational research and writing. This work, based on positivist assumptions, is referred to in contemporary social science and education literature as behaviorism or reductionism.

The Overreliance of the Social Sciences on Positivism   Efforts to develop scientific methods in human matters were frustrated by the complexity of human experience.

Human institutions—economic systems, school systems, cultures—are so complex that it is often impossible to create quality experimental designs and to isolate variables. In response to frustration, social scientists continually refined their "scientific methods," their proof processes, and statistical processes. Social scientists who depended on the philosophy of positivism adopted a faith that improved methodology would lead to truth, as it seemed to have done in the natural sciences.

In pursuit of objectivity, psychologists and other social scientists developed increasingly precise methods of controlling variables. Unfortunately, psychologists usually dealt with these variables under isolated laboratory conditions, and sociologists used statistical manipulation, rather than directly studying real life. In this manner they were able to describe correlations and to imply causation. Psychologists and educational researchers limited and restricted what they considered appropriate topics for study.

Over time, social scientists developed the separate disciplines of geography, economics, political science, psychology, and sociology. Each of these disciplines developed from positivist origins. Most practitioners in these disciplines sought objectivity and believed that the scientific method and processes offered methodological neutrality. Researchers working within the assumptions of positivism presumed that if they continued to refine their research methods they would eventually achieve their goals of developing universal laws and predictive explanations. In part in response to their claims of being based on "scientific research," psychology and psychological perspectives came to dominate educational research and teacher preparation.

The philosophical limitations of positivism have been examined by Giroux (1979). He argues that the culture of positivism seeks to put aside the normative, value-laden issues, the issues of supreme importance to the teacher. These value-laden issues are central to an effort to reconstruct schools in a democratic manner that would empower minority students. For an excellent analysis of these trends see Torres and Mitchell (1998), specifically Popkewitz's (1998) chapter within.

Behaviorism

Social scientific research based on positivist assumptions emphasizes work that is quantifiable, measurable, and verifiable. By the 1960s, the so-called "behaviorist" school of social sciences developed. *Behaviorism*, based on the work of Edward Thorndike and B. F. Skinner, emphasizes control of behavior and is predicated on the belief that one may correctly identify and diagnose inner physical and mental states by studying outward behavior. The researchers in this tradition seek to monitor behavior that is observed and measurable. They tend to ignore or cast aside idealism, consciousness, ethics, and faith because they cannot be measured. Behaviorism became the dominant trend in educational psychology and sociology in the 1970s. Applications of behaviorism in education include behavioral objectives, audio–lingual approaches to language acquisition, and the Madeline Hunter model of Direct Teaching.[1]

[1]For more on behaviorism and education, see Bowers and Flanders (1990), Hartoonian (1991), Popkewitz (1998), Torres and Mitchell (1998), and Wexler (1989).

Behaviorism and cognitive psychology both provide hypotheses about how students learn basic skills. Some students do learn basic skills when teachers use these behaviorist strategies. Behaviorist research and behavioral psychology serve reasonably well to describe how a rat or a pigeon learns (Weinberg & Reidford, 1972). However, you probably have never met a rat or a pigeon that could speak a language or do mathematics. Behaviorism also describes strategies to socialize mostly middle-class students to a culturally congruent classroom. But behaviorism can do little to teach students to succeed in the chaotic, decaying social structure of inner-city schools and neighborhoods. Behaviorism also does not serve democracy well, because a preference for democracy is not reducible to isolated parts. Behaviorism offers few insights for the oppressed. Behaviorism, for example, teaches students from the lower classes to conform to the existing social system, but it does not teach them to use their education to struggle for better schools, educational opportunities, and a more just distribution of wealth and income.

Reductionism

Clearly, applying scientific methods to the natural sciences has led to great advancements in modern society. The use of scientific methods in the social and behavior sciences led to similar major advancements, but these methods are now reaching significant limitations. One version of the scientific method developed a tendency termed objectivism, or reductionism.

Reductionism occurs when a complex problem is "reduced" to an issue that can be measured, even though the entire problem is quite complex. For example, learning to read is a complex problem. Children learn many skills of reading. An emphasis on phonemic awareness measures one of those skills only. But if researchers reduce and restrict their attention only to phonemic awareness, they will fail to understand the complex problems of learning to read.

Reductionism distorts comprehensive observation and limits both the analytical and explanatory powers of much school research. The conceptual framework or research paradigms of objectivists, behaviorists, and to a lesser degree, cognitive psychologists, led them to isolate variables and to study learning behavior out of the real context of schools.

In the pursuit of objectivity, behaviorist and reductionist research has ignored vast amounts of important information on the purposes and intents of learning as well as on the importance of quality relationships between students and teachers. At present, behaviorist and reductionist experimental designs reveal few new useful insights into learning behavior. The effort to be objective, to be empirical rather than normative, directed these research designs away from important issues of power. The pursuit of objectivity and methodological precision distorted and limited research in education and the social sciences. As a consequence, the present unequal distribution of wealth, power, and opportunity in our society and in our schools was usually not considered an appropriate subject of study by researchers committed to procedural objectivity and neutrality.

Objectivist and reductionist psychologies, restricted by positivist assumptions, avoid questions of oppression and domination as research topics in explaining school failure of students of color. Giroux (1979) describes the problem as follows:

> Wrapped in the logic of fragmentation and specialization, positivist rationality divorces fact from its social context and ends up glorifying scientific methodology at the expense of more rational modes of thinking . . . more important, it leaves unquestioned those economic and social structures that shape our daily lives. (p. 271)

In particular, these research efforts leave unquestioned cultural domination and race and gender bias in teaching, learning, and curricula.

Objectivists' and behaviorists' thought processes dominated most research in education well into the 1980s. The behaviorists' view of learning produced reductionist forms of teaching and curricula, particularly in compensatory programs for children from poverty-stricken neighborhoods. The conservative school reform effort and their faith in allegedly objective testing and a test-driven curriculum are direct results of this narrow and restricted view of research (Valdés & Figueroa, 1994).

The errors or distortions of positivism have led to some very specific school intervention strategies. For example, in the controversy in reading education between phonics and whole language, many phonics proponents base their stance largely on a limited, behaviorist view of linguistics. These advocates regularly assert that theirs is the only reading system based on research. The linguistics used to support the phonics approach to reading result from looking only at very limited, controlled data (reductionism). Phonemic awareness research reveals some reading problems, and phonics is a useful approach on some issues. The behaviorist and reductionist research approach has helped teachers to recognize the important role of phonemic awareness. Behaviorism adds important knowledge, but also ignores critical information, tending to negate both the importance of students' own constructions of meaning and the value of a student speaking a second or third language.

The best summaries of reading research at the present time argue for a balanced approach that includes both phonics and an emphasis on encouraging reading in a complex context (Eldredge, 1995; "Every Child Reading," 1998). Note also that while no one strategy for teaching of reading works for all students, students who speak a second language or a divergent dialect of English need strategies for reading that build on the language they already know. We discuss this issue further in Chapter 11.

Taylor (1993) describes this limitation on reductionist research processes that has led to overemphasis on phonics and phonetics in reading education. For more on this issue see Taylor's writings, particularly *From the Child's Point of View* (1993).

Alternatives to Reductionism

A countervailing tradition of reporting and analysis has developed in four arenas: clinical psychology and counseling, the sociology of knowledge, the politically informed movements of empowerment, and in the research process of ethnography.

Gestalt therapy, humanistic psychology, and Rogerian counseling have contributed to the understanding of interpersonal relations and communication styles. Practitioners have developed new, alternative ways of understanding human psychology, emotions, and behavior that do not draw all of their conceptual framework from positivism (Weinberg & Reidford, 1972). In *The Culture of Education* (1996), Jerome Bruner, one of the preeminent psychologists in the United States, describes how culture informs and directs psychological processes. These important concepts provide a conceptual framework for human relations teaching strategies.

Over the last several decades, educational anthropologists and linguists have developed ethnographic approaches to describe in detail the sociocultural and linguistic context of classroom teaching and learning. In contrast to positivist psychologists who, following traditional scientific research formats, usually sought to isolate variables for study, ethnologists discovered new insights by focusing on the dynamic, complex, and often subtle nuances found in diverse classrooms (Heath, 1995; Ladson-Billings, 1994a; Trueba, 1989).

Rather than look for improvement in student achievement as a result of a single intervention, such as the use of a new curriculum or teaching strategy, educational ethnographers incorporate "classic" anthropological research tools to examine the day-to-day phenomena unfolding in schools and classrooms. Foremost among these tools is the use of extended participant observation (often over several years) and informant interviews (usually teachers, administrators, staff, parents, and at times, even students).

In one ethnographic effort, Trueba, Rodriguez, Zou, and Cintrón (1993) studied a northern California rural school district and a specific school therein to describe the rise to political power of a Chicano community and how this affected school language policies and practices at a local elementary Spanish immersion school. In seeking to describe the development of excellence in bilingual school reform at Beamer Park Elementary School, Cintrón (1993) analyzed the more established quantitative measures employed by the school and then extended the analysis by using ethnographic research methods. The qualitative approach revealed a myriad of interesting findings, including the significance and type of teacher preparation at the school; the inherent reward systems within the school culture; faculty self-identity; immersion teacher relationships with non-immersion colleagues, administration, and students; and parental attitudes toward the school and immersion program in particular.

In *The Dreamkeepers: Successful Teachers of African American Children*, Ladson-Billings (1994a) describes the context and the cultural perspectives of eight teachers, both European American and African American, who regularly encouraged excellence from their mostly African American students.

Both the work of Trueba et al. (1993) and of Ladson-Billings (1994a, 1994b) reveal that a broader, ethnographic framework provides a more complex, detailed, and more interactive description of school realities than does the limited reductionist approach common in prior educational research.

Developments in the sociology of knowledge first brought into question the domination of positivism within educational research and its role in fragmenting and segregating knowledge. Torres and Mitchell (1998) and Popkewitz (1998), among others, have critiqued popular understandings of the role of research and pointed out the improbability of scientific neutrality. Through careful reasoning, workers in the sociology of knowledge have demonstrated the intertwined nature of empirical data collection and value judgments. This important theoretical development recognizes that, within the social sciences, ideology and science are inextricably interconnected. Ideas originally developed within political movements, for example on the complex interaction of race, class, gender, and identity, are explained to university audiences by sociologists such as Torres.

In Brazil, Paulo Freire and his coworkers taught peasants to read in about 30 hours using cultural circles. They developed a theory to explain their action. The theory required praxis, an interaction of consciousness, and social action on the side of the poor (Freire, 1972). Freire was not neutral, nor was he "objective." He and teams of cultural workers engaged peasants in dialogue to develop literacy and to democratize knowledge, culture, and power in their societies (I discuss Freire's work in Chapter 7). In the United States, developments in psychology, ethnography, and the sociology of knowledge translated Freire's insights into the language of U.S. academics.

Consciousness, a central concept in Freire's work, is an awareness of one's own existence and of the environment. Both philosophy and experience demonstrate that consciousness exists. Gestalt psychology argues that consciousness is centrally important to understanding human behavior. Studies of the feminist movement and the struggles of people of color testify to the importance of consciousness raising. Behaviorist educational researchers are unable to measure the role of consciousness. Because they cannot quantify it, they fail to use this important concept in developing educational programs. But failures of measurement do not deny the importance of awareness of self, consciousness, and self-knowledge.

On the contrary, the best strategies designed for empowering students depend on an understanding of consciousness. The teacher's choice to promote either equality or inequality in the classroom is a product of the teacher's awareness and consciousness. Positivist, reductionist, and objectivist research designs that cannot explain issues of context, classroom ecology and social relations, and consciousness, among other topics, are too limited and unrealistic to provide a basis for developing multicultural education (Bowers & Flanders, 1990).

Human relations theory provides important insight into the process of whether teachers motivate students or alienate and discourage them. Teachers promote either equality or inequality through their interaction with students. Some teachers are supportive, motivating, and demanding while others are tentative, distant, disengaged, and, at times, oppressive. These different interaction styles significantly influence student motivation and achievement.

Differences between interaction styles are substantially a result of the human qualities and cultural competence of the teacher. Interaction styles are subject to study and improvement. Ethnographic studies add significant power to educational research by focusing on the interaction, context, and the characteristics and the consciousness of both teacher and students (Ladson-Billings, 1994a; Mehan, Lintz, Okamotoa, & Wills, 1995; Trueba, 1989).

Interaction styles and communication among teachers and students consist of far more than words and sentences. Communication improves when teachers and students respect each other, when they know each other's realities, are aware of the assumptions they hold, and when they can "read" each other's body language and tones. Communication styles differ among cultures and between genders. For example, positivist, quantitative research methodologies do not measure the educational effect of the manner in which a teacher responds to an Appalachian or Mexican accent, or the status of the teacher's own accent. Ethnographic research points to women and Latino teachers and researchers placing more importance on the quality of relationships between teachers and students, while researchers trained in the positivist tradition were satisfied with measuring the number of questions, the nature of the questions asked, and the frequency of responses (Foster 1995; E. Garcia, 1995).

A growing body of research based on observations of classrooms and of clients in therapy contends against positivism's narrow, empiricist tradition to better describe the complexity of human learning (Bruner, 1996). The observations produce a new paradigm of learning to help teachers understand classroom interaction (Figure 6.2).

Students' classroom experience improves when teachers design their instruction and interaction using insights from both of the models, or paradigms, shown in Figure 6.2. Exclusive use of the information in paradigm A may result in improvements in instructional technology, but it will not inform or significantly assist in student

Figure 6.2   Models of Classroom Interaction Research Paradigms

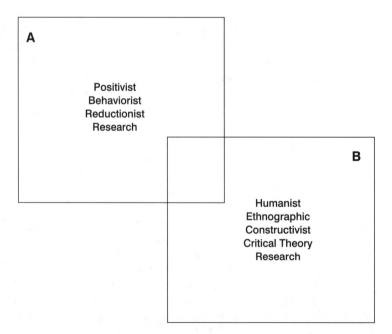

A

Positivist
Behaviorist
Reductionist
Research

B

Humanist
Ethnographic
Constructivist
Critical Theory
Research

human relation empowerment. Paradigm B works from the hypothesis that, for some students, the quality of student–teacher relationships is as important to student achievement as the instructional materials, texts, and teaching strategies. In fact, the quality of the student–teacher relationship may be even more important.

In the humanist, constructivist model (B), teachers are concerned with the quality of their interactions with students. Both teachers and students enter the classroom with motivational styles that are, in part, culturally influenced (Ramirez & Castañeda, 1974). For example, research summarized by E. Garcia (1994) asserts that, while many children achieve well in our increasingly formalized, depersonalized classrooms, young Latino children learn more when the teacher provides a positive, supportive, human interaction. Research summarized by Bennett (1986) asserts that African American children tend to learn better in an oral-interactive environment rather than in situations in which they individually read a text and write answers to worksheets. J. E. King (1995) and Ladson-Billings (1994a) have researched the attributes of teachers who are successful with African American children. Native American children may learn more in cooperative settings and where observation and listening are respected. When teachers use communication and motivation styles that respect students, the relationship is improved. To recognize and participate in multiple communication styles require cultural competence on the part of the teacher.

Teachers as Cultural Mediators

The role of teachers in society varies across cultures. Immigrant children from Latin America and Southeast Asia and migrant students from the South and Southwest come from societies where teachers usually receive far more respect from working people than do teachers in the rest of the United States. Many immigrant students are confused—and at times, appalled—at much of the disrespectful student behavior in our schools.

In our own country, some members of dominated cultural groups (such as African Americans, Puerto Ricans, Chicanos, Native Americans) have learned to perceive teachers as outsiders (Ogbu, 1995). They recognize teachers as people who dominate and enforce the rules of a school system in which family members and friends have been failed. As young people, these students are subjected to teacher authority as a price for staying in school. By adolescence, some of these students become rebellious and engage in a struggle for self-worth and identity. They refuse to accept teacher authority, and struggle against norms expected by the school and usually enforced by teachers (Ogbu, 1995).

Schools reward compliance with a promise of future success. This promise is too remote and often unrealistic for many children. Neither our consumer culture nor students' life experiences prepare them to work for long-term educational goals (West, 1993b). Students vaguely sense that African American males who graduate from college earn less money than European American high school graduates. When the teacher's role is primarily one of domination, older students (grades 6 through 12) will respond by struggling for their own arenas of power, such as gangs, sports teams, bathrooms, and play areas.

Quality interpersonal relations between teachers and students are particularly problematic in marginalized neighborhoods. Too few teachers live in the neighborhood of the school and participate in the cultures of the students. The teaching profession and teacher preparation programs remain predominantly centered on the European American experience. A cultural and communication gap exists between many teachers and the several communities of color.

When communities suffer economic distress, students' stress levels require even more supportive teacher–student relationships. Quality schools in marginalized neighborhoods must provide a positive alternative to the decaying urban social order. In the primary grades, teachers establish positive relationships with their students by directly teaching appropriate role behavior and communication systems. The social skills of being a productive student are taught rather than assumed. Effective teachers repeatedly encourage rather than demand cooperation between the student, the home, and the school.

James P. Comer and the School Development Program, based in New Haven, Connecticut and at Yale University, developed an extensive system of schools working closely with communities to produce a positive, child-friendly school environment. The program teaches children and teachers positive social and emotional skills. This approach of concentrating on the safety and environment of the school for all of its participants—students, staff, teachers, parents, and so on—produced remarkably positive results in about one-third of the schools. The Comer School Development Program concentrates on developing positive and nurturing adult–student relationships (O'Neil, 1997). I discuss the program and other similar approaches in more detail in Chapters 8 and 13.

Improving the quality of teacher–student relationships and reducing depersonalization are essential to school reform, particularly in middle schools and high schools. Teachers facilitate a democratic relationship by respecting students' rights and by encouraging them to display responsible behavior. At the same time, teachers need to discourage and prevent abusive and disrespectful behavior. (Additional strategies for positive classroom management appear in Chapter 8.)

Schools in low-income areas are brimming with students in crisis. Successful teachers serve as cultural mediators or even cultural therapists for these students (Spindler & Spindler, 1991). They assist students in their often-painful transition from secure members of their home culture to effective participators in the larger economy and society. Many students are at risk and suffer from crises of poverty and oppression. Confronted by society and by failure in school, many students respond with adolescent—at times, destructive—rebellion.

Even suburban and affluent districts need programs to build positive social and emotional support systems for students. The crisis of the inner cities has become the crisis of the suburbs. Gangs, alcohol and drugs, violence, alienation, early pregnancy, and student suicide now are found in suburban and affluent schools as well as in marginalized neighborhoods. The drugs and violence of choice may change, but the destructive alienation is expressed by young people of many cultures and social classes.

The several crises in our society make students more and more isolated and alienated. They blame themselves, other ethnic groups, and politicians for their loss of equal opportunity. As the authority and legitimacy of government officials and institutional leaders decline, a growing portion of students adopt a cynical, even nihilistic, worldview clearly revealed in some popular music (West, 1993b). At the same time, schools and the knowledge and credentials they control are ever more important to students from the working classes. Alienation from school is ever more damaging to their economic future. Teachers committed to democracy must help students to fashion a way out of this growing cynicism and defeat.

As explained in Chapters 1 and 2, schools both transmit the dominant culture and socialize students to that culture. Schools are transitional institutions where society insists that students adjust to the social stratification of the emerging global economy (Thurow, 1996). For many in oppressed communities, this emerging economy offers poverty, drugs, underemployment, crime, and alienation or a low-level, poorly paid job with little future.

When curriculum by omission or commission attacks a student's culture or gender, it attacks the student's self. In particular, invisibility, intimidation, and failure in the school attack the student's "enduring self" (Spindler & Spindler, 1991). The teacher as a mediator must help students identify and work toward more positive alternatives.

Students need to learn effective resistance to economic and racial oppression. Students best succeed when they understand the changing society and how to pursue individual and community progress. They succeed when they understand their own culture and the forces of assimilation, and when they know how to choose new strategies and when to adapt past practices to new situations. Effective teachers help, coach, and guide students through this turmoil.

By middle school, the curriculum should study issues of youth alienation and cultural and racial conflict. For example, in Lee Middle School in Woodland, California, Enrique Sepulveda in 1998 conducted a special class one day a week for students alienated from school and prone to joining gangs (personal communication, February 1998). They deal with real issues such as personal responsibility for pregnancy and for staying in school, and peer group pressures to act out in school. Separate classes are held for boys and girls, with a female counselor facilitating the girls' classes. Alienated young people need to know that some adults care, that some listen, and that school is a place where they can learn to work through their very real problems of adolescence. Young people need counselors in the schools. Studying these conflicts helps students to comprehend and validate their own reality and to fashion productive responses. Teachers as mediators encourage students to find alternatives. Cultural mediation and cultural therapy help students draw on their own cultures and experiences as resources, as sources of knowledge for developing strategies to overcome the barriers of an often hostile society.

Teachers who are emotionally well adjusted and comfortable with themselves are able to establish a healthy classroom environment that promotes quality relationships among students and that promotes quality teaching. Being well adjusted in an urban school includes being comfortable with one's own ethnicity and the complexity of one's own culture. Well-adjusted teachers are not overstressed by fear of others or by guilt. Teachers are not responsible for the general societal oppressions of people of color or for the inadequate funding of most urban schools. Teachers *are* responsible for promoting high achievement and educational opportunity for the students in their classes.

Teachers help most by encouraging students. Human relations theory is helpful for teachers as well as for students. Teachers must concern themselves with their own mental health, biases, and perceptions. Teachers need to view themselves and their students in generally positive ways if they are to establish positive relationships. Both teachers and students need to consider each other as being successful and able persons with dignity.

Maria Delgado—A Teacher Serving as a Cultural Mediator

The case of Maria Delgado, a Mexican American (Chicana) high school teacher in Texas, illustrates the importance of positive social relationships between teachers and students. Because her presence at the school establishes the idea that Chicanas can go to college and become teachers, Maria serves as a positive role model to young Chicanas. She can be particularly helpful and sensitive to other students.

Maria makes close personal contact with some of her students. She looks for opportunities to talk privately and supportively with her students. She uses a little Spanish, the endearment "Mija," and some friendly advice to establish rapport with her female students. Expressions of empathy and understanding as well as active listening skills serve her well. Students often need to talk and explore ideas and emotions with adults other than their parents. When a safe, student-friendly environment is established, many students approach the teacher for advice.

Maria's female students perceive her as a woman who "understands" that their daily turmoil and conflicts—dress, looks, boyfriends, parents, rules—all are critical issues. Most of these conflicts are personal rather than academic. Maria's own training as a counselor taught her to use active listening skills to establish empathy. With over 160 students per day, each week three or four students need help. She can put her arms around a young girl and give her a hug and reassurance. She can provide them with important information on crisis intervention, dating, birth control clinics, and counseling support for family crises.

It helps that Maria is a Chicana, but teachers do not have to be Chicano to encourage Chicano students or African American to encourage African American students. Two of Maria's mentors were European Americans.

Support behavior, both verbal and nonverbal, is often culturally specific and precise. Family supervision styles often vary across cultures and are changing. A female European American may lose contact with some of her Mexican American students if she fails to comprehend or respect traditional Mexican American values of close family supervision or Catholic values on birth control. A European American female teacher could provide most of the support that Maria provides. Indeed, it was a European American teacher—not a Mexican American—who first encouraged Maria to go to college.

Some teachers from other cultures learn about Chicano culture, work closely with the Mexican American community for years, and become a part of the community. They are seen in the neighborhoods and get invited to family rituals such as baptisms, first communions, and weddings. They become a friendly and supportive aunt or uncle, padrino or madrina—a significant and accepted member of the community. These teachers and many teacher assistants provide desperately needed guidance for students and important communication between home and school (E. Garcia, 1994).

Being Chicana is not a guarantee of empathy with Chicana students, nor is being black a guarantee of support for African American students. Some Mexican American teachers choose to remain apart, uninvolved in their students' lives. All individuals, including teachers, respond uniquely to their life circumstances. The teachers' personal goals and the major differences within the culture, between generations, language usage, and degrees of assimilation divide some students and teachers.

The lack of male role models in elementary school produces a particular problem for young boys of several cultures. By the middle school years, coaches and a few male teachers provide an additional support system and guidance for boys. Female teachers and principals may extend themselves to assist boys, but the gender difference creates barriers that only more self-assured or more desperate male students will cross.

The increased incidence of harassment charges and actual sexual molestation makes it more difficult today for teachers to use hugs and physical comforting with students of the opposite sex. Racism, racial fears about sexuality, and homophobia frighten many teachers. Lawsuits, abuse charges, and many district policies prohibit teachers from using even small amounts of physical force to direct a child (such as holding onto a child's arm while scolding him or physically breaking up a fight). What seems a simple, obvious, and supportive touch to you as the teacher, may cause concern among a small number of parents. Some children, and unfortunately some teachers, are immature and prone to exaggerate. Children often have little comprehension or concern for the consequences of their accusations. As a new teacher, particularly if you are a male teacher in elementary or middle school, you should exercise care while learning the professional and safety guidelines for touch in your particular school district.

There is cause for professional caution. Sexual abuse, molestation, and unprofessional conduct charges against a very few teachers have frightened others. In addition to a few abusive adults, young children and teenagers in times of crisis develop vivid imaginations. Too few counselors are available. Not all parents are reasonable, rational, and supportive. In our society, where many children need more attention, more comforting, and even more encouraging touch, we have yet to develop new guidelines and reasonable procedures.

Teaching Social Skills

Children and adolescents need to be taught to work together cooperatively and to respect one another. These goals are not attained unless they are taught and promoted by specific teaching strategies.

For kindergarten and first grade, social skill development is a normal part of the social studies curriculum. Human relations lessons work well for teachers in teaching social skill development.

Teaching role behavior, respectful, positive communication styles, and other social skills is an important component of cooperative learning (described in Chapter 10). Such instruction should begin by at least second grade and continue thereafter. In classes with a mix of cultures and in schools serving economically marginalized neighborhoods, social skills, human relations, and the study of conflict resolution strategies help teachers achieve a positive classroom environment and improve school social climate.

As a result of social decay in some neighborhoods, the crises in our cities and families, and the drug crisis, many young students are dysfunctional in the classroom. They do not use appropriate or respectful communication processes with the teacher or with other students. Skills and attitudes promoting positive communication and positive human relationships must be taught. I discuss strategies for teaching positive social skills in Chapter 8.

Some older students do not use respectful communication because their life and school experiences have not taught them to value the use of positive communications. An increasing number of young people have not accepted their role as students and have not learned to interact positively with schools and teachers. Meanwhile, their peer-group experiences on the streets reinforce aggression, competition, and disdain and disrespect for many school norms.[2]

These same students are clearly able to learn under certain conditions. Gangs are, in themselves, schools that teach role relationships and communication styles, albeit negative ones. If the school and family do not offer positive alternatives, the street culture in many cities offers incentives, communication, and motivation styles that are opposed to school success. The economic results of student alienation from school have already reached crisis proportions. The crime results are staggering.

Teachers using human relations help students to work together and to assist one another in the classroom. Social skill lessons teach respect, cooperative social behavior, and problem-solving techniques. Teachers can use assigned roles in cooperative learning groups to help all students to belong to positive social groups in the classroom. Additional human relation lessons may deal with stereotyping and scapegoating—long identified as problems that contribute to inter-ethnic conflict.

---

[2]It is important to not overgeneralize. Many students have learned appropriate role behavior at home, and they may also have learned aggressiveness and rebellion at school. This conflict is not unique to disenfranchised students or students of color.

Teachers present a model of positive human relations when they treat students with dignity and respect and when they insist that students treat each other with dignity and respect. By middle school, adolescent alienation and nihilism often dominate peer-group exchanges. Human relations lessons teach students how to develop positive communication and supportive relationships.

Promoting Positive Self-Esteem

The theories of promotion of positive self-esteem derive primarily from a humanistic psychology that has taken too-limited notice of cultural differences. Behavior that would illustrate a positive self-concept in one culture, such as assertiveness, might be interpreted as a sign of poor education in another (Bruner, 1996). Separately from this debate, teachers have developed a series of classroom strategies to encourage students to conduct themselves appropriately.

Safety and Security

Most students need a strong sense of comfort and safety from both physical and emotional abuse and criticism in their classroom. Teachers need to have enough order that students do not intimidate, insult, or overly criticize each other. You achieve this sense of positive order by teaching and developing positive social skills. Students do well when they believe that they can depend on the teacher and their classmates. This comfort is achieved by rules and regulations in the classroom that are sensible and consistently enforced (see Chapter 8). Teachers build a trusting relationship by helping and encouraging students and by stopping inappropriate behavior such as racial and gender harassment.

At all ages, students are very sensitive to what they perceive as unequal treatment. When students believe that their teacher favors some students over others, conflict grows in the classroom and their trust in the teacher declines.

In secondary schools, teachers have more students and therefore know them less well. Secondary teachers place more emphasis on teaching subject matter and tend to place less emphasis on serving as coach, mentor, counselor, and cultural mediator. The lack of opportunity to develop personal relationships and the variety of teacher and student personalities create disharmony. Students want to be listened to and respected as human beings with wants, desires, fears, and emotions.

Over the years, students need to develop a strong sense of security, and they should have the opportunity to develop a trusting personal relationship with some teachers and students. Teams, clubs, and student government projects contribute to this important sense of belonging. Each student should encounter at least one teacher or counselor who is interesting and motivating each day. If this does not occur, the school will lose the student. Without positive, personal relationships, schools become warehouses for students rather than learning centers.

Teachers and students without a sense of security develop symptoms of stress and anxiety. They resist change. When schools are full of inter-ethnic conflict or sexual harassment, the violent environment prevents many students from learning. Human relations lessons and strategies, such as those found in the curriculum *The Wonderful World of Difference* (B'nai B'rith Antidefamation League, 1986), help to build classrooms where students feel safe and comfortable. This curriculum offers more than 100 lessons emphasizing positive human relations strategies.

Self-Worth

When schools serve students well, students develop a sense of self-worth and competence and come to expect to succeed at classroom and social projects. By adolescence, students can recognize their own strengths and can develop plans to overcome their weaknesses. The curriculum should be planned and presented so that all students succeed.

Teachers can promote a positive sense of self by providing frequent opportunities to succeed in classroom work. In the primary years students should learn to read. If they are not successful readers, additional support of increased teacher time, tutors, and special instruction along with a rich variety of reading strategies must be provided so that students learn to love reading, and so they do not fall behind (Slavin, 1998). Learning successful reading skills and acquiring joy and interest in reading contribute to a positive sense of self-worth in school.

Failure to develop essential reading skills leads to failure in other subject areas and failure in the upper grades. Human relations lessons should complement, support, and include reading instruction. Human relations and multicultural lessons are not substitutes for important reading skill development. Skilled teachers use many strategies to improve reading, including spending time each day reading, developing comprehension strategies, and providing interesting and useful reading materials.

A strong relationship exists between poverty (social class) and reading scores. Teachers of grades 4–8 need to assist students to improve their reading. Lessons in history, science, and literature should systematically include high-interest literature, allow students choice, and emphasize skill development. Improving students' reading skills, whether through explicit instruction or through coaching (see Chapters 7 and 8), will lead to more school success and a positive sense of self-worth.

Upper elementary (grades 4–6) and middle-grade students (grades 6–8) also improve their sense of self-worth by learning to set immediate, accomplishable goals and establishing clear criteria for achieving them. With clear goals and lessons, students can recognize and improve their study and interpersonal skills. Quality literature and guest speakers can regularly present positive lifestyle choices to students.

Students who believe themselves competent become more willing to take risks. They generally feel successful at important tasks and school subjects. Such students are willing to share their ideas and opinions and to recognize the accomplishments of other students. Too often teachers use theories of motivation based on the competitive nature of the macroculture and poorly informed teacher folk knowledge about testing, measurement, and curve grading. Overreliance on competition obstructs the goal of developing a positive sense of self-worth for all students. Teachers who notice that their students are dependent, frustrated, or withdrawn need to change their assessment systems. (For a thorough discussion of these and other assessment issues, see Stiggins, 1997.)

Students in supportive environments develop a positive sense of self. Violence, drug use, and alienation among teenagers indicate that school or society is failing them. During adolescence, many students struggle with *individuation,* becoming self-aware as an individual. Adolescents try on many roles and traverse many role changes. Developing an accurate and realistic view of their self is important for students, even as that self changes frequently (Elkind, 1988; K. Gordon, 1991). Students bridging two or more cultures and identities suffer increased stress and conflict. Literature and lessons about teen conflicts, challenges, and successes offer opportunities for support. Students need to find themselves and recognize their conflicts in the curriculum, and literature used must include teens from the cultures represented in the classroom (Bushman & Bushman, 1997).

Troubled students overuse negative statements in describing themselves and others, and are uncomfortable with praise. Schools with adequate counseling staffs establish programs to supplement the classroom in helping students to question and redefine their identity. Budget cuts that reduce counseling support leave students even more reliant on an often negative peer culture. Peer culture may of course at times be positive, but it certainly should be supplemented by adult direction.

The sense of self is highly dependent on cultural frames of reference and individual family situations. Descriptions of "normal" behavior and "normal" rebellion should always be tested from within the cultural viewpoint. The ideas of students studying the nature of culture given in Chapter 2 provide important cautions to the assumed universality of many theories of self (Spindler & Spindler, 1992).

Sense of Belonging

Students at all ages have a strong need to belong to groups. The desire to fit in provides a major source of motivation and—at times—challenges to school rules (see Chapter 8). Students may feel conflicting desires to belong to an ethnic or cultural group, girls' or boys' athletic teams, or any one of a number of other groups. Learning to work positively within a social group is important to maturity.

Students strengthen their sense of self-worth when they receive recognition, approval, appreciation, and respect from their peers. A human relations approach to multicultural education uses lessons to promote inclusion and acceptance of all students. You can promote these important feelings in the classroom by using cooperative and collaborative learning and classroom projects. Lessons should draw on the diversity of languages and skills students bring to school. Make every attempt to recognize leaders, authors, scientists, literature, and teachers from all cultural groups.

Deliberately developing peer support groups and recognizing the diversity of talents—for language, music, math, social leadership, and so on—help students to develop a sense of belonging to one or more of the groups in school.

By adolescence, group affiliation can at times contest against school rules and norms. Teen culture, like African American, Latino, or teacher culture, must be respected. If schools set themselves against teenage culture, the conflict will destroy many students. Only negative aspects of teen culture, such as drugs, violence, or theft, should be opposed. In the many classrooms and schools that seek to impose a Euro-centered culture and also seek to defeat teen culture, conflict and opposition by students can reach destructive levels. Students resist the imposition of a dominating culture in a number of ways. Some forms of resistance, such as developing their own styles of dress, their own music, and their own humor, are not cause for concern. But many young people join negative groups, such as gangs. In some neighborhoods, gangs have become the dominant political force, forcing students to either join or fear them. Others young people may turn to drugs and/or alcohol. Still other students withdraw from school and peers; they become isolated and lonely.

Unfortunately, some public schools must now use desperately short funds to offer programs to assist students to leave the gang and drug cultures dominating their neighborhoods. Principals have turned to peer conflict resolution and gang and narcotics units of police departments to augment inadequate resources. Students need to be recruited and encouraged to support the positive aspects of school through clubs, team building, conflict resolution, and leadership development programs.

The school must become a student-friendly, safe environment. To achieve this goal, we must both respect and celebrate the cultures of students. Peer coaching, peer counseling, and tutoring programs help individual students deal with the many conflicts of adolescence.

Sense of Direction

While young students often accept the direction of their parents and the school, by adolescence many students are redefining their roles and their choices. Some students need repeated lessons on goal setting and establishing their own sense of responsibility and direction. Students can learn to make decisions and identify consequences. Experiential education programs and outdoor programs help students with goal setting and motivation. Coaching and counseling by teachers can help students make preliminary career and college choices. Teachers serving as advisors to clubs—such as MECHA, MAYA, African American clubs, ski clubs, teams, and journalism—often play important roles in helping students to define and to select their future. By talking with students and supporting them in areas that interest them, you often help them to develop their own sense of self and to deal with the turmoil in their lives.

Sense of Purpose

Students succeed more when they have a sense of purpose to their school life. Essentially, success at school is their job. School needs to prove its worth to them. Students benefit from lessons and experiences of decision making and cooperative problem solving. By the middle grades, and throughout high school, students benefit from lessons on goal setting and accepting their own responsibilities and consequences. These lessons can be taught in combination with study skills lessons or with peer support groups, drug education, and sex education programs.

You encourage positive self-esteem when you recognize, validate, and respect students' own cultures. Cooperative learning and other human relations strategies teach students positive interdependence and how to create and maintain a cooperative group working environment. Students learn the rewards of shared responsibility and cooperation. These lessons help to create a classroom environment that is safe and supportive, where students may both achieve recognition of their self-worth and validate other students as capable, worthy, and confident (see Chapter 10).

Many students need this validation of their self-worth, particularly during adolescence. Some schools are experimenting with all-girl math classes to overcome the recognized loss of self-confidence among middle-school girls in math. Other school districts, where de facto segregation creates all–African American schools, have created all-male primary schools to promote positive self-esteem for black males in school (African American Male Task Force of Milwaukee Public Schools, 1990).

Teachers make decisions to structure their classrooms in ways that encourage learning and cooperation, or they make decisions that produce anxiety, frustration, competition, failure and disruption. In particular, a highly competitive classroom environment discourages trust and cooperation. Some students always lose, and these students legitimately feel alienated and angry. Students must come to trust that the teacher has their own best interests at heart, even in difficult times. Teachers achieve this goal by demonstrating their respect for the fundamental dignity and worth of each student.

Stopping Demeaning Comments

Too often, particularly in grades 4 through 10, classrooms are the scene of intolerance and demeaning comments among students. All students deserve a safe environment in which to learn. Teachers should prohibit demeaning and derogatory comments, particularly those that invite racial and gender conflict (see Chapter 8). Teachers need to work against this intolerance by presenting lessons and activities on tolerance and respect and lessons opposing scapegoating. These positive social values are required first steps in instruction for cooperative learning (see Chapter 10). The curriculum *The Wonderful World of Difference* (B'nai B'rith Antidefamation League, 1986) is also useful in promoting these values.

You improve your classroom climate by modeling positive, supportive communications skills and by teaching these skills to students. The great majority of interactions in classrooms are among students. You can influence these interactions and encourage respect in these interactions by teaching positive skills. Lessons in active listening, using "I" messages, and negotiating conflicts show students how to treat each other with respect. These lessons are desperately needed in our increasingly alienating culture.

Teaching democratic participation and decision making encourages positive self-esteem. Students can participate in making important decisions about classroom rules. (see Chapter 8).

Resolving Conflicts

Students and teachers encounter stress, anger, and fear in their lives. Life in many urban neighborhoods makes one angry or fearful. Intergroup conflict is frequent. Physical danger is a reality on the streets and often in schools. This conflict, anger, and fear must be dealt with, not silenced or ignored. Suppressing or not talking about these problems may create an even more dangerous setting.

Many schools have successfully taught groups of students and parents to serve as conflict mediators, allowing teachers to invest more time in teaching. Developments in the area of peace studies and conflict resolution have become increasingly valuable for teachers. Classroom management systems work when the general atmosphere of the school, the neighborhood, and family life is positive, helpful, and supportive. But management alone, even skillfully applied management, will not resolve deeply rooted conflicts of poverty, racism, and schools that rely on authoritarianism to respond to adolescent growth and change.

Classroom conflict can be caused by a number of events: an overemphasis on competition, intolerance learned at home or on the streets, bullies and criminals in schools, teachers and students using poor communication skills, and lack of practice in conflict resolution.

Teachers who make irrational or impossible demands on students also contribute to classroom violence. The present conservative school reform movement has advocated raising standards, and certainly standards should be raised in those schools presently failing. But high standards must always be accompanied by support and encouragement. Simply raising standards and failing more students, as advocated by many, without restructuring the curriculum and teaching to provide opportunities for students to learn will only lead to increased school failure. Failure and leaving school do not serve students or society well.

Teaching Conflict Resolution in the Social Studies

Many elementary teachers, restricted in part by the limits of their own university preparation, have responded to the demand to improve reading and math skills by reducing the time spent on social studies. This is an unwise choice. The field of social studies provides students with an opportunity to be proud of who they are and healthy in who they are becoming. Quality social studies encourages students to develop the social skills necessary to cooperate with others and to resolve problems. Social studies lessons should encourage students to analyze their own environment and their society, and to plan and prepare to take charge of their own future. In schools in impoverished areas, where governmental services are inadequate and voter turnout usually low, students need additional assistance to learn to believe in, to value, and to advocate for a democratic society and to overcome cynicism (Acuña, 1996). Young people can learn these things by studying the history of African Americans', Latinos', women's, and working peoples' struggles for justice, dignity, and democracy.

By middle school (grades 6–8), many schools have taught positive communication skills and conflict resolution skills to reduce violence, power struggles, and rebellion. This instruction begins with a recognition that feelings are important. Dealing with our feelings in a positive, constructive manner is an important part of schooling.

Teachers and students gain from preparation in conflict resolution. The level of conflict students experience may reach dangerous and unhealthy levels. Teachers alone cannot "control" the violence that comes into the schools from outside. They need to enlist students in a cooperative effort to reduce violence, at least in school. One way to lessen the impact of these stresses is for students to learn clear communication skills. Students learn alternative, nonviolent strategies for reducing conflict. They learn mediation skills. Most importantly, they learn that even major social problems such as conflict can be faced and dealt with within a cooperative community.

Teachers' choices of what to teach in social studies and in literature can contribute to reducing stereotyping, misunderstanding, and unnecessary conflict. They should introduce discussions of race, ethnic, class and gender relations. Students live in a world of intersecting demands. Studying these demands, and multiple perspectives on these demands, assists students to make deliberate and wise choices. In community action projects, they can learn to advocate skillfully for their own interests. It strengthens community to learn to resolve conflicts in a democratic and cooperative manner.

Violence increases when student conflicts are depersonalized or cast into a "we versus they" format. Excellent violence reduction programs have been developed that work even with tough gang members, using outdoor and experiential education programs where former enemies learn to rely on one another (see, for example, Dear, 1995; Tennessee Education Association & Appalachian Educational Laboratory, 1993).

Many classes require a time of trust building and attention to issues of group dynamics. Continued attention to trust building is called for in our increasingly polarized society, in which major changes in populations and power relationships are occurring. Schools should be places where children learn to work and play together. They should be places where children learn to judge others on their merit and on their actions, rather than on stereotypes, fear, and mistrust. A long period of working together on sports teams, in classrooms, and in student leadership programs can significantly reduce intergroup hostilities.

By converting the violence of adolescent lives into something to study, to analyze, teachers moves from coercive power to adult authority. Fr. Greg Boyle in Los Angeles argues that many adolescents need additional amounts of adult authority in their lives. Students need guidance. They need help making fateful choices. Students are full of fear about joining gangs, using drugs, bringing weapons, sexual identity and similar explosive matters. If the school is silent, or ignores these issues, issues that are consuming children, then the school becomes an accomplice in the violence and terror in parts of our society (Fremon, 1995).

Schools must be about developing positive and respectful relationships. Classrooms, forums, and clubs should discuss values central to democratic living, such as respect for the opinions of your opponents, fairness, honesty, and willingness to listen to others. The curriculum and the school culture can be shaped to give students practice in democratic, open decision making.

If certain communities of parents do not participate in the school, outreach workers should be employed to recruit and foster parent participation. Lacking funding, teachers oriented to community participation can create parental participation systems. Local universities' social work departments and teacher preparation programs may assist. Many parents in immigrant communities literally do not know how to participate. Schools can sponsor workshops by community leaders, religious leaders, and migrant education specialists to teach the fundamental skills of parent participation as well as hold English as a Second Language classes (Olsen & Dowell, 1997).

There are several emerging strategies for resolving conflict. One, classroom meetings, is described in Chapter 8. Johnson and Johnson (1992) describe successful efforts in Edina, Minnesota, to develop a peer mediation program in the schools. Similar programs are emerging in schools across the country. Some programs focus on improving communication skills, while others prepare specially skilled mediators.

Communication skills taught to students include the following:

1. Checking for understanding of the opposing viewpoint
2. Clearly stating one's own position
3. Sharing one's needs, feelings, and interests in the conflict

Mediators can assist by doing the following:

1. Recognizing negotiable and less negotiable conflicts
2. Helping to restate conflicts in negotiable forms
3. Reframing the issues (talking about the issues in a new, nonpolarized manner)
4. Seeking rather than suppressing solutions to conflict

School administrations must state clear rules for conflict management in schools.

The report *Reducing School Violence: Schools Teaching Peace,* by the Tennessee Education Association and the Appalachian Educational Laboratory (1993), concludes by stating, "Training and practice in conflict resolution can give students the skills to explore peacefully the differences among them. Tolerance and empathy can be taught, and, at a time when incidents of violence and hate are at an all-time high, the need has never been greater" (p. 9).

Curricula have developed to assist classrooms and mediators with training. For more information on conflict resolution efforts, contact the following organizations:

Educators for Social Responsibility
475 Riverside Dr.
Room 450
New York, NY 10115

International Chapter for Conflict Resolution
Box 53
Teachers College, Columbia University
New York, NY 10027

Teachers using the work of Spencer Kagan (1985) to help students improve their communications skills have posted charts displaying a list of alternative behaviors available to students under stress. Students practice and role play these alternatives. Then, when conflicts arise, they have a choice of responses. Kagan suggests using and posting on the classroom wall the following methods for resolving conflicts:

- Share
- Take turns
- Compromise
- Change
- Seek outside help
- Postpone
- Avoid
- Use humor

The coaching practices described in Chapters 7 and 8 describe a useful strategy for helping the increasing number of students with extremely high stress and conflict levels.

Teacher Self-Confidence

Many teachers, particularly during their first year, too often experience the frustration of failure. These feelings cause many new teachers to transfer schools or to leave teaching altogether.

Several aspects of teachers' work roles—disruptive students, undermotivated students, feelings of failing as a teacher, and demeaning professional work conditions—may combine to attack a teacher's self-confidence. Both teachers and students respond to attacks on their self-concepts in a defensive and at times hostile manner. Parents may expect that teachers can teach responsibility in a society characterized by self-indulgence, immediate rewards, and consumerism. This expectation is unrealistic and represents an overreliance on schools. As the now well-known traditional African proverb contends, "It takes an entire village to raise a child."

The clash between teacher and student can be quite a power struggle, and often produces an unfortunate, nonproductive, and conflictive environment for both parties in the classroom. Adolescent conflicts are particularly severe in at-risk schools where both the number of students suffering in their home lives and the number of new, inexperienced teachers increase.

Tense conditions and persistent failure for both students and teachers in desperately underfunded schools encourage the development of stereotypes, conflicts, and cultural clashes. Teachers, schools, and university teacher preparation programs have sufficient power to defend their cultural domination. But students have less power. Students who refuse to be dominated defend themselves by refusing to go along with school culture or by dropping out. Both resisting and leaving school lead to a long-term economic crisis for the student and the community.

Multicultural education offers an alternative form of resistance. Students can be incorporated into a cooperative, positive school culture. They can learn to respect communities and cultures. Successful students contribute to their community's health and safety rather than leave school to join a gang (O'Neil, 1997).

In schools all across the country, hundreds of involved, positive teachers of all cultural groups engage and motivate students. Unfortunately, many students also encounter rigid, alienated, resentful teachers who produce troubled, conflict-filled classrooms. In positive classrooms, both the teachers and students gain; in negative classrooms, both teachers and students lose.

Building Supportive Relationships

Cultural Competence

Understanding their position as cultural mediators helps teachers work with students to establish positive interpersonal relationships. When teachers are comfortable with their own cultural perspectives, they can accept cultural conflicts as normal. Students need instruction in the culture of schools. Some students need to learn to negotiate cultural conflicts and to seek positive, respectful resolutions. When formal, hierarchical relationships in schools are rigidly maintained, small conflicts between students become power struggles. Winning, losing, and revenge injure the positive interpersonal relationships needed in the classroom. Culturally competent teachers are able to help to resolve student conflicts. They do not waste their energy in endless struggles for power and control.

A teacher's real power to manage a classroom productively comes from cultural competence, experience, and maturity—not from using punishment and physical force. Teachers committed to empowerment for students of color help students to analyze and resolve their own cultural conflicts.

Teachers are a unique cultural group. Like other cultural groups, teachers tend to communicate well with and accept students who share their culture and agree with the norms and values of the school. Most students want to be treated fairly. Fairness helps to establish an environment in which it becomes easier to teach appropriate school behavior.

Many students learn in school. There are hundreds of success stories as a result of schooling poor and minority students (see Olsen et al., 1994; Olsen & Mullen, 1990). Students learn best when teachers believe in them. But for teachers to have confidence in students, teachers must first have confidence in themselves. Teachers must model and teach the value of education and of social service. Encouragement and guidance help students win the difficult struggle to develop a positive, productive life.

Most middle schools and secondary schools are larger than elementary schools and use more hierarchical, impersonal, and formal control mechanisms. The formality of the schools and rigidity of controls produce more conflict and win–lose situations. Teachers establish personalized and supportive relationships in their classes to work against the problems of size and rigidity. Students and teachers under great stress at times need an accepting, even therapeutic relationship. Young people need the opportunity to belong, to be successful in school life even while they make errors. They are, after all, children or adolescents. For maximum success, middle and secondary schools in inner cities should be broken up into smaller units. To address the many social needs of the students, we need to reestablish teacher guidance, coaching, and counseling time in addition to subject-matter instruction (McPartland & Slavin, 1990).

Teachers assist students by developing supportive relationships—particularly with those students who are resisting the depersonalization and hierarchical structure of the school. Teachers can talk with students and explore current crises in their lives.

When a School Emphasizes Human Relations

Central Park East School (CPE) in New York City is one of those few effective schools serving diverse social classes and multiple ethnic groups. The three Central Park East schools are located in "El Barrio," one of the original Puerto Rican settlement areas of the city. Large numbers of students from the Dominican Republic and Mexico are moving into the area and bringing a distinctly new need for English language acquisition and Spanish language maintenance. In spite of the severe economic poverty of the area, students come from other parts of the city to enroll in the community-based schools of Central Park East. Former principal Debbie Meier and the teachers in CPE have achieved many positive student–teacher relationships. Their remarkable and delightful story is told in *The Power of Their Ideas: Lessons for America from a Small School in Harlem* (Meier, 1995). In a report on the school, Bensman (1987) describes the efforts to develop a positive discipline system:

> CPE staff tried to develop an approach to discipline that stressed mutual respect rather than fear and punishment. Teachers spent time explaining to children why certain types of behav-

ior made it impossible for others to do their work, they tried to teach children to empathize with others, to understand the impact of their own actions on other children . . . (p. 13)

A CPE student described the experience:

I think that kind of open classroom situation was so much better. I liked it because it wasn't formal. When you came from public school to CPE, it was so different because at CPE you could be friends with your teacher. I think you want to learn because you have a friend instead of somebody who's dictating all the time. (Bensman, 1987, p. 12)

Summary

Improving the quality of the human relationships between teachers and students is central to multicultural education. The dominant trend of positivism in education and the behavioral sciences has not been helpful in developing cross-cultural, positive teacher–student relationships. Multicultural education and ethnographic research offer new strategies in developing positive relationships.

The diverse cultures of teachers and students affect their interactions and the classroom climate. Multicultural education encourages teachers to become culturally competent. Dedicated teachers can learn about cultural conflict and improve their skills as cultural mediators.

Questions Over the Chapter

1. What are four important goals of the human relations approach?
2. Describe why children from the working class need a human relations teaching approach in primary grades.
3. How can a teacher influence the quality of the student–teacher relationship?
4. List four social skills appropriate to teach in grades 1 and 2.
5. List four communication skills appropriate to teach in grades 6 through 10.
6. Define *cultural mediator.*
7. Define *cultural competence.*
8. Which cultures do you feel competent within?
9. In which cultures do you feel confused or out of place? Recall your experiences in the game BAFA BAFA.

Activities for Further Study of Human Relations

1. Interview a student about the teachers who most influenced him or her. What are the characteristics of the influential teacher? Ask the student to compare this teacher with another who was less influential. What are the characteristics of the noninfluential teacher?

2. Conduct library research on experiential teaching strategies and simulation activities. Then present your findings to the class.

3. Role play a coaching session between a student and a teacher. Brainstorm a range of responses to problems. (See Chapters 7 and 8 for more on coaching.)

4. Conduct library research on teacher stress, its symptoms, causes, and consequences. Prepare a written summary of your findings.

5. A group of student teachers can role play the culture of teachers in school. Create a hypothetical faculty room. What are the concerns and issues discussed? Have observers comment on the behavior as a separate culture. Compare this culture to gang behavior. What are the similarities and differences?

Teaching Strategies

Teaching strategies for human relations vary somewhat according to students' age level and maturity.

At the Primary Level

1. Select a student of the week. Have students bring in pictures of themselves and their families. Feature one student each week.

2. Consistently use positive statements. Try to make a positive statement to each child each day. Start each day with a positive statement.

In Intermediate Grades

1. Designate one of the bulletin boards in the class for student work. Groups of students can take turns, and responsibility, for the materials on the board. Create bulletin boards that feature student work.

2. Have students write their autobiographies. Use Writers Workshop or other strategies to edit and improve these autobiographies. Take pictures of the students and post the writings with the pictures.

3. Deliberately create a positive classroom spirit. Use a banner, a mural, a class newspaper to create a positive view of the classroom. Be careful to not compare your classroom with others so as to avoid unintentionally encouraging your students to feel superior to other students.

4. Involve parents and other community members in your class. Invite parents to come in and to make presentations. Inform parents of what is happening in the class. Perhaps produce a classroom newspaper to facilitate this effort.

5. Identify, recognize, and build on students' strengths. Emphasize the skills they have learned.

In Middle School and High School

1. Invite a guest speaker to address the issue of gangs. Encourage the speaker to discuss why young people are attracted to gangs. Ask the speaker to compare gangs to other formal groupings in the school (sports teams, cheerleaders, student government). Why do young people join groups? What are the advantages and disadvantages?

2. Assign students to view the video *American Me* (MCA Universal, 1992). This video is a chilling description of the brutality of gang and prison life among Mexican Americans.

3. Make a list of classroom activities that promote and respect diversity. Perhaps have students make murals or posters of these behaviors, and then display the posters prominently.

4. Practice clarifying responses and paraphrasing in discussions with students. Consider altering your daily schedule to increase the time available for small-group discussion, where these skills best function.

At All Grade Levels

1. Ask students to list their favorite three movies or television shows. View these programs for insights into student interests.

2. Record a current music video. Transcribe the words to the song. Play the song in class and read the words. Analyze the themes of the song.

3. Select a student in your class who is not actively involved in class discussions. Make an effort to talk to this student informally before or after class at least three times per week. If the student finds the experience uncomfortable, change to another student.

Chapter 7

Teaching to Empower Students

Cuando somos realmente honestos con nosotros mismos debemos admitir que nuestras vidas son todo lo que verdaderamente nos pertenecen. Por lo tanto, es como usamos nuestras vidas lo que determina que clase de hombres somos. Es mi creencia mas profunda que solamente con dar nuestra vida encontramos la vida. Estoy convencido de que el acto mas verdadero de valor . . . es el de sacrificarnos por los demas en una lucha por la justicia totalmente no violenta.

When we are really honest with ourselves, we must admit that our lives are all that really belongs to us. So it is how we use our lives that determines what kind of people we are. It is my deepest belief that only by giving our lives do we find life. I am convinced that the truest act of courage . . . is to sacrifice ourselves for others in a totally nonviolent struggle for justice.[1]

—César Chávez (1927–1993)

---

[1]Statement made at the termination of a 25-day fast for nonviolence, 10 March 1968, Delano, California. From Cesar Chavez Foundation (in press). Reprinted by permission.

César Chávez (1927–1993)
Photo: National Archives

Four Approaches to Multicultural Education

At least four major approaches to multicultural education are commonly used in U.S. public schools. Each approach has both strengths and weaknesses. Some efforts concentrate on making the curriculum more inclusive, others on raising academic achievement, and still others on improving intergroup relations. Often the discussion of multicultural education becomes confused by mixing references to the different approaches as if they were aspects of one program. They are not.

In Chapter 2 we described an approach termed "the nature of culture," which incorporates the best of a recent anthropological perspective to overcome the limits of an earlier and very limited educational approach frequently called "teaching the culturally different."

Sleeter and Grant (1999) develop a typology of approaches to multicultural education, as does Gibson (1987). Both of these typologies recognize a human relations approach. Human relations approaches (such as those described in Chapter 6) have been popular among teachers since the 1960s. These approaches include valuable materials and techniques for breaking down habits of thought that lead to prejudice, stereotyping, and discrimination. Human relations and intergroup relations strategies are an important part of a good curriculum, particularly for the primary grades and for students from the macroculture. However, as demonstrated in Chapter 3, the worst damages of racism and sexism are structural or institutional. Human relations strategies of teaching students to eliminate their individual prejudices, though an essential part of an enlightened curriculum, are by themselves inadequate for meeting the crisis of our increasingly divided society.

An approach called "single-group studies" or "ethnic studies/women's studies" has led to major debates in the popular media over appropriate curricula or "canons" of study in the college curriculum. The descriptions in Chapter 3 detailing the diversity of U.S. ethnic and cultural experience are a strong argument for the usefulness of single-group studies. Students need and deserve to know their own histories, and many are empowered by this information. But ethnic studies and women's studies have primarily served only the target groups; they have added new specializations but have not recast the macroculture's basic conceptual framework of history, literature, and the social sciences. The great majority of students in the United States are still learning the macroculture's worldview. The single-group studies approach has challenged, but not revised, the canons of the academic disciplines.

Choosing Democracy argues for multicultural education in a "strong sense," as a process that engages students in building a more democratic society. *Strong-sense multicultural education* is similar to the humanist approach, but it also emphasizes social responsibility. As Sleeter and Grant (1999) point out, strong-sense multicultural education incorporates ideas and strategies from each of the prior traditions and adds the philosophy of *social reconstruction*, the idea that schools should participate in efforts to create a more just and a more democratic society. The reconstructionist position can also be termed *antiracism education*. In the remainder of this chapter, I will argue that a social reconstructionist position on multicultural education offers the best hope for achieving educational equality and cultural democracy.

Unlike other approaches, multicultural education that is social reconstructionist deals directly and forcefully with social and structural inequities in our society including racism, sexism, and class prejudice. It prepares students from oppressed groups to succeed in spite of existing inequalities. This approach argues for a bold commitment to democracy in schooling based on a belief in the learning potential of students from all races and classes, and both genders.

In 1990, the National Governors' Conference (cochaired by then-governor Bill Clinton) made a call for equal access to high-quality education. In 1991, President Bush adopted the goals of the Governors' Conference in the report *America 2000: An Education Strategy.* The authors of these goals claim a consensus. The goals can serve as a starting point for pursuing high-quality, democratic education. The report stated the following:

> American students will leave grades 4, 8, and 12 having demonstrated competency in challenging subject matter including English, mathematics, science, history, and geography; and every school in America will ensure that all students learn to use their minds well, so they may be prepared for responsible citizenship, further learning, and productive employment in our modern economy. (U.S. Department of Education, 1991, p. 3)

These are fine goals, and were adopted as U.S. policy by Congress in 1993 (see Chapter 13). There is little evidence, however, that a significant number of U.S. schools have made progress toward these goals.

Changing—or restructuring— schools in pursuit of these goals requires ending tracking and rigid ability grouping. Students from all cultural groups deserve the opportunity to learn democratic principles and skills. Our commitment to democratic opportunity requires that we reform all schools—particularly those where students are presently failing in substantial numbers. Violence is done to democratic opportunity when students in "honors" classes and magnet schools receive quality instruction utilizing forums, debates, and critical thinking, while low-income, mostly urban kids receive remedial drills and practice sheets. Inadequate school funding, current teacher recruitment practices, and the folk culture of schools encourage teachers to accept the school failure and to select and teach to the "good" students. Strong-sense multicultural education rejects this process and instead chooses to engage all students in critical analysis and the pursuit of excellence.

Goals for Democratic Schools

The Public Education Information Network (1985), a group of educators interested in developing more democratic schools, offers the following description of appropriate goals for schools:

> In briefest terms, the three aspects of a democratic curriculum are as follows:
> - **Critical Literacy:** This goes beyond learning to read and write to include the motivation and capacity to be critical of what one reads, sees, and hears; to probe beyond surface appearances and question the common wisdom.
> - **Knowledge and Understanding of the Diverse Intellectual, Cultural, and Scientific Traditions:** We refer not only to the more familiar academic disciplines and traditions of high culture, but to the histories and cultural perspectives of those people, including women and minorities, traditionally excluded from formal study.
> - **Ability to Use Knowledge and Skills:** to pursue one's own interests; to make informed personal and political decisions; and to work for the welfare of the community. (p. 3)

Working toward these goals will require substantial changes in the folkways and teaching practices of schools. In Chapter 4, I detail how schools contribute to class stratification when working-class students and students of color are often pushed out of school and tracked out of future economic opportunity. Teachers face the choice of continuing the present school system with its 50 percent dropout rate for many urban students of color, or they can choose alternative teaching strategies based on a multicultural social reconstructionist position that empowers students to achieve democratic goals for society.

Critical Theory and Critical Pedagogy

During the 1970s, a new approach to schooling for student empowerment developed in the United States. This alternative intellectual tradition, known as *critical theory*, developed from the ideas and works of Antonio Gramsci, an Italian Marxist intellectual and activist. Critical theory and critical pedagogy in the United States had four major historical contributors: the work and influence of Paulo Freire; the work and influence of scholars who followed the lead of Althusser (Aronowitz & Giroux, 1985); feminist scholars who were searching for alternative understandings of gender relationships; and the political movements of empowerment, from the

Mississippi Freedom Schools to current struggles to rebuild the schools for democratic citizenship.

Critical Theory

Educators, using critical theory, assume that men, women and children have a moral imperative toward developing humanness and freedom. This assumption differs from the "scientific" positivist or empiricist scholarly tradition, where researchers assume the need for neutrality and objectivity of investigation (see Chapter 6). Critical theorists further assume that the current problems of any society are subject to investigation and change. They assume that individuals and groups can and should work together to build a more democratic education system and a more democratic society.

Educational writers urging the use of critical theory in the United States include Paulo Freire, Henry Giroux, Peter McLaren, Lois Weis, Alma Flor Ada, Jim Cummins, Kathleen Weiler, and Stanley Aronowitz.[2]

The following concepts are central to critical theory, and are useful in trying to comprehend and analyze your own teaching experience:

Consciousness. Awareness of yourself and your environment. Consciousness includes self-awareness. Multicultural consciousness refers to a recognition of the ethnic, racial, and social divisions in our society.

Culture. The collective knowledge of a group of people (described extensively in Chapter 2). Please note that European American critical theorists have tended to rely on European authors for descriptions of culture, authors who tend to emphasize class differences and to pay less attention to differences among cultures and ethnic groups.

Domination. The act of controlling a group of people.

Empowerment. Educational processes that lead to political courage and political efficacy. Empowerment strategies teach students to analyze and to act on their analyses. Empowerment strategies also help students gain social, political, and economic power, including the power to make their own decisions.

Ethics. Normative preferences and decisions based on values rather than exclusively on objective research.

Hegemony. The overwhelming domination of ideologies or economic systems by a single group or source of power. Often ideological hegemony leaves learners unaware of alternative viewpoints. For example, most schools and teachers have an unexamined commitment to competitive grading.

---

[2]See in particular Aronowitz and Giroux (1985), Freire (1997), Freire and Macedo (1987), Giroux (1988), McLaren (1989), and Weiler (1988).

Hidden curriculum. The variety of values and ideas taught informally in schools. These attitudes and assumptions permeate school but rarely reveal themselves in lesson plans or tests. For example, U.S. schools commonly teach individualism, competitiveness, and a European American perspective on our nation's history.

Ideological domination. Controlling the ideas presented to students by, for example, selecting the content of textbooks.

Ideologies. A series of interrelated ideas, such as racism or cultural pluralism. A dominant ideology is often taught in schools as if it were the only truth. For example, we are taught that the United States has a democratic government. Our system is then presented as the definition of democracy: two competing parties, regular elections, a free press, and limited government intervention in the economy. There are other models of democracy, but our particular system is taught as an ideology. In similar fashion, we are taught an ideology that our schools are politically neutral, even though they are clearly committed to the maintenance of the present power system.

Social class. A group identified by its economic position in the society, that is, working class, poor, wealthy owners of production. There are several contending descriptions of classes in the United States (see Chapter 4).

Social construction of knowledge. The observation that most knowledge is created by persons. What we regard as knowledge has a purpose. The concept of the social construction of knowledge treats knowledge as purposeful and as serving particular interests rather than as neutral and merely discovered. For example, IQ tests were generated for a particular purpose, to predict school success. They do not define intelligence; rather, they measure a specific kind of mental aptitude in relation to a specific purpose. As an alternative, Gardner (1983) proposes that the concept of multiple intelligences provides a different, more useful description of thinking processes.

Critical Pedagogy

At the turn of the last century, John Dewey (1859–1952) argued that critical analysis and learning by doing were essential for the preparation of citizens in a democracy (Dewey, 1916/1966). Influenced by the massive European immigration from 1900 to1920, Dewey was not an advocate of multicultural education as we presently know it. Like Jefferson before him, Dewey favored having schools lead the nation in developing a new, idealized, democratic American. Today, in a parallel period of massive immigration, Dewey's works provide a partial foundation for the ideological position that schools can serve in the cause of social reconstruction.

In the 1970s, the Brazilian educator Paulo Freire contributed to a rebirth and extension of Dewey's ideas in the field of advancing a pluralistic democracy. Freire's work revolves around a socially responsible humanism. Like Dewey, he believed that education has a central role in building a democratic society. But Freire's writings offered a new and fresh view of education's role in liberating the oppressed, which he saw as essential to the process of building a democratic, participatory community.

Freire first gained attention for the methodology he and his colleagues developed to teach literacy to the impoverished people of the Recife area of northeast Brazil. His first major book, *A Pedagogy of the Oppressed* (1972), described a revolutionary educational and social change process for the poor in Latin America. Freire believed that educational workers could help empower students by engaging in dialogue with them rather than falling into traditional teacher–student roles. The Brazilian government's official response to his work was to arrest him in 1964. After his imprisonment and eventual deportation, he worked for the World Council of Churches in Geneva. *Pedagogy of the Oppressed* was soon being read and discussed throughout Latin America and among small circles of intellectuals in the United States and Europe (Freire, n.d., 1985; McFadden, 1975). In it Freire describes the oppressive and colonizing functions served by traditional teacher-dominated education. Freire's ideas have important ramifications for understanding the education of oppressed cultural and class groups in U.S. schools.

Prior to Freire's work, most published educational research and university work in social science education in the United States had suggested only technical improvements to the existing school curriculum. The "scientific study" of schools, common in the 1970s and 1980s, used positivist, reductionist research methods (see Chapter 6). This research generally strengthened the school's role in the domination of oppressed communities. Freire's writings suggested new analytical concepts to describe the experiences of students. His work offered new hope and insight for teachers working with alienated and oppressed students in our own society. Teachers and activists searched his works and found alternative strategies for work with immigrant and working-class students. Freire's work proposed solutions to the structural failure of poor children in U.S. schools, while the narrow research paradigms of positivism avoided the critical questions of race and class.

Freire openly acknowledged that his views included a political pedagogy. He revealed the political and class dimensions underlying any educational system. Education and schools could reinforce the domination of the existing structure or they could introduce persons to citizenship and freedom. Education could help young people to lead free and self-empowering lives. Following Freire's lead, educational teams in Brazil, Chile, Venezuela, and Nicaragua taught the poor to read by helping community members analyze their life situations. Poor peasants engaged in community organizing to effect social change. Freire used the term *praxis* to describe the process of critical analysis leading to action. The experience of praxis empowers people to participate in democratic struggles. Strong-sense multicultural education applies the principles of cultural action and praxis to U.S. public schools, particularly schools serving students of oppressed classes and cultures.

Conservative scholars accuse advocates of multicultural education of politicizing the curriculum. This charge has intimidated some multicultural education advocates and placed them on the defensive. Yet clearly the writings of John Dewey were profoundly political. Critics attack the political dimension of both Freire's work and multicultural educational theory while refusing to acknowledge that Dewey's major works provide the intellectual foundations of social reconstruction. Dewey argued that the schools should promote immigrant assimilation and build a democratic society. These are political goals. Freire's work, like Dewey's, recognizes the essentially political nature of education.

Both the present Eurocentric curriculum and its multicultural alternatives are highly political. Realistically, a teacher's choice is not between being political or neutral. Claiming political neutrality for schools actually supports the continuation of the current tracked, starkly unequal system—a profoundly political position.

The teaching strategies and attitudes described by Freire and adapted for multicultural education in the United States begin by respecting the prior cultural knowledge that all students bring to the classroom. Freire, like Dewey, argued for rooting the educational experience in students' real experiences. Freire believed that speech, language, and literacy can be understood only in a social context and that students learn language and literacy best in the context of their social experience. He worked with a number of adult literacy campaigns that have applied this principle and that have had enormous impact in societies seeking transition to democracy. Cultural action in literacy contributed to social change in Brazil, Chile, Guinea-Bissau, and Nicaragua (Freire, 1997). In his writings, Freire also applauded successful efforts in the United States—notably the Foxfire project and Highlander Folk School in Tennessee.

Culturally Relevant Pedagogy

Freire's work occurred at the same time as the field of ethnography developed within anthropology. Both movements were influenced by research efforts in Latin America. Ethnography revises one aspect of positivist scientific methods: Instead of breaking a research problem into parts and subcategories, ethnography stresses observing the community, classroom, or school as a complex whole; describing an event in context; and seeking to understand the culture of the participants or a classroom (Trueba, 1989). Both ethnographic research and Freire's work in Latin America considered culture as a field of struggle, not as a fixed or static object. In this view, developing an understanding of their culture helps students to respect themselves, to learn from the past, and to participate in the active creation of a democratic future. The literacy programs designed by Freire and his colleagues used an ethnographic perspective to assist peasants in learning about their culture as a means of empowering them (Freire & Macedo, 1987). In a similar manner, students and teachers from oppressed communities of color in the United States need to recover and recognize their own cultures.

Outstanding work has been done in the United States using ethnographic perspectives. King (1995) has developed an extensive and powerful argument that African

American studies offers new insights into how to overcome the current crisis in education for African American students. Dr. King served on the California Department of Education committee that drafted the *History–Social Science Framework for California Public Schools* (see Chapter 12) and argues that deep biases control the way textbook publishers select what knowledge is important to teach to students.

She proposes that African American cultural knowledge will assist teachers to redesign educational processes for success. Referring back to Carter B. Woodson's important 1933 essay, King argues that African American young people are miseducated as a result of the current social construction of knowledge and the curriculum: "As Black students move through the educational system, they face 'the school's undermining doubt about their ability.' Their dignity and positive group identity may be further undermined by hegemonic school knowledge and curricula that traumatize and humiliate many Black students" (King, 1995, p. 283).

King focused on intellectual traditions in the African American community. Ladson-Billings (1994a) performed case studies to describe a culturally relevant pedagogy for teachers working with African American students. Based on her studies, she argues that effective teachers for African American students

- Have high self-esteem and high regard for others
- "see themselves as a part of the local community and see their work as contributing, or giving back to the community" (p. 38)
- "believe that all students can succeed, and organize their lessons based upon this belief" (p. 44)
- "help students to make connections between their own community and national and global identities" (p. 49)
- See their work as "digging knowledge out of the students" (p. 52) rather than imposing new knowledge on them
- See their goals as creating a "community of learners" (p. 69) and building positive relationships with students, their families, and their communities

Ladson-Billings (1994a) tells the tales of eight effective teachers, five African Americans and three European Americans, who have established successful close working relationships with their students and the students' families. Her case studies approach provides new teachers with many diverse insights into how high-quality teaching relationships are established.

Eugene Garcia, formerly director of the Office of Bilingual Education for the U.S. Department of Education, and currently dean of education at the University of California at Berkeley, reviewed extensive literature to summarize a list of characteristics of effective teachers working with Mexican-American students. His review of literature found that effective teachers shared many characteristics, including the following (E. Garcia, 1995):

- Perceived themselves as effective teachers
- Were autonomous decision makers about instructional activities

- Used a communications-based approach to language
- Usually favored thematic curricula and cooperative groupwork
- Had a strong commitment to home–school relationships
- Held high academic expectations for themselves and for their students
- Served as advocates for their students
- "Adopted" their students and were in close, often familylike, relationships with their students' families

Empowerment as a Goal

Once students recognize their own cultural context, they can learn to think critically about it and make meaningful decisions about their life opportunities. Critical pedagogy, or problem-posing education, seeks to help students understand the world they live in and to critically analyze their real-life situations. Critical analysis, practical skills, and self-confidence lead to empowerment. Participation in community development helps students develop the political courage to work toward the resolution of their real problems. Community action teams working with preliterate peasants in Latin America helped them to learn to read and perhaps to create a labor union or farmer cooperative. For students from oppressed or marginalized groups in the United States, the goals might be gaining admission to college, receiving a good-quality high school preparation for work, or counteracting crime in their communities.

The strong democratic reconstructionist form of multicultural education has adopted the goal of empowerment as central to educational reform. By urging that schools help students build a more democratic society, multicultural education moves away from positivism's stress on being an objective observer of events. Educational projects designed for empowerment help students to take a stand. They provide opportunities for students to intervene in their own families and communities; to analyze situations, decide, act, and then to analyze their actions anew. Empowerment is taught to overcome disempowerment.

The multicultural education movement, incorporating Freire's insights with those of ethnography, argues that because culture is constantly changing, and because cultures adapt through education, then community development is always available as an alternative to oppression. Analysis (praxis), social participation, and student action teach skills, confidence, and political courage for community development.

How the Present Curriculum Fails Students

The present curriculum is often divorced from students' actual experience. Lessons in the social studies should provide a natural starting place for students to engage in multicultural education. However, since the 1970s, the pressure to raise scores on standardized tests, particularly in math and reading, has intensified. As a result, social studies in the primary grades have been practically eliminated. Additional reading, language, and math time have been given priority.

In the elementary grades, schools too often rely on haphazard and fragmentary approaches to supplement the textbooks. These intermittent units that touch on cultural holidays, heroes, "foods of other lands," and similar activities may be fun, but they hardly amount to multicultural education. Instead of providing an intellectually defensible view of a multicultural society, many middle and secondary schools are even further distanced from students' reality. They generally follow the canons of establishment history and culture imposed by universities and textbook publishers and often avoid a rigorous analysis of race, culture, class, and gender even though many students' daily lives are immersed in these conflict areas.

Teacher preparation programs and the present public school curriculum generally reflect and promote the majority culture's view of reality, reproducing ideological domination. Students need empowerment strategies to counteract the pervasive influence of disempowerment. These strategies should include goal clarification and establishing clear measures of progress. For example, immigrant students want to acquire fluent English, but many give up and accept low levels of language learning. Their failure is not from a lack of goals, nor of practice. Failure develops from school experiences that do not provide frequent confirmation of measurable progress toward language mastery. Language acquisition programs fail when they approach lessons as if language were only a skill. Attitudes toward language, toward culture, and toward self all influence language acquisition (Freire & Macedo, 1987). Positive experiences with language use and reflective thinking about cultural conflict and assimilation encourage students to stay in school and continue toward graduation.

The conservative school reform movement of the 1980s successfully convinced social studies textbook buyers and publishers to focus on history and geography—avoiding the more open-ended social sciences of economics and sociology as well as social and controversial issues. In the upper grades, middle schools, and secondary schools, inadequate and unrealistic texts predominate. Instead of engaging students' interests, most history texts offer a sterile, inaccurate, and incomplete view of our society in boring prose. Teachers resort to grades, tests, and worksheets to motivate students to pay attention. Some teachers have become wardens, forcing rote memorization on reluctant students, adding to the students' growing impression that school, particularly history, is irrelevant to life. Empowerment strategies reverse this debasement of history and reintroduce the social studies (Campbell, 1987; Task Force on Minorities, 1989).

Our society cannot afford further deterioration in the preparation of its youth. When we fail to teach children from diverse cultures about their own heritage, we reap a harvest of low self-esteem, greater alienation from school, and higher dropout rates. We must offer students the opportunity to learn the beauty and refinement of their own cultural heritage.

In addition, the multicultural curriculum must include academic skill development. To succeed in school or to get a better job, students need to improve their reading and writing skills. It is better for students to develop reading and math skills in fourth or even eighth grade rather than to struggle with remedial classes in high school or college. Practice in reading and writing helps students to experience more school success and to develop a positive attitude toward school. Lesson plans and curricula should include developing improved study skills as attainable, measurable goals appropriate to young people and directly related to economic success and opportunity.

Despite the need for continued improvements in the areas just discussed, our society has changed. There is more equality in 2000 than there was in 1950. Economic opportunities for the well-educated African American, Latino, Native American, or Asian have appreciably improved. The success of individuals from each of these communities reveals that instruction that starts with the students' home and community experiences provides the basis for strategies to convert frustration into determination, and prior defeat in school into hope.

Selecting Themes

New teachers often do not know where to begin to find themes rooted in students' own experiences. A theme can be a topic or subject that recurs frequently in the life of a child. The process of studying themes from their own reality validates students' cultures and helps them to recognize the importance of school.

To help students understand that school and lessons are valuable, school lessons should help to explain real life. Teachers err when they assume that the relevance of their lessons is obvious. On the contrary, teachers should explain and re-explain the relevance of lessons both to students' lives and to prior lessons.

Selecting Themes for Kindergarten Through Grade 3

Many good teachers begin the process of discovering their students' interests by observing and listening. What do they do? What do they talk about? You can also ask parents what the most important things are for their children. In particular, you should ask the parents of a child that is mildly off-task or disruptive to share some of the activities and interests the child responds to at home.

If you provide children with a free choice of books, those they choose will suggest themes. Popular magazines written for their level, such as *My Weekly Reader, Highlights for Children,* and *National Geographic World,* also cover themes of importance to children. You will find it useful to read the special teacher's editions of these magazines.

Providing students with time to draw and fantasize also reveals themes of interest to them. During sharing time, they can explain their drawings to others, revealing even more themes. An excellent series of books has been written and cooperatively published by parents and children in the Literatura Infantil program near Watsonville, California. The books and lesson plans are now available for $8.95 commercially from

Children's Book Press
5925 Doyle Street, Suite U
Emeryville, CA 94608
415-655-3395

New teachers often get ideas for themes by watching *Sesame Street, Square One,* and other children's television shows to observe what interests children. These programs are excellent, and can greatly enhance learning when integrated with regular lessons. Computers, hypermedia, and instructional television can also provide you with important time to work with one or two children while other students interact in more self-directed learning.

Student teachers should begin to collect supplementary materials, bulletin board ideas, charts, and other supplies during their practice teaching.

Selecting Themes for Intermediate Grades 4 Through 6

At this level, you can start with inventories of student interests. One example, created by Sidney Simon and his colleagues (Simon, Howe, & Kirschenbaum, 1972), is the values clarification exercise shown in Figure 7.1.

In the original exercise, the list was kept private. The teacher then guided students through the process of values analysis, calculating factors of risk, cost, and parental influence for each item on their lists (Simon et al., 1972). Changing the exercise and collecting the lists provide you with an excellent source of themes in students' lives.

A similar exercise has students list their favorite TV shows. You or the students compile the lists, which you then analyze. Analysis of television viewing can provide important curriculum themes.

Free-choice literature selections often reveal what children are interested in. Many teachers assign students to interview community leaders and then write up the results as group exercises. New themes often emerge from this writing. While student groups work on the interviews, you can circulate around the room and listen to their conversations for additional themes.

You also may discover student themes by attending student events, talking to experienced teachers, and reading teaching periodicals such as *Teaching Tolerance* and *Rethinking Schools.* You can also provide students with imaginary moral dilemmas or other incomplete conflict situations and assign students to describe the most effective responses. Their descriptions will reveal new themes for the day.

These efforts do not abandon the curriculum in search of student interest. Instead, you are searching for themes in students' lives that make the curriculum valuable, useful, and motivational.

Lessons should have a context and a sequence. Because students benefit from knowing what teachers are going to teach next and why, explain your organization of the lessons. Writing the day's agenda on the chalkboard is one way to inform students about what you will cover so they can see the progress they are making.

Figure 7.1 Values Clarification Exercise

The students prepare a paper by listing the numbers 1 through 20 down one side. The exercise calls for students to make a rapid list of their favorite activities. The teacher explains in advance that she will collect the paper. Students should not write intimate items on this paper. Names are not needed on the paper.

When the teacher gives the signal, the students make a rapid list of the items they would most like to do. The items are not listed in any priority.

Example:

Things I Would Most Like To Do

1.
2.
3.
4.
5.
6.
7.
8.
9.
10.
11.
12.
13.
14.
15.
16.
17.
18.
19.
20.

Note. Adapted from *Values Clarification* (p. 30), by S. B. Simon, L. W. Howe, and H. Kirschenbaum, 1972, New York: Hart.

Selecting Themes for Grades 8 through 12

The examples of student inventories, literature, and values clarification lessons described for grades 4 through 6 also apply to grades 8 through 12. However, for these grades, teenage students will also need validation of their own experiences and cultures. Because adolescents often feel as if they are under attack, they may benefit from talking about their frustrations, conflicts, and anxieties. Teachers should listen to the problems of adolescents in a rapidly changing and often dangerous society. Students' own problems constitute important themes for study.

Your choices of what to teach in social studies and in literature can contribute to empowering students. Race, ethnic, class, and gender relations should be studied. Your students live in a world of intersecting demands. Studying multiple perspectives on these demands assists students to make deliberate and wise choices. Students will not necessarily make positive choices by themselves. They have to be taught. That is why we require schooling.

You may select your content from the textbook, or from a district curriculum guide. You may also choose to take the time and effort to teach units in social studies on the cultures represented by students in your school, the cultural conflicts common in your school, and the personal development skills your students will need in an increasingly divisive society. These themes should not be left to informal learning while classroom instruction focuses on the Roman Empire. Like gang behavior and drugs, it is best to bring these topics into the open, to study and discuss them.

Open discussion of race, gender, and class conflicts may reduce the physical conflict in your school, but may increase the level of disagreement in your classroom. Some teachers are uncomfortable even discussing these topics with students. Your own self-confidence and recognition of your role as a cultural mediator permit you to openly discuss volatile issues. Discussions of these topics, and closely related issues such as affirmative action and bilingual education, is too-often avoided.

As with grades 4 to 6, you may have students list their favorite TV shows and movies. View as many as you can, looking for themes to connect to classroom lessons. Writing the lyrics of a popular song on the chalkboard can stimulate a dynamic discussion. You might pose such questions as, What is the message? Do you agree with the message? Do your friends agree? To extend the discussion to a homework assignment, you might ask students to explore in an essay one or two of the issues revealed in the lyrics. Additional topics that encourage valuable discussion include, What struggles do you have with your parents? Are you prepared for sex? Do you need more information? Where can you get information about drugs?

Analyzing advertising aimed at young people reveals additional themes. For instance, many clothing advertisements encourage teenagers to believe that a certain look will win them access to a desired social group. Some advertisements for clothing encourage conformity, some aggressive sexuality, while others encourage eccentricity. These themes are ever-present in students' lives. Initially, students may deny advertising's effectiveness, but more thoughtful examination usually reveals its function in defining "the good life."

Teenagers particularly respond to stereotypes about teenagers. Often the stereotypes are revealed in name calling and group forming. Gangs for the poor and exploited, and cliques and fraternities for the middle class, are expressions of young people's need to belong to a group. Social studies classes should study the roles and functions of gangs and cliques.

State education departments and local school districts provide teachers with curriculum guides and even textbooks. These materials reflect adult decisions about what a student should know. These decisions are often valid, but adolescents must be convinced of the value. We can no longer assume that teenagers accept and participate in the values expressed in the curriculum and the school. One of the roles of school is to introduce students to the real world—the world beyond adolescent movies, music, and fantasy.

Students become bored when learning makes no apparent difference in their lives. Schools need to encourage young people to study, to prepare for adult life, and to talk about what matters to them. The skills of articulate communication are important for professional careers, but the present school system often fails to teach these skills to low-income students, tracking them instead into nonprofessional employment. These skills can be learned. Many migrant farmworkers have learned English to fight their bosses, and African American students learned the discipline of nonviolence to overthrow "Jim Crow" laws in the South. People in these cases learned quickly and effectively because they had concrete reasons for developing new skills and acquiring new knowledge. Developing a willingness to analyze problems, formulate plans, and then to act on the plans prepares young people for self-governance.

Reality—Its Place in the Classroom

In spite of the national ideal of promoting pluralism, racism and discrimination remain realities of our society. While human relations approaches may be sufficient for kindergarten through grade 3 and for European American students, students of color need more powerful strategies to prepare them to overcome the institutionalized inequality in our schools and our society. An inaccurate, utopian view of our society and our government invalidates students' own life experiences as sources of knowledge. An empowerment curriculum should offer the opportunity for students to study racism and pluralism and encourage them to search for new democratic alternatives.

The violence of racism, sexism, and class oppression provide important subjects for study and analysis. By studying oppression in historical settings and analyzing its constituent parts, students develop a perspective that stops placing the blame on the victim. In empowerment classes, this sort of critical analysis leads to planning for social change. By middle school (grades 6 through 8) students should be encouraged to consider empowerment strategies, including seeking individual advancement through education and collective advancement through political struggle.

Current opportunities for schooling are unequal, but educational opportunities are more equal than are economic or housing opportunities. From at least 1900 until

1970, schooling was considered a preparation for life and an opportunity to earn a better standard of living. Advocacy groups fought long and hard for educational opportunity culminating in *Brown v. Board of Education* (1954), *Lau v. Nichols* (1971), and the Civil Rights Movement of the 1950s and 1960s. An empowerment curriculum seeks to bring the results and the orientation of these struggles for equality into the classroom. Present school tracking by "ability groups" promotes the ideology of meritocracy and strengthens discrimination (Oakes, 1985). Students in the upper college-bound tracks have an inherent advantage. Low-income students in the middle and lower tracks need to understand the school system they are subject to and become more mature and more goal oriented in order to gain equal educational opportunity. The study of racism, sexism, and class oppression in schools helps students comprehend this unequal system and to make personal decisions to take advantage of their school experience to prepare for the future.

Television and the youth culture present a competing, less mature, more immediate, self-indulgent life philosophy. The abundance of wealth in our society bestows on middle-class students the luxury of extended adolescence. They can get serious about growing up later in college or after college. But working-class students may sacrifice their future educational opportunities when they substitute the value of the commercial youth culture for hard work in school. These young people especially need adults to present a commonsense, real-world perspective on opportunity.

Social Participation in Schools

Anthropologists refer to two aspects of school curriculum—the formal and the informal. The *formal curriculum* consists of the goals, course outlines, strategies, and materials used to teach and evaluate lessons and skills. The *informal curriculum* includes the messages conveyed by a combination of rules, regulations, procedures, and practices, including the attitudes of teachers, staff, and administrators. The formal and the informal curricula sometimes conflict. The formal curriculum may encourage students to take a position and to defend that position with argument, but students are seldom coached and supported for taking action on controversial issues in schools such as tracking, alienation, and violence.

Schools have long recognized the value of participation in student councils and student governments, but these structures typically serve a small, select few. It is not an accident that middle-class schools have numerous opportunities for participation while inner-city schools tend to emphasize administrative control of the student population. Such differences betray attitudes that are potentially harmful to many students: A small portion of the middle class is taught to lead while the poor are contained and controlled. The informal curriculum of many schools serving working-class students discourages these students from getting involved in self-governance. The cultural democratic alternative argues that because all students need preparation for democracy, all students should be engaged in decision making.

Humans learn best by doing. Yet schools often seek to teach citizenship to students from dominated cultural groups through passive methods such as readings, discussions, films, and worksheets. To prepare students to participate in our democracy, we must make room in the curriculum for more active strategies that teach democratic participation. Active strategies expose students to meaningful social and political choices and give them opportunities to act as responsible citizens. For example, in 1996 and in 1998 California students participated in election campaigns in support of affirmative action and in defense of bilingual education. We know how to reach the "good" students who are already committed to schooling. We need new strategies to reach the isolated, alienated students who are potential dropouts. These reluctant and passive students are in greater need of participatory strategies than are the academically successful.

Schools encourage democratic behavior when students engage in substantial decision making. Some teachers achieve this by having students participate in management decisions and discipline systems in classroom meetings. Many elementary, middle, and secondary schools have engaged student teams in conflict resolution and violence reduction strategies. This strategy of teaching democratic behavior, attitudes, and analysis through encouraging students to participate in social controversy and social movements is called *social participation*. Introducing social participation into the curriculum in the upper grades produces a positive, prodemocratic effect on both formal and informal curricula (Beane, 1990).[3]

Teachers promote social participation by encouraging projects at a level of safety and controversy appropriate to each school community. Social participation projects offer excellent ways to complete thematic units that integrate two or more subjects. For example, fourth-grade students might design a campaign to rid the school of litter. Sixth-grade and older students can participate in conflict resolution training to reduce violence on the school grounds. Tenth-grade students might want to lobby for auto insurance reform or school financing of intramural athletics. Urban students can work to make their school grounds or neighborhood a drug- and violence-free zone. Students learn academic skills and increase their sense of efficacy and self-worth when they study issues, make decisions, and then take action that helps to eliminate problems they have identified. You will find excellent ideas for student-centered educational projects in Hoose (1993).

Through skillful training in decision-making and problem-solving processes, students can learn to accurately predict the possibility of achieving specific changes. Teachers guide students in conducting research on topics and appropriately selecting targets for their efforts. Later, students analyze their results to measure the accuracy of their predictions and the effectiveness of their chosen strategies.

Multicultural curriculum reform often includes civic and community participation projects. Students develop social and work skills along with prodemocratic values

---

[3]Unfortunately, most of the research on effectiveness of these strategies is limited to its effect on students from the European American culture. See Leming (1985).

through active, guided participation with community service agencies. By working with a range of groups, such as antipoverty agencies, political parties, and labor organizations, 11th- and 12th-grade students can gain a realistic and diverse view of their community and of the political process. Social participation develops both the skills and the sense of political courage needed to overcome the present alienation between many students of color and the schools (Banks, 1997; Quality Education for Minorities Project, 1990).

Too many working-class students have been trained for defeat. Sitting in classes completing endless worksheets confirms their cynical belief that schooling and education make little real difference in life. On the other hand, social participation empowers students and provides a means to break out of these defeatist patterns. Work in community agencies gives students a realistic view of the processes of change. Adult community activists serve as mentors to students and encourage them to complete their education. Students begin their transition to the world of work and return to school more mature and focused on improving their own education.

Interaction with life, work, racism, and poverty will convince many students of the value of education. Students gain a sense of social responsibility when they participate in projects that actually contribute to the health of their own communities. It is important to select social participation activities that provide both safety and success. Some schools have fifth-grade students become "buddies" who are responsible for helping first-graders adjust to school. In other schools, 10th-grade students staff tutoring centers to help seventh- and eighth-grade students complete their homework. Students, the school, and the community gain by these efforts. Students learn to work to achieve goals. Social participation teaches that we can accept responsibility and control our own lives, an important step toward believing in the value of education.

In earlier decades, some of the finest traditions of the social studies were built on a conception of curriculum that stressed social participation. Dewey (1916/1966) stressed the need to create a new society by democratic participation in the construction of such a society. Aronstein and Olsen (1974) describe how to get students involved in productive community service projects as integral parts of their classroom experiences. Shaver and others (Shaver, 1977) advocate further development of the ideas of participation.

The ideological assault on schools, curricula, and school boards carried out by socially and politically conservative forces from the 1970s to the present, however, has eliminated or neutralized social participation efforts in many communities. Conservative forces favor the presentation of an "approved" curriculum, often sterile and irrelevant academic lessons that continue the current ideological hegemony. These lessons teach many students apathy and alienation from school and from society. Conservatives blame the home and the neighborhood for school failure, ignoring the irrelevance of much of the curriculum. Conservatives often consider social and political participation strategies in multicultural education as radical attempts to "politicize" the schools (Campbell, 1980; Ravitch, 1990).

Over 50 percent of the adults in our nation do not vote in general elections. Even fewer vote in local and school board elections. Nonvoters tend to be poor and are frequently African American, Latino, and Asian (Figure 7.2). By not voting, they participate in their own disenfranchisement. In turn, schools, roads, and social services in their communities are the most neglected, resulting in steadily fewer resources for their children.

Social reconstructionism, or antiracism education, like other educational philosophies, is political. Multicultural education that is social reconstructionist uses participation as a strategy to develop a critical consciousness about the roles of race, class, and gender in structuring our society and controlling our schools. Students from working-class communities engage in advancing democracy and advancing their own education. Future citizens from *all* cultures and classes deserve to learn the skills and acquire the political courage needed to make government work for their interests.

Empowerment Strategies

Empowering students is central to the social reconstructionist philosophy of developing a multicultural curriculum. Many schools empower middle-class students. And even though problems of drugs, suicide, and violence clearly indicate that not all middle-class students are empowered in school, most are taught the skills, attitudes, and behavior patterns needed to succeed in our society.

Schools presently empower students from dominant classes and disempower working-class students and selected cultural and gender groups. As Trueba (Trueba, Rodriguez, Zou, & Cintrón, 1993) explains, empowerment contests with disempowerment. Schools systematically disempower cultural minority groups by silencing students, by denying the validity of their culture, or rendering their culture and language useless in school.

Trueba describes the process as follows:

In this context of cultural contacts between mainstream persons and those from different linguistic and cultural backgrounds (such as between teachers and students), the least

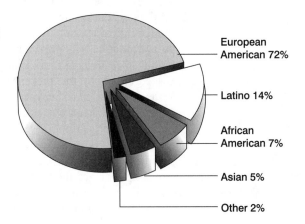

Figure 7.2   Voter Participation and Ethnicity in California, 1998

Note. From *Los Angeles Times* poll, 1998.

European American 72%

Latino 14%

African American 7%

Asian 5%

Other 2%

conflictive position is taken by those persons who adopt multicultural responses. Yet, cultural therapy, as a means to compare and contrast cultural values and understandings, can enhance communication and resolve conflicts arising from misunderstandings in inter-ethnic and intercultural exchanges. There are at least two main ways in which cultural therapy can help. First, it can help develop a strong personal identity based on a better known and better understood cultural background. Second, cultural therapy can also increase the ability to identify areas of value conflict, differences in interpretations of messages and expectations, range of acceptable etiquette, preferential protocol, and other expected behavioral responses.

A strong personal cultural or ethnic identity is providing the individual with legitimacy and recognition for his or her enduring self. The psychological justification for retaining a personal framework for self-understanding and for self-acceptance, the setting to which we feel attached as children—the quintessence of what we are in our own eyes, our enduring self—remains justified and unchanged regardless of other adjustments. This is the basis for deeper emotional peace and stability. In contrast, being forced to abandon this inner frame of enduring self, especially when the home language is lost, isolates a child from the world of his dreams, the world of his affection. How can a child deal with two different worlds and transfer information from one to the other, if the bridge between the two worlds (the language) is broken? How can a child retain a measure of psychological integrity if he is not allowed to reconcile conflicting values from home and school? How can a child enrich his home learning environment if going home is seen as degrading? How can a child seek emotional and cognitive support from parents who are seen as unworthy and despicable? Sooner or later, a child will comprehend that the rejection of one's own language and culture is ultimately the rejection of one's own self. (pp. 147–149)

The Congressional Black Caucus (1991) describes the crisis for students of color as follows:

We must recognize that our nation will be ill prepared to enter the 21st century if our children cannot read, write, and calculate mathematics, much less understand the high-tech world they are about to inherit. We must recognize that a nation that condemns its children to hopelessness, and the lure of drug abuse, is a nation that cannot begin to hope to remain economically competitive or morally strong. (p. 3)

For our democracy to survive and prosper, schools serving students of color need a fundamental shift in emphasis. Democratic teachers will design teaching strategies to empower all students. Schools should teach all students to read and provide them with the skills needed for employment, as well as to gain access to both higher education and the knowledge industries of the future. Students from all social classes and ethnic groups deserve to learn the skills of analysis and organization, as well as to develop the self-confidence needed to engage in struggles for political equality (Freire & Macedo, 1987; Hechinger, 1992; Washington, 1986; W. J. Wilson, 1996).

Students from minority cultures and linguistic groups who have been excluded from democratic participation particularly deserve education designed for empowerment (Cummins, 1986). We can summarize the main strategies for empowerment as follows:

1. Study the nature of culture.
2. Study the nature of cultural conflicts and value conflicts.

3. Study the powerful analytic concepts that reveal students' real culture and current status (see Chapter 2).

4. Use students' home, school, and community experiences as source material for curricula and as a basis for analysis.

5. Compare racism and pluralism as options for the individual and the society.

6. Plan lessons to use success as a strategy. All students deserve the opportunity to succeed.

7. Teach critical thinking (reflective thinking) (see Chapter 9).

8. Use problem-posing education (see Chapter 9).

9. Critically examine students' own social realities and help them plan for change.

10. Develop critical literacy.

11. Use coaching (see following section).

12. Use cooperative learning strategies (see Chapter 10).

13. Respect children's home languages (see Chapter 11).

14. Encourage social participation and praxis as part of the curriculum.

Subsequent chapters in this book provide you with practical advice for these empowerment strategies.

The Teacher as Coach

We need not restrict our view of teaching and learning to large-group instruction. Often educational encounters that empower occur between a teacher and one or two students. A teacher question, a comment, or a few words of encouragement sometimes help students to continue their struggle for an education.

Students who experience regular success in school receive affirmation and support from their daily school experiences. Unfortunately, many students simply pass through school. They seldom reflect on their experiences or consider taking charge of their educational and economic future.

When a teacher coaches a student, a simple comment or a student conference can lead the student to reconsider his skills or behavior and lead to plans for improvement. Good teachers use coaching to conduct conferences on motivation and skill development. A pedagogy for empowerment should make coaching a deliberate, planned series of experiences for all students.

Coaching is begun by teachers analyzing the performance of their students. Students who are performing well should be encouraged to continue. Students who are performing poorly might consider changing their study strategies. Students who are in the middle seldom get noticed. A carefully thought-out strategy of coaching will encourage the success of *all* students (Figure 7.3).

Figure 7.3   A Coaching Process for Teachers

---

1. Identify the issue or individual of concern.

2. Set time aside for coaching. Meet with the student individually.

3. Establish clear goals for the coaching. Your role as coach is to assist the student to achieve the student's goal. Coaching is inappropriate for punishment (see Chapter 8).

4. Cooperatively analyze specific steps that student can take to achieve her goal.

5. Break the task down into manageable steps.

6. Support and encourage the student in taking each step.

7. Meet regularly. Encourage continued effort.

8. Establish a means or criteria for evaluation.

9. Check back with the student on progress.

Set a goal of getting to know one student per week by talking with the student and listening to the student's perception of reality. A suggestion, a prompt, a little praise can encourage students to consider themselves important and to make changes in their study habits. Teachers make time for coaching by planning lessons that provide the opportunities for one-on-one interaction (see Chapter 10).

Working in Teams

Students and adults in many communities are divided and isolated. They quarrel with each other and are frequently alienated from government and society. But when residents of low-income communities work together on projects ranging from crime control to school improvement, both communities and their members gain power.

Structure activities in group work, decision making, consensus seeking, and group evaluation that can prepare students for community leadership development. Some social action projects should require students to work together in teams. Working in groups helps students learn interpersonal skills and increases their chances of experiencing success. Working in groups helps students learn to practice behavior that supports the values of cooperation, noncompetitiveness, sharing of resources, and peer respect.

Cohen (1986) argues that there is an urgent need to structure groups purposefully so that cooperation and caring emerge, because American youngsters are so heavily influenced by forces leading to individualism and competitiveness. Students, particularly in the middle school years (grades 6–8), want to belong to groups to overcome the alienation and fear of rejection common in their lives. Schools that build on group values make important and vital connections with students' concerns. A curriculum of social participation and empowerment can support group values while redirecting students away from gang fights and crime.

Teams of students can work together to combine analysis and action on the following projects:

1. Changing the classroom environment (such as bulletin boards or seating arrangements)
2. Helping to solve neighborhood problems (such as preventing teenage pregnancy, tutoring, or eliminating litter)
3. Visiting the aged, helping in food lockers and kitchens for the homeless
4. Volunteering at daycare centers and breakfast programs
5. Participating in political party efforts
6. Joining with student groups to support union and civil rights organizations

In Chapter 8 we discuss in detail developing teams and processing their work.

Summary

It is important for students to learn that study and analysis in school can help them make life decisions. Positive school experiences that make a difference in students' lives lead them to conclude that further schooling can provide an entrance into the dynamic sectors of our economy. Empowerment strategies derived from critical theory ideology recognize that public schools have served as an important vehicle for the growth of our democracy and our economy. Analysis, social participation, and social action skills teach confidence and political courage. The process of critical analysis leading to positive action (praxis) teaches students that they can take real steps to improve their lives. Multicultural education that is social reconstructionist encourages students to participate in the long and difficult effort to build a more democratic society.

Questions Over the Chapter

1. What are the differences between literacy and critical literacy?
2. List two of Paulo Freire's pedagogical ideas that are similar to those of U.S. philosopher John Dewey.
3. What are at least two examples of Freire's statement that all education is political? What are the political dimensions of your current teacher preparation program?
4. Positivism strives for the neutrality or "objectivity" of the researcher. Critical theory and the work of Freire recognize the political nature of schools and all pedagogy. Is objectivity possible? What are its advantages and disadvantages? What are the advantages and disadvantages of political commitment by teachers?
5. Describe the power relationships in your current school or current program. Who has power? Who does not? What is the nature of power in your school?
6. The basic ideas of critical pedagogy were developed in working with adults. Which ideas would you change when working with young students?

7. Define *social reconstructionism*.
8. List four ways that your curriculum may not be politically neutral.
9. What are the goals of empowerment?
10. What would be important empowerment goals for a group of five immigrant students?

11. List four examples of social participation projects appropriate to the specific grade level you intend to teach.

Activities for Further Study of Empowerment

1. List social participation opportunities that you can relate to some element of your curriculum. Work out a strategy with your students for one of these and guide them in implementing it. Evaluate the results.
2. Role play a coaching session in your university class. Encourage a student to work to improve his or her study skills.
3. Investigate portfolio assessment techniques. They can be powerful tools in evaluating social participation. (For more information on portfolio assessment see Stiggins, 1997.)
4. Write a specific lesson plan for the following student objectives. Choose two objectives from each group.

Grades 1–3
Students will do the following:
a. Assume responsibility for decorating one area of the classroom.
b. Volunteer to assist a limited-English-speaking student with her lessons.
c. Participate in class meetings about student behavior.

Grades 4–8
Students will do the following:
a. Work as a volunteer tutor with younger students.
b. Learn negotiation strategies for conflict resolution.
c. Serve as a conflict resolution monitor in school.
d. Make an educational plan to improve their own reading and writing skills.
e. Interview school volunteers about their work.
f. Assist the teacher with classroom tasks.

Grades 8–12
Students will do the following:
a. Work as volunteers feeding the hungry.
b. Describe *hopelessness* from two or more points of view.
c. Make an educational plan leading toward higher education or a career.
d. Follow through on the first steps of the educational plan.
e. Identify and analyze their own specific academic skills.
f. Plan and practice to overcome a specific skill weakness (for example, writing a paragraph).
g. Conduct research comparing learning conditions in an affluent suburban school and a school serving low-income students.
h. Interview an appropriate elected official concerning unequal funding among school districts in their area.
i. Work as a team within a community service organization. Analyze and improve the team's work.
j. Interview a community activist about what forces prevent community agencies from achieving increased success.
k. Complete a study of conflict resolution strategies. Establish a student-run system of conflict resolution in the school.
5. Provide students with a list of local community agencies accepting volunteers. Help students identify an area they may like to experience, help them identify the appropriate agency, and encourage them to participate in its activities.

Teaching Strategies

1. Present units on culture, cultural conflict, and value conflict.
2. Use students' home, school, and community experiences as sources for your curriculum.
3. Plan community participation and social participation as part of your curriculum.
4. Investigate the present reading and writing levels of your students. Generate plans to advance them at least 1.5 years in one year. (Your goal will be to get low-achieving students up to their actual grade level in two years.)
5. Integrate reading, writing, and language development into all aspects of your curriculum.
6. Plan lessons on the value of staying in school, value clarity, and developing skills to achieve success in school.

Chapter 8

Democracy and Classroom Management

Of all the civil rights for which the world has struggled and fought for 5,000 years, the right to learn is undoubtedly the most fundamental. . . . The freedom to learn . . . has been bought by bitter sacrifice. And whatever we may think of the curtailment of other civil rights, we should fight to the last ditch to keep open the right to learn, the right to have examined in our schools not only what we believe, but what we do not believe; not only what our leaders say, but what the leaders of other groups and nations, and the leaders of other centuries have said. We must insist upon this to give our children the fairness of a start which will equip them with such an array of facts and such an attitude toward truth that they can have a real chance to judge what the world is and what its greater minds have thought it might be.

—W. E. B. Du Bois, "The Freedom to Learn" (in *Foner*, 1970, pp. 230–231)

For many students, schools are not safe. In California, for example, over 10,000 weapons (including 1,131 guns) were confiscated from students in a single year. Florida witnessed a 40 percent increase in gun incidents. New York City reported 1,800 weapons violations in one year. In Birmingham, Alabama, suspensions for

Safety in the classroom (handwritten note in left margin)

possession of firearms increased from 30 to 85 incidents in a two-year period (Hechinger, 1992).

Such statistics illustrate in part a clear response to the loss of economic prosperity and political opportunity throughout U.S. society. Acts of violence and disruption have increased among working- and middle-class citizens. The economic decline of the last 30 years for working people and the decline of effectiveness of schools in preparing working-class young people for economic success has substantially eroded teacher and school authority.

The United States has the highest homicide rate of any modern, industrialized country. The number of youth placed in prisons has grown dramatically. Aspects of life in our society are teaching some young people and adults that violence and force are useful and practical instruments. Many conservatives allege that the "decline of order" is directly related to television and "liberal" social policies. Other authors describe current U.S. society as a "postmodern" culture (Aronowitz & Giroux, 1985).

In the 1980s and 1990s, order declined in our society, particularly in urban areas. Middle school and high school students increasingly challenged the legitimacy of schools and the roles of teachers. Youth gangs became a major problem for schools and gang members had more and more powerful weapons. Gangs are not only a problem for their members; over 380,000 students carried weapons to school in one year, usually, in their view, to protect themselves from the violence of others (Hechinger, 1992). Each year over 300,000 high school students are physically attacked (Hechinger, 1992). The firearm homicide rate for young people more than doubled between 1985 and 1992 (Carnegie Council on Adolescent Development, 1995). An increasingly disorderly environment in many schools demoralized even the most dedicated students and teachers.

Increased racial and class divisions between teachers and the communities they serve isolate and divide teachers from effective family and neighborhood influence. Young people need schools and families working together to reduce violence. The increase in street crime parallels increased disruptions in school. Both are produced by the growth of poverty, marginal employment, and unemployment, and neither crime nor chaos in the schools can be cured by school practices alone (Jackson, 1993–1994; Miller, 1992).

During the 1990s some school districts and communities began to create programs to reverse the violence and to allow schools to return to their educational mission. An important part of regaining control is for schools to create caring and supportive relationships among students. A California report (Dear, 1995) states, "Severe acts of violence such as shootings, rape and assault are best handled by law enforcement and the criminal justice system. The school's focus should be on basic academic development and, to a lesser extent, personal and social enhancement" (p. 2).

While writing reports is valuable, actions speak louder than words. The city of Boston began to address the rise of youth violence in 1982 by forming collaboratives of neighborhood groups, social service organizations, police, and local agencies. By the 1990s, a network of organizations and social service groups working with the police were able to reduce violence significantly; 16 children were murdered in Boston in 1993, six in 1994, four in 1995, and one in 1996 (Children's Defense Fund, 1997). Violence can be reduced when people are willing to work at the problem.

Developing Democracy in Schools

James Banks, a leader in the field of multicultural education, argues (1997), "A fundamental premise of a democratic society is that citizens will participate in the governing of the nation and that the nation-state will reflect the hopes, dreams, and possibilities of its people. People are not born democrats. Consequently, an important goal of the schools in a democratic society is to help students acquire the knowledge, values, and skills needed to participate effectively in public communities. Educating students to be democrats is a challenge in any kind of society. It is a serious challenge in a society characterized by cultural, ethnic, racial, and language diversity, especially when these variables are used to privilege some individuals from some groups and to deny others equal opportunities to participate" (p. 1).

In Chapter 1 I argued that the promotion of democracy should be a central goal of schooling. Teachers should promote and cultivate democratic values. One way we promote democracy is to teach about civic responsibility, the electoral process, and the U.S. Constitution. A second way is to teach using social participation strategies: encouraging students to work with student government and local social service agencies, and on local issues and elections (see Chapter 7). A third way to promote democracy in the classroom is by developing in students a preference for fairness, justice, and mutual respect; these are issues of classroom management. A fourth way is to teach students to work together to resolve problems and to achieve goals (see Chapter 10). Such participatory teaching requires well-developed skills of management and coaching.

In Chapter 7 we defined *empowerment* as a goal for students, and stressed the empowerment of students currently marginalized in our society. In this chapter I will argue that empowerment is often encouraged by creating a classroom environment of civility and is nurtured by the quality of relationships among students and teachers as well as by the themes, concepts, and strategies of the curriculum.

Democratic values are usually studied in the formal curriculum of history and the social studies. Our commitment to developing democracy derives from an ideology espoused by Thomas Jefferson, John Dewey, and many others. We believe that democracy is good. Rule of law is superior to arbitrary power or rule by an elite. Teaching students to have a commitment to a common set of democratic values provides one of the main cohesive forces in our society. Developing democratic values and skills in young people is, along with teaching reading, writing, and arithmetic, a primary reason we build public schools.

Youth Culture

Schools need to respond to postmodern youth culture to help young people develop life-supporting community values. Documents such as the Carnegie Council on Adolescent Development's *Great Transitions: Preparing Adolescents for the 21st Century* (1995) offer a thoughtful perspective on contemporary youth culture.

The development of this culture has significant impact on school attendance, classroom management, and discipline for younger students. Some young people see little reason to attend school. When at school they often miss class, or ignore instruction in the classes they do attend. Some students miss up to 20 classes per semester, making it difficult for their teachers to teach them and establish relationships with them.

Promoting Democratic Values

Teachers learn to either promote democratic values, or promote obedience, or promote anarchy and destruction in their classrooms. Obedience is necessary; you cannot teach math or chemistry if you cannot get students to sit in their seats and to allow you to present information. But reliance on force and obedience and compliance, particularly in urban schools, has led to refusal to learn and disruption on the part of many students. Schools are microcommunities, where students learn how real-world communities both do and should work. Think of the schools you have visited. Do they present positive, goal-oriented introductions to the emerging economy and society or dreary, policed, control-oriented negative views of the students' own future? Teachers need to develop strategies and use management techniques to teach democracy, tolerance, respect, and human dignity.

Students and teachers promote a democratic community when they develop an inclusive classroom and school environment, one where all students can participate with fairness and justice. We promote democracy when students learn to work together, to respect one another, and to resolve conflicts and achieve community goals. These vital lessons are taught on sports fields, in student government, and in the day-to-day management of each classroom. Where these lessons are not learned, schools become dreary warehouses, and teachers spend most of their time managing and controlling young people, rather than teaching them.

Classroom management is necessary for schools to function. By redirecting management toward democracy and empowerment, strong-sense multicultural education promotes a very clear set of values, ones concerned with fairness and justice for all.

Instead of using force and threats of force, we need to develop school societies where democracy is nourished (O'Neil, 1997). Such positive school societies nurture the democratic ethos of community building. Students in safe schools learn to prefer democratic values of justice and fairness because they live with these values in school. For example, the curriculum in such schools offers students opportunities to reflect on their values and behavior, and teaches them to think critically (see Chapter 9).

To better serve alienated and marginalized students, schools must formally teach democracy and fairness as a part of the curriculum. Schools should be places where children experience safety, trust, and respect. When gangs operate as terrorists, and when the police serve as a virtual occupation force, young people seldom learn to respect the law or to respect each other. Life is teaching them violence and revenge, while schools are preaching about respect. In our current society many schools must contend with the increased violence, alienation, and disruption of street culture.

Too often, schools in marginalized and oppressed areas have too many new teachers and too many teachers on "emergency" credentials who are just learning classroom management. New teachers tend to respond to discipline crises either by withdrawing or by resorting to force and control. Over 80 percent of new teachers are European Americans, and many harbor unfortunate misunderstandings and stereotypes about student behavior (see Chapters 2–4). Some of these teachers even fear their own students.

The use of coercive power may serve to control a class for a few hours, but it will not teach democratic values. Coercive power will allow teachers to survive day to day, but leads directly to overlarge numbers of new teachers quitting the profession within the first three years (Riley, 1998).

Some school districts assist new teachers by having mentor teachers and local school experts show them how to manage classrooms. But teachers need both to develop a management system and to promote students' democratic empowerment, particularly for students of cultural and linguistic minority groups. They need to develop consistent, respectful relationships with students in order to help them learn.

Democratic values are not promoted by only presenting social studies lessons about democracy. We must also construct the school environment to teach the important values of mutual respect and tolerance for differences. It is difficult for a single teacher to create a democratic community in a school. Teachers must work together.

In this chapter, we will explore classroom management styles that permit schools to function and teachers to teach. Teachers, even new teachers, have the power of adult expertise, and must learn to manage their classrooms so that students are safe, and are willing and able to learn.

A Safe and Orderly Environment

Children learn best in a safe and orderly environment. Research on "effective schools," common sense, and teacher experience indicate the need for a reasonable and supportive classroom environment. Both teachers and students need order in the classroom (Goodlad, 1984). Teachers want order to encourage learning. Excessive disciplining and lack of classroom order cause extensive waste of teaching time and learning time. Violence and intergroup conflict, combined with academic failure and the many problems of young people, deny many students a classroom environment that supports learning (National Coalition of Advocates for Students, 1991).

When teachers are unable to create a positive atmosphere, when they fail in their attempts to productively manage their classroom, students lose instructional time. Most off-task student behavior is not dangerous, confrontational, or violent, but it is a frustrating waste of academic learning time. Students who are off task tend to become disruptive. The disruptions are cumulative, in that talking and other inappropriate behavior spread from student to student. Students who are off task learn less, and fail more. In many neighborhood schools in poverty areas, a cycle develops of off-task behavior leading to failure, failure leading to discouragement, and discouragement providing a further incentive to get off task.

Constant discipline and management problems frustrate and discourage teachers. Teachers prefer to teach, but classroom conditions require them to manage disruptive behavior. They pay a price in lower self-esteem and less professional satisfaction. For many teachers in difficult schools, the price soon becomes intolerable: some transfer, some quit, some give in to student pressure, demanding little and expecting even less.

Acquiring the skills of effective classroom management takes first priority for most new teachers. These skills are best acquired in a public school classroom with supportive supervision; they are difficult to learn in a college classroom. When cultural differences divide teacher and students, or when cultural and ethnic conflict is common among students, conflict resolution and management skills become even more necessary.

When new teachers fail, they fail more often in their attempts to produce classroom control and motivation than in instruction. This chapter will provide you with detailed and specific ideas for establishing and maintaining positive, democratic classroom management. The principles and goals of democratic classroom management have long been accepted, but classroom practice suffers from frequent conflict and failure. Too many teachers, particularly new teachers, struggle and are frustrated in their vain attempts to control students, particularly in schools in marginalized neighborhoods. Disruptive and rebellious students demand so much of the teacher's time and energy that little remains for teaching. Teachers can reduce discipline problems and design their classrooms for better democratic control by (a) creating a positive classroom environment, (b) promoting student choice, (c) promoting on-task behavior, and (d) promoting positive teacher–student communications. We discuss these concepts throughout the following sections.

Reducing Discipline Problems

You probably chose to enter teaching to make positive contributions to students' lives—not to control unruly kids. But when teachers fail to achieve classroom control—and new teachers fail often—a common response is to seek more power, more control. A major problem in this struggle is that teachers—and future teachers—have a great deal of experience with authoritarian practices and very little with democratic alternatives. They soon discover that their efforts to gain more control through power strategies fail. Endless power struggles exhaust them and remove much of their motivation for teaching. Teachers and students alike pay an enormous price in lost instructional time and damaged self-esteem.

To reverse this unwelcome state of affairs, democratic teachers learn strategies that promote learning and deal effectively with disruptive students. One way to begin effective classroom management and reduce discipline problems is by creating a positive classroom environment in which students feel safe and secure.

Beyond Rewards and Punishment.   The behavior management systems of Fred Jones, Lee Canter, and others may serve a useful purpose to get control of an unruly class. At times, teachers may need to use these techniques (see "A Guide for New Teachers" later in this chapter). However, once control and reasonable rules have been established, teachers should move on to systems that teach students democracy, empowerment, and how to accept responsibility for their own conduct.

Teachers should decide on their own orientation toward class management by reflecting on their core values as they apply in the specific neighborhood in which they teach. Throughout this book, I argue that a central value of schools should be to promote democratic behavior and responsibility. Democracy is not anarchy. Nor is it a laissez-faire approach. Democracy includes the development of a series of fair rules and a respect for the rights of all members of the classroom. In a democracy, citizens (the students) participate in setting up the rules within the limits established by a social contract or a constitution (school policy). Then students are made responsible for keeping their own rules and for complying with reasonable class norms. Teachers and the students need to work together to establish norms for acceptable behavior, to encourage respect for all, and to develop sanctions for those who do not cooperate.

Creating a Positive Classroom Environment

Choose Instructional Strategies That Encourage Success.   One thing successful teachers do to create a positive environment is to choose instructional strategies that help students to feel confident. Students need to believe that they are acquiring important information and skills. Success builds confidence, whereas failure produces anxiety and hopelessness. The environment and the curriculum should produce success.

You can ensure the success of instructional strategies by selecting quality curriculum and demonstrating to students the value and usefulness of the subjects they are studying. An interesting, culturally relevant curriculum assists class management, whereas a boring curriculum invites students to respond with boredom, indifference, and disruption.

Communicate a Belief in Students' Ability to Succeed.   The failure to reinforce for students the idea that they each can succeed in their own unique ways can sometimes have disastrous results. Students who have poorly developed study skills frequently encounter a failure-filled, tense, anxious environment. Unfortunately, experience has taught many teachers to have *low expectations*, to *accept* the failure of poor and minority children as normal. But failure seldom helps to achieve instructional objectives with young people. Failure produces tension and anxiety and interferes with learning. Currently popular proposals to end "social promotion" fail to offer an alternative to persistent failure.

Give Positive Feedback to Students.   When classrooms are chaotic, full of tension and conflict, and students are fearful that teachers will respond to them with insults, the classroom is not a safe environment. Young people who fear sarcasm and demeaning comments from teachers or other students respond with anxiety and frustration. Arbitrary enforcement or settlements imposed by power and bullying do not promote democracy. Such classrooms produce failure for both students and teachers.

Communicating positive feedback to students, however, helps both you and your students. Students get further confirmation that you are there to help them succeed, they receive feedback on *how* to succeed, and because their needs for success are being met, they are less likely to be abusive and critical of other students. When these conditions are met, you have fewer discipline problems and can spend more time on actual instruction.

Your task then is to learn to create a positive, productive environment that enhances the lives of both you and your students. Democratic teachers set up structures and systems that guide students toward positive interpersonal behavior and toward appropriate school behavior.

Arbitrary power and control will not teach democratic lifestyles and will not achieve a positive environment. You need to recruit students and encourage them to cooperate in creating a positive classroom environment.

Promoting Student Choice

Free and responsible choice is at the heart of democratic behavior. While some mistakenly believe that they enter teaching only to instruct students in math, or biology, such a limited view of the teacher's role seldom succeeds. Teachers must also help students learn democratic behavior by assisting them to make responsible choices. Students learn to make responsible choices, or they learn to comply, or they learn to resist.

Not all issues in school are subject to choice. For example, students may not choose to disrupt your class without consequence. But they may choose to either work cooperatively in class or leave. And you, the teacher, may choose to help them learn constructive behavior or to subject them to the school disciplinary system.

Problems and conflicts occur daily in school. Problems provide teachers with opportunities to instruct students in responsibility. They provide opportunities to teach prodemocratic behaviors. Whenever possible, convert the problem into a choice situation, rather than suppressing or trying to control the conflict or allowing a power struggle to develop.

For example, student A hits student B. Student B must choose whether to respond, to walk away, or to move on to conflict resolution. Through role play and discussion, students can learn to evaluate a conflict or violent situation and to make their own choices, including choosing safety for themselves and others. Students should learn decision making and leadership skills to direct conflicts toward nonviolent resolutions. There are a number of available curriculum packages for teaching nonviolent conflict resolution (see the section, "Conflict Resolution," in Chapter 6).

Teachers assist students by making their choices conscious. Students need to be aware of the choices they are making. Discussion of conflict and choice should be a part of your curriculum. You can create and examine scenarios and practice alternative responses. Such practice can assist students to deal with violence in the school or neighborhood. Students are empowered when they have thought through in advance potentially violent situations.

Students can be engaged in planning and creating a safe school or a safe classroom. You can encourage your students to take leadership roles in decision making by advocating school policies that lead to mutual respect and democracy.

Lessons and discussions are appropriate on self-control, setting boundaries, and impulse or anger management. Lessons are appropriate on self-determination and recognizing those realms in which students have decision-making responsibility. For example, if a student initiates a conflict, you can take her aside and explain, "You have a choice. You may choose to cooperate in this class, or you may choose to disrupt it. If you insist on obstructing class, I will ask you to leave." Responding to conflict by providing choice opens opportunities for coaching (discussed later in this chapter).

Particularly after the primary grades, students need to learn take ownership of their own behavior. Self-evaluation and self-regulation are far superior to teacher control. Counseling theory provides you with a powerful instrument in the understanding that you usually cannot change a student or force him to change. You may force compliance, but this is usually temporary, and requires a great deal of your effort to maintain. Forced compliance, at times necessary for the safety of others, seldom leads to learning responsible, democratic behavior.

You can, however, provide powerful assistance to help students to change when they want to change. You can encourage change through coaching and through maintaining a safe, democratic environment, helping students to make responsible choices. You gain additional influence by making contact with students' homes. Teachers and parents need to work together to guide young people. Unless home and school can learn to work together, the urban education crisis will continue (Children's Defense Fund, 1997; Meier, 1995). Your curriculum should include opportunities for students to actively work toward making their own community and school safe and productive places. This may include parental and/or community engagement projects and volunteering with community service agencies (see Chapter 7).

Promoting On-Task Behavior

Positive use of classroom time is a critical issue. Students waste a great deal of time. Researchers have reported that they are off-task, not studying, and not learning up to 50 percent of the time (Charles, 1989; Costa, 1985; Squires, Huitt, & Segars,

1983). Older students are often off task because they believe that what they are being asked to study is boring or irrelevant to their lives. Teachers promote on-task behavior by demonstrating the relevance of lessons to students.

Demonstrate the Relevance of Lessons to Students.   One way that you can show students how schoolwork relates to their lives is by allowing some student choice and choosing student-centered projects. You may find excellent ideas for student-centered educational projects in *It's Our World, Too! Stories of Young People Who Are Making a Difference* (Hoose, 1993) and in *Open Minds to Equality* (Schniedewind & Davidson, 1998). At other times you will need to teach the approved curriculum and teach to state or district standards (see Chapter 12). A well-informed teacher who is a cultural mediator will emphasize those elements of the standard curriculum that have practical or current relevance to students.

Use Positive, Managed Intervention Strategies.   Teachers need to learn skills to assist students to stay on task and to pursue goals. Effective teachers plan for and manage potential conflicts and discipline problems before they even arise. Positive classroom management keeps students working on interesting, useful, and rewarding tasks.

In the elementary grades, when students are off task, effective teachers intervene early and frequently to call on students to return to the learning task. In grades 4 through 8, early interventions produce success and can be employed with low levels of power, thus avoiding failure and confrontation.

Some teachers respond to off-task behavior by becoming more authoritarian and more aggressive toward students. Their efforts may achieve control, but authoritarian action interferes with efforts to provide the safe and supportive environment students need for success. Often, aggressive teacher behavior is self-defeating because it produces more control problems, exhausts teachers, and interferes with productive learning—a cycle of frustration, failure, and repression. For many students during adolescence, constant power struggles between student and teacher disrupt the learning environment and encourage more off-task behavior, even for those students interested in learning.

Frequent, low-level, managed intervention provides an alternative. Teachers learn to use eye contact, body language, physical proximity, facial expression, and gestures to structure and manage the class and keep everyone on task. This strategy combines commonsense teaching practices with rewards. Reward students for increased on-task learning time by giving them planned leisure and recreation time. Interventions can be effective and nondisruptive, encouraging students to return to the task at hand. Once classroom order is established, and at least by sixth grade, democratic management systems should be used.

Try Task Analysis.   Task analysis permits teachers to design a positive environment and to teach students how to succeed. For example, numerous studies have demonstrated that cooperative learning is a helpful strategy, particularly for African American, Latino, and Native American children (E. Garcia, 1995; Ladson-Billings, 1994b). Both children and adults need instruction in how to work cooperatively. As teachers begin to use cooperative learning, they must teach the skills necessary for cooperative work (see Chapter 10).

Task analysis separates the skills of cooperative work into several teachable, learnable sets. For example, essential skills for a fourth- to eighth-grade class might include moving chairs, selecting persons for roles (e.g., monitor, checker, encourager), staying on the subject, listening to one another, taking turns, and supporting the authority of a student leader. Each of these skills is isolated, taught, practiced, and evaluated to improve the quality of cooperative work and classroom relationships.

Direct Instruction.   Madeline Hunter of UCLA developed a process known as *direct instruction* that is useful and effective in teaching students new behaviors (Hunter, 1982). The format works well both for behavior issues and for introducing new concepts in lessons. Direct instruction is most appropriate when teaching clear, identifiable behavior or a specific concept, and is far more effective than criticizing and punishing students for inappropriate behavior.

To use direct instruction, you would first identify the specific behavior you want to change. For example, you might want all students in their seats when class begins, or want students to raise their hands before talking. You would then plan lessons on the behavior. Dr. Hunter has developed a sequential series of steps for direct instruction. Figure 8.1 illustrates Dr. Hunter's steps applied to the issue of students raising their hands before talking.

Figure 8.1   Direct Instruction

1. *Anticipatory set.* Get students' attention to the subject. Start with an example from their own lives, or an example of the problem that just occurred.

2. *Explanation.* Explain the lesson objective clearly. Tell students what they are going to learn and why it is important.

3. *Input.* Give students more information on the task. Explain why it is important for everyone to raise their hands before speaking. Explain the consequences of not establishing rules for polite discourse.

4. *Modeling.* Demonstrate, or have students demonstrate, the actual behavior you are trying to teach. It is essential that students see the actual behavior, not just talk about it.

5. *Check for understanding.* Ask students to explain the reasons for establishing the behavior. Perhaps have two or three students explain or model the behavior.

6. *Guided practice.* Have students actually practice the behavior. For example, several students could simultaneously attempt to answer a question you pose. You may want to repeat this practice two or three times.

7. *Independent practice.* Monitor and comment on the behavior for the next several days. If there are any problems, return to step 4 and repeat the process.

8. *Closure.* Summarize the lesson. Review its importance. Thank students for their participation.

Promoting Positive Teacher–Student Communications

Teacher behavior either contributes to or detracts from the building of a positive classroom environment. Studies indicate that the average teacher uses negative comments and commands much more often than positive comments. Positive communications strategies are important at all levels. They become increasingly important during adolescence. Violence and domination teach violence and domination, while respect teaches respect. Good teachers contribute to a positive environment by practicing positive comments that guide and structure student behavior (Figure 8.2).

Learn to Describe Positive Behavior.   Successful teachers learn to describe positive behavior. Consistent repetition of positive directions guides most students to respond without increasing defensiveness. Such repetition directs student behavior and lowers the anxiety and frustration levels in the classroom. Teachers often produce success through encouragement and cooperation.

Redirect Students' Nonhelpful Behavior.   Effective teachers practice the skill of redirecting students from nonhelpful to helpful behavior by clearly describing precisely *how* to perform a task. Primary teachers often model the task rather than rely on oral instructions. In grades 4 through 8, role playing and physical practice of a task reduce the need for criticism. A clear explanation of how to perform a task provides students with a positive alternative to criticism. Teachers who rely on criticism and correction attack students' self-esteem and make them feel hostile, defeated, alienated, or self-doubting. Because defeat and criticism only rarely lead to intensified effort, it is best to avoid strategies built on negative responses.

Give Clear Directions.   Teachers frequently need to give instructions and commands on how to perform tasks. Giving clear, brief instructions provides a structure within which students can succeed. When a few students do not carry out the instruction, repeating the command is often more effective than criticizing them (e.g., say simply, "Open your books now. Please open your books to page 45.").

Giving clear, appropriate instructions is essential to managing your class. But when instructions are demeaning or issued in an attacking manner, they become criticism and students receive them defensively. Of course, in real classrooms, you

Figure 8.2   Alternatives to Negative Comments

Instead of:	Alternatives:
"Stop talking and get busy."	"Open your book now."
"You haven't started yet?"	"How did you answer question one?"
"Why aren't you working?"	"Can I help you with the first problem?"

occasionally will need to criticize. It often helps to explain your reasoning when critiquing a student's response. Effective teachers try to call students' attention to the purpose behind the instructions. When it is evident that you give your instructions out of concern for the welfare of the class, even criticism can be heard in safety and can lead to positive student behavior. For example, saying, "Please stop talking, I want to go on with the lesson," works better than saying only, "Please stop talking."

Use a Supportive, Encouraging Speaking Style.   Democratic teachers seek to give instructions, even commands, without using an aggressive or dominating style. They seek to replace divisive and demeaning communication with encouraging students to cooperate and support one another. Positive communication contributes to the positive social climate in the classroom necessary to promote personal and social growth.

For students beyond grade 6, *feedback*—or constructive direction—is a useful instructional strategy. The following guidelines promote positive, nurturing communication:

1. Concentrate on criticizing the act or the idea—not the person. Personalizing criticism is worse than useless because it interferes with the possibility of future positive communication.
2. Practice giving feedback and correction when the action occurs and then move on. Repeatedly reminding students of past offenses (nagging) frustrates both teachers and students. No one can change the past. Students cannot undo past mistakes. Concentrate on the present and the future.
3. Feedback and correction should be as specific and concrete as possible. Telling students to be respectful or to behave does not provide the information they need to change their behavior. The best feedback tells students precisely what they can begin doing correctly rather than offering negative evaluations of what they have done.
4. Labeling students and using sarcasm are not helpful. They seldom contribute to behavioral change or instruction.
5. Encouragement always works better than criticism because it helps students to build self-esteem.

Classroom management systems enable teachers to design student success. Unfortunately, not all students will respond to a positive environment. Prior school and home experiences may have taught some students to disrupt and to resist learning.

For students from low-status cultural groups experiencing cultural conflict in schools, the intensity of criticism can reinforce a desire to withdraw from participation and to flee school. Others resist even reasonable school norms. Teenagers frequently experience self-doubt and lack of confidence. Teachers and other students overusing negative messages alienates and divorces some students from schooling.

Respect Students.   Young people can be cruel and critical of each other. It is a mistake for the adults in a school to enter into the teenage culture of putdowns and sar-

casm (Kagan, 1986). Even when a specific student appears arrogant or overconfi-
dent, public sarcasm is damaging, because it intimidates and injures other students.
Although students may have developed apparent defenses against sarcasm from
other students, too much criticism from teachers can be devastating. The consistent
application of positive communication helps students develop a positive attitude.
Respecting students encourages them to internalize new values supportive of civility
and of classroom instruction.

Schools were established to instruct youth in information, values, and skills. The
teacher has a right and a responsibility to establish a positive classroom atmosphere.
Students do not have a right to be disruptive or disrespectful. The school and the
classroom need clear, reasonable parameters of appropriate behavior, and effective
teachers enforce the rules. Democratic behavior can best be encouraged within a
safe environment. When teachers and the school administration fail to consistently
enforce a positive, appropriate, fair structure of discipline, peer group pressures will
disrupt the school. Young people deserve and need adults in charge who will establish and maintain reasonable standards of school-appropriate behavior (Figure 8.3).

Isolate Disruptive School Groups and Provide Appropriate Intervention.   Classes tend to
have several student-centered groups, some supportive of instruction and a positive
school climate, others disruptive. By the middle grades (6–8), most students will want
to belong to a group. Peer-group influences become increasingly important. If peer-
group behavior is positive and supports instruction, most new students will accommo-
date the group. A major teaching task is to establish a positive, productive atmosphere
and then to encourage and recruit the majority of the students to cooperate.

**Figure 8.3   Simple and Clear
Rules Help to Establish a Safe
and Productive Classroom Climate**

Based on suggestions made in *The
good common school: Making the
vision work for all children. A comprehensive guide to elementary
school restructuring* by National
Coalition of Advocates for Students,
1991, Boston, MA: Author.

1. Everyone affected should have a voice in determining school rules. Language barriers to full participation should be removed.
2. Rules should be clearly stated in behavioral terms.
3. Rules should be reasonable.
4. Rules should be enforceable.
5. Rules should be easily understood.
6. Rules should be taught as part of the curriculum.
7. Rules should be communicated to parents in the language spoken in the home.
8. Rules should be consistently enforced by teachers.
9. Rules should be perceived by students as being fair.
10. Rules that disproportionately impact any one group of students should be changed.

By the teenage years, peer-group and gang pressures can dominate a class. Teachers who encounter difficulties with gang members in classes should seek support and additional resources from the school administration and from parent groups.

Individual teachers cannot resolve problems of gangs, resistance, drugs, and violence. In fact, the isolation of teachers from each other and from parents encourages and supports gang behavior in schools. Student groups dedicated to disruptive behavior must first be isolated from influence and then redirected with strong intervention systems, including the police if necessary.

Reteach Appropriate School Behaviors if Necessary.   Young students often need to be taught appropriate behavior. Even adolescents at times need to be retaught basic interpersonal skills, such as talking to others without making "putdowns." You identify and teach the skills of positive behavior just as you would teach the skill of writing a sentence. If you want students to move from a large group into smaller groups, clear directions and rehearsing will help students learn the skills involved. In the primary and intermediate grades, practicing class-appropriate behavior helps students to belong within a positive group and to participate in creating a positive environment. In middle schools and secondary classrooms, you need clear instruction and practice time early in each semester to establish the appropriate behavior for your class.

Provide time for teaching, practicing, and evaluating social skills. Make teaching school-appropriate behavior a part of your curriculum. You and your students will experience success from teaching and practicing appropriate behavior. Instruction and practice lead to change. Management and punishment lead to control that is always temporary.

Major, lasting changes in student behavior occur slowly. Disruptive behavior in class may be the result of years of experience in school and at home. Producing major changes in classroom behavior for some difficult students often requires months and supplementary counseling resources.

Extending the Teacher's Influence Through Coaching

Our society has become increasingly depersonalized in the modern era. Many children have less positive supervision by parents. Some disruptive children literally need more parenting. In our troubled society, many students need guides, coaches, and counselors.

Coaching and conferencing extend teachers' influence in managing the classroom. Successful democratic teachers use conferencing and coaching with those students who continue disruptive and off-task behavior. Coaching strategies provide monitoring, advising, and instruction particularly important to students in the middle grades (6–8), as well as in high school. Students need positive, adult interaction and interventions in school. Setting up coaching and advising sessions helps teachers to guide classroom behavior and build important connections between students and the school (Comer, 1988).

Teachers plan and implement coaching processes when students need weeks of reinforcement and instruction. Just as planning improves instructional delivery in math, science, and the social studies, systematic planning of coaching will improve most students' behaviors, and eventually, their attitudes.

Effective teachers need an intervention system to redirect disruptive students toward prosocial and constructive classroom behavior. A counseling and coaching strategy provides such a system. The system of Individual Psychology, as developed by Alfred Adler, Rudolph Dreikurs, and subsequent researchers, provides an effective democratic approach for helping students to move away from disturbing and destructive school behavior.

A Theory of Antisocial Student Behavior

The Dreikurs system (Dreikurs, Greenwald, & Pepper, 1971; Dreikurs & Stoltz, 1964) proposes a theory of how students learn their worldviews and role behavior and assists in developing an intervention system. Martinez (1978) describes the theory of Adlerian psychology and of Dreikurs intervention systems as follows:

> From infancy, the individual begins to formulate a cognitive representation, a picture of himself/herself, the world, and the individual's place in that world. This view is like a multi-dimensional puzzle with many sides and levels. The child perceives pieces of data and like a puzzle, he/she puts the pieces into some kind of picture (world view). This picture becomes a map which gives direction and purpose to the child's life. Children observe the environment, evaluate it, and arrive at conclusions about themselves, their worth, their potency, and their place in the environment. They decide on a view of what the world demands of them and how they can acquire a sense of belonging to or a sense of being part of that world. The family is the first social group the child encounters. (p. 59)

Martinez quotes Mosak and Dreikurs (1973) to say that through the child's interaction with the family

> [each child] stakes out for himself a piece of territory which includes the attributes of abilities that he hopes will give him a feeling of belonging, a feeling of having a place. If, through his evaluation of his own potency (abilities, courage and confidence), he is convinced that he can achieve this place through useful endeavors, he will pursue the useful side of life. Should he feel that he cannot attain the goal of having a place in this fashion, he will become a discouraged child and engage in disturbed or disturbing behavior in his effort to find a place. For the Adlerian, the "maladjusted" child is not a "sick" child, he is a "discouraged" child. Dreikurs classifies the goals of the discouraged child into four groups: attention-getting, power-seeking, revenge-taking, and declaring deficiency or defeat. It should be emphasized that Dreikurs is speaking of immediate, rather than long-range goals. These are the goals of children's "misbehavior," not of all child behavior. (quoted in Martinez, 1978, p. 117)

Life, like culture, is dynamic rather than static. The world around children is continually changing, and they are changing. Children are continually confronted with new information. Some new data agree with their existing worldviews. Other new information conflicts.

Conflicting information presents the recipient with two alternatives. She can incorporate it in her worldview in place of old information, and thus alter her view of the role she is playing in the classroom. Or she may reject or distort the new information so that it appears consistent with her existing self-image.

Worldviews and views of self serve as cognitive maps, guiding students in their actions. Immaturity, perceptual biases, distortions, and incomplete data make students' worldviews incomplete, but they appear adequate to their holders.

Students behave based on their worldviews and their perceptions of reality. A student's cognitive map and worldview guide her in comprehending new information. These perceptions are culturally influenced and largely subconscious. Students are aware of their behavior, but usually unaware of its underlying worldview, cultural frame of reference, perceptual set, and motivation.

In his helpful guide to teachers and counselors, Martinez (1978) says that, as students move through life toward adulthood, they encounter three major tasks posed by society. Students must face social life and the necessity of achieving: (a) cooperative social adjustment, (b) defined work roles, and (c) sex roles. Mosak and Dreikurs (1973), important contributors to Adlerian theory, argue as follows:

> Since man must live among his fellow man, the individual must come to realize that we live life together, and are responsible for each other. To the extent that the individual assumes this responsibility, he becomes socially contributive, interested in the common welfare. Secondly, the individual must define his sex roles, partly on the basis of cultural definition and stereotypes. He must learn to relate to the other sex, not as the opposite sex, for other people of the opposite sex do not represent the enemy, but rather they are his fellows with whom he must learn to cooperate. Third, since no man can claim self-sufficiency, we are interdependent and division of labor becomes a life requirement. Each of us is dependent upon our contribution. Work, thus, becomes essential for human survival. (quoted in Martinez, 1978, p. 118)

Dreikurs and Stoltz (1964) argue that when teachers share these assumptions, they respond to disruptive students as if the students are discouraged. Children's prior life in and out of school may not have provided them with either the strategies for successful classroom behavior or the motivation to succeed. Prior experience has taught them to pursue short-term self-interest, such as attention-getting through disruption or fighting. Children need to learn to pursue their own long-term self-interest by contributing to a positive social environment where they can experience support and success.

Class Meetings

Teachers using the democratic recommendations of Alfred Adler (1870–1937) and of Dreikurs and Stoltz (1964) have developed classroom meetings as an important aspect of problem solving to improve behavior. Democratic teachers provide leadership and structure to assist students in taking responsibility for resolving some class problems.

Students as young as first graders are taught to clearly identify the problem-causing disruption. In many classrooms, from grades 1 through 8, students set an agenda for the next classroom meeting by listing a problem behavior on an agenda sheet. At a specified time of the day or week, a classroom meeting is called. Classroom meetings work best when students have been prepared in cooperative learning skills (discussed in Chapter 10). The teacher and students together examine the problem behavior, and the students work together to suggest potential solutions. The teacher provides a structure for the meeting by insisting that all solutions must be reasonable, related, and respectful. Suggesting solutions does not resolve problems; students need to agree on the nature of the problem, and they need to agree on the solution.

Class meetings are useful at all grade levels, although rules for conducting them should change based on students' maturity. Typical rules for grades 1 through 4 include to give compliments as meeting starters, to use the agenda to keep focused on the problems, and to identify logical consequences for misbehavior rather than punishment (Figure 8.4).

Classroom meetings work particularly well above grade 4 when combined with training teams of students in mediation and conflict resolution (Tennessee Education Association & Appalachian Educational Laboratory, 1993) (see Chapter 6). Meetings alone will not resolve all conflicts in the classroom. When combined with an empowerment curriculum that encourages students to belong, to work cooperatively in groups, to be successful, and to be effective, problem-solving classroom meetings are very effective in improving classroom behavior, encouraging students to develop democratic behavior, and getting students to accept responsibility for their own actions.

Perhaps as a consequence of John Dewey's strong influence of educational theory, most teachers want to assist students in practicing democratic behavior even though they frequently do not know how to advocate for these positions. In classroom meetings, strategies for empowerment and for cooperative learning combine to provide teachers with powerful strategies for encouraging democratic behavior.

Figure 8.4   Sample Problem-Solving Scenario

The students in Mrs. G's fourth-grade class have practiced classroom meetings. They know the rules and the skills to facilitate conflict resolution. Mary places Heather's name on the agenda for the next meeting. At meeting time, the students sit in a circle. Mrs. G serves as a facilitator. She asks Mary to explain what is the issue. Mary says that Heather constantly calls her a "dirty Mexican." She wants the name calling stopped.

Several classmates confirm that they have heard this name calling. The class discusses name calling and stereotypes. They decide that children often repeat what they hear from adults. But at school, all children deserve respect. The teacher guides the children in role-playing name-calling events to clarify the issues.

After a time, the subject changes to consequences.

Coaching Using Dreikurs's Ideas

Classroom meetings use the powerful motivations of group cohesion and group belonging to encourage students to learn cooperation, but some students will resist. Many individual students have strong desires to disrupt or to seek control of the classroom agenda. These powerful drives at times are too complex to simply turn the problem over to a problem-solving group; coaching and conferencing are additional strategies for you as a democratic teacher.

Even though students frequently bring enormous conflicts from their home and peer lives into school, your first task is to redirect their behavior to help them succeed and to function effectively in the classroom. Set up a coaching/counseling session to redirect the behavior of consistently disruptive students. The coaching-counseling relationship will encourage them to learn the motivation and strategies necessary to operate positively within your classroom environment.

Harried student teachers may quickly protest that they do not have the time or skills to arrange for counseling and coaching. Only a few urban schools have adequate counseling and support resources. Several leading educators advocate that teachers deserve substantial additional support and assistance to deal with the several children per class who are potentially disruptive, particularly in communities suffering a high degree of economic and social stress (Comer, 1997; O'Neil, 1997).

But, in the face of few resources, teachers have little choice. They must respond. The continued use of power and force for discipline does not resolve conflicts. Power only temporarily suppresses students' disruptive behavior. The conflicts will emerge or explode at other times when teachers will be unprepared to manage the problems. If teachers do not develop effective response systems, such as coaching, students will continue to disrupt their classrooms.

As a teacher-coach, you first schedule a meeting with a disruptive student to analyze the problem and to plan for behavioral change. Initiate a positive, therapeutic relationship so that your coaching process can move forward. Typically, you and the student can agree on some fundamentals. You are in charge of the class. Disruptive behavior is not acceptable. You want to set up a system in which the student is not disruptive. After clearly explaining these fundamentals, analyze together the specific behavioral problem displayed in class and attempt to identify the problem's relationship to the student's own goals.

When you have established a safe relationship and a clear goal for coaching, the student can openly examine his behavior and select alternatives that will help him belong positively to the class. Work together with the student to give up the disruptive behavior and practice appropriate behavior. Successful coaching often requires a number of sessions to help a student gain a more positive and productive control over his classroom behavior. Detailed analysis and practice of each step help you direct most students toward constructive behavior (Figure 8.5).

In our violence-prone society, teachers will encounter a few students who, as a result of a dysfunctional family life, drug abuse, or similar trauma, refuse to permit the classroom to function. The school administrator must provide alternative

Figure 8.5 **When a Disruption Occurs**

1. Talk to the student privately.
2. Remove the student from the scene.
3. Establish a coaching relationship.
4. Teach the appropriate behavior rather than punish inappropriate behavior.
5. Have the student practice the behavior.
6. Contact the parents. Ask for their assistance.

resource classrooms or other resources for such students. Teachers seldom have the time or skills for therapy, but they can advocate for and demand additional staff with appropriate skills.

When children in elementary school are taught self-direction and social cooperation skills, they improve school achievement and develop strong self-esteem. By 10 to 12 years of age, disruptive behavior may become a way of school life, and ever more sophisticated and powerful intervention systems are needed. Fortunately, older students can conceptualize, discuss, and relearn school-appropriate behavior. Respect and safety cannot be assumed, they must be taught.

The Work of James P. Comer

James P. Comer (1997) has developed a psychotherapeutic perspective to assist educators in creating nourishing and safe environments for schools and communities. Such a community-building approach, while beneficial for any school, is particularly important for schools in disenfranchised and marginalized communities.

The failure of schools to attend to safety problems and teach positive social behavior is quite expensive, leading eventually to students leaving school and often entering the far more expensive criminal justice system.

Comer and his associates have stressed the importance of teachers themselves being both healthy and culturally competent to deal with the stresses of urban education. Creating positive, nurturing relationships for children requires a positive and supportive environment for adults, as well as a close working relationship between home and school.

No one psychotherapeutic theory has proven adequate and useful to teachers in all situations. Nor has adequate quantifiable data validated any one theory's explanation of student behavior. Meanwhile, teachers need a strategy to work within on a daily basis. The Adler-Dreikurs theories presented are the theories most connected to the practice and extension of democracy. The promotion of democracy in the classroom is difficult and substantially underdeveloped (Banks, 1997; Cagan, 1978; Gross & Dynneson, 1991).

Drug Interventions

Students in their adolescent years are often trying out new identities. For many it is a dangerous world, and gang affiliation and crime often appear as attractive options. Schools need to offer alternative, positive affiliations through sports, clubs, service groups, and clinics. These supplemental services require the support of parents, church groups, and civic groups. Where these positive alternatives are not available, and encouraged and made attractive, students seeking more affiliation may become alienated, or drift into gang membership and drug use.

Schools are among the most dangerous locales in many communities. An alert visitor to many campuses can quickly identify areas of a school where discontented students "hang out." Smoking and drug sales may be common there. These areas place many students' lives at risk (Hechinger, 1992). Teachers, principals, and security personnel know these areas, and in most cases can identify those students who are placing themselves and others in danger.

School personnel must be willing to intervene and to stop illegal drug sales and pre-gang activity on school grounds, rather than trying only to control the behavior. As a first step, the school should not permit drug use and weapons under any conditions. Administrators who allow such developments must be replaced by educational leaders willing to work hard to create positive environments for students. School personnel unwilling to help implement plans to ban drugs and weapons should be removed from the school. Employee unions and parents alike should support such actions to protect the safety of students, faculty, and staff. Schools cannot allow young people to make life-threatening decisions. It may be true that in some areas governmental authorities have not provided sufficient police and probation support. In that case, educational leaders need to recruit parents and civic groups to stop this introduction to self-destruction.

In addition to strategies for controlling behavior problems, a principal, vice principal, or a respected teacher should set up a class, with mandatory attendance, for all students in this alienated group. The class can study drug abuse, physical abuse, and violence the students experience. Local antidrug and antigang community groups, such as Narcotics Anonymous and Alcoholics Anonymous, and the local probation department may also become involved. The teacher may choose to hold separate classes for boys and girls to facilitate free discussion of issues of physical abuse, sexual practices, and other sensitive topics. By converting the violence of adolescents' lives into something for them to study and analyze, the teacher moves from coercive power to adult authority.

Many adolescents go through a period of exploring a drug- or gang-related identity. During this time they are alienated from their families. With appropriate support, most will mature to become productive citizens. However, ongoing crises in many families require that schools provide assertive leadership roles, substitute parent roles, for some young people. We cannot simply assert that this is not the school's job, that the school is to teach only subject matter, not life skills. Many adolescents need additional amounts of adult authority in their lives. Students need

guidance. They need help making fateful choices. They are full of fear about gangs, drugs, weapons, sexual identity, and similar explosive matters. Unless these students are helped, they will disrupt school and endanger their own lives (Fremon, 1995; Hechinger, 1992). If schools are silent, or ignore these issues, issues that are consuming students, then they become accomplices to the violence and terror of that part of society.

A Guide for New Teachers

Schools in minority neighborhoods have a high proportion of new teachers. Many experienced teachers transfer out of such schools to places where they can spend more time teaching and less time managing the classroom. Initially, new teachers experience a difficult time of trial and error. Their teaching skills are learned on the job through practice (Figure 8.6).

New teachers in difficult schools face a number of hardships, and students inevitably suffer from having less experienced teachers. New teachers often suffer from having to learn to teach with the most difficult students (Bradley, 1994).

As a new teacher, you will work with children from diverse cultures, and can benefit from getting to know the school community. Prior to the first day of school, you should travel around the community, visit its churches, its youth clubs, its neighborhoods. It helps to visit your school early to acquaint yourself with the principal, the secretary, and the resources you will need.

The school is not an island apart from the community. Teachers who arrive at school, spend their time teaching, and leave just after school will misunderstand their students. In the past, prior to the current concern for multicultural education, some teachers displayed an offensive colonial attitude in their relationship to school. They entered the community to teach. They received pay from the community, but they did not respect the community. They appeared like missionaries bringing out-

Figure 8.6   New Teachers Can Learn the Skills of Classroom Management

Effective teachers
*   communicate clearly and positively with students.
*   demonstrate concern for students' many conflicts, including gender and cultural issues, peer pressure, and academic success.
*   are respected and trusted by students for their fairness and equity.
*   set clear, consistent limits.
*   defuse or divert many potential disruptive situations with coaching or with conflict resolution.

side culture to the natives. This colonial attitude led to misunderstanding, hostility, and resentment. Most parents know that education and schooling are important to economic success, but a colonial relationship prevents mutual support and respect between teachers and parents. When a gap exists between parents and schools, younger children suffer. Older students and gangs exploit the communication gap to resist school. To avoid such strained relationships, teachers should think of themselves as employees of the community and make it their responsibility to learn about the community so they can use community resources and culture to support the educational program (Olsen & Dowell, 1997).

Instruction isolated from a community context too often fails. Quality teaching requires understanding children's reality, rather than holding a series of stereotypes. Knowing students' reality allows you to select experiences in their lives to build on.

One of the fundamental differences between successful middle-class schools and failing schools is that middle-class teachers in middle-class schools share the reality of their students. They draw from a common source of experiences for reading, writing, and skill development. When teachers draw from students' own experiences, it validates and empowers the students. In contrast, teachers with a colonial attitude seek to impose curriculum content on students. This imposition of culture invalidates and negates students' own experiences and culture. They are made to feel inadequate. They do not learn confidence in themselves, their families, or their cultural competencies.

For students to succeed, your classroom must be reasonably orderly. Teachers and students have varying tolerances for disorder. Teaching should start on time, and the classroom needs to provide a safe and orderly environment, an environment that encourages learning. You need to provide students with successful learning experiences, particularly in the first few days of instruction. You should start with a well-organized, firm process of management and discipline. When you are able to minimize disruptive behavior, you gain time on task, learning time (Figure 8.7). When

Figure 8.7 Minimizing Disruptive Behavior

1. Teach positive rules.
2. Teach positive roles.
3. Respond to small disruptions.
4. Teach responsibility.
5. Share responsibility with students through cooperative strategies.
6. Try to avoid power struggles. Provide students with a cooling-off period.
7. Maintain your adult composure and decision-making skills.

you have established order and have learned more about students' individual characteristics and personalities, you can move toward a more democratic environment.

All teachers benefit from personalizing their teaching. Personal influence, personal knowledge, personal contact provide you with your best instruments of instruction as well as the best instruments of classroom control. When you know students and communicate with them in ways that acknowledge their selfhood, such as learning a few words of their home language, your classroom environment improves dramatically.

You can be more helpful when you know your students well. Elementary school teachers master this problem with ease, while middle school and secondary school teachers facing 150+ students per day have difficulty. Instructors who do not learn about individual students are reduced to giving commands and instructions. This command relationship, in turn, produces student resistance. Such depersonalized relationships produce a significant portion of the discipline and conflict management problems of upper-grade teachers. Important school reforms suggested by the Carnegie Foundation for the Advancement of Teaching (1988) include breaking middle schools down into smaller schools of 250 students each. Such subschools could personalize teacher–student relationships and thus provide coaching and guidance.

Small steps, such as calling students by name and asking them about their interests, personalize your interchanges. You can use transitions between activities and time provided by cooperative learning to talk with students about their lives and interests. Students from cultures that value reinforcing interpersonal relations before engaging in business and task exchanges (such as Latinos, Asians, Arabs, and Native Americans) will particularly benefit from your efforts to personalize your teaching.

Teachers acquire a powerful set of connections when they get to know students individually. You will soon get to know the "good" students. To improve classroom control, make an effort to get to know the potentially disruptive student, the clown, the resister. Talk to them. Telephone their parents or guardians. This individual contact will give you information that will help you direct them toward cooperative rather than disruptive behavior.

Your efforts to personalize your interactions with students will help make your classroom a safe environment. Students respond more positively, more respectfully to teachers who treat them with respect.

It is easier for you, a new teacher, to establish a positive environment in the first few days than it is to dominate the class. A tense environment where commands are common and cooperation is minimal produces resistance and disruptions. Beyond grade 6, trying to win consent exclusively through the use of power is seldom effective with students, particularly when some are skilled in resistance.

This is not to argue for a hands-off, laissez-faire approach. Most students, except for those in kindergarten and first grade, already have experience with school and teachers. Students evaluate new teachers during the first few days to decide what kind of classroom to expect and to determine what they can get away with. It helps to make your goals clear: a safe and orderly classroom, clear and reasonable rules, a high degree of on-task learning time, and a personalized classroom where students and teacher all respect one another.

On the first few days of school, establish a few basic rules and post them where all students can read them. Rules commonly used by primary teachers include the following:

1. Only one student out of seat at a time.
2. Raise your hand to speak.
3. Keep your hands and feet to yourself.

Rules common to middle school students include the following (note the overlap with the primary school list):

1. Only one student out of seat at a time.
2. Raise your hand to speak.
3. No putdowns or negative personal comments.

Establishing a positive, productive classroom climate is particularly difficult in schools with large numbers of at-risk children. By adolescence, the cultural gaps between teacher and students are greater, producing miscommunication and conflicting expectations. Establishing a positive, personal, supportive environment can turn an ineffective classroom into an effective one.

You have both a right and a responsibility to provide an organized, calm classroom. Once you have established rules, enforce them. Students require more than just reading and discussing rules. Demonstrate, model, and practice appropriate behavior. If lack of respect for a particular rule becomes a generalized problem, reteach the rule and practice the behavior again. You will save yourself important time and energy by teaching and reteaching rules instead of trying to manage and control each individual child.

Try to identify management problems within the first few days of class. Some teachers have difficulty because six students need to sharpen their pencils just before an assignment, or four students come to them for assistance at the same time, or the noise level becomes intolerable when asking students to move into groups.

When problems appear, isolate and analyze them. Try to identify the precise behavior that is causing disruption, and then develop a process for teaching the appropriate skill and practicing the appropriate behavior. Learning school-appropriate behavior is like learning to play soccer; it takes practice. Practice improves student performance far more than does criticism and making demands.

As a new teacher, you can gain valuable insight by recruiting an experienced teacher as a mentor, someone who can answer the hundreds of simple questions you will have. You also benefit from recruiting an ally, someone with whom you can share frustrations and anxieties. If there are no other new teachers in the school, consider taking a course at a nearby university where you can discuss your concerns with other teachers.

There are a number of good guides for new teachers. For primary teachers, Bonnie Williamson's *A First-Year Teacher's Guidebook for Success* (1988) contains many useful ideas. Interested readers can find an excellent guide to classroom management in C. M. Charles's *Building Classroom Discipline: From Models to Practice* (1989).

Summary

Teachers need to use classroom management skills with a commitment to cultural and social democracy. Without this commitment, management skills lead to control, not to student empowerment. Neither teacher domination nor chaos and anarchy prepare young people to live responsible, democratic lives. Teachers can use management skills to promote a democratic, trusting, caring environment in the classroom.

Questions Over the Chapter

1. List three classroom rules that would reduce interpersonal conflict.
2. What three student behaviors in your classroom produce the most off-task time for students? What steps could you take to prevent these behaviors in the future?
3. Define *coaching*.
4. How can a teacher get enough work time for coaching?

5. What does Dreikurs describe as the four major goals of disruptive behavior by discouraged students?
6. Give two examples of personalizing the interaction between students and teachers.
7. List areas of authority where teachers should assert their adult-teacher responsibilities.
8. What are major in-school causes of class management problems?

Activities for Further Study of Classroom Management and Power

1. Consider a democratic approach to class management. Read Hoover and Kindsvatter (1997).
2. If you are having difficulty with class control, enroll in a workshop for assertive class management.
3. Consider new forms of student assessment (see Stiggins, 1997).
4. Attend a teen Nar Anon (Narcotics Anonymous) or similar self-help group meeting. Find out if there is such a group in your school. Listen to teens discuss their own experiences and dependency on drugs.

5. Observe a teacher conducting a classroom meeting at your grade level.
6. Contact your local probation department. Investigate what programs they have for schools, and for drug or gang intervention.
7. Role play a coaching session with a student.
8. Observe and participate in training for conflict mediators in a school district. Learn these skills.

Teaching Strategies

1. Decide on your three most important classroom rules. Post them. Teach them. Consistently enforce them.
2. After completing strategy 1, add no more than one new rule per week. Clearly describe and practice appropriate behavior.
3. Isolate off-task behavior and reteach the rule and appropriate behavior to those who are off task.
4. Step out of power struggles. Refer to strategies 1 through 3.
5. Use positive communications whenever possible. (See the suggestions given in this chapter.)
6. Teach and practice appropriate social skills.
7. Plan and implement a coaching strategy.
8. Teach the skills of conflict resolution to students.
9. Reread Figures 8.5, 8.6, and 8.7. Identify and practice ways to integrate these concepts into your relationships with students.

Chapter 9

Promoting Critical Thinking

The educational literature is full of terms such as *reflective thinking, inquiry, decision making, critical thinking, higher-level cognitive skills,* and *evaluation.* Educational researchers use such terms to describe multiple aspects of complex thought processes. Most educators agree that students gain from instruction in these critical-thinking skills. Such instruction teaches students to carefully consider ideas and to examine the assumptions they are based on. This instruction also teaches students to process evidence, to draw precise conclusions, and to limit their conclusions. A variety of instructional strategies exists to teach students a number of processes for gathering evidence, determining patterns among data, and stating the results of analysis or conclusions.

It is the classroom teacher who makes the most important decisions concerning teaching these processes. Teachers choose daily whether to stress equality or inequality, content coverage, skill development, or critical thinking. And teachers choose based on their own view of students and their learning potential, and their own view of society.

Teachers dedicated to building a democratic classroom recognize that teaching critical thinking plays a central role in moving away from inequality and toward cultural pluralism. Based on their own values and philosophy of democracy in education, teachers can make the important decision to emphasize critical-thinking strategies.

This chapter provides an overview of critical thinking, of critical-thinking skills and how, in many schools, low expectations for students and an overreliance on drill and practice activities have hindered the development of such critical thinking. Finally, this chapter will describe several strategies for teaching critical-thinking skills.

Critical Thinking Defined

Descriptions of the processes of thinking were developed in the modern era by William James (1842–1910) and converted into educational theory by John Dewey (1859–1952). They based their theories on the developing field of psychology and on philosophical works dating back to Plato. Philosophers, beginning with Plato, have argued that quality education should move beyond memorization of facts to teach the processes of learning. An inquiring mind and spirit are admired and promoted. Modern philosophers of education have advanced the idea that development of rational thinking should be a primary goal of schools (Arnstine, 1995).

Cognitive psychologists, notably Jerome Bruner and Jean Piaget, used observation as a primary research technique to further advance the theory that cognitive processes develop based on experience. Vygotsky (1978) amplifies and clarifies the important relationship among experience, social relationships, and learning.

Most teachers would agree that schools should teach students to solve problems, to make decisions, and to arrive at conclusions based on evidence and reasoning. The formal written goals of most schools and many curriculum guides include providing students with experiences in developing critical-thinking skills. A central task of multicultural education is to extend the teaching of critical thinking to all students so that our several communities can participate in the political process and vote to develop inclusive, democratic public policy for our highly diverse society.

We can begin to define *critical thinking* with Beyer's (1988) definition: "Our graduates should be able to make well-reasoned decisions, solve problems skillfully, and make carefully thought-out judgments about the worth, accuracy, and value of information, ideas, claims, and propositions" (p. 1). Paul (1988) clarifies further:

> A passionate drive for clarity, accuracy, and fair-mindedness, a fervor for getting to the bottom of things, to the deepest root issues, for listening sympathetically to opposite points of view, a compelling drive to seek out evidence, and intense aversion to contradiction, sloppy thinking, inconsistent application of standards, a devotion to truth as against self-interest—these are the essential components of a rational person. (p. 2)

A group associated with Paul's work, the National Council for Excellence in Critical Thinking (Scriven & Paul, 1994), defines critical thinking as follows:

> Critical thinking is the intellectually disciplined process of actively and skillfully conceptualizing, applying, analyzing, synthesizing, and evaluating information gathered from, or generated by, observation, experience, reflection, reasoning, or communication, as a guide to belief and action. In its exemplary form, it is based on universal intellectual values that transcend subject matter divisions: clarity, accuracy, precision, consistency, relevance, sound evidence, good reasons, depth, breadth, and fairness. It entails proficiency in the examination of those structures or elements of thought implicit in all reasoning: purpose, problem or questions-at-issue, assumptions, concepts, empirical grounding, reasoning

leading to conclusions, implications and consequences, objections from alternative view-points, and frame of reference. Critical thinking—in being responsive to variable subject matter, issues, and purposes—is incorporated in a family of interwoven modes of thinking, among them: scientific thinking, mathematical thinking, historical thinking, anthropological thinking, economic thinking, moral thinking, and philosophical thinking.

Critical thinking can be seen as having two components: 1) a set of information and belief generating and processing skills and abilities; and 2) the habit, based on intellectual commitment, of using those skills and abilities to guide behavior. It is thus to be contrasted with: 1) the mere acquisition and retention of information or beliefs alone, because it involves a particular way in which information and beliefs are attained and held; 2) the mere possession of a set of skills, because it involves the continual use of them; and 3) the mere use of those skills ("as an exercise") without acceptance of their results. (p. 2)

Conservative scholar E. D. Hirsch (1996) dismisses much of the emphasis on critical-thinking skills as romantic and unscientific nonsense. Darling-Hammond (1997), on the other hand, whose own work is in the areas of educational evaluation and policy studies, argues that Hirsch is wrong about the research evidence he cites and wrong about common school practices.

Critical Thinking for All

A recent focus of research on critical thinking has been on how "experts" reason and make judgments in comparison to how "nonexperts" reason. When monitored, experts in a field use a variety of testing strategies and intuitive leaps demonstrating more skillful performances than amateurs. A great deal of speculation on critical thinking, however, is egocentric on the part of the educated. Professionals describe and admire their own preferred behavior. What they actually describe is how they prefer to see themselves. Analysis of the behavior of self-described intellectuals (including college professors, philosophers and advocates of critical thinking) in a variety of situations, including university committee work and interpersonal relations, reveals that the traits commonly expressed as positive indicators of intellectual life are not always demonstrated in their lives or the life of the academy (Ryan & Sackrey, 1984).

Evidence has not yet demonstrated that the life of the university demonstrates more rational thought processes than say, the life of a corporation or a professional baseball team. Reflective thought resembles the process scholars admire, write about, and prefer to believe they engage in.

This romanticized egocentric view, coupled with the lack of precise analysis, leads to a common folk culture of schooling from middle school through the university. If the teacher presents the material and students learn, then the students are considered capable and intelligent. If the teacher presents the material and students fail to learn, then the students are considered limited or not bright. Many teachers respond to students they consider "not bright" by selecting for them drill, practice, and testing strategies rather than critical-thinking strategies.

This inaccurate and simplistic view of learning ignores numerous intervening factors including poverty, inadequate school resources, and the important subjective interaction between the instructor's communication and motivation styles and the corresponding communication and motivation styles of students (Bruner, 1996). Since these styles are learned in cultures, conflict between teacher and learner styles frequently produce failure in learning (Anderson, 1988; Ramirez & Castañeda, 1974). Because of the power relationship between teacher and learner, failure to master the material is blamed on the student and too often attributed to limited intellectual capabilities—an often inaccurate analysis.

Nonacademic Sources of Rational Intelligence

Most authors and teachers assume, without much evidence, that a critical, rational life develops in school. The Italian intellectual Antonio Gramsci (Aronowitz & Giroux, 1985; Giroux, 1988) supplemented school-based definitions by describing the role of "organic intellectuals" as those in the working class who demonstrate intellect based on their life experience, usually without being subservient to schools or university norms. Gramsci described persons without formal training who often develop the reflective ideal and assist others in reconceptualizing world–work relationships. Some parent activists and community organizers fit Gramsci's description of "organic intellectuals."

People are expert in a variety of fields. The rice farmer in Africa is an expert in measuring and planting rice. His approach to problem solving offers solutions not available to a novice planter, even if she were college educated. The pursuit of intellectual excellence is not an exclusive domain of schools and formal schooling.

If we are cautious to not confuse the lifestyle and culture of professionals with intellect, we can still agree that it is useful to pursue rational analysis and critical awareness. It remains a normative assumption that schools should promote intellectual life and intellectual integrity.

Although philosophers since Plato, and U.S. schools since Dewey, have been promoting critical thinking and rational processes, researchers do not yet know enough about human brain activity to describe the processes adequately. We operate from a series of hunches. One important body of work argues that instead of the recent focus on one, fixed definition of intelligence, derived from reductionist views of psychology, teachers should adopt the theory of "multiple intelligences" to explain the variety of student thinking patterns (Gardner, 1993). Developments in so-called "brain-based research" are beginning to suggest that teachers can select teaching and language strategies that are more compatible with the human mind, and which enhance learning (Pool, 1997).

Overcoming Low Expectations

Schools in poverty areas commonly use more drill and practice and place less emphasis on teaching intellectual processes than do middle-class schools. Drill and practice exercises keep children quiet, and they complete their work. Since many poor and minority children score low on standardized exams, a myth has emerged that these children are less capable of advanced thinking. A series of rationalizations, each based on biased or incompetent research or applications, developed to demonstrate the alleged limited abilities of poor children (Banks, 1997). Even some well-meaning research on cognitive styles has been abused to reach conclusions not based on evidence. There is no reason to assume that children from diverse subcultures have any less need for training in critical thinking (DeAvila, 1987; Miller-Jones, 1991; Rist, 1970). Teachers in multicultural settings face important decisions about what to emphasize in their classrooms. Too often these teachers are forced to choose between compensatory education strategies of drill and remediation, and critical-thinking strategies. This choice is one of the most fundamental decisions in choosing democracy. The power to choose lies fundamentally in the hands of each teacher. In this important arena of students' lives, teachers have more power than the legislature, school board members, principals, or unions. The choice for critical thinking is an expression of teacher power and a rejection of biased research, and reaffirms basic democratic values and your reasons for becoming a teacher.

The pattern of stressing drill and practice over critical thinking in de facto segregated schools has major social consequences. Under slavery, Africans brought to this country were prohibited from learning to read as a form of social control. In our present schools, social control is further advanced when students living in poverty areas, particularly students of color, are directed away from classes that encourage critical thinking and decision making and into classes that emphasize drill and practice and remediation. Promoting the development and practice of critical thinking must be a major concern in school reform (Adler, 1982; Boyer, 1983; Goodlad & Keating, 1990).

Critical thinking, or reflective decision making, should be central to the agenda of multicultural educational reform. Whereas many schools have not stressed thinking skills and processes enough, students of color and working-class students receive the least training in these areas. Many urban schools have an honors track or a magnet program in which thinking skills and processes are taught and a basic track in which students are incorrectly assumed to be incapable of abstract thought. Poor and minority students are regularly assigned to the basic track (Goodlad & Keating, 1990).

The process at C. Wright Mills High School (situated in a large urban district) illustrates how students of color are scheduled away from critical-thinking classes.[1] Mills is an integrated school: 23 percent Asian, 22 percent African American, 20 percent European American, and 35 percent Latino. Mills has a "magnet" program emphasizing the humanities and fine arts. Students in the program receive an excellent education stressing critical thinking and college preparation. Visitors to the magnet program are surprised to find 90 percent of the students are European American and Asian in an otherwise integrated school. Visits to the military science (ROTC) and vocational programs reveal over 80 percent Latino and African American stu-

---

[1]The name "C. Wright Mills" is a pseudonym for an actual school I have often visited.

dents. In this manner, a legally integrated school has tracks based on race, and students of color are tracked away from classes likely to stress critical thinking. Internal school tracking practices are common throughout the nation (Oakes, 1985).

We know that effective schools that serve working-class children emphasize higher-level cognitive processes (critical thinking) (Olson, 1986). Yet, in most schools with students from poverty-stricken areas, drill and practice exercises abound. Teachers respond to student failure by turning to behaviorism and reductionism and away from critical thinking. Worksheets and control replace efforts to motivate and encourage divergent thinking.

Teachers with low expectations of students design their classes in ways that produce students with low achievement (Oakes & Lypton, 1990). Low expectations include not expecting students to excel in reading and writing and not engaging students in tasks that require higher-order thinking. Low expectations are a primary factor in school failure. They are displayed in low cognitive-level instruction such as that demonstrated by an overreliance on worksheets and drill and practice. Combined with other school barriers to success, teachers' low expectations communicate to students not to expect much of themselves or their future.

No significant evidence demonstrates that children from minority cultures have less ability to perform high-demand cognitive tasks (critical thinking). Children from all cultures benefit from instruction in critical thinking and the related higher-order thinking areas. Schools and curricula need to develop learning experiences in which children's own repertoire of knowledge is used to stimulate their intellectual processes (DeAvila, 1987).

Instead of passively accepting the folk culture of low expectations for poor and minority students, try to develop strategies to teach critical-thinking processes. Failure in the areas of abstract thinking is most often a result of inappropriate or insufficient clarity in the presentation and practice of skills necessary for the process.

Teachers may ask questions from the textbook or teacher's manual and silence follows. Communication barriers may be caused by lack of attention to cross-cultural learning and motivational styles. Rather than assume a disability in the students, you need to examine the structure and pattern of your questions. When questions seek data from students' own experiences and are clearly organized on a retrieval chart, students from all racial, cultural, and class groups readily perform higher cognitive functions such as predicting and evaluating. Teaching that blames students for apparent weakness in reasoning is damaging and ineffectual. Rather than blame students, accept your responsibility to plan questions and lessons that help students to learn critical-thinking processes.

The Need for Teaching Strategies to Develop Critical Thinking

The "back to basics" movement of the 1980s most often led poor and minority schools to emphasize skill remediation and rote practice rather than problem solving. In spite of its importance, schools often pay little attention to critical thinking and seldom evaluate the development of critical-thinking skills. At present there is no conclusive evidence of success in teaching thinking skills (Brant, 1990; Cornbleth, 1985).

There are many reasons for schools' failure to focus on teaching critical thinking. The most obvious is that most schools have seldom tried. Teachers are hired and given a job to teach a specific body of content. University professors seldom model critical thinking in their content courses. Few students are trained to teach critical-thinking skills. Further, college courses are usually divided into content areas, and exams largely emphasize content. This problem is made even more difficult when districts hire "intern" teachers who have neither teacher preparation nor a major in the field they are teaching. Untrained teachers tend to teach without reflection. In schools where discipline is a problem, there is little motivation for teachers to believe in their students' potential and to emphasize critical thinking.

The growing emphasis on standardized testing influences the curriculum toward content memorization. Few tests exist that measure higher-order thinking skills, and those tests are expensive to employ (Hirsch, 1996; Popham, 1999).

When schools successfully teach critical thinking, students make well-reasoned judgments and solve problems skillfully. They also learn to make evaluative judgments about the worth, accuracy, and value of information. They learn to analyze claims, ideas, and ideologies.

Clearly, learning to think is not the incidental outcome of classroom study directed at subject matter such as history, math, or literature. Rather, development of critical thinking can best be approached by a direct study of the skills involved. In the primary grades, students should learn skills such as sequence, grouping, and categorization. These can be taught in one subject matter (e.g., reading or social studies) and generalized to another (e.g., science).

By fourth grade, critical-thinking skills become more specialized by subject field. Each discipline area can teach the appropriate skills with attention to their transferability. For example, the sciences can focus on observation, the use of data, and recognition of cause and effect. History and social studies can focus on identification of bias and propaganda. Reading and literature can focus on similarities and differences, point of view, and prediction.

The California Department of Education has delineated by grade level a precise set of critical-thinking skills for history and the social sciences (Figure 9.1). The California model is useful in identifying the subskills needed for critical thinking. Important elements missing from the California chart, however, include the processes of decision making and the more powerful conceptions of inquiry that move beyond individual skills practice.

Teachers used to assume that by teaching content they were also teaching the operations and skills needed to learn or process the material. There is, however, little evidence to support this assumption. From elementary school to the university, teachers have failed to teach the process of learning. Our citizens do not demonstrate a passion for fair-mindedness and accuracy. Our political processes are not typified by a willingness to explore difficult issues, a propensity for open-mindedness. We are not, in general, willing to suspend judgment and to listen sympathetically to opposing points of view. Particularly troubling, if we teach middle-class chil-

Figure 9.1   Critical-Thinking Skill Continuum for History–Social Science—California

3rd Grade	6th Grade	8th Grade

I. Defining and Clarifying Problems
  a. Makes careful observations
  b. Identifies and expresses main ideas, problems, or central issues
  c. Identifies similarities and differences
  d. Organizes items into defined categories
  e. Defines categories for unclassified information
  f. Identifies information relevant to a problem
  g. Formulates questions
  h. Recognizes different points of view
 	
II. Judging Information Related to the Problem
  a. Identifies obvious stereotypes
  b. Distinguishes between fact and opinion
  c. Identifies and explains sequence and prioritizing
  d. Identifies evidence that supports (or is related to) a main idea
  e. Identifies obvious assumptions
  f. Identifies obvious inconsistency and contradiction
  g. Identifies cause-and-effect relationships
 	
III. Solving Problems/Drawing Conclusions
  a. Recognizes the adequacy of data
  b. Identifies cause-and-effect relationships
  c. Draws conclusions from evidence
  d. Puts simple hypotheses into *if, then* sentences
	I. Defining and Clarifying Problems
	  a. Identifies central issues or problems
	  b. Identifies similarities and differences
	  c. Understands the concept of relevance and irrelevance
	  d. Formulates appropriate questions
	  e. Expresses problems and issues
	  f. Recognizes obvious individual and group value orientations and ideologies
	
	II. Judging Information Related to the Problem
	  a. Identifies stereotypes and cliches
	  b. Identifies obvious bias, propaganda, and semantic slanting
	  c. Identifies facts, opinions, and reasoned judgments
	  d. Identifies inconsistency and contradiction
	  e. Identifies assumptions
	  f. Identifies evidence
	
	III. Solving Problems/Drawing Conclusions
	  a. Recognizes the adequacy of data
	  b. Identifies cause-and-effect relationships
	  c. Draws conclusions from evidence
	  d. Predicts consequences
	  e. Hypothesizes
	  f. Reasons with analogies and generalizations
		I. Defining and Clarifying Problems
		  a. Identifies central issues or problems
		  b. Compares similarities and differences
		  c. Determines which information is relevant
		  d. Formulates appropriate questions
		  e. Expresses problems clearly and concisely
		
		II. Judging Information Related to the Problem
		  a. Distinguishes among fact, opinion, and reasoned judgment
		  b. Checks consistency
		  c. Identifies unstated assumptions
		  d. Recognizes stereotypes and cliches
		  e. Recognizes bias, emotional factors, propaganda, and semantic slanting
		  f. Recognizes value orientations and ideologies
		
		III. Solving Problems/Drawing Conclusions
		  a. Recognizes the adequacy of data
		  b. Identifies reasonable alternatives
		  c. Tests conclusions or hypotheses
		  d. Predicts probable consequences

Note. From *Assessment of Critical Thinking in History–Social Sciences* (pp. 231–236) by California Assessment Program, 1985, Sacramento, CA: California Assessment Program.

Figure 9.1 *continued*

10th Grade	12th Grade

I. Defining and Clarifying Problems
   a. Delineates controversy components
   b. Identifies criteria that serve to organize data
   c. Identifies fallacies of relevance
   d. Formulates appropriate questions
   e. Paraphrases accurately
   f. Distinguishes among diverse viewpoints
 	
II. Judging Information Related to the Problem
   a. Recognizes subtle manifestations of stereotypes and cliches
   b. Recognizes subtle manifestations of emotional factors, propaganda, and semantic slanting
   c. Distinguishes among fact, opinion, and reasoned judgment
   d. Recognizes subtle or indirect inconsistencies
   e. Demonstrates a sensitivity to questionable assumptions
   f. Recognizes subtle differences in judging the sufficiency of data
 	
III. Solving Problems/Drawing Conclusions
   a. Justifies the selection of an alternative
   b. Distinguishes between possible and probable consequences
   c. Concludes only what is justified by the evidence
   d. Understands opposing points of view and reasons with them
   e. Recognizes fundamental problems in causal reasoning, generalizing, and arguing by analogy
   f. Recognizes indirect or extended implications
	I. Defining and Clarifying Problems
	   a. Identifies central issues or problems
	     1. Distinguishes real and stated issues
	   b. Compares similarities and differences
	     1. Analyzes system similarities and differences
	   c. Determines which information is relevant
	     1. Evaluates degrees of relevance
	     2. Assesses different interpretations of data
	     3. Summarizes positions and their supporting evidence
	   d. Formulates appropriate questions
	   e. Expresses problems clearly and concisely
	
	II. Judging Information Related to the Problem
	   a. Distinguishes among fact, opinion, and reasoned judgment
	   b. Checks consistency
	     1. Recognizes subtle consistencies and inconsistencies
	   c. Identifies unstated assumptions
	     1. Recognizes unstated fundamental assumptions
	   d. Recognizes bias
	     1. Identifies emotional factors, propaganda, semantic slanting, stereotypes, and cliches
	     2. Converts biased materials into unbiased form
	   e. Recognizes value orientations and ideologies
	   f. Distinguishes between false and accurate images
	
	III. Solving Problems/Drawing Conclusions
	   a. Recognizes and assesses cause and effect and multiple causation
	   b. Draws warranted conclusions
	   c. Identifies reasonable alternatives
	   d. Tests conclusions or hypotheses
	   e. Predicts probable consequences
	     1. Assesses desirable and undesirable consequences
	   f. Demonstrates the ability to come to a reasoned judgment in reading, writing, and speech

dren higher cognitive processes, and working-class children drill and remediation, we are using the schools to promote social control and class stratification rather than democracy.

Instead of critical thinking, teachers often simply exhort working-class students to work harder. Criticism and exhortation have not served as effective critical-thinking teaching strategies for these students. Instead, teachers deserve assistance in planning their instructional approaches to encourage students to learn the skills of thinking. Emphasis on content, on processing content, on questions, and on worksheets do not, by themselves, help students improve their thinking. Questions may encourage thinking and, at times, may even provoke thinking, but they do not teach the skills of reflective inquiry.

The Constructivist Perspective

In the 1960s through the 1980s, advocates of critical thinking would term their psychological perspective cognitive psychology. Today they are more likely to term it constructivism. *Constructivism* presumes that teachers cannot give knowledge to students. Instead, students use received information to construct knowledge, and give it meaning, in their own minds. Teachers facilitate this process by using strategies that make information meaningful and relevant, by teaching students to use critical-thinking or metacognitive skills, and by encouraging discovery learning. The essential insight is that we cannot transfer knowledge from one person to another; rather, we can only assist students to construct their own.

We will use this text as an example. In Chapter 2 we discussed the nature of culture; in Chapter 3, race; in Chapter 4, class; and in Chapter 5, gender. These presentations, and your teacher's accompanying lectures, videos, and activities, did not give you a comprehension of culture, race, class, and gender. You did not accept completely what the text or your instructor said. Instead, you received examples and concepts, and developed your own definitions based on how your prior experience blended with the information received. Each student in your class defined these key issues differently. A constructivist psychologist would say that each of you constructed your own knowledge about culture, race, class and gender.

The constructivist perspective draws its psychology from the works of Piaget and Vygotsky on the social nature of learning, and from Bruner and cognitive psychology on the importance of discovery learning. Bruner (1996) describes the constructivist tenet as follows:

> The reality that we impute to the "worlds" we inhabit is a constructed one. To paraphrase Nelson Goodman, "reality is made, not found." Reality construction is the product of meaning making shaped by traditions and by a culture's toolkit of ways of thought. In this sense, education must be conceived as aiding young humans in learning to use the tools of meaning making and reality construction, to better adapt to the world in which they find themselves and to help in the process of changing it as required. (p. 20)

Direct Instruction in Critical Thinking

Cultural and linguistic minorities, like all students, should receive direct instruction in developing thinking skills. Separating the many facets of critical thinking into clearly identifiable skills allows each skill to be focused on, taught, practiced, and evaluated. In Chapter 8 you were introduced to the strategy of direct instruction to teach a new behavior. Direct instruction also works well with the initial steps of teaching critical thinking. To use direct instruction to introduce a critical-thinking skill, follow this strategy:

1. Select the skill.
2. Give clear and precise instructions.
3. Model the skill for students.
4. Have students practice systematically.
5. Provide students opportunities for practice under your guidance.
6. Assess students' abilities with the skill.
7. Have students practice independently.

Direct instruction is a useful strategy for initial critical thinking, cooperative learning, classroom management, and other lessons. Used in conjunction with other strategies, it provides a good place to teach essential skills. When students have acquired the necessary skills, you can vary your strategies. For example, you may use direct instruction to teach a student to compare. The student may then use comparison as a skill within more extended problem-solving tasks. Direct instruction can teach appropriate group roles for cooperative learning, after which the group can explore divergent and imaginative social participation projects. In the midst of an active project of experiential learning, you may want to reteach some basic skill, such as writing a paragraph, using direct instruction.

Sample Critical-Thinking Strategies

Grades K Through 2.   In grades K through 2, we should teach students lessons on grouping and categorizing. You can use students themselves as participants by categorizing them into groups, such as those with brown hair or red shoes or girls and boys. (Some teachers use ethnic groups as one of several categories for grouping, but it causes much confusion!)

Lessons on sequencing can also be taught. For example, students should recognize the opening, body, and ending of stories. Teachers can direct discussions about the concepts of cause and effect with students in literature, science, and other subjects.

The following lesson is from a split kindergarten/first-grade bilingual class in Woodland, California. The teacher was Lisette Estrella-Henderson. She describes the events:

The leg of the reading table which we had been using since the beginning of the year fell off one day without any warning. All of our materials went flying, and by the time we had finished cleaning up the mess, there was no time left to do the activity which the students had been looking forward to. Needless to say, my students were upset and frustrated—not to mention how angry I was, since I had asked the secretary to tell the maintenance department about the problem two weeks before!

I finally realized that the only way I was going to get any action was by illustrating to the administrators how their apathy directly affected my students. I engaged my students in a discussion about what they thought we could do about the problem. (They knew that I had already asked for the leg to be fixed once before.) It was wonderful and enlightening for me to see how their ideas developed and evolved as a result of thinking out loud and putting their ideas together.

The final consensus was to write a class letter explaining our problem and sending it not only to the principal but to the maintenance department and the superintendent as well. The students also drew pictures illustrating the situation and took them home to show their parents as they explained the situation to them. I had the parents and mainte-nance department at my door the very next day to fix the table, not to mention the visit from the principal and the call from the superintendent. I asked the parents and the main-tenance department to let us borrow their tools, and the children fixed the table leg them-selves! I could not have come up with a better problem-solving lesson that promoted higher-level thinking skills if I had planned it.

The students really learned that by combining their brains, physical power, and the skills of working cooperatively, they really could make a difference.[2]

Grades 3 Through 6.   To teach critical thinking in grades 3 through 6, teachers inte-grate lessons on evidence, cause and effect, stereotypes, and similar skills into the cur-riculum. For example, you could show a portion of the film *Amistad* and then have one group of students write a description from the point of view of the African cap-tives. Have a second group write a description of slavery from the point of view pre-sented in their textbooks. Each group should support its point of view with evidence.

As another example, after you give direct instruction on the concepts of sequence and character, students can read a work of literature and describe a sequence of events from the perspective of various characters.

Grades 6 Through 8.   Students can build a retrieval chart to compare the experi-ences of European immigrants with those of Native Americans, Mexican Americans, and African Americans in previous centuries and in the present (Figure 9.2).

By this age you can teach a decision-making process like the following:

1. Identify a problem and clarify the issues.
    *   Is the conflict definitional?
    *   Is the conflict empirical?
    *   Is the conflict value based?
2. Suggest alternative solutions.
    a. Have teams evaluate each proposed solution.

[2]From L. Estrella-Henderson, Woodland, California. Used with permission.

Figure 9.2 Sample Retrieval Chart

	American Indian	Mexican	African American	European American Northern/Southern
Reason for coming?	Already here.	Already in Southwest when Europeans arrived.	Slavery, brought in chains by force.	Economic opportunity and religious persecution.
To what degree is the group a victim of racism and discrimination?	Faced genocide. Still face some discrimination.	Forced off of their land. Still face some discrimination.	Enslaved until the 19th century. Still face discrimination. Terrorism used to oppress.	Incidents of discrimination have decreased after one generation.
Present status?	High suicide rate. Many continue to live on reservations. 50% urban	High school drop out rate is high. Current attempts being made to limit additional immigration.	High unemployment in urban areas. Some political power.	Assimilated into mainstream.

- • State probable outcomes.
  b. Plan a criteria system for evaluating each alternative.
3. Implement the preferred alternative.
4. Evaluate the outcomes.
5. Have students give an oral or written report on the process of problem solving.

At these grade levels, students might also develop a plan to assist immigrant students in their classroom or in the school. Then they may implement and evaluate it.

Grades 10 Through 12.   Divide students into teams. Provide students with titles of ethnic group and women's history texts available in your school or community library. Have each team select a period of U.S. history, and compare the histories of Native Americans, Latinos, Asians, African Americans, and women as given in their textbooks with the information in the library books. Students should consider omissions, assumptions, and the effect of learning a particular point of view in history.

Critical Theory and Critical Thinking

Critical theory, as described in Chapter 7, incorporates critical-thinking strategies and extends them beyond their positivist roots to include empowerment of students and oppressed peoples. Critical theory raises issues of concern with ideology and the social control of knowledge. When teachers raise this issue of the ideological loading of education and the curriculum, the political right often counterattacks with vehemence and vigor, accusing them of "politicizing" the curriculum.

The conservative school reform movement of the last two decades displaced liberal concerns of human relations and civil rights with emphases on "core knowledge" and standards in discussions of schooling and the curriculum. When social reconstructionists and critical theorists discuss the political and ideological content of current curricula, and when they emphasize critical thinking and the values of democracy and pluralism, this offends or frightens the conservative forces in education (Hirsch, 1996). Many of the most divisive battles over textbooks and curricula were provoked by the challenge of multicultural education advocates revealing the ideological control of the present curriculum (Apple & Christian Smith, 1991; Cornbleth & Waugh, 1995).

Critical theory encourages learners to always look at facts and theories in their context. Our educational systems, including universities, public schools, and teacher preparation programs, not only teach facts, they also teach norms, values, and acceptance of the existing relationship between schools and the economy (Bruner, 1996).

Critical theory denies that social systems such as schools are neutral, but assumes that, as systems designed by people, schools contain within themselves the values of the designers. The same is true of textbooks and of teacher education programs. Think about it for a moment. Is your teacher preparation program neutral, or is it based on a specific worldview and a specific set of values and assumptions? Critical theory seeks to uncover and to reveal these perspectives, these worldviews, and to reveal the hidden curriculum of schools (Carnoy & Levin, 1985; Darder, 1991; B. M. Gordon, 1995). For examples, see Loewen (1995) and Zinn (1990).

Critical theory adds two additional concepts to the discussion of how we know things: student voice and praxis.

Student Voice

Both critical theory and feminist pedagogy have added important ideas about the role of student voice in the classroom. In order to learn powerful knowledge, students need opportunities to enter into dialogue with other students, with teachers, and with other members of the community. Encouraging students' expression of opinion, of concern, is fundamental to developing their democratic interests. For example, having students write narratives, and then analyzing them in class, provides excellent opportunities for developing habits of critical and reflective thinking (Darder, 1991; Freire & Macedo, 1987).

Many language arts curriculum efforts have focused on developing and encouraging student voice. For immigrant students, this development is often in their native language; for African American students, voice may be expressed in Black English (Ebonics) (see Chapter 11). Language instruction has recently been substantially reconstructed based on recognizing the power inherent in students sharing their own ideas. The importance of voice, of adolescent voice, extends beyond language instruction to all areas of the academic and arts curriculum. Progressive teachers encourage expanding student dialogue and reflecting on student ideas (Wink, 1997).

We think through language; we cannot think or express thoughts we have no words for. Students with limited mastery of English express their most powerful and most intimate ideas in their home language. Teachers who use only English will prohibit the expression of student voice on many issues.

Freire's work in Brazil and elsewhere, along with the powerful messages of Martin Luther King, Jr., Cesar Chavez, Ernesto Cardenal, and others illustrate that when people find their own voices, when they can name their own realities, they begin an empowering process of problem-posing education. Students from silenced cultures begin a revolutionized form of reflective education through finding their own voice (Freire & Macedo, 1987; Freire & Shore, 1987).

Meier (1995) describes the important development of "habits of the mind" when schools encourage mutual respect between students and teachers, and encourage diversity and disagreement of intellectual issues. She describes her students learning to focus on ideas and themes across the curriculum. They do not find that critical thinking or reflective thinking is a product of a single subject matter area. Teachers work to integrate the school curriculum so that students can understand the unity of experience and knowledge.

Lawrence-Lightfoot (1994) provides dialogues and narrative about six prominent African American citizens. By reading their stories, by hearing their narratives, students and teachers learn about perspectives and about those persons who have been left out of history and literature.

Praxis

The concept of praxis is a second powerful critical-thinking tool that developed from critical theory. *Praxis* is the process of learning by doing and then reflecting on the activity (see Chapter 7).

As a learning process, praxis introduces students to critical theory. You learn to read by reading, to write by writing, to teach by teaching. But action alone, work and experience as a teacher alone, will not necessarily improve your teaching. Praxis is learning by doing, and then reflecting on (analyzing) and improving your efforts. Figure 9.3 diagrams the process.

Problem-Posing Education

Teachers encourage praxis though a process known as problem-posing education. Problem-posing education engages students in analysis and action on a problem (Friere, 1972). The problem might be anything from racial or gender stereotypes

Figure 9.3   Praxis

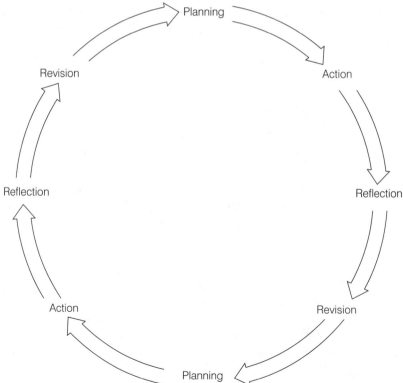

among students to an apparently irrelevant curriculum. Students set up a project to investigate the problem. Then, based on their investigation, they take a selected action.

For example, your students might believe that their math class is not relevant to the jobs available in their community. They could investigate the local job market, and compare math requirements there to the curriculum. Then, they may draft ideas about how the math curriculum could be made more relevant. This process will necessarily teach them more about math. Planning and posing curriculum revisions in an intellectually honest way will require significant math expertise. As they test their proposed revisions, they will learn even more. And so the process continues, with you serving throughout as coach, guide, and fellow investigator.

Multicultural education designed for empowerment should go beyond teaching isolated critical-thinking skills to encompass decision-making problem-posing education (Freire & Shore, 1987). Praxis and problem-posing education are powerful forms of intellectual development that involve more than acquiring a series of isolated skills. Problem-posing education encourages acquiring both skills and attitudes that support inquiry, discovery, and decision making. Problem-posing education assumes the radical, democratic stance that all students *and* adults can resolve their own problems and make their own decisions.

Knowledge as Design

Democratic multicultural education, building on the insights of critical theory, seeks to reveal the ideological domination that keeps political and cultural power in the hands of a small segment of society. Psychologist David Perkins developed a critical-thinking system termed *Knowledge as Design* that is useful for grades 4 through college to reveal ideological control and domination (Perkins, 1986).

The *Knowledge as Design* system begins by assuming that knowledge is purposeful. Most discoveries were made for a purpose. For example, Galileo described the solar system to explain a pattern he observed. The purpose of Galileo's theories was to explain. The purpose of Louis Pasteur's theories was to find a cure for disease.

After recognizing this general assumption, *Knowledge as Design* sets out to have students discover the purposes of *particular* knowledge. The system is especially useful and helpful with controversial issues and with issues of value conflicts.

You, as the teacher, help students to analyze an issue by pursuing the following questions.

Critical Thinking About the Social Construction of Knowledge.

Knowledge as Design:
1. "For what purpose?" (Perkins, 1986, p. 5)
2. "What is its structure?" (p. 5)
3. "What are some models or cases of the design?" (p. 5)
4. What is the history of the design?

5. "What are some of the connected assumptions?" (p. 5)

6. What are arguments that explain and evaluate the design?

7. If the design achieved its purpose, how would you know?

8. If the design achieved its purpose, what other purposes would it serve?

You can discover the value of the *Knowledge as Design* system and explore the social construction of knowledge. Simply apply the listed questions to some of the most controversial issues in your own teacher preparation program or in this course. For example, consider the variation in reading scores among African American, Latino, and European American youth presented in Chapter 1. Now, assume that this variation is not an accident or an error. Assume, for the purpose of analysis, that it is deliberate—it is a design. Using this assumption, look for answers to the *Knowledge as Design* questions.

Follow the same procedure with the preponderance of women in elementary teaching, teachers' salaries, the failure of inner-city schools, the preservation of European American domination of the curriculum to this time, or other value-laden or controversial issues.

When working as a teacher with students in school, you can save time by dividing the questions among several groups. Have a recorder from each group report on the group's findings. That is, if you assume that reading achievement variation is purposeful (a design), what purposes could it serve? You do not need to ask all eight questions about each topic, but it is important to ask at least four. Following this process will allow your class to move beyond mere repetition of opinions and advocacy of previously held positions to analysis.

Summary

In many schools, low expectations and overreliance on drill and practice activities have prevented students in poverty areas and students of color from developing critical-thinking skills. It is vitally important that teachers in multicultural settings choose to emphasize direct instruction of critical thinking rather than rely on compensatory education strategies. Teachers committed to establishing democratic classrooms can use the sample critical-thinking strategies described in this chapter to help their students develop the skills necessary for processing evidence, drawing accurate conclusions, and solving problems skillfully.

Questions Over the Chapter

1. What is the relationship between low expectations and teaching critical thinking?

2. List four critical-thinking skills appropriate to your grade level.

3. Researchers have noted that teachers in schools serving low-income areas and people of color frequently rely more on drill and practice and less on teaching critical thinking. How would teachers you know justify this decision? What are some consequences of this decision?

4. Which value positions or value orientations support teaching critical thinking in schools?

5. Why would the objectives and strategies of critical-thinking lessons be different in grades 1 and 2 and grades 10 through 12?

6. This chapter urges teaching separate critical-thinking skills in grades K through 6 and then teaching a decision-making process in grades 7 through 12. What are the differences between these two strategies? Do you agree or disagree with this approach? Explain your answer.

Activities for Further Study of Critical Thinking

1. Write objectives for critical-thinking skills about topics in multicultural education. (See the example in Teaching Strategies, following.)

2. Write lesson plans or unit plans that include the teaching of at least one specific critical-thinking skill.

3. Plan the evaluation of critical-thinking skills.

4. In a small group, research critical thinking. A good starting point is *Developing a Thinking Skills Program* by Barry K. Beyer (1988). This work offers a comprehensive and systematic approach to the topic. Report to the class on the potential integration of critical thinking and multicultural education.

5. A team of students can plan a multicultural education program without including critical thinking. Have the team compare their work with the work of the group that responded to activity 4.

6. In a small group of students, study the *Knowledge as Design* system as developed by Perkins (1986) and discussed in this chapter. Then, have each team member respond to the questions from *Knowledge as Design* about selected controversial issues in your university or classroom. Select someone from your group to report your group's findings to the class.

7. Prepare lessons for students to analyze their own K through 12 textbooks. Students can compare how the books portray African Americans, Latinos, Asian Americans, or women in literature or history. Have students write a comprehensive, multicultural, inclusive history of a week or a month in their classroom. Students will need to deal with significance, evidence, point of view, and similar problems.

Teaching Strategies

Critical-Thinking Lesson Plans

The following list of objectives will help you begin to plan critical-thinking lessons. Students will be able to

1. Cite evidence to support a stereotype.

2. Cite evidence to contradict a stereotype.

3. Form a conclusion about stereotypes.

4. Analyze school inequality from two points of view.

5. Analyze school inequality using the *Knowledge as Design* questions.

You may use a variety of lesson plans based on the theories of instruction that you favor. There is no one correct form or format. An actual lesson would include additional objectives and strategies to achieve human relations or empowerment goals in addition to critical thinking.

The following lesson plans are provided to help you as a new teacher get started in planning critical thinking. Your instructor may want to add additional components. For example, many teachers include a component on evaluation.

Sample Lesson Plan for Grades 2–4

Students will be able to

1. Categorize data as learned or inherited.
2. Group data based on the categories provided.
3. Recognize that students learn both at home and at school.
4. Recognize that culture is learned behavior.
5. Read words on the board.

First list the following categories on butcher paper or the chalkboard:

Things I Learned	Things I Inherited
language	hair color
food preferences	skin color

Then provide students with some clear examples of each category. In class discussion, have students categorize the skills and characteristics as either learned or inherited.

After students have made the first categorization, list the following categories on butcher paper or the chalkboard:

Things I Learned at Home	Things I Learned at School
language	reading

Then have teams of students meet to create lists using this second group of headings. A reporter from each team should share the ideas from that group. You then record the students' ideas on butcher paper or chalkboard.

As you summarize the information students generate, provide the conclusion that students learn both at home and at school. This conclusion is important to their understanding lessons on culture. See Chapter 2.

Sample Lesson Plan for Grades 8–12

Students will be able to

1. State a thesis and support it with evidence.
2. Arrive at a conclusion based on evidence.

First, introduce the subject of inequality and review the process of using evidence to support a position. Provide students with a model by stating a conclusion, supporting it with evidence, and then formulating a thesis. For example, you might use this thesis: Students suffer from unequal funding of schools.

Through class discussion, have students offer evidence to support this thesis. After a class discussion, have students draft a series of thesis statements on inequality. Record the theses on butcher paper.

Assign teams of students to collect evidence to support each thesis. Ask students to research responses to the *Knowledge as Design* questions focused on inequality (see the chapter). Allow each team 30 minutes to 3 days to collect evidence to support its position, depending on the subtlety of the inequality in question.

Have each team prepare a report on its research responses to the *Knowledge as Design* questions about inequality. Each report should begin with a thesis statement followed by the evidence the team has gathered to support it. Finally, each team reports its conclusions and supporting evidence to the class. Provide time in class for feedback.

Have each team write a short essay (1 to 3 paragraphs) using its thesis as its main idea, and presenting its supporting evidence. Allow each team to edit and improve its essay prior to submission.

Finally, offer a summary of the importance of using evidence to support a conclusion.

Chapter 10

Cooperative Learning and Multicultural Education

Teachers generally have chosen to structure classrooms in a win or lose manner, where competition and individual effort are rewarded or punished. As shown in prior chapters, the working-class students and students of color systematically lose in this system. As a part of the response to the challenge of teaching in the multicultural classroom, some teachers have developed strategies whereby pairs and small groups of students work together, learn from each other, and master the material while building respect, solidarity, and a sense of community. These strategies collectively are called *cooperative* or *collaborative learning*.

Cooperative learning strategies engage students from diverse cultures who may be alienated from the macroculture. This high-energy approach also has shown success with students across social classes whose interest in learning may have been dulled by rapid changes in society and an increasing dependence on television. Teachers can no longer assume that the home has nurtured in the student positive attitudes toward school and toward working with others. Using the cooperative learning approach, we can teach students how to build positive relationships with other students and with adults.

A variety of teaching strategies exist to encourage social interaction and collaborative learning, including learning buddies, jigsaw study, literature response groups, reciprocal teaching, and cooperative group work. (I discuss reciprocal teaching later in the chapter. For more on cooperative learning strategies, see Johnson & Johnson, 1991.) Practice and success in these activities develops what Gardner has termed "intrapersonal intelligence," a highly useful perspective for students' social, political, and economic future (Gardner, 1993). Development of intrapersonal intelligence and collaborative skills empowers students, parents, and communities.

Collaborative learning strategies take advantage of the complex relationship dynamics that exist in all classrooms—teachers instructing students and students interacting with each other. Students learn more when they talk about a subject, explain an idea to other students, and even argue about an idea, than when they hear a lecture or read a book. Rather than trying to suppress student-to-student interaction in the interest of "classroom order," teachers who use collaborative learning regard such interaction as an important learning resource, and they present strategies to capture this energy to support and strengthen learning. The total amount of teacher talk is reduced, and the amount of teacher-directed student-to-student interaction, and thus student learning, increases.

Cooperative learning provides both elementary and secondary teachers with strategies to teach positive social skills, such as listening, sharing, and working together. These lessons are particularly needed in depressed neighborhoods, where economic and social stresses combine to thwart student achievement. The process of improving group interaction is enormously interesting to young people, and they soon become engaged in creating a positive supporting classroom environment. They learn from one another.

Groupwork conducted within multicultural classes encourages students to exchange viewpoints, check their validity, and gradually engage in dialogue. It teaches students to work together, and reduces prejudice in the classroom (Slavin, 1995). Groupwork can move the class away from seatwork and worksheets to cognitively demanding instruction. Well-planned collaborative learning also encourages students to take responsibility for their own education.

Ladson-Billings (1994a) argues that collaborative structures and team building are important elements used by effective teachers of African American students. She states the issue thusly, "Culturally relevant teaching encourages students to learn collaboratively and expects them to teach each other and take responsibility for each other" (p. 70). The teachers in her study found significant improvement in their students' conduct when they taught collaborative skills. E. Garcia (1995) similarly asserts that consistently effective teachers of Mexican American children organized so as to ensure small collaborative academic activities requiring a high degree of heterogeneously grouped student-to-student social (and particularly linguistic) interaction.

Skilled teachers use cooperative groups to break down the effects of ability grouping and to establish high expectations for all. Cooperative strategies counter traditional tracking and ability-grouping strategies, which undercut student perceptions about equality of opportunity and democratic principles. Kagan (1986) cites evidence to suggest that cooperative learning can equalize achievement among students in subjects such as math and science, providing a needed step toward equal educational opportunity.

The use of cooperative learning results in improved academic achievement for many underachieving students. While cooperative strategies are valuable in all schools, they are particularly important in a multicultural environment because they produce high achievement levels for all, promote equal-status interaction among students, and teach students to work together to resolve problems (Johnson & Johnson, 1991). Cooperative learning is a direct way to teach positive intergroup relations. Kagan's (1986) research indicates that when students are taught how to cooperate and are placed in teams, student friendship and respect across racial lines increase.

The Tracking Debate

A sharp debate has developed around the nation over ability grouping and tracking. (Recall that in Chapter 1 we defined *tracking* as a system wherein individuals are identified according to specified physiological, cultural, socioeconomic, or academic criteria and placed in academic course schedules [tracks] designed to fulfill select educational prerequisites, develop a specific skill set, or prepare them for specific careers. See also "Tracking Female Students" in Chapter 5.) Most multicultural education advocates oppose tracking. They see classes for the gifted and for low-track students as contributing to the problems of unequal access to the curriculum. Significant evidence supports this view (Oakes, 1985). Advocates of programs for the gifted and talented argue that heterogeneous classes prohibit "bright" students from seeking educational excellence. They, too, have substantial research to support their position (Darling-Hammond, 1995).

While excellent work is being done by a minority of teachers to oppose tracking, most take ability grouping for granted. High school teachers accept that some students are college bound and others are not. Teachers often avoid low-track classes, and principals assign these classes to the newest faculty. Teachers in low-track classes find it difficult to establish positive, productive learning environments because many of the students recognize their low status and conform to the schools' low expectations. Students exhibit defeatism, alienation, and resistance to academic work. Soon both teachers and students develop low expectations of these classes. There is more authoritarian teacher behavior and more student-to-student violence in these classes. In racially integrated schools, low-track classes have an overrepresentation of African American, Latino, and Native American students (Darling-Hammond, 1995).

Not only are students tracked, schools and teachers—particularly new teachers—are as well. Schools in low income areas of cities often have fewer resources, and fewer fully credentialed teachers than do schools in more affluent areas. Schools in low income areas have more teachers instructing in a field other than their major (e.g., physical education majors teaching social studies). Meanwhile, affluent schools have only math majors instructing math, and science majors instructing science classes. Tracking occurs when schools considered difficult have eight classes of general English or math and only one class of honors or advanced English or math.

Even bright, motivated students in such schools will not have access to a demanding curriculum. When these students graduate, they compete for access to universities with students from schools where most students took advanced placement history, math, and English (Darling-Hammond, 1995).

You must consider several important issues when developing a professional view on tracking and ability grouping. Substantial evidence indicates that students are frequently identified and placed into ability groups based on poor measures and inadequate placement decisions (Oakes, 1985). Oakes and others have demonstrated that race and social class strongly influence the placement of individuals. High-track programs are available in middle-class schools, whereas urban schools have a preponderance of low-track, remedial, and terminal programs. The placement process itself is unequal and unfair (Darling-Hammond, 1995).

A major problem is that placement in low-track classes or low-ability groups is unnecessarily and inappropriately rigid. Students change and mature. Schools help students to learn. But rigid placement systems punish students for poorly informed or biased decisions made by students and faculty in prior years. The rigidity of ability grouping reduces the value of hard work. A fixed conception of ability and intelligence has long been abandoned by most serious researchers.

Being placed in a low track contributes to the several attacks on self-esteem that devastate many students—particularly adolescents, girls, and students of color. Ability grouping, as presently practiced, frequently contributes to racial, ethnic, and class isolation. Lawsuits in Boston, San Francisco, and other cities have challenged school integration plans that guarantee access for African Americans and Latinos to prestigious high schools by limiting access for European American and Asian students (Guthrie & Brazil, 1999; Walsh, 1999).

If these criticisms of tracking are true, then what about the arguments of advocates for gifted and talented programs? Aren't bright students bored and held back in "regular" classes? Haven't magnet schools and programs for the "gifted" kept European American students in urban public schools when they would have otherwise fled? These arguments also have merit. Changing to homogenous classes will not, by itself, overcome the failure to motivate and interest students common in too many classrooms. Without other significant improvements in the quality of education, ending ability grouping might simply bore all students equally.

In real-world classrooms, the two positions on ability grouping should not be treated as only polar opposites. Concern for equal opportunity leads to the conclusion that students should be primarily taught in heterogeneous classes. Teachers can change their teaching strategies to encourage all students to learn. Cooperative learning strategies are some of the fundamental strategies for teaching in heterogeneous classes (Cohen & Lotan, 1997).

In a few subjects that are highly sequential, such as math, students can be grouped based on their demonstrated abilities. That is, some students can study math while others study calculus. But these groupings are less harmful if they are not rigid. That is, while the students may be placed in a "gifted" class for math, they should be in a homogenous class for social studies, physical education, and other less sequential courses. Schools should offer advanced classes in art, music, and other subjects where students might also be "gifted." Also, students with special needs sometimes require special services to gain access to the mainstream curriculum. For example, limited-English-speaking students might be separated for part of the day to give them increased opportunity to learn and practice English. At other times, these students might be in a class that studies literature or some other appropriate subject in Spanish.

A change to a less tracked curriculum requires teachers to adjust their strategies. Most importantly, teachers need to consider multiple definitions of intelligence (Gardner, 1993) and abandon current fixed and static views.

Language-Minority Students

Collaborative strategies are particularly helpful in a classroom where some students have limited English skills. Placing students in teams provides second-language learners with a significantly improved learning environment by dramatically increasing the number of student-to-student exchanges. Those learning a second language usually understand these exchanges better than they comprehend teacher-to-student talk. Dialogue among students provides context cues and opportunities for comprehension checking missing from most formal teacher presentations. (In Chapter 11, I present additional strategies for oral language development through collaborative learning.)

Not only does groupwork stimulate the development of language skills, but it also increases learning across all subject matter. A teacher's professional vocabulary and interests often create a gap between presented material and students' prior knowledge. This gap interferes with learning. The student-to-student exchanges common in cooperative learning help to close the gap by allowing students to discuss presented material using terms and contextual clues that are meaningful to them (Vygotsky, 1978).

As you know, traditional strategies of competition do encourage some students to work. Collaborative learning does not replace the competitive approach, but it does add additional strategies to encourage the participation of students who may not flourish under individual, competitive practices. There is no evidence to show that time spent on cooperative interaction slows down academically talented students. These students actually learn more—not less—as they interact with the material in group discussions and explain difficult sections to others.

When students have practiced cooperative learning and have learned a few basic rules and roles (see Figure 10.2), groupwork resolves many classroom management problems. For example, students can learn to work independently on clearly defined tasks. One student per team serves as a task monitor to assist the teacher in keeping students involved in their team project. The teacher serves as monitor, helper, and coach.

Teachers in the middle grades (6–8) particularly benefit because they can spend less time trying to control the class and more time working with individuals. Well-run cooperative groups allow teachers the time and freedom to build the positive human relationships required for effective teaching.

Preparing a Class for Cooperative Learning

You must take four initial steps to prepare a class for cooperative learning:

1. Design the environment.
2. Select appropriate tasks.
3. Teach appropriate roles.
4. Encourage positive interdependence.

Designing the Environment

Students need to be *taught* to work together. Learning how to work in groups requires instruction and practice. To prepare for teamwork, design practice sessions so students can learn new roles and new social skills. Long-range projects covering a week or two are appropriate only after students have developed skills of coopera- tion and processing.

For very young students and for students new to cooperation, instruction often begins with extended practice working in pairs. In these early stages of cooperative learning, select tasks students can complete within 5 to 10 minutes. Later, combine pairs to create teams of four to six students, groups small enough so each student can participate. Assign one student per team as team recorder and have all teams document their activities.

Reorganize and rotate team membership every two to four weeks. Form separate teams for different subjects so students do not think that the teams are ability groups.

Require frequent oral progress reports from each team. These reports encourage high expectations. Any member of the team can use the recorder's notes and report for the team. You may say, for example, "The person to the left of the recorder will make the report." Distributing the reporting function helps to keep the entire team responsible for quality work. Encourage and monitor student participation by regu- larly collecting and reviewing team notes.

Teaching students how to engage in cooperative learning takes time, but there are no shortcuts. A lecture on role behavior is no substitute for practice. You must define the roles, help students practice those roles, evaluate the practice, and then help students improve their role behavior. Some teachers may be reluctant to divert valuable class time to this training, but time so used will result in time saved over the school year. Students who have learned on-task behavior and know how to work in teams to pursue independent study projects will more than make up for the time spent in learning these skills.

Teachers have developed a variety of team-building exercises to begin instruction in cooperative learning. Guides to these exercises can be found in Kagan (1989), in the video by Heredia-Arriaga and Campbell (1991), and in the "Teaching Strategies" at the end of this chapter.

Selecting Appropriate Tasks

Collaborative assignments work best when they provide intrinsic and immediate rewards based on successful completion of appropriately challenging tasks. These tasks should require multiple skills and encourage students to take diverse viewpoints. Whenever possible, draw on students' personal experiences as subjects for study.

Effective tasks for cooperative learning should involve conceptual thinking rather than a group search for a single right answer (Figure 10.1). Creative problem solving also works well.

Not all tasks are appropriate to group investigation. Groupwork lends itself to problem solving rather than to rote memorization of predetermined material. You can use a group structure for memorizing the definitions of adverbs and nouns, but it is more useful in helping students to edit their own writing. Groupwork is of marginal value in memorizing historical or geographical facts, but very useful for teaching critical thinking in the course of a history or social science investigation.

Teaching Appropriate Roles

You begin cooperative learning by teaching appropriate role behavior. The roles suggested in Figure 10.2 have proven useful in many classrooms.

Figure 10.1 Suggested Cooperative Tasks

Primary
Share feelings
Language practice

Upper Elementary Grades 3–5
Math problems
Language practice
Science projects
Reciprocal teaching

Middle Grades 6-8
Process writing
Language practice

Secondary Grades 9–12
Discussion of controversial issues
Process writing
Student governance
Social participation projects

Figure 10.2   **Suggested Roles for Cooperative Learning**

Checker: This student checks for agreement in the group and makes certain all students understand the answers.

Praiser: This student praises the students' efforts, ideas, and role behavior.

Recorder: This student records ideas and decisions and shares the final product with the class.

Task Monitor: This student keeps the group on the assigned task and monitors time.

Gate Keeper: This student encourages all students to participate and keeps any one person from dominating.

The several tasks of group maintenance are too complex to assign to a single individual. Assigning multiple roles allows all students to learn and practice leadership skills. Rotate role assignments within the group to ensure that each student acquires the skills necessary for each role.

Science and math projects often involve handling materials and objects, and it is helpful to assign some additional roles to group members. The Finding Out/Descubrimiento Project uses a "gofer," a safety monitor, and a cleanup director (Cohen, 1986). The gofer has the task of getting all materials to the work area. Assigning this role discourages dozens of students from getting out of their seats to get materials. The safety monitor remains alert for sharp objects, spills, and other safety concerns. The cleanup director supervises and monitors the cleanup activities for all team members. Once established, such roles assist the teacher and reduce stress.

Encouraging Positive Interdependence

When you use cooperative learning, you seek to establish positive interdependence among students. Arrange tasks and evaluation so the group does better when it cooperates. The task of broken circles is a good example (Figure 10.3). Students in a group are supplied with a series of parts to circles. Each group has all the parts necessary for all members to make complete circles. Group members are expected to assist their teammates in completing their circles. However, if a few students seek only their own success and ignore the needs of others, they will complete their circles using parts that their teammates need to complete theirs, thus preventing the group as a whole from completing the task.

Projects in which the entire group receives a common grade engender positive interdependence. Encourage teams to look for ways in which they can use to their advantage the artistic or mechanical aptitude of apparent underachievers. Kagan (1989) describes ways teachers encourage positive interdependence by establishing a grading system in which bonus points go to the team that has the fewest members

Figure 10.3   Simple Broken Circles

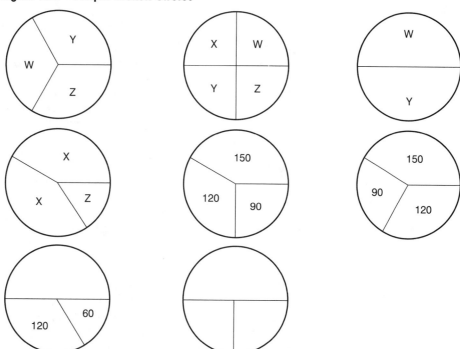

Note. From *Designing Groupwork: Strategies for the Heterogeneous Classroom* (p. 162) by E. Cohen, 1986, New York: Teachers College Press.

with low scores. He notes that students helping teammates to review basic multiplication and division improves the teammate's score, the team score, and all students' math competence.

Traditionally, grading systems and curricula of most schools have emphasized competition and the resultant sorting of students into winners and losers. Cooperative learning, and particularly group grading, counteract these school folkways (Figure 10.4) (Johnson & Johnson, 1991).

Reciprocal teaching is a strategy for assisting students to work in teams for reading, writing, and math. Teams regularly use collaborative strategies to improve members' reading and research skills. Each team member has a task for helping the others become more proficient. Students engage in dialogue and serve as monitors for each others' work (C. J. Carter, 1997).

Teamwork serves particularly well for social action projects in middle and high schools. The ideas and diversity of a four- to six-member student team bring originality, intellect, and creativity to bear on resolving real-life problems of classrooms, agencies, service organizations, and community groups. Teamwork skills developed in social action projects, like development of critical thinking, prepare students for employment in the growing world of knowledge-based industries. Projects provide a

Figure 10.4   **Differences Between Traditional Groups and Cooperative Groups**

Cooperative Learning Groups	Traditional Learning Groups
Positive interdependence	Little interdependence
Group accountability	Individual accountability
Heterogeneous	Homogeneous
Shared leadership	One appointed leader
Shared responsibility for each other	Responsibility only for self
Task and group maintenance emphasized	Task emphasized
Social skills directly taught	Social skills assumed
Teacher observes and intervenes	Focus on task
Groups process their effectiveness	Little or no focus on group processes

Note. From *Circles of Learning* (p. 10) by D. W. Johnson, R. T. Johnson, E. J. Holubec, and P. Roy, 1984, Alexandria, VA: Association for Supervision and Curriculum Development.

bridge from the passive-receptive behavior common to students in teacher-centered classrooms to the active and responsible behavior required in the adult world of work.

The proliferation of computers in classrooms offers opportunities to enhance collaborative work. Students often perform better research by working together in teams on computers, and can assist one another with technology problems. A collaborative, team approach to computer use encourages students to verbalize their thought processes.

Periodic evaluation of teamwork is critical. Teams should regularly monitor their processes and work on improving team skills. Figure 10.5 shows a sample evaluation sheet.

A Classroom Example

Miguel Hernandez teaches eighth-grade social studies in Merced, California, a medium-sized city in California's Central Valley. He wants his students to think about the world of work and their own future job prospects, to recognize the advantages of staying in school, and to improve their writing skills.

Miguel initiates the project by first discussing these issues and sharing a short autobiographical paper he wrote on schooling and his own job. He encourages students to comment on the paper and to critically evaluate its ideas.

Miguel directs students to move into their prearranged small groups. Each group spends about 8 minutes reacting to Miguel's paper and recording suggestions for improvement. Then Miguel refocuses the discussion. He tells each group to brainstorm ideas and issues the members could use in papers of their own. Each group delegates a recorder to write down all of the ideas. This brainstorming might last 10 to 15 minutes. Each team member makes a copy of the ideas from the recorder.

Figure 10.5   Evaluation of Small-Group Work

In addition to the information and ideas discussed, you should be learning to improve the processes of group work. The questions below were selected to assist you in evaluating your progress.

A. How well is the group working toward solving the problem?	Very Far		Not Far
defining the task?			
gathering information?			
sharing information from several sources?			
making a decision?			

B. What issues were discussed?
    Was agreement reached on any issues?

C. What strategies or behaviors helped to move the discussion along toward your goal?
    What strategies or behaviors interfered with progress?

D. How well are members of the group helping each other? Are members:	Very Well		Poorly
sharing?			
expressing different points of view?			
seeking solutions to problems?			
encouraging each other?			

After brainstorming, group members write a draft of an outline for their individual papers. Each student must record three to five ideas. Students are allowed to share and discuss their ideas during this time. If students have difficulty, the team helps them to draft their initial ideas. Miguel monitors progress during this time, visiting each group and offering his assistance if needed.

Once rough outlines are done, each student writes an opening paragraph based on the outline. Paragraphs are then revised to improve spelling and sentence structure.

Back in their groups, team members read their opening paragraphs aloud. This is called a *read-around*. The other team members comment and make helpful suggestions. They are encouraged to offer ideas on content, clarity, and style. Team members may also make "me, too" comments to affirm a writer's themes. Team members suggest additional ideas that might illustrate or support the themes. The writer takes notes and considers the teammates' ideas.

After all opening paragraphs have been discussed in the teams, each writer prepares an initial draft of the paper. Usually the drafts are short, one to two pages. Writers prepares their draft for further discussion by correcting spelling and sentences. If a photocopier is available, each author makes four copies of the paper.

The team now takes the time to read each paper and to make marginal notes. Members discuss each paper while the author takes notes, focusing on its main ideas, clarity of expression, and communication. At times, Miguel assigns tasks such as having one student provide feedback on sentences or paragraphs while another provides feedback on clarity.

At this point, Miguel groups the writers in pairs to rewrite, proofread, and edit a final copy of each paper. Once that is done, the papers are "published" on a copy machine. Finally, Miguel reads the papers, grades them, and confers with each student on how he or she is developing as a writer. Miguel's strategy for conducting a cooperative learning writing project is shown in Figure 10.6 in outline form.

After students complete the project, Miguel further guides them in processing the experience and in selecting social skills for future development.

Confronting Racism and Sexism Through Equal-Status Interaction

Cooperative learning helps teachers to deal with the societal problems of racism and sexism. It provides excellent strategies for directly working against different forms of prejudice.

Figure 10.6 Outline for Cooperative Learning Writing Project in Miguel Hernandez's Class

1. Brainstorm on themes	(Small group, 2–4 students)
2. Build an outline	(Cooperative)
3. Write first draft	(Individual)
4. Read-around	(Small group, 2–4 students)
5. Critique draft	(Small group, 2–4 students)
6. Redraft	(Individual)
7. Edit	(Pairs—Writer and team member)
8. Rewrite	(Individual)
9. Second read-around	(Cooperative)
10. Edit or rewrite	(Individual)
11. Publish/print	(Cooperative)
12. Distribute	(Cooperative)

Children Learn Prejudice

In a society such as ours, where racial, sexual, and homophobic ideologies contend with more liberal and humanistic philosophies, prejudice is easy to learn. Children learn prejudice, often at an early age from their parents and peers.

For students from stressed and disrupted families, where safety and security are often missing, misinformation and prejudice are often projected onto groups who serve as convenient targets to blame for problems in the family, the neighborhood, or the economy. In other families, the burden of learned racism is passed down from generation to generation.

Teaching students positive human relations helps to reduce prejudice by providing the support and self-esteem they need. Teachers must themselves provide a consistent model of behavior that respects the diverse cultures and abilities in the classroom. Your modeling will contend against other examples in society. You can bring up these issues by presenting accurate information, rather than stereotypes, about all cultural groups. The empowerment strategies described in Chapter 7 reduce prejudice by moving the potential victim out of the position of oppression. When students achieve equality, it is very difficult for oppressors to maintain their prejudices except by the most distorted logic.

Cooperation and mutual respect are central goals of the multicultural curriculum. You should plan for and work toward these goals rather than only hope that they will emerge in your classroom. Gordon Allport, in his classic work, *The Nature of Prejudice* (1979), says, "Prejudice (unless deeply rooted in the character structure of the individual) may be reduced by equal status contact between majority and minority group members in pursuit of common goals" (p. 281).

Cooperative learning that includes equal-status interaction strategies works against prejudice by providing students with regular experiences of mutual support, dependence, and caring. You consciously plan the control of status in your class. To achieve equal-status interaction, carefully teach the roles of group behavior (see previous section). Select group members and integrate each group to the degree possible by race, ethnicity, gender, observed talents, and perceived ability. Once learned, rotate role positions so that all students have an important function in helping the group achieve its common goals.

A substantial body of research shows that cooperative learning reduces prejudiced behavior in the classroom when teachers use planned interventions to control for social status. The effects of these cooperative efforts are strong and long lasting (Slavin, 1995). Few or no other strategies have as strong a claim to prejudice reduction, although combinations of strategies can promote school reform (Levine & Lezotte, 1995).

Students who initially do not perform well or who lack academic or cooperation skills are given extra instruction and assistance rather than criticism and avoidance. Place students who might be low status in high-status positions for group projects and assist them in performing there. Try to design cooperative groups in ways that ensure the distribution of high status to all, particularly to those who might otherwise be left out. Further, evaluate and consistently improve groupwork. Expect students to function well. This activity requires caring for and supporting all group members (Cohen, Lotan, & Whitcomb, 1992).

Consistent planning of role-playing simulation games and rotating roles within cooperative learning, along with planning status interventions, will significantly reduce the stereotyping, prejudice, and social distance between students in your class.

Students with strong acquired prejudices may resist working cooperatively in groups, but you should exercise leadership and insist on positive, democratic behavior in your classroom and in the school. Do not permit prejudices brought from outside to structure your classroom interaction. If some students resist even more, you may want to use coaching (see Chapter 8) to encourage them to behave cooperatively and respectfully.

Certain cooperative learning programs have developed a sophisticated approach to equal-status interaction among ethnic groups and between genders. Through careful planning and monitoring, students participate in equal-status role relationships rather than hierarchical or oppressive relationships. Prejudices tend to be reduced when students working cooperatively succeed at a mutual task (Cohen, 1986).

One of these programs was developed by Elizabeth Cohen, Ed DeAvila, and their associates at Stanford University. Called Finding Out/Descubrimiento, this program combines curricula, teaching strategies, and evaluations to effectively establish equal-status interaction. This bilingual math/science curriculum project provides numerous insights into critical thinking, classroom management, and group processes (DeAvila, 1987).

By rotating students through roles, all students practice and develop the skills of leading and assisting others. Students learn to participate with and depend on students from diverse ethnic and cultural backgrounds. The teacher arranges tasks so students must turn to all of their peers, not just the ones they may feel most comfortable with.

Planned cooperative learning encourages students to use the multiple talents in the group. Some cooperative learning tasks may require a good artist, some a good negotiator, and others a bilingual advocate. Cooperative projects demonstrate the slogan, "All of us together know more than any of us apart."

If you are teaching in a class with two to six (or more) children with limited English skills, design role relationships that place bilingual children in roles as experts. For example, bilingual children could serve as a translators from English to the target languages and from them to English for the group, allowing all students to learn. Bilingual children gain status by using two languages to communicate, while students learning English in the group are assisted in comprehending and participating in group tasks. Using bilingual translators in cooperative groups creates a win-win situation for students.

Most countries other than the United States use the metric system, and many immigrant children can excel in tasks related to metric measurement. You can enlist the assistance of immigrant children as experts when teaching this system. English-dominant students on a team reciprocate by helping these students with their English.

During the Civil Rights Movement (1954–1968), young people working together to solve problems of segregation and injustice learned to believe in their own worth and to make demands on the government for redress of grievances. Today, students from low-income areas and students of color seldom encounter opportunities to work successfully together for positive, constructive purposes. Teamwork in schools that focuses on social service and participation tasks provides the instruction in morals and values necessary to extend our democracy to include, rather than exclude, students from low-income families and ethnic minorities from public participation. Teamwork also involves students in social issues vital to their own future by helping them learn to respect diversity of skills, talents, perspectives, and the values essential to community building.

Cooperative learning empowers both teachers and students. Students learn problem-solving strategies. Student teams identify problems, draft solutions, consider possible outcomes of each proposed solution, implement a solution, and then work to overcome barriers. Teams working toward problem resolution provide excellent preparation for participation in a democratic society.

Classroom Management

Teaching cooperative learning in an increasingly self-centered, individualistic, and competitive society is difficult. Many children are not prepared to cooperate. You must teach the skills of cooperation and the attitudes supporting cooperation. You will need to use the classroom management strategies described in Chapter 8 to teach and promote cooperation.

Two groups of students are particularly resistant to adopting collaborative learning strategies: those who consistently win in the competitive classroom and those who have mastered the art of avoiding teacher attention and scrutiny. You must use a balance of cooperative and individualized learning to provide both competitive and cooperative students with an environment where they can succeed.

When a small number of students fail at cooperation, carefully reteach the skills and roles of cooperative learning. Teaching and insisting on role behavior sometimes need to be done assertively, especially in the early stages of learning cooperation. Later, once the groups are functioning well, new students can receive orientation and skill training from other students in the group (Johnson & Johnson, 1991).

You, the teacher, should address major problems of management, alienation, or nonparticipation by a few students, not assign them to the group. When one student refuses to work, it frustrates other group members. The task of correcting student behavior is potentially very divisive to the group, as most students have little or no experience in conflict resolution. They may resort to brutal and severe strategies. After several weeks of cooperative learning, these problems will decrease as groupwork becomes rewarding and students learn to prefer working together.

Heterogeneous grouping works best for most collaborative learning. After practicing roles, structure the groups for integration of ethnic, gender, class, and perceived ability levels within the teams. When cooperative work is initiated prior to second grade, interethnic tensions are quickly reduced. Interethnic cooperation may take time with older children.

In communities where racial hostility is significant, weeks of student preparation and extended social skill practice will enhance the success of cooperative groups. For example, in a recently integrated school or in a school to which children of different ethnicities are bussed long distances, students need clear goals and rules of conduct for working together. They need to practice social skills as a part of preparation for collaborative work. Team-building activities can contribute to the creation of an equal status, integrated environment. Systematic development of cooperative learning in the classroom will reduce ethnic divisions in class and contribute to reducing violence in the school.

Cooperative learning produces a change in classroom management. The noise level often increases in classrooms using groupwork. Teachers and administrators learn to distinguish between productive, on-task noise and idle chatter. As students develop increasing skills in cooperation, your role changes from one of struggling for control to one of giving direction and guidance. You will spend more time establishing the cooperative environment and designing tasks for it and less time criticizing students for their behavior. Initially, designing appropriate tasks takes a great deal of time and ingenuity. Fortunately, once designed, the tasks are useful year after year. You will gain time, ideas, and support by working with other teachers—cooperating—in project design.

Summary

Schools and teachers need additional strategies to respond to the growing diversity of U.S. society and the growing alienation of some students. The recent development of collaborative and cooperative teaching strategies provides a direct and interesting approach to democratic, multicultural education. Cooperative learning empowers students and teaches self-confidence as well as a sense of responsibility for the welfare of others. It also teaches students to listen, to share, and to advocate for their own interests. Cooperative learning strategies change the relationship between teacher and student to promote person-to-person dialogue and a sharing community in the classroom.

Questions Over the Chapter

1. What are some skills for grades K through 3 that are taught through collaborative learning?
2. Define *tracking*. Are there examples of tracking in your school?
3. What are the results of tracking?
4. Give examples of groupings that are not tracked.
5. Why do many teachers assume that tracking is beneficial?
6. As a student teacher, would you rather work in a high-tracked class or a mixed-ability class? Explain your preference.
7. How would you prepare differently for teaching the two different classes?

8. Do you support special classes for the gifted? Explain.
9. Do you support "magnet" programs? Explain.
10. How can cooperative learning provide an alternative to tracking?
11. What new social skills do students need to learn as a teacher "de-tracks" a class?
12. What are advantages of heterogeneous grouping?

Activities for Further Study of Cooperative Learning

1. Teach the cooperative skills lessons presented in this chapter to your students. Plan lesson plans for your class using cooperative strategies.
2. After teaching cooperative skills to your students, periodically assess their use of cooperation (see Figure 10.5) and identify skills you need to reteach.
3. Use coaching sessions to teach the skills of cooperation to a group of students in your class who will serve as assistants and tutors for language-minority students. Plan time for them to work together to advance language learning.
4. Investigate and use the strategies for assigning status within cooperative learning as developed by Cohen and Lotan (1997).

Teaching Strategies

Sample Objectives for Cooperative Learning Lessons
Students will
1. Work cooperatively in a group.
2. Share materials with others.
3. Stay on the subject while working in the group.
4. Listen to other members of the group.
5. Gather information by listening to others.
6. Contribute ideas to others in the group.
7. Accurately report on the group's progress.
8. Assist other members of the group.
9. Serve in a specific role (for example, checker, task monitor, etc.).
10. Contribute to improving the process of the group.
11. Select a skill for the group to work on next.
12. Evaluate the effectiveness of the group.
13. Plan and practice group improvement.

Sample Lesson Plans for Cooperative Learning
Lessons in cooperative learning teach values, skills, content, and critical thinking while using cooperative strategies. The following lessons focus only on the cooperative strategies. You should add content, values, and skills to these preliminary lessons.

Grades 1–3
Students will
1. Listen to others.
2. Work in a group (or pairs).
3. Get to know other students in the class.
   Have students line up based on height (from shortest to tallest). Other variables for lineups might include number of brothers and sisters, birth dates, etc. Once lined up, the person at one end steps forward and walks to the opposite end. The persons second from the end will follow in a line.
   The students are now facing a partner. Designate which line of students should share their ideas first. Select some easy-to-answer question, such as What is your favorite ice cream, food, television show, sport, or game? or What do you like to do after school?

Students in the first line share their responses to your questions. Then students in the second line share their responses to the same questions.

Have students return to their seats and pose to them sample discussion questions such as these: What is one thing you learned about your classmate? What did you do to show you were a good listener? Praise students who exhibit specific examples of positive social and academic skills during the activity.

Grades 4–8
Students will
1. Work cooperatively in a group.
2. Stay on the subject while working in a group.
3. Practice specific role behavior (checker, task monitor, etc.).
4. Contribute to improving the group's functioning.

Present the specific roles shown in Figure 10.2. Describe and discuss each role.

Provide the task. Each group will discuss cooperation. Each group should make a list of the advantages and disadvantages of cooperation. The assigned persons will practice their roles within each group.

After an eight-minute work session, each group reports on their list. Each member of the group gives one evaluative remark to the checker. The group plans to improve the practice of working as a team. Rotate the roles one person to the right, so each group member has a new role to practice.

The group discusses improved group functioning, with each student practicing the new role. Provide an evaluation system in advance. Have the students evaluate how well the group members are sharing opinions and how well they respect the points of view of others.

Evaluate the discussion. Then summarize the skills practiced this day. Use these skills with discussions again the next day.

Grades 8–12
Students will
1. Work cooperatively in a group.
2. Define the task prior to beginning work.
3. Consider the viewpoints of others.
4. Give feedback to each other.
5. Decide to reduce the name calling in class.

Divide the class into small groups and assign appropriate roles. Instruct students on the importance of clearly defining the task prior to initiating group discussion.

Provide the task. Each group is to decide on three suggestions for reducing the use of derogatory names in class. In a small-group discussion, each group member should suggest ideas.

Each person should practice their assigned role. Have the reporter from each group report on the group's ideas. Record the ideas on the chalkboard. Later, students could make charts of these ideas for posting in the class.

Select the three to five most common or most interesting suggestions. Assign two groups this task: Describe the positive and negative consequences of these suggestions.

Assign two other groups this task: List the influences that will assist or prevent students from following these suggestions.

Have the recorder in each group report for the group.

Have the groups evaluate their work, using a form like that shown in Figure 10.5.

As the teacher, you should comment on positive and helpful behavior observed while the groups were working. Remind students of the importance of having a clear definition of the task prior to beginning work.

Chapter 11

Teaching Language-Minority Populations

with Kathryn Singh and Diane Cordero de Noriega

Do you think that "English is under attack?" If so, from whom?

What should you as a teacher do when you have three or four students in your class who do not speak English well? What assistance, and what special skills, do you need?

This chapter will provide information for teachers working with language-minority students. Helping these students to learn English and to succeed in school requires you to both have accurate information and develop new teaching strategies.

Language-Minority Students in the Schools

In periodic waves in the 1980s and 1990s, immigration and immigrants became a focus of concern in the nation and our schools. Worldwide economic restructuring, increased ease of transportation, and changes in U.S. immigration law produced major increases in immigration to the United States. While in the 1970s the United States received some 400,000 immigrants per year, by 1997 that figure increased to over 900,000 per year. Even though the number of immigrants has increased significantly, current immigration is proportionally less than European immigration of the late nineteenth century. In 1910 immigrants made up 15 percent of the national population, while today they make up only 9. 3 percent (U.S. Bureau of the Census, 1998a).

Schools and employment are the entrance points into our society for many new immigrants. Some immigrants bring families with them. Children born here of immigrant parents are immediately citizens of the United States and are eligible for all school services. Recent immigrant populations, particularly Latino and Asian, are young people and usually have a higher number of children entering school than do U.S.-born European Americans (Fix & Passel, 1994). Each year thousands of new immigrant children enter school speaking a home language other than English.

The 1990 U.S. Census estimated that over 5 million students in our schools speak native languages other than English (U.S. Bureau of the Census, 1993). Although Spanish was the predominant language after English (54%), more than 20 other languages have significant numbers of speakers concentrated within specific communities. The number of schoolage children (ages 5–17) living in households where a non-English language is spoken was 7.9 million, or 14 percent of the total schoolage population. Language representation was as follows: 54.4 percent Spanish, 8.8 percent French, 7.3 percent Chinese, 6.5 percent Vietnamese, 2.5 percent Native American, 1.7 percent Cambodian, 1.6 percent Pilipino/Tagalog, 1.5 percent Hmong, 1.3 percent Korean, and 14.5 percent other (Pérez, 1998).

For almost 100 years, schools served as the primary vehicle to "Americanize" immigrants. They taught the children of immigrants to speak English. From the 1870s until the 1940s, many—even most—immigrants failed in school and left school prior to eighth grade (Rothstein, 1998). In an industrializing economy, there were jobs for unskilled labor. Today, the rapid change toward a technology-based economy has eliminated many of these jobs and lowered the wage scale for unskilled labor. School dropouts no longer have access to well-paying industrial jobs and economic opportunity. Schools must now prepare immigrant students for entrance into the new, high-technology economy.

Immigrant and language-minority students have unique educational needs that, when met, result in their successful integration into the rapidly changing economy. Immigrant students primarily learn the structure and rules of the dominant culture—particularly the English language—in school. Schools in certain states (New York, Florida, Illinois, Massachusetts, Hawaii, California, and Texas) are heavily affected by the rapid growth of the limited-English-speaking population. New immigrants and new language-minority children are a fact of life in schools throughout the nation.

Immigrant students bring enormous language and cultural skills to our classrooms. They arrive at school with the knowledge and wisdom of many cultures. They and their families have learned to survive in many lands. Classrooms with immigrant students are filled with knowledge about societies, customs, and languages that English-speaking students need to study. All immigrant students can and should learn English. Many will become bilingual, speaking both English and their home language. Bilingualism, particularly literate bilingualism, provides these students with a distinct advantage in the emerging global marketplace. As Cummins (1996) asks, by what peculiar twist of logic have these immigrant students and their language resources been construed as a problem to our schools?

Recent linguistic research indicates that instruction provided by bilingual teachers and sheltered English programs (modified instruction that is comprehensible to English-language learners) offer the best way to encourage students toward academic success and employment (Collier, 1995; Ramirez, Yuen, & Ramey, 1991). However, none of the states with large concentrations of immigrant students has an adequate number of bilingual teachers to serve the rapidly growing student populations.

Each immigrant group, each language group, has its own culture and experiences. Language, experiences, traditions, and cultures all vary dramatically. Even within a cultural group, children who have spent most of their lives in the United States have experiences substantially different from those of recent immigrant students (Figure 11.1).

A movement called "English First" has emerged in the United States. Proponents believe that diversity in schools is a new "problem" and that it should not be addressed by providing bilingual instruction. English First advocates believe that bilingual education is a new, unproven approach and that current and future students should follow the path of past immigrants who just jumped in and learned English through a "sink or swim" approach (Crawford, 1991). Unfortunately, we have learned through the experiences of numerous students and educators that immersion can be a very painful and unsuccessful process for learning English and for acquiring academic material. Those who were immersed in the pool of English did not always succeed.

Adaljiza Sosa Riddle, currently a Ph.D. professor of political science at the University of California at Davis, tells what the sink-or-swim programs were like for her as a young child (personal communication, 18 May 1998):

> I speak as a child of immigrants who attended a public school system in southern California in the 1940s–1950s prior to the development of bilingual programs. I, along with 2530 other poor children of Mexican immigrants, entered kindergarten speaking only Spanish. We did not know how to read or write anything. We learned a second language by coercion, fear, intimidation, punishment, shame, and the need to survive. There was no pleasure in anything we did in school. Even making valentines was a dreaded activity. It seemed to us as if teachers stayed up late to devise new means to torture us. It was no wonder that only half of my classmates finished high school and none went to college, even when they were clearly capable.
>
> Our acquisition of English was uneven within each class, and even within each family. Our ability to learn Spanish beyond the level of a 5-year-old was completely thwarted. I was lucky because my parents and my oldest sister had taught themselves to read and write Spanish and they in turn taught me as best they could. This was very difficult in a family of nine children and extreme poverty. The loss of talent was indeed great, unhealthy, and destructive. I don't praise myself for surviving that. Instead, I am brought to tears remembering all those years.

Figure 11.1   **Success Stories**

Miguel Perez

After fleeing with his mother from the war in El Salvador, Miguel Perez entered the United States illegally. He struggled for years to learn English and to stay in this country. Soon after he came to the United States, his mother died. Once he was even ordered deported by the Immigration and Naturalization Service. However, in 1992 he graduated as valedictorian of his class from California State University–Dominguez Hills and is currently studying health education in Pennsylvania. He won his case with the INS and received permanent resident status. When eligible, he wants to become a U.S. citizen.

Moa Vang

At age nine, Moa and his family walked three weeks to flee the invasion of their village in Laos. Half of his family died en route to the refugee camps in Thailand. After four years in the camps, Moa and one brother were allowed to come to the United States. A sponsor took him in and helped him to succeed in school. As a refugee, he did not have the fear of deportation experienced by Miguel. Now 34, Moa has spent over a decade getting permission for other family members to immigrate. The war, the refugee camps, the difficulty of immigration and adjustment have devastated his family and much of his community. After working for three years as a teacher assistant, Moa began the long, difficult task of becoming a teacher.

Ann Ngo Tran

As a young girl, Ann remembers life in Vietnam. Then, she and her family had to flee. Because her father worked in the military, they were able to fly out of Saigon. Many members of her family were left behind. When she arrived in Portland, Oregon, Ann spoke only a few words of English, but she was able to attend school and struggled to learn English. The stresses of migration and learning to live in this country have produced great divisions in her family. One brother is a gang member. But Ann is a respectful daughter. She has watched her generation achieve and has watched her parents' generation struggle with their loss. She has now graduated from college and become a bilingual teacher, hoping to assist other immigrant students with their difficult transitions.

The descriptions of Moa and Ann are composites drawn from the experiences of several students in the bilingual program at California State University, Sacramento.

History of Bilingualism in the United States

Bilingualism has a long history in our nation of immigrants. Forms of bilingual education were common practice in the early years of the nation. The framers of the Constitution considered guaranteeing German language rights. Spanish language rights were implied in the Treaty of Guadalupe Hidalgo (1848, by which the United States acquired the Southwest from Mexico) and were explicit in California's and New Mexico's first state constitutions (Crawford, 1991).

From 1880 to 1910, the United States experienced massive migration from Europe and Mexico. In response, fraternal and social organizations were formed to limit immigration and to insist on the dominance of English. During World War I, government-sponsored anti-German pressures led to the cancellation of German language schools, and several states passed laws restricting schools to using English only. Public schools were charged to promote rapid assimilation of immigrants and to encourage the use of the "American" language (Crawford, 1991).

Policies to eliminate ethnic enclaves and use of foreign languages were advocated as good for students. Crude and inaccurate racial theories developed, based on early Darwinism, to argue for the superiority of Anglo Saxon culture against Greeks, Slavs, Italians, Mexicans, and other immigrants (Crawford, 1991; Omi & Winant, 1986). A legend began circulating that U.S. schools served as the vehicle for immigrant opportunity, in spite of significant evidence to the contrary (Aronowitz, 1973; Boyer & Morais, 1955; Colin, 1975; Davis, 1986). In this period, leaving school early was not viewed as a crisis; a young person could get a job in industry with little formal schooling or preparation.

In a diverse, fragmented, and at times divisive society, language uniformity became an important political movement advocated by conservative business groups. Crawford (1991) notes that Henry Ford made attendance at Americanization classes mandatory for foreign-born workers. If immigrants used Polish, Yiddish, or Finnish to organize radical unions, conservatives used their control of government to promote "Americanism" by developing language uniformity. Insistence on speaking English was an important mechanism for weakening ethnic group loyalty and group support for labor unions. Speaking English became the approved way for immigrants to "Americanize" their families (Crawford, 1991; Davis, 1986).

During the 1920s, in response to these pressures and partly in reaction to World War I, prior academic interest in "foreign languages" declined and English became the exclusive language of the educated in the United States. Speaking a second or third language lost status and value. Instead of considering the language abilities of immigrants as important resources, teachers urged immigrant children to speak English and to forget the language of their parents and family. Greek immigrants were discouraged from teaching their native language to their children while university doctoral candidates struggled to learn Greek to read the Bible, Plato, and Aristotle. The Bureau of Indian Affairs operated boarding schools and applied harsh measures to promote English over tribal languages (Crawford, 1991).

Language domination became closely connected with "Americanism" in popular culture until the 1950s. Only the competition with the Soviets in the Cold War finally called into question these English-only and English-first policies. In 1959, a rebel army led by Fidel Castro wrested control of Cuba from the U.S.-backed Batista government. The new Castro government turned to the Soviet Union for support and adopted a Soviet-style authoritarian government. Over 100,000 Cubans fled to the United States. The U.S. government rushed to provide substantial resettlement costs to anticommunist Cuban refugees and their families, including provisions for temporary bilingual schools in Florida (Crawford, 1991).

In the same era as the Cuban exodus, the Civil Rights Movement (1954–1968) in the United States emphasized educational reform as a strategy to gain equal economic opportunity for minorities. A Mexican American political movement and an emerging Chicano student movement in the Southwest (1958–1980) demanded bilingual education programs to overcome the educational barriers faced by Spanish-speaking children (U.S. Commission on Civil Rights, 1975). Legislators were convinced to include provisions prohibiting the denial of state services and voting rights on the basis of language in the 1964 Civil Rights Act. The language provisions of this act became the legal basis for bilingual education in the United States.

In 1974, in *Lau v. Nichols*, a federal judge ruled that the San Francisco School District violated the 1964 Civil Rights Act. The judge ordered the district to provide instruction that Chinese-speaking children could understand, establishing the principle that children have a right to instruction that they can understand in the public schools. The court ordered the district to develop remedies to overcome existing inequalities of opportunity.

The *Lau* decision did not require a school district to implement any specific remedy, such as bilingual education. It listed bilingual education as one of several available legal options. Subsequent federal court decisions, such as *Castañeda v. Pickard* (1974) and *Keyes v. School District #1* (1983), further required that districts provide a quality program, with trained teachers, that would provide students with equal access to the regular curriculum, and that programs collect data to demonstrate their adequacy (Crawford, 1991).

Bilingual Education in California

State laws were established to guide school districts in providing special programs for limited English proficient (LEP) students. By 1976, California had one of the strongest bilingual education laws in the nation. Even with this law, some 50 percent of children legally eligible for bilingual assistance received only Individualized Learning Programs (ILP) (Crawford, 1991). These individualized programs pulled children from their regular classrooms for a very limited amount of time, for a special class in English as a second language. For the rest of the day, they were submerged in an English-only environment. Few of these "bilingual programs," had a consistent and organized approach to language acquisition.

In 1976, the California Legislature passed a bilingual education law with a 10-year authorization. In 1986, the required reauthorization bill passed both houses of the legislature and was then vetoed by the Republican governor. Since then, revisions to the bill have passed the legislature four times, only to be vetoed each time by the governor. The present legal status of bilingual education in California relies on federal court decisions. The California experience is representative of the attacks on bilingual education in several states. Bilingual education laws vary considerably from state to state and language practices vary from classroom to classroom.

The immigration waves of the 1970s and 1980s, resulting in part from wars in Indochina and then in Central America, changed bilingual programs. Now schools often include students from five or six different language groups rather than two. California alone has over 90 different language groups (California Department of Education, 1997). Schools seldom finance bilingual education for language groups when only a few students speak a specific language. Most bilingual programs are Spanish-English bilingual classes (Gándara, 1997). In some areas, Cantonese-speaking and Navajo-speaking groups are sufficiently concentrated to justify bilingual classes.

According to a 1997 report to the California Legislature by Dr. Patricia Gándara, one in four students in California are English-language learners, and an estimated 40 percent of students in kindergarten and first grade are learning English as a second language. Gándara (1997) states, "Approximately 30% of LEP students are taught in classrooms with primary language instruction in academic subjects and English-language development—or what most people would refer to as bilingual classrooms. . . . Seventy percent (70%) of LEP students (in California) are educated in English-only classrooms without academic instruction in the primary language. Of these, about 20 percent may receive some *informal* help in their primary language principally from an instructional aide to help decipher a lesson that is taught in English" (p. 3).

In 1998, California voters passed Proposition 227, eliminating the state requirement for bilingual language support. Federal court decisions determine the legal minimums required of all states and school districts and may be in conflict with the new California law.

The Need to Learn English

Most immigrant students recognize the need to immediately learn English. Children want to learn English to fit into their new society. Substantial evidence indicates that students who were educated in their homeland and acquired school skills there readily transfer their academic skills to U.S. schools (National Research Council, 1997).

English competence facilitates including students in school and including students' families in society. Despite the clearly recognized need and school districts' legal obligations, almost one in four students who enter our schools with limited English receive no special instruction. They are placed in classes with teachers who lack preparation for promoting English acquisition. These students are expected to sink or swim. Only learning English offers them access to the rest of the curriculum.

In meeting the needs of these students, teachers cannot simply turn to their own English–language arts preparation. Learning English as a second language is not the same as learning English as a native speaker. Heath (1986) argues as follows:

> Language learning is cultural learning: Children do not learn merely the building blocks of their mother tongue—its sounds, words, and order; they learn also how to use language to get what they want, protect themselves, express their wonderings and worries, and ask questions about the world. The learning of language takes place within the political, economic, social, ideological, religious, and aesthetic web of relationships of each community whose members see themselves as belonging to a particular culture. (pp. 145–146)

Serving language-minority students effectively requires knowledge of cultural elements, linguistic factors, methodology that allows teachers to modify the curriculum, and an awareness of social and political issues that play a role in education. Just knowing English and having effective English-language teaching techniques in general is not enough. As a teacher, you need to examine your attitudes toward language-minority students, learn about how these students learn, and redefine your classroom, if necessary, to meet the needs of this large segment of the U.S. school population.

Language-Minority Students

Language-minority students arrive at your classroom door with experiences that may or may not be similar to their native-English-speaking classmates. You should not assume that students have totally different experiences or that they are culturally or linguistically deficient. It is important that you provide a comfortable environment that supports all students and that you find out as soon as possible about the experiences that students do bring. Building shared experiences into instructional activities makes sure that all are "on the same page" and serves as a strong base for lessons to come. It helps to keep the following in mind:

- Not all bilingual students are alike. Each comes from a unique background and has her own abilities, needs, interests, and goals. It is important for educators to find out about each student in order to best meet her needs and to be as supportive as possible.

- Instructional strategies and materials must be modified to assure that language-minority students can comprehend and make connections with material. Without modifications, students are faced with lessons that they cannot absorb.

- Language-minority students need social and emotional support. They find themselves in a setting that may not be aligned with their experiences. They may face discrimination and exclusion due to their language, race, or ethnicity.

When second-language learners come to school, they usually do not have the luxury of taking time out to learn English while putting content acquisition aside, nor is that advisable. While they are developing the structures and meanings of English they must also learn math, science, social studies, and language arts with their classmates.

Factors Affecting the Acquisition of English

The Language Acquisition Process

Krashen (1981) argues that language needs to be acquired rather than learned. In acquiring a language, students follow much of the same patterns and strategies used in learning a first language (California Department of Education, Bilingual Education Office, 1986; Crawford, 1991; Krashen & Terrell, 1983). Terrell (Krashen &

Terrell, 1983) terms this alternative process of fostering second-language acquisition the "natural approach," since it seeks to follow seemingly natural language acquisition patterns of children. Students acquire language when they understand the language. The focus in language acquisition must be on communication, not rules of grammar.

Krashen (Krashen & Terrell, 1983) also suggests an "input" hypothesis. He argues that only comprehensible "input," or comprehensible language, will help students acquire a second language. This hypothesis suggests that language fluency in students emerges naturally, over time, as a result of communication. Fluency emerges under conditions of comprehensible input and low anxiety. Teachers promote a low-anxiety environment by avoiding overcorrection of language errors. Constant correction impedes and frustrates communication in the classroom. Soon many students are reluctant to volunteer and to speak. Overcorrection actually slows down language acquisition. Students learning English or any second language, like children learning a first language, will hear and correct many of their own errors as they seek improved communication.

Comprehension precedes production. Receptive language is usually stronger than expressive language; second-language learners will usually understand more than they can produce themselves. It is usually easier to listen or read than to speak or write.

Language Acquisition Stages.   *Preproduction*, also known as the *silent period*, is when students are observing and trying to "make sense" of the new language. They can understand a limited amount but are not yet ready to speak. At this stage, students need to be involved with activities that allow them to listen and to respond nonverbally. They need to build vocabulary and start to learn basic grammatical structures. Reading and writing should be limited to one to two words at a time.

Early production involves utterances of one to two words with many errors. Receptive language is still much stronger than expressive. Students at this stage can answer simple questions or make statements with one- to two-word answers. Structures need to be kept very simple, preferably in present tense and in active, not passive, form. Reading and writing can include basic sentences.

Speech emergence is when learners are able to produce longer utterances with fewer errors, although still noticeably nonfluent in nature. At this point, students can answer with complete sentences, can ask questions, and can make more complex statements. Reading and writing can reach a higher level, with students being able to write paragraphs, even simple essays.

With *intermediate fluency*, utterances are of longer length and are often grammatically correct. There may be some subtle errors, such as misunderstanding idioms or incorrectly choosing a word. Intermediate fluency students can be introduced to reading and writing at their grade level with some assistance. You should not expect these students to function at the same level as native speakers, although they may appear to be fairly proficient in English.

Fluency is when learners have begun using language at a level that approximates a native speaker. Not all learners reach this level. At this level students can read and write at the same level as native speakers. Occasionally, some words or structures will continue to pose difficulties.

Communicative focus facilitates acquisition. When English-language learners negotiate meaning in a relevant setting that focuses on getting the message across rather than on grammar or syntax, they tend to acquire the language easier and retain it longer. Past approaches to language instruction have often focused on narrow aspects of language, not on allowing students to use it for authentic purposes.

The Contributions of Jim Cummins.   Jim Cummins (California Department of Education, Bilingual Education Office, 1981) is a Canadian researcher who has contributed significantly to our understanding of language acquisition. He focuses on how language use is related to the empowerment of students and their families and looks at how different types of language are developed. He emphasizes the role of the first language and culture in the process.

1. *Types of language:* Cummins writes about two types of language, social and academic. *Social* language is used by second-language speakers to perform day-to-day tasks such as greeting, taking leave, initiating conversation, apologizing, making excuses, explaining what one did over the weekend, and so on. *Academic* language is a higher level of language needed in order to function in content classes such as math or science. Academic language takes approximately five to seven years to acquire.

2. *Context and cognitive demand:* Tasks can be examined in terms of how embedded they are in context and how cognitively demanding they are. Teachers must provide greater context when working with students who are limited in English. An example of this would be involving students in a demonstration where they actually see one form of matter change into another (such as making ice cream) rather than just talking about solids, liquids, and gases and their ability to change form. Limitations in English do not indicate limitations in cognitive ability.

3. *Transfer:* Once someone learns something in his first language, he can transfer the knowledge and skills to his second language. An example would be learning how to find the main idea in a paragraph. Once you learn how to do that you don't need to learn the skill again in another language, you just need to learn the language.

Other Factors Affecting Language Acquisition

Personal factors include age, motivation, aptitude, self-esteem, degree of risk taking, and personality. When students want to learn a new language, they can. When second-language acquisition brings prestige and new opportunities, students learn quickly. When learning a second language is mixed with criticism, ridicule, cultural conflict, and self-doubt, language acquisition is slowed (Brown, 1987; Gardner & Lambert, 1972; Horwitz, Horwitz, & Cope, 1991).

English itself presents a number of issues: dealing with a new sound system, tackling a possibly different syntax or word order, figuring out rules for putting words together, and discovering subtle meanings connected to verbal and nonverbal messages. It will be easier to learn English if the primary language is similar to English.

Culture conflict is the frustration experienced by children trying to learn a new language, and is evident in the following excerpts from *Immigrant Students and the California Public Schools: Crossing the Schoolhouse Border* (California Tomorrow, 1988):

> I just sat in my classes and didn't understand anything. Sometimes I would try to look like I knew what was going on; sometimes I would just try to think about a happy time when I didn't feel stupid. My teachers never called on me or talked to me. I think they either forgot I was there or else wished I wasn't. I waited and waited, thinking that someday I will know English. (Ninth-grade Mexican girl who immigrated at age 13, p. 62)

> You don't know anything. You don't even know what to eat when you go to the lunch room. The day I started school, all the kids stared at me like I was from a different planet. I wanted to go home with my Dad, but he said I had to stay. I was very shy and scared. I didn't know where to sit or eat or where the bathroom was or how to eat the food. . . . I felt so out of place that I felt sick. Now I know more, but I still sit and watch and try to understand. I want to know what is this place and how must I act? (Eighth-grade Vietnamese girl who immigrated at age 9, p. 71)

Learning English for school survival requires learning about a new culture. For students from immigrant communities treated as low status, acquiring English requires redefining their own cultural frame of reference or worldview. The anxiety produced by cultural conflicts impedes English acquisition. Success for language-minority students in school depends on both academic language mastery and students' comprehension of schools' cultural systems. Self-confident immigrants can direct and influence their own language acquisition. You, the teacher, can reduce conflict and anxiety by providing conditions that facilitate learning and by studying cultural conflict (described in Chapter 2).

Language lessons can explore the following:

- Why do I want to learn this language?
- What is the value of learning the language?
- How will other people who are important to me perceive me if I study, practice, and learn this language?
- How do I feel when I fail to use English properly?
- What steps can I take to acquire English without giving up my language, culture, family, and friends?

Support and Empowerment

Cummins (1989) has combined the insights of critical theory in the sociology of education with current theories of second-language acquisition. He lists the major components of a language empowerment strategy:

1. A genuine dialogue between student and teacher in both oral and written modalities,
2. Guidance and facilitation rather than control of student learning by the teacher,
3. Encouragement of student–student talk in a collaborative learning context,
4. Encouragement of meaningful language use by students rather than correctness of surface forms,
5. Conscious integration of language use and development with all curricular content rather than teaching language and other content as isolated subjects,
6. A focus on developing higher level cognitive skills rather than factual recall, and
7. Task presentation that generates intrinsic rather than extrinsic motivation. (p. 64)

Educators play an important role in helping or encouraging students and their families to become empowered. Empowerment means that an individual has control over her destiny and is able to make changes. Cummins (1996) expresses the concern that we often see students' native language and culture as being inferior, not worthy of being used as tools in the school setting. In fact, when we do not allow students to build on their existing base, we and they lose a great deal of richness and value, and we perpetuate the myth that non-English languages are not school languages.

Compliance: What Must Educators Legally Do?

Educators are required by federal law to provide language-minority students with specific services and to involve them and their parents in the educational process. These legal requirements are also supported by a number of court rulings, a major one being *Lau v. Nichols* (1974).

- Students must be identified and classified in terms of their language.
- Students must be tested in both English and their primary language.
- Students whose tests indicate limited English proficiency (LEP) should be placed in a setting where they can get the assistance necessary for school success.
- Limited English proficient students should receive services that allow them access to the curriculum.
- There should be a sufficient number of qualified teachers available to teach language-minority students. Some states require teachers to have special certification in the area of working with second-language learners.

Program Configurations

Language-minority students can receive services through a variety of program options, depending on their primary language, their proficiency in English, their parents' wishes, legal regulations, and district philosophy and resources. Programs range from complete submersion in English to full dual-immersion in a two-language program that strives to promote bilingualism and biliteracy.

English-Only Programs

Submersion (All English).   Most English-language learners in the United States are involved in submersion. This is a regular classroom in which the teacher (an English speaker with little or no second-language skills) provides instruction completely in English. Strategies and materials are not modified to any great extent to meet the needs of English-language learners. Students will either "sink or swim," managing to be successful because of or despite the all-English approach, or failing because they cannot grasp content or attain a sense of success and positive self-esteem. With this approach, students quickly learn that English is the high-status language and the only language valued by the school. Many children learn to avoid their home language, even to the extreme of avoiding talking with their own parents in public.

English Plus English Language Development (ELD).   In this classroom, the teacher provides instruction in English and provides English language development (ELD), or English as a second language (ESL) instruction, either within the classroom or through a pull-out program. In *pull-out programs*, students are taken out of the classroom and are served by a specialist, certified teacher, or an instructional aide closely supervised by a teacher. Students are expected to work in the English class for most of the day. They do get some support when English language development lessons are offered and materials are tailored to their language level. This approach provides some support to students who are learning English but only for a very limited part of the day. After students achieve an ability to communicate and perform in English, planned and organized English language development lessons should continue for up to five years to provide students with access to higher levels of social and academic English.

English Language Development (ELD).   In ELD, also called English as a second language (ESL), classes, the first priority is to teach students to communicate in English so they can survive in school as well as to provide the basic language needed for understanding academic instruction. To be successful in subject-matter lessons, students must have specific vocabulary and be aware of certain language structures (such as the expression, "How much?" in mathematics). The teacher achieves comprehension by carefully developing the context of language through interactive, experiential lessons. Teaching English as a second language is not language arts, it is a well-developed sequence of lessons that allows students to develop vocabulary and grammatical structures in a meaningful context. English can be taught through direct language lessons (focus on vocabulary or grammar) or through content-based experiences such as planting seeds, collecting items of various shapes, or interviewing a family member about moving to the United States.

Typical strategies used for ELD lessons may include role play, poetry, readers' theater, chants, songs, total physical response (responding by movement to commands given by teacher or other students and gradually building grammatical structures and vocabulary), art projects, games, predictable literature, interviews, matching words with pictures, and computer games.

National Standards for ELD.   The organization Teachers of English to Speakers of Other Languages (TESOL) has developed a set of Pre-K–12 standards for ESL. The standards are based on the following assumptions (TESOL, 1998):

- Language is communication.
- Language is learned through meaningful use.
- Bilingualism and multilingualism are valuable.
- Native language plays an important role. It serves as a base for learning English.
- Language and academic development involve cognitive, social and cultural processes.
- Assessment must be tailored to respect linguistic and cultural diversity.

TESOL sets the following three goals for English-language learning:

Goal 1: To use English to communicate in social settings . . .

Standards for Goal 1
Students will:
- participate in social interaction
- interact in, through, and with spoken and written English for personal expression and enjoyment
- use learning strategies to extend communicative competence

Goal 2: To use English to achieve academically in all content areas.

Standards for Goal 2
Students will:
- use English to interact in the classroom
- use English to obtain, process, construct, and provide subject-matter information in spoken and written form
- use appropriate learning strategies to construct and apply academic knowledge

Goal 3: To use English in socially and culturally appropriate ways

Standards for Goal 3
Students will:
- use appropriate language variety, register, and genre according to audience, purpose, and setting
- use nonverbal communication appropriate to audience, purpose, and setting
- use appropriate learning strategies to extend sociolinguistic and sociocultural competence (pp. 9–10)

The TESOL document emphasizes that the development of English, in both spoken and written forms, is one part of a total educational program.

Modified Instruction in English Plus ELD.   Modified classrooms are becoming more common as districts scramble to meet legal compliance requirements for specially trained teachers. In this type of classroom, the instruction is completely in English, although the teacher has gone through specific training that allows her to be more aware of and sensitive to the needs of English-language learners and to modify instruction using SDAIE (specially designed academic instruction in English) techniques.

SDAIE.   Specially designed academic instruction in English (SDAIE), also known as sheltered English, involves teaching in modified English so that English-language learners can comprehend and participate successfully in the classroom. SDAIE strategies are appropriate only after students have reached an intermediate level of English. Unfortunately, in many schools, students do not have the benefit of primary-language instruction and a well-organized ELD program that prepares them for a sheltered experience.

SDAIE strategies include the following:

- Extracting the important points of a lesson or unit and focusing on them rather than on numerous details
- Modifying text
- Simplifying teacher talk (e. g., shorter and less complex sentences, more consistent work choice, face-to-face communication, use of active rather than passive voice)
- Involving students more actively in hands-on activities
- Providing supports such as buddies or cooperative groups
- Providing a great deal of context through gestures, visuals, and other graphic tools
- Tapping into and building on students' background knowledge
- Finding alternative ways to check for understanding and measure final outcomes of lessons

Instruction with SDAIE strategies should begin in context-rich subjects such as art, physical education, and music, eventually moving on to math and science where demonstrations, modeling, and experiential learning are common. Final stages of implementation would include social studies and language arts, both "word-intensive," subjects whose texts at times have few illustrations or graphic depictions.

SDAIE has as its goals achievement in the subject field and improved usage of English. It does not consist of watered-down courses made easy. Teaching in a SDAIE mode requires thoughtful selection of objectives, building in of active student participation, delivery in a very concrete and inclusive way, and evaluation using techniques that allow students of limited English ability to show what they have understood.

Literacy and the Language Experience Approach

English literacy development for second-language learners continues to provoke considerable controversy ("Every Child Reading," 1998). Educators question whether it is more appropriate to develop reading skills in children's home languages or in English. Many districts decide that primary-language literacy development is not feasible due to multiple languages present in classrooms. These districts promote English-language literacy even when students are not yet fluent.

A major concern is deciding when it is appropriate to introduce reading in English to students who are already reading in their primary language. Teachers find that even students literate in their first language and who speak English adequately may have difficulty learning to read in English. Comprehension is always a problem. Second-language learners seldom have all the sight vocabulary of typical English speakers. Researchers claim extensive evidence of the value of phonemic awareness for reading, but in your teaching you will quickly learn that there are numerous exceptions to this claim of phonemic regularity (Adams, Foorman, Lundberg, & Beeler, 1998). For example, students who are literate in Spanish are accustomed to its regular sound–symbol relationship. Learning to read English, with its extensive irregular use of vowels, may be difficult and confusing for such children.

The language experience approach to reading was introduced in the United States in the 1920s. Disused for decades, was rediscovered by Roach Van Allen, who observed the method being used in Texas with bilingual Spanish-speaking children. The basic premise, as explained by Van Allen (Van Allen & Allen, 1976), is simple: What I think about, I can say. What I say I can write. I can read what I have written. I can read what others have written for me to read. Research on the language experience approach to reading reveals positive results (M. Hall, 1981). It offers several useful steps to assist English-language learners.

Procedure.   Teaching English as a second language and developing literacy in English-language learners involves several critical factors. Teachers should introduce reading in English as part of English as a second language (ESL) classes. One of the mistakes teachers most often make is to immediately place limited English proficient students in a reading group with English-only peers, usually the lowest-ability reading group in the class. This is not only discouraging to these students, it is unfair to everyone in the group. Limited-English-speaking students are not slow learners, they are limited in their English-language skills. Their problems are significantly different from English-speaking students with reading problems.

Krashen and Terrell (1983) argue that students "acquire" rather than "learn" a language. While students acquire language, they learn to read (Green, 1998). In the language experience approach, readers "write" their own story. They use their own words to write about their own experience. This real-life experience becomes their context for reading, and they comprehend all of what they read.

For example, one elementary teacher scheduled a field trip to provide a common experience for his class. He and the class then made an "experience chart." He asked students questions about the trip and wrote their answers on the chart. The children then "read" the story aloud. Such chart stories are widely used in kindergarten and elementary classrooms to introduce children to reading in a way that ensures comprehension and to motivate them by making the story their own.

For students participating in this approach, there is no right or wrong language; the contribution of every child is valued whether it is grammatically correct or complete. Error correction is kept to a minimum. For students struggling to learn to decode in English, language experience lessons provide an opportunity to move into reading English with comprehension supported by experience.

Language experience lessons allow you to be very creative. The methods motivate students. Children love to read stories about themselves, and these are not only stories about them, they wrote them themselves. With computers and programs such as *Bilingual Writing Center,* you and your class can print high-quality and visually appealing stories to share with students' families.

You also may expand on the traditional language experience approach to include teaching phonemic awareness, grammar, and other skills necessary to enable English-language learners to be successful readers.

Teaching Phonemic Awareness.   For phonemic awareness lessons, whether with language experience or phonics-based reading programs, you must make yourself aware of the phonemic structures of other languages. For example, children who read Spanish are accustomed to its regular series of vowels, while English constructs a diverse series of phonemes from its vowels. Children who speak Asian languages are accustomed to several distinct phonemes that may interfere with their recognition of English phonemes.

English-language learners may have difficulty hearing and recognizing English sounds and phonemes because equivalent sounds may not exist in their language. Spanish speakers, for example, may have difficulty recognizing the English sounds /sh/ as in *shirt,* or initial /s/ as in *skirt.* Simply adding more drill will not resolve the problem. You must stop, explain the language differences, and help students hear the phonemes.

When using the language experience approach to reading for English-language learners, you need to be mindful of both the skills of teaching English as a second language—listening, speaking, reading, and writing—and of the reading skills of vocabulary development, word attack, and comprehension. A language experience story always includes oral discussion, brainstorming, listening, and speaking during its initial construction. It is a "natural" process in the sense that everything occurs at learners' vocabulary levels.

Teaching Grammar.   Older or more advanced students may be ready to refine their language by paying attention to points of grammar with their written language experience stories. They can look for verbs, and then edit for correct tense and person. Students can look for adjectives in their story and add descriptive words or change those already there. They may develop new vocabulary in this fashion. Some students may find English's irregular plurals difficult to master. A good exercise for them is to find all the nouns in their stories, write them down, and list their singular and plural forms. Prepositions are also difficult, and are developed late in the sequence of English-language acquisition. Students can look for prepositional phrases and edit them for correctness.

These are only a few ways that you can adapt the language experience approach to reading to help your limited-English-speaking students. The approach is appropriate for students at any age or level who are beginning to read in English.

Bilingual Education

Bilingual education is a series of instructional strategies for teaching students school subjects, in part in their home language, and for teaching English. In bilingual classes, the instruction might be in Spanish or another language for part of the day and English for another part. In this manner, the student learns math, reading, and other subjects while acquiring English. Bilingual education uses ELD strategies to help students acquire English. Bilingual education encourages the development of bilingual and biliteracy skills in both languages—valuable assets in our increasingly international economy.

It is difficult for children to learn when the instruction is in a language they barely understand. Bilingual education teaches other academic subjects as it teaches English. While children are learning English, they are also taught the difficult tasks of reading, math, and science in the language they best understand. After two or more years (preferably five to seven) of instruction and practice in English, instruction in most subject areas gradually changes to all English.

Most states have been unable to provide a sufficient number of bilingual teachers to provide native language instruction for students who need it. In areas of a high concentration of a specific language group (such as Cantonese, Navajo, or Spanish), school districts can organize classrooms to provide bilingual instruction. All students need education in a language they can comprehend. They deserve an environment that encourages their enthusiasm, an environment that makes them independent and autonomous learners. The U.S. Office of Education estimated in 1992 that only 11 percent of students who have a legal right to bilingual education actually receive bilingual services (McKeon, 1994).

Both bilingual instruction and English-language development respond to students' needs to learn English. By law and by practice, well over 80 percent of all bilingual programs are transitional; that is, they use the home language for only a few years while the student learns English. A few bilingual programs also maintain and develop academic skill in the home language as well as English. Rarely do primary language skills get preserved and developed in sheltered English programs, ignoring and negating tremendous language skills these students bring to school. In an increasingly international economy, our society needs to preserve and develop language skills in primary languages.

Bilingual education and extended use of sheltered English allow students time for transition to all-English instruction. A common underlying language proficiency and common learning skills facilitate rapid progress once English has been acquired (California Department of Education, Bilingual Education Office, 1981). Students may have learned important concepts in school in their home country. For example, children need to learn to read or learn math only once. Most reading and math skills learned in another language readily transfer to English.

Native-language instruction is vital for young children and adolescents. Children receive their primary instruction about respect, motivation, and life from their families. They need extended and consistent guidance. At times, school personnel who are poorly informed about language acquisition have urged families to stop talking to their children in their home language. This has usually proven to be a disastrous recommendation. Children respond best to positive communication. Lack of communication, even in the home language, impedes children's learning of concepts and skills.

The misguided advice to stop speaking Spanish, Cantonese, or Hmong results in reduced talk and communication between parents and children. School pressure divides children from their home, and they lose their major source of instruction for cooperation, fairness, personal responsibility, and attitudes toward work. They may become alienated from both home and school (Wong-Filmore, 1991).

Teachers and language specialists have developed several approaches to bilingual education. Districts and schools select which program to use based on the language philosophy of the district, the languages and proficiencies of their students, and the expertise of their faculty. Programs differ based on (a) how much the primary language is used, and (b) how long the primary language is used for academic instruction.

Transitional Bilingual Education (TBE).   In this program, students receive instruction in the primary language until they are ready to make the transition to English. The model allows for a greater amount of primary language at the beginning, with the amount gradually decreasing until an all-English model is reached. Students usually begin the program with 50 to 90 percent of their instruction in the primary language. Within a few years, classrooms use 100 percent English for instruction. In addition to primary language instruction, TBE also includes English-language development (ELD). The goal of TBE is to use the primary language for a limited period of time, creating a strong base for transition to English. Unfortunately, students are often left at a second- or third-grade reading level in their primary language due to the gradual shift to English. Transitional programs may contribute to the loss of true bilingualism.

Maintenance Bilingual Education.   Students are taught in their primary language with ELD instruction and gradual introduction to content in English. The difference between this type of program and transitional bilingual education is that the primary language is maintained and supported for as long as possible. The goal is to create a truly bilingual individual. Both languages are used for instruction, and students may use either one to accomplish social and academic tasks. Medina has demonstrated that use of the primary language significantly increases the probability of becoming skilled in both the first and second languages (Medina & Escamilla, 1992).

Immersion (One Way, Two Way).   Students in a dual-immersion classroom are taught in two languages, with one being used for a greater part of the day than the other. Usually, as students start in kindergarten there is more of the second language with some of the first language (90% to 10%). Eventually, the percentage shifts to approximately 50:50 by grade 5 or 6. Dual-immersion programs teach, for example, Spanish to English speakers and English to Spanish speakers, so both groups of students become bilingual.

Attacks on Bilingual Education

Unfortunately, even though bilingual education has provided a positive and supportive environment for the academic and social growth of many language-minority students, politically motivated opposition to bilingual education continues to grow. The mobilization of conservative forces throughout the nation in the 1970s and 1980s attacked taxes, schools, and bilingual education. In the 1990s, these same groups frequently attack multicultural education as divisive to national unity. Some English speakers are offended that immigrant children are taught in their native tongue for part of the day. Political leaders argue that bilingualism handicaps children.

Conservative business and educational activists make ongoing efforts to reverse the move toward cultural and linguistic diversity. They seek to reestablish the dominance of the viewpoints of the English-first movements of the early twentieth century. Their arguments ignore the data on immigrants' school performance and the need for educational remedies to respond to students' need to learn English (Rothstein, 1998).

For example, Porter (1998) argues, "Bilingual education is a classic example of an experiment that was begun with the best of humanitarian intentions, but has turned out to be terribly wrongheaded. . . . The accumulated research of the past thirty years reveals almost no justification for teaching children in their native languages to help them learn either English or other subjects" (pp. 28–30). Like the debates on affirmative action, conservatives have created the deception that minorities are gaining an advantage, that bilingual education is discrimination against European Americans (Krashen, 1996). The attacks on bilingualism continue with voters in several states voting for "English as the Official Language" bills.

In June 1998, California's electorate (69% European American) responded to crisis in the state's educational system by passing Proposition 227, which effectively abolishes bilingual education for immigrant children (whose parents are often not citizens and cannot vote) by making the use of other languages in schools illegal except under special circumstances. Latinos make up 29.4 percent of the population, and over 36 percent of schoolage children, but only 12 percent of voters. The decision to eliminate California's bilingual education programs is currently being challenged in the courts as a violation of the *Lau v. Nichols* (1974) decision and the Fourteenth Amendment to the U.S. Constitution.

Exit polls conducted by the *Los Angeles Times* indicate that the vote on Proposition 227 by ethnic group was as follows:

	Yes	No
European American	67%	33%
Latino	37	63
Asian[1]	57	43
African American	48	52

Bilingual education is under assault in a number of cities including Denver, Albuquerque, and Chicago. Often the assault is assisted or initiated by Linda Chavez' Center for Economic Opportunity (http://www.ceousa.org/) and U.S. English (http://www.us-english.org/). There has been no move by other states with large immigrant populations, such as Texas and New York, to repeal bilingual education. Texas educational officials note that bilingualism is considered an economic asset in Texas and an important component of educational preparation for students entering the global economy (Florio, 1998).

The public debate on bilingual education often deals with a false dichotomy of choosing either English or the home language. All immigrant parents want their children to learn English. Both languages are valuable. Bilingual advocates urge that the nation should gain from the language resources of its immigrant communities while antibilingual advocates stress the need for national cohesion through one language.

In spite of the conservative political mobilization against bilingualism, the rapidly growing language minority populations require schools to respond to the needs of their children. Professional groups, such as the National Association for Bilingual Education and the California Association for Bilingual Education, have joined with voter coalitions and teachers' unions to present the case for educational equity for second-language students.

Effective Bilingual Programs

High-quality, effective bilingual programs have been created in a number of schools, such as El Paso and Isleta in Texas and in the Calexico School District in California (Cummins, 1996; Krashen, 1996). Bilingual education by itself, however, cannot overcome the student achievement crisis of public schools within failing school systems (such as in Oakland, Los Angeles, Sacramento, Chicago, or New York).

---

[1]The Asian vote, less than 4 percent of the total, is widely diverse, from Chinese American to Vietnamese. Useful conclusions cannot be drawn from this limited sample.

As a consequence of political controversies, bilingual education faces unusual and rigorous demands for evidence to support its claims. Substantial and adequate research has been collected in the last two decades to support bilingual strategies. The study by Ramirez et al. (1991) is one of a long series of supportive research reports. More recently, Green, of the University of Texas at Austin, conducted a meta-analysis of 11 studies (after ruling out others due to their methodological problems). His study clearly shows that bilingual programs help students increase their scores on standardized tests measured in English (Green, 1998). Resistance to bilingualism is usually a political issue, not an educational issue.

Classroom Goals

How can you support students as they move through a bilingual or ELD/SDAIE schooling process? How can you make services to language-minority students effective? Overarching goals can include providing a supportive environment, delivering content effectively, developing both English and home languages, and empowering students and their families.

You may achieve a *supportive environment* both in terms of the physical setup of the classroom and the way in which business takes place there. A classroom that is bright, colorful, full of student work, print rich, personalized, and comfortable will allow students to function in a positive way. Seating students in groups rather than rows allows them to interact and to support each other academically. Making materials accessible to students means that the classroom is student centered. Having routines that are consistent, fair, and owned by all allows second-language learners to know what to expect and to participate in the daily events in their classroom. The way in which you and your students interact with each other also has an effect on the environment. In positive environments, teachers talk less and allow students to talk more, show that they truly care about their students, are fair, expect the best of everyone, show flexibility, see learning as a process that needs support and patience, and demonstrate that they are both human and lifelong learners.

Effective content delivery is extremely important. Students spend most of their day studying subject-matter material. If you do not plan and organize this instruction and deliver it in a way that is comprehensible and interesting, much will be lost. You should know what you are teaching over the course of the year, plan cohesive units that integrate material (preferably under a theme), and make sure that each lesson allows students to actively participate, approaching learning from a variety of learning styles. You can use SDAIE, or sheltered English techniques, to ensure that instruction is comprehensible.

Development of primary language should be in place for all language-minority students. Unfortunately, there are not enough teachers to provide this type of instruction. Some students are in bilingual classrooms but the majority are in all-English classrooms with support ranging from a great deal to none. You should help students develop their primary language because (a) it is their dominant form of communication both at school and home, (b) they can use it as a tool for acquiring content knowledge and skills, (c) it can act as a base or springboard for them as they move into English instruction (a strong first-language base leads to a stronger transition to English), and (d) it is a tragedy for anyone to lose their language. Teachers who do not speak the primary language of their students can still validate and support students' first languages. Native language support builds a cooperative relationship among students, their parents, and the school. We need a closer home–school relationship to reduce crime, school dropouts, and growing social decay in many cities.

English is necessary for both social and academic transactions. You can develop students' English in a number of ways: through daily interaction and your teaching environment, through English language development (English as a second language) instruction, and through content instruction using SDAIE/sheltered English. In other words, you can promote English throughout the day. As students see word banks, read language experience stories, look at labeled classroom objects, work with classmates in cooperative groups, participate in circle sharing time, and take part in a science or social studies field trip, they are exposed to English. As long as that English is comprehensible and able to get past students' anxiety and be retained, then they will acquire it. When you give them opportunities to use English in a supportive, negotiable way, their knowledge will grow.

Getting Started

What are some things that you, as a teacher, can do to provide a positive and productive experience for language-minority students and their families?

1. *Find out as much you can about your students and their families.* Do not fall into the "all foreigners are alike" trap! Talk with your students and their parents, try to visit their homes, attend community events, read, see films or documentaries, talk with other teachers about their experiences.

2. *Provide a positive physical, social, and academic classroom environment.* Students should feel wonderful from the minute they walk in the door to the minute they go home. As the primary adult throughout the major part of their day, your attitude and actions make a difference. You are also responsible for making sure that all students are included, respected, and validated. Work on status issues, deal head on with racist or sexist comments or actions, incorporate other cultures and languages into your daily classroom life.

3. *Use your classroom and its routines to teach English.* Label, post word banks, build patterns into your routines (such as circle time, calendar), post procedures for doing things (such as writing process, heads together, share with a partner, etc.).

4. *Provide English language development (ELD) time daily to your language learners.* Do not assume that students will pick up English through language arts or through classroom routines alone. Language

learners need a block of time with you, or occasionally with an instructional assistant or volunteer, during which they can be exposed to and can practice vocabulary and structures. Make sure you teach both social and academic language. Respect the stages of language development, tailoring your ELD lessons to the students and what they are comfortable doing. Use fun, engaging activities that focus on meaning rather than form. Try to get students listening, speaking, reading, and writing in a natural setting. Be kind with error correction.

5. *Scaffold! Scaffold! Scaffold!* Many teachers have adopted the strategies of scaffolding as a process to help students learn English. Scaffolding is a metaphor. Think of repairing a major building. First, workers build a scaffold so that they can reach and work on the building. A significant amount of language work has been influenced by Vygotsky (1836–1934) and his view of the "proximal zone of development" (Vygotsky, 1978). Scaffolding in a classroom is when the teacher assists students to understand a concept by gestures, objects, questions, and responses. The teacher helps them to use English to describe an event or an opinion. She may ask questions that require students to reflect on their experiences and use English words to describe them. The teacher accepts students' tentative use of English and then elaborates or extends the descriptions by supplying more descriptive and useful words.

   Find out as much as you can about specially designed academic instruction in English (SDAIE). SDAIE consists basically of doing whatever it takes to make sure that content is relevant, interesting, and comprehensible to students. As a beginning, cover the main points, not every little detail. Provide as much context as you can to guarantee that concepts come alive. Be consistent with your vocabulary and watch the complexity of your speech. Look at students when you talk—do not face the board or look down if you can avoid it, as students lose your facial expressions. Structure lessons so that students can work together.

6. *Find ways in which to involve your students* in decision making, taking responsibility for their learning and for the classroom in general. (See Chapters 7 and 8.)

7. *Involve parents in meaningful ways.* Find out how to get parents to school if they are not already coming to the site. Provide translation.

8. *Work closely with anyone at the school providing assistance to language-minority students,* such as language specialists or ESL teachers, instructional assistants, volunteers, peer tutors, and those working with Title I programs and afterschool tutoring programs.

9. *Provide support in the form of peer or cross-age buddies* who can help language-minority students with finding their way around campus as well as providing assistance with school work.

10. *Promote understanding and cooperation by taking the time to talk and listen to new students.* In the first few weeks, it is important to check in

with new students each day. Chat before school, during recess, or a lunch. You gain insight into students' viewpoints and culture by listening to their views of how well they are adjusting to the new language and the new school.

Summary

Teaching language-minority populations is an exciting and perspective-widening challenge. Schools have developed a variety of strategies in response to the needs of immigrant students, including English language development (ELD, also called English as a second language [ESL]), specially designed instruction in English (SDAIE, also called sheltered English), and bilingual education. All bilingual programs are designed to teach students English. These transitional programs offer one-way bilingualism. Few programs encourage the development of the language resources of immigrant populations. U.S. schools have yet to recognize the advantages of bilingualism.

Language acquisition and a multicultural curriculum should provide students with meaningful, comprehensible, challenging, and substantive school opportunities. Bilingual education and sheltered English instruction teach students from cultural and linguistic minorities the macrocultural values and language necessary for survival in the public schools.

Questions Over the Chapter

1. Schools often "Americanize" immigrants. In what ways is this Americanization appropriate? Give examples of inappropriate Americanization.
2. In what ways is learning a second language like learning a first language? In what ways is it different?
3. Which strategies help teachers stress communication rather than formal language rules?
4. What are some advantages to teachers of becoming bilingual?
5. The *Lau v. Nichols* (1974) decision requires that all students be provided with access to the mainstream curriculum. Which teaching strategies help provide immigrant students with access to the curriculum?

Activities for Further Study of Language Acquisition

1. Make a list of the advantages to becoming bilingual.
2. If you have studied a second language, describe to a classmate your experiences in trying to learn it. How did you respond to your teacher's correction of language errors? Based on your own language experiences, what strategies would you employ as a teacher to help your students learn a second language?

about their experiences
bout the support they
ir first language and
d in a bilingual pro-
experience positive?
ypes of bilingual programs
your area. Do the schools provide
transitional, maintenance, or immersion? Which
languages are served?

5. Observe a sheltered classroom. What types of strategies does the teacher use to make sure that students are included and able to participate?

6. Investigate your district to find out what efforts are made to include parents in the education of their language-minority children. What types of

committees are in place? How are parents encouraged to take part in school functions, both special and ongoing?

7. Take a look at some programs commonly used for teaching English as a second language. How are they structured? What do they include? What types of activities are used? Are they meaningful, focusing on communication rather than on grammatical correctness? Is language developed in a natural way?

8. Visit a bilingual classroom. How are the two languages used? How are students encouraged to develop both languages? Are parents involved? What are the goals of this particular program?

Teaching Strategies

1. Create and maintain a low-anxiety environment.
2. Focus on communication rather than on correct language form.
3. Be tolerant of errors, and minimize correcting them.
4. Simplify information whenever possible to make it comprehensible. Use pictures, movement, simple language (see 5c), and other strategies.
5. Use sheltered instructional strategies, such as the following:
   a. Extract the important points of a lesson or unit and focus on them rather than on numerous details.
   b. Modify text.
   c. Simplify teacher talk (use shorter and less complex sentences, use words consistently, communicate face to face, use active rather than passive voice).
   d. Involve students more actively in hands-on activities.
   e. Provide supports such as buddies or cooperative groups.
   f. Provide a great deal of context through gestures, visuals, and other graphic tools.
   g. Tap into and build on students' background knowledge.
   h. Find alternative ways to check for understanding and measure final outcomes of lessons.
6. Focus on concepts. Evaluate, reuse, and expand concept lessons.
7. Provide students with visible context for ideas and concepts: pictures, videos, field trips, role playing.
8. Scaffold students' communication and your own.

Part 3

The Dialogue Between Democracy and Multicultural Education

Chapter 12

Curriculum and Multicultural Education

with Velma Villegas

The most potent weapon in the hands of the oppressor is the mind of the oppressed.
—Steve Biko

Multicultural education is part of an ideological movement whose aim is to make schools more democratically inclusive. Its intellectual roots lie in the civil rights struggles of the 1960s, the ethnic studies movements of the 1970s, and in the struggles for bilingual education (Banks, 1992). Multicultural education responds to a resistance among some students and increased alienation, failure, and school leaving among others.

In the 1980s, conservatives distorted the debate by raising an "alarm" concerning writings arguing for an Afrocentric curriculum. The debate over Afrocentrism continues, but multicultural education is not the same as Afrocentrism. Racism in the United States is inadequately described with a black–white paradigm. There are multiple races and even more cultures, each of which deserves study. A part of the effort of multicultural education is to rewrite the curriculum and textbooks so that all students—members of the United States's diverse communities—recognize their own role in building the U.S. society and economy.

Curriculum content, expressed in standards and textbooks, is very important. These materials direct and shape what students read and often outline the teaching strategies to be employed. Most school systems assume that teachers will follow a curriculum provided to them by the district or by a text publisher. Lacking sufficient preparation time and support services, teachers simply do not have the time to write their own curricula. Additionally, many teachers feel they do not have the expertise to design a math or science curriculum, so they rely on state or district standards, textbooks, and curriculum guides to organize their lessons. Throughout our school system, most teachers accept the decisions made by distant writers and publishers for many curriculum and teaching decisions.

Teachers' reliance on textbooks makes their content and structure very important. In some school districts, teachers enjoy a great deal of latitude in selecting and using materials. In these districts, principals and other administrators consider the teachers professionals and hesitate to impose decisions from outside the classroom. In other schools and districts, administrators closely monitor the curriculum. Schools and districts where test scores are low often insist on a uniform curriculum and a blanket set of rules governing homework and tests as a strategy to improve achievement. The strategy seldom works.

The failure of schools to prepare all students for entrance into the economic and political life of the nation and to achieve equal educational opportunity, and the increased diversity of our society require multicultural curriculum reform. The following guidelines for reform are suggested by the National Coalition of Advocates for Students (1991) and Olsen and Mullen (1990). Textbooks and curricula should be changed to do the following:

1. Eliminate bias and stereotypes in instructional material.
2. Eliminate tracking.
3. Reduce overreliance on worksheets and other materials of questionable educational merit.
4. Reduce reliance on materials and strategies that focus primarily on direct teacher instruction.
5. Include higher-order thinking skills (critical thinking) in the curriculum for all students.
6. Provide time for teachers to prepare enriching instructional material.
7. Revise texts and materials for all students to tell a comprehensive, complete, and inclusive view of society and its history.
8. Encourage cooperative learning, sharing, and helping one another.
9. Base materials on students' life experiences.
10. Emphasize the development of language and communication skills.
11. Develop materials that explore cultural and national differences and that teach students to analyze diverse viewpoints.

12. Provide all students with introductions to the rich contributions of many cultures.

13. Build on and extend students' experiences.

14. Build on and extend students' languages.

15. Promote dialogue between teachers and students.

16. Help students analyze and comprehend their real-life situations; that is, peer groups, gangs, drugs, violence, romance, youth culture, and music.

Most existing textbooks do not meet these minimum criteria.

The Debate Over Textbooks

Glazer (1993) points out that multicultural school wars are far from new. Battles over the place of ethnic groups, history, and culture in the curriculum date back at least to 1840. Further, he notes that

> none of the leading critics of a multicultural curriculum—neither Arthur Schlesinger, Jr., author of *The Disuniting of America,* nor Diane Ravitch, the educational historian and former assistant secretary of education, nor Albert Shanker, former president of the American Federation of Teachers—argues against a healthy diversity that acknowledges the varied sources of the American people and its culture. Still, all see a multicultural curriculum as a threat to the way we live together in a common nation. (p. 1)

Ravitch (1974), a leading critic of multicultural education, documents the battles in the New York City schools. Prior generations battled over the role of Irish Catholics, of Germans and German languages, and the appropriate manner in which to accomplish the "Americanization" of immigrant groups. The past 20 years have witnessed a resumption of these battles over textbooks, state curriculum adoptions, and the appropriate inclusion of multicultural and gay and lesbian lifestyles in literature. (For a good description of the politically conservative educational agenda, see Carlson, 1992, and Lowe & Miner, 1996.)

Ravitch (1974) describes the conflict as follows:

> Questions of race, ethnicity and religion have been a perennial source of conflict in American education. The schools have often attracted the zealous attention of those who wish to influence the future, as well as those who wish to change the way we view the past. . . .
>
> The rising tide of particularism (multicultural education) encourages the politicization of all curricula in the schools. If education bureaucrats bend to the political and ideological winds, as is their wont, we can anticipate a generation of struggle over the content of the curriculum in mathematics, science, literature and history. . . .
>
> The spread of particularism throws into question the very idea of American public education. (pp. 331, 357)

In her writings, Ravitch supports the inclusion of a limited amount of multiracial history within U.S. history, but she uses a narrow and restrictive framework for considering what history is important or significant.

Similarly, Gitlin (1995), who considers himself a progressive, offers a sympathetic view of textbook authors, and an unsympathetic view of teachers as multicultural critics in the conflict over textbooks in Oakland, California: "The debate was not about actual textbooks, to be used as practical instruments of schooling but about symbols, overloaded with emotional meaning, totems of moral conviction" (p. 23).

Textbook battles frequently occur over religious, sexual preference, and women's issues as well as multicultural education. Texas, for example, has a long history of struggles by a group of religious conservatives to edit, censor, and ban specific references in textbooks. Groups such as Citizens for Excellence in Education have supported local religious evangelists in challenging curriculum materials in Pennsylvania, Michigan, Colorado, and California. In 1993, religious conservatives organized along with many working-class Latino and African American parents to force the dismissal of New York City Schools Chancellor Joe Fernandez, and they sought control of the school board to prevent use of a "Rainbow Curriculum," which they alleged included children's stories about families with gay and lesbian parents (Karp, 1993). In 1997, when Mexican American teachers Patsy and Nadine Cordova in Vaughn, New Mexico, tried to supplement their approved text with Chicano history, they were fired by the Hispanic-led school board (Hill, 1997).

Efforts to achieve comprehensive representation of diverse cultures often are rancorous and frequently are opposed by textbook writers (often college professors) and commercial publishers. The conflicts reveal the underlying struggle for power in education. When long-hidden issues are unmasked, persons who have enjoyed undeserved and unwarranted privileges of defining "history" and literature react with alarm. Presently, state curriculum committees and textbook publishers control the selection of common knowledge. King (1995) points that control of knowledge determines who controls the future. Changing the control of knowledge is central to school reform (Glazer, 1991; King, 1995).

Apple (1988) and Carnoy and Levin (1985) discuss the importance of control of knowledge. Apple contends that control of knowledge has been a primary factor in controlling women and devaluing women's work in the field of education. Critical theorists have paid particular attention to ideological control and domination within education, arguing that the historical record has been persistently slanted to support ideological control and institutional racism (Apple, 1993). When scholars use a multicultural perspective to reveal historical biases, when they criticize narrow definitions and perspectives on history, they frequently encounter hostile responses and a vigorous defense of a European American–centered viewpoint as the only truth (Gitlin, 1995; Schlesinger, 1992; Sewell, 1991).

Textbook struggles in California and New York reveal the opposing viewpoints. The view that won out in California was crafted by neoconservative historian Diane Ravitch and supported by Paul Gagnon and former California State Superintendent of Public Instruction Bill Honig, among others. (See "Writing the California Framework for History and Social Science," later in this chapter.)

Their view argues that textbooks and a common history should provide the glue that unites our society. Historical themes and interpretations are selected in books to create unity in a diverse and divided society. This viewpoint assigns to schools the task of creating a common culture. In reality, television and military service may do more to create a common culture than do schools and books. Neoconservatives assign the task of cultural assimilation to schools, with particular emphasis on the history, social science, and literature curricula. Historians advocating consensus write textbooks that downplay the roles of slavery, class, racism, genocide, and imperialism in our history. They focus on ethnicity and assimilation, on the success of achieving political reform, representative government, and economic opportunity for European American workers and immigrants.

In arguing for this unity, the authors consistently tell only one viewpoint of historical events. They select heroes that champion unity and events that support their theses, while ignoring heroes that champion diversity or class struggle (Figure 12.1). Loewen (1995) and Weatherford (1988) illustrate the narrow misrepresentations of history favored by this group (see also the discussion in Chapter 3).

Ravitch, Schlesinger, Gagnon, and other opponents of most multicultural curriculum reform contend that teaching a common history—albeit an incomplete one—has served to build unity out of diversity. They present a European American assimilation model as the norm for all people. This *consensus viewpoint* dominates textbook publishing, but these partial and incomplete histories do not empower working-class students or students of color. By recounting primarily a consensual,

Figure 12.1 Common History Textbook Heroes

Unity Heroes	*Diversity Heroes*
Alexander Hamilton	Daniel Shay Patrick Henry
Andrew Jackson	Chief Pontiac Chief Tecumseh
Stephen F. Austin	Gregorio Cortez
Abraham Lincoln	John Brown
General Custer	Sojourner Truth Sitting Bull
Samuel Gompers	Eugene Debs
Teddy Roosevelt	Big Bill Haywood Emma Goldman
George Washington Carver	W. E. B. Du Bois Elizabeth Cady Stanton Jane Addams Alice Paul Lucia Gonzales Parsons
Martin Luther King, Jr.	Malcolm X M. L. King, 1967–1968

European American view, history and literature extend and reconstruct current racist, sexist, and class biases in our society (King, 1995). When texts or teachers tell only part of the story, schools foster intellectual colonialism, an ideological domination that contributes to the subjugation and oppression of women and communities of color.

The New York State Social Studies Review and Development Committee (1991) argues against continued ideological domination and for diversity in the curriculum:

> If the United States is to continue to prosper in the 21st century, then all of its citizens, whatever their race or ethnicity, must believe that they and their ancestors have shared in the building of the country and have a stake in its success. (p. 1)

Consensus advocate and historian Arthur Schlesinger (1991a) wrote a strong dissent from the committee position.

The differences between these two positions are profound. The views differ both on what happened and whose knowledge gets validated. Young people have their own background knowledge. They have a worldview based on their experiences each day in their homes, among their friends, and on the streets. If the curriculum reaches out to build on and extend this knowledge, then they feel validated as part of the larger society. Students need to see themselves and their lives as part of history. A curriculum of diversity and inclusion treats them as members of the community. Inclusion encourages all students to participate in building a more tolerant, more just, and more democratic community.

Students of color encountering the neoconservative consensus view find their own history discounted or ignored. When their background knowledge is ignored, they are invalidated. They are made invisible. The discounting of working-class history, significantly a history of people of color, combined with economic subjugation, leads to the pain and rage that periodically explode in crime, in violence on school grounds, and occasionally in urban riots.

The struggle between the two viewpoints is a struggle over worldviews, as explained in Chapter 2. The new multicultural worldview contends against the existing Eurocentric view. Both sides can marshal evidence, and both sides have competent historians. Both sides have advocates who refuse to give a fair rendition or just consideration to the viewpoints and evidence of their opponents (Gagnon, 1995; Gitlin, 1995).

Rather than just choosing sides, or using only a consensus text, the journal *Rethinking Schools* gives numerous examples of critical teachers recognizing that the interpretation and analysis of history and the social sciences are a continuous project in which students can participate. In a special publication, *Rethinking Columbus*, the journal demonstrates that there is not historical consensus on a single viewpoint. To present only the conclusions of the unity advocates in textbooks encourages poor scholarship and limits students' freedom of thought (Rethinking Schools, 1998).

Each worldview selects specific concepts to present and specific content to cover. Power relationships, along with research, are expressed in the defining and selecting of categories (King 1995; Popkewitz, 1987). Teachers need to know about several views and their nuances in order to present materials that provide academic balance and that supplement commercial textbooks.

Democratic multicultural education works to transform the curriculum to achieve the goals previously listed, and to present an inclusive curriculum. For example, most U.S. and state histories use the concept of the *frontier* in telling the story of the conquering of the Midwest and the West. Textbooks portray European settlers as bringing civilization to a previously uncivilized land and people. Any reasonable analysis of the lifestyle of gold miners, cattlemen, and others, in comparison to Native American lives, reveals that the settlers were not "more civilized" and the Native Americans "less civilized," even though textbooks frequently perpetuate these views. The Europeans were not less violent, more family oriented, or more respectful of life, social mores, and other community values. They were better armed and more numerous. And they won. Most public school texts present a romanticized, Eurocentric view of the frontier and civilization (Foner & Werner, 1991). A similar misapplication of the concepts of frontiers and civilization occurred in recording the Europeans' conquering Africa and initiating the transatlantic slave trade. Textbooks often portray the expansion of European culture as a historical inevitability, as natural. The resultant destruction of peaceful societies and the deaths of millions are dismissed as historically insignificant.

When teachers, parents, and others seek to balance textbooks to offer a less Eurocentric view of territorial expansion, they can expect to be attacked by neoconservatives in education, government, and private foundations. Although neoconservatives do not totally control the public discussion, their network of professors, institutes, and foundations is effective in getting media attention (Asante, 1991; Ravitch, 1991; Sowell, 1991; "Splits on the Right," 1996).

Attacks on multicultural education often mix criticisms of university and public school curricula in a way that distracts public attention from the most important issues (Gitlin, 1995). The university debate has been about proposals to require ethnic studies or women's studies courses or revising the "canon" of survey courses in history, humanities, and literature. This debate is interesting. As Meier (1995) points out, more vital to the survival of our democratic society is the call for a radical improvement in the quality of public school education for students of color and students living in poverty. While the university debate rages in academic journals and the popular press, another generation of African American, Latino, Asian, and Native American children has entered grades K through 3 in inadequate, underfunded, failing schools. And another generation of students in our major cities has entered ninth grade, where over half of them will drop out prior to graduation.

Beyond the Melting Pot Myth

Most educational leaders continue to accept the "melting pot" point of view. They believe in a legend of how the public schools served European immigrant groups (Banks, 1992; Greer, 1972). The view of history presented in books conflicts with the multiethnic reality students see around them.

The *melting pot* thesis, dominant until the 1990s, held that these "new" populations should melt into the majority group, becoming as much like the European

American majority as possible. The dominant culture was assumed to be superior and worth the pain of assimilation. Many European immigrants chose this path to "Americanism" (see Chapter 4).

While all groups clearly accept the educational goals of mastering the English language and acquiring work skills, advocates of multicultural education reject the thesis that it is also schools' function to force cultural assimilation on students.

The multicultural worldview insists on developing a more comprehensive and inclusive view of history, the social sciences, and the humanities than has been presented in curricula thus far. The absence of a people's history from the curriculum is usually a product of lack of power, a lack of political and educational capital. It is *not* a product of having contributed little to the development of our communities and nation.

The domination of the language and literacy curriculum by researchers familiar only with the macroculture leads to teaching strategies that fail many students (Heath, 1986). The majority of strategies and materials used for language arts instruction were developed based on assumptions of working with English-dominant students (Au, 1993).

Knowledge is required for self-identity (King 1995; Ladson-Billings, 1994a; Tetreault, 1989). The existing curriculum rests on the false assumption that experiences of the European American male adequately represent all of our history and culture. It assumes that the European American male experience provides sufficient basis for generalizing about society as a whole. Today several communities refuse to be rendered invisible in textbooks as if they had not contributed to the development of the United States.

The battle over what history and literature to study in the university has been hotly contested and shamelessly distorted. The standard university curriculum provides future teachers with the canons of "appropriate" knowledge. During the Reagan administration (1980–1988), Secretary of Education William Bennett and then-Director of the National Endowment for the Humanities Lynne Cheney charged that the curriculum was being diluted by "tenured radicals" because, after two years of debate, Stanford University decided to add one book written from a non-Western viewpoint to the 10 books required in a freshman world civilization course (Cheney, 1987).

The struggles over the content of public school curricula are of far greater significance. Interest groups arguing for multicultural education must contend with the established and preferential political power of the publishers and many educators. The case of history and social science textbook adoptions in California in 1990 illustrates the complexities of the struggle.

Writing the California Framework for History and Social Science

California has the largest population of any state, with over 5,640,000 students in school. California students make up over 11 percent of the U.S. total. California, along with some 16 other states, adopts textbooks for the entire state rather than district by district. This makes the California adoption the largest single textbook sale in the nation. Many publishers write and edit their books in a targeted attempt to win control of this lucrative market. In an effort to increase their profits, publishers promote and try to sell throughout the nation books developed for California.

The election of 1982 began 16 years of conservative, Republican control of the California governorship. Governors appoint the members of the State Board of Education. Their control changed the history–social science, language, and reading curricula and textbooks for the state, and influenced textbook decisions throughout the United States.

On election as California's superintendent of public instruction in 1982, Bill Honig agreed with the *Paideia Proposal* (Adler, 1982) that a classical academic curriculum, such as that taught in elite academies, was appropriate for all students. This position neglects the academic and vocational interests of a majority of students in inner-city schools. The classical, Eurocentric curriculum inaccurately represents history and the humanities, discounting or ignoring the contributions of people of color. Honig proceeded to direct the redrafting of the *History–Social Science Framework for California Public Schools* (California Department of Education, 1987), the state's guidelines for social studies teaching and textbook selection.

The draft excluded an accurate history of Latino and Native American settlement of the Southwest and did not cover the substantial Asian history in the West (see Almaguer, 1994). By electing to concentrate on a melting pot, consensus point of view, the *Framework* assumes that telling the history of European immigrants adequately explains the experiences of Mexicans, Native Americans, and Asians.

The *Framework* does not describe the displacement and destruction of Native American, Mexican, and Mexican American communities from 1850 to 1930 throughout the Southwest, including in Los Angeles and San Diego. The *Framework* ignores how American settlers used land laws to steal land from Californios (Californians of Spanish descent) and Mexican settlers and reduce landowners to the status of day laborers. The authors, among them historian Diane Ravitch, failed to note that the present mosaic of Southwest culture was created by the subjugation and domination of previously existing groups, both Native American and Mexican American.

The California document won the praise of conservative educators. Honig and Ravitch cited it in their writings and speeches as a positive example of multicultural inclusion. The *History–Social Science Framework for California Public Schools* was one of several documents that pushed forward the neoconservative position on school reform in the 1980s and engaged the broad ideological battle to define the direction of curriculum reform.

U.S. history books submitted for the 1990 California adoption, and readopted in 1998, expanded African American, Native American, and women's history coverage, but were totally inadequate in their coverage of Latinos and Asians—both significant population groups in the development of western history. (Asians and Latinos make up 44 percent of California's student population.) Coverage of Native Americans in fourth-grade books was embarrassingly Eurocentric. The treatment in seventh- and eighth-grade texts of the history and cultures of Africa and the U.S. slave system was promptly challenged by members of the African American community

(King, 1992). The history of African Americans was presented as if it was not central to understanding U.S. history. The books did not accurately describe the interactive and interdependent nature of the African, European, Native American, Latino, and Asian communities.

African American legislators as well as Latino and Asian groups criticized the texts and asked for a delay in adoption to insist on revisions. Superintendent Honig decided not to attend the hearings. He displayed his intolerant views on the inclusion of multicultural history and the demands of non-European groups when he said, "A lot is at stake here. . . . Do we try to keep this society together or do we split up into *tribal warfare?* [emphasis added]" (Trombly, 1990). Ignoring written testimony and the protests of a range of scholars, teachers, and community activists, the conservative-controlled California Board of Education unanimously approved the books (Olsen, 1992). The books were distributed to all schools, although Oakland schools and a few other districts declined to use them. (For a detailed analysis of this curriculum conflict, see Cornbleth & Waugh, 1995. For an opposing view of the Oakland fight, see Gitlin, 1995.)

Curriculum Commissioner Charlotte Crabtree and textbook series author Dr. Gary Nash subsequently received a $1.5 million grant to establish a National Center for History in the Schools at the University of California at Los Angeles. This center has taken the lead in writing much-criticized national standards for U.S. and World History. Ironically, these standards have been attacked as being too inclusive and too multicultural (Gagnon, 1995; Olson, 1995).

In 1998, California adopted new reading–language arts guidelines that focus intensely on phonics instruction for grades K–3. The reading (and math) scores of California's children had dropped perilously from 1982 to 1994, as the state struggled with an economic crisis and critically underfunded its schools. Class sizes mushroomed to over 33 students per teacher. Conservatives blamed falling reading scores on the "whole language" approach to reading education and on inadequately prepared teachers. The state board of education and the legislature held hearings, where only phonics advocates were allowed to present their ideas. Almost none of their research has been with language-minority children, who constitute 1.4 million, or nearly 30 percent, of the total student population (Taylor, 1988).

Taylor (1998) describes how research was abused and ignored and academic careers created in the successful right-wing campaign to change reading instruction. The legislature, ill informed on reading and language instruction, passed laws requiring phonics lessons in new textbooks, smaller class sizes in the primary grades, and phonics training for all new teachers. Former Superintendent Honig was one of several advocates claiming that research showed phonics instruction would improve the schools. (They did not explain the similarly dismal math scores.)

The New York Curriculum of Inclusion

Similar textbook and curriculum struggles have occurred elsewhere in the United States. In 1987, the New York Commissioner of Education, Thomas Sobol, convened a task force, "Minorities: Equity and Excellence," to evaluate the progress of New York's schools toward meeting a series of state requirements on inclusiveness. In July 1989, the task force published *A Curriculum of Inclusion* (Task Force on Minorities, 1989), calling for substantial revision of the New York state curriculum. The report began as follows:

> African Americans, Asian Americans, Puerto Ricans/Latinos, and Native Americans have all been the victims of intellectual and educational oppression that has characterized the culture and institutions of the United States and the European American world for centuries. (p. iii)

The report was quickly attacked and criticized as extreme by the neoconservative network of education advocates, as well as by several major newspaper columnists.

After considering the criticism, the New York Commissioner's office drew together a new review committee, whose members included several eminent scholars. This second committee wrote *One Nation, Many Peoples: A Declaration of Cultural Interdependence* (New York State Social Studies Review and Development Committee, 1991). This document offers extensive guides and suggestions to teachers to supplement the inadequate textbooks available. Once again, the report was attacked as extremist. Arthur Schlesinger, Jr., resigned from the committee in protest, while historian Oscar Handlin and others defended the report. In their attacks on the New York efforts, the network of conservative scholars repeatedly cited the *California Framework* as a preferred example of curriculum response to the demands of inclusive history (Cornbleth & Waugh, 1995). The California State Board of Education had adopted a "consensus" view, and the New York Board of Regents had adopted an "inclusion" view.

Unfortunately, to date, an integrated, comprehensive U.S. history suitable for public school use has not been published. Nor do adequate supplementary materials exist for teachers. This gap between current scholarship and available textbooks contributes significantly to students' alienation from history and social science courses (Tyson-Bernstein, 1988).

The problems of textbooks and the problems revealed in the battles over them are not accidental; nor are the relentless political attacks to restrict and defund bilingual education. These struggles are the product of past choices by people in power to use the teaching of history to promote a specific worldview. This worldview is being challenged by both the evangelical Christian right and from the left by the multicultural education movement. The views that pass for a consensus history have been developed in history departments in universities and influenced by the current distribution of political and ideological power.

Cornbleth and Waugh (1995) describe the process of opinion shaping and media control as follows:

> Also noteworthy is the organizational location of individual members (of the conservative network) which lent status and authority to their pronouncements. One speaks not for oneself but for a committee, commission, council or center or a university or federal government agency. Network members supported one another and their reform cause by praising each other's work in public statements and journal articles, appointing one

another to advisory boards, hiring one another as consultants for their various projects, and helping to fund these projects. (p. 18)

These institutions and networks resist emerging multicultural perspectives. In many cases, members of this political stratum choose to remain unaware of the dramatic changes occurring in our economy and society. They are holding on to the past because in the past they were "leaders," respected, and financially successful. The emerging multicultural society challenges the traditional distribution of power (Apple, 1993).

The curriculum should help students understand society and their place in it, and it should prepare them for a positive, productive future. To achieve these goals, a democratic multicultural perspective argues that students' histories should not be left out of the curriculum. All students need to learn that they belong, that they are participants in the democratic project. The curriculum should help students to learn that they are important. They need to learn the skills, information, and attitudes that will protect and extend democracy and allow them to participate in the twenty-first century economy.

Clearly, U.S. society is more democratic today than it was in 1776. It became more democratic as a result of popular struggles to expand democracy, such as the Civil Rights Movement (1954–1968). Textbooks and curricula should tell the stories of struggles for democracy: for women's right to vote; against slavery; and for labor unions, civil rights, and economic justice. The curriculum can help empower students by teaching them that past struggles have made our society more democratic. In studying these events, students learn that conflict is a normal and natural way to make change and that progress is the result of hard work.

Beyond the Text

Some textbooks are interesting, others are boring; some sell well, others do not. A universally acceptable, ideologically neutral body of knowledge that all students should learn does not exist. Nor can any teacher be expert in all areas. Textbooks serve as guides. They are a particular selection of knowledge. This selection delivers power to some people—those who are in charge of writing, publishing, and selecting textbooks. While authors, publishers, and adoption committees are often in conflict over textbook content, a Eurocentric viewpoint consistently dominates the U.S. market. This viewpoint creates an ideological preference for a consensus worldview (see Apple & Christian Smith, 1991).

Teachers interested in promoting democratic multicultural education seldom have textbooks on their side. But you can use existing texts, helping students to study them for what they are—a particular point of view on history, literature, or language. One good method is to analyze and compare two or more texts on the same issue. This strategy requires that you skip some material and cover other material in depth. You and your students can bring in current news reports from multiple perspectives and compare them with the texts.

After learning critical thinking skills, students can analyze the textbook presentations (see Chapter 9). Using texts as critical thinking subjects demystifies the books. Students interact actively with the books rather than merely read and repeat the ideas of others.

Because current books usually inadequately present the histories and cultures of minority groups, you must become a resource for your students. The curriculum *The Wonderful World of Difference,* by the B'nai B'rith Antidefamation League (1986), provides interesting human relations lessons. You will need to locate and use Latino, African American, and Asian bookstores in your community to gather additional material. Regular reading of newspapers and magazines written for each community will provide students with substantial resources. You can gain the necessary background by taking ethnic studies classes at a local university.

Cooperation among teachers also provides useful materials. Access to the Internet and the World Wide Web has revolutionized our ability to find exciting, interesting, and accurate information. Look on the Web for the Hmong home page (http://www.hmongnet.org/), for example, where you will find links to a variety of information. Native American, Latino, and Asian resources on the Web are seemingly limitless. There are Web pages and resource guides for all. (The Web changes rapidly, and pages listed here may become out of date. You need to use a search engine and look for materials.) There are over 100,000 lesson plans on the Web. Good places to start are www.rethinkingschools.org and www.nea.org. The problem is not lack of material, but developing the skill of selecting good material over poor.

Setting students to work on searching for new material will reduce your own stress. Two starting points are Steen, Roddy, Sheffield, and Stout's (1995) *Teaching with the Internet* and Williams's (1995) *The Internet for Teachers.* A particularly valuable tool is Cummins and Sayers's (1995) *Brave New Schools: Challenging Cultural Illiteracy Through Global Learning Networks.*

Creating Your Own Materials

Teachers and students produce some of the most effective materials themselves. Writing their own curriculum empowers students and their community, whether or not they achieve the graphic quality and professional look of commercial materials. You can download thousands of interesting materials and lessons from the Internet. To begin, see Vaughan (1997), *Web Trek: Social Studies Internet Directory.*

Young students can research and record the history of their classroom. Middle-grade students (grades 6–8) can interview neighborhood residents and research local communities. With the help of computer programs, students can now write their conclusions and leave their studies for next year's class, when students can read and add to the material. In Sacramento, California, for example, immigrant students from Cambodia, Laos, and El Salvador have written textbooks of their own stories of migration and adjustment to U.S. life. These tales, researched, written, edited, and published by students, provide preparation, writing, and language practice. They also provide far more accurate analyses of the society of young people than most textbooks offer.

Students can write multiple perspectives on an event and compare their conclusions to those provided in their textbooks. Soon students question their books' authors. They become historians, and begin to understand the process of content selection and perspective that has excluded many histories, and perhaps their own, from the books.

The *Foxfire* project and books and the Highlander Folk School in Tennessee both have a long history of validating culture while supporting young people in the recording of the history and culture of Appalachian areas. A group called Aspectos Culturales in Santa Fe, New Mexico, records local histories that complement inadequate official texts. Web page designers have recorded countless quality materials. These projective history and cultural recovery efforts offer outstanding guides to the creation of dynamic, living history. Students develop cultural knowledge and perspective, reading and writing skills, and self-confidence by producing their own curriculum and by, when possible, writing their own Web pages. Often this material is of higher intellectual quality than that of commercial textbooks. Through this kind of participatory curriculum development, multicultural education can help unite our racially divided nation.

Stages of Improvement in Instructional Materials

Changing textbooks and curriculums for gender, racial, and cultural equity requires a long-range struggle. Figure 12.2 illustrates the levels of curriculum reform necessary for integrating the curriculum.

Contributions Approach

A few books have taken the first step—a contributions approach. In the *contributions* approach, publishers and teachers add a few ethnic heroes and subjects to the present curriculum. The primary grades use biographies, literature, and holidays to "integrate" the curriculum.

Typically the school selects a few important dates, such as El Cinco de Mayo and Martin Luther King, Jr.'s birthday. Students participate in lessons, pageants, and celebrations of the events. The contributions approach, combined with human relations strategies such as those described in Chapter 6, is the most common approach to multicultural education. Multicultural curriculum reform in the sciences and math has focused primarily on a contributions approach.

With Internet access, however, students can pursue much more lively and participatory history. For example, there are several websites devoted to Martin Luther King, Jr. Students can read and download texts and photos, often of King's efforts in their own cities. A similar collection is being assembled about Cesar Chavez. These news stories are more detailed and interesting, include more conflict, and contain more evidence, than the rather sterile descriptions of King and Chavez that

Figure 12.2   Banks's Approaches to Multicultural Curriculum Reform

```
                    ┌─────────────────────────────────────────┐
                    │              Level 4                     │
                    │      The Social Action Approach          │
                    │                                          │
                    │  Students make decisions on important    │
                    │  social issues and take actions to help  │
                    │  solve them.                             │
                    └─────────────────────────────────────────┘
         ┌─────────────────────────────────────────┐
         │              Level 3                     │
         │      The Transformation Approach         │
         │                                          │
         │  The structure of the curriculum is      │
         │  changed to enable students to view      │
         │  concepts, issues, events, and themes    │
         │  from the perspectives of diverse ethnic │
         │  and cultural groups.                    │
         └─────────────────────────────────────────┘
   ┌─────────────────────────────────────────┐
   │              Level 2                     │
   │        The Additive Approach             │
   │                                          │
   │  Content, concepts, themes, and          │
   │  perspectives are added to the           │
   │  curriculum without changing its         │
   │  structure.                              │
   └─────────────────────────────────────────┘
┌─────────────────────────────────────────┐
│              Level 1                     │
│      The Contributions Approach          │
│                                          │
│  Focuses on heroes, holidays, and        │
│  discrete cultural elements.             │
└─────────────────────────────────────────┘
```

Note. From *An Introduction to Multicultural Education*, 2nd ed. (p. 31) by James Banks, 1999, Boston: Allyn & Bacon. Reprinted by permission.

make it into published textbooks. Students with computer access can go around the limits of most published textbooks (including this one).

The contributions approach, however, has several limitations. It leaves the existing curriculum unchanged and unchallenged. Children are first taught the main story, history, and literature of society from a mainstream European American point of view. Then a few interesting stories are added. The authors of New York's *Curriculum of Inclusion* criticize this approach as "multiculturalism [that] is additive and not at the center of the endeavors" (Task Force on Minorities, 1989, p. 21). The contributions approach does little to validate students' culture and background knowledge. Most students still find their own histories left out of the story. Because students do not look at society from several perspectives, they fail to learn the concept of *multiple perspectives*. The contributions approach declines to recognize that the mainstream curriculum carries a fundamental ideological slanting.

Heroes and holidays of the contributions approach tend to isolate the story of people of color from inclusion in the development of our society. The Houghton Mifflin history texts authored by Gary Nash, for example, adopted first for use in California and subsequently for schools around the nation, are particularly limited by the contributions approach. While dances, music, and celebrations are interesting, this focus tends to present non-European cultures as exotic or unusual. Usually the dances, foods, and dress are of a romanticized, idealized culture from another country. Of course, recognition of ideal culture is important to all students. The stories of historical figures such as Abe Lincoln, George Washington, and Betsy Ross describe ideal culture for the European American macroculture. But ideal culture should be clearly distinguished from dynamic, real culture. For students in the middle grades and high school, the history of African American, Latino, Asian, and indigenous cultures would more accurately be presented in a context of the struggle against racism and the struggle for decent jobs in society, rather than through a heroes and holidays approach.

Ethnic Additive Approach

Several textbooks, school districts, and curriculum guides now offer units and materials on specific ethnic groups—this is the ethnic additive approach. While moving one step beyond the contributions approach, this approach continues to isolate ethnic history and society from the mainstream curriculum. School districts using this approach add ethnic content and units without restructuring the curriculum.

The *ethnic additive* approach assumes that the present conceptual framework and viewpoints of society are accurate but incomplete. Teachers or curriculum guides add some African American or Chicano history or literature. Like the contributions approach, the ethnic additive approach views the history and culture of the United States from the mainstream perspective. Writers select heroes and contributions to supplement and support mainstream views. For example, students will study the Civil Rights Movement and Martin Luther King, Jr., but they will seldom study the separatist challenge of Malcolm X or the radicalization of King's own ideas from civil rights to economic justice in the last three years of his life.

Native American nations and African slaves certainly had a different view of history than those presented in most textbooks. For example, Native Americans were not considered citizens of the United States until 1924. They were residents of domestic, occupied, defeated nations. The Native American viewpoint of the expansion of European America cannot be adequately presented in a single chapter or reference. From Jamestown to Hawaii, native peoples and cultures were displaced and destroyed by the advancing "Christian civilization."

In typical U.S. history books, the period from 1800 to1850 is presented as a conflict between the "North" and the "South", but what is studied about the West? Major developments were occurring in California and New Mexico. And, what was happening among the Kiowa, Comanche, Cheyenne, Arapaho, and the Lakota (Sioux) on the high plains? These events were shaped by westward expansion, and they significantly determined the direction of development for the West, but they are ignored in most textbooks.

The ethnic additive approach rarely helps students to understand the diverse perspectives of native peoples. Minority groups and minority languages become a problem, an unexamined opposition to majority "progress."

The New York efforts of *A Curriculum of Inclusion* and *One Nation, Many Peoples* were based on the ethnic additive approach. This move beyond the California contributions approach was vehemently attacked by established European American historians and advocates of the melting pot thesis of consensus history.

Transformative Approach

Just as European American power established the Eurocentered curriculum, the political shift to democratic empowerment of all peoples in this multiethnic nation requires shifting to a multicultural curriculum. The *transformative approach* to multicultural curricula recognizes that present textbooks are a product of past power, not a reflection of "truth" or neutral or "objective" analysis. Transformation of the curriculum involves reconsidering basic themes, units, and courses.

The transformative approach, at times informed by critical theory, becomes appropriate and even necessary for the educational survival of many working-class students and students of color. Studies in history, social sciences, language, and the humanities would break with current content coverage to assist students in defining themselves and their own worldview.

Popkewitz (1987) describes the issue well:

> The social sciences are social productions, being neither neutral, disinterested, nor unrelated to their political context. . . . The methods and procedures of science are produced often in response to particular social agendas. The modern testing and measurement industry has its origins in a political movement of eugenics to improve the quality of racial stock. . . . The values underlying our science help us to understand that there is no one notion of science but multiple traditions for understanding and interpreting. Our social sciences contain paradigms or different constellations of value, commitment, methods and procedures. (pp. 338–339)

In a transformative curriculum, students study the relationship of knowledge to power. They learn that there is a strong relationship between whose knowledge gets validated and whose power is respected. The transformative curriculum involves students in considering the social, cultural, and political interests of those who select "school" knowledge and who define success.

Teachers require a great deal of assistance in transforming the curriculum. Their university coursework prepares them for admission into the field of teaching but, because of its Eurocentric bias, seldom provides them with an adequate background for curriculum revision. New books and new course outlines are needed. To transform the curriculum, teachers must have taken a number of ethnic studies courses and become cross-culturally competent in their disciplines. Such a transformation requires teachers to work with students to continually reconstruct the curriculum.

The Portland, Oregon, African-American Baseline Essays are the best-known examples of a transformative curriculum. These essays provide one of the few applications of Afrocentrism as advocated by Asante (1991). Conservatives insist that these essays, organized by Asa Hilliard, include some problems of historical accuracy. The few efforts at maintenance or dual immersion bilingualism are based on a transformative approach. *Rethinking Columbus* (Rethinking Schools, 1998) provides excellent and interesting models of transformative education about the experience of European colonization of the Americas. Several school districts have sought to develop African American schools for males and Afrocentric studies in response to the destruction of life opportunities for young African American males.

Social Action Approach

The social action approach applies the ideas of social participation and uses the empowerment strategies described in Chapters 7 and 11. Only a few teachers, programs, and schools have attempted social action approaches to reconstruct the curriculum. The best known is the *Foxfire* curriculum development projects for Appalachian students. (For information, contact the Foxfire Fund, P.O. Box 541, Mountain City, GA 30562.) Many English as a second language (ESL) classes for immigrant students have used whole language lessons and a social action approach to record students' own histories of immigration. The Writers' Workshops and the computer program *Bilingual Writing Center* (1993) teach students to write, edit, and publish their own stories. These materials add transformative elements to the curriculum.

The social action approach goes further than the other approaches to include important critical-thinking and decision-making processes. Critical-thinking education is essential to multicultural curriculum reform.

The social action approach recognizes and confronts the political nature of the mainstream curriculum. Public school officials rarely acknowledge openly the degree to which ideology shapes the curriculum. The social action approach often develops from local curriculum development efforts, such as Ojibwa in Northern Wisconsin and the SNCC (Student Nonviolent Coordinating Committee) Freedom Schools in 1965.

Social action curriculum reform happens when teachers move outside of textbooks. The economics of textbook publishing dictate that commercial texts will be slow to respond to social change. Emerging computer technology already permits high-quality, low-cost printing of student-created materials. Students learn from well-organized class discussions of current and vital issues in their communities. Particularly by middle school (grades 6–8), students need places to discuss their concerns about race, violence, fear, sex, power, and drugs. Rather than simply relying on textbooks, you can use the numerous materials already available to promote an authentic and hopeful dialogue.

What Can Teachers Do With Eurocentric Texts?

The battle over textbooks continues. Despite more than 20 years of struggle, few districts have a pluralistic curriculum. New teachers frequently encounter terrible texts selected by a state or district committee.

Teachers rely on textbooks because the teachers are overworked rather than because the current texts are useful tools for instruction. Existing texts have a number of structural problems including that they are usually boring, unreliable, and frequently unreadable. The history–social studies texts written for California in 1990 and for Texas in 1994 were written by committees and editors trying to include both everything acceptable to conservative critics and a trivialized view of multiculturalism. The result was dry, uninteresting, incoherent writing. Such writing does not motivate alienated young people to read. Few teachers have written textbooks. Few textbooks have been improved by testing them with students. Most are written to impress textbook committees (Stille, 1998).

In your first year of teaching, you will probably not have an opportunity to influence textbook selections. But in your classroom, you can go beyond the texts to pursue critical thinking, cooperative learning, and a transformative pedagogy.

Improving Student Achievement

The single most important thing a teacher can do is to help students succeed with *whatever* materials they use. Revising the curriculum to overcome the current Eurocentric bias is important, but to achieve equality we need to develop democratic schools. For students in underfinanced, poverty-stricken schools, we also need to improve academic achievement. Our goal should be to eliminate student failure.

Successful strategies include establishing clear curriculum goals. Then, administration, faculty, and staff together must develop comprehensive systems of assessment and accountability. In many areas this goal setting is connected to establishing standards (see the following section).

The journal *Education Week* annually evaluates U.S. schools. In 1998 its editors wrote, "It's hard to exaggerate the education crisis in America's cities. Words like scandal, failure, corruption, and despair echo in the pages of the nation's newspapers. They are words that aptly describe many urban districts, and the schools within them" ("Quality Counts," 1998, p. 6).

Making the curriculum multicultural and will not, by itself, improve these schools. Simply being a student in an urban district with low academic standards, large administrative bureaucracy, crumbling buildings, and a lack of safety also lowers academic achievement. "Quality Counts" (1998) reports, "In urban schools where most of the students are poor, two-thirds or more of the children fail to reach even the 'basic' level on national tests" (p. 6).

Teachers also must plan to improve academic achievement. This requires selecting goals, discipline, and planning and assessment. For example, if the district has a focus on reading, then teachers need assistance with designing reading lessons. Improvement of basic reading and writing skills must be part of any multicultural curriculum.

Imaginative teachers design their curriculum around the life experiences of their students, using newspapers, magazines, literature, videotape, and other sources (sometimes at great personal expense) to supplement textbooks.

By working together, teachers can produce their own curriculum materials. Teacher teams select empowering themes that bridge across disciplines. For example, when studying discrimination, students can use reading skills to learn the history of discrimination, writing skills to compose essays and letters, and math skills to calculate and demonstrate tracking, voting patterns, and income inequalities. They can make presentations and video recordings of their work. Teachers can share planning and read samples of student work in other classes. Teachers, not textbooks or curriculum plans, establish high expectation levels.

The Standards Movement

A direct result of the conservative school reform efforts of the 1990s was an emphasis on establishing new academic standards. In many cases, government officials did not know how to improve instruction and were unwilling to invest new money, and so called for standards as a substitute for real reform of failing schools. Elected officials and area employers called for "clear" standards, and school districts and professional organizations responded. State departments of education, professional organizations, and most local school districts embraced the new standards movement with a passion. Writing standards became a growth industry for policy advocates and staff and leaders of educational organizations.

National organizations, such as the National Council for Teachers of English to Speakers of Other Languages and the National Council of Teachers of Mathematics each developed standards models. There are now standards in math, geography, history, English, English as a second language, the sciences, and most core curriculum areas, and all demand more, often much more, of schoolchildren than previously. While this may help middle-class districts, ironically, most impoverished districts were already not meeting the previous low, poorly defined standards.

To understand standards, let's take an example. A district decides that fourth-grade students should be able to read and do math at a fourth-grade level. (There are, of course, problems with how to define this level.) This district defines a fourth-grade level as the 50th percentile on a nationally normed test, the average work for fourth graders nationwide.

Then a group of professors, advocates, and teachers get together and try to define what student work appropriately demonstrates mastery at this level. This definition becomes the *standard*. Using this standard, committees of advocates and professionals define what reading and math to include in the fourth-grade curriculum.

In Massachusetts, Texas, California, and other states, proposed standards sparked intense battles over whole language versus phonics approaches to reading, hands-on math versus drill-oriented math, and whose history was going to be taught (see Taylor, 1998). Standards became a new battleground in the curriculum wars. In California, proposed new history–social science standards led Native American historian Jack Forbes to say, "For many years our curriculum has insulted non-whites and neglected women while giving preferential treatment to persons of Anglo-European ancestry and male gender. . . . I must say in all frankness that I find [the proposed new standards] outrageously biased and fundamentally racist" (personal communication, 12 September 1998).

Once standards were established, the next step was to develop assessment instruments to measure student work. In most cases, states and districts purchased commercial tests. (The test production industry in the United States is a highly profitable enterprise.) As a result, a shift occurred in many states. Test scores became more important, or as important as teachers' grades. Some states, such as Texas, decreed that students must pass state tests to move on to the next grade or to graduate from high school. Because almost all tests include some cultural bias, new high-stakes tests particularly affected students from language minorities and students who had attended underfinanced inner-city and rural schools. In Texas, for example, many Mexican American and African American high school students did not pass the state test, and therefore did not graduate. The Mexican American Legal Defense and Education Fund is suing Texas in hopes of barring the use of state tests to deny high school graduation ("Texas Test Sued," 1997).

In California, the state Department of Education and local districts developed extensive "world-class" standards. The governor insisted that testing be implemented in 1998, but no test had been written to correspond to the new standards. So, a test was purchased, the SAT/9, to be used to measure teachers' and students' success. For political reasons, the governor insisted that all students be tested in English, even though they may not yet speak it. This will obviously adversely affect the scores of schools and classrooms with numerous limited-English speaking students (California Department of Education, 1998).

Assessment must be aligned with the curriculum in order to improve student achievement (Popham, 1999). For example, if the state adopts a standard that fifth graders should know a specific skill, then teachers should teach that skill, and tests should measure it. Tests not aligned with curricula will measure student performance on skills they have never been taught, such as teaching students addition and multiplication and then testing them on square roots.

Teachers and Accountability

New standards and tests have begun to establish a new system of teacher accountability. Prior to the standards movement, teachers could teach poorly and have virtually no measure of their skills except their ability to control a classroom. Standards, tests, and accountability programs begin to change this situation. Experiences in Texas reveal that some teachers in low-performing schools simply are not successful with students. They will not raise their standards and they will not do the extra preparation required to assist all students to learn. With standards and accountability, these teachers can be identified, coached, and provided with opportunities to improve their teaching.

A Positive Experience in Texas

Two Texas school districts illustrate how standards and accountability, along with other forces, can lead to substantive school reform. Coauthor Dr. Villegas was an associate superintendent in Harlandale, Texas, during the 1990s. She tells the story as follows:

Several school districts in Texas, with concentrations of students from high-poverty areas, have made dramatic improvements in student achievement in recent years, as evidenced by the Texas Assessment of Academic Skills (TAAS). In the Ysleta Independent School District in El Paso and the Harlandale Independent School District in San Antonio, entire schools have made significant gains in student achievement. In 1993, these districts were like many low-income districts; high dropout rates, low attendance, low morale, and low student achievement. Now, some of the schools offer their students a high-quality education, an equal opportunity to enter the world of work, and have reached "Recognized" or "Exemplary" status in the Texas state rating system.

These districts focused on high standards for all students, accountability with strong alignment to the written, taught, and state-tested curricula, and strategies and structures that engendered strong dedication to school improvement in all the stakeholders in those systems (stakeholders are discussed in Chapter 13). These processes, strategies, and structures were key to the change and to the high results of the students (Olson & Hendrie, 1998).

Since 1993, the Texas Education Agency has worked closely with districts to develop an integrated accountability system using a district's accreditation status, campus ratings, recognition for high performance, and campus-, district-, and state-level reports. The Academic Excellence Indicator System (AEIS) serves as the basis for all accountability ratings, rewards, and reports. The AEIS report also includes student attendance and dropout rates.

Each site and campus is rated based on its TAAS performance, which currently assesses student achievement data on reading, writing, and math. Performance standards for TAAS have gradually increased each year. The assessment is aligned with the Texas Essential Knowledge and Skills, the grade-level standards for each content area of the state curriculum. The curriculum is both process and content based. District and campus improvements follow a three-year plan focusing on problem areas identified by the state, district, and/or school. These plans become the blueprint for implementing initiatives, strategies, and structures to increase student academic performance and the percentage of students taking and passing the SAT and ACT tests, reduce the dropout rate, and increase student attendance.

Performance reports are provided to each district and school for the following student categories: Hispanic, African American, White, and Economically Disadvantaged. For a rating of "Recognized" at least 75 percent of all students and each student group must have passed each section of the TAAS. For a rating of "Acceptable" at least 40 percent of all students and each student group must have passed (Figure 12.3).

Following are profiles of student achievement data in two high-poverty Texas school districts.

The Ysleta Independent School District is located in El Paso, Texas, adjacent to the Cuidad Juarez, Mexican border. Of 46,860 students enrolled, 70 percent are low income, approximately 85 percent are Hispanic, and 32 percent are limited English proficient. It is a highly concentrated, low-wealth district.

In 1993, the district had 7 "Academically Unacceptable" campuses. All other campuses were identified "Acceptable"; there were no "Recognized" or "Exemplary" campuses. Ysleta was rated at the bottom of the "Big 8" districts in Texas and above the state average in only 1 of 20 categories. By 1997, Ysleta's achievement levels had changed. There were now no "Academically Unacceptable" campuses, 22 "Recognized" campuses, and 2 "Exemplary" campuses. They were also above the state average in 17 of 20 categories and ranked first or second in the Texas "Big 8."

The AEIS data shown in Table 12.1 reflect the district's improved student achievement picture in 1997 and 1998 by grade level in reading, math, and writing in comparison to passing percentages statewide. District percentages exceed statewide percentages in all categories.

Figure 12.3 Accountability Ratings

Note. From *Accountability Manual* (Table 1) by Texas Education Agency, 1998. Retrieved 15 February 1999 from the World Wide Web: http://www.tea.stste.tx.us/perfreport/account/98/manual98.pdf

Exemplary: 90% of the students are passing all TAAS tests taken; 1.0% dropout rate; 94% attendance

Recognized: 75% of the students are passing all TAAS tests taken; 3.5% dropout rate; 94% attendance

Academically Acceptable: 40% of the students are passing all TAAS tests taken; 6.0% dropout rate; 94% attendance

Academically Unacceptable: Less than 40% of the students passing TAAS tests; 7.0% dropout rate; 94% attendance

Table 12.1 **Texas Education Agency Academic Excellence Indicator System: Comparison of Average District Performance and Ysleta Independent School District**

	State Average	Ysleta
Grade 8		
Reading		
1997	81.5	85.6%
1998	82.3	87.1%
Math		
1997	76.3	76.5%
1998	83.8	87.7%
Grade 6		
Reading		
1997	84.6%	88.5%
1998	85.6%	89.1%
Math		
1997	81.8%	89.1%
1998	86.1%	93.7%

The Harlandale Independent School District in San Antonio, Texas, has an enrollment of 16,000 students. The student population is 92 percent Hispanic. The district is in one of the highest-poverty areas in San Antonio, with 86 percent of students identified as "low socioeconomic status." The district went from having nine "Academically Unacceptable" schools in 1993 to achieving five "Recognized" schools by 1997, two of which were "Academically Unacceptable" in 1993. All other schools were rated "Acceptable."

From 1994 to 1997, all grades assessed (3–8, and 10), showed a 50 percent or higher increase of students passing "all tests taken."

Strategies, Structures, and Processes That Worked. Districts and schools with a high percentage of students in poverty who have achieved high AEIS ratings have implemented assessment, alignment, and collaborative processes that have resulted in significant student performance gains for all students.

In the Ysleta and Harlandale school districts, an initial step of understanding their student achievement levels through graphic presentations of data was key. All stakeholders were involved in analyzing the data and identifying instructional targets.

The Harlandale district focused on five major strategies and structures for student achievement: (a) a districtwide K–12 assessment program, (b) alignment of the written, taught, and tested curricula, (c) vertical and horizontal curriculum articulation by grade level and subject area, (d) academic rigor and focus for all students, and (e) extended-day, extended-year structures to academically support students in literacy, math, college preparation, and other core areas such as algebra and biology.

Similarly, the Ysleta district established assessment and support teams to focus on and support those campuses needing resources to improve their student achievement. The majority of available resources were devoted to the targeted campuses. The support teams played a critical role in interpreting data for each site, facilitating districtwide assessment, and monitoring student progress. Schools were given a great deal of autonomy in their efforts to improve their TAAS scores.

The Reform Process.   In both the Harlandale and Ysleta school districts, the following courses of action were factors in producing improved student achievement:

1. All stakeholders were involved in processes that allowed them to understand student achievement and the reason for change.
2. The superintendent and school board clearly defined expectations and consequences.
3. Data collection and analysis (by teachers, administrators, and support personnel) led to changes in curriculum materials, schedules, and teaching strategies.
4. Assessment of students, feedback, and accountability were ongoing districtwide.
5. A healthy climate existed, in which all stakeholders were included in decision making.
6. Support structures such as resource teams, teacher leader-facilitators, curriculum support sessions, and staff development and coaching were made accessible to schools and teachers.
7. All students were expected to achieve, and support structures were created to ensure their success.
8. Parents and the community were involved in all implementation.
9. Plans were developed to ensure focus, continuity, and financial support for a minimum of three years.

Summary

We face a massive challenge—to create a new curriculum based on the full participation of all students. Creating schools that are equitable across race, class, and gender, and that provide high-quality education appropriate to a rapidly changing economy requires fundamentally rewriting the curriculum.

There are two distinct curriculum reform movements. The neoconservative school reform of the 1980s stressed raising standards, increasing testing, and creating a common culture through textbook selection and publication. Neoconservative reform stressed aligning schools and curricula more clearly with business interests and corporate productivity. The multicultural curriculum reform movement developed from a different worldview and holds a different theory of the appropriate role of schooling in society. Multicultural reform seeks to make the curriculum more inclusive, and to transform it to empower all students for economic and political participation. School and curriculum reform can play a role in uniting—in healing—a divided nation.

Improving students' level of achievement of both content and skills is an important component of multicultural curriculum reform. Harlandale and Ysleta, Texas, are examples of school districts that have used standards and teacher accountability measures to significantly improve student performance.

Questions Over the Chapter

1. What do you believe are the differences between a conservative and a multicultural approach to curriculum?
2. Under what conditions is it appropriate for a group of European American children to study African American history? Under what conditions should African American students study European American history?
3. Explain why there have been major conflicts between scholars over history and literature books, but fewer conflicts about multicultural content in math and science texts.
4. Define the *melting pot* thesis. What are the goals of assimilation?
5. Many advocates of multicultural education reject the melting pot thesis. What are their arguments?
6. Describe your own experiences in reading history and literature. Were your textbooks inclusive and pluralistic? Do you now comprehend the basic historical narrative of the nation's major cultural groups? Of women?
7. How are textbooks selected or adopted in your school, district, and state?
8. Using a transformative approach to textbooks, how would you change this textbook?

Activities for Further Study of Curriculum

1. How accurate and complete do you think the textbooks you used in school were? Compare your views with those of a person from another cultural group.
2. Conduct historical research on one of the diversity heroes listed in Figure 12.1. In your opinion, should this person be included in general U.S. history texts? Why do you think the person was left out?
3. Read James Loewen's *Lies My Teacher Told Me: Everything Your American History Textbook Got Wrong* (New York: New Press, 1995). Write a short essay on the significance of omissions from history books.
4. List three ways you could use a textbook in your classroom if the book inadequately covered its subject.
5. Design two examples of a transformative approach to curriculum. Share your ideas with your class. What obstacles would prevent you from using a transformative approach?

6. Create a list of social action projects appropriate to the grade level you are working with. Share your list with your class. (Be cautious about the safety level of any project.)

Teaching Strategies

1. Find out your district or state standards for your intended teaching level.
2. Plan lessons to teach to the level of the standards.
3. Assess your students' abilities to perform at the level of the standards.
4. Modify your instruction, using strategies from Part Two of this text, so that your students can successfully work meet the standards.
5. Provide supplementary skill development (reading, writing) when necessary.
6. Teach using critical-thinking strategies.
7. Frequently assess and revise your curriculum. Compare your students' performance to the standards. Change instructional strategies where necessary.
8. Decide on substantial reductions in the content coverage—not the skill level—of your curriculum. Remove material to make time for a transformative, multicultural approach to your subject(s).

Chapter 13

Democratic School Reform:
How Do We Get from Here to There?

with Pia Lindquist Wong

Power concedes nothing without demand. It never did and it never will.

—Frederick Douglass

A Brief History Of Educational Reforms

Public education in the United States is a relatively young system, but its importance has grown throughout its existence. Until the late 1800s, schooling was an activity pursued primarily by children from elite families. At the turn of the twentieth century, approximately 60 percent of schoolage children were enrolled in schools (Carnoy & Levin, 1985). Waves of immigration and a newly industrializing economy in the early 1900s made mass public schooling a more important priority, as schools became useful in the dual processes of "assimilating" newcomers and "training" an industrial workforce. By 1920, most states had passed compulsory education laws, and about 80 percent of schoolage children were enrolled in schools. By the 1970s over 90 percent of schoolage children were enrolled in school and three-quarters of them were graduating from high school (Carnoy & Levin, 1985).

Since the time that public school became a mass education project, widely available in all communities, educational policy and reforms have vacillated between two primary agendas: preparation for citizenship in a democracy and preparation for a capitalist workforce. Carnoy and Levin (1985) argue that schools are

> subject to tension between two conflicting dynamics attempting to influence the control, purpose and operation of the schools. On the one hand, schools have traditionally reproduced the unequal, hierarchical relations of [the] capitalist workplace; on the other, they have represented the expansion of economic opportunity to subordinate groups and the extension of basic human rights. (p. 14)

A brief overview of the major educational reforms of the twentieth century highlights this ideological tension. The formative period of our current public education system was roughly between 1900 and 1940, when many of the basic practices and organizational modes were developed. A central concept that emerged during this period was that of *tracking*, placing students into starkly differentiated programs that used distinct curricula and instructional strategies and espoused very different goals and objectives for students. Ostensibly, these different tracks were designed to enhance the efficiency of the system by providing students with a program of study that "best" suited their abilities and imagined future goals and employment. During this formative period, then, the primary concern of educational policy makers was to tailor the education system to meet the needs of the workplace.

Business and economic demands on schools receded somewhat following World War II, when economic prosperity and New Deal legislation (such as the G.I. Bill) ushered in programs that greatly expanded educational opportunities. Student enrollment at all levels of education, including higher education, exploded. Because resources were relatively abundant, equity concerns rather than efficiency and workplace concerns came into sharper focus. This period was cut short by the launching of the Soviet space probe, Sputnik, in 1957. This historical event prompted calls for educational reforms to improve America's economic, scientific and military competitiveness. Policy makers and politicians demanded that schools pay more attention to accountability and student achievement in math and science. Efforts to train the "best and the brightest" students were paramount. Thus, policy makers and school reformers turned their sights back on issues of competitiveness and efficiency.

Responding to intense pressure from grassroots civil rights movements and spurred by such studies as that of Coleman (1966), a new wave of educational reforms was introduced in the 1960s, designed to ensure that goals of equity and equal opportunity were met (Labaree, 1997). The landmark U.S. Supreme Court decision of *Brown v. Board of Education* (1954), the Civil Rights Act (1964), and other legislation brought about by the Civil Rights Movement (e.g., Title I, Title VII, and Title IX of the 1968 Elementary and Secondary Education Authorization Act) were pillars in the national effort to make equal educational opportunity a reality. Court decisions and national legislation legitimized grassroots demands for a more equitable education system. During this period such innovations as multicultural education, bilingual education programs, and gender equity efforts were initiated.

This new focus on equity issues led to research into "effective schools" (see, for example, Edmonds, 1979) undertaken between 1976 and 1987, some of it problematic (Levine & Lezotte, 1995), which identified characteristics of schools where working-class students and students of color perform at national and state averages (Figure 13.1). Effective schools research offered hope in that it demonstrated that some schools (about 1.6%) in impacted areas worked well to promote student achievement.

By the mid 1980s, however, policy makers began waging a new battle in the terrain of educational reform. Fueled by the conservative renaissance that began during the Reagan administration, politicians and academics such as William Bennett and Diane Ravitch focused on standards and used the rhetoric of competition and "back-to-basics" to reform schools, students, and teachers. Increased resources were decried as wasteful and leading to a bloated administration. These reformers claimed to be concerned about "mediocrity," which they used in reference to student achievement in particular, but also often as an indirect way of criticizing teachers, and their

Figure 13.1 Summary of Characteristics of Effective Schools

A. A well-functioning total system producing a school social climate that promotes positive student outcomes

B. Specific characteristics crucial to the development of effectiveness and thus to a positive school social climate
  1. A safe and orderly school environment
  2. Positive leadership, usually from the formal leaders
  3. Common agreement on a strong academic orientation
      a. Clearly stated academic goals, objectives, and plans
      b. Well-organized classrooms
  4. Well-functioning methods to monitor school inputs and student outputs

C. A positive school social climate
  1. High staff expectations for children and the instructional program
  2. Strong demand for academic performance
  3. High staff morale
      a. Strong internal support
      b. Consensus building
      c. Job satisfaction
      d. Sense of personal efficacy
      e. Sense that the system works
      f. Sense of ownership
      g. Well-defined roles and responsibilities
      h. Belief and practice that resources are best expended on people rather than on education software and hardware

Note. From "Effective Bilingual Schools: Implications for Theory and Practice" (n.p.) by T. Carter & M. Chatfield, 1986, November, *American Journal of Education,* pp. 200–231. Reprinted by permission.

training and performance. They viewed school improvement as a management issue, and presented school failure as a technical problem, subject to a new science (Chubb & Moe, 1989; Weiss, Cambone, & Wyeth, 1992). New school bureaucracies were created to manage students and teachers. Business administration ideas were advocated and applied. Reformers argued that new management and control systems, along with an emphasis on remedial drills and skill development, would improve schools for all students (Carlson, 1992). Common reforms of the 1980s included standards, vouchers, charter schools, and site-based management or decentralization.

In 1988, George Bush pledged to be the "Education President." Much fanfare accompanied his major educational initiative, *Goals 2000*. It is our contention that the reforms of the Reagan and Bush administrations called on schools to abandon a commitment to equity and presented a narrow and inaccurate understanding of the role of schools in our society. With other scholars (Olsen et al., 1994; Sarason, 1990) we argue that these reforms have failed to improve schools, particularly those that serve traditionally marginalized students.

Standards

Educational standards have been an important component of conservative reform efforts since the 1980s. Again, industry-related concepts of "performance" and "accountability" factor in heavily in the standards movement. The key idea behind standards is the notion of "systemic reform" (Smith & O'Day, 1993). *Systemic reform* is a process in which high-quality objectives and goals are clearly spelled out, and curriculum and assessments redesigned or realigned to lead to them. The expected result of such a "seamless" system is improved levels of student performance.

The standards movement has both supporters and detractors. Standards can be a powerful tool for school reform, as evidenced by the Texas experiences described in Chapter 12. At the same time, the prevailing understanding and enactment of standards tends to sidestep issues of equity and multicultural education, as discussed here.

Odden (1992) cites *America 2000: An Education Strategy* (U.S. Department of Education, 1991) to assert support for educational standards. He outlines a structure for systemic reform in which standards are the central component:

- Set clear student learning outcomes.
- Have a high quality curriculum program.
- Implement site-based management, allowing teachers to have a major influence and power over implementation.
- Have an assessment or monitoring system calibrated to world class standards that indicates the degree to which objectives are being accomplished.
- Have a sharp-edged accountability system with rewards and sanctions. (Odden, 1992, p. 12)

In 1996, at the National Education Summit, governors and business leaders concluded that "efforts to set clear, common . . . academic standards for students in a given school district or state are necessary to improve academic performance" ("Quality Counts," 1997, p. 32). The drumbeat to raise academic standards began with the publication of such advocacy pieces as *A Nation A Risk* (National Commission on Excellence in Education, 1983), which raised the alarm that our schools were failing. By 1998 virtually all states and most school districts had adopted some form of standards as central to their efforts to improve student achievement ("Quality Counts," 1998).

Nevertheless, two main arguments are put forth in almost every critique of standards. First, standards developed at the federal level, such as *Goals 2000* or *America 2000,* are voluntary (Figure 13.2). Because of strong history of state-based control of education in the United States, there is little precedent to support the idea that states will respond to voluntary mandates or that they will adhere to national standards. In fact, although there limited additional funding is available for states to participate in *Goals 2000* projects, adherence to the national standards has not become commonplace. Though such decentralization is not inherently problematic, in states such as California, where the political and bureaucratic commitment to issues of equity and affirmative action have been abandoned, as evidenced by recently approved initiatives

Figure 13.2   Goals 2000: Educate America Act (Public Law 103-227)

Goals 2000, an educational plan forwarded to then–President Bush in 1989 by the nation's governors, proposed a set of objectives for all schools to pursue by the year 2000.

In March 1993, Congress passed the Goals 2000: Educate America Act (PL 103-227), excerpted here. (Note: Goals 7 and 8 were added in 1993 to the original 1989 proposal).

1. All children in America will start school ready to learn.

2. The high school graduation rate will increase to at least 90 percent.

3. American students will leave grades four, eight, and twelve having demonstrated competence in challenging subject matter including English, mathematics, science, history and geography; and every school in America will ensure that all students learn to use their minds well, so they may be prepared for responsible citizenship, further learning, and productive employment in a modern economy.

4. U.S. students will be first in the world in science and mathematics achievement.

5. Every adult American will be literate and will possess the knowledge and skills necessary to compete in a global economy and exercise the rights and responsibilities of citizenship.

6. Every school in America will be free of drugs and violence and will offer a disciplined environment conducive to learning.

7. The Nation's teaching force will have access to programs for the continued improvement of their professional skills and the opportunity to acquire the knowledge and skills needed to instruct and prepare all American students for the next century.

8. Every school will promote partnerships that will increase parental involvement and participation in promoting the social, emotional, and academic growth of children.

Congress further declared that "the gap in high school graduation rates between American students from minority backgrounds and their non-minority counterparts will be eliminated."

to dismantle affirmative action (Proposition 209) and disband bilingual education programs (Proposition 227), it is difficult to imagine that the development of standards will lead to school improvement for marginalized students.

In addition, current rhetoric tends to focus exclusively on two types of standards: learner standards (e.g., student skills) and content standards (e.g., student knowledge). Elliot Eisner, professor of education at Stanford University and an authority on school reform, critiques these types of standards as "a 'superficial distraction' from the real work of making schools better places for teachers and students. . . . What do you do if the children do not achieve the standards?" (Eisner, 1994, p. 6). If the answer to his question is that substandard schools must then search for more ways to engage, motivate, and stimulate students and for broader ways to involve parents and families in their children's education—as has been the case in some high-achieving Texas schools—then perhaps standards can serve a worthwhile purpose in democratic school reform. If the answer is that substandard schools and their students once again become mere statistics, then, as Eisner states, standards are just one more in a series of reforms that have failed poor and minority children.

Because of this concern, many critics of standards have urged the inclusion of "opportunity to learn" standards (McGee Banks, 1997). Such standards would force district, state, and federal programs to take a hard look at the distribution of resources, funding, materials, and capital outlays among schools. In doing so, they would initiate discussion and action related to issues of equity and access.

By setting goals and standards, and refusing to consider opportunity to learn standards, members of Congress and other policy makers appear to respond to the school crisis while making few real changes in those schools that systematically fail a substantial portion of our children, particularly poor students and students of color. By passing goals without allocating sufficient resources, elected officials avoid the issues of raising taxes and spending money that any serious effort to provide equal opportunity would require. Finally, controversy has also erupted over how to assess states' achievement of any national goals, and with no evaluation tool it is difficult to determine whether state and district efforts are actually making a difference.

Vouchers

In 1993, conservative organizations in several states campaigned for school "choice" systems. After more than a decade of federal budget deficits and state budget crises, schools were underfunded. Achievement scores were declining as new immigrant populations entered schools. Since some schools were failing, conservatives argued for "breaking the monopoly" of public education. They wanted to use tax monies to finance private, even religious schools. For example, Chubb and Moe's (1989) proposal for school vouchers envisioned a "choice" system in which demand for high-quality public education would weed out subpar schools. Major support for these measures comes from supporters of religious-based parochial and private schools (People for the American Way, 1996). Advocates of voucher systems particularly seek support from low-income families, particularly African American and Latino parents, pointing to the failure of public schools to provide quality education in these neighborhoods (Shokraii, 1996; U.S. Congress, 1992). Minnesota and Wisconsin have adopted limited "choice" programs. With strong union financial and volunteer efforts, Colorado and California voters defeated similar proposals that would have challenged the current system of public education.

The rhetoric of such voucher advocates as Chubb and Moe paints a rosy picture in which parents are empowered and given resources to make real educational choices for their children. But the reality of most voucher systems is that they perpetuate the current unequal system because of their unwillingness to give poor families the necessary means to compete in this new educational market (Coons & Sugarman, 1978). For example, most prominent school choice programs suggest that all families will be provided with a voucher of equal value for each schoolage child. Schools will use these vouchers to fund their programs. At the same time, under most of these plans, schools will not be prevented from creating additional requirements or developing exclusionary restrictions for admission (Coons & Sugarman, 1978). Thus, schools could require additional fees, parent volunteering, and student purchase of extra tests and other supplies as conditions of acceptance in addition to a child's voucher. They could also create prerequisites and other acceptance criteria. Further, these plans tend to be mute on such subjects as providing services to students who have disabilities, limited proficiency in English, special transportation needs, and so on.

There is little evidence of the success of voucher systems in improving the delivery of education or in improving student achievement. The limited research available suggests that voucher systems have tended to accentuate segregation in school systems and that those parents currently disenfranchised by the public school system remain so under voucher programs (Bomotti, 1998; Carnoy, 1998; Jimerson, 1998; Lowe & Miner, 1996).

Many educators oppose vouchers as attacking the very essence of public schools and for taking desperately needed funds from public schools to be used in private ones. In addition, voucher advocates attempt to appeal to disenfranchised parents, but their proposals do not specifically address the particular failure of schools to educate their children, as discussed in prior chapters. For voucher proponents, the strategy for fixing schools is to create a less monopolistic environment where public, private, and parochial schools must compete against each other to attract students. Schools may attract students using any number of public relations strategies, but ensuring that they learn and achieve in an equitable manner must be pursued through multicultural approaches that focus on the serious issues of race, class, tracking, low expectations, and improved funding. These latter issues are not on the agenda of voucher advocates. Voucher efforts seek to privatize schools rather than to reform schools for the democratic common good. Although there is ample evidence of bureaucratic administrative mismanagement of school systems, particularly in New York, Chicago, Philadelphia, Boston, and other major cities, the competition model espoused by the voucher system in our opinion is not the most direct way to pare down these bureaucracies. It is important to keep in mind that competition always produces winners and losers. In a society stratified by race and class, the poor and racial minorities consistently lose.

Charter Schools

Charter schools have been another state-level effort initiated to bring about school reform. The charter school movement has been particularly strong in states such as California, where state legislation authorized the creation of 100 new charter schools. Based on the notion of deregulation, charter school legislation allows schools, under certain conditions, to comply with only the most minimal of state health and safety laws (Schwartz, 1996). Charter school legislation lifts what are considered burdensome state and federal regulations. In turn, the creative and innovative energies of administrators, teachers, parents, and students should be freed and focused towards school improvement. Charter schools must garner the full support of their teachers, parents, and students and collectively develop a school charter that outlines the major educational premises of the school and benchmarks for assessing progress and student gains. Local school boards must annually review and approve charter schools. Though many charter schools can be found in urban settings, they tend to serve a more homogeneous and Caucasian population (Schwartz, 1996). Their effects on improving student achievement are not yet documented (Saks, 1997; Schwartz, 1996).

Site-Based Management, Restructuring, and Decentralization

The restructuring movement in education is a direct reflection of broad changes proposed in industry in the late 1980s. In response to decreasing productivity and profitability experienced by many corporations in the 1980s, attention was increasingly turned to new forms of organization and management in the industrial sector. Several experiments emerged at this time, including employee-owned stock plans and production teams. The objective of employee-owned stock plans is to give workers added incentive to boost their productivity by allowing them to share in a portion of the profits reaped from that increased productivity. Production teams, modeled in large part after Japanese manufacturing organizations, break with the assembly line model of production by including all workers, at all levels of the hierarchy, in decisions about the many stages and aspects of product design and production. By playing a role in the entire production process—from product conception to product completion—it is anticipated that workers will feel more invested in the work that they do, thereby increasing productivity.

The ideas embodied in production teams resonated with research on policy implementation, which focused on the ineffectiveness of top-down reform strategies for education (Hannaway & Carnoy, 1993; McLaughlin, 1991; Odden, 1991). Mandates from above, be they from district offices, state departments of education, or the federal government, have often been met with teacher resistance, frequently because these mandates, envisioned as one-size-fits-all policies, bear little relation to the realities at individual school sites. These experiences pointed to new strategies that would involve those at the ground level—teachers, parents, and in some cases students—in developing and implementing policies and programs. It was hoped that greater involvement in decision making would accomplish two objectives: first, input from those in daily contact with classrooms and schools (teachers, parents, and students) would ensure authentic and relevant information and ideas; second, participation in crafting programs and other policies would encourage more faithful, enthusiastic, and knowledgeable implementation. *Site-based decision making, restructuring,* and *decentralization* are all terms that refer to a similar practice of devolving decision-making powers to school sites and creating at those sites bodies with broad representation.

These new forms of governance and decision making for school sites are intriguing innovations and have the potential to create exciting new structures and programs for schools. Initial responses to this reform were enthusiastic. But time and experience has shown that restructuring is not a panacea. It requires teachers, administrators, and district personnel alike to learn significant new skills in such areas as budget management, group process, and goal setting, which are often not directly linked to their initial professional training. Moreover, training is rarely provided to help school staffs develop these skills. As a result, restructured schools have created very little real change. In fact, studies of site-based decision making and restructuring reveal that while teachers in restructured schools report an increased sense of commitment and interest in school issues, the impact on classrooms has been minimal in terms of changes in teaching and improvements in student learning (Marks & Louis, 1997; Weiss et al., 1992). More importantly, issues key to improving schools for low-income and minority students have been largely overlooked when restructuring schools. Studies by a California school advocacy group (Olsen et al., 1994) conclude, "Based on our look at schools, multicultural curriculum is not a feature of the school restructuring movement, despite the presence of an increasingly diverse population. . . . The bilingual education field remains largely marginalized from the school restructuring field" (pp. 182, 218).

The directions taken in the 1980s for school reform suppressed the ideological issue of equality of opportunity. Conservative school reform advocates portrayed bilingual and multicultural education as divisive and as a "distraction" from important issues (Bloom, 1987; Hirsch, 1987). Not surprisingly, the important equity goals embodied in the reforms of the 1960s and 1970s fell by the wayside, deemed unimportant or promised as trickle-down byproducts of current efforts to raise standards. These efforts focused more on school management than on the actual dynamics of teaching and learning in classrooms. Moreover, few conservative reform efforts attended specifically to schools that were failing to meet the needs of poor and cultural minority students. At the same time, liberal responses to conservative initiatives tended towards the piecemeal, suggesting the inclusion of representative heroes and authors or the hiring of minority role models as teachers.

The Carnegie Foundation for the Advancement of Teaching (1988) analyzed the accomplishments of the 1980s reforms in this way:

> We are deeply troubled that a reform movement launched to upgrade the education of all students is irrelevant to many children—largely black and Hispanic—in our urban schools. In almost every big city, dropout rates are high, morale is low, facilities often are old and unattractive, and school leadership is crippled by a web of regulations. There is, in short, a disturbing gap between reform rhetoric and results.
>
> The failure to educate adequately urban children is a shortcoming of such magnitude that many people have simply written off city schools as little more than human storehouses to keep young people off the streets. We find it disgraceful that in the most affluent country in the world so many of our children are so poorly served. (p. xi)

Education Week's editors write, "Despite 15 years of earnest efforts to improve public schools and raise student achievement, states haven't made much progress" ("Quality Counts," 1997, p. 3). In fact, these 1980s conservative reform efforts show pitiful results. In 1996, states earned an average "grade" of "C" for quality of teaching, based on poor preparation and professional support and development opportunities; "C–" for overall school climate; and "B–" for funding equity and "C–" for funding directed at teaching and learning activities. Given our concerns with such issues as funding equity and school climate, this "report card" delivers appalling news. In such states as California, Texas, and Massachusetts, with tremendous student diversity, schools received grades of "D" and "D+" for funding equity and "C's" and "D–'s" for school climate ("Quality Counts," 1997).

During the 1990s, federal education policy directed by the Clinton administration has proceeded in fits and starts. Early on, it appeared that many of the ideas initiated during the conservative reform would be maintained. President Clinton continued to pursue national standards as a key educational reform, despite growing dissension about the content of those standards and how to assess them. As Clinton represented the more conservative wing of the Democratic Party, his initial reforms basically echoed those proposed during the Bush administration. However, a more progressive stance on educational issues emerged during the latter half of Clinton's first term (Smith & Scoll, 1995), where the administration focused on early childhood objectives (e.g., immunizations, nutrition, and preschool programs); reauthorization of the Elementary and Secondary Education Act (PL 103-382, renamed the Improving America's Schools Act of 1994), which emphasized high standards for all students, site-based programmatic flexibility, technology, and professional development opportunities for teachers, administrators, and parents; and improved school-to-work transitions (through the School-to-Work Opportunities Act). Additional initiatives during this period included expanded access to higher education through the Americorps program (the National Service Act), which allowed students to earn college credits through community service), and the Federal Direct Loan Program, designed to offer more flexible student loan repayment packages.

Because poverty is directly related to school achievement, the Welfare Reform Act of 1996 (PL 104-193), passed by Congress and approved by President Clinton, may have significant negative impact on school children and their families. This act dramatically reduced social service benefits allocated for children. At the same time, by 1998 a prospering economy led to 67 percent increase in public assistance to the poor, raises in the minimum wage helped the working poor, and the earned income tax credit produced significant tax savings for low-income workers. Once again, the Clinton administration seems to be traveling in opposite directions at the same time. As of this writing we cannot make a conclusive statement on the balance of resources for the poor. The impact of the Welfare Reform Act will begin to be felt between 1998 and 2001.

The federal focus on national standards continues and is accompanied by piecemeal efforts to rectify educational concerns. For example, part of Clinton's 1998 budget proposal included funds for 100,000 new teachers and bond measures for significant new building programs. However, the federal government has not articulated a clear set of educational objectives or reforms and has not progressed beyond the call for adherence to the national standards expressed in *Goals 2000* (see Figure 13.2).

Schooling For Poor Students and Students of Color in Urban and Rural Settings

While conservatives blamed teachers and ethnic minorities for school failure, Joe Fernandez, formerly chancellor of New York City's public schools, argues in *Tales Out of School* (Fernandez & Underwood, 1993) that any serious analysis of school reform must begin by looking at budget priorities. In many ways, federal policies have exacerbated the problems of urban areas and of urban schools. One U.S. House of Representatives study (Moynihan, 1993–1994) states:

> Between 1970 and 1991, the value of AFDC (Aid to Families with Dependent Children) benefits declined by 41 percent. In spite of the proven success of Head Start, only 28 percent of the eligible children are being served. As of 1990, more than 18 billion dollars in child support went uncollected. At the same time, the poverty rate among single-parent families with children under 18 was 44 percent. Between 1980 and 1990 the rate of growth of the total federal budget was four times greater than the rate of growth of children's programs. (p. 13)

Bob Chase, president of the National Education Association, notes that "the richest nation in the world has yet to muster the political willpower to provide every child with a decent chance at quality education. At least 15 million children in America attend substandard schools. . . . That's why the states must level up funding for the poorest public schools, especially inner city and rural schools" (Chase, 1997, p. 2). He says further, "To set high academic standards for all students nationally, without providing the resources to meet them, would be a cruel joke. As cruel a joke as promising to treat each child equally and never living up to that promise" (p. 2).

We spend less per student than 16 other modern, industrialized countries (Slavin, 1998). Moreover, of these, we are the only country that does not actively promote equality of educational opportunity. In the Netherlands, for example, schools receive 25 percent more funding for each lower-income child and 90 percent more funding for each minority child than in the United States (Slavin, 1998). Clearly, schools serving working-class students and cultural minorities fail in large part because our nation refuses to invest in its children. Our economy needs well-educated workers. We cannot permit schools to continue to fail students of color. When schools succeed for the middle class and fail for working-class students and students of color, schools contribute to a crippling division along economic and racial lines in our society. Schools, as public institutions, must find ways to offer all children equal educational opportunity. Yet reformed schools are more exceptions than the common pattern, particularly in our urban areas.

The following portrait (adapted from Wong, in press) paints an image of the disparities among schools within a single district—disparities that play out on a larger scale when one looks across districts. A typical school in the eastern part of this urban district boasts a well-maintained facility with experienced and effective teachers. Classrooms are cheerful, colorful, and enlivened places where students are enthusiastic about their learning. Student work adorns walls and hallways. Classrooms buzz with activity and students proudly explain their thoughts and opinions. Parents are actively involved and organize fundraisers and other special events to benefit the school. Numerous indicators reflect the school's positive environment and related successes. 1994 student scores on the Comprehensive Test of Basic Skills (CTBS) were 16 and 20 percentiles above the national median in third- and sixth-grade reading, respectively, and 10 and 21 percentiles above the national median in third- and sixth-grade mathematics. There was a 3 percent retention rate in 1993 and no students were suspended. No students come from families that receive AFDC, and only 9 percent qualify for the free/reduced lunch program.

A mile or two away on the western edge of the same district students study under vastly different circumstances. The school here has leaking roofs, rusty playground equipment, and boarded-over windows that hide bullet holes and glass broken by recent acts of vandalism. Classrooms are often overcrowded. Student learning and classwork is rarely displayed. Many of the district's least experienced or least successful teachers can be found concentrated here. School staff tend to be disdainful of parents; not surprisingly, parent participation is limited. The overall environment reflects a high rate of student poverty, with over half the students qualifying for the free/reduced lunch program and coming from families that receive AFDC. Disruptions and inadequate academic progress appear to be rampant: the suspension rate in 1993 was 36 percent and the retention rate was 7 percent. Student achievement in this school is disturbingly low. Third-grade CTBS reading scores have historically been at least 10 percentiles below the national median, and mathematics scores are as low as 25 percentiles below their national median. Sixth-grade scores, on average, are even lower. The majority of the students in the first school are Anglo and from middle-class families; the majority of students in the second school are cultural- and language-minority children from working-class and poor families.

Theoretically, because these two schools are located in the same district, they have the same resources. But, careful scrutiny challenges this assumption. First, the age and condition of the physical plants warrants different treatment and resources;

the first school is newer and has fewer current needs for repairs or upgrades. Tangentially, a more pleasant working environment often serves as an incentive for attracting better qualified teachers. Second, the middle-class families in the first school are also in a more privileged position to contribute to their children's school in material and nonmaterial (e.g., volunteering in classrooms, appearing as guest speakers, etc.) ways. Third, neighborhood location plays a crucial role in that students in the first school also have easier access (because of proximity and parents' ability to provide rides) to a range of educationally supportive resources such as libraries, museums, and so on.

Let us be clear about the reality of schools in our nation. Some middle-class schools could benefit from reform, but most middle-class schools work. Most schools in urban areas, however, are unable to provide the equal educational opportunity called for by our national ideals and by constitutional law. There will be no significant change in the quality of urban education without substantial new funds allocated to these schools. As the NEA's Chase has noted, children in these schools need and deserve the same quality of buildings, teachers, materials, and resources as do students from affluent neighborhoods.

New Goals for Democratic School Reform

As we have documented in this volume, the U.S. public education system has consistently failed low-income students, many African American, Latino, and Native American students, and some Asian American students. Many reforms have been initiated, yet few have articulated an agenda that specifically seeks to hold the system accountable for providing equal educational opportunities for all students. A democratic agenda for school reform is long overdue and is imperative for the future health of our society.

Macedo (1993) summarizes some of the results of continuing the present school system:

> It is indeed ironic that in the United States, a country that prides itself on being the first and most advanced within the so-called "first-world," over sixty million people are illiterate or functionally illiterate. . . . To the sixty million illiterates we should add the sizable groups who learn to read but are, by and large, incapable of developing independent and critical thought.
>
>   . . . I believe that, instead of the democratic education we claim to have, what we really have in place is a sophisticated colonial model of education designed primarily to train state functionaries and commissars while denying access to millions, a situation which further exacerbates the equity gap already victimizing a great number of so-called "minority" students. Even the education provided to those with class rights and privileges is devoid of the intellectual dimension of true teaching, since the major objective of a colonial education is to further deskill teachers and students so as to reduce them to mere technical agents who are destined to walk unreflectively through a labyrinth of procedures. What we have in the United States is not a system to encourage independent thought and critical

thinking. Our colonial literacy model is designed to domesticate so as to enable the "manufacture of consent." (p. 203)

Too often, school reform is approached piecemeal, implementing one reform at a time. This approach has proven less than productive. Only systematic reform will work. We should be clear about our assumptions and the directions of reform we support if we hope to design safe and effective schools in those neighborhoods where schools are currently failing. The following arguments underlie the case for equity-based educational reform. We need to select interventions and reform proposals consistent with these arguments that advance long-range, equity-based change.

1. In a changing economy, education in specific skills and work habits is necessary for a decent standard of living. Students learn these skills, habits, and knowledge through their own efforts. It is not enough for teachers and school leaders to plan a new curriculum. Equity-based reform requires students to modify their behavior, to make more effort. Our task is to help students, especially those from marginalized communities, to acquire the maturity and discipline to take their educational future into their own hands, using coaching and other proactive strategies (see Chapter 8).

2. The real results of not getting a good education and dropping out of school are poverty, family disintegration, and lost opportunity. Students need to learn why it is important to stay in school. Equity-based school reform includes teaching students the values of staying in school and of getting a good education. Teachers cannot assume that students have internalized these values. It is not enough to simply present them with the current math, science, literature curriculum, adding in contributions of major ethnic groups. Lessons in social studies and literature should focus on the value of the education. Coaching and counseling would be appropriate for the most alienated students (see Chapter 8).

3. Schools and other institutions must organize to help students to move out of poverty toward work and democratic participation. School-to-work programs, career shadowing, and opportunities to earn an income in high school should become part of the curriculum.

4. Crime, drugs, gangs, teenage pregnancy, and dropping out of school are destructive to students' lives and to their opportunities for quality education. We cannot allow the negative aspects of teen culture to go unchallenged. Our task is to prepare these students for the future. We cannot continue to accept high dropout and unemployment rates in U.S. cities.

5. Through democracy, people can fashion a political-economic system with good jobs, a decent standard of living, provisions for good health, and education for all. We need to teach realistic hope. We do not achieve this by preaching, but by teaching students skills and helping them to move toward democracy and productive employment. Stu-

dents learn to internalize hope through cooperative learning and by working together successfully on projects (see Chapter 10).

6. Individual students can choose to work for their education and against crime, social destructiveness, and poverty. For many students, in many schools, in many neighborhoods, life is difficult. But, individual decision making can lead them toward constructing a positive life for themselves and their families, even when their school or their family is in crisis. These decisions require maturity and clarity. Schools in at-risk neighborhoods need strategies and programs (such as Al Ateen, special classes for mothers, crisis counseling, and other targeted services) to help students learn to make these decisions.

7. Students and adults have a right to seek improved standards of living—and to change the structures that prevent their development. Too often we accept as inevitable that large numbers of students will be alienated by school, or large numbers will drop out, or our building needs repair and the district says it has no money. We create a positive future orientation by approaching these issues as challenges, as problem-posing issues (see Chapter 9).

8. Not all school failure is due to individuals' lack of effort or ability. You can examine school practices and change them to promote success and equal opportunity. If your school tracks, students in lower tracks may be being prepared for failure. When an entire school has low achievement scores, as many do, then the structure of the school itself needs re-examination and reform (see Chapter 12). Students and parents have a right to oppose tracking, to demand counselors and health clinics, and college or career preparation programs. They have a right to schools where all students learn.

9. Comprehensive secondary schools, including community colleges, should allow students to make career decisions, change their directions, and work toward economic opportunity.

These ideas pose ambitious goals for school reform, including that schools should contribute to building a democratic society. Of course, some in the United States do not in fact prefer a more democratic society, and certainly do not want schools promoting more political participation.

Views of Reforming Schools

The following vignettes, adapted from McLeod (1996), illustrate the work of schools that are already pursuing an agenda of democratic school reform for poor and minority students, and highlight practices that make their work successful.

At Wiggs Middle School in Texas, integrated thematic curriculum is a powerful tool. Drawing on the local Mexican and Chicano culture, one curriculum unit was organized around the study of chili. Social studies classes focused on the chili crop and tensions created by it between Mexico and New Mexico during the nineteenth century. Students developed math skills by graphing the relative hotness of different chilies, analyzing chili production in different regions of the world, and computing the yield of chilies by acre in their neighboring communities. Students learned about the biology of chilies in science class, and used literature about the chili god to create their own myths related to this potent plant.

At Sierra Accelerated Elementary School in northern California, the Options classes offered every Thursday afternoon bring excitement and wonder. During Options time, teachers and parents offer minicourses geared towards specific topics and skills; students self-select into these courses for a four-week period. Options time provides important opportunities for staff and community to work together on activities that build on their strengths and enhance their relationships. In addition, students are exposed to information and material not typically covered in their curriculum and have the chance to work with adults in unconventional ways. This school has also taken an aggressive stance towards parent involvement: meetings are held at times convenient to working parents' schedules— before 8:00 A.M. and after 5:00 P.M.

Staff at Graham and Parks Middle School in Massachusetts have found ways to maximize instructional time and minimize disruptions. Core academic subjects are taught in an interdisciplinary manner and organized around extended blocks. Students take a two-hour block of language arts/social studies and another two-hour block of mathematics/science. These longer time periods make projects and multiple activities more feasible.

At Linda Vista Elementary School in southern California, bilingual and monolingual English-speaking teachers teach together in teams. This gives all students exposure to English and Spanish instructional models. It increases the status of Spanish among English-speaking students and it eases the transition to an all-English environment for Spanish-speaking students. In addition, students at this school work together to design and produce multimedia book reports that incorporate computer software. Students delegate and share tasks—graphics design, text composition, use of the software, and final oral presentation. Students are encouraged to complete these tasks in the language with which they are most comfortable; thus a mixture of English and Spanish can be heard in their discussions.

At Hanshaw Elementary School in central California, the principal interviewed 500 local families prior to the opening of school to determine the types of expectations they had for their children and to understand the extent of their knowledge of the school system. In addition, he took his teachers on a bus tour of the school neighborhood. Through both efforts, this school was able to bridge the previously considerable gap between the staff's perceptions of the out-of-school environment and the concrete realities of students' and their families' lives. Through these processes, the school has been able to develop programs that more accurately reflect students' concerns and needs while also supporting parents' aspirations for their children's futures.

Hollibrook Elementary School in Texas offers "continuum classes" that allow students and teachers to stay together for several years. This continuum gives teachers an opportunity to see the full range of growth of their students while also allowing students and teachers to develop strong and caring relationships.

At Zavala Elementary School in Texas a coalition of parents, teachers, and administrators developed proposals that linked school sites and municipal departments in an efforts to provide afterschool activities for students. At Zavala, the teacher-coordinators of this afterschool program developed courses that promoted each of the seven different types of intelligences identified by Gardner (1983). Offerings included a math club, an authors' club, cooking, computers, sewing, and magic.

The practices described here worked for these schools, given their mix of staff, students, and community members and their local conditions and situations. While specific activities or processes initiated at these sites may not work in all situations, it is important to highlight the underlying practices, which can be crafted to fit any school site.

The following list is not meant to be used as a checklist for things to do to improve a school. Rather, the items are ideas you may use to initiate discussions, spark dialogue, and frame inquiry and investigation. View them as broad guidelines, some of which may be applicable to particular schools and particular situations (McLeod, 1996):

1. Include language-minority students by providing opportunities for and supporting their participation in all activities in the regular curriculum.

2. Provide a rich and enriching curriculum and academic program to all students, principally through the use of heterogeneous groups, cooperative learning, and use of students' native languages.

3. Help to make your school internally motivated to make improvements.

4. Be flexible in your instructional and organizational practices but try to implement programs and activities in a coordinated manner both within and between grade levels.

5. Protect and extend learning time.

6. Encourage your school to provide all teachers with training, support, mentoring, and planning time to develop and use effective and innovative teaching strategies.

7. Involve parents in their children's education.

8. Create school and classroom environments that nurture and encourage all aspects (cognitive, social, emotional, etc.) of students' development.

Who Is Involved in Democratic School Reform?

Democratic school reform will require the creation of a new coalition of teachers and parents, and new political forces. As described in the beginning of this chapter, the history of educational reform is replete with federal, state, and district mandates. But these mandates alone have not worked. We must begin to mobilize for educational improvement at the grassroots level: with parents, students, teachers, administrators, teachers' unions, and other community members. All must become stakeholders in this critical process.

Parents as Stakeholders

Increasing numbers of parents are giving up on schools. Some place their children in "safe" private (often church-supported) schools, others initiate home schooling, some support school "choice" plans, and still others support the establishment of all-male or predominantly black academies. These are the responses of a population that doubts the effectiveness of public schools for its children. Middle-class parents achieve the same ends by moving to the suburbs, to "better" neighborhoods, and by establishing "magnet" schools for their children.

Successful school improvement efforts result, in part, from new relationships and partnerships with parents and other community members. Decentralized decision making, site-based management, and an effective school–home communication system all assist in increasing parent participation, and make it possible for parents to actually assume leadership roles in school reform. Involving parents in the important decisions of the school brings them in as partners in the education equation. Schools can find ways to help parents and teachers articulate and define together the types of knowledge and skills they would like students to develop. Dialogue between parents and teachers will help to solidify their understanding of these goals and their collaborative commitment to reaching them. Individual teachers can be very effective in reaching out to parents, in part by initiating frequent and respectful communication. They can learn the different community resources available to children and their families and serve as information conduits, passing on important contacts and phone numbers to parents and community service providers. Conversely, parents can bring much-needed resources into classrooms. They can serve as volunteers, tutors, role models, and counselors, they can help with conflict resolution, and they can join teachers as advocates for youth.

Unfortunately, parents and teachers often find themselves in an unproductive trap of blaming each other for student underachievement. Parents in major urban districts are usually aware of the failure of their schools to provide a safe environment and a quality education for their children. Parents are often accurate in their perception of school failure to provide their children with equal educational opportunity. Angry parents tend to blame the school district, the teacher's union, or the teachers. This anger can create a group of parents easily mobilized against both tax increases and school programs, such as reading, math, or bilingual education.

On the other hand, teachers who are faced with rebellious students may blame parents for failing to teach their children proper behavior and respect. This often hostile or distant relationship between teachers and parents is the result of long and complex histories of miscommunication and school failure. Only frequent and positive contacts between the school and parents will improve these relationships; such a close working relationship is required for school reform. In addition, educators must begin to realize that most parents are concerned about their children's education, though they may have varying skills in expressing their concerns and in making the school system address them (Figure 13.3).

Figure 13.3   Example of an Effective School Site Council

When a School Site Council Works

While raising six children, Ella sat on her share of school/parent advisory groups. She soon learned that parents usually don't have much power; paid professionals dominate decision making. Ella is relieved that parents are the majority on this council. Some folks have reservations about parents having the most votes, but not Ella. In her mind, numbers aren't the real issue. The real issue is parity.

Ella knows—and others are learning—that although the council sets policies, principals and teachers run the school all day long, day in and day out. For professional educators, running a school is both a career and a full-time job. They needn't worry about staying well informed; they are automatically inside the information loop. And information is power.

For real negotiations to occur between the community and the school, a more equitable sharing of power is necessary. Even very active parents spend relatively little time at the school—almost always after meeting the demands of his or her own employment. A parent's involvement with school is usually limited to the amount of time his or her child attends it. Having a majority of parents on the council is one way to offset this inherent power imbalance.

In addition to Ella, council membership includes five other parents, two community representatives, two teachers, and the principal. Ella knows educating children requires a strong partnership between parents and professional educators, and she works hard to build it. Because Ella deeply values a true partnership, she is determined that the shared decision making of the council not play itself out as "anti-teacher." She knows this would sabotage the school's ability to support the academic success of its students.

She always perseveres until consensus can be reached at council meetings—even when the agenda is full and meetings run overtime. In fact, the council has agreed to not adjourn until all disagreements are settled. She is also very clear about the council's role. It sets policy. It hires the principal. It develops a plan that sets priorities for school improvement. It prepares and approves a budget supporting the school improvement plan.

The school's professional staff has a strong voice in helping to shape policy and is responsible for its implementation. A professional advisory committee works closely with elected teacher members of the council who carry staff views on various issues to council meetings. The professional advisory committee plays a large role in determining the content of curriculum and rethinking teaching methods.

Note. From *The Good Common School: Making the Vision Work for All Children* (pp. 12–14) by National Coalition of Advocates for Students, 1991, Boston: Author. Reprinted by permission.

Students as Stakeholders

A primary focus of democratic educational reform is on student empowerment, helping young people to see themselves as having the power and knowledge to shape the direction of their own lives. Because of this basic premise, democratic school reform must include students and their voices, opinions, and ideas in charting the future course of education. This is particularly true for students who are presently marginalized and disenfranchised. Students can be powerful members of governance and decision-making bodies. Their experiences and attitudes can form the basis for concrete changes to make schools more engaging and inviting places to learn. Understanding their hopes and dreams can be a suitable starting point for developing new programs and curricula. Students can be trained to be influential leaders, helping their peers and younger students to develop good study habits, make informed life choices, and participate in extracurricular activities.

Traditionally, students have participated in schools through tracks such as student council that parallel adult decision-making processes but have considerably lower status and importance. In democratic school reform, these activities would be important, but students would also be involved in key decisions about school policies and programs; after all, along with the teachers, they are the ones most affected by these actions. More importantly, however, such involvement teaches important life and civic skills. Students need to learn about democracy, responsibility, decision making, and empowerment by experiencing them and reflecting on them, not by reading about them in a book or being told by an adult about their importance. The more structured activities students have that involve them in thinking about and making important decisions, the better.

In a society that increasingly legislates against nonmainstream groups (such as through the 1996 Federal Welfare Reform Act; Congressional efforts to restrict affirmative action; and California's propositions 187, to eliminate services to undocumented immigrants, 209, to dismantle affirmative action, and 227, to restrict bilingual education), it becomes ever more urgent for students from marginalized communities to learn democratic empowerment skills by participating early and often in struggles to defend and develop their schools and communities (see Chapter 7).

Teachers as Stakeholders

Anyone serious about democratic educational reform should address their concerns first to teachers. Teachers are the major resource available for improving education. Teachers' salaries are the largest part of any school budget. It is teachers—not administrators—who conduct the basic educational process. Most teachers want to do better and would welcome an opportunity to help more students to succeed. Reformers interested in improving the educational opportunities for working-class students should first look to help teachers perform their jobs better.

Over the years, various efforts have been made to produce curriculum and instructional strategies that are "teacher proof"; that is, the authors script and monitor each step a teacher might take in delivering a lesson, hoping that strictly charting teacher action will guarantee student outcomes. (For example, several recent phonics-based reading curriculum packages use this approach.) But a history of research, with a landmark milestone in Lortie's *Schoolteacher* (1975), has revealed that good teaching is a highly individual and creative act, based as much on instinct and experience as on theory and philosophy. Even the most organized and innovative curriculum can become monotonous in the hands of mediocre teacher; highly skilled teachers can transform drill and practice into activities that students find engaging and productive.

Recent reform efforts have sought to capitalize on teachers' "wisdom of practice" (Shulman, 1987) by empowering them to participate more fully in policy development and other important decisions. School improvement programs such as the Accelerated Schools Project seek to empower teachers while also expanding their responsibility for the development and implementation of educational decisions (Hopfenberg et al., 1993). Restructuring efforts, mentioned earlier, attempt to create site-based decision making that opens school governance to those most affected by it: teachers.

Increased involvement of teachers has had many benefits, including more practical and better-implemented policies as well as renewed enthusiasm and interest in teaching on the part of educators. Thus, recognition and acknowledgment of teacher voice, experience, knowledge, and wisdom can create momentum for school change. At the same time, we must consider several important factors when thinking of teachers as stakeholders in democratic school reform.

Teachers in general are highly committed to their students and care about their education and overall welfare. Educational reforms and reform movements should capitalize on this commitment by focusing their efforts on the matters of most importance to teachers: learning and teaching in the classroom. A recent study at Stanford University (McLaughlin & Talbert, 1993) found that, across the country, reforms that support teacher learning by providing time for study, reflection, and inservice training on concrete classroom issues will have the most chances for improving student learning. Reforms that provide teachers with supportive environments in which to innovate and try new practices will help to unleash the creative ideas that are typically quashed by the more standard "teacher-proof" curriculum. Reforms that connect teachers to teachers and involve them in a network that can provide a flow of new ideas, new questions, new strategies, and other forms of renewal will solidify in teachers a spirit of continual improvement, accountability, and high standards.

Teachers need improved organizational and material conditions in order to be active participants in democratic reform efforts. Most teachers work in conditions that would be deemed unacceptable by other professionals. They have little more than an hour or two per week to plan and develop lessons, they often spend much of their own salaries for basic materials, and in a majority of urban schools they work in classrooms with leaky roofs, broken glass, insufficient lighting, and limited access to telephones. These conditions are demoralizing, and devalue the skills and talents that most teachers have developed. It is also essential that democratic school reform grapple with the personnel dimensions of school change. As discussed in earlier chapters, the teacher corps in the United States is overwhelmingly female, Caucasian, middle class, and monolingual. There is nothing about this profile that prohibits effective teaching. But, with a school population that is becoming increasingly multicultural and multilingual, these teachers will need special knowledge and training to work successfully. In addition, it is becoming more important than ever to actively recruit and mentor bilingual teachers and teachers from minority communities. Adding their voices to those already active in democratic school reform will only strengthen these movements.

Administrators as Stakeholders

Each element of schools has its own culture: students, teachers, support staff, and administrators. Administrators develop their own sense of their position, values, and rewards and punishments connected to those values. New administrators acquire these viewpoints both as they study to become administrators and as they experience their first few years of leadership responsibility.

An important part of the administrative worldview is the need to get things done. Administrators want to fix the broken window, deal with the disruptive child, and locate the substitute teacher, and they want to perform in a manner respected by their supervisors in central administration.

This "tyranny of the urgent" is particularly evident in dysfunctional schools where school plants are deteriorating or the community permits violence in the surrounding neighborhoods. The need to respond to a neverending series of crises keeps many administrators from becoming leaders.

To address this situation, administrators must learn new skills and behaviors if they are to be effective partners in democratic school reform. They must begin to see themselves less as managers and more as facilitators. At the same time, because they do have official power and authority, they must consistently model a commitment to ideals of equity, social justice, and quality teaching and learning. They can do this by jealously guarding time and resources for instruction and teacher renewal. They also adopt many of the practices we have suggested for teachers. They should recognize the many talents and strengths of their staff members and create structures and opportunities that promote these qualities. They need to learn to make decisions collaboratively by ensuring that staff members have channels through which to voice their opinions and concerns as well as access to data and information needed to make well-informed and thoughtful decisions. They will benefit their schools by taking an active role in supporting teachers, having frequent positive contact with students, understanding the classroom issues that face teachers, and providing the resources, programs, and leadership for them to create effective and engaging classrooms. Administrators are in an almost ideal position to become strong liaisons with community groups and organizations, thus initiating the types of networks and coalitions needed to involve important community support in the process of democratic school reform.

Finally, site administrators will need to rethink their role *vis á vis* their supervisors at the district office. Schools involved in democratic school reform challenge the norm and the status quo. Site administrators must be prepared to fight for the resources and special considerations their schools may need while also protecting them from many of the normal district demands that might retard or divert their efforts. For example, a school that has established a democratic decision-making process involving a range of stakeholders (students, families, teachers, etc.) will require a longer timeline to make decisions than one in which the administrator is the sole decision maker. The administrator will need to convey the importance of the extended timeline rather than bypassing the school stakeholders in the rush to meet district deadlines. Similarly, a school involved in democratic reform may need a different set of professional development workshops than those typically pre-scribed by the district. In these situations, the administrator may have to make a special case with district personnel for a waiver or consideration to follow a site-spe-cific plan. Such instances require administrators adept not only at representing and advocating for their school but also at successfully negotiating district politics.

Teacher Unions and School Reform

Over 75 percent of teachers in the United States are represented by unions (National Education Association, 1996). Teachers responded to the growth of educational man-agement and bureaucracy in the 1960s and 1970s by forming unions. In the interven-ing decades unions have become increasingly politically active, using their organiza-tion and money to protect their members' interests. Organized teachers' unions have often protected school funding in the midst of public fiscal crises. Serious effort at school reform must engage teachers through their unions, and teachers interested in school reform need to enlist their unions' aid. Unions have the organization and politi-cal capital that can assist or defeat efforts to democratize public schools.

For example, in the wake of the California tax revolt of 1978, which limited the growth of the state budget, California teachers' unions in 1988 led a successful cam-paign to pass Proposition 98, protecting school funding from cuts ("Quality Counts," 1997). In California, Michigan, Illinois, Massachusetts, and many other states, pro-longed economic crisis stopped most efforts at school reform. In 1992, teachers' unions, particularly the National Education Association (NEA) devoted substantial resources in a successful effort to defeat George Bush and elect Bill Clinton as Presi-dent of the United States. Both unions (NEA and AFT) contributed substantially to Clinton's 1996 reelection campaign (Burkins & Simpson, 1996; Pitsch, 1996).

While unions have led the efforts to protect school funding and to elect pro-educa-tion legislators and a new president, they have not provided substantial leadership in the struggle to improve the quality of education in our poor rural and urban educa-tional crisis areas. When schools are under attack, unions provide a vital and vigorous defense. But, in our experience, when only poor schools suffer ruinous underfunding, unions have often been reluctant to commit their resources to the struggle for equality of opportunity. Teacher-activists concerned with producing equal educational opportunity for children from urban districts will have to reconceptualize the roles of their unions. Negotiations with an entrenched management may produce improved benefits, but may not produce educational improvement for urban students.

A beginning was made toward union activism on educational reform in August 1994, in Portland, Oregon, at a meeting of the National Coalition of Educational Activists. A document produced at this meeting, entitled, "Social Justice Unionism," (National Coalition of Educational Activists, 1994) contains the following statement:

> Public education is at a crossroads and so, too, are our unions. Our society's children face deepening poverty and social dislocation, challenges and higher expectations with declining resources. . . . As the organized core of the teaching profession, education unions remain central to resolving these crises. (p. 12)

More positive evidence comes from recent developments in the National Education Association, which has begun to challenge funding disparities and has adopted a new orientation towards school reform.

There are many teacher and administrator organizations. The largest are the unions, the National Education Association (NEA) (http://www.nea.org/), the American Federation of Teachers (AFT) (http://www.aft.org/), and their state affiliates. These organizations have professional development goals, staff, and resources. As unions, they advance the interests of their members. In 1998 these two organizations voted to eventually merge into one national teachers union. Several academic disciplines also have their own organizations, such as the National Council for Social Studies (http://www.ncss.org/), the National Council of Teachers of English (http://www.ncte.org/), and so on, with their state affiliates. In addition, organizations exist whose purpose is to improve opportunities for marginalized students, such as The National Association of Bilingual Education (http://www.nabe.org/) and the National Association of Multicultural Education.

These organizations often work in concert with established citizen groups (Figure 13.4). In any school reform effort, these organizations and others have roles they could play. Clearly, reformers would benefit by drawing on their expertise.

The Process of School Reform

In many ways, the term *school reform* is misleading because it can evoke images of new programs, new activities, and new materials. In fact, new learning is probably the most important element of school reform, though it is frequently underestimated or overlooked. As highlighted by Banks (1994) and discussed in Chapter 12, multicultural education reform is a complex and multidimensional transformation, one that requires all participating adults and youth to think, act, and respond in new ways. Successful participants will need to unlearn practices and beliefs and to learn different ones. Just as educators put time, energy, creativity, and resources into creating powerful learning environments for students, similar care must be invested to create situations that stimulate and sustain the new learning required for school

Figure 13.4   **The Industrial Areas Foundation**

The Industrial Areas Foundation (IAF) is a cornerstone organization of a national network of broad-based, multiethnic, interfaith organizations that work primarily in poor and low-income communities. This network has been in operation for over 50 years and works to further the vision of its founder, Saul Alinsky, in building the competence and confidence of ordinary citizens to change the relationships of power and politics in their communities (Cortés, 1996) As the IAF contends,

> Any effort to improve the quality of early care and education must be connected to the revitalization of the social and political institutions in our communities. . . . In every community throughout the nation there are literally thousands of people with the potential to participate successfully in public life. Reform strategies won't work unless they recognize and draw upon the resources of these people and their ties to community institutions. (p. 2–6)

Building from this belief, the IAF has worked in numerous communities to mobilize support for fundamental educational reforms. Their efforts have been highly successful, yielding not only substantial improvements in local schools but compelling insights about the nature of broad-based networks. They observe that parents' (particularly immigrant parents or those with their own negative schooling experiences) and community leaders' initial forays into school reform highlights how unfamiliar they are with basic aspects of school structure and organization. Because they do not yet understand how schools operate or possess skills for effectively working in this arena, they are often ineffective advocates and participants in decision making. IAF organizers use careful and consistent mentoring to help build parents' and community members' skills at such endeavors as identifying and researching issues, organizing action teams, and engaging in public debate and negotiation. As their self-esteem and self-confidence increase, parents become active participants in the reform process who not only respond to but actually shape the efforts to improve their schools.

IAF has been most active in school reform in the Southwest. Through the Alliance Schools Initiative, a Texas partnership of districts, cities and IAF organizations, many schools have seen test scores and attendance rates increase, dropout rates decrease, and parent participation escalate dramatically. In these cases, a compelling cultural shift has occurred: "Principals no longer see themselves as compliance officers of the district, but as leaders of a team. Teachers learn how to negotiate rules and regulations and can contribute their creative ideas to the classroom. Parents learn how to be equal decision-makers at the table with teachers, principals, and officials" (Cortés, 1996, p. 13). During an era when politics and social movements can seem fractured by narrow group interests, the IAF highlights the importance and effectiveness of cross-group coalitions.

reform. As Darling-Hammond (1997) observes, "Teachers teach from what they know. If policy makers want to change teaching, they must pay attention to teacher knowledge [and make] investments in those things that allow teachers . . . to grapple with transformations of ideas and behavior" (p. 339).

Until the mid 1970s, the research and study of school reform tended to focus on descriptions of programs and policies and analyses of their outcomes and products, ignoring important contextual factors that affect implementation such as grade level, subject matter, characteristics of the student population, and so on (McLaughlin & Talbert, 1993). As a result, when program outcomes failed to meet expectations, teacher resistance, lack of training, and resource shortages were often blamed.

Studies in the 1980s and 1990s have analyzed the process of school reform implementation, uncovering important insights into factors that shape institutional and individual responses. We summarize and elaborate on this research here. These conclusions can be applied to all involved in the change process—teachers, administrators, parents, and students alike.

New learning must have a clearly defined purpose. In most cases, this means that participants must recognize a need for new learning or changes (T. P. Carter, 1990).

Multicultural education reform requires democratic educators to recognize the value-laden nature of present curriculum and school-funding decisions, which support the current unequal distribution of knowledge, wealth, power, and authority in U.S. society.

The National Coalition of Educational Activists (1994) argues, "We must address the negative impact of racism—both on U.S. education and within the educational reform movement. Schools must give a high priority to confronting the long history of racism that has shaped our education system" (pp. 12–13).

To strengthen our democracy, we must defeat racism, sexism, and class bias. Schools, because they are public institutions, have an obligation to provide equal educational opportunity and to promote prodemocratic values. Whenever and wherever schools or school districts fail the test of equal opportunity, they must be changed.

New learning should be embedded in everyday practices, focused on the concrete teaching and learning issues and questions that emerge from daily classroom and school situations (Case & Bereiter, 1984; Lieberman, 1995; McLaughlin & Talbert, 1993; Tharp & Gallimore, 1988).

Most educators, students, and community members care deeply about their local schools and the future of the students that attend them. The reform process should start with school site realities and participants' understandings of and explanations for them. This taps into their priority concerns as well as their passions. Reflection on these realities can initiate dialogue and discussion about what participants value, what they want changed, and how they think about possible changes.

New learning must focus on using new or revised materials, new teaching approaches and *altering pedagogical beliefs and assumptions* (Fullan, 1991).

If teachers continue to believe that boys are better than girls at math, even the most gender-neutral or gender-affirming curriculum will not allow them to garner high math achievement from their female students. Similarly, if Anglo parents continue to view bilingual education as something that gives immigrant children special status, while immigrant parents wonder if their children are learning English, political groups will continue to mobilize against democratic reform for these children (see Chapter 11). If administrators define "good teaching" as a quiet classroom, innovative math manipulatives and hands-on science kits that require interactive and often noisy groupwork will remain boxed up on shelves. As stated by the Commission on Chapter 1 (1993):

The fact is that we know how to educate poor and minority children of all kinds—racial, ethnic, and language—to high levels. Some teachers and entire schools do it every day, year in and year out with outstanding results. But the nation as a whole has not yet acted on that knowledge, even though we need each and every one of our young people to master high-level knowledge and skills. (pp. 46–47)

New learning must be supported and encouraged in numerous ways, including internal networks (e.g., grade-level, cross-disciplinary, and circuit teams) and external networks (e.g., professional organizations and partnerships) (Lieberman, 1995; McLaughlin & Talbert, 1993).

School reform is a process, not an event. In fact, school reform is actually a learning process. Like other learning processes, the work of school reform requires structures and networks to guide, support, and sustain it. When reform participants can interact with each other around important school or classroom issues, they gain insights, identify colleagues' strengths, and receive encouragement. Similarly, engagement with such external networks as school–university partnerships, school reform organizations, and subject matter groups, provides an infusion of new ideas, objective feedback on ideas and activities, and solidarity with others involved in similar efforts.

New learning is a long-term process with many aspects: building new roles (e.g., teacher leaders); inventing relationships (e.g., peer coaching); creating structures (e.g., site-based decision making); working on new tasks (e.g., proposal writing, creating standards, completing school site performance quality reviews); and creating a culture of inquiry (Lieberman, 1995).

Reformers must understand the changes that will occur as well as the nature of the change process (T. P. Carter, 1990; Fullan, 1991). They must be able to perceive the small changes that happen on an individual level, with particular teachers or students, comprehend the larger changes that affect the school structure and culture, and recognize the ways in which these small and large changes interact (Hopfenberg et al., 1993; Sarason, 1990).

For example, in one Accelerated school, a staff person reflected on the relationship between two teachers at year's end: "Ms. Smith and Mr. Jones now talk with one another." On its face, it is somewhat humorous. This is not what we expect when we think about school reform. But this simple statement, the fact that they had learned to talk with one another, was significant on a personal level—they had made changes and compromises that allowed for collaboration where animosity had previously existed. Equally significant was the fact that Ms. Smith and Mr. Jones taught different grade levels. Their increased collaboration was actually symbolic of larger changes in the school structure that were making cross-grade communication and planning more common. Additionally, this combination of individual and structural changes was mutually reinforcing. The breakthroughs Ms. Smith and Mr. Jones had with each other gave them the confidence to enter into other partnerships that they might not have entertained previously, and it encouraged others to try to overcome historic differences for the purposes of working on common challenges and issues at the school.

To succeed, these new learning processes must involve teachers and parents working together to set new goals and develop a new vision of the possible (Figure 13.5). Positive experiences of planning and improving the school culture can lead to nour-

**Figure 13.5   The Interactive
Change Process**

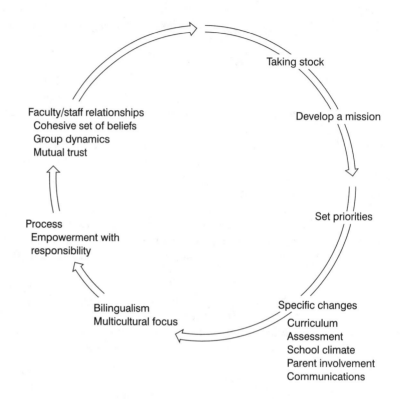

Taking stock

Develop a mission

Set priorities

Specific changes
Curriculum
Assessment
School climate
Parent involvement
Communications

Bilingualism
Multicultural focus

Process
Empowerment with
responsibility

Faculty/staff relationships
Cohesive set of beliefs
Group dynamics
Mutual trust

ishing experiences for teachers and to a healthier work life for all. Positive experiences with community or parent councils improve communication and develop trust and respect. Development of mutual respect contributes to a safe environment for children and teachers and dispels and reduces destructive personal conflicts.

Pertinent Reform Questions

As an educator, you will experience firsthand the forceful winds of change. The 1990s ushered in one of the most active periods of school reform to date (McLaughlin & Oberman, 1996). Calls for school reform are likely to increase as we experience more rapid economic and social change. You will likely be asked to consider different reforms and to participate in various reform projects. It will be crucial that you base your decision on serious and probing questioning of these reforms and their objectives. You may consider using the following questions to determine the ability of proposed reforms to meet democratic and multicultural education objectives.

Do the proposed reforms (curricula, materials, strategies, reorganization ideas, etc.) do any or all of the following:

- Build on the cultural and linguistic strengths of students?
- Teach students to develop positive human relations?
- Incorporate meaningful cooperative learning strategies into daily routines?
- Develop students' critical-thinking skills?
- Provide coaching and encouragement for students?
- Structure in opportunities for meaningful dialogue and exchange among participants (teachers, administrators, parents, students, etc.)?
- Address key local issues identified as priorities by participants?
- Create structures of democratic empowerment for all school stakeholders?

School Reform Alternatives

A range of educational reforms are currently being implemented at district and state levels across the United States. Some of them explicitly pursue equity-related goals, while others tend to further conservative agendas as framed in the 1980s.

School Reform Networks.   One pathway to pursuing multicultural and democratic school reform can be found through the efforts of educators and researchers outside of state departments and districts who have developed powerful intervention strategies. Building on the ideas of "effective schools" (see Figure 13.1), such efforts as the Comer School Development Program, the Accelerated Schools Project, the Child Development Project, and the Coalition for Essential Schools offer innovative models for school improvement. For reform efforts like the Comer School Development Program and the Accelerated Schools Project, both rising out of collaboration between school districts and major research universities (Yale University and Stanford University, respectively), changing school governance structures to include a broader group of stakeholders—that is, parents, community, teachers, and students—is a key component. The Comer program also concentrates on underlying issues of mental and emotional health that often prevent urban students, impacted by poverty, violence, substance abuse, and lack of physical safety, from concentrating on their academics (Mintrop, Wong, Gamson, & Oberman, 1996). The Accelerated Schools Project adds a focus on raising teacher expectations of students and empowering both teachers and students to demand and maintain enriched and challenging educational programs. Both of these reform efforts operate large national networks (more than 300 Comer schools and more than 700 Accelerated schools). Their schools are found primarily in low-income urban and rural settings.

The Child Development Project combines a strong commitment to ethical and prosocial curricula, with broader changes in school governance and decision making (Mintrop et al., 1996). This program, which has a specific focus on schools serving poor students and students of color, focuses intensively on assisting teachers to transform their instructional attitudes and strategies along with adopting new curricula, structured heavily around literature and language arts. In addition, the project introduces more democratic and participatory forms of school governance. The Coalition of Essential Schools, founded by Theodore Sizer and affiliated with Brown University, uses a limited set of "essential principles" around which school communities transform their school (Mintrop et al., 1996). These principles include such ideas as, "small is better" and "student knowledge should be demonstrated." This is one of the larger networks and offers participating schools a number of attractive professional development opportunities including national conferences, regional conferences, and a partner school that acts as a "critical friend." This reform model is considered most appropriate for high schools; early participants tended to be primarily suburban schools, though the network has been expanded recently to include more schools serving diverse populations.

A New Teacher's Survival Guide

You are entering teaching at a time of great controversy and discussion of school reform. New teachers are central to school improvement. New teachers enter the profession with high expectations and optimism. The following guidelines are offered to assist you to maintain your optimism while working in a very difficult environment.

1. Have confidence in yourself. Build and support that confidence.
2. Maintain a positive attitude by focusing on your students. Many schools have some teachers who say no to all initiatives and new ideas, who will tell you that there are no new ideas, just old failed ideas recycled. Don't let them get you down.
3. Pick a problem to work on, limiting yourself to one (at most, two) of the most important. Select problems that you can actually do something about. For example, you can change name calling in your classroom, but in your first year of teaching, you probably cannot change the district or state textbook selection. Choose problems that will help you to build a teacher support group.
4. Break problems into pieces. Start small. Pick issues you can win on; for example, starting a clothes closet or English as a second language classes for parents. Your victories will lead to more self-confidence and greater personal power.
5. Take an inquiry approach to classroom challenges. Reflect on root causes rather than superficial behaviors or symptoms. Get the facts. Prepare yourself. Research issues and develop solutions. Ask for assistance and team up with like-minded folks. Often a mentor teacher or a peer teacher can assist you with learning how other teachers have resolved this issue.
6. Learn who has the power to change things. Identify decision makers and persons with influence in your school. What decisions can the

principal make? What decisions do experienced teachers make? Does the Parent-Teacher Association have influence? Who is your union representative? What decisions are covered by your contract? Keep a list of names, addresses, and phone numbers.

7. Plan. Sort through your information and decide what you want. What are achievable goals? Who is responsible for providing resources? Be certain to regularly recruit new supporters. Insist that your union join you in the effort. Don't try to change the school by yourself. Who in the community may be willing to assist you and support your teacher network?

8. Develop a range of improvements. Start with recommendations that can be acted on immediately, within existing laws and programs, with little or no money. For those of you teaching in underfunded schools, develop a long-range plan that will require resources to bring your school up to equal financial support for your state. Real reform costs money.

9. Start changing things. Begin with the person closest to the problem. It may be you as the teacher in the classroom. Do not assume that other teachers or administrators are against you until they have actually demonstrated their opposition. Many teachers and administrators are simply used to the way things are. They have each tried their own innovations in their time and may have become discouraged.

10. Be a smart and informed consumer of educational ideas and programs. Be cautious of initiatives that ask teachers to work harder. Instead, try to find ways to help teachers work smarter. For example, cooperative learning strategies give teachers both assistance with management and more teaching time. Ask questions of reform or program promoters, such as: What theory of instructional improvement underlies the design? How good is the evidence? Are the claimed effects sustained over time? Have the effects served language-minority and working-class students, or are the effects only measured at a few, middle-class institutions? Under what conditions has the program failed to produce positive effects? Are there existing programs that can be visited or involved teachers that can be interviewed? For more information, see the Consortium for Policy Research in Education on the World Wide Web (http://www.upenn.edu/gse/cpre/).

11. Develop a support network of people with similar ideas and goals. Never underestimate the value of such professional and emotional support!

12. Do not give up. Change in a school is a slow process.

A Choice Between Two Futures

Greider (1992) describes the political deadlock and economic crises facing our nation. In this deadlock, schools can continue as they are. A segment of society will be well educated, another segment will continue to fail. The economic crisis for working people and people of color will continue to grow (Coleman, 1987; Lowe & Miner, 1996; Mishel, Bernstein, & Schmitt, 1999).

Marshall and Tucker (1992) contend that "there is every reason to believe that if we continue on our current path, our national prosperity will evaporate. A rising portion of our people will sink into poverty and the well being of our middle class will slowly decline, thereby rending the political fabric of America, perhaps beyond repair" (p. xiv).

Within this scenario there will continue to be a few effective schools serving poor and minority students and a few effective classrooms created by dedicated teachers and administrators.

As an alternative, teachers, parents, and activists could organize a political coalition of conscience and caring that revitalizes our communities. Nonvoters and disenfranchised voters would begin to participate politically as advocates for their children, their schools, and their communities. A progressive agenda for school reform would insist on equality of opportunity.

A bold democratic agenda raises the fundamental political issue of providing equal funding. Our commitment to democracy permits nothing less. This scenario would develop one community at a time. Some neighborhoods and some schools in San Antonio, El Paso, Los Angeles, Oakland, Chicago, New York, Corpus Christi, Albuquerque, and in other cities are already making progress.

The possibility for change exists. The present class- and race-stratified system of publicly funded higher education transfers significant resources from the working poor to a professional elite. Currently popular proposals such as school choice and using public monies to fund private education (Chubb & Moe, 1989) will not lead to democratic reform. Rather than continue these privileges, a reform movement must build on working people's beliefs in progress and equality of opportunity. These traditional values can triumph over the hostility and violence produced by racism, sexism, and class bias presently accepted as "normal" and natural in our schools.

The growth of the African American, Asian, and Latino middle class—a direct result of the Civil Rights Movement's use of political power to reduce discrimination based on race—provides powerful evidence that racism can be combated through education and public policy. Frederick Douglass spoke to this issue in 1849, when he wrote the following:

The whole history of the progress of human liberty shows that all concessions yet made to her august claims have been born of earnest struggle. The conflict has been exciting, agitating, all absorbing, and for the time being putting all other tumults to silence. It must do this or it does nothing. If there is no struggle there is no progress. Those who profess to favor freedom, and yet depreciate agitation, are men who want crops without plowing up the ground. They want rain without thunder and lightning. They want the ocean without the awful roar of its many waters. This struggle may be a moral one; or it may be a physically one; or it may be both moral and physical; but it must be a struggle. Power concedes nothing without demand. It never did and it never will. (Douglass, 1849/1991, p. vii)

Summary

Advocates for democratic multicultural education challenge those social forces acting to preserve the present inequalities and injustices in our society. We consider schools as sites for the struggle for or against more democracy in our society. In schools, teachers and parents can participate in creating a more democratic society. Carnoy and Levin (1985) describe it in this way:

> Democratic struggles [by parents and teachers] are important for achieving the types of schools and economy that serve the broadest needs of our society and our citizenry. Even under the present circumstances—when the quest for improved educational services for minorities, the poor, and the handicapped is under attack by conservative interests—it is the marshaling of social movements and the democratic forces that places limits on the retrenchment and makes the battle costly for the other side. But beyond this resistance, the struggle enables the tide of hegemony of the narrow interests of the wealthy to be countered in the courts, at the polls, in the media, and on the streets. Continuing struggle, together with the failures of existing policies to meet the larger concerns of democracy, will increase the power of democratic coalitions for fairness, equity, and participation. (p. 267)

The first edition of the present text was written in 1994, at a time of severe economic crisis. Elected officials then claimed that we could not afford to improve the schools in this time of belt tightening. School budgets were trimmed, teachers laid off, buildings were not repaired.

Now (1999), both the nation and the states have new money from a growing economy, and still many elected officials claim that we can not afford to improve the schools. For example, in 1998, California Governor Pete Wilson argued that proposals to spend that state's 4.1 billion-dollar budget surplus to bring that state's per-pupil expenditures up to the national average were unreasonably expensive. Instead he favored a tax reduction for auto licenses (Smith, 1998). While there is much talk of school reform, few elected officials in other states are willing to discuss providing the funding necessary to bring our urban schools up to minimum building, safety, and student achievement standards.

Democratic educators must constantly respond to two fundamental questions, as posed by Brazilian educator Paulo Freire: Education for whom? Education in the service of what? (Freire, forthcoming). The struggle for educational improvement and educational equality is a struggle for or against democratic participation. The struggle for multicultural education, based in democratic theory, is an important part of the general struggle against race, class, and gender oppression.

Schools serving urban and impoverished populations need fundamental change. These schools do not open the doors to economic opportunity. They usually do not promote equality. Instead, they recycle inequality. They prepare less than 50 percent of their students for entrance into the economy and society. A democratic agenda for school reform includes insisting on fair taxation and equal funding for all children. We cannot build a safe, just, and prosperous society while we leave so many young people behind.

We know which schools need improvement, and we know how to improve them. Teachers can pursue democracy with instruction in multicultural education, critical thinking, cooperative learning, improved reading and language skills, and empowerment. Teachers and parents together face a political choice. Shall we continue providing high-quality schools only for the middle and upper classes, and underfunded, understaffed schools for the poor? Or, shall we work together to improve schools that are presently failing? Without justice there will be no peace.

Questions Over the Chapter

1. Define *equal educational opportunity*. What are the legal bases for this goal?
2. Why do you think there are so many diverse reform efforts rather than a single agreed-on reform plan?
3. Most school reform reports recognize a need for new skills. What skills are needed for entrance into the emerging economy? What attitudes and values are most urgently in need of clarification among our young people (for example, those promoting violence, drugs, and crime)?
4. In 1989, President Bush proposed *America 2000: An Education Strategy*, enacted into law in 1993 (see Figure 13.2). What evidence indicates that we are closer to, or further from, achieving any of these goals today? Has further legislation advanced these goals?

Activities for Further Study of School Reform

1. Explain the federal role in education. What percentage of local school budgets come from the federal government?
2. List three reasons that some parents are frustrated with schools. Share your list with your class. Brainstorm ideas for addressing these concerns.
3. If you are working in a school, would you be pleased to have your own child attend this school? Share your answer with your class.
4. List three activities parents could assist with at your school site.
5. If you are a resident of a state with an ongoing school funding conflict, investigate how the dispute is affecting school budgets. Present your findings to your class.
6. Decide on the three most urgent reforms you could initiate as a student teacher (language support, coaching, or conflict resolution, for example). Make a plan for initiating one of these efforts.
7. Decide on three urgent reforms you would initiate as a tenured, experienced teacher. What are the differences between the answer to this question and that for question 6?
8. Do you plan to join a teachers' union? Explain your choice. What are the advantages and disadvantages of each choice?
9. Contact one of the following organizations and request materials. Determine whether their recommendations (if any) are appropriate to your school. Discuss in class how you would present them at a faculty, staff, or other schoolwide meeting.
   Accelerated School Project. Henry M. Levin, Director. Stanford University, Ceras 109, Stanford, CA 94305-3084. Telephone 415-725-1676.

Association for Effective Schools. Ben A. Birdsell, President. 8250 Sharpton Rd., R.D. Box 143, Stuyvesant, NY 12173. Telephone 518-758-9828.

California Tomorrow. Laurie Olsen, Director. Fort Mason Center, Building B, San Francisco, CA 94123. Telephone 415-441-7631.

Coalition of Essential Schools. Theodore Sizer, Chairman. Brown University, Box 1969, Providence, RI 02912. Telephone 401-863-3384.

Foxfire Fund. Kim Cannon, Director. P.O. Box 541, Mountain City, GA 30562. Telephone 706-746-5318.

Success for All. Robert Slavin, Director. Center on Research on Effective Schools for Disadvantaged Students, Johns Hopkins University, 3505 N. Charles Street, Baltimore, MD 21218. Telephone 410-516-8809.

Appendix

A: A Brief Guide to African American History

Prior to 1500: Africans live in diverse cultures and communities in Africa. Several societies are as advanced as their European counterparts, except they do not have firearms.

1619: The first Africans arrive in the English colonies of North America.

1619–1800: Africans endure massive slave trade and forced migration to North, Central, and South America and the Caribbean.

1783: Slavery is recognized in the U.S. Constitution.

1808: Importation of free Africans as slaves is made illegal, but slave trade continues illegally. Societies made up of former slaves dominate parts of the Caribbean and coastal areas of Central and South America.

1817: Frederick Douglass is born.

1831: Nat Turner leads a slave rebellion.

1857: Dred Scott case is decided in the U.S. Supreme Court; racist and anti-African violence is common in the North.

1861–1865: U.S. is engaged in Civil War.

1863: January 1, President Lincoln issues the Emancipation Proclamation. All slaves in states fighting against the Union are declared free.

1865: Thirteenth Amendment to the U.S. Constitution abolishes slavery.

1866: Fourteenth Amendment to the U.S. Constitution recognizes as citizens all persons born in the United States or naturalized.

1866–1876: Reconstructionist state governments develop populist cooperation for public schools and other reforms.

1870: Fifteenth Amendment to the U.S. Constitution grants most African American males the right to vote.

1875–1880: Reconstructionist governments in the South are overthrown by racial conflicts, intimidation, and economic pressure. African American colleges are established (Tuskegee, Fisk, Morehouse, and Howard) to prepare black leadership.

1887: Marcus Garvey is born August 17.

1896: In *Plessy v. Ferguson,* Supreme Court rules "separate but equal" facilities are constitutional.

1905: W. E. B. Du Bois and others establish an African American scholarly tradition.

1909: National Association for the Advancement of Colored People (NAACP) and other civil rights organizations form in response to anti-black violence, lynchings, and intimidation.

1914: Marcus Garvey organizes the Universal Negro Improvement Association, establishing a black nationalism position.

1916–1919: African American troops participate in the invasion of Mexico and in World War I.

1919: W. E. B. Du Bois organizes the First Pan-African Congress. Race riots against Negroes in Chicago, Arkansas, and Washington, D.C.

1921: The Harlem Renaissance, a cultural and literary movement, flourishes in New York.

1929: Martin Luther King, Jr., is born.

1942: Congress of Racial Equality (CORE) is founded.

1943–1946: Violence against African Americans leads to a series of "race riots" in Texas, Detroit, Harlem, Athens, and Philadelphia.

1950: Ralph Bunche awarded Nobel Peace Prize for service to the United Nations.

1954: In *Brown v. Board of Education* the Supreme Court rules school segregation is illegal.

1955: Rosa Parks' refusal to yield her seat on a bus ignites the Montgomery Bus Boycott in Alabama.

1957: The Southern Christian Leadership Conference (SCLC) is organized by Dr. Martin Luther King, Jr., and other clergy. President Eisenhower sends U.S. troops to Little Rock, to prevent interference with school integration.

1960: Sit-in movement starts in Greensboro, N.C., and spreads quickly. Over 1,000 arrested throughout the South.

1961: CORE organizes Freedom Riders to integrate bus facilities throughout the South.

1963: More than 250,000 persons participate in march on Washington, D.C. Civil rights demonstrators are attacked by police in Birmingham. Dr. Martin Luther King, Jr., and hundreds more are arrested. A landmark civil rights bill passes. Medger Evers, NAACP leader is murdered in his home in Jackson, Miss. Four girls are killed Sept.15, in the bombing of the Sixteenth Street Baptist Church, Birmingham, Ala.

1964: Three civil rights workers are murdered in Mississippi. Malcolm X (Malcolm Little) leads a complex movement of cultural integrity and independent black political action. Civil Rights Act signed by President Johnson on July 2.

1964–1971: The rise of black nationalist forces and culture redefines the Civil Rights movement.

1965: Feb.21, Malcolm X is assassinated. Campaigns of nonviolent direct action lead to the passing of the Voting Rights Act of 1965, allowing African Americans to register and vote in the South. Later court decisions based on the bill encourage voting by Latinos and other minorities.

1966: Dr. Martin Luther King, Jr., leads a protest demonstration of 125,000 in New York against the war in Vietnam.

1968: Dr. Martin Luther King, Jr., assisting striking sanitation workers in Memphis, Tennessee, is assassinated. Riots follow in over 100 major cities. Poor People's Campaign creates a Resurrection City in front of the White House to protest poverty in the United States. Black and Latino parents struggle for community control of schools in Oceanhill-Brownsville district of New York. Community control defeated by a citywide teachers' union strike in New York City. Black students demanding black studies departments take over buildings at Columbia University. U.S. athletes Tommie Smith and John Carlos give Black Power salutes while receiving Olympic medals in Mexico City. Third World (People of Color) strike begins at San Francisco State University, over demands for ethnic studies classes.

1969: Assassination of Fred Hampton in Chicago. Destruction of the Black Panther Party by police infiltration and violence. COINTELPRO program of FBI.

1970–1979: Major increase in the number of black elected officials. Black college enrollment expands from 92,200 in 1960 to 341,000 in 1975. Emergence of black feminist movement.

1971: Black and Afro-American Studies programs established at predominantly white universities.

1972: National Black Political Assembly in Gary, Indiana. Shirley Chisholm is a candidate for Vice President in the Democratic Party primary. Coalition of Black Trade Unionists founded. Against strong resistance, federal judge orders integration of Boston Public Schools.

1976: Democratic Party Convention has 508 elected black delegates; 310 are women. Jimmy Carter appoints Andrew Young as Ambassador to the United Nations. William Julius Wilson publishes *The Declining Significance of Race*.

1980: Miami riots, a repetition of black revolts in earlier decades, occur. Changing federal policies place traditionally black colleges at risk for survival. Election of Reagan ends a decade of black political progress. Black industrial working class impacted by economic shift from manufacturing to service industries. Black Congressional Caucus provides a unified electoral agenda.

1982: Recession accelerates loss of good-paying jobs for African American industrial workers.

1983: After years of pressure, Dr. Martin Luther King, Jr.'s birthday becomes a national holiday. Harold Washington elected mayor of Chicago.

1984: Rev. Jesse Jackson organizes the National Rainbow Coalition within the Democratic Party.

1988: Rev. Jesse Jackson becomes a leading contender in the Democratic primaries.

1989: Ron Brown becomes chairperson of National Democratic Party. Continued dramatic growth of numbers of black elected officials. Michael Wilder elected governor of Virginia. African Americans elected as mayors of New York, Seattle, and Denver. National economic policies take funds from anti-poverty programs. Inner-city schools become increasingly segregated. Disparities of funding between urban and suburban districts reach crisis proportions.

1991: Clarence Thomas replaces Thurgood Marshall on the U.S. Supreme Court. Black conservatives gain media attention. The nation becomes increasingly racially polarized. Ku Klux Klan, Aryan Nation, and other white racist groups gain membership. Ex-Klan leader David Duke runs for governor of Louisiana in the Republican Party and receives 40% of the vote. Ron Daniels, former National Director of the Rainbow Coalition, runs for President as an independent candidate. Detroit, New York, Milwaukee, and other large school districts experiment with all-African male elementary schools in grades 1 through 3 to reduce the crisis of black males. April 28–May 3: Lack of hope and economic opportunity combined with police brutality lead to urban riots and rebellion in Los Angeles, soon followed in other cities. At least 51 people are killed and thousands arrested; 50% of the dead and 35% of those arrested are African Americans. Carol Moseley Braun becomes the first African American woman elected to the U.S. Senate.

1993: Benjamin Chavez becomes head of the NAACP. A new generation of African American intellectuals and leaders emerges. Cornel West publishes *Race Matters.* African Americans serve in the President's cabinet. Congressman Ron Dellums chairs the Armed Services Committee.

1994: *The Bell Curve,* by Charles Murray and Richard Herrnstein, is published and widely debated. The book cites data that its authors allege demonstrate the old and often disproved thesis that African Americans tend to have lower IQ scores than the national average. While Democrats lose heavily in the fall elections, African Americans continue to hold 38 seats in Congress, 19% of the Democratic party total.

1995: Myrle Evers Williams, wife of slain civil rights leader Medgar Evers, is elected as Chair of the Board of the NAACP. Affirmative action programs come under attack in many states and at the national level. Oct. 16: Million Man March. Almost 1,000,000 African American males march in Washington, D.C., to protest living and work conditions. This was the largest public gathering of African American people ever. Conflict occurred over the role of Louis Farrakhan and the exclusion of women.

1996: Ward Connerly leads the effort to pass California Proposition 209 to ban affirmative action in public education and contracting. A nationwide movement against affirmative action is organized within the Republican Party. Welfare Reform Act of 1996 is significantly targeted at African American women and mothers.

1997: Oakland, California, school board votes to recognize Ebonics (black English) as an aid to improving the instruction of African American children. After the media firestorm and congressional hearings, the policy is withdrawn. NAACP settles case of Piscataway public schools suit over affirmative action out of court rather than risk a loss. President Clinton appoints a National Commission on Race Relations with historian John Hope Franklin as chair. The task of the Commission is to initiate a dialogue on race relations.

1998: Imposition of Prop. 209 in California, and related policies, leads to a dramatic decline in enrollment of African Americans in the professional schools of the University of California. African American scholarship receives new attention at Harvard University with the assembling of significant scholars including Henry Louis Gates, Cornel West, William Julius Wilson, and others. In Chicago, African American political groups organize the Black Radical Congress to recreate a progressive coalition within the African American community. Dr. Manning Marable is one of several leaders.

B: A Brief Guide to Mexican American (Chicano) History

200–800 A.D.: Mayan civilization flourishes with advanced agriculture and cities.

1400: Aztec civilization conquers the several major civilizations of what is now Mexico, and forces them all to pay tribute.

1521: Hernán Cortés, leading the Spaniards with thousands of Indian allies, defeats the Aztecs.

1598: Juan de Onante establishes a Spanish city near present-day Santa Fe, New Mexico. First European settlement of the area.

1610: First Catholic church in what is now the United States is established at Santa Fe.

1630: Some 30 small settlements and missions are established along the trail to Santa Fe.

1680: Poet Sor Juana Ines de la Cruz becomes the Americas' first published feminist writer in Mexico City. Pueblo Indians revolt against brutality and slavery imposed by the Spanish, and drive the Spanish from the Southwest. Pueblos maintain their cultures and societies. Some of the Isleta Pueblo forced to retreat and serve the Spanish.

1692: The Spanish return with superior military power and occupy Santa Fe. Resistance continues to Spanish conquest. The Spanish control the cities and a few missions. They survive, at times, by raiding and stealing from pueblos.

1718: Missions and presidios are established in San Antonio, Texas.

1769: Fray Junipero Serra and the Franciscans establish the San Diego Mission and Presidio and, later, 21 California missions.

1810: Father Miguel Hidalgo is major leader of the Mexican War of Independence from Spain.

1821: Mexico bans slavery in Mexican territory, including present-day Texas and the Southwest.

1836: Anglo Texas settlers, seeking to maintain and extend slavery, rebel against Mexican rule. Anglo-Texans win the rebellion and declare Texas an independent republic. Eight Mexicans die in the Alamo on the side of the Texans.

1845: The United States annexes Texas.

1846: The U.S. invades Mexican territory and begins the Mexican American War. Mexico is deeply divided by internal strife. The U.S. seizes California with the assistance of Californio leaders.

1848: The Treaty of Guadalupe Hidalgo ends the war. Mexico is forced to give up one third of its territory. The Southwest becomes a part of the United States by conquest. The treaty promises that Mexican culture, language, and property rights will be respected.

1850: California becomes a state. The first constitution promises a bilingual California. Eight leading Californios, descendants of Spanish settlers, sign the constitution.

1850–1880: Mexican citizens in the Southwest are systematically deprived of property and political participation by terrorism and court decisions.

1853: The U.S. purchases 45,532 square miles of Mexican land in the Gadsden Purchase.

1859: Juan N. Cortina leads a rebellion against Anglo domination in the Rio Grande Valley of South Texas.

1862: Battle of Puebla. Mexican forces defeat the French. Independence regained on Cinco de Mayo.

1870–1920: Texas Rangers control and harass Mexicans and keep them from civic participation. Poll taxes, etc., exclude Mexicans from voting.

1877: Mexicans rebel against Anglo privatization of the salt beds in the El Paso Salt War.

1886–1889: Armed resistance efforts against Anglo land seizures occur in northern New Mexico.

1910: Revolution in Mexico causes extreme hardship. Over a million people migrate to the Southwest. Revolutionary leadership surfaces in the Southwest, particularly the brothers Ricardo and Enrique Flores-Magon.

1912: New Mexico is granted statehood. Status is delayed by Congress in objection to New Mexico's official bilingualism and large Spanish-speaking population.

1916: The United States invades Mexico at Vera Cruz. U.S. policy helps determine the winning side of the Mexican Revolution.

1924: The U.S. Border Patrol is established along the Mexican border to control immigration.

1929: League of United Latin American Citizens (LULAC) is formed to defend civil rights of Mexican Americans.

1929–1935: Thousands of Mexican immigrants and U.S. citizens of Mexican descent are deported to Mexico during the Great Depression.

1930: Mexicans are forced to attend segregated schools in Texas and California. Emma Tenayuca Brooks leads pecan shellers' strike in Texas.

1932: Extensive Mexican labor union activity occurs in agriculture and mining.

1938: El Congreso de Pueblos de Habla Español organized. Luisa Morena, leader of the California Congress of Industrial Organization (UCA-PAWA), is elected as Chair.

1942: The United States and Mexico sign an agreement to import temporary workers for wartime labor—Braceros.

1943: The "Sleepy Lagoon Case" leads to anti-Mexican attacks in Los Angeles (Zoot Suit riots). Sailors and others attack Mexican American residents of Los Angeles area.

1946–1950: Luisa Morena and hundreds of Mexican labor leaders are purged and deported, often accused of being communists.

1950–1960: Numerous attempts are made to organize farmworkers.

1954: Immigration Service begins "Operation Wetback," a massive program to deport Mexican laborers.

1965: Grape strike initiated by Filipinos, combines with Mexican union to create the United Farmworkers Union (AFL-CIO). Multiracial organizing is critical for success. Rodolfo "Corky" Gonzales forms the Crusade for Justice in Denver. Change in U.S. immigration law sets the stage for dramatic increases in future immigration.

1966: Reies Tijerina and others are arrested for seeking to reclaim land in New Mexico taken from their ancestors at Tierra Amarilla. Mexican American Political Association (MAPA) is founded to contend for respect within the Democratic Party.

1966–1972: United Farmworkers Union uses consumer boycott to win contracts. UFW trains generations of union organizers. César Chávez and Dolores Huerta are leaders of U.F.W.

1968: Over 1,000 high school students walk out of classes in Los Angeles protesting inadequate educational opportunities. Protests spread to other cities in the Southwest.

1969: El Plan de Santa Barbara sets out a program to develop Chicano self-determination in education. Chicanos participate in Third World Strike in San Francisco. Over 20,000 Chicanos march in Los Angeles to protest Chicano deaths in the Vietnam War. Police attack the march, resulting in a three-day battle between police and the community; three are killed.

1970: La Raza Unida Party organized in Crystal City, Texas, by Jose Angel Gutierrez and others. Chicano nationalism becomes prominent. U.S. Census begins using the term *Hispanic origin*. Chicano studies programs are established on university campuses. Chicana feminist movement is organized.

1971–1972: Community organizations seize buildings and public property to establish Chicano community organizations in Seattle and Santa Barbara.

1976: After years of boycott pressure, a farm labor law is signed in California, providing free, supervised elections in the fields. This is the first legal protection of farmworkers' rights. Jerry Apodaca and Raul Castro are elected as governors of New Mexico and Arizona. Meaningful bilingual education law passed in California. Mexican immigrants and Chicanos work together to protect the rights of undocumented immigrants.

1980: After Republican electoral victories, Mexican and Chicano programs are assaulted. Previous legislative gains are reversed (e.g., farmworkers' rights, bilingual education). A Decade of the Hispanic is declared. Henry Cisneros is elected Mayor of San Antonio.

1982: Severe economic recession particularly impacts Latino families. Texas authorities try to deny admission to school for children of some immigrant parents. The U.S. Supreme Court decides in *Plyler v. Doe* that Texas must allow all children to attend school.

1984: Latino votes are critical to the election of Harold Washington in Chicago. Enrollment in Chicano studies declines. Albar Pena is elected Mayor of Denver, Colorado. Latino organizations participate in the Rainbow Coalition. Major growth occurs in new organizations, National Association for Bilingual Education (NABE) and CABE, to extend and protect bilingual education.

1987: Growth of Hispanic conservative forces with Richard Rodriguez and Linda Chavez as prominent spokespersons.

1988: Several states with large Latino populations pass English-as-Official-Language statutes. MALDEF serves as a major litigant.

1989: Latino votes are critical to the election of Mayor David Dinkins of New York. Federal courts overturn prejudicial voting districts in Texas and Watsonville, California.

1990: A federal judge rules that the Los Angeles County Board of Supervisors has deliberately drawn electoral districts to discriminate against Latinos. The decision affects 8.5 million residents, and Los Angeles is forced to redistrict.

Poverty increases, and society becomes increasingly divided by class and by race. Neighborhood violence, lack of hope, economic decline, and police brutality toward an African American ignite an urban insurrection and riot in Los Angeles. Twenty of the 51 killed and over 50% of those arrested were Latinos—mostly from immigrant neighborhoods. Government response is minimal. Latino participation in the rebellion is ignored by policy makers. Hispanic Congressional Caucus grows to 16. The Mexican Government (PRI) and the Bush administration propose a free trade agreement between the United States, Mexico, and Canada. NAFTA (North American Free Trade Agreement) accelerates the integration of U.S., Mexican, and Canadian economics. Lucille Roybal-Allard, a Chicana, is elected Vice Chair of the Congressional Hispanic Caucus.

1993: César Chávez, President of the United Farmworkers of America (AFL-CIO), dies in May. California Governor Pete Wilson, U.S. Attorney General Janet Reno, and others declare a crisis of immigration. Over 1 million immigrants arrive. Major concerns are raised about "illegal" immigration. Over 40 people are killed along the U.S./Mexican border. Proposals are made to amend the U.S. Constitution to restrict rights of immigrant children.

1994: California Governor Pete Wilson leads an anti-immigrant initiative (Prop. 187) seeking to deny education to children without legal documents. Anti-immigrant, anti-Mexican campaign reaches intense animosity—the worst since the 1950s. By a margin of 62% to 38%, California voters support Proposition 187, a measure to restrict and punish illegal immigration. Governor Wilson focuses his reelection efforts on this anti-immigrant campaign. The California electorate polarizes along racial and ethnic lines. Latinos vote 3 to 1 against Prop. 187; African Americans and Asians vote against by about 52% each, and European American voters (80% of the total) supported the measure by 60%. Anti-immigrant campaigns spread from California to other states.

All but one provision of Prop. 187 are blocked from enforcement by the federal courts, citing U.S. constitutional protections. Court decisions forcing equalization of school funding in Texas promise increased funding for the Mexican American areas in the Rio Grande Valley.

1995: The New Mexico legislature passes a resolution denouncing anti-immigrant campaigns similar to California Prop. 187. In Texas, similar campaigns have little support. Mexico's economy suffers a major financial crisis, which produces increased immigration into the United States. In public schools, high rates of failure and drop outs/push outs continue for Latino students. In Texas, the Industrial Areas Foundation, led by Ernesto Cortes, organizes parents into a potent political force demanding school improvement.

1996: Immigration Reform Act passed by U.S. Congress provides for immigration limits and increased border enforcement. Welfare Reform Act passed by Republican Congress and signed by President Bill Clinton, cuts many social services to immigrant communities. These two acts impact both Latino and Asian communities. October 12: Over 100,000 Latinos march in Washington, D.C., protesting increasingly anti-immigrant politics. November: California passes Prop. 209 to eliminate affirmative action in education and in state contracting, a major loss of opportunities to women as well as people of color. Lorretta Sanchez (D) defeats Bob Dorman to become the first Latina Congresswoman from conservative Orange County, Calif. Hispanic Caucus in the U.S. House reaches 16 Democrats and 3 Republicans. B. Dorman challenges the election of Sanchez in Congress, alleging illegal aliens voted. In December, Cruz Bustamante becomes Speaker of the California Assembly. Over 14 Latinos elected to California Legislature.

1997: The United Farmworkers Union launches its Strawberry Workers campaign with a march of over 30,000 supporters in Watsonville, California. Efforts are made to abolish bilingual education programs in Denver, Chicago, and Albuquerque. Linda Chavez is a key advocate of abolition. Nadine and Patsy Cordova are dismissed from teaching positions in Vaughn, New Mexico, by a Hispanic majority school board, for teaching Chicano history to students.

1998: California voters pass Prop. 227 by 61% to 39% to eliminate bilingual education in California schools. Jaime Escalante is the Yes Campaign co-chair. Latinos make up 14% of the total state electorate. Latinos vote 2 to 1 against Prop. 227. Latino enrollment at University of California declines by 18% as a result of the end of affirmative action (Prop. 209).

C: A Multicultural History of Women in the United States

1500: Iroquois Confederation women participate in substantial decision making. Women select the leaders of the nations.

1680: Mestizo culture comes to the Southwest (New Mexico, Texas, California), bringing ideas

of community property, and protects the legal status of women to own property.

1690: Sor Juana Inez de La Cruz—poet and feminist—receives education, publishes, and advocates for education of women and teachers.

1700: In English colonies, women are excluded from voting and political participation. African American women, as slaves, have substantial responsibilities as heads of families.

1776: Women help plan the Boston Tea Party. Women participate in American Revolution (War of Independence). European American women's legal and social states are not affected by the revolution. There are few records of protest, with exceptions of Abigail Adams and Mercy Otis Warren. Abigail Adams warns her husband, John Adams, to grant women's rights in the drafting of the U.S. Constitution. Settlement of colonial population destroys Iroquois Confederation and their tradition of women's active participation.

1820: Large New England textile mills begin factory system. Women organize strikes to improve working conditions. In Mexico (current U.S. Southwest), women enjoy community property rights and legal status. Women participate and lead anti-slavery agitation (L. Mott, the Grimke sisters, Sojourner Truth, and others). Women and children become dominant work force in factories. Difficult working conditions and long hours are normal.

1833: Oberlin College is founded as coeducational institution.

1837: First college for women is founded at Mt. Holyoke, Mass.

1840: Chinese immigration begins. Chinese women are specifically excluded from immigration as a form of labor and social control.

1845: Women form first trade unions such as the Lowell Female Reform Association.

1848: Seneca Falls Women Rights Convention. First national organization of women. Women demand right to vote and other reforms.

1850: Coeducational public elementary schools are developed. U.S. forces conquer the Southwest: Texas, California, New Mexico, and Arizona. Traditional community property laws and legal status for women weaken as a result.

1850s–1870s: Women's Rights Conventions continue. Several women's colleges are established to promote education: Smith, Vassar.

1860: Upper-class women begin to gain leisure time through domestic help and labor-saving devices. Women are admitted to higher education institutions. More women's colleges are established. Elizabeth Gurley Flynn and Mother Jones work as labor organizers.

1886: Establishment of Hull House by Jane Addams. Lucy Gonzales Parson gains fame as organizer of Haymarket Square Defense Committee. Later, she helps found Industrial Workers of the World.

1890: Women in most states achieve legal status and property rights equal to men. This is an era of intense reform and development of settlement houses. Socialists and populists lead demands for expansion of democracy. Helen Keller leads anti-imperialist movement. Clara Zitkin becomes a leader of Garment Workers Union. May Elizabeth Lease organizes the Populist Party.

1910: Eighty percent of elementary and secondary teachers are women. Women found and lead several peace organizations. Flores Magonistas provide substantial feminist perspective and feminist leadership in Mexican Revolution and the Southwest. Sara Estela Ramirez is a writer and activist in Partido Liberal Mexicano.

1920: Outstanding women such as Emma Goldman and Alice Paul serve as leaders of radical politics. Ida Wells Barnet leads anti-lynching campaign. National Women's Political Party is founded. Nineteenth Amendment to the U.S. Constitution gives women the right to vote. Southern male senators are assured by suffrage advocates this doesn't mean black women can vote.

1928: Emma Tennayuca organizes pecan shellers' strike in San Antonio, Texas.

1930: This is an intense period of union activity and organizing for women. CIO increases its membership of women to 800,000.

1936: Luisa Moreno serves as President of UCAPAWA (CIO). Frances Perkins becomes the first female member of the Cabinet as Secretary of Labor. Women provide critical support for the Flint Sit Down Strike, establishing the United Auto Workers Union. Eleanor Roosevelt uses her position as First Lady to advocate for women's rights.

1940: Masses of women enter war industries and unions. After the war, they are "encouraged" to return home. Programs for child care, national health, and other "women's issues" get pushed off the national agenda.

1948: Margaret Chase Smith becomes first woman to serve in both houses of Congress.

1950: One in three women works outside the home.

1955: Rosa Parks initiates Montgomery Bus Boycott. Ella Baker organizes for SNCC and Congress of Racial Equality.

1964: Dolores Huerta becomes a leader of National Farm Workers Association, and later, Vice President of United Farmworkers Union (AFL-CIO).

1963: *Feminine Mystique* is published. New forms of gender oppression are identified and articulated. Equal Pay Act is passed.

1964: Fannie Lou Hammar leads the Mississippi Freedom Democratic party to challenge white control of Democratic Party. Patsy Takemoto Mink of Hawaii (D) is the first Japanese American (Nisei) woman elected to U.S. House of Representatives. Title VII of the Civil Rights Act prohibits discrimination.

1965: Executive Order 11246, signed into law by President Johnson, bars discrimination on the basis of race, color, religion, or national origin by federal contractors.

1966: National Organization for Women (NOW) is founded.

1967: Executive Order 11375 expands the definition of nondiscrimination to include women. These orders are the basis for affirmative action.

1969: Shirley Chisholm becomes first African American woman to serve in Congress.

1970: Third major women's movement grows. Women's studies become established as university courses. Fifty thousand women march for equal rights in New York City.

1971: National Women's Political Caucus (NWPC) is established.

1972: *Ms.* magazine is established as forum for new women's movement. Shirley Chisholm runs for president.

1973: Equal Rights Amendment to the U.S. Constitution passes Congress, but fails to get two-thirds of state legislature to ratify. U.S. Supreme Court *(Roe v. Wade)* rules that a woman may choose to terminate a pregnancy, based on her constitutional right to privacy from government intervention. *Our Bodies/Our Selves* is published.

1974: Women form the Coalition of Labor Union Women (CLUW). Ella Grasso is elected governor of Connecticut.

1975: International Woman's Year proclaimed by the United Nations.

1980s: The pill and other forms of birth control give women more choices. Anti-feminist political forces organize in the Republican Party under the name of pro-family. Women make up 40% of all union members. Clerical and government services become unionized. Mary Furtrell leads the National Education Association as major spokesperson for liberal causes. Sandra Day O'Connor becomes first woman in the U.S. Supreme Court.

1983: Sally Ride is the first woman on the space shuttle.

1984: Geraldine Ferraro receives Democratic nomination for Vice President of the U.S.

1986: Wilma Mankiller is the first female Chief of Cherokee nation.

1990: *Ms.* magazine reborn. Between 1970 and 1990, the number of women physicians doubled from 7.6% to 16.9% of the total, a result, in part, of affirmative action.

1991: Sexual harassment becomes national issue in the confirmation hearings for Supreme Court Justice Clarence Thomas. NOW commission recommends exploration of a third political party after concluding that neither major political party is responsive to women's needs.

1992: Carol Moseley Braun becomes the first African American woman elected to the U.S. Senate, one of 5 women Senators. Women's Caucuses in the House of Representatives and Senate are increasingly effective. Congressperson Patricia Schroeder leads criticism of the Navy for sexual harassment. Marian Wright Edelman is founder and President of the Children's Defense Fund. The American Association of University Women publishes *How Schools Shortchange Girls,* initiating a new dialogue on gender equity in classrooms.

1993: African American author Toni Morrison receives the Nobel Prize for Literature.

1994: Affirmative action programs are attacked in California and other states, with opposition increasingly a campaign issue in the Republican party. Organizations opposed to choice on abortion rights become increasingly militant and aggressive. Women's health clinics are bombed and shut down. Two doctors and health workers are killed by terrorists. Conservative leaders, such as Diane Ravitch, oppose funding for gender-equity efforts in the federal education budget.

1995: After significant congressional victories by Republicans, federal budgets are cut for children's programs, school lunches, and AFDC. Since over 60% of all welfare recipients are women or their children, the assault on welfare is interpreted by major organizations such as NOW as an assault on women. Congress adopts the Gender Equity in Education Act to train teachers, promote math and science learning by girls, and prevent sexual harassment. Sixty million employed women in the U.S. represent 46.1% of all employed workers.

1996: California passes Prop. 209 which eliminates affirmative action in education and in government contracting. Women had been the chief beneficiaries of affirmative action. Under affirmative action the number of women in executive and managerial positions in the U.S. had risen from 17.6% of the total to 42.7% in 1995. The percentage of women physicians had grown from 10% in 1972 to 24.4% in 1995. (Bureau of Census). Linda Chavez Thompson is elected Vice President of the AFL-CIO. U.S. women's teams at the Summer Olympics win 19 gold medals, 10 silver, 9 bronze, a result of changes in sports resources mandated by Title IX. *United States v. Virginia* requires that the Virginia Military Academy admit women into their tax supported school.

1997: AFL-CIO holds Working Women's Conference. Establishes Working Women's Department. Madeline Albright becomes U.S. Secretary of State, the first woman to hold such a high post. Janet Reno remains Secretary of the Justice Dept.

1998: NOW wins protection of women's health clinics and doctors from violence and bombings, in *NOW v. Schneider*. Women's organizations celebrate the 150-year anniversary of the Seneca Falls convention. National Women's History Project produces quality materials for classroom use.

D: A Brief History of Japanese Americans

1868: Over 100 Japanese contract laborers begin to work in Hawaii. Japanese are recruited to break the power of Chinese workers.

1869: Japanese immigrants arrive in California and establish a colony at Gold Hill (Coloma, California—near present-day Sacramento).

1882: Chinese Exclusion Act passes Congress.

1884: Japan permits legal emigration.

1885: Men, women, and children immigrate to Hawaii.

1894: *Nishimura v. U.S.* leads to an agreement that the United States shall protect the rights of Japanese living in this country.

1900: San Francisco school board establishes segregated schools for 93 Japanese school children. The order is rescinded in 1907. The United States and Japan agree to restrict Japanese immigration to the United States.

1910: Naturalization Act of 1870 is expanded to exclude all Asians from Citizenship. Japanese are banned from marrying non-Orientals. Practice of arranging for picture brides begins.

1913: California legislature makes it difficult for Japanese to own land. California Alien Land Act.

1922: Supreme Court declares Asian immigrants ineligible for naturalization *(Ozawa v. U.S.)*.

1924: Asian Exclusion Act prohibits most Japanese immigration.

1930s: Anti-Japanese propaganda common in U.S.

1930: Japanese American Citizens League founded.

1940s: U.S. soldiers of Japanese descent fight valiantly in World War II in a segregated unit.

Three hundred and ten Nisei women serve in the Armed Forces.

1941: Japanese bomb Pearl Harbor in Hawaii. The United States enters war with Japan.

1942: President Roosevelt signs Executive Order #9066 establishing forced relocation camps (internment camps) for all Japanese Americans on the mainland.

1944: U.S. Supreme Court rules that the removal and detentions are legal (Korematsu case).

1945: United States drops atomic bombs on Hiroshima and Nagasaki, ending World War II. On December 28, President Truman signs War Brides Act allowing GIs to bring wives back to the U.S.

1946: Four hundred thirty-six persons of Japanese ancestry are repatriated or deported to Japan. Internment camps are closed.

1948: U.S. Supreme Court declares the California law banning interracial marriages unconstitutional.

1952: McCarren-Walter Immigration Act permits new immigration and naturalization.

1964: Patsy Takemoto Mink of Hawaii (D) becomes first Nisei woman elected to U.S. House of Representatives.

1965: Immigration and Naturalization Act of 1965 abolishes prior national origin quotas. Allows increase in Asian immigration.

1968: Third World Strike at San Francisco State Univ. in California establishes Asian American Studies programs.

1970s: Robert Matsui, Patricia Saiki, and Norm Mineta—all Japanese Americans—are elected to

Congress. Daniel Inouye is elected to U.S. Senate from Hawaii. Japanese American (Nisei) and Chinese American politics become majority politics in state of Hawaii. S. I. Hayakawa is elected to the U.S. Senate from California.

1975: A wave of new immigration from Southeast Asian begins after the U.S. withdraws from the war in Vietnam in 1972.

1980: Commission on Wartime Relocation is created by President Carter. It recommends a formal apology, monetary redress, and educational funds for Japanese Americans interned during World War II. Anti-Japan feeling is revived in United States based on economic dislocation and competition. Vincent Chinn is murdered because Detroit auto workers thought he was Japanese.

1988: President Reagan signs redress bill for Japanese Americans who had been interned.

1989: Ronald Takaki publishes *Strangers from a Different Shore: A History of Asian Americans.*

1990: Japanese Americans are granted reparations for World War II incarceration. Asian Americans dramatically improve their rates of participation in higher education.

1992: Urban riot and rebellion in Los Angeles include an anti-Korean component. Poor African American communities are, at times, polarized against Koreans and other Asians. Six Asian Americans are elected to Congress.

1997: A coalition of Asian American groups files a 27 page petition seeking U.S. commission on civil rights hearings on anti-Asian violence.

E: A Brief History of Chinese Americans

With assistance from Eric Mar, Northern California Coalition for Immigrants' Rights.

1640: Chinese immigrants go to Philippines, Mexico, Brazil, Peru, and the United States.

1839: British troops occupy Canton and create oppression in China, resulting in the Anglo-Chinese War.

1840: Chinese immigrate to Hawaii as contract labor. Yankee missionaries and traders live in China.

1848: First Chinese immigrants arrive in San Francisco.

1849: Gold Rush spurs Chinese workers, like many others, to move to California.

1851: Cantonese immigrants form Chinese Association.

1852: Anti-Chinese activism is common in California.

1854: A Chinese worker rejected as a witness in court against a white person in *People v. Hall.*

1855: California passes tax on Chinese workers. Twenty-four thousand Chinese work in the mines.

1864: Chinese workers labor on the Union Pacific-Central Pacific transcontinental railroad.

1866: Chinese workers work through the winter building railroads through the Sierra Mountains. Chinese workers strike for higher wages.

1868: Businesses seek Chinese immigrants as cheap labor.

1869: Chinese farmers develop the San Joaquin and Sacramento River delta. Chinese are the primary agricultural laborers in California. Chinese become workers in southern United States. Anti-Chinese riots occur in San Francisco.

1870: Sixty-three thousand Chinese live in United States, 50,000 in California. California prohibits immigration of most Chinese women. Naturalization act excludes Chinese from U.S. citizenship.

1871: Anti-Chinese attacks in Los Angeles by more than 500 whites. Fifteen Chinese hung, 4 more shot to death.

1877: Anti-Chinese "riots" in San Francisco.

1880: California law prohibits intermarriage between whites and Chinese.

1882: Chinese Exclusion Act, the first openly racial U.S. immigration law, prohibits further immigration.

1885: In Rock Springs, Wyoming, miners murder 28 Chinese American miners.

1893: Anti-Chinese violence and ethnic conflicts occur in labor force.

1906: Earthquake in San Francisco destroys most immigration records. After 1907, thousands of new immigrants arrive.

1910: Chinese move to cities to resist oppression and violence. Chinatowns are established in San Francisco and Sacramento. Anti-Chinese violence drives Chinese from agriculture to Los Angeles, Oakland, Chicago, Seattle, and Portland.

1920: Chinese develop urban professions such as laundry services. Urban ghettos develop.

1923: Education becomes a major process for Chinese American advancement for second- and third-generation Chinese Americans.

1935: Chinatown develops into tourist attraction in San Francisco. Higher education leads to few job opportunities.

1939: Chinese, as World War II allies, improve U.S. attitudes toward Chinese Americans.

1943: Public response to Chinese as allies in World War II. Chinese Exclusionary Laws are repealed. Chinese again are admitted as immigrants to the United States.

1949: Communists win control of mainland China. Political divisions are deep in Chinese American community.

1959: Hiram L. Fong becomes first U.S. Senator of Asian ancestry (D-Hawaii).

1970s: Asian Americans build some political ties between Japanese and Chinese communities. Chinese Americans establish successful positions in higher education.

1974: Nationalist Chinese government seeks to influence U.S. Chinese communities. In *Lau v. Nichols,* the U.S. Courts found that San Francisco Unified Schools were denying Chinese American students a "meaningful opportunity to participate in public educational programs." This court case established the legal foundations for most bilingual education programs. Hong Kong, Taiwan, and Singapore become major commercial centers in Asia.

1976: Ethnic Chinese from Vietnam immigrate to the U.S. as refugees. Existing bilingual education programs assist their assimilation into society.

1980: A reforming China allows extensive travel and study. U.S. government establishes closer relationships with Chinese government.

1989: Chinese government crushes the "pro-democracy" movement at Tienanmen Square in Beijing. Chinese Americans respond with support for the dissidents.

1993: Hundreds of Chinese seek to enter the U.S. illegally, fleeing poverty in their homeland. A crisis of "illegal immigration" targets Latinos, Chinese, and Arabs. Eight Chinese drown trying to reach the U.S. from boats.

1994: Anti-immigrant campaigns in California affect the Chinese community. Attempts to build Asian support for immigration and bilingual education struggle to deal with the diversity of the Asian population: Chinese, Korean, Japanese, Vietnamese, Khmer, Hmong, and others. New groups refer to themselves as inclusive of Asian/Pacific Islanders.

1995: Campaigns against affirmative action divide the Chinese community by generation, and at times divide the community from other immigrant groups. Chinese, Vietnamese, and some other Asian groups have more representation in the Republican party, while other immigrant communities are traditionally Democratic.

1996: Welfare reform legislation signed by President Clinton results in draconian cuts in food stamps, SSI, etc., to thousands of immigrants and dramatic increases in citizenship applications in the Chinese and other immigrant communities. Backlogs of people waiting to become citizens grow quickly. Chinese Americans protest the new anti-immigrant legislation, which is eventually signed by President Clinton. Gary Locke is elected governor of Washington state.

1994–1997: Garment Workers Justice campaign: grassroots community groups like Asian Immigrant Women Advocates and others nationwide challenge sweatshop conditions and large clothing manufacturers like Jessica McClintock.

1997: El Monte, Calif., Asian Americans and human rights activists fight sweatshop conditions and the involuntary servitude of dozens of Thai workers. As a result, other organizations launch nationwide campaigns against sweatshop conditions in the U.S. and link these struggles with those of workers in Asia. Anti-Asian violence: April 29, Kuan Chung Kao is shot and killed in front of his family by a Rohnert Park police officer. Thousands attend demonstrations and forums at Santa Rosa and San Francisco. Angela Oh (Korean American attorney) is appointed to the President's Commission on Racial dialogue. She argues that racism in the United States cannot be understood in only a black-white paradigm.

1998: The U.S. Commission on Civil Rights and a state Advisory Committee hold hearings in Santa Rosa, Calif. Asian Americans successfully link Kao's killing to other incidents of police brutality throughout northern California. Chinese Americans are very active in the California No on Proposition 209 and No on 227 campaigns. In response to stereotypes and media portrayals by the Republicans as well as Democratic National Committee, Asian-surnamed donors to political campaigns are scrutinized. The stereotyping of the community brings protests. UC Berkeley Prof.

Ling Chi Wang and others organize Asian Americans for Campaign Finance Reform.

F: A Brief History of Puerto Ricans

Arawak and Taino people live on the Island of Puerto Rico.

1493: Columbus lands on Puerto Rico.

1508: Juan Ponce de León becomes Spanish Governor of Puerto Rico.

1511: The Taino people rebel against forced labor and are defeated.

1513: African slaves are brought to work on plantations in the United States.

1868: El Grito de Lares—Puerto Rican revolutionaries—attempt a revolt for independence.

1873: Slavery is abolished in Puerto Rico.

1898: The United States invades Puerto Rico as a battle in the Spanish-Cuban-American War. In the Treaty of Paris, Spain cedes Puerto Rico to the United States.

1899: League of Patriots of Puerto Rico seeks a plebiscite on the island to test if the people accept U.S. control.

1900: Congress passes Foraker Organic Act, bringing Puerto Rico under U.S. administrative control. The U.S. President appoints the Governor and Executive Council. The people are allowed to elect a House of Delegates.

1917: In March, the Jones Organic Act is passed. Puerto Ricans are given U.S. citizenship. The government of Puerto Rico, imposed by the United States, allows some local self-government. Presidential appointees control the major posts. Puerto Ricans are subject to U.S. Selective Service (the draft) in World War I.

1918: President Wilson proclaims natural self-determination is "an imperative principle of action." Wilson prevents the plebiscite in Puerto Rico and invades Mexico, Nicaragua, and Haiti.

1920: Puerto Ricans living on U.S. mainland total 11,800.

1930–1937: The Nationalist Party demands immediate U.S. withdrawal from Puerto Rico.

1933: President Roosevelt transfers jurisdiction over Puerto Rico from the War Department to the Department of the Interior.

1935: Puerto Ricans living on U.S. mainland now total 58,000.

1936: The United States suppresses the Nationalist Party and jails its leaders.

1945: Puerto Rican legislature proposes the people be given a free choice of independence, statehood, or dominion status. The U.S. military opposes the plan "for national security reasons."

1947: U.S. Congress approves an Elective Governor Act for Puerto Rico. Luis Muñoz Marin, a Puerto Rican, is elected governor.

1950: Nationalists attempt a revolution on Puerto Rico.

1951: A plebiscite is held; the voters of Puerto Rico choose a commonwealth status.

1952: Puerto Rico becomes a commonwealth, defined as "an Associated Free State."

1953: The U.S. is challenged in the United Nations for its continued colonial relationship with Puerto Rico. Rapid urbanization and light industrialization change Puerto Rico. Hundreds of thousands of displaced workers migrate to the U.S. mainland in search of jobs.

1959: Puerto Rico presents the Fernó-Murray Bill in the U.S. Congress, requesting a clearer definition of the status of a commonwealth.

1960: Puerto Ricans do not fit into the racial categories of *white* or *black* that are commonly used in the United States.

1962: The United Nations considers the case of decolonizing Puerto Rico.

1965: The U.S. Civil Rights Act allows Puerto Ricans living in the United States to vote without passing an English literacy test.

1967: Puerto Ricans vote in a plebiscite to maintain their commonwealth status.

1969: The Oceanhill-Brownsville dispute in New York divides Puerto Rican and black parents from the leadership of the American Federation of Teachers.

1972: The United Nations Committee on Decolonization approves a resolution supporting the self-determination and independence of Puerto Rico. Bilingual education programs offer improved educational opportunities for Puerto Rican children.

1973–1975: A "New Pact of Association" is drafted and presented to the U.S. Congress. Puerto Ricans begin to hold important posts in labor unions.

1978: President Jimmy Carter promises to respect the principle of self-determination and to support a referendum for the Puerto Rican people to decide on their status.

1980: Over 2,000,000 Puerto Ricans live in the United States; 3,187,000 live in Puerto Rico.

1982: Puerto Rican votes are critical to the election of Harold Washington in Chicago.

1989: Puerto Rican votes and community organizations are determining factor in the election of David Dinkins in New York. The U.S. Senate Committee on Natural Resources prepares a bill for a plebiscite to establish a plebiscite on statehood or independence (S-172).

1992: A Puerto Rican woman, Nydia Velasquez, is elected to the U.S. Congress.

1993: Puerto Ricans on the island vote to become a state in a preference poll. José E. Serrano (D-New York) is elected chair of the Congressional Hispanic Caucus.

1996: Welfare reform legislation leads to intense conflicts over New York City Mayor Giuliani's programs to hire former welfare recipients for city work, replacing union employees.

1997: Over 100,000 Puerto Ricans march in protest against their governments' plan to sell the publicly owned telephone company to a private corporation (privatization). Combined Latino and black enrollment at the City University of New York plunges from 26,000 students in 1995 to 14,510 in 1997. Budget cuts and attempts to eliminate remedial programs are blamed.

1998: A bill for Puerto Rican statehood passes the U.S. Congress 209–208, without requiring that English be established as the official language. Congresspersons of Puerto Rican descent split on the bill due to other provisions. Over 140,000 public workers in Puerto Rico gain the right to collective bargaining and union contracts. Puerto Ricans, Dominicans, and others in New York retain bilingual education programs in public schools.

G: A Brief History of Native Peoples

With the assistance of Denis Minamora.

A history of the native peoples of North America must take a distinctly different form than that of the preceding sections. There was not one American Indian experience. There were over 120 tribes, each with its own culture, history, and language. This work is divided into 6 areas: Northeast, Southeast, Plains, Southwest, Far West, and Northwest Coast. Each group of native peoples has its own history.

Northeast

Woodland societies predate the arrival of the Europeans. There were several large groupings of nations, including the Penobscots, Pennacooks, Pequots, and Wampanoags. The Iroquois Confederation included the Mohawks, Oneidas, Onondagas, Senacas, and others. Along the Ohio River Valley lived the Eries, Sauk and Fox, Kickapoos, Shawnees, Peorias, and others. Many tribes spoke languages related to Algonquian. Primary foodstuffs were the animals of the forest.

500–1000 A.D.: Reliance on hunting, fishing and trading.

1400–1600: The Iroquois create a confederacy, the Five Nations, also known as the League of the Iroquois. The constitution of the Iroquois Confederation later serves as a model for the Constitution of the United States.

1620: First encounter English settlers after Plymouth.

1637: Connecticut colonists kill over 500 Pequot tribespeople. The governor of the colony declares a day of thanksgiving.

1675: Chief Metacom (called King Philip), a Wampanoag chief, organizes several tribes to resist English colonial expansion. They are destroyed.

1754-1763: The French recruit Indians to join them in a war against the English. Pontiac, of the Ottowa, is betrayed by his French allies at the siege of Detroit and loses the Great Lakes territory.

1775: The English recruit Native Americans as allies against the colonists. In each of these wars, defeat usually led to the destruction of the tribe or its banishment to a restricted territory. Wars between the European powers and the colonists eventually destroy the Iroquois confederation.

1789: The U.S. Congress passes the Northwest Territory Ordinance, which promises that "The utmost good faith shall always be observed toward the Indians, their lands and property shall never be taken from them without consent; and in their property rights and liberty, they shall never be invaded or disturbed. The U.S. would sign some 389 treaties with various Indian nations.

1832: Black Hawk War drives Indian people out of Ohio, west to Iowa. The expansion of U.S. society drove many tribes west onto the plains.

1879: Carlisle Indian School is established in Pennsylvania. Indian schools are used to forcibly assimilate young Indians into white society and to take them away from their tribes.

Southeast

1500 B.C.–700 A.D.: Early inhabitants are a society of mound builders. They settle large cities in areas near the Mississippi, trade with native nations in all directions, and grow corn and other crops. Tribes include the Cherokee, Seminole, Choctaw, Chickasaw, Creek, and Alabaman. The Cherokee nation is a matrilineal society; wealth is inherited along the woman's family lineage.

1513: Juan Ponce de Leon lands in Florida.

1565: Spanish establish a colony at St. Augustine in Florida.

1609: English establish a colony at Jamestown, Virginia.

1622: Powhatans tries to stop the land growth of English tobacco farmers in the Chesapeake Bay region. This society was being devastated by European diseases. English settlers respond to the war with devastating attacks. Most native peoples in the Chesapeake Bay area are exterminated.

1644: Powhatans tries again to limit English expansion through war; but they are destroyed.

1750: English colonies such as South Carolina exist alongside powerful native nations such as the Cherokee and the Choctaw. In most cases, the English colonists could recruit one tribe to serve as warriors against another tribe.

1775: In the War of Independence, native peoples often were recruited to support the English against the colonists.

1802: Georgia Compact. The U.S. government promises to extinguish Indian title to lands in Georgia with Indian consent.

1808, 1810: Cherokees cede tracts of land in Georgia, Alabama, Tennessee to the advancing colonists. The Cherokee migrate west.

1814: Battle of Horseshoe Bend. Andrew Jackson becomes famous as an Indian fighter

1814–1830: Cherokee leaders adopt the ways of the colonists, speaking English and sending their children to school. Some practice slavery. Sequoyah develops written Cherokee language and publishes a newspaper.

1817–1819: Cherokees are forced to cede more lands.

1827: Cherokee constitution is adopted, which gives the vote only to free men. This event ends women's political influence in the Cherokee nation.

1830: Gold is discovered on Cherokee land.

1832: President Andrew Jackson orders the Cherokee, Choctaw, and other tribes to leave the U.S. and move west to Oklahoma.

1835: Some Cherokee men sign the treaty of New Echota, promising to leave their lands and move west. Women, who traditionally held the property, did not sign the treaty.

1838: Osceola (Seminole) dies in U.S. prison at age of 34. His nation never surrenders. The Seminoles, Chickasaws, and Cherokees, over 60,000 people, are forced to leave. Thousands die along the way from the harsh conditions.

1839: Cherokee nation is removed by force and terror, and driven west by armed forces. Hundreds of infants and the old die along the way, which became known as the Trail of Tears.

1900: Treaty with the Cherokees by the Dawes Commission.

Plains

Societies of Native Americans had long lived on the plains. Mandans and others constructed earthen homes. Lewis and Clark encountered them on their journey west. Among the major groups are the Blackfeet, Crow, Cheyenne, Arapaho, Pawnee, Kiowa, and the Sioux or Lakota people. The buffalo is the primary source of food for many. Villages also grow crops, including squash, corn, and beans.

About 1600: Cultures on the plains change dramatically with the arrival of horses.

1830: Congress, with the blessing of President Andrew Jackson (veteran of the Indian Wars) passes the Indian Removal Act that leads to moving all Indians to lands west of the Mississippi. Subsequently the line is changed from the Mississippi to the 95th meridian. In the far western plains, the Dakotas and Montana, native peoples remain migratory.

1864: Colorado militia under the command of a Col. J. M. Chivington attacks a village of peaceful Cheyenne and Arapaho at Sand Creek, killing 105 women and children as well as 28 men.

1865: An alliance of Cheyenne, Arapaho, and Sioux carry out raids along the South Platte River, burning the town of Julesburg in retaliation for the Sand Creek massacre. Chief Red Cloud declares war on the United States.

1868: Captain William J. Fetterman declares, "Give me a hundred men and I can ride through the whole Sioux Nation!" On Dec. 21 Fetterman's entire command is wiped out. The U.S. Government admits defeat and withdraws all troops from the Powder River country, burning the forts behind them. Red Cloud is to be the only Indian to win a war against the United States. Black Kettle's Southern Cheyenne village is attacked at their winter quarters on the Washita River. Fort Laramie Treaty cedes the Black Hills of the Dakota Territory to the Lakota nation. "No white person or persons shall be permitted to settle upon or occupy any portion of the territory, or without the consent of the Indians to pass through the same."

1872: An expedition led by George Armstrong Custer discovers gold in the Black Hills. Miners flood into the area. Under pressure by politicians and railroad builders, the cavalry is sent in to protect the miners. All Indians are to be placed on reservations.

1876: Sioux and Cheyenne tribes, under the strategic leadership of Sitting Bull and the tactical guidance of Crazy Horse, wipe out the 7th Cavalry led by George A. Custer.

1889: Paiute spiritual leader Wovoka begins the Ghost Dance religion, which preaches peaceful dance to encourage the return of ancestors and the disappearance of the white invader.

1890: Followers of the Ghost Dance are branded as renegades. The 7th Cavalry is sent to arrest them. Three hundred Lakota men, women and children are killed at Wounded Knee Creek in South Dakota. The Sioux are forced onto reservations. This is the last major resistance on the plains.

Southwest

One early language group was the Hohokam. They planted and harvested corn, squash, and beans. The Anazasi (200–1100 A.D.) seem to have been the ancestors of the Pueblo peoples. They created vast cities and irrigation systems in the Southwest and developed means of managing scarce water. Their cliff dwellings and cities can be viewed today at Chaco Canyon, Mesa Verde, and other sites. By 1100 A.D. over 90 distinct Pueblo societies had developed. Major groups in the Southwest included the Pueblos and the Navajo.

1540: Coronado travels to the Pueblos in search of the fabled cities of gold. He has an army of 300 Spaniards and 1000 Indians from Mexico.

1598: Juan de Oñate establishes control of the pueblos through terror and military domination. Following a brutal occupation, Spaniards attempt to Christianize the Indians and make them work for the Spanish authority. Fransicans establish missions near San Antonio, Texas.

1680: Pueblos revolt against the Spaniards. The revolt is crushed ten years later.

1683: Retreating Spaniards establish missions at Ysleta and Socorro, now El Paso, Texas.

1690: Spanish military and missions are reestablished, controlling some of the territory of New Mexico until the arrival of U.S. forces.

1848: In the Treaty of Guadalupe Hildalgo ending the Mexican-American War, the U.S. promises protection of all Native American land rights in the ceded area, a provision consistently violated.

1863: Kit Carson and the U.S. army use a "scorched earth policy" to drive the Navajo from their lands.

1864: Major groups of Navajo surrender on January 31. They are forced to march through deep snow to Texas; over 190 die en route.

1868: Navajo are allowed to return after signing a new treaty, ceding large amounts of their lands to the U.S. Navajo are forced to live on reservations.

1886: Geronimo, an Apache leader, is forced to surrender to U.S. troops. His defeat marks the end of most resistance in the Southwest.

1887: Congress passes the Dawes Severalty Act, designed to break up tribal authority. It proves disastrous to native peoples.

1900: Many Indians intermarry with Mexican-Americans and pass as Mexican-Americans, since the discrimination and brutality against Mexicans is less than that faced by Indian peoples.

Far West

Native California peoples have an abundance of food and live in small villages of less than 200. They are a largely peaceful people. Groups include the Yuroks, Salinas, Miwoks, Wintun, and many more. Many become noted for their basket weaving. Many catch fish from the ocean. Others hunt in a manner similar to eastern forest tribes.

1769: Spain establishes missions in San Diego and Monterey, later developing a chain of 21 missions. The missions depend upon Indian labor. Forced work and slavery are practiced.
1830: European diseases kill over two-thirds of the native people in California.
1832: The missions are secularized, and the Indians "released." Many work on California ranches.
1849: The Gold Rush brings thousands of Europeans to California. They kill most of the remaining Indians. By 1900, only 15,000 native people are left in California.
1854: Seattle (Seathl), Dwamish chief, surrenders their territory in Washington state to the U.S.
1873: Captain Jack (Kintpuash) leads Modocs in resisting being forced onto reservations in California.
1910: Indian children from many tribes are sent to Stewart Indian School in Carson City, Nev., and the Sherman Indian School in Riverside, Calif. They are "Americanized": separated from their tribes, their language, and their cultures.

Northwest Coast

Greatly developed fishing and hunting societies. Salmon was a major food source. Some hunt whales. Chinooks, Umpquas, Coos, and other groups live near the sea and build large canoes for fishing. Kwakiutle and others are known for artwork and the potlatch ceremony. Tlingits are known for fishing and totem poles. The early contacts are with Russians and English seeking furs.

1877: The Nez Perce with Chief Joseph are driven from their homes in Oregon by soldiers. They attempt to reach Canada but are defeated.

Mexico

Several major distinct civilizations lived in the area presently known as Mexico, including the Maya, Olmec, Aztec, Monte Alban, and numerous others.

Native societies dominated Mexico. Intermarriage with Spanish conquerors was common. Persons migrating north to the United States are often meztiso or part Indian.

General

1871: Congress prohibits the further making of treaties with tribes. Many existing treaties are not recognized by Congress.
1887: The Dawes Severalty Act requires the division of communal land and seeks to terminate the special relationship of Indians with the U.S. government, despite existing treaties.
1924: Citizenship Act declares Indians are citizens of the United States.
1934: The Wheeler Howard Act allows Indians to reestablish their tribal culture and lands.
1943–1945: During World War II, Navajo "code talkers" use their own language as an unbreakable communications code to assist U.S. army operations in the Pacific.
1954: Congressional action terminates the relationship between the federal government and several tribes, including the Klamath in Oregon and several California groups.
1961: Menominee Tribe and reservation (Wisconsin) "terminated" by Act of Congress.
1969: Indians occupy Alcatraz Island and insist that it and other abandoned federal lands be returned to native ownership. Navajos officially designate themselves a nation at Window Rock, Arizona.
1970: New conflicts emerge in Washington state over tribal rights to fish, guaranteed by earlier treaties. Valerie Bridges found dead in the river.
1971: Indians vacate Alcatraz Island.
1973: Members of the American Indian Movement and others occupy Wounded Knee in South Dakota for 71 days to resist the imposed tribal government. Federal police and National Guards are used to force the end of the occupation.
1970s: A series of Indian-run colleges are established. Schools on reservations become Indian led. Mining corporations seek coal on Navajo and Hopi land at Black Mesa.

References

Acuña, R. F. (1972). *Occupied America: The Chicano's struggle toward liberation.* San Francisco: Canfield.

Acuña, R. F. (1981). *Occupied America: The Chicano's struggle toward liberation* (2nd ed.). San Francisco: Canfield.

Acuña, R. F. (1996). *Anything but Mexican: Chicanos in contemporary Los Angeles.* London and New York: Verso.

Adams, J. (1995). Proposition 187: What's to be learned? *Race File,* pp. 19–29. Oakland, CA: Applied Research Center.

Adams, M. J., Foorman, B. R., Lundberg, I., & Beeler, T. (1998). The elusive phoneme. *American Educator, 22*(1–2), 18–29.

Adler, M. (1982). *The Paideia proposal: An educational manifesto.* New York: Macmillan.

AFL-CIO. (1998). *Working Women.* Retrieved 5 March 1999 from the World Wide Web: http://www.aflcio.org/women/wwfacts.htm

African American Male Task Force of Milwaukee Public Schools. (1990, May). *Educating African American males: A dream deferred.* Milwaukee, WI: Milwaukee Public Schools.

Allport, G. W. (1979). *The nature of prejudice.* Reading, MA: Addison-Wesley.

Almaguer, T. (1994). *Racial fault lines: The historical origins of white supremacy in California.* Berkeley, CA: University of California Press.

Al-Qazzaz, A. (1996). The Arab lobby: Political identity and participation. In Wilbur C. Rich (Ed.), *The politics of minority coalitions: Race, ethnicity and shared uncertainties* (n.p.). Westport, CT: Praeger.

America on trial: Fire and fury. (1992, 11 May). *Newsweek,* pp. 24–29.

American Anthropological Association. (1997, November). *Anthropology Newsletter, 38*(11), 1.

American Association of Physical Anthropologists. (1996). *American Journal of Physical Anthropology, 101,* 569–570.

American Association of University Women (AAUW). (1992). *How schools shortchange girls.* Washington, DC: Author.

Amott, T. L., & Matthaei, J. A. (1991). *Race, gender and work: A multicultural economic history of women in the United States.* Boston: South End.

Anderson, J. A. (1988, January–February). Cognitive styles and multicultural populations. *Journal of Teacher Education,* pp. 2–9.

Annie E. Case Foundation. (1997). *Kids count data book.* Baltimore, MD: Author.

Anzaldúa, G. (1987). *Borderlands/La Frontera: The new Mestiza.* San Francisco: Spinsters/Aunt Lute.

Apple, M. (1988). *Teachers and texts: A political economy of class and gender relations in education.* New York: Routledge & Kegan Paul.

Apple, M. (1993). *Official knowledge: Democratic education in a conservative age.* New York: Routledge & Kegan Paul.

Apple, M., & Christian Smith, L. K. (1991). *The politics of the textbook.* New York: Routledge.

Armor, D. J. (1995, 2 August). Can desegregation alone close the achievement gap? *Education Week,* p. 68.

Arnstine, D. (1995). *Democracy and the arts of schooling*. Albany, NY: State University of New York Press.

Aronowitz, S. (1973). *False promises: The shaping of American working class consciousness*. New York: McGraw-Hill.

Aronowitz, S., & Giroux, H. (1985). *Education under siege: The conservative, liberal, and radical debate over schooling*. South Hadley, MA: Bergin & Garvey.

Aronstein, M., & Olsen, E. (1974). *Action learning: Student community services projects*. Washington, DC: Association for Supervision and Curriculum Development.

Asante, M. K. (1991, Spring). Multiculturalism: An exchange. *American Scholar*, pp. 267–272.

Association for Supervision and Curriculum Development. (1988). *Dimensions in thinking*. Alexandria, VA: Author.

Association for Supervision and Curriculum Development. (1992). The core curriculum conundrum. *Education Update, 34*(2), 1.

Au, K. H. (1993). *Literacy instruction in multicultural settings*. New York: Harcourt Brace Jovanovich.

Au, K. H., & Kawakami, A. (1994). Cultural congruence in instruction. In E. R. Hollins, J. King, & W. Hayman. (Eds.), *Teaching diverse populations: Formulating a knowledge base* (pp. 5–23). Albany, NY: State University of New York Press.

Banks, J. A. (1984). *Teaching strategies for ethnic studies* (3rd ed.). Needham Heights, MA: Allyn & Bacon.

Banks, J. A. (1988). Approaches to multicultural reform. *Multicultural Leader, 1*(2), 1–3.

Banks, J. A. (1989). Multicultural education: Characteristics and goals. In J. A. Banks & C. A. McGee Banks (Eds.), *Multicultural education: Issues and perspectives* (pp. 2–3). Needham Heights, MA: Allyn & Bacon.

Banks, J. A. (1992). African American scholarship and the evolution of multicultural education. *Journal of Negro Education, 61*(3), 273–285.

Banks, J. A. (1994). *An introduction to multicultural education*. Needham Heights, MA: Allyn & Bacon.

Banks, J. A. (1995). Multicultural education: Historical development, dimensions, and practice. In J. A. Banks & C. A. McGee Banks (Eds.), *Handbook of research on multicultural education* (pp. 1–24). New York: Simon & Schuster/Macmillan.

Banks, J. A. (1997). *Educating citizens in a multicultural society*. New York: Teachers College Press.

Banks, J. A., & McGee Banks, C. A. (Eds.). (1989). *Multicultural education: Issues and perspectives*. Needham Heights, MA: Allyn & Bacon.

Banks, J. A., & McGee Banks, C. A. (Eds.). (1995). *Handbook of research on multicultural education*. New York: Simon & Schuster/Macmillan.

Bartlett, D. L., & Steele, J. B. (1992). *America: What went wrong?* Kansas City, MO: Andrews & McMeel.

Bastian, A., Fruchter, N., Gittell, M., Greer, C., & Hoskins, K. (1985). *Choosing equality: The case for democratic schooling*. Philadelphia: Temple University Press.

Beane, J. A. (1990). *Affect in the curriculum: Toward democracy, dignity and diversity*. New York: Teachers College Press.

Bell, D. (1992). *Faces at the bottom of the well*. New York: HarperCollins.

Bennett, C. (1986). *Comprehensive multicultural education: Theory and practice*. Needham Heights, MA: Allyn & Bacon.

Bensman, D. (1987). *Quality education in the inner city: The story of Central Park East schools*. New York: New York Community Trust.

Bernstein, B. (1977). *Class, codes, and control*. London: Routledge & Kegan Paul.

Beyer, B. (1988). *Developing a thinking skills program*. Needham Heights, MA: Allyn & Bacon.

Bilingual Writing Center. (1993). [Computer program]. The Learning Company. Available on the World Wide Web at http://www.shoptlc.com/

Bliatout, B. T., Downing, B. T., Lewis, J., & Yang, D. (1988). *Handbook for teaching Hmong-speaking students*. Folsom, CA: Southeast Asia Community Resource Center, Folsom Cordova Unified School District.

Bloom, A. (1987). *The closing of the American mind: How higher education has failed democracy and impoverished the souls of today's students*. New York: Simon & Schuster.

B'nai B'rith Antidefamation League. (1986). *The wonderful world of difference: A human relations program for grades K–8*. New York: Author.

Bobo, K., Kendall, J., & Max, S. (1991). *Organizing for social change: A manual for activity in the 1990s*. Washington, DC: Seven Locks.

Bomotti, S. (1998). School choice: Complexities, cross-currents, and conflicts. Paper presented at

American Educational Research Association Annual Meeting, 13–17 April.

Bowers, C. A., & Flanders, D. J. (1990). *Responsive teaching: An ecological approach to classroom patterns of language, culture and thought.* New York: Teachers College Press.

Bowles, S., & Gintis, H. (1976). *Schooling in capitalist America: Educational reform and the contradictions of economic life.* New York: Basic Books.

Boyer, E. (1983). *High school: A report on secondary education in America.* Princeton, NJ: Carnegie Foundation for the Advancement of Teaching.

Boyer, R. O., & Morais, H. M. (1955). *Labor's untold story.* New York: United Electrical Workers.

Bradley, A. (1994, 14 September). Education for equality: The story of Ron Rodriguez. *Education Week*, pp. 28–32.

Brant, R. (1990, February). On knowledge and cognitive skills: A conversation with David Perkins. *ASCD Educational Leadership*, pp. 50–54.

Brown, D. (1987). *Principles of language learning: Theory and practice* (2nd ed.). Upper Saddle River, NJ: Prentice-Hall.

Brown, P. A., & Haycock, K. (1984). *Excellence for whom? A report of the planning committee for the Achievement Council.* Oakland, CA: Achievement Council.

Bruner, J. (1996). *The culture of education.* Cambridge: Harvard University Press.

Bruner, J., & Cole, M. (1973). Cultural differences and inferences about psychological processes. In J. M. Anglin (Ed.), *Jerome S. Bruner: Beyond the information given: Studies in the psychology of knowing* (pp. 452–467). New York: W. W. Norton.

Burkins, G., & Simpson, G. R. (1996). As Democrats meet, the teachers' unions will show their clout. *Wall Street Journal, 128*(39), A1.

Bushman, J. H., & Bushman, K. P. (1997). *Using young adult literature in the English classroom* (2nd ed.). Upper Saddle River, NJ: Merrill/Prentice Hall.

Buteyn, R. J. (1989). *Gender and academic achievement in education.* (Report No. 313103). Washington, DC: U.S. Department of Education. (ERIC Document Reproduction Service No. ED 313 103)

Butler, J. E. (1989). Transforming the curriculum: Teaching about women of color. In J. A. Banks & C. A. McGee Banks (Eds.), *Multicultural education: Issues and perspectives* (pp. 145–163). Needham Heights, MA: Allyn & Bacon.

Cagan, E. (1978, May). Individualism, collectivism, and radical educational reform. *Harvard Educational Review*, pp. 227–266.

California Department of Education. (1987). *History–social science framework for California public schools: Kindergarten through grade twelve.* Sacramento, CA: Author.

California Department of Education. (1994–1995). *Fact book.* Sacramento, CA: Author.

California Department of Education. (1997). *Language census report for California public schools, 1997.* Sacramento, CA: Educational Demographics Unit, California Department of Education.

California Department of Education, Bilingual Education Office. (1981). *Schooling and language minority students: A theoretical framework.* Los Angeles: California State University, Evaluation, Dissemination, and Assessment Center.

California Department of Education, Bilingual Education Office (1986). *Beyond language: Social & cultural factors in schooling of language minority students.* Los Angeles: California State University, Evaluation, Dissemination, and Assessment Center.

California Senate Office of Research. (1995). *The status of affirmative action.* Sacramento, CA: Author.

California Tomorrow. (1988). *Immigrant students and the California public schools: Crossing the schoolhouse border.* San Francisco, CA: Author.

California Tomorrow. (1994). *The unfinished journey: Restructuring schools in a diverse society.* San Francisco, CA: Author.

Cameron, S. C., & Wycoff, S. M. (1998, Summer). The destructive nature of the term *race*: Growing beyond a false paradigm. *Journal of Counseling and Development, 76*, 277–285.

Campbell, D. E. (1980). *Education for a democratic society: Curriculum ideas for teachers.* Cambridge, MA: Schenkman.

Campbell, D. E. (1987). How the Grinch stole the social sciences: Moving teaching to the right in California. *Journal of the Association of Mexican American Educators*, pp. 43–49.

Campbell, J. R., Donahue, P. L., Reese, C. M., & Philips, G. W. (1996). *NAEP 1994 reading report card for the nation and the states.* Washington,

DC: National Center for Education Statistics, U.S. Department of Education.

Carlson, D. (1992). *Teachers and crisis: Urban school reform and teachers' work culture*. New York & London: Routledge.

Carnegie Council on Adolescent Development. (1995). *Great transitions: Preparing adolescents for the 21st century*. New York: Carnegie Corporation of New York.

Carnegie Foundation for the Advancement of Teaching. (1988). *An imperiled generation: Saving urban schools*. Lawrenceville, NJ: Princeton University Press.

Carnoy, M. (1989). Education, state, and culture. In H. A. Giroux and P. McLarne, (Eds.), *Critical pedagogy, the state, and cultural struggle* (pp. 3–23). Albany: State University of New York Press.

Carnoy, M. (1994). *Faded dreams: The politics and economics of race in America*. Cambridge, England: Cambridge University Press.

Carnoy, M. (1998). National voucher plans in Chile and Sweden: Did privatization reforms make for better education? *Comparative Education Review, 42*(3), 309–337.

Carnoy, M., & Levin, H. M. (1985). *Schooling and work in the democratic state*. Stanford, CA: Stanford University Press.

Carter, C. J. (1997, March). Why reciprocal teaching? *Educational Leadership*, pp. 64–68.

Carter, T. P. (1990). *Effective schools and the process of change*. Unpublished manuscript, Sacramento, CA: California State University—Sacramento.

Carter, T. P., & Chatfield, M. L. (1986). Effective bilingual schools: Implications for policy and practice. *American Journal of Education, 95*(1), 200–232.

Carter, T. P., & Segura, R. (1979). *Mexican Americans in school: A decade of change*. New York: College Entrance Exam Board.

Case, R., & Bereiter, C. (1984). From behaviorism to cognitive behaviorism to cognitive development: Steps in the evolution of instructional design. *Instructional Science, 13*, 141–158.

Center for Civic Education. (1991). *Civitas: A framework for civic education*. Calabasas, CA: Author.

Center for Popular Economics. (1987). *A field guide to the U.S. economy*. New York: Pantheon Books.

Center for Popular Economics. (1995). *The new field guide to the U.S. economy, 1985–1995* (2nd ed.). New York: New Press.

Cesar Chavez Foundation (Ed.). (in press). *Education of the heart: Cesar E. Chavez in his own words*. Keene, CA: Author.

Charles, C. M. (1989). *Building classroom discipline: From models to practice* (3rd ed.). New York: Longman.

Chase, R. (1997, 27 April). All children are equal: But some children are more equal than others. *NEA Today*, p. 2.

Chávez, L. (1998). *The color bind: California's battle to end affirmative action*. Berkeley, CA: University of California Press.

Chavez Comeron, S., & Macias Wycoff, S. (1998, Summer). The meaninglessness of race: Growing beyond an artificial paradigm. *Journal of Counseling and Development*, pp. 277–285.

Cheney, L. V. (1987). *American memory: A report on the humanities in the nation's public schools*. Washington, DC: National Endowment for the Humanities.

Children's Defense Fund. (1997). *The state of America's children: Yearbook, 1997*. Washington, DC: Author.

Children's Defense Fund. (1998). *The state of America's children: Yearbook, 1998*. Washington, DC: Author.

Chubb, J. E., & Moe, T. M. (1989). *Politics, markets and America's schools*. Washington, DC: Brookings Institution.

Cintrón, J. (1993). A school in change: The empowerment of minority teachers. In H. T. Trueba, C. Rodriguez, Y. Zou, & J. Cintrón (Eds.), *Healing multicultural America: Mexican immigrants rise to power in rural California* (pp. 115–132). Washington, DC: Falmer.

Cohen, E. (1986). *Designing groupwork: Strategies for the heterogeneous classroom*. New York: Teachers College Press.

Cohen, E., & Lotan R. A. (1997). *Working for equity in homogeneous classrooms: Sociological theory in practice*. New York: Teachers College Press.

Cohen, E., Lotan, R. A., & Whitcomb, J. A. (1992). Complex instruction in the social studies classroom. In R. J. Stahl & R. L. Van Sickle (Eds.), *Cooperative learning in the social studies* (p. 87). Washington, DC: National Council for the Social Studies.

Coleman, J. (1966). *Equality of educational opportunity*. Office of Education of the United States Department of Health, Education, and Welfare. Washington, D.C.: U.S. Government Printing Office.

Coleman, J. (1987). *Public and private high schools: The impact of communities*. New York: Basic Books.

Coleman, J. (1990). *Equality and achievement in education*. Boulder, CO: Westview.

Colin, G. (1975). *The great school legend: A revisionist interpretation of American public education*. New York: Basic Books.

Collier, V. (1995). *Promoting academic success for E.S.L. students: Understanding second language acquisition for school*. Elizabeth, NJ: Teachers of English to Speakers of Other Languages—Bilingual Educators.

Colvin, R. L. (1998, 19 May). Too many teachers are ill prepared. *Los Angeles Times*, pp. R1, R5, R6.

Comer, J. P. (1988). *Is parenting essential to good teaching?* Washington, DC: National Education Association.

Comer, J. P. (1997). *Waiting for a miracle: Why schools can't solve our problems—and how we can*. New York: E. P. Dutton.

Commission on Chapter 1. (1993, 13 January). Making schools work for children in poverty. *Education Week*, pp. 47–51.

Congressional Black Caucus. (1991). *Quality of life budget, FY 1991*. Executive summary. Washington, DC: Author.

Consortium for Policy Research in Education. (1998, May). States and districts and comprehensive reform. *CPRE Policy Briefs RB–24*. Philadelphia: University of Pennsylvania.

Coons, J. E., & Sugarman, D. S. (1978). *Education by choice: The case for family control*. Berkeley, CA: University of California Press.

Cornbleth, C. (1985). Critical thinking and cognitive process. *Review of Research in Social Studies Education: 1976–1983, bulletin 75*, pp. 11–55.

Cornbleth, C., & Waugh, D. (1995). *The great speckled bird: Multicultural politics and education policymaking*. New York: St. Martin's.

Cortés, E. (1996). *The IAF and education reform: Organizing citizens for change* (Mimeograph). Dallas, TX: Industrial Areas Foundation.

Costa, A. (1985). *Teaching for intelligent behavior*. Orangevale, CA: Search Models Unlimited.

Cotton, K. (1989). *Expectations and student outcomes*. Portland, OR: Northwest Regional Laboratory.

Crawford, J. (1991). *Bilingual education: History, politics, theory and practice* (2nd ed.). Los Angeles, CA: Bilingual Educational Services.

Crawford, J. (1992). *Hold your tongue: Bilingualism and the politics of "English only."* Reading, MA: Addison-Wesley.

Cummins, J. (1986). Empowering minority students: A framework for intervention. *Harvard Educational Review, 56*(1), 18–36.

Cummins, J. (1989). *Empowering language minority students*. Ontario, CA: California Association for Bilingual Education.

Cummins, J. (1996). *Negotiating identities: Education for empowerment in a diverse society*. Ontario, CA: California Association for Bilingual Education.

Cummins, J., & Sayers, D. (1995). *Brave new schools: Challenging cultural illiteracy through global learning networks*. New York: St. Martin's.

A curriculum of inclusion: Commissioner's Task Force on Minorities: Equity and excellence. (1989, July). Albany, NY: New York State Education Department.

Dahl, R. (1985). *A preface to economic democracy*. Berkeley, CA: University of California Press.

Darder, A. (1991). *Culture and power in the classroom: A critical foundation for bicultural education*. New York: Bergin & Garvey.

Darling-Hammond, L. (1990). Instructional policy into practice: The power of the bottom over the top. *Educational Evaluation and Policy Analysis, 12*(3), 339–348.

Darling-Hammond, L. (1995). Inequity and access to knowledge. In J. A. Banks & C. A. McGee Banks (Eds.), *Handbook of research on multicultural education* (pp. 465–470). New York: Simon & Schuster/Macmillan.

Darling-Hammond, L. (1997). *The right to learn: A blueprint for creating schools that work*. San Francisco: Jossey-Bass.

Darling-Hammond, L., & Ancess, J. (1996). Democracy and access to education. In R. Soder (Ed.), *Democracy, education and the schools* (pp. 151–181). San Francisco: Jossey-Bass.

Davis, M. (1986). *Prisoners of the American dream: Politics and economy in the U.S. working class*. London: Verso.

Dear, J. (1995). *Creating caring relationships to foster academic excellence: Recommendations for reducing violence in California schools.* Sacramento, CA: Advisory Panel on School Violence, Commission on Teacher Credentialing.

DeAvila, E. (1987). *Finding out: Descubrimiento, teacher's guide.* Northvale, NJ: Santillana.

DeAvila, E. (1990). Assessment of language minority students: Political, technical, practical, and moral imperatives. Paper delivered at the National Symposium on Limited English Proficient Students, Washington, DC, 10 September.

DeParle, J. (1994, 31 March). Sharp increases along borders of poverty. *New York Times,* p. A-18.

Dewey, J. (1916/1966). *Democracy and education: An introduction to the philosophy of education.* New York: The Free Press/Macmillan.

DeWitt, K. (1994, 19 December). Have suburbs, especially in the South, become the source of American political power? *New York Times,* p. B9.

Douglass, F. (1849/1991). Letter to an abolitionist associate. In K. Bobo, J. Kendall, & S. Max (Eds.), *Organizing for social change: A manual of activity in the 1990s* (cover page). Washington, DC: Seven Locks.

Dreikurs, R., Greenwald, B., & Pepper, F. (1971). *Maintaining sanity in the classroom.* New York: Harper & Row.

Dreikurs, R., & Stoltz, V. (1964). *Children: The challenge.* New York: Hawthorn.

Du Bois, W. E. B. (1975). *Color and democracy: Colonies and peace.* Millwood, NY: Kraus-Thompson.

Dweck, C. (1977). Learned helplessness and negative evaluation. *Educator, 19*(2), 44–49.

Edmonds, R. (1979). Effective schools for the urban poor. *Educational Leadership, 37*(1), 15–24.

Edmonds, R. (1982). Programs for school improvement: An overview. *Educational Leadership, 40*(3), 4–12.

Education Week (1997). Quality counts: A report card on the condition of public education in the 50 states. A supplement to *Education Week, 16*(January 22).

Education Week (1998). Quality counts 98: The urban challenge: Public education in the 50 states. A supplement to *Education Week, 17*(January 8).

Ehrenreich, B. (1989). *Fear of falling: The inner life of the middle class.* New York: Pantheon.

Ehrenreich, B., & Ehrenreich, J. (1979). The professional-managerial class. In P. Walker (Ed.), *Between labor and capital* (pp. 5–45). Boston: South End.

Eisner, E. (1994). *Education update.* Alexandria, VA: Association for Supervision and Curriculum Development.

Eldredge, J. L. (1995). *Teaching decoding in holistic classrooms.* Upper Saddle River, NJ: Merrill/Prentice Hall.

Elkind, D. (1988). *The hurried child: Growing up too fast too soon.* Reading, MA: Addison-Wesley.

Eller-Powell, R. (1994). Teaching for change in Appalachia. In E. R. Hollins, J. E. King, & W. G. Hayman (Eds.), *Teaching diverse populations: Formulating a knowledge base* (pp. 61–75). Albany, NY: State University of New York Press.

Equity Resource Center Digest. (1997). Newton, MA: WEEA Resource Center at Education Development Canter, Inc.

Every child reading: An action plan of the Learning First Alliance. (1998). *American Educator, 22*(1–2), 52–63.

Faludi, S. (1991). *Backlash: The undeclared war against American women.* New York: Crown.

Fernandez, J., & Underwood, J. (1993). *Tales out of school: Joseph Fernandez's crusade to rescue American education.* Boston: Little, Brown.

Fine, M. (1993). Sexuality, schooling, and adolescent females: The missing discourse of desire. In L. Weis & M. Fine (Eds.), *Beyond silenced voices; Class, race, and gender in United States schools* (pp. 75–99). Albany, NY: State University of New York Press.

Fix, M., & Passel, J. (1994). *Immigration and immigrants: Setting the record straight.* Washington, DC: Urban Institute.

Florio, G. (1998, 8 June). Bilingual classes are a hit in Texas: There is no plan to cut back. *Philadelphia Inquirer,* p. 1.

Foner, E., & Werner, J. (1991, July). Fighting for the West. *The Nation,* pp. 163–166.

Foner, P. P. (Ed.). (1970). *W. E. B. Du Bois speaks: Speeches and addresses, 1920–1963.* New York: Pathfinder.

Forbes. (1999). Retrieved 15 February 1999 from the World Wide Web: http://www.forbes.com/tools/toolbox/rich400

Fordham, S. (1988). Racelessness as a factor in black students' success: Pragmatic strategy or

Pyrrhic victory? *Harvard Education Review, 58*(1), 54–84.

Foster, M. (1994). Effective black teachers: A literature review. In E. R. Hollins, J. King, & W. Hayman (Eds.), *Teaching diverse populations: Formulating a knowledge base* (pp. 225–241). Albany: State University of New York Press.

Foster, M. (1995). African American teachers and culturally relevant pedagogy. In J. A. Banks & C. A. McGee Banks (Eds.), *Handbook of research on multicultural education* (pp. 570–581). New York: Simon & Schuster/Macmillan.

Freire, P. (n.d.). *Conscienticizing as a way of liberating*. Washington, DC: LADOC, Division for Latin America.

Freire, P. (1972). *A pedagogy of the oppressed*. New York: Continuum.

Freire, P. (1985). *The politics of education: Culture, power, and liberation*. New York: Bergin & Garvey.

Freire, P. (1997). *Pedagogy of hope: Reliving pedagogy of the oppressed*. New York: Continuum.

Freire, P. (forthcoming) *Politics and education* (P. L. Wong, Trans.). Los Angeles: UCLA, Latin American Center. (Original work published 1993)

Freire, P., & Macedo, D. (1987). *Literacy: Reading the word and the world*. South Hadley, MA: Bergin & Garvey.

Freire, P., & Shore, I. (1987). *A pedagogy for liberation: Dialogues on transforming education*. South Hadley, MA: Bergin & Garvey.

Fremon, C. (1995). *Father Greg & the home boys*. New York: Hyperion.

Friend, R. A. (1993). Choices, not closets: Heterosexism and homophobia in school. In L. Weis & M. Fine (Eds.), *Beyond silenced voices: Class, race and gender in United States schools* (pp. 209–235). Albany: State University of New York Press.

Fullan, M. (1991). *The new meaning of educational change* (2nd ed.). New York: Teachers College Press.

Gagnon, P. (1995). What should children learn? *Atlantic Monthly, 276*(6), 65–73.

Gándara, P. (1995). *Over ivy walls: The educational mobility of low-income Chicanos*. Albany, NY: State University of New York Press.

Gándara, P. (1997). *Review of the research on instruction of limited English proficient students:*

A report to the California Legislature. Davis, CA: University of California at Davis, Linguistic Minority Research Institute, Education Policy Center.

Garcia, E. (1994). Attributes of effective schools for language minority students. In E. Hollins, J. King, & W. Hayman (Eds.), *Teaching diverse populations: Formulating a knowledge base* (pp. 93–104). Albany, NY: State University of New York Press.

Garcia, E. (1995). Educating Mexican American students: Past treatment and recent developments in theory, research, policy, and practice. In J. A. Banks & C. A. McGee Banks (Eds.), *Handbook of research on multicultural education* (pp. 372–387). New York: Simon & Schuster/Macmillan.

Garcia, M. T. (1994). *Memories of Chicano history: The life and narrative of Bert Corona*. Berkeley, CA: University of California Press.

Gardner, H. (1983). *Frames of mind: The theory of multiple intelligences*. New York: Basic Books.

Gardner, H. (1993). *Multiple intelligences: The theory in practice*. New York: Basic Books/HarperCollins.

Gardner, R., & Lambert, W. (1972). *Attitudes and motivation in second language learning*. Rowley, MA: Newbury.

Gibson, M. (1976). Approaches to multicultural education in the United States: Some concepts and assumptions. *Anthropology and Education Quarterly, 7*(4), 7–18.

Gibson, M. (1987). The school performance of immigrant students: A comparative view. *Anthropology and Education Quarterly, 18*(4), 262–275.

Gilligan, C. (1982). *In a different voice*. Cambridge: Harvard University Press.

Giroux, H. A. (1979). Schooling and the culture of positivism: Notes on the death of history. *Educational Theory, 29*(4), 263–284.

Giroux, H. A. (1988). *Teachers as intellectuals: Toward a critical pedagogy of learning*. New York: Bergin & Garvey.

Gitlin, T. (1995). *The twilight of common dreams: Why America is wracked by cultural wars*. New York: Henry Holt.

Glazer, N. (1991, September). In defense of multiculturalism. *The New Republic*, pp. 18–20.

Glazer, N. (1993, 28 November). Multicultural school wars. *Sacramento Bee*, p. 1.

Goodlad, J. (1984). *A place called school: Prospects for the future.* New York: McGraw-Hill.

Goodlad, J., & Keating, P. (Eds.). (1990). *Access to knowledge: An agenda for our nation's schools.* New York: College Entrance Examination Board.

Gordon, B. M. (1995). Knowledge construction, competing critical theories, and education. In J. A. Banks & C. A. McGee Banks (Eds.), *Handbook of research on multicultural education* (pp. 184–199). New York: Simon & Schuster/Macmillan.

Gordon, K. (1991). *When good kids do bad things: A survival guide for parents.* New York: W. W. Norton.

Green, J. F. (1998, Spring–Summer). Another chance. *American Educator,* pp. 74–79.

Greer, C. (1972). *The great school legend: A revisionist interpretation of American public education.* New York: Basic Books.

Greider, W. (1992). *Who will tell the people? The betrayal of American democracy.* New York: Simon & Schuster.

Grelle, B., & Metzger, D. (1996). Beyond socialization and multiculturalism: Rethinking the task of citizenship education in a pluralistic society. *Social Education, 60*(3), 147–151.

Grey, P. (1991, 8 July). Whose America? *Time,* pp. 12–17.

Grisold del Castillo, R. (1979). *The Los Angeles barrio: 1860–1890: A social history.* Berkeley, CA: University of California Press.

Gross, R. E., & Dynneson, T. L. (1991). *Social science perspectives on citizenship education.* New York: Teachers College Press.

Guthrie, J., & Brazil, E. (1999, 16 February). Tentative deal settles suit before trial. *San Francisco Examiner,* p. 1. Retrieved 18 February 1999 from the World Wide Web: http://www.examiner/archive/1999/02/12news

Hacker, A. (1992). *Two nations: Black, white, separate, hostile, unequal.* New York: Scribner's.

Hall, E. E. (1994). *California K–12 report card.* Sacramento, CA: California Legislative Analyst Office.

Hall, M. (1981). *Teaching reading as a language experience.* Columbus, OH: Merrill. Cited in J. L. Eldredge, *Teaching decoding in holistic classrooms* (p. 9). Upper Saddle River, NJ: Merrill/Prentice Hall, 1995.

Handlin, O. (1957). *Race and nationality in American life.* Garden City, NY: Doubleday.

Hannaway, J., & Carnoy, M. (Eds.). (1993). *Decentralization and school improvement: Can we fulfill the promise?* San Francisco: Jossey-Bass.

Hansen, J. F. (1979). *Sociocultural perspectives on human learning: Foundations of educational anthropology.* Upper Saddle River, NJ: Prentice Hall.

Harrington, M. (1963). *The other America: Poverty in the United States.* New York: Macmillan.

Harrington, M. (1989). The new American poverty. Lecture delivered at Haverford College, Haverford, PA, May.

Hartoonian, H. M. (1991). The role of philosophy in the education of democratic citizens. In R. E. Gross & T. L. Dynneson (Eds.), *Social science perspectives on citizenship education* (pp. 195–219). New York: Teachers College Press.

Heath, S. B. (1986). Sociocultural contexts of language development. In California Department of Education, Bilingual Education Office (Ed.), *Beyond language: Social & cultural factors in schooling of language minority students* (pp. 143–186). Los Angeles: California State University, Evaluation, Dissemination, and Assessment Center.

Heath, S. B. (1995). Ethnography in communities: Learning the everyday life of America's subordinated youth. In J. A. Banks & C. A. McGee Banks (Eds.), *Handbook of research on multicultural education* (pp. 114–128). New York: Simon & Schuster/Macmillan.

Hechinger, F. M. (1992). *Fateful choices: Healthy youth for the 21st century.* New York: Carnegie Council on Adolescent Development.

Henry, W. A. III. (1990, April). Beyond the melting pot (the browning of America will alter everything). *Time,* pp. 28–31.

Heredia-Arriaga, S., & Campbell, D. (1991). *How to integrate cooperative learning for the elementary teacher: Video and training program.* Carson City, NV: Superior Learning Programs.

Herrnstein, R. J., & Murray, C. (1994). *The bell curve: Intelligence and class structure in American life.* New York: Free Press.

High standards for all—experienced teachers for some. (1998). *Reforming Middle School & Schools Systems, 2*(2), 1–2.

Hill, D. (1997, August–September). Sisters in arms. *Education Week,* p. 1.

Hirsch, E. D., Jr. (1987). *Cultural literacy.* New York: Houghton Mifflin.

Hirsch, E. D., Jr. (1996). *The schools we need, and why we don't have them.* New York: Doubleday.

Hoffman, D. M. (1996). Culture and self in multicultural education: Reflections on discourse, text, and practice. *American Educational Research Journal, 33*(3), 545–569.

Hollins, E. R., King, J. E., & Hayman, W. C. (Eds.). (1994). *Teaching diverse populations: Formulating a knowledge base.* Albany, NY: State University of New York Press.

hooks, b. (1994). *Teaching to transgress: Education as the practice of freedom.* New York: Routledge.

Hoose, P. (1993). *It's our world, too! Stories of young people who are making a difference.* Boston: Little, Brown.

Hoover, R. L., & Kindsvatter, R. (1997). *Democratic discipline: Foundations & practice.* Upper Saddle River, NJ: Merrill/Prentice Hall.

Hopfenberg, W. S., Levin, H. M., Chase, C., Christensen, G., Moore, M., Soler, P., Brunner, I., Keller, B., & Rodriguez, G. (1993). *The accelerated schools resource guide.* San Francisco: Jossey-Bass.

Horwitz, E., Horwitz, M., & Cope, J. (1991). Foreign language classroom anxiety. In E. Horwitz & D. Young (Eds.), *Language anxiety: From theory and research to classroom implications* (pp. 27–36). Upper Saddle River, NJ: Prentice Hall.

Hunter, M. (1982). *Mastery teaching.* El Segundo, CA: TIP.

Ignatiev, N. (1995). *How the Irish became white.* New York: Routledge.

Institute for Puerto Rican Policy. (1991). *The Puerto Rican exception: Persistent poverty and the conservative social policy of Linda Chavez.* New York: Author.

Jackson, T. (1993–1994). Everyday school violence: How disorder fuels it. *American Educator, 17*(4), 4–9.

Jargowsky, P. A., & Bane, M. J. (1991). Ghetto poverty in the U.S., 1970–1980. In C. Jenks & P. E. Peterson (Eds.), *The urban underclass* (pp. 235–273). Washington, DC: Brookings Institution.

Jensen, A. S. (1969). How much can we boost IQ and scholastic achievement? *Harvard Educational Review, 39*(1), 1–123.

Jimerson, L. (1998). The students "left behind": School choice and social stratification in nonurban districts. Paper presented at the annual meeting of the American Educational Research Association, San Diego, CA, 13–17 April.

Johnson, D. W., & Johnson, R. T. (1991). *Learning together and alone: Cooperative competitive and individualistic learning* (3rd ed.). Upper Saddle River, NJ: Prentice Hall.

Johnson, D. W., & Johnson, R. T. (1992, September). Teaching students to be peer mediators. *Educational Leadership,* pp. 10–18.

Johnston, R. C. (1998, 8 April). Minority admissions drop sharply at California universities. *Education Week,* p. 1.

Joint Economic Committee, U.S. Congress. (1992). *Families on a treadmill: Work and income in the 1980s.* Washington, DC: U.S. Government Printing Office.

Kagan, S. (1985). *Cooperative learning.* San Juan Capistrano, CA: Author.

Kagan, S. (1986). Cooperative learning and sociocultural factors in schooling. In California Department of Education, Bilingual Education Office (Ed.), *Beyond language: Social & cultural factors in schooling of language minority students* (pp. 231–298). Los Angeles: California State University, Evaluation, Dissemination, and Assessment Center.

Kagan, S. (1989). *Cooperative learning, resources for teachers.* San Juan Capistrano, CA: Resources for Teachers.

Karp, S. (1993, March). Trouble over the rainbow. *Z,* pp. 48–54.

King, J. E. (1992). Diaspora literacy and consciousness in the struggle against miseducation in the black community. *Journal of Negro Education, 61*(3), 317–335.

King, J. E. (1995). Culture-centered knowledge: Black studies, curriculum transformation, and social action. In J. A. Banks & C. A. McGee Banks (Eds.), *Handbook of research on multicultural education* (pp. 265–293). New York: Simon & Schuster/Macmillan.

King, K. C., & Jackson, R. L. (1997, 12 September). Asian Americans charge fund-raising scandal bias. *Los Angeles Times,* p. 1.

King, M. L., Jr. (1986). Speech to clergy and laity concerned. In J. Washington (Ed.), *Testament of hope: The essential writings and speeches of Martin Luther King, Jr.* (pp. 313–328). San Francisco: Harper.

Kozol, J. (1991). *Savage inequalities: Children in America's schools.* New York: Crown.

Krashen, S. D. (1996). *Under attack: The case against bilingual education.* Culver City, CA: Language Education Associates.

Krashen, S. D., & Terrell, T. D. (1983). *The natural approach: Language acquisition in the classroom.* Hayward, CA: Alemany.

Kuhn, T. S. (1970). *The structure of scientific revolutions* (2nd ed.). Chicago: University of Chicago Press.

Labaree, D. F. (1997). Public goods, private goals: the American struggle over educational goals. *American Educational Research Journal, 34*(1), 39–81.

Labov, W. (1970). *The study of nonstandard English.* Champaign, IL: National Council of Teachers of English.

Ladson-Billings, G. (1992, September). The multicultural mission: Unity and diversity. *Social Education,* pp. 308–311.

Ladson-Billings, G. (1994a). *The dreamkeepers: Successful teachers of African American children.* San Francisco: Jossey-Bass.

Ladson-Billings, G. (1994b). Who will teach our children? Preparing teachers to successfully teach African American students. In E. Hollins, J. King, & W. Hayman (Eds.), *Teaching diverse populations: Formulating a knowledge base* (pp. 129–135). Albany, NY: State University of New York Press.

Lawrence-Lightfoot, S. (1994). *I've known rivers: Lives of loss and liberation.* Reading, MA: Addison-Wesley.

Leming, J. S. (1985). Research on social studies curriculum instruction: Interventions and outcomes in the socio-moral domain. In W. B. Stanley (Ed.), *Review of research in social studies education, 1976–1983* (pp. 123–194). Washington, DC: National Council for the Social Studies.

Levin, H. (1994, Spring). Powerful learning in accelerated schools. *Accelerated Schools Project Newsletter,* pp. 14–18.

Levine, D. U., & Lezotte, L. W. (1995). Effective schools research. In J. A. Banks & C. A. McGee Banks (Eds.), *Handbook of research on multicultural education* (pp. 525–547). New York: Simon & Schuster/Macmillan.

Lewis, O. (1968). Culture of poverty. *Scientific American, 215*(4), 19–24.

Lieberman, A. (Ed.). (1995). *The work of restructuring schools: Building from the ground up.* New York: Teachers College Press.

Limerick, P. N. (1988). *The legacy of conquest: The unbroken past of the American West.* New York: W. W. Norton.

Llanes, J. (1982). *Cuban Americans: Masters of survival.* Cambridge, MA: Abbott.

Loewen, J. W. (1995). *Lies my teacher told me: Everything your American history textbook got wrong.* New York: New Press.

Lortie, D. (1975). *Schoolteacher.* Chicago: University of Chicago Press.

Los Angeles County Office of Education. (1991). *The condition of public education in Los Angeles County, 1990–1991.* Los Angeles, CA: Author.

Lowe, R., & Miner, B. (Eds.). (1996). *Selling out our schools: Vouchers, markets, and the future of public education.* Milwaukee, WI: Rethinking Schools.

Luhman, R. (1996). *The sociological outlook* (5th ed.). San Diego, CA: Collegiate.

Macedo, D. P. (1993, Summer). Literacy for stupification: The pedagogy of big lies. *Harvard Educational Review,* pp. 183–204.

MacLeod, J. (1987). *Ain't no making it: Leveled aspirations in a low-income neighborhood.* Boulder, CO: Westview.

A man of Flint: How General Motors lost the loyalty of its workers in Flint, Michigan. (1998). *The Economist, 347*(8073), 79.

Marable, M. (1985). *Black American politics: From the Washington march to Jesse Jackson.* London: Verso.

Marable, M. (1992). Multicultural democracy: The emerging majority for justice and peace. In M. Marable, *The crisis of color and democracy: Essays on race, class and power* (pp. 249–251). Monroe, ME: Common Courage.

Marks, H. M., & Louis, K. S. (1997). Does teacher empowerment affect the classroom? The implication of teacher empowerment for instructional practice and student academic performance. *Educational Evaluation and Policy Analysis, 19*(3), 245–275.

Marshall, R., & Tucker, M. (1992). *Thinking for a living: Education and the wealth of nations.* New York: Basic Books.

Martinez, M. (1978). *Self concept and behavioral change through counseling, consulting interven-*

tions. Unpublished doctoral dissertation. Lubbock, TX: Texas Tech University.

McCarthey, K. F., & Vernez, G. (1997). *New immigrants, new needs: The California experience* (Publication No. RB-8015). Santa Monica, CA: Rand Institute on Education and Training.

McCarthy, J. D., & Yencey, W. L. (1971). Uncle Tom and Mr. Charlie: Metaphysical pathos in the study of racism and personal disorganization. *American Institute of Sociology, 76*, 648–672.

McDermott, R. P. (1974). Achieving school failure: An anthropological approach to illiteracy and school stratification. In G. Spindler (Ed.), *Education and Cultural Process* (pp. 173–209). New York: Holt.

McDermott, R., & Varenne, H. (1995). Culture as disability. *Anthropology and Education Quarterly, 26*(3), 324–328.

McFadden, J. (1975). *Consciousness and social change: The pedagogy of Paulo Freire*. Unpublished doctoral dissertation. Santa Cruz, CA: University of California at Santa Cruz.

McGee Banks, C. A. (1997, Spring). The challenge of national standards in a multicultural society. *Education Horizons*, pp. 126–132.

McKenna, G. (1992, 27 March). Heartware, not hardware. *Los Angeles Times*, p. A11.

McKeon, D. (1994, May). When meeting "common" standards is uncommonly difficult. *Educational Leadership*, pp. 45–49.

McLaren, P. (1989). *Life in schools: An introduction to critical pedagogy in the foundations of education*. New York: Longman.

McLaughlin, M. W. (1991). The Rand change agent study: Ten years later. In A. Odden (Ed.), *Educational policy implementation* (pp. 143–156). Albany: State University of New York Press.

McLaughlin, M. W., & Oberman, I. (Eds.). (1996). *Teacher learning: New policies, new practices*. New York: Teachers College Press.

McLaughlin, M. W., & Talbert, J. (1993). *Contexts that matter for teaching and learning: Strategic opportunities for meeting the nation's educational goals*. Stanford, CA: Center for Research on the Context of Secondary School Teaching.

McLeod, B. (1996). *School reform and student diversity: Exemplary schooling for language minority students*. Washington, DC: George Washington University, National Clearinghouse for Bilingual Education, Institute for the Study of Language and Education.

McPartland, J. M., & Slavin, R. E. (1990). *Increasing achievement of at-risk students at each grade level*. Washington, DC: U.S. Office of Education.

Medina, M., & Escamilla, K. (1992). Evaluation of transitional and maintenance bilingual programs. *Urban Education, 27*(3), 263–290.

Mehan, H. (1992). Understanding inequality in schools: The contributions of interpretive studies. *Sociology of Education, 65*(1), 1–20.

Mehan, H., Lintz, A., Okamotoa, D., & Wills, J. S. (1995). Ethnographic studies of multicultural education in classrooms and schools. In J. A. Banks & C. A. McGee Banks (Eds.), *Handbook of research on multicultural education* (pp. 129–145). New York: Simon & Schuster/Macmillan.

Meier, D. (1995). *The power of their ideas: Lessons for America from a small school in Harlem*. Boston: Beacon.

Miller, J. (1992, April). Silent depression. *Dollars and Sense*, p. 6.

Miller-Jones, D. (1991). Informal reasoning in inner-city children. In J. F. Voss, D. N. Perkins, & J. S. Segal (Eds.), *Informal reasoning and education* (pp. 107–130). Hillsdale, NJ: Lawrence Erlbaum Associates.

Mintrop, H., Wong, P., Gamson, D., & Oberman, I. (1996). *Evaluation of the San Francisco Foundation school reform portfolio*. San Francisco: San Francisco Foundation.

Mishel, L., & Bernstein, J. (1995). *The state of working America, 1994–1995*. Armonk, NY: M. E. Sharpe.

Mishel, L., Bernstein, J., & Schmitt, J. (1999). *The state of working America, 1998–1999*. Ithaca, NY: Cornell University Press.

Mishel, L., & Frankel, M. (1997). *The state of working America, 1996–1997*. Armonk, NY: Economic Policy Institute.

Moll, L. C., Vélez-Ibañez, C., & Greenberg, J. (1992). *Community knowledge and classroom practice: Combining resources for literacy instruction: A handbook for teachers and planners*. Arlington, VA: Development Associates, Inc.

Moore, J. (1988, April). *An assessment of Hispanic poverty: Is there an Hispanic underclass?* San Antonio, TX: Thomas Rivera Center.

Moraga, C., & Anzaldúa, G. (Eds.). (1981). *This bridge called my back.* New York: Kitchen Table, Women of Color Press.

Mosak, H., & Dreikurs, R. (1973). Adlerian psychology. Originally published in R. Corsini (Ed.), *Current psychotherapies* (pp. 35–84), Itasca, IL: Peacock. Quoted in Martinez, M., *Self concept and behavioral change through counseling, consulting interventions* (pp. 35–84). Unpublished doctoral dissertation. Lubbock, TX: Texas Tech University, 1978.

Moynihan, D. P. (1993–1994, Winter). Defining deviancy down. *American Educator,* pp. 10–18.

Münch, R., & Smelser, N. J. (Eds.). (1992). *Theory of culture.* Berkeley, CA: University of California Press.

Nathan, J. (1996–1997). Progressives should support charter public schools. *Rethinking Schools, 11*(2), 20–21.

National Center for Children in Poverty. (1991). *News and issues.* New York: Columbia University School of Public Health.

National Center for Education Statistics. (1995). *The educational progress of Hispanic students.* Washington, DC: U.S. Department of Education.

National Center for Education Statistics. (1997). *The condition of education 1997: The social context of education* (NCES 97-981). Washington, DC: U.S. Department of Education.

National Center for Education Statistics. (1998). *Characteristics of the 100 largest public elementary and secondary school districts in the United States.* Washington, DC: U.S. Department of Education. Retrieved from the World Wide Web: http://www.nces.gov/pubs/98/98214.pdf

National Center for Immigrants' Rights. (1979). *Immigration defense manual.* Los Angeles: Author.

National Coalition of Advocates for Students. (1991). *The good common school: Making the vision work for all children. A comprehensive guide to elementary school restructuring.* Boston, MA: Author.

National Coalition of Educational Activists. (1994, Autumn). Social justice unionism. *Rethinking Schools, 9*(1) 8, 12–13.

National Commission on Excellence in Education. (1983). *A nation at risk.* Washington, DC: U.S. Government Printing Office.

National Education Association. *Status of the American public school teacher.* Washington, DC: Author.

National Education Association. (1990). *Tracking: Report of the NEA Executive Committee on academic tracking.* Washington, DC: Author.

National Education Association. (1998). *American education statistics at a glance: NEA research, March 1998.* Washington, DC: Author. Retrieved 5 February 1999 from the World Wide Web: http://www.nea.org/society/edstat98.pdf

National Geographic Society. (1993). *The world of the American Indian.* Washington, DC: Author.

National Labor Committee. (1996). *The U.S. in Haiti: How to get rich on 11 cents an hour.* Report of the NLC Education Fund. New York: Author.

National Research Council. (1997). *Schooling for language minority children.* Washington, DC: Author.

New York State Social Studies Review and Development Committee. (1991). *One nation, many peoples: A declaration of cultural interdependence.* New York: New York State Education Department.

Njeri, I. (1991, 13 January). Beyond the melting pot. *Los Angeles Times,* pp. E1, E8, E9.

Oakes, J. (1985). *Keeping track: How schools structure inequality.* New Haven, CT: Yale University Press.

Oakes, J. (1988). Tracking in mathematics and science education: A structural contribution to unequal schooling. In L. Weis (Ed.), *Class, race and gender in American education* (pp. 106–125). Albany: State University of New York Press.

Oakes, J., & Lypton, M. (1990). Tracking and ability grouping: A structural barrier to access and achievement. In J. Goodlad & P. Keating. (Eds.), *Access to knowledge: An agenda for our nation's schools.* New York: The College Entrance Examination Board.

O'Day, J., & Smith, M. S. (1993). Systemic reform and educational opportunity. In S. Fuhrman (Ed.), *Designing coherent educational policy: Improving the system.* San Francisco: Jossey-Bass.

Odden, A. (Ed.). (1991). *Educational policy implementation.* Albany, NY: State University of New York Press.

Odden, A. (1992). School finance and educational reform. In A. Odden (Ed.), *Rethinking School Finance: An Agenda for the 1990s* (pp. 1–40). San Francisco, CA: Jossey-Bass.

Ogbu, J. U. (1978). *Minority education and caste: The American system in cross cultural perspective.* New York: Academic Press.

Ogbu, J. U. (1995). Understanding cultural diversity and learning. In J. A. Banks & C. A. McGee Banks (Eds.), *Handbook of research on multicultural education* (pp. 582–596). New York: Simon & Schuster/Macmillan.

Olsen, L. (1988). *Crossing the schoolhouse border: Immigrant students and the California public schools.* San Francisco, CA: California Tomorrow.

Olsen, L. (1992, Fall). Whose curriculum is this? Whose curriculum will it be? *California Perspectives, California Tomorrow,* p. 3B.

Olsen, L., , Chang, H., De La Rosa Salazar, D., Leong, C., McCall Perez, Z., McClain, G., & Raffel, L. (1994). *The unfinished journey: Restructuring schools in a diverse society.* San Francisco: California Tomorrow.

Olsen, L., & Dowell, C. (1997). *The schools we need now: How parents, families and communities can change schools* (Published simultaneously in Spanish as *Las escuelas que necesitamos hoy: De cómo los padres, las familias y las comunidades pueden participar in el cambio escolar*). San Francisco: California Tomorrow.

Olsen, L., & Mullen, N. (1990). *Embracing diversity: Teachers' voices from California.* San Francisco: California Tomorrow.

Olson, L. (1986, January). Effective schools. *Education Week,* pp. 11–21.

Olson, L. (1995, 11 January). Looks cloudy for standards certification. *Education Week,* p. 12.

Olson, L. (1997, 22 January). Keeping tabs on quality. *Education Week* (Special issue), pp. 7–17.

Olson, L., & Hendrie, C. (1998, 8 January). Pathways to progress. *Education Week,* pp. 32–34.

Omi, M., & Winant, H. (1986). *Racial formation in the United States: From the 1960s to the 1980s.* New York & London: Routledge & Kegan Paul.

O'Neil, J. (1997). Building schools as communities: A conversation with James Comer. *Educational Leadership, 54*(8), 6–10.

Orfield, G., & Ashkinage, C. (1991). *The closing door: Conservative policy and black opportunity.* Chicago: University of Chicago Press.

Orfield, G., Bachmeier, M., James, D. R., & Eitle, T. (1997). *Deepening segregation in American public schools.* Cambridge, MA: Harvard University, Harvard Project on School Desegregation.

Orfield, G., Eaton, S. E., & the Harvard Project on School Desegregation. (1996). *Dismantling desegregation: The quiet reversal of Brown v. Board of Education.* New York: New Press.

Osborne, A. B. (1996). Practice into theory into practice: Culturally relevant pedagogy for students we have marginalized and normalized. *Anthropology and Education Quarterly, 27*(3), 285–314.

Padilla, A. M., & Lindholm, K. J. (1995). Quantitative educational research with ethnic minorities. In J. A. Banks & C. A. McGee Banks (Eds.), *Handbook of research on multicultural education* (pp. 97–113). New York: Simon & Schuster/Macmillan.

Parker, R. (1972). *The myth of the middle class.* New York: Harper & Row.

Pastor, M. (1993). *Latinos and the Los Angeles uprising: The economic context.* Claremont, CA: Thomas Rivera Center.

Paul, R. (1988). Program for the fourth international conference on critical thinking and educational reform, Sonoma State University, Rohnert Park, CA. In R. J. Marzano, R. Brandt, C. S. Hughes, B. F. Jones, B. Z. Presseisen, S. C. Rankin, & C. Suhor (Eds.), *Dimensions of thinking: A framework for curriculum and instruction* (pp. 18–22). Alexandria, VA: Association for Supervision and Curriculum Development.

People for the American Way. (1996). *Parental rights: The Trojan horse of the religious right attack on public education.* Washington, DC: Author.

Pérez, B. (1998). *Sociocultural contexts of language and literacy.* Mahwah, NJ: Lawrence Erlbaum Associates.

Perkins, D. (1986). *Knowledge as design.* Hillsdale, NJ: Lawrence Erlbaum Associates.

Perry, T., & Delpit, L. (Eds.). (1997). The real Ebonics debate: Power, language, and education of African American children. *Rethinking Schools, 12*(1), 1–34.

Pickney, A. (1990). *The myth of black progress.* Cambridge, MA: Cambridge University Press.

Pipher, M. (1994). *Reviving Ophelia: Saving the selves of adolescent girls.* New York: Ballantine.

Pitsch, M. (1996, 7 August). Dole speeches plug vouchers, plaster unions. *Education Week*, p. 27.

Pogrow, S. (1996, June). Reforming the wannabe reformers: Why education reforms almost always end up making things worse. *Phi Delta Kappan*, pp. 656–663.

Pool, C. R. (1997, March). Maximizing learning: a conversation with Renate Nummela Caine. *Educational Leadership*, pp. 11–16.

Popham, W. J. (1999, March). Why standardized tests don't measure educational quality. *Educational Leadership*, pp. 8–15.

Popkewitz, T. S. (1987). Knowledge and interest in curriculum. In T. Popkewitz (Ed.), *Critical studies in teacher education: Its folklore, theory, and practice* (pp. 338–339). London, England: Falmer.

Popkewitz, T. S. (1998). Restructuring of social and political theory: Foucault, the linguistic turn, and education. In C. A. Torres & T. R. Mitchell (Eds.), *Sociology of education: Emerging perspectives* (pp. 47–89). Albany, NY: State University of New York Press.

Popkewitz, T. S., Tabachnick, B. R., & Wehlage, G. (1982). *The myth of educational reform.* Madison, WI: University of Wisconsin Press.

Porter, R. P. (1998, May). The case against bilingual education. *Atlantic Monthly*, pp. 28–29, 38–39.

The President's Initiative on Race. (1998, 18 September). *One America in the 21st century: Forging a new future.* The Advisory Board's Report to the President. Washington, DC: The White House.

Quality counts: A report card on the condition of public education in the 50 states. (1997, 22 January). *Education Week* (Special issue).

Quality counts: The urban challenge. (1998, 8 January). *Education Week* (Special issue).

Quality Education for Minorities Project. (1990). *Education that works: An action plan for the education of minorities.* Cambridge, MA: MIT Press.

Ramirez, J. D., Yuen, S. D., & Ramey, D. R. (1991). *Final report: Longitudinal study of structured English immersion strategy, early-exit and late-exit transitional bilingual education programs for language-minority children.* Washington, DC: U.S. Department of Education.

Ramirez, M., III, & Castañeda, A. (1974). *Cultural democracy: Bicognitive development and education.* New York: Academic Press.

Rasell, M. E., & Mishel, L. (1990). *Shortchanging education: How U.S. spending on grades K–12 lags behind other industrialized nations.* Armonk, NY: Economic Policy Institute.

Ratnesar, R. (1998, 20 July). The bite on teachers. *Time*, p. 23.

Ravitch, D. (1974). *The great schools wars.* New York: Basic Books.

Ravitch, D. (1990, Spring). Diversity and democracy: Multicultural education in America. *American Educator*, pp. 16–48.

Ravitch, D. (1991, Spring). Multiculturalism: E. pluribus plures. *American Scholar*, pp. 337–354.

Ravitch, D. (1997). *Student performance today* (Brookings Policy Brief No. 23). Washington, DC: Brookings Institution.

Ravitch, D., & Viteritti, J. P. (1997). *New schools for a new century: The redesign of urban education.* New Haven, CT: Yale University Press.

Raymond, C. (1991, 30 October). Results from a Chicago project lead social scientists to a rethinking of the urban underclass. *Chronicle of Higher Education*, p. A9.

Reese, C. M., Miller, K. E., Mazzeo, J., & Dossey, J. (1997). *NAEP 1996 mathematics: Report card for the nation and the states. Findings from the National Assessment of Educational Progress.* Washington, DC: National Center for Education Statistics, U.S. Department of Education.

Reich, R. B. (1991a, 20 January). Secession of the successful. *New York Times Magazine*, p. 44.

Reich, R. B. (1991b). *The work of nations: Preparing ourselves for 21st century capitalism.* New York: Alfred E. Knopf.

Reich, R. B. (1997, May–June). Up from bipartisanship. *American Prospect*, pp. 27–35.

Reidford, R. (1972). Educational research. In C. Weinberg (Ed.), *Humanistic foundations of education* (pp. 257–280). Upper Saddle River, NJ: Prentice Hall.

Resolving a crisis in education: Latino teachers for tomorrow's classrooms. (1993). Claremont, CA: Tomas Rivera Center.

Rethinking Schools. (1998). *Rethinking Columbus* (2nd ed.). Milwaukee, WI: Author.

Riley, R. W. (1998). *The challenge for America: A high-quality teacher in every classroom.* Annual Back-to-School Address, National Press Club, 15 September.

Washington, DC: National Press Club. Retrieved 15 February 1999 from the World Wide Web: http://www.ed.gov/speeches/980915.html

Rist, R. C. (1970, August). Student social class and teacher expectations: The self-fulfilling prophecy in ghetto education. *Harvard Educational Review*, pp. 411–451.

Rose, P. (1974). *They and we: Racial and ethnic relations in the United States* (2nd ed.). New York: Random House.

Rose, S. (1992). *Social stratification in the United States: The American profile poster* (rev. ed.). New York: New Press.

Rothstein, R. (1993, Spring). The myth of public school failure. *The American Prospect*, pp. 20–34.

Rothstein, R. (1998, May). Bilingual education: The controversy. *Phi Delta Kappan*, pp. 672–678. Retrieved 31 March 1998 from the World Wide Web: http://www.pdkintl.org/kappan/krot9805.htm

Ryan, J., & Sackrey, C. (1984). *Strangers in paradise: Academics from the working class*. Boston, MA: South End.

Sadker, M., Sadker, D., & Long, L. (1989). Gender and educational equality. In J. Banks and C. H. M. Banks. *Multicultural education: Issues and perspectives* (pp. 106–123). Needham Heights, MA: Allyn & Bacon.

Saks, J. (1997). *The basics of charter schools: A school board primer*. Alexandria, VA: National School Boards Association.

Sanchez, R. (1997, 13 October). Mixed results on gifts to education. *Washington Post*, p. A01.

Sarason, S. B. (1990). *The predictable failure of educational reform: Can we change course before it is too late?* San Francisco: Jossey-Bass.

Sawicky, M. B. (1991). *The roots of the public sector fiscal crisis*. Washington, DC: Economic Policy Institute.

Schlesinger, A. M., Jr. (1991a). A dissenting opinion. *One nation, many peoples: A declaration of cultural interdependence* (Appendix to Report of the New York State Social Studies Review and Development Committee). New York: State Education Department.

Schlesinger, A. M., Jr. (1991b, Winter). The disuniting of America. *American Educator*, pp. 57–61.

Schlesinger, A. M., Jr. (1992). *The disuniting of America*. New York: W. W. Norton.

Schmidt, P. (1994, 28 September). Idea of "gender gap" in schools under attack. *Education Week*, pp. 1, 16.

Schnaiberg, L. (1997, 5 March). The politics of language. *Education Week*, pp. 25–27.

Schniedewind, N., & Davidson, E. (1998). *Open minds to equality: A sourcebook of learning activities to affirm diversity and promote equity*. Boston: Allyn & Bacon.

School finance: State efforts to reduce funding gaps between poor and wealthy districts. (1997, February). (GAO/HEHS 97–31). Washington, DC: U.S. General Accounting Office.

Schwartz, W. (1996). How well are charter schools serving urban and minority students? Teachers College, NY: ERIC Clearinghouse on Urban Education, Institute for Urban and Minority Education. *ERIC/CUC Digest* (No. 119).

Scriven, M., & Paul, R. (1994). Defining critical thinking. Draft statement for the National Council for Excellence in Critical Thinking Instruction, Sonoma State University, Rohnert Park, CA.

Sewell, G. T. (1991). *Social studies review*. New York: American Textbook Council.

Sharp, R. (1993, 14 September). Losing ground: In latest recession only blacks suffered net employment loss. *Wall Street Journal*, pp. A1, 12, 13.

Shaver, J. (Ed.). (1977). *Building rationales for citizenship education* (Bulletin No. 52). Arlington, VA: National Council of the Social Studies.

Shokraii, N. (1996, December). Free at last: Black America signs up for school choice. *Policy Review, 80*, 20–26.

Shorris, E. (1992). Latinos: The complexity of identity. *NACLA Report on the Americas, 26*(2), n.p.

Shulman, L. (1987). Knowledge and teaching: Foundations of the new reform. *Harvard Educational Review, 57*(1), 1–22.

The siege of L.A.: Special report. (1992, 11 May). *Newsweek*, pp. 30–37.

Simon, S. B., Howe, L. W., & Kirschenbaum, H. (1972). *Values clarification*. New York: Hart.

Slavin, R. E. (1995). Cooperative learning and intergroup relations. In J. A. Banks & C. A. McGee Banks (Eds.), *Handbook of research on multicultural education* (pp. 628–634). New York: Simon & Schuster/Macmillan.

Slavin, R. E. (1998, January). Can education reduce social inequity? *Educational Leadership*, pp. 6–10.

Sleeter, C., & Grant, C. (1999). *Making choices for multicultural education: Five approaches to race, class, and gender* (3rd ed.). Upper Saddle River, NJ: Merrill/Prentice Hall.

Smith, D. (1998, 21 August). Governor signs state's biggest tax-cutting bill. *Sacramento Bee*, p. 1.

Smith, M., & Scoll, B. (1995). The Clinton human capital agenda. *Teachers College Record, 96*(3), 389–403.

Snider, W. (1990, 21 February). Schools are re-opened in Selma amid continuing racial strife. *Education Week*.

Sowell, T. (1991, May–June). Cultural diversity: A world view. *American Enterprise*, pp. 45–54.

Spindler, G., & Spindler, L. (1991). *The process of culture and person: Multicultural classrooms and cultural therapy*. Paper presented at the Cultural Diversity Working Conference, Stanford University School of Education, Stanford, CA, October.

Spindler, L., & Spindler, G. (1992, April). *The enduring and the situated self*. Paper presented at California State University, Sacramento, CA.

Sping, J. (1988). *Conflict of interests: The politics of American education*. New York: Longman.

Splits on the right: What do they mean for education? (1996). *Rethinking Schools, 10*(3), 11–18.

Spradley, J. P., & McCurdy, D. W. (1994). *Conformity & conflict: Readings in cultural anthropology* (8th ed.). Boston: Little, Brown.

Squires, D. A., Huitt, W. G., & Segars, J. K. (1983). *Effective schools and classrooms: A research-based perspective*. Alexandria, VA: Association for Supervision and Curriculum Development.

Steen, D. R., Roddy, M. R., Sheffield, D., & Stout, M. (1995). *Teaching with the Internet: Putting teachers before technology*. New York: Resolution Business Press.

Stiggins, R. J. (1997). *Student-centered classroom assessment* (2nd ed.). Upper Saddle River, NJ: Merrill/Prentice Hall.

Stille, A. (1998, 11 June). The betrayal of history. *New York Review*, pp. 15–20.

Sullivan, M., & Miller, D. (1990, February). Cincinnati's Urban Appalachian Council and Appalachian identity. *Harvard Educational Review*, pp. 105–124.

Takaki, R. (1989). *Strangers from a different shore: A history of Asian Americans*. Boston: Little, Brown.

Tannen, D. (1990). *You just don't understand: Women and men in conversation*. New York: Ballantine.

Task Force on Minorities. (1989). *A curriculum of inclusion. Report of the Commissioner's Task Force on Minorities: Equality and excellence, July, 1989*. (Mimeograph). Albany, NY: New York State Education Department.

Tate, K. (1992). Invisible woman. *American Prospect, 8*(1), 74–81.

Tavris, C. (1992). *The mismeasure of woman: Why women are not the better sex, the inferior sex, or the opposite sex*. New York: Simon & Schuster.

Taylor, D. (1993). *From the child's point of view*. Portsmouth, NH: Heinemann.

Taylor, D. (1998). *Beginning to read and the spin doctors of science: The political campaign to change America's mind about how children learn to read*. Urbana, IL: National Council of Teachers of English.

Tennessee Education Association, & Appalachian Educational Laboratory. (1993). *Reducing school violence: Schools teaching peace*. Charleston, WV: Appalachian Educational Laboratory.

TESOL. (1998). *ESL standards for pre-K–12 students*. Washington, DC: Teachers of English to Speakers of Other Languages, Inc.

Tetreault, M. K. T. (1989). Integrating content about women and gender into the curriculum. In J. A. Banks & C. A. McGee Banks, (Eds.), *Multicultural education: Issues and perspectives* (pp. 124–144). Needham Heights, MA: Allyn & Bacon.

Texas test sued in federal court. (1997, Fall). *Fair Text Examiner*. Retrieved 12 February 1998 from the World Wide Web: http://www.fairtext.org/exam-arts/fall/97.texas.htm

Tharp, R. G., & Gallimore, R. (1988). *Rousing minds to life: Teaching learning and schooling in social context*. Cambridge, England: Cambridge University Press.

Thurow, L. C. (1996). *The future of capitalism: How today's economic forces shape tomorrow's world*. New York: William Morrow.

Tienda, M., & Stier, H. (1991). Joblessness and shiftlessness: Labor force activity in Chicago's inner city. In C. Jenks & P. E. Peterson (Eds.), *The urban underclass* (pp. 135–154). Washington, DC: Brookings Institution.

Toby, J. (1993–1994, Winter). Everyday school violence: How disorder fuels it. *American Educator,* pp. 4–9, 44–48.

Torres, C. A., & Mitchell, T. R. (Eds.). (1998). *Sociology of education: Emerging perspectives.* Albany, NY: State University of New York Press.

Trombly, W. (1990, 13 September). Honig defends textbooks of real history. *Los Angeles Times,* p. A3.

Trueba, H. T. (1989). *Raising silent voices: Educating linguistic minorities for the 21st century.* Boston: Heine & Heine.

Trueba, H. T., Rodriguez, C., Zou, Y., & Cintrón, J. (1993). *Healing multicultural America: Mexican immigrants rise to power in rural California.* Washington, DC: Falmer.

Tyson-Bernstein, H. (1988). *A conspiracy of good intentions.* Washington, DC: Council on Basic Education.

UNESCO. (1993). *The progress of nations.* New York: United Nations.

UNICEF. (1997). *The state of the world's children, 1997.* New York: United Nations.

U.S. Bureau of the Census. (1981). *1980 Census.* Washington, DC: U.S. Government Printing Office.

U.S. Bureau of the Census. (1991). *The Hispanic population of the United States.* Washington, DC: U.S. Government Printing Office.

U.S. Bureau of the Census. (1992). *Population and Housing, 1990.* Summary Tape File 3c (CD-ROM). Washington, DC: U.S. Government Printing Office.

U.S. Bureau of the Census. (1993). *We the American . . . foreign born.* Washington, DC: U.S. Government Printing Office.

U.S. Bureau of the Census. (1996a). *Current Population Survey, 1996.* Washington, DC: U.S. Government Printing Office.

U.S. Bureau of the Census. (1996b). *Poverty in the United States: 1995* (P 60-194). Washington, DC: U.S. Government Printing Office. Retrieved 17 February 1999 from the World Wide Web: http://www.census.gov:80/prod/2/poverty95/p60-194

U.S. Bureau of the Census. (1997a). *Educational attainment in the United States: March 1997* (P 20-505). Washington, DC: U.S. Government Printing Office.

U.S. Bureau of the Census. (1997b). *Poverty in the United States: 1996 Highlights* (P 60-198). Washington, DC: U.S. Government Printing Office.

U.S. Bureau of the Census. (1997c). *Population projections of the United States by age, sex, race, and Hispanic origin: 1995 to 2050* (P 25-1130). Washington, DC: U.S. Government Printing Office.

U.S. Bureau of the Census. (1998a). *Foreign born population* (CB 98-57). Washington, DC: U.S. Government Printing Office.

U.S. Bureau of the Census. (1998b). *Poverty in the United States: 1997* (P 60-201). Washington, DC: U.S. Government Printing Office.

U.S. Commission on Civil Rights. (1975). *A better chance to learn: Bilingual-bicultural education* (Publication 51). Washington, DC: Author.

U.S. Congress. (1992, 12 March). Empowering our nation's low-income communities: Hearing before the Committee on Small Business. House of Representatives, 105th Congress, 1st Session, Washington, DC.

U.S. Department of Education. (1987). *Schools that work: Educating disadvantaged children.* Washington, DC: U.S. Government Printing Office.

U.S. Department of Education. (1991). *America 2000: An education strategy.* Washington, DC: U.S. Government Printing Office.

U.S. Department of Education. (1996). *Digest of education statistics, 1996.* Washington, DC: U.S. Department of Education, Office for Civil Rights.

U.S. Immigration and Naturalization Service. (1997). *Statistical yearbook, 1996.* Washington, DC: U.S. Government Printing Office.

Valdés, G. (1996). *Con respeto: Bridging the distances between culturally diverse families and schools: An ethnographic portrait.* New York: Teachers College Press.

Valdés, G., & Figueroa, R. (1994). *Bilingualism and testing: A special case of bias.* Norwood, NJ: Ablex.

Valentine, C. A. (1968). *Culture and poverty: Critique and counter-proposals.* Chicago: University of Chicago Press.

Van Allen, R., & Allen, C. (1976). *Language experience activities.* Boston: Houghton Mifflin.

Vaughan, P. (1997). *Web trek: Social studies Internet directory.* Vallejo, CA: Web Trek.

Vygotsky, L. S. (1978). *Mind in society: The development of higher psychological processes* (M. Cole, J. Teiner, S. Scribner, & E. Sauberman, Eds.). Cambridge, MA: Harvard University Press.

Walker, P. (Ed.). (1979). *Between labor and capital.* Boston: South End Press.

Walsh, J. (1999). A new racial era for San Francisco schools. *Salon Magazine.* Retrieved 18 February 1999 from the World Wide Web: http://salon-magazine.com/news/1999/02/18news.html

Warner, W. L. (1949). *Democracy in Jonesville: A study in quality and inequality.* New York: Harper & Brothers.

Washington, J. M. (Ed.). (1986). *Testament of hope: The essential writings and speeches of Martin Luther King, Jr.* San Francisco: Harper.

Weatherford, J. (1988). *Indian givers: How the Indians of the Americas transformed the world.* New York: Crown.

Weber, D. J. (1973). *Foreigners in their native lands: The historical roots of the Mexican Americans.* Albuquerque, NM: University of New Mexico Press.

Weiler, K. (1988). *Women teaching for change: Gender, class & power.* South Hadley, MA: Bergin & Garvey.

Weinberg, C., & Reidford, R. (1972). Humanistic educational psychology. In C. Weinberg & R. Reidford (Eds.), *Humanistic foundations of education* (pp. 104–132). Upper Saddle River, NJ: Prentice Hall.

Weis, L. (1988). High school girls in a de-industrializing economy. In L. Weis (Ed.), *Class, race and gender in American education* (pp. 183–208). Albany: State University of New York Press.

Weis, L. (1990). *Working class without work.* New York: Routledge.

Weis, L., & Fine, M. (Eds.). (1993). *Beyond silenced voices: Class, race and gender in United States schools.* Albany, NY: State University of New York Press.

Weiss, C. H., Cambone, J., & Wyeth, A. (1992). Trouble in paradise: Teacher conflicts in shared decision-making. *Educational Administration Quarterly, 28*(3), 350–367.

West, C. (1993a). *Prophetic thought in postmodern times: Beyond Eurocentrism and multiculturalism* (Vol. 1). Monroe, ME: Common Courage.

West, C. (1993b). *Race matters.* Boston: Beacon.

Westminster School District of Orange County et al. v. Mindez et al., 161 F.2d 744 (Ninth Cir. 1947).

Wexler, P. (1989). Curriculum in the closed society. In H. Giroux & P. McClaren (Eds.), *Critical pedagogy, the state, and cultural struggle* (pp. 92–104). Albany, NY: State University of New York Press.

Whitmore, K., & Crowell, C. (1994). *Inventing a classroom: Life in a bilingual, whole language learning community.* York, ME: Stenhouse.

Whose culture? (1992, January). *Educational Leadership* [Special issue].

Wilbur, G. (1992). Gender-fair curriculum. Research report prepared for Wellesley College Research on Women. In American Association of University Women, *How schools shortchange girls* (p. 112). Washington, DC: AAUW.

Williams, B. (1995). *The Internet for teachers* (2nd ed.). Foster City, CA: IDG Books Worldwide.

Williamson, B. (1988). *A first-year teacher's guidebook for success: A step-by-step educational recipe book from September to June.* Sacramento, CA: Dynamic Teaching Company.

Wilson, E. D. (1994). *California's legislature.* Sacramento, CA: California State Legislature.

Wilson, W. J. (1978). *The declining significance of race.* Chicago: University of Chicago Press.

Wilson, W. J. (1987). *The truly disadvantaged: The inner city, the underclass and public policy.* Chicago: University of Chicago Press.

Wilson, W. J. (1988, May–June). The ghetto underclass and the social transformation of the inner city. *Black Scholar,* pp. 10–17.

Wilson, W. J. (1996). *When work disappears: The world of the new urban poor.* New York, Alfred A. Knopf.

Wink, J. (1997). *Critical pedagogy: Notes from the real world.* New York: Longman.

Wolf, N. (1991). *The beauty myth: How images of beauty are used against women.* New York: Doubleday.

Women's Equity Resource Center. (1997, August). 25 years of Title IX. *WERC Digest,* pp. 1–12.

Wong, P. (in press). Negotiating conflicts and constraints. In J. Hannaway & M. Carnoy (Eds.), *Differential demands and models of management.* Washington, DC: Urban Institute.

Wong-Filmore, L. (1991). When learning a second language means losing the first. *Early Childhood Research Quarterly, 6*(3), 323–346.

Zinn, H. (1990). *Declarations of independence: Cross-examining American ideology*. New York: Harper.

Name Index

Subject Index